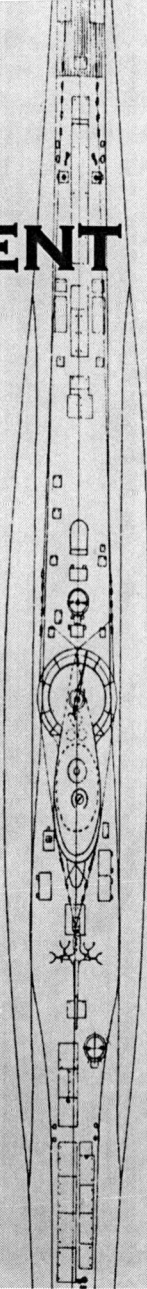

VERTICAL DESCENT

STEVE TURLEY

Vertical Descent

ISBN-13: 978-1-906628-02-4

Published by CheckPoint Press, Ireland

CheckPoint Press
Quality Fiction - Quality Reading

CHECKPOINT PRESS, DOOAGH, ACHILL ISLAND, WESTPORT, CO. MAYO,

REPUBLIC OF IRELAND

TEL: 098 43779   International +353 9843779

EMAIL: EDITOR@CHECKPOINTPRESS.COM

www.checkpointpress.com

This book is available via major online bookstores, and directly from the publisher at bulk discount rates of 30%

Author's Note

U602 last made radio contact with UbD (U-boat Control Centre) from a position north of Oran, Algeria on the 19th April 1943. Although there are many theories as to her eventual fate and final resting place, at the time of writing, she is still officially listed as missing in action.

This book is a work of fiction, and there is no suggestion that U602 was engaged in anything other than routine patrols at the time of her disappearance.

Diving, especially deep diving, can be a dangerous activity without correct training and competent supervision.

Acknowledgements

Thanks go to the survey team at the Bristol Port Company for answering all my questions about modern sounding technology, Leigh Cunningham for being 'sweet as' when giving technical advice, Donna Chabanne for her keen photographic eye and all the tireless U-boat enthusiasts who maintain such fascinating and informative web sites.

Special thanks go to my talented wife Louise, for her artwork and more importantly for her patience, support and understanding during the writing of this book.

For general information and an accompanying online fish

guide visit: VerticalDescent.co.uk

For all enquiries: mail@verticaldescent.co.uk

For Cleo and Charley

An ocean of adventure awaits you!

Prologue

Propriano, Corsica

T he tall German looked much like any of the other summer season tourists, but his reason for visiting this unglamorous quarter of Propriano was certainly not to discover its authentic suburban charm. If it had been, he would have been greatly disappointed.

Glancing down at the piece of paper in his hand, he compared the name written on it with the one that was painted in fading letters above the neglected bar which now stood in front of him. It was undoubtedly the one which he had been looking for. His discerning taste was more suited to the chic cocktail bars of Hamburg and the Côte d'Azur, but it was not for the purpose of entertainment that he was drawn towards this dismal establishment.

Ignoring the curious stares of two threadbare old men who were sitting at a plastic table outside, he pushed open a fingerprint smeared glass door and was met by the lingering odour of stale tobacco as a tinny chime announced his entrance. He felt his skin crawl as his eyes searched the solemn, dark interior before coming to rest on a serving counter at the rear. Behind it stood a surly looking man whose disapproving regard suggested that his intrusion was about as welcome as that of a penniless beggar. Ignoring the cold reception, the tall German walked confidently across the room towards him and stood next to the only other customer in the bar; a thin faced, sly looking character who was busily eyeing his diamond studded Cartier watch.

'*Bonjour Monsieur, un verre d'Armagnac s'il vous plait.*'

The thickly bearded proprietor gave the slightest of nods and began to serve him the glass of Armagnac which he'd asked for.

'*Putain, même les Bosches,*' muttered the gaunt man to his right. Having an excellent command of French, the German visitor understood the racist slur and struggled to control his anger. Not so very long ago, his father would have had a man shot for such a remark. He calmed himself as the proprietor pushed a glass containing a dark yellow spirit towards him.

'*Six euros.*'

The tall German looked up in surprise at the unusually high price and seemed ready to protest. Instead, he calmly pulled out a ten Euro note and appeared amused as he placed it beside the glass.

'*Gardez la monnaie* - keep the change.'

The surly proprietor raised his eyebrows, took the banknote without a word and turned towards the cash register.

'You are Jean-Claude Santorini, are you not?'

The proprietor froze and placed his hand over the pistol which he kept loaded and taped beneath the counter.

'Who wants to know?' he barked.

The tall German paused, enjoying the sudden psychological advantage which he had over the man in front of him.

'Let us just say that a friend of yours is a friend of mine,' he said with an enigmatic and self-assured smile. The proprietor eyed him warily.

'What do you want here?' he challenged.

The tall German visitor took a sip of Armagnac and carefully replaced the glass on the counter in front of him.

'My contact has informed me that you and your associates are very knowledgeable about the coastline here and that you are also competent divers. Is that true?'

The proprietor narrowed his eyes. The tall German seemed to know a little too much about his affairs for his liking.

'You seem to be well informed. What interest would it be to you if we were?'

'If what my contact tells me is true, then I have an interesting proposition for you,' he said, looking directly into the proprietor's dark, intelligent eyes.

'And what would that be?'

The tall German motioned to the man standing to his right with a dismissive jerk of the head. 'Is he a close...how shall we say...comrade, of yours?'

'He can be trusted if that's what you mean,' snapped the proprietor.

'Good. Then let me get right to the point.'

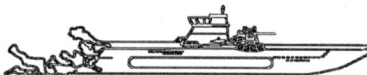

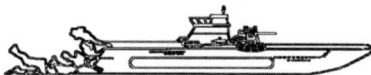

1

Somewhere off the East Coast of Sardinia, April 1943

K apitänleutnant Rolf Sturmann, was in his private quarters. Not that there was anything particularly private about them, but then any concession to personal comfort was to be appreciated when living in the cramped interior of a 67 metre long steel tube. For Rolf was a U-boat Captain and although most *Kriegsmarine* officers preferred the command of vessels which remained on the surface, Rolf and his crew had learned to take comfort in the comradeship and bravery which bound them together beneath it.

At present Rolf was deep in thought, studying the progress of his vessel on his private chart in the hope that it would throw some light on recent events.

A little more than three weeks ago, he'd been on shore-leave on the west coast of France, after returning from a successful patrol of the Atlantic. Like the majority of *Kriegsmarine* officers, he had spent his time on shore celebrating in the lively bars and restaurants of the port of Lorient, while trying to resist the undoubted charms of its less reputable ladies. On the morning of his return to active duty, however, his mood of optimism quickly began to fade. Having reported, as usual, to the *Grossadmiral's* office at Lorient's Kéroman U-boat base, he had been fully expecting to re-join his colleagues of the Weddigen Wolf-Pack fleet out patrolling in the Atlantic, but the unusual presence of a *Brigadeführer* of the *Waffen SS* was the first sign that his new orders were unlikely to be routine.

Now, inexplicably, Rolf found himself consigned to the Mediterranean, expressly forbidden to engage the enemy and being treated more like the skipper of a supply vessel than an elite commander of a hunter killer submarine. He wondered what he and his crew had done to deserve such ill treatment.

Rolf consoled himself with a sip of the precious supply of Calvados which he kept hidden away in the wooden locker next to his bunk. As he breathed in the rich apple and oak infused vapours, he caught a glimpse of his piercing grey-blue eyes and finely chiselled features in the shaving mirror that was fixed to the opposite bulkhead. His dark, short cropped beard and unruly jet black hair were proof that the mirror rarely served its true purpose while at sea, but Rolf cut an imposing figure none the less. The *Grossadmiral* regarded him as something of a maverick; a dangerous individualist even, but the incontestable success of his unconventional approach had earned him both the admiration of his contemporaries and the unflinching loyalty of his crew. And yet three weeks ago, when he had reluctantly dismissed sixteen of his men and watched them trudge despondently back along the quays of the U-boat hangar, he had felt more like a traitor than a hero. It might have been easier if he could have given them a reasonable explanation for their dismissal; but he was just as mystified as they were. He recalled that there was a strange sense of foreboding amongst the remaining crew when he had finally ordered the moorings to be slipped and the sleek hull of the VIIC U-boat began to slice through the cold choppy waters of the Atlantic.

Rolf's musings were interrupted by a voice outside his quarters.

'Herr Kapitän?'

Rolf quickly hid his glass and pulled back the thick curtain which separated his quarters from the passageway outside. Berndt, the *Leitender Ingenieur*, stood before him with an apologetic look on his face. The Chief Engineer was a stout, hairy man with a bushy red beard and a gruff temperament which had earned him the nickname *Der Grizzlybär*.

'Ah Berndt, I haven't seen you since we left Tunis.'

'No sir. *Oberleutnant* Grünwald asked us to avoid disturbing you.'

Rolf nodded and smiled at the thoughtfulness of his Second in Command.

'There's no need to worry about that Berndt. I'm just trying to keep my head down at the moment.'

'That's understandable sir.'

Rolf tilted his head when he noticed that one of Berndt's dark brown eyes had distinctive black and yellow shading around it.

'Berndt, did you have an argument with someone by any chance?'

The Chief Engineer shuffled uncomfortably.

'Er, no sir – I was actually trying to break up a fight between one of our men and a *Wehrmacht* soldier while we were in port.'

'Oh really? And one of them hit you did he?'

'Well, yes sir. The soldier called me a *Kriegsmarine schwein* and I let loose and then his friends joined in and...well you can probably guess the rest.'

'Yes Berndt, I can well imagine. Now you know that I can't condone that sort of behaviour don't you?'

'Yes Captain, I - er - sorry sir.'

'That's fine Berndt...so did we at least give the *Wehrmacht* boys a good seeing to?' asked Rolf, breaking into a conspiratorial smile.

'Oh yes sir,' replied Berndt, with a broad grin. 'We had them running through the streets of Tunis.'

'Excellent! Now what can I do for you?'

The Chief Engineer screwed up his eyes and wrung his hands.

'It's that pig of an SS officer sir, if you'll excuse me for saying so. I need to get access to the engine room to change the fuel filters, but he won't let me past because he says that I've spent far too much time in there already today.'

Rolf sighed heavily. He had met *Oberführer* Blickmann for the first time only three days ago and like Berndt had disliked him almost immediately. The order to accommodate the *Waffen SS* Officer in the stern section of the U-boat along with a cargo of ammunition cases and five armed guards had consequently met with little enthusiasm.

'Couldn't you have changed them while we were in port Berndt?' asked Rolf irritably.

'Well, yes sir, but we were eager to have a look around Tunis while we had the chance. And of course I had no idea that we would have our access restricted when we got back on board.'

'No, neither did I Berndt – nobody did. Can't it wait a couple of days?'

'I dare say that it can sir, but if we run out of power while we've got a Destroyer on our tail.' Berndt left the statement hanging in the air.

Rolf scratched his coarse beard contemplatively.

'Leave it with me Berndt; I'll see what I can do.'

'Very well sir,' said Berndt, nodding curtly before dismissing himself.

Rolf was left wondering what Blickmann could be transporting in those damned ammunition cases to warrant such intense security. It had to be something vital to the war effort to justify the sacrifice of a U-boat so desperately needed in the battle for the control of the Atlantic. He stared wistfully at his chart, knowing that his command would never join her sister ships of the Weddigen fleet again. The powerful incoming currents at the Straits of Gibraltar would now condemn her to remain in the Mediterranean until the end of the war. And perhaps for all eternity.

He breathed a sigh of resignation and began to fold away his chart. As he was doing so, the Radio Operator came over from the communications area and coughed politely to gain his attention.

'*Herr Kapitän.* I'm sorry to disturb you, but we have just received this message from U-boat Control.' The young Radio Operator handed Rolf a sheet of paper printed with lines of coded script.

'Thank you Johann. You may go.'

Frowning concernedly, Rolf went directly to the hidden Enigma decoder and began to decipher the encrypted transmission. As the original message began to emerge from the printer, Rolf could not believe what he was reading. Infuriated by its content, he exited the communications area, slipped horizontally through the forward hatch and stormed past the men who were on duty in the control room. Heads craned as he halted in front of the stern access hatch, hunched down next to it and calmly asked the guard on duty behind it to fetch *Oberführer* Blickmann. The stony-faced soldier unhurriedly shouted to a colleague further back and a minute later *Oberführer* Blickmann's pink, bloated face appeared at the hatch, looking tired and irritable.

'What is it *Kapitän?*'

'I need to speak to you in private.'

Blickmann sighed wearily.

'Fine; where do you suggest?'

'We'll go aloft; I'll ask the men on watch to wait below decks.'

'Very well *Kapitän*. Lead the way.'

Rolf climbed the ladder to the bridge and emerged into the warmth of a late afternoon sun, with Blickmann following close behind. Once he had dismissed the Watchkeepers, Rolf closed the hatch without locking it and turned to face the cold grey eyes of the SS Officer.

'You told me that we were bound for La Spezia...Italy!'

'That is correct.'

'Then why have I just received the order to proceed to Toulon?'

'Ah yes,' said Blickmann with a condescending smile, 'I was expecting it.'

'You were expecting it! Then why in God's name wasn't I informed?' Rolf barked.

It was Blickmann's turn to be vexed.

'If you needed to be told then I would already have told you,' he said scathingly.

'Do you question my trust?' asked Rolf.

'The *Waffen* SS trusts no one outside of its highest ranks. It was as important for you to believe that we were going to La Spezia as it was for our enemies. On your present course even a second rate Navigator could guess at your intended destination.' Rolf was taken aback.

'Do you seriously believe that there could be a traitor amongst my crew?'

'*Kapitän*, with the sensitive nature of this operation, we are not prepared to take any risks. And if that means keeping a few ragged looking sailors in the dark for a few days, then that is what we will do. Now are you going to take this vessel to Toulon or do I have to relieve you of your command and find someone who will?'

Rolf seethed, but was forced to hold his tongue. Blickmann outranked him. And he could see from the set of his jaw that he was clearly prepared to carry out his threat.

'Well my Chief Engineer is certainly no traitor and if you don't allow him to change the fuel filters this very evening, I give you no guarantee that we will make it to Toulon.'

Blickmann snorted, studying Rolf from head to toe.

'Very well *Kapitän*. If you are so very concerned, I will allow your engineer a further hour to complete his work.'

It was a minor victory, but Rolf was not prepared to stand idly by while the reputation of his crew was brought into question.

'In that case I will order a change of course. If all goes well we should reach the French Coast by tomorrow evening.'

'Excellent, keep me informed of our progress.'

Rolf nodded curtly and gestured to Blickmann to descend. There was an uneasy silence in the control room as Blickmann returned aft and Rolf walked stiffly away in the opposite direction. Once through the forward hatch, Rolf went directly to the navigation room and unfurled a small scale chart of the Mediterranean. He spread it out on the table in front of him and studied it intently. After a moment his fist suddenly came down hard beside it.

'*Natürlich!* – Of course!' he bellowed. The young Navigator, who had stepped aside to accommodate Rolf, flinched nervously, feeling decidedly uncomfortable in the confined space along with his Commanding Officer. Rolf turned towards the young man and put him at ease with a rakish smile.

'It's an old trick Gustav. Whatever we are carrying, they must be very afraid of losing it to the Allies.'

'*Herr Kapitän?*'

'Never mind Gustav; you may retire for the evening; I'll take over from here.'

'Very good sir,' stuttered the young Navigator, confusion clouding his face.

When Rolf was alone, he returned his attention to the chart. It was now strikingly obvious to him why he'd received the new orders; it was a tactical diversion. If anyone had been planning to intercept them on their present course, then the logical place to do so would be in the narrowing passage of the Tyrrhenian Sea between Corsica and the Italian mainland. But since their new course obliged them to pass through the Straits of Bonifacio, they would now be able to slip quietly away into the relative safety of the Balearic Basin. Rolf smiled at the ruse as he modified his course to pass west between the *Arcipelago Della Maddalena* and the *Iles Lavezzi* which spread across the entrance to the straits.

Two hours later, Rolf was out on the bridge, surveying the passage ahead. Night had fallen, yet the two groups of islands were still clearly visible, bathed in moonlight, like ghostly icebergs floating menacingly on the horizon. Rolf ordered a minor course correction and glanced skyward as the U-boat sliced quietly through the glistening surface of a gently undulating sea. The stars shimmered brilliantly from between high cirrus clouds and Rolf picked out the major constellations while enjoying the sweetness of the cool evening air; so invigorating after the dank fetidness which lingered below decks.

An hour passed by and the dangers of the notorious Lavezzi Islands were at last behind them. Rolf breathed a sigh of relief, mindful of the long list of vessels which had met an untimely end there. Cape Pertusato now lay ahead of them and beyond it Bonifacio, the lights of which were visible, high amongst the ancient buildings which perched precariously on the edge of vertical sea cliffs. As they passed Cape Feno and advanced northwards along the coast of Corsica, the view of the moonlit mountains to the east was breath-taking. Inspired by the perfect conditions, Rolf modified his course to bring the U-boat closer to shore; an indulgence for which he felt no guilt after the way he had been treated. Staring down from the bridge, he noticed tiny electric-blue sparks of bioluminescence lighting up the sides of the dark hull below the waterline. It gave the whole scene a surreal quality as the glow of the tiny organisms danced amongst the dazzling pinpricks of starlight which reflected from the oily surface of the sea. Rolf smiled to himself, thinking that this unexpected detour towards the French Coast might not be so unpleasant after all. But his optimism was about to prove unfounded.

The skies were clear apart from a scattering of feathery clouds which caught the moonlight like frosted webs on a winter's morning. The sea, far below, was gently ruffled by the sweeping approaches of a light north westerly breeze.

Since leaving the air base in Malta, they had kept well south of the island of Sicily, skirted around the southern tip of Sardinia and then followed a wide arc out into the Balearic Basin. After failing to locate a target and drawing close to the limits of their fuel range, they had decided to call it a day and head east towards the coast of Corsica. Half an hour later, a high mountain range came into view.

Wing Commander John Rossland pulled the joystick to the right and settled the Wellington Night Bomber onto a southerly heading, running parallel to the coast.

To his left, Smithy, the Navigator, was studying the coastline and attempting to relate it to his charts.

'Are you sure that you've got the right island there Smithy?' asked John.

'Of course I have Skip, look it's written here on the chart: Corsica.'

'I was actually referring to that big mountainous thing on your left.'

'Oh that! Yes, I suppose so.'

'Now you're sure aren't you, because I'm really not too keen on Italian food.'

'Don't worry Skip, if we land in enemy territory, I promise I'll go to the local chippy for you.'

'What? You mean one of those world renowned Italian fish and chips shops?'

'Of course Skip. After all, it's a country renowned for its culture is Italy.'

'You're such a Philistine Smithy.'

'Thank you sir.' Smithy grinned as he glanced out of the cockpit window and watched a ribbon of moonlight race over the sea ahead. On the coast below he spotted a long, white stretch of beach and wondered if it would look quite so tempting by the light of day. As his eyes flicked lazily back to the thin band of moonlit sea, a smooth, dark object suddenly cut across it at speed and the unmistakable shape of a turret was momentarily cast into silhouette.

'Shit...shit! U-boat Skip....just went by on the port flank, heading north.'

'Are you sure?'

'I'm positive.'

'OK, battle positions everyone,' shouted John, while gently pushing the joystick to the right. His instincts immediately kicked in as he banked sharply to starboard and planned an arc in his head which would bring them around and onto an attacking approach from the sea.

'Smithy did you get a visual reference – anything at all?'

'Yes Skip, there was a long stretch of beach with an odd looking outcrop next to it.'

'Good, we'll come in low against the moonlight. See if you can spot them again.'

The wind whistled against the canvas fuselage as the Wellington levelled out and hurtled back towards the coast.

'There's the beach,' shouted Smithy, pointing, 'and the promontory to the right of it.'

'Well spotted. Dropping down to attack altitude.'

John's eyes burned with concentration as he scanned the sea in front of him, but it was Mitch, manning the guns in the front turret who was the first to spot the target.

'I see her Skip, go right,' he shouted. John nudged the joystick to starboard and then back again.

'She's dead ahead.'

Smithy pulled a pair of binoculars away from his eyes and pointed.

'There Skip do you see her?'

'Yes, I'm going in! Select torpedoes and stand by with charges.'

'Aye Captain,' called Billy, the Bomb Aimer, lying prostrate on the bombing couch. 'Doors open, target sighted, go left-left....steady....right.' There was a sudden deafening rattle from below as Mitch opened fire with tracer bullets. John gritted his teeth and levelled out at 65 feet – a dangerously low but essential manoeuvre for effective aerial torpedo attacks.

Rolf was in the control room, speaking with his Second in Command, *Oberleutnant* Grünwald, when he heard the shout from above.

'*Flug! Flug!*'

'Stop the engines!' Rolf shouted, aware that their foaming bow wave would be highly conspicuous under such calm conditions. He bolted up the ladder and emerged from the hatch in time to see the dark underside of an aircraft flash past on the port side.

'Was it ours?' asked one of the Watchkeepers anxiously.

'I don't know,' replied Rolf, 'I didn't get a good enough look at it. Man the anti-aircraft guns and keep a silent watch.'

The two men quickly took up their positions and strained their ears in silent concentration as the distant drone receded to the south. Rolf winced as the sound of Blickmann's angry voice cut through the quiet in the control room below.

'*Was passiert? Antworten Sie mich!* – What's happening? Answer me!'

'Silence down there!' Rolf shouted through the hatch. In the control room below he heard *Oberleutnant* Grünwald arguing with Blickmann and attempting to prevent him from mounting the ladder.

'*Scheiße!*' Rolf swore as his Second in Command's warnings went unheeded and Blickmann's swollen face appeared at the hatch.

'Please *Oberführer*, you cannot come up here, it is not allowed...it is not safe,' he implored.

'Nonsense!' countered Blickmann, pushing himself defiantly to his feet.

'It's coming back *Kapitän*; there at 8 o'clock,' shouted the younger of the two Watchkeepers from his gun post. Rolf saw a glint of moonlight reflected from the cockpit of the incoming aircraft and felt a sudden surge of adrenaline course through his body. 'Fire when ready!' he ordered before dropping to one knee and screaming down the hatch. 'We're under attack; full speed ahead. Inform U-boat Control.'

'Why do you not give the order to dive *Kapitän*?' asked Blickmann, his eyes wide with concern.

'I would have done if you'd remained below decks,' said Rolf through gritted teeth, 'Their depth charges would blow us from the sea if we tried to dive now.'

'Torpedoes in the water!' came a sudden shout from below. A second later the U-boat's 2cm and 3.7cm automatic anti-aircraft guns burst into life, drowning out any further conversation. Rolf climbed midway down the control room access ladder.

'Hard rudder to port!' he bawled, over the deafening rattle from above. The Helmsman responded swiftly and the U-boat slowly swung through the water to face the direction of the oncoming torpedoes.

John kept one eye trained unerringly on his altimeter as he corrected for turbulence and responded to Billy's heading corrections. There was a tinkling of glass as bullets streamed around the cockpit, tearing holes through the flimsy skin which covered the wings and fuselage. He steeled himself, bravely ignoring the imminent mortal danger to himself and his crew as he advanced towards his target. Billy, sighting along the drift wires pressed the bomb release at a range of 800 metres. 'Torpedoes away!' he shouted.

'Pulling out!' John yelled as he eased the joystick back and to the right. The Wellington banked into a tight rising arc, exposing its underbelly momentarily. A stream of bullets passed clean through the tail section but she was soon moving too fast for the U-boat's anti-aircraft guns to track her. John levelled out along the coast and then banked again to starboard to bring them back onto an attack heading.

Rolf saw the bomber begin to bank away as the last rounds of tracer fire ricocheted off the steel hull. It was the moment which he'd been waiting for.

'*Tauchen*! – Dive!' he shouted through the hatch. The two Watch-keepers immediately left their gun posts and slid expertly down the ladder into the control room below. Rolf heard the hiss of air boiling out of the ballast tanks seconds before two huge towers of water shot up from the sea 50 meters behind the U-boat's stern; confirmation that his evasive tactics had been a success. He stumbled as the force of the detonating torpedoes shook the hull, but swiftly regained his footing, knowing that each passing second was now critical. Searching desperately for Blickmann, he found him kneeling beneath the rails of the turret, dazed and frozen to the spot.

'You must descend now!' Rolf shouted, pointing resolutely towards the open hatch. There was no movement from Blickmann.

'If you don't come this instant, I swear I will leave you here to drown.' Blickmann hesitated and then in a sudden flurry of activity, scrambled clumsily towards the hatch. As he dropped into the ladder well his gun holster caught on the lip of the hatch and Rolf agonised as precious seconds were wasted. In growing frustration he kicked the holster free and pushed down forcefully on Blickmann's shoulders.

'*Unten*! – Get down!' he shouted angrily.

The decks were now completely submerged and the sea was lapping hungrily at the base of the conning tower. Rolf flinched when he heard the sound of renewed tracer fire; they had been spotted and it was too late to do anything about it. He cursed his misfortune and jumped down the ladder well, landing hard on Blickmann's arm in the process. The SS Officer's scream rang out, but was almost immediately stifled as water swamped the bridge and began to surge down into the ladder well. Rolf quickly dragged the hatch cover down and turned the locking wheel, sealing it against the inrushing torrent.

'I fear that we may have cut it a little fine this time *Kapitän*,' said *Oberleutnant* Grünwald from his position by the periscope.

'Our only mistake was to carry out our orders,' Rolf replied flatly as he stepped from the ladder and stared gloomily at the needle of the depth gauge. Blickmann was left rolling around in agony, swearing profusely as he cradled his injured arm.

'You imbecile!' he shouted, as he rolled onto his knees and pushed himself to his feet. Rolf ignored the insults and walked towards the hydrophone listening post. The tension in the air was palpable as he ordered the watertight hatches to be closed and sealed.

'Target in range!' shouted Billy as John fought to level the Wellington.

'She's diving,' shouted Smithy, squinting through binoculars at the dark shape in the sea ahead.

'Perfect!' smiled John. 'Select the Torpex charges and activate for 5 metres.'

'Aye Skip,' acknowledged Billy, as two towering white columns rose skyward, just beyond the stricken vessel. The sound of the double detonation hit them a fraction of a second later.

'Damn it!' cursed Smithy, we'd have had them with sonic torpedoes.'

'We'll have them yet,' roared Billy from the bombing couch, lining up the guide wires again.

Blickmann pushed his way towards Rolf, his face burning with outrage. 'You nearly broke my arm, you *arschlocke!*'

'You are fortunate that I didn't leave you up there to die,' replied Rolf unperturbed.

Incensed, Blickmann drew a handgun and pointed it at Rolf's chest.

'I am a senior officer of the *Waffen SS* and I will not...' Before he could finish his sentence, the Hydrophone Operator suddenly turned around and with terror in his eyes shouted, '*wasserbomben!* – depth charges!'

Rolf and his crew instinctively grabbed the nearest hand holds, seconds before a powerful detonation sent the vessel reeling. There were yells of pain as the men were thrown around the cramped interior, crashing into instruments and stumbling against one another. Most of Rolf's crew managed to regain their footing as the violent shuddering began to ease, but it was of little consequence when a second, more powerful explosion tore deep into the hull, sending debris hurtling across the control room and plunging the whole vessel into darkness.

Torn cables spat and hissed like angry snakes, intermittently lighting up the destruction that was all around them. Creaking and crashing sounds reverberated eerily through the length of the hull before the emergency lights finally flickered on. Rolf opened his eyes to find himself lying on his side, light-headed and with the taste of blood in his mouth. His clothes were sodden and there was the disconcerting sensation of cold water creeping around his body. Half choking on the acrid smoke, he staggered to his feet and suddenly became aware of the carnage that surrounded him. Trails of dark fluid trickled from the ears and noses of motionless bodies and mixed with rising seawater.

Amongst the ragged remains of bodies, Rolf spotted Blickmann, sprawled awkwardly on his side, his hair matted with blood, but took no pleasure in seeing the dark wetness that oozed from a crushed eye socket. Spray from a powerful jet of water spewing out from the base of the conning tower hit Rolf in the face and brought some measure of lucidity to his mind. Now standing knee deep in water, he realised that he and anyone else who might still be alive in there would have only the briefest of reprieves unless the U-boat surfaced immediately. Stepping over a naked, headless torso, he reached for a hand-set and made a call to the engine room. To his immense relief the call was answered and with undisguised anguish in his voice, he screamed the order to surface. At the other end of the line, Berndt, the Chief Engineer acknowledged the request in a rasping voice.

'I'll do my best sir, but there's a fire raging back here.'

Deafened by the blast, Rolf could make no sense of the answer.

'I can't hear you,' he shouted in desperation. 'For God's sake surface or we'll all drown!'

A moment later, Rolf was standing waist deep in water, consoling a dying member of his crew, when he felt the vessel suddenly lurch forwards and break surface. The jet of water streaming from the gash in the conning tower eased to a steady trickle and Rolf silently thanked whoever had answered his desperate plea in the engine room. Sensing that salvation was near, he climbed the bridge ladder and attempted to open the hatch, only to find that the locking wheel had seized. As he was fighting to free it, a huge explosion ripped into the U-boat's stern, sending Rolf hurtling back into the water again. He groped his way to the surface through the mass of floating bodies and emerged, winded and gasping for air. There was a terrible creaking and cracking sound as the bulkhead opposite began to rise up and over him. As he began to realise the full horror of what was happening, the emergency lights flickered and then failed altogether. He lunged for the ladder in desperation, his outstretched fingers helplessly flailing the air. Once more, a torrent of water began to blast in through the hole at the base of the conning tower, swamping out the screaming and banging sounds that were coming from behind the forward hatch. Rolf began to choke as he struggled to keep his head above the surface of the rising water. Groping blindly for a way out in the darkness, he began to reach the limits of his endurance. He cried out in angry frustration, defiant in the face of death, but his screams were lost in the swirling turmoil. He inhaled water deep into his lungs and after a final desperate struggle to escape his fate, a strange calm suddenly came over him. Floating in the silence of a dark emptiness, he found himself once again at the bridge of the VIIC U-boat, surrounded by his loyal crew and advancing victoriously towards an ocean of liquid light.

John passed directly over the disturbed patch of sea where the U-boat had been sighted just seconds earlier. He felt the Wellington lift as the charges were released and then he pulled clear, climbing steeply up towards the coast. Four white plumes rose up vertically behind him and moments later the surface of the sea began to boil. He banked to port high over the barren hills beyond the coast and then back out to sea again, returning to the point where the charges had detonated.

'Look Skip, she's surfacing; she's been hit,' shouted Smithy, excitedly.

John eased the nose of the Wellington down and began to circle the stricken U-boat.

'It looks like we've crippled her,' agreed John, 'I can't see any sign of surrender though.'

'We should finish her off,' proposed Smithy.

'We couldn't even if we tried. We're out of ordnance. Besides I don't think we should risk staying around here any longer; we'll just make a note of her position and report...'

Before John could finish his sentence, a huge explosion erupted from the stern of the U-boat and a ball of orange flames leapt high into the air.

'Bloody hell! Looks like we got her after all,' said Smithy, grinning.

'Nice work Billy,' yelled John. 'That was probably her munitions going off. She'll drop like a stone now.'

'Yep, she's already going,' said Smithy. 'I still can't see anyone on deck though; they must all be trapped inside, poor bastards. Better them than me.'

'Quite!' agreed John as he watched the U-boat slip back into the dark embrace of the sea, surrounded by a funeral wreath of white foaming water.

'Nice bit of flying that Skip,' commented Smithy as John banked away and continued south along his original heading. 'I think I'll treat you to a nice Italian meal when we get back.'

On a barren coastal hillside, three drunken old men stood in the middle of the road, arguing excitedly amongst themselves as they pointed towards the bomber that was circling the bay.

'*Je vous l'avais dit; c'est les Britanniques* - I told you so; it's the British,' cried one of them in triumph, as it roared past overhead. He waved his cloth cap above his head and shouted encouragement to its crew as the bomber banked and headed out to sea again. Moments later there was a sharp intake of breath as a huge explosion lit up the sea, revealing the dark silhouette of a sleek hulled vessel.

'*Un sous-marin*! - A submarine!' they gasped, in astonishment.

The three men began to cheer and slap each other on the back as they watched towering flames rise high above the stricken vessel only to die down and disappear again as the submarine upended and slipped back into the sea. Suitably entertained, they stumbled back to the bar, laughing and joking and needing little excuse to share the exaggerated details of their story with anyone foolish enough to provide them with an audience.

2

Southern Corsica, present day

I t was one of those beautifully calm, warm summer days, typical of the Western Mediterranean. The rustling sea breeze brought with it the heady fragrances of tree heather, rock rose and wild mint which grew in profusion along the rugged coastline of the island. The cries of animals, insects and birds filled the air, as they gathered in the abundant natural harvest and competed tirelessly for the attention of mates, while in the silence of the background, the shimmering blue Mediterranean was awesome in its immensity and seeming impenetrability.

Mike Summers was blissfully reclined in a hammock, staring out to sea and feeling at one with the beauty of his surroundings. His head nodded gently to the suitably laid-back tune that was drifting through the earphones of his iPod while he sipped freshly squeezed orange juice from a tall glass. Beneath his shades, his eyes were hazel-green and his finely chiselled nose and full lips were framed by a firm jaw line. The rugged nature of his looks was enhanced by the deep bronze tones of his skin, which like the golden streaks etched into the locks of his naturally light brown hair, were the result of frequent exposure to the sun.

Mike was no stranger to exotic settings and a carefree lifestyle, having spent most of his professional life working as a SCUBA Instructor in the popular resorts of Asia, the Caribbean and the Middle-East.

His adventure started ten years ago, when disillusioned by his timid commuter lifestyle, he had walked into a travel agent after a particularly stressful day at work, booked a ticket to Australia and handed in his notice the following day. Less than a month later, he'd found himself standing at Gatwick's departure terminal, armed with a credit card, a work visa and the bare bones of a plan.

Mike had always wanted to learn to dive and Australia seemed like the perfect place to learn. It had the world's largest reef system, huge expanses of warm, tropical waters and a seemingly inexhaustible supply of gorgeous women. It ticked just about every box that he could think of.

After landing in Sydney, Mike found work and digs at an upmarket hotel in Manley Beach, overlooking the Tasman Sea. Over the next six weeks he spent all of his spare time and much of his hard earned cash learning the basics of diving at a local SCUBA centre. Once his newly acquired skills had been honed, he headed north to Queensland and the diving Mecca of Cairns. And it was there, in between late nights working and partying in the local bars and early mornings spent loading cylinders onto trucks, that he worked his way up through the ranks until he reached the level of guide. After three months, he was penniless and utterly exhausted, but proudly working as a Dive Guide, leading tours out to the world famous Barrier Reef.

One evening, encouraged by a stunning sunset and the contents of several cans of Victoria Bitter, he threw his return ticket into the embers of an impromptu barbecue and vowed never to return to his former life again. Consequently, when his visa expired a few months later, he left Australia with a heavy heart, but armed with the knowledge and experience that would allow him to work his way around the diving hot spots of the world.

Since that time, Mike's semi-nomadic existence had by no means made him wealthy, but in terms of fulfilment, he'd lived a life that many would envy. What is more, he was totally dedicated to his chosen profession and to the protection of the fragile undersea world which he had grown to love.

From the Kitchen of the pretty stone-faced villa he heard the distant clattering of dishes as his friend Thomas rifled through the cupboards in search of clean crockery. He winced and removed his headphones, resigned to the fact that his peaceful start to the morning was over.

Thomas walked out onto the white and grey tiled terrace wearing an old pair of boxer shorts, carrying a cereal bowl full of coffee in one hand and a chunk of *baguette* in the other. He tilted his rounded face up towards the sun and grunted, his striking blue eyes squinting at the intensity of the light.

'Couldn't you find a cup?' asked Mike, with a disapproving glance.

'What do you mean? This is a cup; it's just missing a handle,' protested Thomas. 'Anyway, the others are all dirty.'

Mike rolled his eyes and turned to face the sea again.

'The views from this place are amazing aren't they?'

'Yeah, I have to say that the old lady had pretty good taste.'

Mike watched Thomas dunk bread into his coffee.

'Shame it doesn't run in the family.'

Thomas flicked an index finger at him without raising his head.

'I don't want to sound callous, with your Gran having just passed away and everything, but we were pretty fortunate to get this place.'

'I'm still surprised that my mother let us stay here,' said Thomas, slurping noisily from his bowl. 'I've a strong suspicion that it's so she can keep her eye on me.'

'I can quite understand her concerns,' said Mike, watching him spill coffee onto the terrace table. 'How long did you say we can stay here for?'

'As long as we like; but we'll have to do a bit of work on the place in return.' Thomas reflected on his words and screwed his face up. 'Actually, what I meant to say was, *you'll* have to do a bit of work on the place. I'm not really suited to manual labour.'

'I don't think you're really suited to any kind of labour.'

'True...which is probably why I decided to become a SCUBA Instructor,' said Thomas, grinning.

'And you never know; one day you might actually find something that you're good at.'

Thomas had grown up with the Mediterranean on his doorstep. His parents were both French, his mother being a native of Corsica and his father a mainlander from Marseille. Thomas grew up in *La Pointe Rouge*; the picturesque coastal district on the eastern outskirts of Marseille and spent his teenage years exploring the rich marine environment for which the islands and *calanques* of the area are famous. When he turned 18, he was posted to the diplomatic corps in Amman, Jordan, to complete his military service. The consular work was tedious, but every weekend, he and his colleagues would make the six hour journey south, through dramatic desert landscapes to dive over the pristine corals of the Red Sea's Gulf of Aquaba. Thomas was already an accomplished skin-diver and with his natural underwater ability he took to compressed air diving with ease. By the time that his military service had ended, Thomas was himself a qualified Dive Guide and when an offer of work was put forward by the diving centre which had nurtured his talent, he had no hesitation in agreeing to extend his stay. It was to prove the start of an eventful career that would take him to some of the most challenging and exciting diving destinations in the world.

Thomas and Mike's paths crossed in Dahab; a relaxed Egyptian Red Sea resort on the eastern coast of the Sinai Peninsular. Dahab was considered the Goa of the Middle East, and like it's counterpart in India, was an obligatory stop on the backpacker trail. It was renowned for its Bedouin style charm, cheap food and lodging, a relaxed attitude towards marijuana and some spectacular deep diving. It was a place where you worked and partied in equal amounts.

By then, both Mike and Thomas were highly qualified instructors and had accumulated a wealth of experience between them. Mike had specialised as a Technical Cave Diving Instructor during an extended stay in Mexico's Yucatan Peninsular and Thomas had qualified as an Advanced Trimix Instructor while working in the prestigious resorts of Micronesia. For the past year, they had been working at the same diving centre and become inseparable friends. They often spent their evenings together, sipping Bedouin tea and smoking sweet-smelling shisha pipes while discussing the pros and cons of running their own diving business, but the talking really only became serious when Thomas' grandmother suddenly passed away, leaving her villa in Corsica to his parents.

When Thomas told Mike about the unspoilt natural beauty of Corsica, with its deep crystalline waters and unique fauna and flora protected by marine national parks, he was naturally intrigued. One evening as they sat on Bedouin rugs, staring out towards the moonlit coast of Saudi Arabia,

they agreed to take a few months out to visit Corsica and research the
practicalities of setting up a technical diving facility there. The following
month, much to their own surprise, their bags were packed and they were
boarding a Corsair flight to Ajaccio.

They had now been on the island for two days.

Mike sat across the table from Thomas and began to flick through the
pages of a guide book.

'Well I suppose that we ought to do a bit of exploring now that we're
here. How about taking a look at the Lavezzi Islands?'

'We may as well start with the best,' agreed Thomas. 'I want to test my
rebreather out anyway.'

'There's a list of some dive centres in Bonifacio here. Athena in the
harbour area sound OK. They run dives out to the island and according to
this they've got nitrox facilities too.'

'Sounds perfect,' agreed Thomas. 'We could go down there this
morning and get my cylinder filled.'

'That did cross my mind. I'd better give them a call though, just to make
sure that they can do that. Shall I book us in for the Lavezzis too?'

'Yeah, go ahead. And then I'll show you around Bonifacio; maybe we
can have a beer by the harbour too.'

'But of course my chubby friend, just as long as you're sure that it won't
be too much exercise for you all in one day.'

'The day that beer drinking becomes exercise, I'll join a gym.'

Mike laughed and pulled out his mobile phone. He called Athena and
attempted to explain his request in French, but found his vocabulary
lacking. He gave up and spoke English, but even this proved difficult,
mainly due to the fact that there was a demented Frenchman standing in
front of him, wearing his boxer shorts on his head and playing air guitar to
a highly appreciative, but imaginary audience.

By late morning they had loaded their hire car and were bouncing their
way up the rough access track to the point where it joined the busy main
road. They took a right turn and settled down for the 20 minute drive along
the coast towards Bonifacio.

Mike was starting to realise that in Corsica, stunning views were a
normal part of the scenery. From the high mountain ridges in the centre of
the island to the wide valleys which plunged directly into the sea, there was
a certain raw beauty about the place which Mike found captivating. Even
after they had left the coastline behind and entered the historic town of
Bonifacio, Mike was surprised to discover that the dramatic scenery did
not stop there. He opened his window and craned his neck to get a better
view of the Medieval Genoese citadel, perched imposingly above the steep
sided inlet which forms Bonifacio's natural harbour.

'What an amazing place. You've been hiding this from me haven't you?'

'I take it you approve then?'

'Oh yes,' replied Mike as he watched a pretty girl cross the road. 'It all
looks pretty stunning from where I'm sitting.'

'There's the dive shop,' said Thomas with a jerk of the head. 'We'll, leave the car outside.'

Located right on the harbour front, Athena was a slick and professional outfit. Mike and Thomas stepped inside and were immediately greeted by a cheerful young counter assistant who took charge of the rebreather cylinder and helped them to complete the formalities for the following day's dive. Once the paperwork was complete, they decided to take a stroll along the harbour quays, admiring the rows of brightly painted fishing boats that were swaying gently on their moorings.

'Shall we go and visit the citadel now?' asked Thomas.

'Sure, but I think I'll grab something to eat first, just in case you get us lost up there.'

'It's nice to see that you have such faith in me...now where did I put that map?'

Mike spotted a local bakery and bought a Corsican *Libecciu* sandwich, which he despatched hungrily while Thomas led them up the Montée St-Roch to the Port de Gênes; the impressive carved stone entrance gate to the old town within the citadel walls. Once inside, they ambled along one of the many narrow roads which thread their way through the citadel's interior. After passing a succession of historic churches, ancient workshops and terracotta tiled dwellings they arrived at the impressive Place de la Manichella, perched high above sheer limestone sea cliffs. From their elevated vantage point they admired the stunning views over the Bouches de Bonifacio, the straits which separate Corsica from Sardinia, 12 kilometres to the south.

'Wow! Well that was definitely worth the walk,' enthused Mike.

'Yeah, it's a little bit better than Fulham isn't it?' said Thomas with a grin.

Mike stared down the near vertical cliffs to the crashing waves below and let his eyes roam across the vastness of the open space in front of him.

'I've never seen anything like this. Look at those buildings; they're literally hanging over the edge of a precipice.'

'Yeah, you wouldn't want to be a window cleaner around here would you?' chuckled Thomas. 'We could get a better view of the straits from Pertusato Lighthouse; it's about an hour's walk that way,' said Thomas pointing into the distance. 'Of course, if you're not feeling quite so energetic, we could just go and get ourselves a beer by the marina.'

Mike peered into the distance and then turned to face Thomas.

'It would be a shame to try to see everything all at once wouldn't it?'

'You are a very uncultured, but wise person,' smirked Thomas. 'I'll lead the way.'

They retraced their steps back down to the harbour and found a café-bar with a terrace overlooking the quays. On Thomas' advice they each ordered a bottle of the local Serena beer.

'It has quite a strange taste to it,' Mike remarked.

'That's because it's made from chestnut flour.'

'Really?' Mike picked up the bottle to check the ingredients and noticed the unusual design of a black prisoner's head on the label.

'So it does. Weird label too.'

The waiter placed a saucer of mixed olives on the table along with the bill. Mike decided to try a word of Corsican on the waiter.

'*Grazie* - thank you'. To his surprise and embarrassment, the waiter replied pointedly in French;

'*Je vous en prie monsieur* – you're welcome sir.'

'You're wasting your time trying to speak Corsican, just stick to French,' advised Thomas after the waiter had departed.

'Why's that?'

'It's hard to explain, but just try to imagine going to Wales and trying to speak Welsh with the locals. They'd think you were taking the piss. Anyway they're a bit stubborn here, like all islanders, a bit like you British in fact.'

'No, that's not true; we like everyone to speak English.'

'Yeah, but given that it's the only language you *can* speak, that's not really surprising. Anyway, the point is that the mentality is a bit different here and you'll need to learn how to approach the locals without offending them.'

'Jeez, it sounds just like dealing with women.'

'It will require even more of your limited talent for diplomacy my dear friend. You see it's all about honour here; in fact the Corsican clans have a reputation second only to the Sicilians for violent vendettas. That's probably because most of them are descended from powerful Italian families.'

'Wow, maybe I'll stick to French in future then.' Mike took a sip of beer and frowned as a thought crossed his mind. 'Is this vendetta thing likely to be a problem for our business?'

'I doubt that,' replied Thomas. 'There is still some organised crime here, but it's marginal. Most of the gangs these days operate on the mainland where the money is. Of course, the locals are a bit wary of foreign investment, but as long as we don't step on anyone's toes, we'll be fine.'

'But you're almost a local aren't you?'

'No, I'm from the mainland and that makes me a *Pinzuti*.'

'I take it they aren't very keen on the mainland French then?'

'Not really.'

'Excellent! Now I'm starting to warm to them.' Mike smiled smugly at his jibe and changed the subject before Thomas could retaliate.

'Hey look they have boats for hire over there. We should rent one out and do a couple of dives near the villa. What do you think?'

'Yeah, I suppose we could, but it's quite a long way to the villa from here; do you know how to handle a RIB?'

'Of course,' replied Mike, 'I've got a power boat licence. We could pick one up tomorrow after the dive, then I can take the boat back while you return by car.'

'But where will you keep it?'

'Hmm, good point. The shoreline's a bit rocky where we are; I'd have to dive down and tie a mooring...or, what about that bay we passed on the way down from Ajaccio - the one just up the road from the villa?'

'You mean Roccapina? Yeah, I suppose that's a possibility. There are usually one or two boats moored up there during the summer. It's a really nice place too. If you like we could go there and check it out.'

'That sounds like a good idea; let's do it now before we start to lose the light.'

They drained their glasses, left their payment plus a generous tip on the table and headed for the car. Half an hour later they were exiting the main road and carefully avoiding the worst of the potholes as they negotiated the winding track which led down to the stunning turquoise waters below.

'This place looks perfect,' beamed Mike, as they stepped out into the car park. 'Let's climb that headland so we can get a better view.'

'The promontory? That's where the lion rock is; at least the tourist's seem to think it looks like a lion. Personally I think it looks like a rock.'

'What's that tower I saw up there?'

'It's an old watchtower. There are quite a few of them dotted around the coast here.'

'Who were they expecting?'

'Probably an invasion of English tourists.'

'Yeah! No doubt they were afraid we'd steal their women.'

'I think they'd have been more worried about their men,' smirked Thomas.

They set off walking towards the promontory and after several minutes of puffing and panting, arrived at the top, gasping for breath between hoots of delight at the sight of the pure white beaches and stunning, crystal clear bays which lay to either side of them.

'Man, look at the clarity of those shallows down there; they're just perfect for us.'

'It's even better than I remember it,' said Thomas nodding.

'Well I certainly shouldn't have any problems spotting that watchtower from the sea. It makes a perfect navigational reference...which is pretty ironic really.'

'I wonder how deep it is out there,' mused Thomas, staring at the sea beyond.

'According to my chart, you get anything between 18 to 200 metres off the western shore. And in this area right in front of us, there's a relatively shallow shelf which extends way out to a small chain of islands called *Les Moines*. There's definitely plenty of scope for exploration.'

'I can't wait to get started.'

They sat down on the edge of the promontory and watched the sun gradually drop towards the horizon, casting a purple hue across the mackerel skies which were drifting high above them. In the gradually darkening waters below, shoals of mullet and salema meandered about in the shallows, searching for one last meal before being forced to seek refuge against the predators of the night.

'I'm starting to get a really good feeling about this place,' said Mike, while chewing reflectively on a long stalk of grass.

'Yeah, Corsica is like that; it grows on you.'

'I'm starting to understand why the Corsicans are so reluctant to share their island with outsiders...I mean, just look at it! No wonder they call it *l'Isle de Beauté.*'

As they stared out to sea, wondering what adventures might lie in store for them, they were unaware that hidden within its depths lay a secret which was about to tear their lives apart.

Le Bar des Chasseurs was quiet that morning. A handful of locals stood at the bar sipping strong espressos to shake off the last vestiges of sleep before reluctantly trudging off to work, while those who had less pressing concerns, sat around reading the morning papers while discussing betting prospects for the day's big races. Jean-Claude Santorini stood behind the serving counter, wiping away coffee stains with a grimy cloth and stacking empty cups into the sink. He was portly, thickly bearded and crowned with a mop of coarse black hair. Under his thick-set brow, his shifting brown eyes surveyed the clientele, with the same indifference as the wild boar, deer and mountain goat whose heads hung lifelessly from the yellowing walls.

Le Bar des Chasseurs was a bar for Corsicans, or more precisely, Corsican men, and Santorini went out of his way to ensure that it stayed that way. The few outsiders unfortunate enough to stumble across it by accident, were quickly made aware that their custom was tolerated rather than welcomed and invariably left after their first drink. There was no pleasure for Santorini in running the bar and the paltry profits which it generated barely justified the effort that he put into it. In fact the only reason why he continued to do so, was that it served as an effective front for a far more insidious and lucrative operation.

Santorini was a fervent supporter of the separatist cause and held a deep rooted hatred for the French beaurocrats who ran the island. He'd been a member of the armed political wing of the *Front de Libération Nationale de la Corse* since its formation in 1976 and over the years his dedication and allegiance to the FLNC had led him to become a trusted and powerful senior figure. The security services had long suspected his involvement in the organisation of high profile political assassinations and terrorist bombings, both in Corsica and on the mainland, but had never been able to bring a successful conviction against him. The Gendarmes had met with similar frustration in their attempts to link him to the murder of several local businessmen. Santorini's blatant lack of concern at the attempts of the authorities to bring him to justice led many people to believe that his political connections afforded him protection. It would perhaps have been no surprise for them to learn that apart from being an effective money laundering operation, *Le Bar des Chasseurs* served as a refuge for fellow separatists on the run and a place where arms and messages could be safely deposited and retrieved.

Over recent years, Santorini had become increasingly disenchanted with the FLNC however. Their acceptance of narrow political defeat following a referendum over the future status of the island had left him feeling angry and betrayed. Unable to accept that Corsica would remain under the control of parasitic French civil servants, he decided to set up a splinter group, *Libertà Corso*, whose small group of adherents continued to support the use of arms to obtain the island's independence. To fund it, Santorini diverted some of the 'revolutionary taxes' which he collected on behalf of the FLNC into his group's coffers. It was an action that would not go unnoticed for long and Santorini knew that it would only be a matter of time before he found himself isolated and stripped of his power and influence.

A thin, wiry man with thick curls of black hair and a handlebar moustache strolled into the bar.

'*Bunghjornu* Jean-Claude.'

'*Bunghjornu* Michel.'

'Whisky?'

'Why not? Have one yourself.'

'It's a bit early for me thanks. What's new?'

'Oh the usual,' said Michel pulling out a cigarette. 'I'm helping Pascal with some building work at the farm later in the week, but that's about all.'

'What's he having done?'

'He wants to extend the sheds. Get a few more cattle in.'

'A bit more funding from Brussels then?'

'Heh, you know the game Jean-Claude.'

'Only too well Michel, only too well.'

While the whisky was being served, Michel pulled a manilla envelope from his jacket pocket and casually dropped it onto the bar.

'Pichet finally paid up.'

'Did he now?' Santorini picked up the envelope and carefully counted the wad of 50 euro notes that he found inside it. He nodded and tossed a few bills to Michel.

'Well I suppose that saves us from having to burn his shop to the ground.'

'Shame. I was quite looking forward to it,' said Michel with a smirk.

The door chime sounded at that moment and Santorini quickly stashed the envelope beneath the counter.

'Relax; it's Pierre,' said Michel, swivelling in his seat.

A gaunt, shaven-headed man walked briskly towards the bar and gave firm handshakes to both men.

'*Bunghjornu* Pierre. It's a bit early for you isn't it?' asked Santorini, raising a quizzical eyebrow.

The man's small, furtive eyes quickly scanned the room before meeting Santorini's expectant stare.

'I need to speak with you Jean-Claude.'

'Go ahead.'

'I'd prefer to keep this private,' he insisted.

Santorini raised his eyebrows and breathed a grunt.

'Michel, watch the bar for me will you? We'll be in the back.' He invited

Pierre to follow him with a jerk of the head. 'And keep your thieving hands off the whisky.'

Michel smiled and adopted a contrived look of hurt as the two men disappeared into the kitchen area behind the bar.

When Santorini was alone with Pierre, he pulled an unlabelled bottle and two tumblers down from a shelf. He gestured to Pierre to sit at a rough wooden table while he filled each glass with a generous measure of a clear, potent spirit made from local myrtle. In draining it, they entered into an unspoken agreement that what they were about to discuss was to be held in absolute confidence.

'Now what can I do for you Pierre?' asked Santorini, as he refilled their glasses. The gaunt, dark skinned man paused to prepare his delivery.

'You remember that shifty German who came into the bar some time ago and asked us if we knew anything about a U-boat wreck in the area?'

'Ah, you mean the tall bloke who sweated like a pig. Yeah, I remember him.'

'That's the one. He offered us a considerable amount of money if we could locate it.'

'I'm aware of that,' said Santorini wondering where all this was leading, 'but we asked around and there was just some stupid story about a submarine going down in Roccapina during the war. No one believed it...and anyway, we did a few dives around the area and found nothing.'

'Yes, that must have been what - two years ago now?' asked Pierre.

'That sounds about right. Can we get to the point now?'

'I'm getting there,' said Pierre irritably. 'I got talking to someone I know in the bar the other day. He works down at the marina during the week, but in his spare time he makes a bit of money diving for red coral, you know the stuff they make jewellery out of.'

'Yes I know,' said Santorini, rolling his eyes and checking his watch.

'Like I was saying, he does a bit of diving for the stuff, but there's not so much of it around any more, so he has to go a bit deeper. Anyway, a couple of weeks ago he was diving out in front of Roccapina and he came across a strange piece of wreckage.'

'What was strange about it?'

'He thinks that it was some kind of panel or hatch; the type which you might find on a submarine. It still had the rubber seal around it and he says that he could see the sheared remains of the locking bolts.'

'Yeah, well that doesn't tell us very much,' scoffed Santorini. 'It probably fell off a ship. There must be hundreds of vessels which have passed through that way over the years.'

'Yes that's true; but this panel had German writing on it.'

Santorini looked up sharply.

'How does he know that it was German? Does he speak German?'

'No, but he memorised the first word - *vorschtic* or something like that and when he got home he checked it out. It *is* German and it means beware.' Santorini sighed and shook his head.

'It all sounds like a load of drunken talk to me.'

'Anyone else and I'd have agreed with you, but Jeannot is not the kind of person who makes things up just for the sake of it. In any case, I asked him if he could find it again and he said that he could.'

Santorini scratched his beard and stared contemplatively at the table.

'Do you trust this guy?' he asked, his eyes hardening, 'because if we start looking for this thing all over again and I find out that he's messing us around, he's going to seriously regret it.'

'I'm certain that he's telling the truth,' replied Pierre.

Santorini nodded, frowning.

'Well we might as well check it out. That German guy seemed pretty convinced that there was a wreck out there somewhere; and with the amount of money he was prepared to pay us, he must have believed that it was carrying something valuable. But before we start making any plans, I want to meet this friend of yours. Tell him that if he can keep his mouth shut, I'll pay him 100 euros to show us where he found the hatch.'

'OK, but I think it might also be worth considering bringing him in on the deal. After all, he knows the diving around here better than most and he's got a boat, a compressor and several sets of diving equipment.'

'You're right Pierre; he could prove to be very useful to us. Let's get him here first and after I've spoken to him we'll decide what's best. Drink up!'

The two men fixed each other as they raised their glasses in a toast.

'*Indipendenza!*'

Their business concluded, they returned to the bar to find Michel draining a large glass of cognac.

'It's not whisky!' he pointed out, with a mischievous grin.

The oxygen analyser showed 40.2% on the digital read-out. Thomas had requested a 40% blend but 1% either way was considered an acceptable safety margin when diving with oxygen enriched air, better known as nitrox. He was well aware that exposure to elevated levels of oxygen could be potentially fatal at depth, but his rebreather unit required a richer source of oxygen than the 21% that was naturally present in air. To ensure that he would not expose himself to the inherent risks of oxygen toxicity, he and Mike had planned their dive to a depth where the pressure would be unlikely to provoke its effects.

Mike watched Thomas connect the internal regulator to the nitrox cylinder within the rebreather unit and insert the chemical filter that would screen out his exhaled carbon dioxide. Once Thomas had calibrated the rebreather's settings to suit his personal breathing pattern and checked the pressure of the emergency air cylinder, he closed the cover and hauled the unit onto his shoulder.

'It's just as well that we're not in a hurry,' chided Mike.

'The best things come to those who wait,' replied Thomas.

'Not if they're waiting for you. Let's go find our boat.'

Thomas muttered under his breath as he followed Mike towards a fibreglass hulled diving boat that was moored up alongside the quay wall. The guide was already on board, loading cylinders into racks. He came over to introduce himself when he saw Mike and Thomas approaching.

'Hi, I'm Thierry - and you must be the two instructors. Is that right?'

'Yep that's us. I'm Thomas and he's Mike.' said Thomas, pointing with his chin.

'Welcome aboard,' said Thierry. 'I'll be your guide today.'

'Good, because we were told that you're a bit of a local expert.'

'Really? That's news to me,' said Thierry modestly.

'But you know all the names of the fish around here, right?'

'Well I know quite a few of them, yes.'

'Perhaps you'll be able to help us then; we're trying to find a seabass called Claude.'

Thierry put his face in his hands as Mike and Thomas began to laugh.

'Why do I always get the wise guys?' he groaned.

'It had to be done,' chuckled Thomas, 'where do you want this stuff?'

'You can strap the rebreather into the racks. The rest goes underneath the benches.'

'Thanks. And don't worry we're actually pretty easy to please,' said Mike. 'As long as we get to see the odd manta or whale shark, we'll be happy.'

'Hmmm, I hate to tell you this, but we don't actually have enough fuel to get to the Seychelles,' said Thierry, playing him along, 'I might be able to find you a nice grouper or two though.'

'Would that be one of those famous Corsican man-eating groupers?' asked Thomas.

'No, they all got taken by the giant squid I'm afraid,' laughed Thierry, 'but we do have some ordinary ones left.'

'Looks like we're going to have to settle for a nudibranch again then,' said Thomas, feigning disappointment.

'That, I can more or less guarantee.'

Thierry turned to see more clients approaching.

'OK guys, I'll leave you to sort yourselves out. Let me know if you need any help.'

'Sure thing.' Mike watched from the corner of his eye as Thierry welcomed another four divers and checked off their names against his crew-list. A young French couple boarded first and greeted Mike and Thomas with a smile and a polite '*Bonjour!*' They were followed by two pretty girls who spoke French with a very distinctive accent. Thomas sidled over towards Mike.

'French Canadians!' he said under his breath, while raising his eyebrows and breaking into a conspiratorial smile. Mike discreetly checked out their youthful curves.

'Nice country.'

When all the dive bags were neatly stowed away, Thierry gained everyone's attention and began to run through a routine introduction. The Skipper strolled up and climbed unhurriedly aboard, giving a brief nod and a wave to his passengers before busying himself with preparations for departure. Thierry concluded his general orientation and climbed onto the quayside, ready to slip the moorings. The boat's single diesel engine chugged into life with a smoky belch and soon they were on their way. Thomas quickly became engrossed in conversation with the French couple, entertaining them with outlandish diving stories accompanied by random bursts of wild gesticulations. Mike turned his regard towards the citadel and the sheer limestone cliffs which towered high above him on either side of the inlet. The glare of the white rock was dazzling and he slipped on a pair of shades and leaned back against the cylinder racks, listening absently to the voices around him, while enjoying the warmth of the morning sun on his face.

He stirred when he heard a voice nearby and opened his eyes to see one of the Canadian girls attempting to capture his attention. She was very pretty, with long dark hair, blue-green eyes and a deliciously curvaceous figure. Mike found himself staring dumbly at her before realising that she had just asked him a question.

'Sorry what was that?' he blurted before correcting himself and attempting the same phrase in French. *'Excusez-moi...que-est-ce-que...'*

'It's OK I speak English; we're French Canadian,' she said with a smile. 'I was just wondering what type of equipment that is which you're using.'

'You mean this?' asked Mike, pointing. 'It's a rebreather unit.'

'What's different about it?' she asked.

'Well, er...sorry, what was your name?'

'Marianne...and this is my friend Angela,' she said pointing to a blonde haired girl who was at that moment speaking to Thierry. Angela smiled and gave him a brief wave.

'Pleased to meet you. I'm Mike and that freak over there is Thomas,' he said with a jerk of the head. 'To answer your question, Marianne, when you use a rebreather, your exhaled air is recycled and rebreathed - hence the name. The most obvious difference is that it doesn't produce any bubbles...at least, not so many, and as a result you waste less gas than a standard open circuit system like the one you're using.'

'But how can you breathe the air again? Surely you have used up all the oxygen in it?'

'Only about four percent of it actually, but the supply gas in this system is not air; it's nitrox, which is air that has had oxygen added to it. If you did put air in the feed cylinder of a rebreather, the mixture in the counter-lung would rapidly become hypoxic.'

'That means less oxygen than air, right?' asked Marianne.

'Yes, I'm most impressed,' smiled Mike, 'but since we're using nitrox in this system, the oxygen which is lost during normal respiration can be replaced.'

Thomas looked up and noticed that Thierry was now speaking to the Captain. He took his cue to sit next to Angela and join in the conversation.

'The thing that most people are unaware of is that it is actually high levels of carbon dioxide which cause the feeling of suffocation and not low levels of oxygen.'

'My socks must be full of carbon dioxide then,' chuckled Thomas, to Marianne and Angela's amusement. Mike rolled his eyes and continued.

'To prevent this, the rebreather unit has a chemical filter in it which screens out your exhaled carbon dioxide. Of course, the disadvantage of the system is that it is possible to accidentally run out of gas and not be aware of it, because you would continue to breathe comfortably right up until the point where you passed out due to oxygen starvation.'

There were looks of alarm on the faces of the two girls.

'Of course, if you monitor your gas supply correctly, that should never happen.'

'It all sounds a bit complicated to me,' said Angela, frowning.

'Well, it's more complex than conventional SCUBA equipment, for sure, but it's not that difficult to use. I mean, this rig belongs to Thomas after all.'

The girls laughed as Thomas threatened Mike with one of his fins.

'So is it any different to dive with?' asked Marianne.

'It feels strange at first,' said Thomas, taking up the conversation. 'Once you've got used to the way that it affects your buoyancy, you start to notice that it's really quiet and because there are no bubbles, you can get much closer to the fish. It's fantastic for underwater photography and the best thing is that it makes you look really cool.'

'Or not, in your case,' countered Mike.

'It sounds like fun,' said Marianne 'do you think that we could have a go?'

'Unfortunately not,' replied Thomas, shaking his head, 'even if you are both very cute.'

The girls broke into shy smiles.

'The problem is that we are both instructors and for legal and safety reasons we'd have to give you some basic training and fill out a lot of paperwork first.'

'So you're both diving instructors then?' asked Angela impressed.

'Yes, isn't that obvious?' exclaimed Thomas with fake indignation.

'We are not worthy,' sniggered Marianne, bowing her head.

The boat's engines slowed at that moment and Thierry interrupted their conversation to inform them that they were about to arrive at the dive site. After gathering all his guests together at the stern of the boat, he began to run through a detailed dive briefing. Mike and Thomas listened attentively as he gave a general site orientation, spoke knowledgeably about the local flora and fauna and stated the parameters of the dive. After answering a couple of routine questions, Thierry concluded his briefing and invited everyone to start preparing their equipment.

Thomas busied himself with final checks on the rebreather, working from a check-list to ensure that nothing was overlooked. Mike casually pulled on his wetsuit while taking in the surrounding scenery.

The islands themselves were low-lying bare granite outcrops with a sparse covering of coarse vegetation. The extensive shallow waters which surrounded them were a stunning shade of turquoise that wouldn't have seemed out of place in more tropical latitudes. Peering over the side of the boat, Mike could clearly see a cluster of dome shaped boulders deep beneath him. In stark contrast to the barren rock above, the granite substrate below the water supported a richly diverse eco-system. A profusion of colourful algae, sponges and coral polyps covered every inch of the bare rock and in turn attracted a teeming variety of invertebrate and fish species. Mike watched dark scissor-tailed damselfish darting to and fro close to the surface, while a small school of silvery mullet idled by, their flanks intermittently flashing as they caught the sun. There was a small splash as one of the school rose to scoop a morsel from the surface and a brief skirmish ensued as black banded seabream were alerted to the promise of an easy meal.

Mike noticed that most of the divers were starting to run through their final checks and he quickly slipped on the rest of his equipment. A moment later, Thierry began to move everyone towards the stern of the boat, where a low platform extended outwards. Thierry entered the water first and was followed almost immediately by the French couple. The Canadian girls came next, leaving Mike and Thomas to take up the rear. They both inflated their integrated buoyancy jackets and pulled their masks over their heads before plunging feet first into the crystal clear water below. There was a brief glimpse of scattering fish and a patch of sand through the streams of bubbles before their buoyancy jackets brought them swiftly back to the surface. They emerged to find the rest of the group waiting patiently for them a short distance away. When they had joined the others, Thierry gave the signal to descend and there was an immediate chorus of hisses, as air was purged from bulging buoyancy jackets. Once beneath the surface, Mike immediately checked Thomas' rebreather for leaks and gave him the all clear with an OK sign. After consulting their instruments, they relaxed to enjoy the unique thrill of weightlessness as they glided effortlessly through the water, like astronauts floating in the silence of blue space.

While drifting over the huge, submerged granite boulders, Mike began to identify some of the more common Mediterranean fish species. Above and around them, the ever present black banded seabream turned and twisted incessantly, their silver flanks flashing as they darted about in their relentless battle to feed and avoid being fed on themselves. On the rocky substrate below, the bright blue and orange flanks of slender rainbow wrasse flashed by as they competed for scraps with dark, oval shaped damselfish. Tiny, intricately painted blennies poked their heads out from between fissures in the rock, their feathery tentacles giving them an appearance of alarm.

Mike and Thomas slowly distanced themselves from the group and began to encounter large areas of bright yellow coral polyps, like the trumpets of daffodils, contrasting sumptuously against the pervading blue. Multicoloured encrusting sponges and intricate, flower-like anemones competed for space with bright green algae, transparent hydroids and delicate red and orange sea fans. Further down they came across small caves and overhangs where red cardinals swam amongst the secretive lairs of spider crab and spiny lobster. Mike was soon totally engrossed with his surroundings, studying each unfamiliar organism with rapt fascination. He flipped onto his back beneath a cave entrance and was just studying the intricate structure of a bright yellow clathrina sponge, when he suddenly became aware that he was alone. With no immediate concern, he exited the cave and glanced upwards into the filtered rays of sunlight, trying to spot the telltale rise of Thomas' exhaled bubbles. He cursed when he reminded himself that Thomas was using a rebreather, which barely produced a trickle. Shaking his head, he turned to begin searching the surrounding area and froze when he suddenly spotted Thomas' limp body floating face down on the rocks just below him.

Monica Huber awoke to the sound of birds chattering in the plane trees outside her window. She squinted at her alarm clock; it was just before seven thirty in the morning. She gazed distractedly at the hairline cracks in the plaster ceiling above her bed and then let her eyes drift towards the window where sunlight was pushing its way around the heavy curtains. The room was large and comfortable in its rustic simplicity and although it was in need of some attention, Monica found no reason for complaint. In fact she considered herself lucky to have been there at all. She might just as easily have found herself stuck in a damp bog somewhere on one of the many isolated North European digs, living in a tent and wearing clothes which never seemed to fully dry out. Fortunately her expert knowledge of ancient Mediterranean civilisations sometimes reaped its rewards.

She lay back against the plump, white cotton pillows and focused her mind on the day's tasks. Her approach was always detailed and rigorous - some would have said to the point of obsession, but those qualities were part of the reason why, barely into her twenties, she had risen so quickly through the ranks to become Head Archaeological Field Researcher for the University of Zurich's Department of Prehistory.

Time is always an important factor in excavation work and good organisational skills make the difference between success and failure. Only rarely do archaeological research teams have the luxury of both unrestricted site access and unlimited funds to sustain their projects, and consequently researchers who have the ability to deliver results quickly and effectively under such conditions are very highly sought after. Monica had an outstanding track record in the field, but in truth she had few operational concerns for her current assignment; the research site was accessible all year round, her team had been provided with state of the art equipment, and as a result of joint research between the Archaeology Department in Zurich and the *Universita di Corsica Pasquale Paoli* in Corte, full financial backing was assured. This was not to say that Monica had been given an easy task. In fact the chances of her returning with any result at all were extremely remote. Her team were attempting to detect traces of a civilisation about which almost nothing was known in a part of the island where they had almost certainly never set foot.

Once Monica had the morning's tasks and objectives clearly fixed in her mind, she stretched, threw back the thin cotton bed sheets and slipped neatly out of bed. An oversize tee-shirt was lifted smoothly over her head to reveal a lithe figure beneath. She padded barefoot over the red terracotta tiled floor and into the adjoining bathroom. The water which spurted forth from the old-fashioned chrome bath shower was barely luke-warm, but pleasantly refreshing after the sticky heat of the warm summer evening. Monica let the jets pound against her scalp and gently massage the stiffness from her neck and shoulders. She reached for a bar of soap and lathered up her honey coloured skin, following a strict routine which started with her face and ended with her feet. When the last rivulets of soapy water had been rinsed from her shapely legs, she stepped out of the heavy iron bath tub and wrapped herself in a thick white towel. She hand dried and brushed her wavy, shoulder length, ash-blonde hair, pulling it neatly back with her fingers before tying it in place with a hair band. In the bathroom mirror, she noticed that the pale blue of her eyes had begun to intensify as her skin darkened under the influence of the Mediterranean sun. Light freckles were beginning to appear on her sleek nose and the upper part of her high cheek bones. Her lips curled into an indulgent smile; taking unaccustomed pleasure from the subtle transformation. She pulled her eyes away from the distractions of the mirror and returned to the bedroom where she discarded the towel and slipped into a bathing costume. After pulling on a pair of well worn Khaki shorts and an old white polo-necked shirt, she went in search of her colleagues. The smell of fresh coffee led her to the kitchen.

'Morning Bertie. Morning Anna.'

'Morning Monica,' replied her two colleagues.

'Did you sleep well?' asked Anna, her delicate fingers separating thin slices of emmental cheese.

'I slept very well thanks.'

'Good. There's coffee in the jug if you want it and fresh croissants too.'

'Sounds perfect. Is Hubert up?'

'He's...on his way,' replied Bertie hesitantly. 'I'm afraid that he'll probably be a bit fragile this morning. He went to the local bar last night and got back late.'

'Oh great! That's all we need.'

'I did try to warn him,' said Bertie, raising his dark eyebrows, 'but you know how he is.'

'Hmm, well could you go and hurry him along please?' she asked, wrinkling her nose in annoyance.

'I'll do my best,' said Bertie leaving the room.

'He'll be the death of me, that one,' said Monica as she poured herself coffee. 'How are things going between you and Bertie?'

'Oh...everything's fine between us.'

'It didn't seem like that yesterday.'

'No, we had a little disagreement, but we've cleared the air since then.'

'I'm glad to hear that, because I could really do without any more uncomfortable situations during this trip.'

'Yes, I'm really sorry Monica - we both are. It won't happen again, I promise you.'

'I hope so Anna. You know my position on this. If it does become a problem, I'll have to reconsider allowing you both to work with me in future.'

'Yes, I understand that. I think we both do.'

'OK, we'll leave it at that then.'

Monica looked up as Bertie returned to the kitchen accompanied by a tall blonde haired man with glazed eyes and a very sheepish expression on his face.

'Morning,' he grunted, shielding his eyes from the light.

'Are you going to be of any use to us today Hubert?' asked Monica scornfully.

'Yeah, of course; I just need a glass of water...and maybe some coffee.'

'And a doctor by the look of it,' said Anna, while pouring a glass of water for him. 'I don't suppose you'll be wanting any breakfast then?'

'No thanks. Maybe just some Paracetamol.' Anna pushed her thin blonde hair behind her ears and raised her eyebrows as she handed him a glass of water.

'I'll have a look in the first aid kit.'

'Thanks Anna,' said Hubert, before forcing himself to drink the water.

Bertie patted Hubert on the shoulder and chuckled.

'Was it a good night at least?'

'Hmm, it's all a bit vague really, but I do remember being forced to drink some evil, local concoction.' He winced and went pale at the thought of it. Anna handed him two white tablets and he waited for the nausea to subside before swallowing them.

'Right can we run through our preparations now?' asked Monica, eager to get things back on track. Bertie and Hubert nodded as Anna joined Monica at the table.

'OK. Hubert, is the boat fuelled and ready to go?'

'Yes, I did it yesterday evening.'

'Good, do we have enough water on board?'

'There should be, but we ought to get more,' said Anna.

'OK, we'll pick up stores from the supermarket on the way. Bertie did you check all the cylinders?'

'Yes, they're fine. I've checked all the equipment against the inventory. We're ready to start loading the truck.'

'Good, Hubert can help you, but leave his kit behind; he won't be needing it today.'

Hubert looked up sharply.

'But I'm fine,' he protested.

'You're not,' countered Monica sternly. 'Alcohol, dehydration and fatigue are contributory factors to decompression sickness as you well know, and I'm not prepared to take the risk even if *you* are. If you're not happy with that, then next time you'll think twice about getting drunk. You'll be doing surface support today.' Hubert scowled.

'Right. Anna, can you double check that we have the extra quadratic grid poles, data cards, labels, log books and sample containers before we load.'

'Yes I'll see to that right now.'

'Thank you. Bertie, has the computer data been transferred?'

'Yes, of course.'

'Excellent. And where will we be working today?'

'Sector 445R,' replied Bertie. 'There are two potential sites that came up on the sounding profile which I looked at last night. If they both turn out to be false leads then we'll continue excavating the amphorae on 443R and then in the afternoon, we'll begin surveying 446R.'

'OK, that all sounds in order,' said Monica, running her eyes down her checklist. 'I think that's everything covered. Is there anything that I've missed?'

There was a pause before Bertie spoke.

'Carabiners.'

'Yes of course; we were running short weren't we? Where can we get those from?'

'They sell them at the chandlers,' said Hubert, groggily. 'With any luck they might even be open.'

'Hmm, they do seem to be a bit relaxed with their trading hours don't they? We'll just have to take our chances - anything else?'

There was silence as Monica and her team wracked their brains. All of them had at some point experienced the frustration and embarrassment of overlooking a vital piece of field equipment and suffered the inevitable arguments and recriminations which followed. Detailed logging solved most of the problems, but by no means all. Academics were notorious for remembering that one vital piece of high-tech equipment while forgetting about food, weather protection, fuel and even each other. Monica sometimes felt that her role was more that of a surrogate mother than a Field Manager.

'Well, if you're happy that we've covered everything, then I suggest that we make a move.'

'Where exactly are we working today?' asked Hubert, rubbing the tiredness from his eyes.

'445R,' replied Monica. 'The southern bay of Roccapina.'

Five men sat around a dark wooden table in the *Bar des Chasseurs*. It was past midnight and Santorini had unceremoniously turfed out his regular customers, locked the front door and lowered the steel shutters three quarters of the way down to the pavement. The men helped themselves to olives, *brocchia* goat's cheese and thin slices of *salamu* sausage from white enamel serving plates that had been placed in the centre of the table. Two unlabelled bottles of illegally distilled spirit were eagerly passed around and glasses were filled with the fiery yellow liquid. Santorini raised a toast to the future independence of the island and prompted the gathering to drain their glasses dry. Once empty, they were slammed down on the table in a show of unerring conviction, the men's faces struggling to remain impassive as the powerful concoction burned their gullets. Cheered by their bravado as much as the alcohol, they laughed and joked, their camaraderie adding to the eager sense of antic- ipation which surrounded the unusual meeting.

The small weather-beaten man who sat to Santorini's left was the only one who did not share in the atmosphere of conviviality. Jeannot would have much preferred to be in the comfort of his own home at that particular moment, and he almost certainly would have been, if three days past, he had not been in a bar by the port, drunkenly bragging to a person he barely knew, that he'd stumbled across part of a German submarine. If he'd been fully aware of Pierre's connections at the time, he may have had the foresight to hold his tongue. But as it was, he'd woken the following day with a nasty hangover, empty pockets and an obligatory summons to meet with a notorious criminal leader.

As he sat there, nervously stroking his long silver moustache, Jeannot was painfully aware that the 100 euros which were now resting heavily in his breast pocket represented the compulsory purchase of his services. He looked up gloomily as Santorini called the table to order.

'Now you all know why we're here tonight,' began Santorini. 'First of all let me remind you that what is said in this room stays in this room. Is that understood?'

There were murmurs and nods of approval.

'Good, now as you know our friend Jeannot here has been doing a spot of diving off Roccapina and has found a piece of wreckage which might have come from the U-boat that we were searching for a few years ago. Now I've had a little word with Jeannot here and he thinks that he can lead us to the place where he saw this object; a hatch of some sort. We'll arrange to go and take a look at it, and if we're all agreed that it's what we think it is, we'll begin making a search of the surrounding area. Naturally, Jeannot has given me his word of honour that he won't go blabbing about his discovery to anyone else.'

The men smiled at Jeannot, whose face remained decidedly glum.

'Now Jeannot found the wreckage in slightly deeper water than we had anticipated, so it's hardly surprising that we didn't find anything the first time. It's lying at a depth of approximately 45 metres, so what I need to know now, is if diving to that depth raises any concerns?' Santorini scrutinised each face in turn. There was some shifting of feet and one or two exchanged glances, but nobody spoke up.

'Good. Our next issue is equipment; who doesn't have any?'

Michel and Pascal raised their hands.

'I've got one spare set,' said Santorini, 'but I doubt if the wetsuit will fit either of you.'

'Maybe we could both fit into it,' sniggered Michel.

His smile faded when met with the silence of Santorini's glare.

'Don't push your luck Michel.'

'I've got one or two bits of spare equipment and old wetsuits that will probably fit them both,' offered Jeannot. 'I've a couple of cylinders too, which might...'

His voice trailed off when he realised his error.

'Ah, I can see that you are going to be extremely useful to us Jeannot,' said Santorini, smiling. Jeannot bit his lip, cursing his big mouth.

'Well it looks like we'll be able to make a start this weekend then,' said Santorini. 'We'll meet at the port on Saturday morning at 8am sharp. Jeannot, bring along all your spare equipment. You might as well leave it on board, because if all goes to plan we'll be doing this over the next few weekends.'

Jeannot looked up in consternation.

'But I can't do this every weekend,' he said, struggling like a doomed insect caught in a web, 'I have my business to think of.'

Santorini smiled and put a hand on his shoulder in mock consolation.

'Ah business! But of course! We are both businessmen and we know that nothing is gained without risk. Rest assured that if we find what we are looking for, we'll have more than enough money to fund our needs and I dare say a little left over to buy you a new boat...and who knows? Maybe even enough to buy you a nice little jewellery shop, where you can sell your red coral trinkets to those wonderful Parisien *Pinzuti* who invade us during the summer months.'

Santorini's men laughed heartily at Jeannot's expense - but they were unwise to do so. Jeannot was a man who knew when to pick his moment.

Spurred into action, Mike powered his way through the water towards Thomas' prostrate body. He grabbed his arm and wrenched him face upwards to check for signs of breathing. There were none. He pumped air into the rebreather's integrated buoyancy jacket and was preparing to lift him to the surface when Thomas' eyes suddenly sprang open. Mike noticed the amused glint in them before he registered the unmistakable sound of laughing in the breathing loop. Swearing loudly into his regulator, Mike punched Thomas hard on the thigh and pushed him away in annoyance. It was a foolish prank, and one that could easily have backfired on him. He watched in irritation as Thomas executed a dance of childish glee. Shaking his head reproachfully, Mike turned and swam slowly away.

Once he had calmed himself, Mike returned his attention to the study of the surrounding microcosm. A pair of silvery grey flanked sea bass swam swiftly by, forging a winding path between rocks which served as refuge for cardinals and ornate blennies. Painted comber, stood guard over their precious lairs, staring up in suspicion as the clumsy looking invaders passed above them.

The metallic ring of a diving knife gently tapping a cylinder attracted Mike's attention and he turned to see Thomas hovering next to a crevice in the rocks, pointing towards two large conger eels which had taken up residence there. Their slender bodies swayed gently backwards and forwards in the swell, as if they were dancing to the tune of a snake charmer's flute. Thomas drew a figure of eight with his finger in front of their jaws and watched them follow it in coordinated movement. Mike was unsure whether their synchronised dance was motivated more by curiosity or trepidation, but there was certainly no sign of aggression. Thomas left them in peace and followed Mike through a narrow passage between a series of huge boulders. Mike pointed out a well camouflaged red scorpion fish, perched motionless on a rock ledge, waiting patiently for small prey to stray within range of its lightening fast jaws. As Mike watched fledgling damsels pass unwittingly within inches of their lives, he thought about how precarious an existence it must be for small fish in such a predator rich environment. He was aware that the chances of juveniles surviving long enough to reach full reproductive maturity were sometimes as remote as a million to one. And when those odds were further reduced by the effects of pollution and over fishing, it was hardly surprising to Mike that the populations of many Mediterranean species were under threat. Fortunately, Corsican waters seemed to have escaped relatively unharmed and he was pleased to note that the authorities seemed intent on keeping it that way.

Thomas had explained to Mike that the Lavezzi Islands were famous for the abundance of dusky grouper which had taken up residence there. Mike already knew that they could live for as long as 40 years and reach nearly two metres in length if left undisturbed, and yet their prized flesh had almost been the cause of their disappearance from the Mediterranean in the 1980's. Ever since his arrival in Corsica, Mike had been looking forward to seeing these gentle giants, and he was understandably delighted when he and Thomas finally caught up with Thierry and the rest of the group and found them observing a sizeable pair of dusky grouper inside the entrance to a small cave. As Mike watched them hovering almost motionless, making precise alterations of position with graceful movements of their pectoral fins, he felt satisfied in the knowledge that the old brown and white flanked, thick-lipped male, who'd actually started out life as a female, would probably spend the rest of his natural life reproducing under the protection of the *Réserve Naturelle des Bouches de Bonifacio*.

Thierry pointed out several more grouper during the latter part of the dive and it was with a certain amount of reluctance that Mike and Thomas had to finally leave them to their fragile underwater world and return to their own when Thierry signalled the end of the dive. A lush, red and green seaweed covered incline led them up to the shallows, where they spent the last few minutes searching for small invertebrates amongst algae covered rocks. Thierry attracted Mike and Thomas' attention and much to their delight pointed out two 9cm long purple glossodoris nudibranch clinging to an encrusting sponge. Unlike their dull counterparts on land, these hermaphroditic sea-slugs sport bright, lurid colours and bizarre shapes, reflecting the rich diversity of their environment. Mike often thought that they looked good enough to eat, but he was well aware that, like the poison arrow frogs of South America, their bright pigments in fact served as a dire warning of the lethal, defensive toxins stored within their skin.

Thomas showed his appreciation by shaking hands with Thierry, before turning to give Mike an underwater high five. To end the dive in style, Mike and Thomas removed their fins, deflated their buoyancy jackets and returned to the boat by moon-walking along the rocky sea floor. They arrived to find Thierry waiting for them beside the ascent line, laughing silently into his regulator to form an appreciative cloud of bubbles.

The journey back to the dive centre was a relaxed affair. Thierry pulled a plate of freshly cut melon from the ice-box and offered it around while his guests compared notes and chatted animatedly in the glare of a late afternoon sun. Mike and Thomas stripped down their equipment as the boat advanced across a gently swaying blanket of blue towards the contrasting white cliffs of Bonifacio.

'Don't forget that we need to pick up the hire boat when we get back to port,' said Mike.

'Maybe we should leave it until tomorrow,' replied Thomas.

'What's the point? The weather might not be so good tomorrow.'

'Well I was thinking...actually no, you go ahead.' There was a glint in Thomas' eye as he turned towards Marianne and Angela, who were working on their tans nearby. 'Hey girls, do you fancy going for a beer when we get back to Bonifacio?'

'Sure, why not?' replied Angela. Marianne shrugged and nodded in agreement.

Thomas turned towards Mike with a triumphant smile on his face.

'It's a shame you won't be able to join us Mike. I guess I'll be seeing you later at the villa then?'

Mike was left open-mouthed at Thomas' cheek, but he was not to be outdone.

'Marianne, Angela, I think that we can do far better than that. How would you like to come to a barbecue tonight at our exclusive hillside villa, from where you can admire the panoramic views over the bay while enjoying a glass of chilled wine? I'm sure that Thomas here will be happy to pick you up and return you to your place of residence, and being of a generous nature, he'll undoubtedly provide all the food and drink too.'

Marianne and Angela swapped amused smiles as Thomas' face dropped.

'Well how could we refuse such a courteous and generous offer Thomas,' grinned Marianne. 'Thank you very much.'

'It's *his* pleasure,' Thomas replied testily.

'And don't forget to carry their bags Thomas, there's a good chap.'

Thomas raised his index finger and accompanied it with a sardonic smile.

Shortly afterwards, the boat arrived back at the quayside and Thierry's guests thanked him for a great day out before stepping ashore and going their separate ways. Thomas directed Marianne and Angela towards the terrace of a nearby café while he finished rinsing the equipment. Mike took the opportunity to slip away and find a boat for charter. A quarter of an hour later he pulled up next to the quayside and yelled to Thomas from the helm of a bright orange semi-rigid inflatable boat with a single 75hp outboard.

'Hey Thomas, check out the beast.'

'Nice one,' said Thomas, admiring the sturdy little RIB.

'I'm going to head off right away,' shouted Mike. 'I'll call you on the mobile when I arrive so you can come and pick me up. Make sure you have your mobile with you.'

'Yeah, no problem. I'll see you in a couple of hours,' replied Thomas, and then with a sly grin added, 'if the girls will let me out of their hotel room that is.'

'In your dreams,' snorted Mike. 'Catch you later.'

Mike turned the boat around and slowly motored through the pontoons and out into the main channel. Once free of the harbour limits, he opened up the throttle and powered the RIB towards the gap between the two towering vertical cliffs which form Bonifacio's dramatic sea exit. He had read in his guidebook, that the unique double capes at the entrance to the inlet were widely believed to be the same ones described by Homer, from where Ulysses' fleet was bombarded and destroyed by rocks thrown by the native Lestrygonians. Although the Lestrygonians were fictional, Mike was surprised to learn that images found on coins on the island of Ithaca, where his kingdom was thought to be seated, suggest that Ulysses was not. As he stared up at the towering natural gateway, Mike was thrilled to think that he might be retracing the same route taken by the great Achaean hero some 3000 years previously.

Emerging into the *Bouches de Bonifacio*, he headed west towards the tip of *Capo di Feno* and then crossed the *Golfe de Ventilegne* following the rugged coastline to the north. The gently rolling sea made for near perfect conditions and Mike increased his speed to 25 knots, holding a direct course towards the *Anse de Roccapina*. The views of the fractured coastline to the north were magnificent and the lowering sun helped him to pick out his next point of reference well in advance. Mike knew from studying his chart that the *Tour d'Olmeto* was the last Genoese watchtower on the coast before Roccapina and when it finally fell behind him, he blew a sigh of relief.

Now in buoyant mood, he glanced seaward and spotted a grey hump and a dorsal fin breaking the surface a short distance away to port. Encouraged by the fact that he was now on the last leg of his journey, he slowed and veered away to find out what creatures might be accompanying him on his passage. As he approached Mike saw more dorsal fins breaking the surface and soon realised that he was amongst a pod of bottlenose dolphins. A large female with her yearling calf dipped below the surface and swam diagonally through the water towards him. Ribbons of light danced over their sleek bodies as they rose up effortlessly to position themselves on either side of the bow. Another adult appeared, almost as big as the RIB and then a fourth which vied for position and then veered off again when it could find no space. Mike gently increased the throttle and watched the three cetaceans rise and fall, swapping places with astonishing ease, always a march ahead of the bow. He had seen the spectacle many times before, but he never tired of observing the grace and agility with which they moved. He leaned over the bow and saw one of the adults flip onto its side, eyeing him with bold curiosity. It was hard to imagine what their enduring fascination with humans was. It seemed to Mike almost as if they felt duty bound to cheer us up; to show us that life is for having fun. If only we treated them with the same courtesy, he thought, wistfully. He watched in awe as first one and then all three of the enigmatic creatures suddenly veered off like fighter jets peeling away from the pack. Their gently undulating bodies reappeared in the wake of the boat and reverted to a more leisurely cruising pace. Mike respectfully left them to their peace and continued his journey.

Before long he could see the main road snaking along the coast to his right, and up ahead, the watchtower, perched on top of the promontory which separated the twin bays of Roccapina. He passed the point of the headland to the south and eased off the throttle as he entered the smaller and more protected of the two bays. By now it was early evening and several of the moorings had become available. Mike chose one that was close to shore, secured the boat to it and cut the engine. The smell of salt air, pine and wild rosemary filled his nostrils and the shrill cry of thousands of cicadas sizzled in his ears. Mike took his mobile phone out of the boat's dry box and keyed in Thomas' number.

'Yeah?'

'It's me, where are you?'

'Um...I'm still in the bar. Where are you?'

'In Roccapina, waiting to be picked up.'

'Damn, that was quick. It'll take me at least half an hour to get there and...hang on a second.' Mike heard a mumbled conversation in the background.

'Listen Mike, the girls need to go back to their place for about fifteen minutes. Can we pick you up in say 45 minutes?' There was an audible sigh.

'Do I have a choice? Look, just sort the girls out, grab some stuff for the barbecue and meet me at the junction on the main road as soon as you can get there. I'll walk up the track to save you coming down. Do you think that you can handle that responsibility?'

'It's a big ask, but I'll do my best. See you at.....say six thirty?'

'OK, but don't mess around. I don't want to be hanging around all evening.'

'I'm already gone - see you *tout de suite*.'

Mike sighed as he opened the seal of his dry-bag and placed his mobile phone, keys and wallet inside. He added the Tee-shirt that he was wearing and then swung his legs over the inflated sponson and lowered himself gently into the water. It was pleasantly warm and Mike relaxed as he kicked out at a leisurely pace towards the shore, the dry-bag trailing in the water behind him. Soon he was walking waist high in the shallows, watching small swimming crabs scuttling out of the way while tiny shoals of fry darted around close to the surface. At this hour the beach was beginning to empty and Mike followed the retreating day-visitors towards a gap in the juniper bushes which gave access to the car park and the exit route beyond. He recovered his Tee-shirt from the dry-bag and set off walking up the winding track which led to the main road. It was a strenuous uphill climb, but it gave Mike the opportunity to appreciate the rich diversity of the *Maquis* bushland growing profusely on either side of the track. Towards the end, the dryness of the air and the lingering warmth of the sun began to take its toll. With no water to slake his thirst, he was greatly relieved when the junction at the top of the hill finally came into view. By now the sun had dropped towards the horizon and Mike turned to see soft pinkish hues highlighting the exposed rock faces of the distant headlands. He reached the main road, seated himself on a flat boulder and admired the view while he recovered from the long hike. Ten minutes later his peace was interrupted when the sound of tyres braking over loose gravel announced Thomas' arrival. Marianne and Angela, seated in the rear of the Peugeot, squealed like teenagers, much to Thomas' satisfaction. Mike jumped into the front seat and was met by the screaming wail of an electric guitar solo, blasting from the speakers of the CD player. He reached over to turn the volume down.

'What's the matter? I thought you liked rock music,' said Thomas as he turned the car around.

'I like being able to hear more.'

Marianne and Angela giggled in the rear seats.

'I take it you were in the bar for a while then?' said Mike, raising an eyebrow.

Thomas smirked and shrugged his shoulders.

'How was your boat trip?' asked Marianne.

'Excellent thanks; at one point I was even escorted by dolphins.'

'Oh, how cool!' cried the girls.

'I've never seen a wild dolphin before,' said Angela. 'I didn't even know they could be found here.'

'Oh they're around all right,' said Mike. 'There should be more of them actually, but pollution and over-fishing have forced many of them away.'

'That's a real shame,' sighed Marianne.

'It is, and dolphins are not the only victims. Illegal drift nets and floating refuse have had catastrophic effects on the Mediterranean sea turtle, and monk seal populations are rapidly depleting as well.'

Thomas rolled his eyes.

'Jeez, you really know how to get a party going don't you?'

'You're right. Sorry to bore you all, but it's a subject which I feel strongly about. Is there anything to drink back there?'

'There's no need to apologise,' said Marianne, as she passed Mike a cold beer. 'We Canadians are very conscious about the environment.'

'I'm glad to hear it. Here's to the wonderful people of Canada then,' he said, raising the bottle in a show of solidarity before slaking his thirst.

Shortly afterwards Thomas slowed and turned right onto the steep access track which wound its way down to the villa. The Peugeot came to a sliding halt on the loose chippings of the drive and the girls immediately leapt out of the car and ran to the terrace to admire the aftermath of a glowing red sunset. Mike flipped on the outside lights and pulled an old rusting barbecue out from the store. Thomas volunteered to find a CD to play but was censored by the girls, who wisely placed a beer in his hand and banished him to a nearby seat. Soon pulsating Salsa rhythms were drifting out of a portable CD player while Angela and Marianne rustled up a salad and Mike prodded at a selection of spicy sausages and marinated lamb kebabs that were sizzling on the barbecue.

Before long they were seated around the terrace table, laughing and joking as they tucked into the mounds of food which were laid out in front of them. Thomas' exuberance increased in direct proportion to the amount of empty beer bottles which accumulated at the end of the table coupled with the roars of encouragement from his captive audience. Even so, after an attempt to scale the legendary east face of mount villa, eat a kebab with the wooden skewer still in it and snort a diving mask clear of beer, even Thomas' boundless energy seemed to desert him. As the evening began to wind down, Mike found himself sitting opposite Marianne in a hammock, swapping travel stories with her while stroking the back of her calves with his toes. After a lull in the conversation she asked him if he was single.

'Well, that's a bit of a sore point actually,' said Mike regretfully. 'You see I was engaged to this girl - a very smart and attractive girl, but unfortunately a week after I proposed to her, she was involved in a serious car crash. It was a very difficult time, and to be honest I've never really got over it.'

'Really? That's awful. So was she...I guess she was killed, right?'

'What? No she was absolutely fine, but after what she did to my car I ditched the stupid cow.'

Marianne tried unsuccessfully to stifle her laughter.

'Come here you idiot.'

She wrapped her arms around his waist and pressed her lips against his. As their tongues intertwined, she reached her hands beneath his tee-shirt and lightly raked his muscular shoulders with her nails. Mike discreetly opened an eye, cast a glance in Thomas' direction and smiled when he saw that he and Angela were locked in an equally passionate embrace. At that particular moment in time, he was having great difficulty deciding whether he preferred Corsica or Canada.

'Well that was a complete waste of time,' said Santorini, angrily throwing his fins into the boat. Are you sure that you didn't just dream that you found this piece of wreckage?'

'I don't use floats to mark where I've been,' said Jeannot, smarting. 'I take a reference from the shore to get a rough fix on my position. Believe me, it's around here somewhere, but I can't be certain where. I didn't expect to be coming back here after all.'

The remainder of Santorini's men began to climb onto the deck of the *Sampiero Corso*, their faces grim with disappointment.

'I can't believe how much air I've used,' complained Pierre, 'I was only down there a few minutes.'

'These damned wrist computers don't give you much time anyway,' said Pascal. 'And where did you get to Michel?'

'I could ask you the same question. I turned around and found myself on my own down there.'

'Look, we aren't diving in the shallows here,' pointed out Jeannot. 'If you aren't careful about what you're doing down there, you'll all get yourselves killed.'

The men stared at Jeannot in surprise.

'I don't know how much you all know about diving,' continued Jeannot, 'not a great deal from what I've just witnessed and at these depths you can't afford to be negligent. You're getting through your air more quickly because it's being compressed by the weight of the water above you, so obviously the deeper you go, the faster you'll use it up. Also, as you descend, the nitrogen in the air that you're breathing is starting to react with your bodies. For one thing, your judgement and coordination will start to become impaired, due to the effects of nitrogen narcosis, but more importantly, the rate at which the nitrogen is being absorbed into your body increases exponentially as you descend and your dive time decreases as a result. Your computer is actually telling you how long you have left before your tissues reach saturation point, and if you go beyond that limit and ascend too quickly or miss a decompression stop, for whatever reason, that excess nitrogen can come out of solution and give you the bends. Believe me, I've seen people suffering from severe decompression sickness and I wouldn't wish it on anyone. The pain can become so severe that all you can do is curl up into a ball and pray that either the helicopter or death comes swiftly.'

Nervous glances were exchanged.

'Yeah, well we know all that,' said Santorini, dismissively, 'but what I want to know is whether we're wasting our time down there as well as risking our necks.'

'You'll waste far more time if you don't do things properly.'

'OK, so why don't you tell us how we should be doing things, *in your opinion.*'

'I think I've already established that at these depths there's no time for us to play around; we need to be disciplined and organised. At 45 meters there will be mandatory decompression stops for any dive which lasts longer than 8 minutes. If we stay down for the full 8 minutes, we'll get 4 minutes to search each way and enough air left to complete a precautionary stop before surfacing. To be certain of that we'll apply the rule of thirds. As soon as you have used up a third of your total air supply you should return to the anchor line, regardless of the time, so that you will have at least a third left in reserve when you begin your ascent. And remember, if you do run out of air down there, you've only got your fellow divers to turn to, so don't ever lose sight of them. As for the search technique – it's pointless all going off in random directions; we need a system. We've got five people on board, so we should divide into two groups of two with one person remaining on the surface. One of the groups could search to the north of the anchor while the other goes south. If we do two minutes out and back, that will leave us enough time to search east and west before ascending and moving on. That's just my advice, but if you want to do it your own way, that's entirely up to you.'

'There is some logic in what you say Jeannot, I have to agree,' said Santorini after some thought. 'Do you have a compass with you?'

'Yes of course.'

'OK, then let's put your theory to the test. You and Pascal can make up one team and me and Michel will make up the other. Pierre, you can sit this one out. I think that we should be aiming to do at least four dives per day with two hours between dives, is that possible?'

'Yes, I'll have to check, but I think so.'

'Good,' said Santorini. 'We'll jump again in two hours time.'

'Excellent. So that leaves us plenty of time to do a bit of fishing in the national park,' said Michel, beaming.

There was laughter and agreement until Santorini called for quiet.

'So Jeannot, you know what is expected of you. You have three weeks to find your hatch and after that my patience will be at an end.'

The small port of Tizzano was a perfect base for their operations. It was a beautiful backwater port in an isolated cove, like a tiny jewel set amongst a coast studded with far bigger and better known attractions. Its small white sandy beach was overlooked by the ruins of an ancient fort which added to the feeling of remote timelessness. A long finger of land shielded the narrow inlet from the ravages of the westerly swell and made it a perfect little hideaway for the few elegant yachts and motor boats which swayed gently on their moorings in its calm limpid waters.

Hubert reversed the white Toyota half-truck along the small jetty and came to a halt beside the 8 metre twin outboard RIB which served as the teams support vessel. He jumped down from the cab and stepped carefully aboard to run through his pre-start checks while Monica, Bertie and Anna began to unload the equipment. When Hubert gave his nod of approval, Bertie passed the air cylinders to him so that he could secure them in their upright retainers around the central console. Next came the cumbersome nylon cables, used to divide the sea floor into grid sections for recording and referencing purposes. Hubert stowed them along the side decks and wedged them in place beneath the sponsons. The underwater cameras, analysers and laptop followed and were carefully placed in the dry holds under the helm and central console. Next, trays of digging and measuring equipment were stowed in the stern along with a small water suctorial device, used for shifting heavy silt and sand. Finally, heavy crates of diving equipment were placed on the deck and wooden planks laid across them to form makeshift seats.

Once the truck had been emptied, Hubert drove it back along the jetty and parked it along the side of the road. He returned to take up position at the helm, glanced at his instruments and fired up each outboard in turn. As they spluttered into life, Bertie plugged his laptop into the console and activated the differential GPS receiver to check its reported position against the Aeronautical Information System overlay on the screen. When a red triangle appeared in the expected position on his digitalised chart, Bertie gave the thumbs up and Monica and Anna cast off the RIB's lines and pushed the bow away from the quay. Hubert engaged the throttle, bringing the yellow and black RIB around the jetty and out into the main channel. As they progressed towards the exit, under the warmth of the morning sun, they were blissfully unaware of the terrifying events which lay in wait for them.

Mike was first aware of a sticky dry palate and a dull ache around his temples. There was a banging sound coming from somewhere on the edge of his consciousness, which seemed to penetrate his skull and send dull echoes careering around inside it. A muffled voice in the background irritated him, its insistence denying his overwhelming desire to shut out the world.

'Marianne!' the voice was calling, in between repetitive bouts of knocking.

Marianne? Who was she?

In the primitive backwaters of Mike's cortex, synapses began to communicate with one another and a faint memory began to pierce through the foggy void. With his eyes closed shut, he stretched out an exploratory right hand and felt the comforting warmth of soft flesh beside him. A smile crept across his face as he rolled over, wrapping his left arm around Marianne's waist and pulling her firmly towards him. He pressed his face against her neck and breathed in the invigorating perfume of her hair and skin. The insistent voice was there again, coming from the direction of the door. It had to be Angela, he realised. With a huge effort of concentration, he finally translated his thoughts into words.

'I think that's Angela at the door,' he mumbled, his lips brushing against Marianne's ear.

'Wha-what? Oh, uh...yes.' Marianne groaned, shielding the light from her eyes with the back of her hand.

'Just a minute,' she shouted.

Mike recoiled, burying his face in the pillow with a grunt.

'What time is it?' she asked, pushing herself to a seating position while fending off Mike's clutches.

Mike patted the bedside table until his fingers closed around his watch. He brought it to his face and stared at it in bewilderment.

'For God's sake; it's only eight thirty!' he groaned.

'Marianne! Come on we have to go,' called Angela's voice through the door.

Mike watched Marianne's full breasts swing as she slipped out of bed and walked naked towards the door. He felt a rekindling of desire, wanting to bury himself in the firm softness of her flesh, but his arousal was doused, when he suddenly registered what Angela had said.

Go? Go where?

The two girls spoke hurriedly through a gap in the door. Marianne returned and began to get dressed.

'What's happening? Where are you going?'

'I'm sorry Mike, but something's come up. Angela got a text from her boyfriend late last night. He's flying into Marseille this evening and we have to go and meet him.'

'What? But...surely you both don't have to go?' he protested.

'Yes we do,' she replied pointedly. 'I'm sorry Mike, but Angela is my best friend and friends look out for each other. She's had a tough time recently and she needs my support.' Mike sighed resignedly.

'Will you be coming back here?'

'I very much doubt it,' said Marianne, frowning. 'We're flying to Canada from Paris in a week.'

Mike nodded his head in resignation. It was a disappointment, certainly, but he wasn't going to dwell on it. Years of working within the tourism industry had taught him to become thick skinned.

'I expect that you'll need a ride back to your hotel then?'

'We can take a taxi if you'd prefer,' said Marianne, now fully dressed.

'No, there's no need, I'll take you both back. It's the least I can do.'

'That's very kind. You really are a nice guy,' smiled Marianne, 'I have to do this for Angela, you understand. If we'd met a little earlier things might have been different.'

Mike shrugged and inclined his head. His regrets were more physical in nature, but he wisely decided to keep that knowledge to himself.

'It's not a problem; you have to do what you feel is right.'

Marianne placed her arms around his waist and pulled him towards her. He was reticent at first, but his interest grew as she began to kiss him and press her breasts into his chest. Feeling that he had little to lose, he lifted Marianne's skirt and began to fondle her rounded buttocks. She prised his hands away with a reproving look, which Mike countered with an expression of innocence.

'Come on, get dressed. I'll make some coffee to wake the *rest* of you up,' she said, flicking her eyes down with a teasing smile.

When Marianne had left the room, Mike stared longingly at his bed. He was tempted to jump back in and hide from the world a little longer, but it would only have been delaying the inevitable. With a reluctant sigh, he rubbed his eyes and padded naked towards the bathroom. The shower jets washed the stickiness from his skin and returned some measure of vivacity to his numbed senses. Once he had dabbed himself dry, applied a liberal amount of deodorant and pulled a fresh tee-shirt over his head, he felt about as close to normal as was likely under the circumstances.

The smell of fresh ground coffee drew him into the kitchen where he found Marianne busily scrubbing the stains from four mugs. There were voices coming from outside and Mike peered through the open doorway. He saw Angela sitting at the terrace table with mascara streaks staining her cheeks. Thomas was sat opposite her, clutching a large glass of water and looking particularly glum. Mike put on a pair of shades and stepped out onto the terrace to greet them.

'Morning you two.'

'Morning,' Angela answered in a subdued voice. Thomas lifted his head and rolled his eyes when he caught Mike's attention.

'So what's the problem Angela?' Mike enquired.

'It's my boyfriend...well my ex actually; he's flying to France today.'

'I see. And I take it you're not too happy about that?'

'Yes. No! I don't know,' said Angela, frowning. 'I wanted to be here without him; to think things over a little. The thing is, we were engaged - until I found out he'd cheated on me.'

Angela's bottom lip began to tremble and then she hid her face in her hands. Mike and Thomas stared at each other in bemused silence.

'I'm sorry Thomas,' she said between stuttering intakes of breath, 'but I think I'm still in love with him. I came here to try and get over him, but I don't think I can. He's been calling me every day since I left Canada and now he's flying out to see me. I have to give him a chance.'

'Doesn't sound like he deserves one,' said Mike. Marianne placed a coffee in front of him and fixed him with a harsh stare.

'But there's probably a perfectly reasonable explanation for his behaviour,' he quickly added, before excusing himself and strolling over to the kitchen. He reappeared holding a piece of softened baguette stuffed with leftover sausages from the barbecue.

'Anyone hungry?'

'No, but I'll have a beer if there's any left,' replied Thomas, ignoring the looks of disapproval from the girls.

'You're an animal,' said Mike, in smiling admiration.

'We really ought to get going if you don't mind,' said Marianne, in a tone which left little room for discussion.

Mike looked at the pitiful state of Angela and agreed that the party was well and truly over.

'OK let's make tracks. You coming along Thomas?'

'Yeah, why not? I need to go to Bonifacio to hire some cylinders for my twin set.'

'You wanna do a deco dive today?' asked Mike, incredulous.

'No, I just want to have it all set up for tomorrow.'

'Fair enough.'

'Is that all you two can think about right now?' interrupted Marianne.

'No, of course not,' said Thomas defensively. He turned to face Mike and dropped his voice. 'I've got some gas left in the rebreather for today.'

Marianne shot Thomas a warning glance. Mike tried with difficulty to stifle a laugh.

'Have you got all your stuff together Angela?' asked Marianne.

'Yes I think so.'

'Right, well I'm going to get my bag and then I think we can leave.'

Mike sighed and followed her into the villa to fetch his wallet and keys. When he returned, Marianne and Angela were already waiting for him beside the car, but Thomas was nowhere to be seen. Mike unlocked the doors of the Peugeot and then returned to the villa to look for him. He found him coming out of the toilet, looking decidedly green around the gills.

'Are you OK?'

Thomas groaned and placed a hand on his forehead.

'Not really. I think it must be something I ate.'

'Nothing to do with the alcohol then?'

'Maybe an allergic reaction.'

'That must be it. Anyway I know the perfect cure for hangovers. Let's drop these two off and then we can go and breathe some nitrox.'

They drove the girls back to their hotel on the outskirts of Bonifacio and said their goodbyes in the car park outside. Marianne gave Mike her E-Mail address and asked him to keep in touch with her. She planted a final, lingering kiss on his lips, pulled away and with a parting smile, turned on her heel and walked coolly into the hotel lobby. Thomas got an apologetic peck on the cheek from Angela.

'I'm sorry for spoiling your evening,' she said, squeezing his hand before turning to follow Marianne inside.

'Well that's that then, I suppose,' said Mike, watching Angela disappear. 'Shall we go and get ourselves some proper breakfast now?'

'Sure,' said Thomas testily, 'just as long as it's not Canadian.'

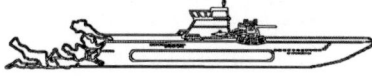

3

H ubert held the RIB's position against the wind while Monica
strapped on her buoyancy jacket and ran through her final
checks. At the bow, Anna attached a lift bag to the eye of the
anchor and stood ready to lower it over the side.

'Ready to dive,' Monica called out, as she pulled the mask strap over her
head.

Bertie studied the marks on his laptop screen.

'OK for position.'

'Stand ready,' called Hubert as he slipped the throttles into neutral.
'OK. Jump!'

Monica placed the regulator in her mouth, pressed the palm of her
hand against her mask and let herself fall backwards into the water. She
re-emerged through a cloud of bubbles to see Anna gently lowering the
anchor into the water with the lift bag billowing out above it. Once it was
safely suspended beneath the surface, Monica gave Anna the standard
thumb touching fingertip OK signal and pulled the air release toggle on the
lift bag. As it began to slip beneath the surface, Monica vented the air from
her buoyancy jacket and followed it. She spotted a flat uniform piece of
sand to her left and made delicate adjustments of the lift bag's buoyancy
so that she could guide the anchor gently down onto it. Once she had
ensured that the flukes were well embedded in the sand, she vented and
detached the lift bag, clipped it to her jacket and then sent a huge column
of bubbles rising up to the surface from her spare regulator. Hubert
spotted the prearranged signal and asked Anna to secure the line before
going astern so that the rope and chain came tight, setting the anchor in.
Bertie activated the GPS alarm function to give ample warning in case the
boat began to drag.

Beneath the surface, Monica made a cursory inspection of the
immediate area, carefully scanning the bottom for traces of man-made

objects while studying the surrounding contours. As if mimicking her actions, colourful ornate wrasse foraged to and fro on the sea floor while red mullet sieved through the sand, searching for hidden prey with their sensitive moustache-like feelers. A solitary flounder abandoned its post as Monica's shadow passed over it and skittered swiftly away across a flat bed of sand. The RIB was now clearly visible, in shimmering silhouette, barely 12 metres above her. Monica glanced at her computer and was about to ascend, when from the corner of her eye she spotted something unusual protruding from the sand.

'I don't like the look of that,' said Santorini, scowling from the wheelhouse of the *Sampiero Corso*. He adjusted the focus of the binoculars as he surveyed the coast, centering them on a small group of divers who were equipped with heavy lifting gear. 'They aren't going for a pleasure dive that's for sure. And if they're spear fishing then they must be expecting to land some pretty big fish. Here take a look Pierre.'

Pierre squinted through the binoculars and scanned the coastline until he spotted a yellow and black RIB equipped with an 'A' frame and lifting gantry. He emitted a low nasal grunt.

'You're right Jean-Claude. That's some pretty serious equipment they have there. They look like a professional salvage team. Do you think they might have caught wind of Jeannot's discovery?'

'I've no idea, but it seems like too much of a coincidence for my liking.' Pierre nodded.

'So what do we do?'

Santorini drummed his fingers on the instrument console and pursed his lips.

Well, there's only one way to find out for sure. Go and get Michel and prepare to pull up the anchor.'

'How much pressure did you say you had left in the rebreather cylinder?' asked Mike, as he and Thomas surveyed the activity in the harbour from the comfort of a *café terrace*.

'About 150 bar.'

Mike made a quick calculation

'So that means you only used 300 litres of gas during that last dive.'

'Yeah. Amazing isn't it?'

'I'm impressed. So does recycling air make you a Greenie?'

'Maybe, but I'm actually a conservative diver,' replied Thomas with a grin.

'I'm more of a radical myself,' chuckled Mike. He took a sip of his *café crème* and a playful smile appeared at the corner of his mouth.

'So did Angela get the text message before or after then?'

'Before or after what?'

'You know what I'm talking about.'

Thomas sighed.

'Can't we just drop the subject?'

'No, not until I've had the full story. Come on you've had plenty of time to lick your wounds.' Thomas' expression grew darker.

'You really can be a pain in the ass sometimes.'

'Ah, so she got the message *before* then.'

Thomas paid the waiter.

'Let's just go and get the cylinders,'

'Hey, don't try to change the subject,' said Mike, enjoying himself.

'Look, if you must know she started getting cold feet before we even got near the bedroom.'

'Bummer! Did she suddenly come to her senses when she saw the skid marks on your underpants?'

'You're so funny,' said Thomas, glowering. 'I knew that I was on to a loser as soon as she started telling me about her stupid fiancé.'

Mike sucked air through his teeth.

'Bad sign...very bad sign indeed,' he agreed, nodding.

'The final blow came when she got the text message. She was convinced that it was some kind of sign; silly cow. In the end I gave up and went to sleep in the hammock.' Mike sniggered.

'I hope you get pox,' scowled Thomas as the waiter brought him his change. 'Come on, let's go.'

Thomas tossed a few coins onto the table, after which he and Mike walked back to the dive shop along the quayside. They were greeted by a young technician dressed in a white polo necked shirt, his skinny legs partially hidden by baggy board shorts.

'I think I have everything that you asked for,' he said, scratching a mop of thick, straw coloured hair. 'Four standard air cylinders plus two eight litre nitrox 40.'

'Yep, that's for our twin-sets and deco slings,' confirmed Thomas.

'Plus a standard twelve litre nitrox 36?'

'That's for me,' said Mike.

'OK, here's the analyser; if you could just check them and sign the log.'

'No problem.'

After testing the oxygen content of the nitrox, Mike and Thomas loaded the cylinders into the car and made their way back to the villa.

'Right lets dump the air cylinders and slings in the store room, grab our gear and head off down to the bay,' proposed Mike.

'Sounds good to me,' agreed Thomas.

An hour later they were standing in shallow water, wearing full equipment in front of a very crowded beach.

'Damn! This place gets busy at the weekends.'

'It's a popular place for both tourists and locals alike,' explained Thomas.

'So it seems. Right, I'm going to swim out to the RIB and bring it close to shore. If you stay here with the gear, I'll bring the boat towards you and then you can pass everything up and fetch the bags from the beach, OK?'

'Something tells me I've got the worst of this arrangement,' said Thomas, jadedly.

'We're just making the most of your talents. Now don't go picking up any Canadians while I'm gone, will you?'

Mike received a blank look.

He shrugged, slipped on his fins and swam swiftly towards the moorings, parting a school of silvery blue anchovies as he went. A moment later he returned at the helm of the RIB and slipped the throttle into neutral as he approached the shallows. Thomas passed up the two SCUBA units, recuperated the dive bags from the beach and then pulled himself up onto the RIB in a single movement.

'Shall we do a quick tour of the bays first?' asked Mike.

'Sure, let's have a good look around.'

'OK, park your ass down there somewhere.'

Mike reversed away from the shallows, turned the boat around and carved a glistening trough through the crystal clear waters of the narrow bay, heading towards open sea.

Once they had cleared the headland, Mike slowed to get a general view of the area. There was rocky coastline to the south, a long white stretch of beach to the north and out to sea a solitary wooden boat pitched gently at anchor. It looked like a fishing boat and Mike took note of its position, knowing that good sites for fishing were often good sites for diving too. He increased his speed, heading northwards, running a course parallel to the mile or so of beach which separated him from the next headland. The white sands were littered with the prostrate bodies of holidaymakers, basking in the heat of the midday sun. Mike had never been fond of lounging around on beaches and felt no compulsion to join the throng. To him beaches were simply the gateways to a more exciting and far less crowded environment.

As they crossed the shallow waters of the bay, Mike watched the changing colour of the water with great concentration. The darker patches indicated areas of seabed covered in posidonia sea-grass or exposed rocks which attracted a wide variety of fish species. The lighter turquoise patches, so stunning to the casual observer, were the result of sunlight reflecting back off bare sand or rock and being poor in nutrients and natural hiding places, were generally barren and of little interest to divers.

The extensive shallows in front of the bay didn't inspire much enthusiasm and Mike continued to the far headland where the rocky shoreline looked to hold more promise. On arrival, Thomas slipped on his mask and fins and jumped over the side to take a look around. After a couple of minutes of swimming back and forth and a tentative dive to the bottom, he returned to the boat.

'It's OK, but nothing special,' he said, throwing his mask into the RIB. 'Just a few big rocks and then lots of bare sand.' Mike nodded.

'Well at least we know now. Climb back onboard and I'll return to the promontory; I thought it looked quite interesting as we passed in front of it.'

Mike took the RIB further away from shore as they doubled back. Thomas leaned over the side, peering into the depths, but saw nothing which inspired him until they reached the steep outcrop of rock at the end of the promontory.

'This looks more like it,' he said, reaching for his mask and fins.

'Just have a quick scout around and if it looks good we'll anchor and kit up.'

Thomas slipped into the water and paddled around on the surface, unhurriedly taking in the spectacle beneath him. After a while he paused motionless, took a couple of deep breaths and flipped his legs into the air before dropping down gracefully into the depths. Mike watched the outline of his body fragment and distort, gradually becoming indistinguishable from the shifting shapes of the submerged rocks below. He looked up when he noticed a large yellow and black RIB anchored just beyond the headland to the south of the promontory. It was displaying a blue and white dive flag; a warning to other boat users to keep their distance. A diver emerged beside the RIB and passed a piece of equipment to someone on board. Mike watched with interest until he heard Thomas break surface nearby, nosily exhaling the stale air from his lungs.

'What's it like down there?' he asked, as Thomas swam back towards the boat.

'It's not bad at all. There's a long ridge which extends way out into deeper water. It looks interesting and there seem to be plenty of fish around too.'

'Sounds good,' said Mike, nodding. 'Just jump on board for now though; there's something I want to check out. I've just spotted a dive boat over there by the headland, so I guess there's a dive site there. We'll pull up alongside and ask.'

Thomas hauled himself out of the water and flipped his legs into the RIB. Mike opened up the throttle and the little boat skittered away, bouncing over small waves that were starting to build up from the west.

A minute later, they were cautiously drifting towards the starboard quarter of a large yellow and black RIB. There were three people on board; a small, light haired woman with a boyish figure and two males; one dark haired, with an unshaven angular face and the other a statuesque blonde of Scandinavian appearance, his eyes hidden behind wraparound shades. A fourth person was just exiting the water, her gender evident from the tight neoprene wetsuit which accentuated a slim hourglass figure. As Mike and Thomas drew close, four blank faces turned towards them and Mike had the immediate impression that their intrusion might not be particularly welcome. The female diver, who had just climbed aboard the yellow and black RIB, threw her mask and fins into a plastic bin and lowered her tank and weight belt onto the deck with practiced ease. Thomas struck up a conversation with the tall, blond haired helmsman while Mike temporarily secured the two boats and cast a curious eye over what looked like specialist salvaging equipment. The yellow and black RIB was evidently no ordinary diving vessel and when Mike overheard the tall blonde helmsman mention the word *archéologique*, he understood the situation well before Thomas turned to translate the conversation.

'I think we're asking the wrong people,' said Thomas. 'They're a Swiss research team involved in archaeological survey work.'

'I can speak English if it makes it any easier for you,' said the blonde haired man, smiling.

'Well your English certainly sounds a lot better than my French,' agreed Mike.

'I imagine that it's better than your Swiss-German too.'

'I wouldn't even know where to start,' admitted Mike, feeling somewhat embarrassed by his lingual inadequacies. He was relieved to see from the man's disarming smile, that there was no judgement intended.

The young woman, who had just climbed aboard, was now crouched down beside the laptop, consulting with her dark haired colleague. She glanced over at Mike and Thomas, stood up and strode confidently towards them.

'Good afternoon gentlemen. Is there something that we can do for you?' she asked in excellent English.

Mike could tell from the young woman's assertiveness that she was the one in charge and although she was wearing a hooded wetsuit, it didn't escape his notice that she was also strikingly attractive.

'I'm sorry if we're disturbing you; we had no idea that you were working,' he said by way of apology.

'That's quite alright; we've just finished work on this site as it happens. What is it that you need?'

'Well to be perfectly honest with you, we thought that you were recreational divers. We're unfamiliar with this area and we just wanted to ask if you know any good places to dive around here.'

'What is it with everyone asking us questions today?'

'Why do you say that?' asked Mike in surprise.

'Earlier this morning we had another group of divers asking us all sorts of strange questions. They're out there in the bay now,' she said with a jerk of the head.

Mike turned to see the same wooden boat which he'd noticed earlier, anchored in open sea.

'Oh yes, I saw it a moment ago. I thought they were fishing.'

There was laughing as Thomas shared a joke with the blonde helmsman.

'Hang on a minute, I can't hear you properly.' The young woman pulled off her diving hood and threw back her tousled hair, sending a shower of fine droplets spraying into the air behind her. When it settled back in place Mike was struck dumb by her beauty.

'Sorry, what did you say?' she asked.

'Ah...I said I was wondering what that boat was doing out there.'

'Diving, I suppose. They're obviously local; no one from outside Corsica would call their boat the *Sampiero Corso*.'

'Why's that?' asked Mike, frowning.

'I guess you haven't read much about Corsica's history then,' said Monica, pretty dimples forming on her cheeks as she smiled. 'Sampiero Corso is a historic figure; a local hero. He was a freedom fighter who struggled to liberate Corsica from the Genoese rulers in the 1600's. He originally fought on the side of the French and then formed his own army of resistance when their interests diverged. He was considered so dangerous to the established authorities that he was eventually assassinated, still fighting at the age of 79.'

'Wow! I don't know if I'm more impressed by *his* military achievements or *your* remarkable knowledge of history.'

'It's a habit of my profession,' Monica replied, self-consciously. 'Sorry, my interests aren't always shared and I do tend to get a bit carried away at times.'

'There's no need to apologise. I'm always eager to learn,' said Mike. 'So what did these people ask you anyway?'

'Well, they wanted to know why we were here, what we were doing and what all this equipment was for. I explained to them that we are Marine Archaeologists searching for traces of pre-Roman history, but I'm not entirely sure that they believed me. One of the men, a huge man with a dark beard, asked me who was sponsoring us, which seemed a very unusual thing to ask. I told him that it was a joint venture between the University of Zurich and the *Universita di Corsica Pasquale Paoli*, which it is - and that seemed to placate him. He then asked me how deep we would be searching and I explained that the deepest that we could practically work with our present equipment was 20 metres. Before they left us, the big, bearded man said that if we found anything unusual we should let him know because it might be worth our while.'

Monica began to laugh and picked something up from the deck.

'When I showed him this rusty old kettle which I found in the sand this morning, he didn't seem to see the funny side of it. He just stared at me like I was an imbecile. So I asked him to be more specific about what he was interested in and he told me that he was a collector of artefacts from the Second World War. It all seemed a little bit odd and to be honest, by that point I just wanted to see the back of them.'

'Are there any Second World War relics to be found around here?' asked Mike, his eyes widening with interest.

'I'm sure that there are one or two, but as far as I know this area was never of any great strategic importance.'

'No. I can't see that it would be either,' agreed Mike. 'So apart from the kettle, did you find anything interesting down there?'

'No, nothing unfortunately. There was just a small group of rocks down there which showed up as a possible site on our survey records. They matched our selection criteria and so we had to investigate.'

'Does that happen often?' asked Mike.

'More often than we would like, but then patience and perseverance are essential qualities in our line of work.'

'Yes I can well imagine.' Mike turned to see Thomas showing his rebreather to Hubert. At the same time Monica found herself passing an admiring eye over Mike's toned torso. She flushed and diverted her eyes when he suddenly turned towards her.

'I'm sorry we haven't introduced ourselves yet. My name is Mike Summers and this is my colleague, Thomas.'

'*Enchanté*,' said Thomas, turning to give a brief salute.

'My name is Monica Huber. I'm pleased to meet you both. That's Hubert who you've just met, Bertie who's working on the laptop and Anna just beside him.'

Bertie and Anna looked up from their work and said a shy hello.

'Bertie also speaks some English,' explained Monica, 'but Anna only speaks a little.' Mike smiled and acknowledged them with a raised hand.

'You referred to Thomas as your colleague,' said Monica, 'does that mean you're not on holiday here?'

'No, we're actually doing a bit of research ourselves. We came to look at the possibility of setting up a technical diving facility here. It's a fast growing sector of the market and we've been deliberating over where to do it for some time. It just so happens that Thomas' parents have inherited a property close by and that obviously influenced our decision to come here. At the moment we're just checking out the potential.'

'Hmm, that all sounds very exciting. I suppose that you're both diving instructors then?'

'Yes, that's correct.'

'Hubert is also a diving instructor, but he gave it up to study Maritime Archaeology. For me it was the opposite; I studied archaeology first and then learned to dive.'

'It sounds like a fascinating profession.'

'It is, but we don't often work in such ideal conditions as this,' said Monica, spreading her arms demonstratively. She smiled briefly and then chewed her lip.

'Well I'm not sure that we're going to be a great deal of help to you Mike. We haven't done any pleasure dives here and we only ever look at the sites which come up on our surveys.'

'But you're searching for remains of wrecks, right?' asked Mike.

'Well yes, in fact we're actually excavating one at the moment. It's a Roman vessel, but it's not really what we're looking for and I doubt if it would be of much interest to you either.'

'Well, any kind of wreck interests me, but I'll take your word for it. What exactly is it that you're looking for then?'

'Are you sure that you want another history lesson?' asked Monica, raising a cautionary eyebrow.

'When it comes from a pretty history teacher like you, I'm all ears,' replied Mike with a grin.

'You're quite a charmer aren't you?' said Monica flushing.

'I would be if I was any good at it,' laughed Mike.

Monica smiled but gave nothing away.

'Have you visited Pagliaju or Stantari yet?'

'No, I can't say that I have.'

'Well if you get the opportunity, do so. They are both Megalithic sites where you'll find standing stones, ancient *dolmens* and *menhirs*, some of which date back as far as 4000BC.'

'Wow, now that is ancient history,' whistled Mike.

Monica inclined her head and continued

'We know almost nothing about the people who erected these structures, but we do know that around 1100BC they were usurped by a group known as the Torréens who carved images of people bearing arms into the stones which they found. The Torréens built their own impressive constructions; towers of stone known as *Torri*, from which they earned their name. They were probably a warrior race, but certainly not unskilled, because some of the huge carved blocks of stone that were used to build the *Torri*, weighed many tons. Very little is known about their culture or what became of it, but it is widely believed that they were actually Shardanes; a group linked to the Sea People. If that is true, then the Torréens were once members of a diverse association of seafaring opportunists which today we would call pirates. The Sea People, as this unlikely group of warriors has become known, allied themselves with the Meshwesh of Libya in 1200BC to launch an attack on Egypt during the reign of Ramses III. We know this, because the battle is recorded in images and hieroglyphics in the Medinat Habu Temple in Luxor, Egypt. Ramses III's army eventually vanquished the alliance and it is believed that once chased back into the sea, the Shardanes split from the other groups and sought refuge in Corsica. Our belief is that if the Shardanes did settle here, then they would almost certainly have used the natural ports of Tizzano and Roccapina to supply the nearby sites of Pagliaju and Stantari. The objective of our mission is therefore to prove beyond doubt that the Torréens actually were Shardanes by finding traces of the vessels that they would have used. If we can find artefacts of Egyptian or Libyan origin, weapons similar to those depicted in the Medinat Habu Temple and pieces of wood which we can carbon date to match the time period, then we will be well on the way to proving the connection. It's an ambitious project, but for the first time ever we can take advantage of advances in mapping technology to save us thousands of hours of painstaking research.'

'That's astonishing,' said Mike. 'What kind of mapping technology are you using?'

'Well Bertie knows better than I do, but basically we use DGPS positioning technology and multibeam sonar scanning to create a 3D colour mesh image of the sea floor. Bertie then runs a software program over it which identifies points on the survey sites which bear a resemblance to the particular criteria which we are looking for.'

'That sounds like exactly what we need to find new dive sites,' said Mike, his eyes widening at the prospect. 'I don't suppose it all fits into your pocket though.'

'Unfortunately not,' said Monica smiling, 'and you would need to have deep pockets too.'

Their conversation was interrupted as Bertie came forward to speak with Monica. Mike listened uncomprehendingly to their exchange in Swiss-German before Monica nodded and turned towards him.

'Well I'm afraid that we need to return to our work now. We still have another site to examine before we continue excavating our Roman wreck.'

Mike nodded and chewed his lip, reluctant to let this beautiful and astonishing woman slip out of his life. He decided to throw caution to the wind.

'I don't suppose that you need any volunteers do you?'

Monica smiled and shook her head.

'I'm afraid that we don't normally allow members of the public to work alongside us for reasons of safety and security. Having said that, I am actually a diver short today. Look I can't promise anything, but how about you go for a dive and come back in an hour or so? You'll find us here inside the small bay to the left,' she said pointing. 'I'll talk to the rest of the team and see how they feel about it. How does that sound?'

'Great,' said Mike. 'I'd love to get the opportunity to see how you Marine Archaeologists work.'

'Good, this might work out well for both of us then. Now about that dive – did you say that you were interested in wrecks?'

'Yes, definitely.'

'Well in that case we might have something interesting for you to take a look at.'

'Come and take a look at this Jean-Claude. There's another RIB lying alongside those Swiss archaeologists. It's been there for the last 20 minutes or so,' said Pascal, handing him the binoculars.

Santorini wiped the saltwater from his eyes with a towel and pressed the lens housings to his face.

'It look's like one of those hire boats from Bonifacio,' said Santorini squinting. 'There are two people on board...and I think they have diving equipment with them.' He watched the small orange RIB break away from the larger vessel and begin to move away.

'Do you think they're part of the group?' asked Pascal.

'I've no idea, but I don't think there's any cause for concern. I'm fairly certain that the Swiss were telling the truth. Besides, they're searching in water which is far too shallow to pose any threat to us.'

'I think we should keep an eye on them all the same. We have no idea who they are.'

'We should be watching every single boat in the area anyway,' said Santorini, still tracking the progress of the smaller RIB, 'especially now that we've found the hatch. If anyone catches wind of what we're doing out here, we'll soon have competition, and anyone who wants a head start will just have to make a note of our position. There's not much that we can do about that except to keep our eyes open and be ready to show that we mean business if anyone starts nosing around.'

Pascal nodded, shielding his eyes from the sun as he stared towards the coast.

'Looks like they're moving to a different spot.'

'They're preparing to drop anchor, so they must be staying put for a while.' Santorini pulled the binoculars from his face and handed them to Pascal.

'Just keep an eye on them.'

'Of course,' replied Pascal, still staring into the distance. 'Do you think that hatch really came from a U-boat?'

Santorini frowned and pinched his nose.

'I don't know Pascal, but for the first time I'm starting to believe that there might be something in it. The writing, the scorch marks, the sheared bolts; it all seems to fit. And of course when someone offers you half a million euros to find something, you have to assume that they have good reason to believe that it's there in the first place. Either way we don't have much to lose; apart from the 100 euros that I gave Jeannot that is, but I reckon he's worth the investment.'

'I'd have to agree with you there. He certainly seems to know his stuff,' said Pascal, eyeing him over his shoulder, 'but do you reckon he can keep his mouth shut?'

'He's no fool. He may have a loose tongue, but I'm sure that he would prefer it to remain firmly attached to the back of his head.'

Mike punched the coordinates which Monica had given him into his handheld GPS, and then navigated towards the resulting waypoint which appeared on the small LCD screen.

'Where are we going?' asked Thomas.

'Not very far. Monica gave me the coordinates of a wreck which they came across earlier in the week. It's just a couple of hundred metres from here.'

'Cool! What type of wreck is it?'

'She's no idea because they only saw it on a sounding profile. Her colleague, Bertie, says that it's not too old, around 15 metres long and appears to be in good condition.'

'Well I guess we'll soon find out,' said Thomas, staring at the scrolling GPS reading. 'I had quite a good chat with Hubert while you were flirting with his boss.' Mike smiled, but refused to rise to the bait. 'He used to work as a guide in Gozo.'

'Yeah, Monica told me he's an instructor. Maltese Islands eh? I've heard there's some good diving there.'

'Sounds like it. He was telling me all about the undersea archways and caves. Apparently there's one site called the Blue Dome; a shallow cavern with a huge curved roof which is illuminated by refracted light and full of seahorses.'

'That sounds awesome.'

'Yeah, we had quite an interesting conversation; unlike you. Since when did you become interested in history anyway?'

'Let me see now; about half an hour ago,' said Mike, a smile creeping across his face. 'You've got to admit that she's stunning.'

'I certainly wouldn't throw her out of bed.'

'You see that's where you let yourself down Thomas; you lack refinement. You wouldn't stand a chance with someone like her.'

'And I suppose you would?' scoffed Thomas.

Mike sucked air through his teeth.

'I have to admit that it's a tough one, even for a man of my charms.' He smiled, watching Thomas cringe from the corner of his eye. 'You know what these scientist types are like; all work and no play. Still, I like a challenge. I'll just have to find her weakness.'

'Yeah, well if it's effeminate men, you're definitely in with a chance.'

'You're just jealous. Anyway, for your information, I've already arranged to meet Monica after this dive. And if all goes well, I'll be working alongside her during the excavation of a historic wreck.'

'Are you joking?'

'Absolutely not, my dear Gallic chum; I'm deadly serious. And you never know, they might even be able find a job for you to do...like clean the boat down or something.'

'Now *that* would be a terrible waste of talent.'

'Let's put it to good use then. Get the anchor ready; we're there.'

The distance to the waypoint gradually scrolled down to zero and a continuous beeping sound was the signal for Thomas to lower the anchor away. After a good length of chain and rope had slipped through the fairlead, Thomas secured it and Mike came astern before killing the engine.

'According to the depth sounder, we've got 15 metres of water here,' said Mike as he leaned over the side. 'I can't see any sign of the wreck though.'

'Me neither. Maybe we should do a quick search over the surface before we descend.'

'Good idea. We could use the rope as a guide until we see the anchor directly below us and then do an expanding square search pattern.'

'OK, I'll take my compass.'

Five minutes later Mike and Thomas were sat facing each other across the decks. A brief exchange of nods was their cue to fall backwards into the water and leave the boat rocking in a pool of swirling bubbles. The cool embrace of the sea was a welcome relief after the heat of the sun on their dark wetsuits. Mike joined Thomas a few metres ahead of the bow and continued to swim forwards, keeping his eyes trained on the descending arc of rope until he saw the anchor lying on the sea bed, directly below.

'This is our starting point,' he said, turning to face Thomas. 'Did you see anything yet?'

'Not a thing. Are you sure we're in the right spot?'

'We're where the GPS says we should be. It's not totally accurate, but we can't be more than 30 metres away.'

'Let's start searching then; I'll do the compass and distance if you do the spotting.'

'OK ready when you are.'

Thomas clamped his teeth back onto the rebreather mouthpiece and swivelled his body in the water until his compass position line pointed due west. He began to swim along the heading, counting ten downward strokes of his right leg before turning northwards and repeating the procedure. Now he turned to face east and doubled the count to 20. He had just reached 14 when Mike suddenly grabbed his ankle. He turned to see Mike pointing downwards and following the line of his vision, picked out the unmistakable outlines of a sunken vessel. Before they dropped below the surface, Mike lifted his head from the water to check their position relative to the RIB and note an approximate return heading from the wreck. After a quick exchange of signals they purged the air from their buoyancy jackets and descended diagonally towards it.

Beneath them was a carpet of lush, green posidonia grass swaying gently in the swell like a ghostly meadow. Shoals of golden striped salema, nomads of the underwater grasslands, paused to graze briefly on the succulent blades before moving on in their relentless search for fresh pastures. Mike and Thomas moved slowly, scanning the leafy undergrowth for slender sea grass pipefish and seahorses, discreet masters of disguise that only trained eyes could differentiate from their environment.

Soon they drew close to the dark hulk of the wreck and began to notice the flashing silver flanks of circling schools of white trevallies and juvenile barracuda.

Lying on its side in a field of shifting posidonia sea grass, Mike could tell from the wreck's deep wooden hull and covered wheelhouse that it was a fishing vessel and one that had clearly been lying there for some time. A multitude of brightly coloured sponges, fine stranded red algae and flower-like zoanthids sprouted from every exposed surface, like an underwater island of life.

As Mike glided over the stern section, he stared into the engine room through a gaping hole in the deck. The charred wood which surrounded the opening was as good a clue as any to the cause of the vessels demise. Moving towards the bow, he and Thomas approached the wheelhouse and watched swarms of black dotted picarel and silver sand smelt twist and turn inside the enclosed space. Thomas entered head-first through an open doorway, causing an immediate explosion of silver flashes as the swarming mass was thrown into panic. Those unfortunate individuals which ventured outside the protection of the cabin became instant prey for the orbiting trevallies, dentex and barracuda which were patiently waiting outside.

Thomas swivelled sideways to match the angle of the boat and took the helm in both hands. Mike stuck his head inside and watched in amusement as Thomas attempted to wrench the throttle lever forwards, screaming orders to an imaginary crew whilst wrestling with heavy seas.

The scattering fish in the wheelhouse must have been convinced that their end was near as this strange predator thrashed about and sent clouds of silt ballooning up around it. Mike retreated from the chaos of the wheelhouse and glided along the outside of the hull to study the organisms which were thriving on the wreck's exterior. Transparent hydroids, orange madrepores, fan worms and flat oysters clung resolutely to whatever foothold they could find, standing their ground against invasive neighbours. Mike came across a group of bright red sea-squirts and marvelled at their simplicity. It was hard to believe that such humble, seemingly inanimate double-valved siphons, which had remained unchanged in their structure for millions of years, were in fact considered to be the origin of all vertebrates.

Thomas came to join Mike as he was studying a colourful nudibranch, crawling over a bright green sponge. They watched its laborious progression in shared fascination until they were distracted by a strange scraping sound nearby. Mike turned his head to scan the immediate area and was surprised to see the exposed beak-like teeth of a parrotfish gnawing at a patch of algae that was growing on the decks. He'd only ever seen parrotfish over coral reefs before and was surprised to find them surviving so far north of the tropics. It was a testament to the adaptability of the diverse wrasse family and yet another example of the many surprises that the underwater world still held in store for him.

Returning to the stern, he and Thomas studied the charred hole in the deck and decided that it was safe to explore the engine room below it. A small group of brown meagre floated lazily on either side of the engine block while swallow tail seaperch and red cardinals loitered in the darker recesses. Mike upended himself and with expert buoyancy control, dipped his head below deck-level to peer into the dark interior. Considering it safe to continue, he placed a steadying finger on the engine block and slid carefully below deck level, with Thomas following close behind. Their eyes adjusted to the light and flicked in all directions, judging the space around them as they moved through the wrecks interior. Disturbed silt, hanging ropes and unstable structures were common hazards for the unwary diver, but both Mike and Thomas had enough experience to know that slow, calculated movements would ensure that they would exit the wreck without incident. It would also greatly improve their chances of seeing anything of interest.

Mike switched on an underwater flashlight and scanned the area ahead of him. Everything inside the hull had taken on a grey-brown colour from years of degradation and silt deposition, but he could still discern the shrouded outlines of coiled ropes, tools, oil cans and numerous lobster pots which all gave a clue to the day to day activities which might have once taken place on this small working boat.

Thomas spotted an octopus crawling deftly between the clutter of fallen objects, extending its tentacles into every crack and crevice in search of small prey. It froze when Mike's light beam centred on it and immediately turned white with fear, shrinking back into the protection of a small hole.

Mike hung motionless, hoping that it would grow confident enough to continue its hunting activities while they watched.

Octopodes were a favourite of Mike and he had read a great deal about them. With excellent vision, astonishing dexterity, a capacity for complex problem solving and a surprisingly good memory, the only flaw in their design appeared to be an unusual circulatory system which leaves them prone to fatigue and cursed with a limited lifespan. As Mike watched the octopus cower, he could just imagine the three separate hearts urgently pumping blue haemocyanin based blood around its terrified body. If it wasn't for such evolutionary peculiarities, Mike wondered just how far these cephalopod molluscs might otherwise have evolved. One way or another, they had certainly come a long way from being the slow-moving, cautious and unimaginative creatures that once filled the world's oceans some 570 million years ago. They had literally come out of their shells.

Thomas drew Mike's attention by tapping a diving knife against his cylinder. He pointed out a large brown moray eel, flecked with gold spots that was protruding from a rusted pipe. Its huge mouth opened and closed as it breathed, revealing an impressive set of razor sharp dentures. Neither Mike nor Thomas showed any sign of alarm, knowing from experience that when left undisturbed, Morays were surprisingly timid creatures. Mike returned his flashlight beam to the place where he had seen the octopus and was not surprised to discover that it had used the opportunity to make its escape. He smiled and continued forwards, watching red shrimp scatter away towards the shadows. After skirting around a pair of black scorpion fish, he followed Thomas up out of the engine room and out into intense blue daylight once more.

The remainder of their dive was spent outside the wreck, where amongst the diverse profusion of organisms, Mike chanced upon a flower-like sea rose and Thomas discovered a pair of beautiful spotted doris nudibranch on a sponge encrusted winch. With their curiosity finally satisfied, they checked their watches and agreed to call it a day. Mike consulted his underwater slate and began to move off along the approximate return heading which he'd noted earlier. Thomas followed beside him as they floated above the endless fields of sea grass, watching small shoals of golden striped salema and bogue rise and fall over the shifting carpet of green, like swooping birds. They passed beside a huge, dark fan mussel, nearly half a metre in length standing erect in the posidonia sea grass like a neglected tomb stone.

After a while, having seen no sign of the anchor line, Mike started to have doubts about the accuracy of his navigation. He turned around, trying to spot the silhouette of the RIB against the surface and was alarmed to see only long white streaks of crashing waves, a sign that the weather had changed for the worse. As he was staring at the surface Thomas suddenly grabbed his shoulder and pointed to a deep gouge that ran straight through the sea grass and disappeared into the distance. Mike realised its significance even before Thomas thrust a slate in front of his face with four urgently scribbled words on it.

The anchor has slipped!

'Well that's it for today, I've had my fill. All we've seen is sand and rock and this wind is going to get worse before it gets better.'

There was a clattering sound as a cylinder fell and began to roll around the deck.

'What do you want to do Jean-Claude?' asked Pierre from the wheelhouse.

'Get us the hell out of here before we get swamped. Michel, go and get the anchor while we lash everything down.'

The diesel engine roared into life with a belch of black smoke and Michel worked his way forwards to the bow, steadying himself on the bulwarks as the boat pitched and yawed in the growing swell. The rolling movement eased as Pierre punched the bow forwards into the oncoming waves allowing Michel to take up slack on the anchor line. When it came up tight, he took a quick turn on the mooring post and the rope began to growl and squeal as the bow was repeatedly lifted into the air. The anchor eventually broke free from its hold and Michel grunted as he strained to haul it in. Jeannot came to add his weight to the task and soon the coil of heavy warp began to pile up on the deck. When the anchor was clear of the water, Jeannot hooked the restraint onto the chain before giving Pierre the signal to move away. They stumbled their way back to the stern deck where they found Pascal leaning over the rail and vomiting noisily into the sea.

Pierre turned the bow of the heavy hulled vessel towards the north-west, but the boat began to roll dangerously and he was unable to hold his course. He cursed and began to tack back and forth against the oncoming waves, making painfully slow progress back towards Propriano. Santorini and Michel stood glumly beside Pierre in the cramped wheelhouse while the others braved the wind and spray outside.

'I don't understand it,' complained Michel, 'we've done four dives today and apart from that panel we've seen nothing at all.'

Santorini accepted the strong *Gitanes* cigarette which Michel offered to him.

'I'm starting to have doubts myself. If the submarine came to rest where it is as a result of an explosion, I would have expected to see other debris by now.'

'Maybe the hatch floated,' suggested Pierre.

'What do you mean, floated,' scoffed Michel, 'it's made of solid steel.'

'Did you see how thick it was?' countered Pierre, 'there's no way that they would have used solid steel.'

'He has a point,' said Santorini. 'The hatch would have been hollow and it's quite possible that it could float, temporarily at least. If there was a small hole or a crack in the casing, which is quite likely after an explosion, it could have slowly filled with water until it sank.'

'Well if were going to start looking into all the possibilities, we could be searching for a very long time,' said Michel scowling.

'I don't like it either, but it's a factor that we have to consider,' pointed out Santorini.

'Maybe it is, but then we have to accept that we have no real idea if we're even looking in the right place.'

'Nobody said this would be a walk in the park Michel, but if we give in now and someone else comes along and finds the wreck right under our noses, we'll be a hell of a lot more frustrated than we are now. We've got to put this into perspective. We could try and rob a bank tomorrow; maybe we'd be successful, maybe we'd end up in jail, or even dead. The point I'm trying to make is that there is no risk involved in attempting to find and loot this submarine. It's not guarded, it's hidden from view and if we take stuff from it, nobody will be any the wiser. Can you think of an easier way to make that kind of money?'

Michel tried and failed to come up with a smart answer.

'At least you know where to find a bank,' he finally grunted, before flicking his cigarette butt out of the doorway.

Santorini scowled as he watched the tip stutter and die on the damp wooden deck.

'We've got to be realistic. It was never going to be easy to find anything this far from shore. Maybe we'll find nothing at all in the end, but at least we'll be able to sleep easy in our beds at night knowing that we gave it our best shot. If anyone wants to give in, that's up to them, but they will forfeit any right to a share in the profits if we find it.'

Santorini let Michel reflect on his words, knowing full well that greed would win him over better than any argument. He inhaled deeply on the remains of his cigarette and flicked the butt into the sea, his eyes never leaving Michel.

Kicking wildly, with his temples pounding, Mike finally caught up with the dragging anchor and forced the flukes into the ground to hold it firm. Thomas arrived close behind him and they quickly began to pull themselves up the chain. After making a cautionary pause at 5 metres, they emerged to a heavy swell and strong, gusting winds. The RIB snatched at the anchor line as the bow was thrown up by the waves, making their exit more difficult than it would normally have been.

Mike slipped off his buoyancy jacket and passed it to Thomas while he pulled himself up over the sponson and onto the deck. He leaned over to retrieve his equipment and then stood ready as Thomas released himself from the rebreather harness. When the next wave approached they used the uplift to wrestle it aboard. Thomas quickly followed.

'Damn, where did this weather come from?' shouted Mike over the howling wind.

'It's probably the...*Mistral*,' replied Thomas, ducking his head as spray crashed over the bow, 'they come on at a moments notice and can sometimes last for days.'

'Great! Well we'd better get the hell out of here before there are two wrecks in the area.'

Mike fired up the engine and punched forward through the waves while Thomas took up the slack line and lifted the anchor free. Once it was safely stowed, he gave the thumbs up and joined Mike at the helm as the RIB came around in a tight arc and followed the rolling swell towards the shore. As Mike was crabbing his way towards the promontory, he spotted the archaeologist's yellow and black RIB crashing through the waves in the opposite direction. Hubert, at the helm, spotted them and eased back on the throttles while Mike approached and held his position close by.

'We're abandoning,' shouted Monica from the port side. 'There's no way that we can continue working in these conditions.' Mike nodded resignedly.

'Yeah, it's pretty messy out here. Where are you heading to?'

'We have a mooring in Tizzano, just up the coast,' replied Monica.

'Is that where you're staying?'

'No we have lodgings in Propriano.'

'Propriano?' repeated Mike, having vague recognition of the name. 'Is that far from here?'

'It take's a good while to get there,' said Monica, evasively.

'By road it's only half an hour away though,' added Hubert.

'Maybe we'll come and pay you a visit sometime then,' said Thomas.

'Sure, come on over anytime,' replied Hubert. 'In fact, if you're interested, there's a band playing in one of the bars tonight.'

Before either Mike or Thomas could answer, Monica admonished Hubert in a torrent of abrasive Swiss-German.

Sensing the friction, Mike thought it wise to decline the offer.

'Thanks for the invitation Hubert, but we've got a deep dive planned for tomorrow; we need to take it easy tonight.'

'No problem,' he replied, visibly smarting from his scolding.

'Yes, I'm sorry, but we're all a little bit tired at the moment and we have some work to catch up on,' said Monica. 'Perhaps some other time?'

'Yes, of course,' said Mike, feigning indifference. 'Are you going to be working in the same area tomorrow?'

'Yes, as long as the weather eases.'

'OK, well maybe we'll drop by on you after our morning dive,' said Mike, 'otherwise we'll catch up with you when the weather improves.'

'Yes, feel free,' said Monica. 'Enjoy your evening.'

'Thanks - and the same to you,' replied Mike.

'Take it easy guys; we'll make a date later on for sure,' shouted Hubert as the larger RIB began to pull away.

'We'll hold you to that,' Thomas called after him.

Mike brought the boat around sharply and headed for the shelter of the small bay. Once inside the protective arm of the promontory, he followed the gently rolling swell towards the shore.

'Well that was a bit of bad luck for you wasn't it? First getting blown out by the storm and then by Monica,' chuckled Thomas.

'I don't think you've got room to talk after last night.'

'Yes, well call it karma, but it's a real pity how that wind suddenly sprang up from nowhere. Monica must have been so relieved to be saved from your pathetic attempts to seduce her.'

'I wasn't trying to seduce her,' countered Mike.

'Well you're wasting your time anyway. It's quite obvious that it's me she likes.'

'What? Oh yes, because she was giving you *all* her attention wasn't she?'

'You see, you know nothing about the subtleties of women. If you did, you'd know that they never talk directly to the one who really interests them. She was just using you to get closer to me; checking me out at a discreet distance and waiting for the moment to give the right signal.'

'What planet are you on? Do you think that you're some kind of love psychologist or something?'

'*Je suis français,*' said Thomas with an amused grin, 'which is more or less the same thing.'

'Oh spare me the drivel,' said Mike, as he eased the throttle into neutral and let the boat drift towards the beach. Thomas began to walk girlishly around the boat squealing in high pitched tones.

'Monica, Monica wherefore art thou Monica?'

Mike made a lunge towards him, but Thomas had been expecting it. Using the sponson as a trampoline, he executed a neat back somersault and landed with a splash into the sea. He emerged at the surface laughing loudly while trying to dodge the wetsuit and fins that Mike was aiming at him.

When they had finished trading insults, Mike left Thomas to transfer the equipment to the beach while he went to tie up the RIB for the evening. By the time that they had loaded the car and made their way back to the villa, it was early evening. Mike closed the shutters, stacked the terrace table and chairs in the store and then collapsed, exhausted on the couch. Thomas, feeling equally exhausted, retired to his room and soon the roar of the gusting wind was competing with the sound of contented snoring.

Mike stirred a few hours later to find himself in semi-darkness. The wind outside had lost some of its intensity and the shutters were no longer rattling against their frames. He glanced at his watch and was surprised to see that it was after 9 o'clock. He was tempted to close his eyes and sleep through until morning, but finally decided against it, knowing that he would probably wake up at some painfully early hour as a consequence. Besides there were things that needed to be taken care of.

A churning stomach reminded him that he'd eaten nothing since breakfast and he went to explore the contents of the fridge. He grabbed a carton of milk, took a slug from it and immediately gagged, spitting out a congealed watery mess into the sink. Cursing loudly, he found a carton of fruit juice and sniffed it cautiously before guzzling it down to wash the bitterness from his mouth. A few crusts of stale bread and some soggy lettuce were all that remained of the previous nights feast, but the freezer compartment held more promise and soon the smells of baking pizza and garlic bread began to fill the house. Lured by the tempting aroma, Thomas emerged from his bedroom, standing in his underwear and sniffing the air like a bloodhound following the scent of a rabbit. Before long Mike and Thomas were tearing into the pizza and squabbling over the scraps like hyenas. Thomas claimed the last crust of garlic bread, rammed it into his mouth and licked his fingers in triumph. Mike sat back on the couch with a sigh of contentment and wiped his hands with a paper napkin.

'Right, I think it's time to make a plan for tomorrow,' he declared, firing up the laptop.

Thomas popped the top off a beer and watched Mike loading a mixed gas, decompression dive planning program.

'Better make this the last one then,' he said regretfully.

'I think you'll find that *is* the last one,' said Mike pointedly, as he opened a fresh file on the screen and studied the parameters.

'Let's see now - environment is saltwater, altitude is zero, maximum CNS oxygen exposure is 1.6 bar, added conservatism...let's say 20%... agreed?'

'Yup.'

'Right, decompression stop size...3 metres on nitrox 40, shallowest stop at 6 metres...,' continued Mike, as he considered and modified each detail of the plan.

'OK let's see what that gives us,' he said, clicking the calculate button.

After a few seconds the schedule appeared on the screen as a list of depths and times.

'Here we go; 50 metres for 20 minutes with a 30 minute decompression schedule and a total run time of 53 minutes. Maximum CNS oxygen exposure will be 1.25 bar and total accumulated oxygen toxicity unit's will be 42; that's all well within the limits.'

'Looks good to me,' agreed Thomas.

'Right, we just need to work out our gas requirements now.'

'I hate doing this bit,' said Thomas as he began tapping values into a calculator.

'Me too, but it has to be done,' said Mike as he quietly stole a few gulps from Thomas' beer.

'OK I think that's it,' said Thomas after a few minutes work. 'We'll need 3,240 litres of air from the total supply of the 4,800 available in the twin cylinders, which leaves us with more than a third in reserve. For the decompression schedule we have 1,600 litres of nitrox available and we only need 1,116 for the plan, so that looks good too.'

'It also matches the gas requirements shown on the software schedule,' pointed out Mike.

'I'm clearly a mathematical genius,' said Thomas, as he dropped his pen on the table and collapsed back against the sofa. He picked up his beer, examined the reduced content with suspicion and then put it permanently out of the way of further temptation.

'Right, now that we've done the hard bit. Where are we going to dive?'

Mike unfolded his maritime chart and laid it out carefully on the table.

'I was thinking of going somewhere around here,' said Mike while pointing at an indistinct spot around a kilometre from the coast.
'Any particular reason?'
'It's deep.'
'I see, and will there be anything to see down there?'
'I have absolutely no idea,' he said grinning.

The leaves of the plane trees were still rustling around the courtyard when Monica awoke. She listened until curiosity got the better of her and then slipped out of bed and pushed back the thick woven curtains. There was a litter of dead leaves and branches lying on the paving stones outside her room. The wind had clearly weakened, although in Monica's opinion it was still far too strong to risk any further excavation work. She shook her head in frustration, aware that she would probably lose a day from her schedule. No one expected miracles from her, but no outside force matched the unrelenting pressure which Monica exerted on herself.

With a heavy sigh, she tied back the curtains, accepting that it was pointless for her to worry about things which were beyond her control. She stepped into the bathroom to take a shower and under the gentle massage of the water jets, let her mind drift until she found herself thinking about her encounter with Mike the previous day. She couldn't deny that she'd found him attractive and had been greatly impressed by his politeness and genuine interest in her work, but there was no question of considering any involvement. There was no room in her life for distractions at the moment. There was far too much at stake. And the emotional wounds inflicted by her last romantic adventure, were constant reminders of the consequences of weakness. As if to drive the point home, she cast her mind back.

His name was Jurgen and he was a junior Professor of Anthropology at the University of Zurich. After months of persistent flattery, Monica finally gave in to his unrelenting pleas and agreed to have dinner with him. It went far better than she had expected and a week later, after drinking a little too much wine, they inevitably ended up in bed together. There followed a passionate two week affair which did wonders for her self-esteem and made her deliriously happy for a while, but unfortunately it was to prove short lived. Jurgen suddenly became distant and for no apparent reason began to go out of his way to avoid contact with her. Soon afterwards, Monica began to notice smiles and winks from male members of staff whom she barely knew. The final humiliation came when a female colleague took her to one side and gently explained to her that she'd been just one of a long list of women who'd fallen for Jurgen's charms, only to be cast off again when his interest turned to fresh conquests. Monica was mortified by his betrayal. She felt used and cheap - and vowed never to let it happen again.

As the memory faded, Monica found herself scratching red marks into her arms. Mike might well be attractive, intelligent and charming, she thought to herself, but that did not exclude him from being just as callous and deceitful as Jurgen. She could get by quite happily without those kinds of disruptions. Her work might seem like a thankless task at times, but it brought her far more reward and satisfaction than any man had been able to provide.

The tiles felt surprisingly cool under foot after the evening chill brought on by the *Mistral*. Mike padded towards the kitchen window and peered outside. The sun was shining in brilliant clear blue skies, despite a persistent breeze that sent pine needles swirling around the confines of the terrace. He blinked in surprise when he caught sight of Thomas crouched on the ground, surrounded by an expanse of tools. Rubbing the tiredness from his eyes, he pushed open the front door and went outside to join him.

'You're a bit keen this morning aren't you?'

Thomas looked up from his work, an adjustable wrench held loosely in one hand.

'Yeah, I woke up early and couldn't get back to sleep again. I thought about playing some loud heavy metal music to wake you up, but tempting as it was, I thought I might do something more productive instead.'

'I'm most grateful to you,' said Mike as he walked towards the edge of the terrace. He shaded his eyes and studied the sea conditions beyond the bay. There were still white caps streaking the surface as far as the eye could see.

'If the weather doesn't calm down a bit, we may have to delay our dive until tomorrow.'

'We'll be fine. We've dived in much worse conditions than that before now.'

'Yes, but we were diving closer to shore. Either that or we had adequate surface support. And after what happened yesterday I'm not too keen to take unnecessary risks.'

'I see your point. Still, maybe we could take our DPV's with us. That way we wouldn't be totally dependant on the boat.'

Mike frowned, unsure if it was wise to use Diver Propulsion Vehicles as emergency back-up.

'You want to take the scooters? I agree that with these onshore winds and incoming waves we'd probably make it back if we had to, but it's risky. After all, there's no guarantee that they won't run out of power midway. And then we'd be in a whole heap of shit.'

'Well if you can't take the excitement old man, then we'll just stay at home, order a pizza and watch a movie.'

Mike sighed in exasperation.

'Fine, have it your way then. We'll load the car up, we'll go down to the beach and I'll take the boat as far as the promontory. But if I come out of that bay and we're jumping around like a jackrabbit on a hotplate, I'm turning around and coming right back in again.'

'You're such a lightweight. Maybe you should take along a nice cushion and a pair of slippers for the boat ride.'

Mike sighed, shook his head despairingly and went to find his cylinder clamps.

'The conditions aren't exactly ideal but we'll have to make do,' said Santorini as he watched the *Sampiero Corso* strain against its moorings. 'Jeannot, I'll need the anchor and warp from your boat. Go and give him a hand Pierre.'

Jeannot's jaw tightened as he turned to walk away. He was tired of being pushed around and forced to sacrifice his time and resources to pursue this foolish enterprise, but what choice did he have? He was slowly but surely being sucked into Santorini's plans.

What had started out as a simple exercise to locate an isolated piece of wreckage had gradually transformed into a full blown search operation, and now Jeannot's knowledge made him indispensable. Yet, as each successive search drew a blank, the mood aboard the *Sampiero Corso* became increasingly ill-humoured and Jeannot seemed to be bearing the brunt of it all. He was thick-skinned enough to bear the taunts; but his loss of income was far harder to shrug off. The 100 euros which Santorini had paid him now seemed like a pittance compared with the amount of money he'd be earning if he was still harvesting red coral.

His weekend enterprise had become a reliable source of income over the years and despite the fact that it was becoming increasingly scarce and more challenging to find, the value of red coral had increased dramatically as a consequence. Jeannot was now one of only a handful of skilled divers in the area who had the knowledge and equipment to reach and collect the precious organism in the deep waters where it could still be found, and that more or less guaranteed him a market. But his trading partners demanded regular supplies and Jeannot was left wondering how long it would be before they turned to his competitors. Clearly, he had to get out of his present predicament as quickly as possible, and as far as he could see there were only two ways of doing it. He could do his utmost to help Santorini's gang search the area, in the hope that they would quickly find what they were looking for, or sit back and wait patiently for them to give up hope. One way or another, Jeannot had much to think about as with the assistance of Pierre, he returned to the *Sampiero Corso* carrying an anchor, a length of chain and a long coil of rope.

'Right everyone on board,' ordered Santorini as they approached, 'we're going to carry on searching for this wreck even if a hurricane comes our way.'

'I don't think that we should attempt it personally. We have a lot of sensitive electronic equipment onboard which could easily get damaged by the salt spray, and then we'd have serious delays to contend with.'

'Yes, I realise that Bertie, but surely there is some other work that we could get on with, which doesn't need the accuracy of the positioning system. The handheld GPS should be enough to get us to an excavation site, and once we're there we could just do some basic clearance.'

'That's true, but there's also the risk of damage to equipment as the boat is being thrown around; the camera and floodlights for example. And I don't think that you should overlook the danger and discomfort for your crew.'

'Yes, perhaps I am being a little unreasonable,' admitted Monica.

Bertie stared out of the kitchen window at the swaying branches of a large plane tree.

'Look, what I suggest is that we pack the truck and go down to Tizzano as usual. Hubert and I will take the boat out unloaded and leave the shelter of the port to assess the conditions outside. If everything looks OK, we'll come back to get you and load the equipment.'

'That sounds reasonable. And if it's still too rough?'

'Then we'll moor up and wait for a break in the weather. The forecast says that it will ease at some point today, so we might as well be ready to move when it does. We could hang out in one of the restaurants there.'

'That's an excellent idea Bertie. I'll go and put it to Anna and Hubert.'

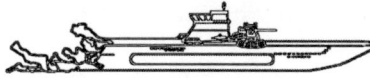

4

Mike cautiously edged his way down the uneven track towards Roccapina, mindful of the heavy equipment that was lying in the trunk. It was late morning and the temperature was rising as the cooling wind fell into retreat. In the distance, Mike watched occasional streaks of white spray form on the backdrop of blue, a sign that the sea conditions were far from perfect. But the weather clearly presented no problem for the handful of intrepid yachtsmen who were now tacking their way out of the bay.

After finding a shaded spot in the car park at the foot of the track, Mike and Thomas stepped out into the fresh, juniper-scented air and opened the hatch of the Peugeot. They pulled out their equipment and were soon sat side by side on the edge of the trunk, strapping on harnesses and clipping their sling tanks into place. Once they were ready, they pushed themselves to their feet, straining under the weight of the extra 35 kilos which they were supporting on their shoulders.

'I doubt if they'll have ever seen anything like this in Roccapina before,' said Thomas, smiling at the mass of equipment which they had strapped to their bodies.

'Yeah, let's see what kind of a reaction we get.'

They walked hunched over like primates, through the car park and across the beach towards the sea, attracting puzzled stares from bemused holidaymakers. A group of giggling children stopped dead in their tracks and ran screaming towards their parents as the strange looking creatures in black space-suits approached. Thomas smiled and waved at two toothless little girls who stared wide-eyed at him from behind the legs of their father. Once over their fear they peeked out and beamed shy, toothless smiles back at him. There were several requests for photographs, but Mike and Thomas paused only for a few seconds as they were keen to relieve the weight of their equipment. They waded out until they were waist deep in the shallows before fully inflating the large capacity, horseshoe shaped buoyancy wings which would support the weight of their multiple cylinders in the water. The expanding tubes grew outwards from their supporting back-plates and puckered as they pushed against the rubber restraints, like huge, black colon-like sausages. Mike sat back in the water and sighed with relief as he unclipped his harness and pushed the floating rig towards Thomas.

'Right hold on to this lot and I'll be back in a tick.'

He slipped on a pair of fins and set off swimming towards the moorings, returning with the RIB shortly afterwards. Once both sets of equipment had been heaved aboard, Thomas went to retrieve the accessory equipment and the two DPV's from the car, his every move scrutinised by a steadily growing audience.

On his return, the crowds parted to let him pass, curiously eying the bright yellow electric propulsion units that he clasped in each hand. A small group of children plucked up the courage to follow Thomas into the water and began to splash noisily around him as he passed the equipment to Mike on the RIB. Before he hauled himself aboard, Thomas turned around and began to laugh like a maniac, chasing after them, to their screams of delighted terror.

'Looks like we've caused quite a stir,' chuckled Mike as Thomas climbed aboard.

'Yeah, I nearly wet myself when I heard one kid asking his dad if we were robots.'

'Excellent! I can already see it in the newspapers: Tourist beach terrorised by invading aliens!'

'I think we impressed the ladies too,' said Thomas, making his eyebrows dance. 'I got one or two admiring glances as I was walking back.'

'French-Canadians again?'

Thomas shot Mike a warning glance.

'OK, OK, water under the bridge and all that,' said Mike, holding his hands up in submission. He pushed the throttle forwards and brought the boat around in a tight curve before heading smoothly out of the bay.

Jeannot sat on the aft deck of the *Sampiero Corso*, puffing distractedly on his pipe with one elbow resting on the rail. He glanced at his wristwatch and scanned the surface of the water to check for the tell-tale columns of rising bubbles which would signify the presence of Santorini and his men. It wasn't easy to keep track of the patches of disturbance in the choppy sea conditions and if Jeannot was honest with himself, he cared little about where they were in any case. It would suit him fine if they all disappeared under the waves and were never heard from again. In fact it had briefly crossed his mind to pull up the two anchors and leave them all behind, stranded at sea. If the consequences of any of them surviving and making it back to shore were not too terrible to contemplate, he might even have seriously considered it. Since there was nothing else to do but wait, he sat back against the gunwale and let the lapping sound of the waves distract him from the dark mood which had descended on him since they'd left Propriano.

While he was reaching over the rail to tap some ash into the sea, he noticed the crashing white plumes of a power boat, punching its way through the incoming waves as it headed out to sea. As the seconds passed, it came ever closer and Jeannot's curiosity turned rapidly to concern when he realised that it was heading directly towards him. Slamming his pipe down on the bench, he jumped to his feet and stared into the depths, willing Santorini and his men to emerge; but there was no sign of them. He cursed, realising that he would have to deal with the incursion alone. If they were officials from the national park, he would probably be safe, but if they were rivals, who'd caught wind of his find, he would have to tread very carefully. As the RIB closed in, Jeannot knew that he had to quickly come up with a plausible reason for being anchored over a kilometre from shore, in close to 50 metres of water, on a boat that was strewn with diving equipment.

The shallow waters of the small bay had taken on a dull milky appearance from the fine sand and sediment that had been churned up by the swell. Past the promontory, as the depth increased, Mike watched the sea's striking cobalt blue colour return. He powered the bow through the gentle swell and pushed westwards towards the open sea. In the distance ahead, he spotted a solitary boat at anchor.

'Hey look, there's the boat Monica was talking about, the one I saw yesterday as we were coming out of the bay.'

'What's so special about it?'

'Well nothing I suppose, apart from the fact that Monica spoke to the people on board and thought they were a bit strange. She did say that they were divers though, so maybe there's a wreck out there.'

'Well, let's go over and ask them. If nothing else, they might at least be able to point us towards another site.'

'That's what I was thinking, but I have to warn you that Monica didn't give them a glowing recommendation. I think I'd better let you do the talking.'

'Great! So I'll be the one who gets punched in the face.'

Mike shrugged and quickly ducked as a burst of spray came over the bow. Thomas, caught unawares, cursed as he wiped the saltwater from his face, much to Mike's amusement. The RIB pushed on relentlessly through the breaking crests until they were within a few boat lengths of the stern of the solitary vessel. She was about twelve metres in length, had a generous beam and a spacious, covered wheelhouse with large open decks. Mike was reminded of Monica's brief history lesson when he saw the name *Sampiero Corso* clearly written across her transom. On closer inspection, he spotted a mobile compressor, a couple of cylinders and five empty equipment bags lying on the decks. They were quickly confronted by a short wiry man in his early fifties, with thinning, untamed hair and a drooping grey moustache which gave him a mournful, wizened appearance. His grey-green eyes peered at them suspiciously from beneath a furrowed brow.

'Bonjour monsieur,' chirped Thomas, 'we were just wondering if by any chance you were diving on a wreck out here.'

There was a flicker of alarm in the man's eyes.

'What makes you think we're diving a wreck?' he asked defensively.

'Well you're diving in pretty deep water, so we assumed that there must be something interesting to see; we're just looking for a place to dive.'

Jeannot passed a professional eye over their equipment and his concern mounted when he saw that they were equipped to conduct prolonged deep dives.

'There's nothing around here, just sand and a few rocks. You'd be better off going to the Lavezzi Islands or Valinco.'

'So why are you diving here if there's nothing to see?' asked Thomas, perplexed.

'We're working. We're diving for red coral.'

Thomas frowned and nodded, barely hiding his contempt.

'Do you know if there are any deep wrecks around here that are worth diving?'

Jeannot fixed Thomas with an unwavering stare, unsure if he was being baited.

'Like I said, it's just rocks and sand here. You're in the wrong place.'

Sensing that he was unlikely to extract any further information, Thomas decided not to press him further.

'*Merci tout de même* - Thanks all the same.' Thomas smiled politely and then pushed the bow of the RIB away from the hull of the other vessel. Jeannot watched them leave in silence.

'Well he seemed like a nice friendly chap,' said Mike as they began to distance themselves.

'Who - Don Quihote there? Yeah he was a fountain of joy,' replied Thomas. 'He says there's nothing to see around here; just sand and rocks.'

I understood that bit, but what did he say they were doing?'

'Collecting red coral.'

'Oh really? A coral killer! I like this guy more and more.' Mike shook his head in despair, knowing that it could take up to 75 years for red coral to fully regenerate. To his mind, these so called collectors were little more than thieves; robbing the sea to satisfy the vanity of those who least understood and respected it.

'There's still something which strikes me as odd though. The other day the crew told Monica that they were interested in Second World War memorabilia. In fact they asked her to contact them if she came across anything unusual. And yet now they say that they're looking for red coral.'

'Well it's possible that they have other interests besides red coral,' pointed out Thomas.

'Yes, I suppose so,' said Mike, 'but I still have a sneaking suspicion that they're not being altogether straight with us. Anyway, I'll soon find out because I recorded their position on the GPS while you were talking. We can come back and check out the site when they're not around.'

'You should get a job with MI5, you know.'

'Nah, you won't catch me wearing a suit - not unless it's made of neoprene anyway.'

'Me neither. These are the only work clothes I ever want to wear.'

Mike took the RIB a couple of hundred metres away from the *Sampiero Corso* and watched the digital depth sounder count down from 44 to 51 metres.

'OK, we'll drop anchor here. It's not where I planned to go, but it's deep enough and probably just as good...or equally bad of course.'

'I guess we'll find out soon enough.'

Thomas paid out the anchor chain followed by two long lengths of rope separated by a heavy weight to reduce the jarring action of the swell. Once the anchor was firmly set in, they seated themselves as best they could on the small deck and began to strap on their heavy equipment. After several minutes of rolling around, cursing and straining, they helped each other to a sitting position and sat facing each other on opposite sides of the RIB. While they were running through their final checks, Mike glanced towards the *Sampiero Corso* and saw divers climbing out of the water and moving about on the aft deck. Some of them began to stare in his and Thomas' direction, clearly surprised by their presence. He pulled his eyes away and returned his attention to the dive schedule written on his slate. Sitting motionless, he tried to block out all distractions as he visualised each step of the plan. When he was satisfied that each detail had been rehearsed and fixed firmly in his mind, he glanced upwards to see Thomas staring expectantly in his direction. A single word was all that was needed to spur them both into action.

'Ready?'

'Ready!'

Hands instinctively went towards masks as, in a blur of fluid motion, they leaned over backwards and fell simultaneously into the water. Their fully inflated buoyancy wings brought them briefly back to the surface where they exchanged rapid signals before purging air and slipping silently below the waves again. At 3 metres they paused and took turns to rotate while being checked for gas leaks. Once they had given each other the all clear, they deflated their wings and commenced a rapid feet-first descent.

They held their relative positions as they fell through the water, making precise position adjustments with their fins. Mike glanced below and was surprised to see a huge shimmering layer beneath him, like a hazy mirage on a hot road. It was a deep thermocline, and the brief visual disturbance as they passed through it was accompanied by a sudden drop in temperature. Fortunately their thick 7mm neoprene wetsuits made the transition less disagreeable.

After seeing nothing but fingers of shifting light reaching down into the obscurity, it was reassuring to see vague, dark shapes starting to form deep beneath them. Mike rotated once, scanning the area all around him and began to see parallel rock ridges running east to west across an otherwise flat, sandy plain. The anchor line was now starting to arc away and Mike quickly took a compass bearing on it before it disappeared into the foggy void. They slowed their descent by adding bursts of air into their buoyancy wings and finally came to a stop at 46 metres, hovering effortlessly above the sea floor.

Mike was aware of the minor effects of nitrogen narcosis on the fringes of his perception. The ambient blue of the filtered daylight seemed to have a crystalline purity to it which had never been apparent at shallower depths. He stared with curiosity at luminous red sponges and orange gorgonian sea fans, knowing full well that the colour which he saw could not be physically discerned at that depth. But there was no time for such distractions. Snapping his mind back into focus, he concentrated his attention on his instruments. Three minutes of time had elapsed, the pressure had dropped by 20 bar on his right cylinder and his current depth was 48 metres.

Conscious that time was passing, he consulted his compass and oriented his body so that he was aligned with the heading he'd taken earlier. Overlooked by a curious grouper that was hovering in a gap between rocks, he attracted Thomas' attention with a single tap on his cylinder. After a brief exchange of signals they unclipped their DPV's and held them out at arms length. Mike flicked the switch to the lower speed setting and immediately felt his body being pulled through the water. Once he'd reassured himself that Thomas was following, he headed towards a marker which he'd identified along the line of his trajectory.

A childlike thrill overtook them both as they were pulled effortlessly through the water, temporarily liberated from the restraints of manual propulsion. Mike soon spotted the heavy line looping down from above and followed it along the seabed until he reached the anchor. Seeing that it was embedded in soft sand, he transferred it to a crevice in the rock where it would gain a better hold. With no further need for the DPV's, they clipped them onto their harnesses out of the way. Thomas attached a reel of line to the anchor and paid it out like a spider's silken thread to maintain a physical link with their point of exit as they began to move away and explore the surrounding area. They had travelled only a few metres when Mike pointed out a marbled moray eel, protruding from a gap beneath a large, flat rock. Being unaccustomed to the scrutiny of such large and fearsome looking creatures, it wriggled its strikingly painted body and retracted warily into the shadows.

Mike glanced at his watch, noting that they were already 6 minutes into their planned run-time with 16 minutes remaining at their maximum depth. A simple calculation told him that with an allowance for delays they would need to start retracing their steps after 7 more minutes had elapsed.

They entered an imposing corridor formed between two parallel ridges of rock; a diverse microcosm of life. A small school of silver sea bream lazily held their position before cautiously peeling away as these strange creatures from another world drew close. Mike saw a lizard fish shoot out from under Thomas as he passed over its territory and then zigzag along the rocks until it found a similar position above a raised ledge. Thomas switched regulators to maintain the equilibrium between his two air cylinders and Mike followed suit. A beautifully delicate sea pen stood erect in the sand ahead of them, feeding invisibly on the surrounding soup of zooplankton like some bizarre alien plant. Spiny seastars and red-black sea urchins clung to the rocky substrate with a multitude of tiny tubular feet while swarms of sand smelt and picarel darted around them in an erratic, predator-confusing dance.

Thomas suddenly grabbed Mike by the arm and pointed towards a disturbance in the sand a few metres ahead. There was a cloud of sediment and the occasional flash of dark undulating wings. When a long, distinctive whip-like tail flicked up out of the disturbed silt, Mike was left in no further doubt as to what they'd had the fortune to stumble across. It was an eagle ray, shovelling its nose into the sand in search of buried molluscs. Mike knew that they could detect the minute electrical impulses of their living prey beneath the sand and then dig them up and crush them to a pulp in their specially adapted teeth plates, shell and all. While the gracious ray was busily attempting to extract its reward, Mike and Thomas managed to approach to within a few metres before it finally spotted them and bolted away, its wide pectoral fins flapping like the wings of some strange prehistoric bird. Mike grinned and patted Thomas on the shoulder in recognition of his discovery.

Looking down at his computer, he saw that the run-time had now reached the 12 minute mark. With only one minute remaining before they would have to turn back, Mike paused to spend time studying unfamiliar anemones and hydroids on a nearby rock platform. As he was hovering close to a large gorgonian sea fan, scouring its intricate web like structure for small invertebrates, he suddenly noticed something unusually geometric in form, lying amongst the organic forms which covered the surrounding substrate. On closer inspection it appeared to be a piece of torn pipework connected to a drum shaped object, the size of a small saucer. It was overgrown with madrepores and calcareous worm casings but came away easily in Mike's hand. He turned the object over and scraped away some of the scale from its surface. There was a shattered glass face on the opposite side and a dial and printed lettering were visible beneath it. With time pressing, Mike deliberated, unsure whether he ought to leave the object where he'd found it. In the end, curiosity got the better of him and he slipped it under the rubber retaining bands of his sling tank so that he could study it later.

Thomas came over to remind him that it was time to turn around and start heading back towards the anchor. Mike acknowledged with an OK signal and fell in beside Thomas as he began to reel his way back along the safety line. While returning through the rock corridor, they came across a stunning, bronze coloured John Dory, a distinctive black spot clearly evident on its large oval flank. The long slender dorsal rays and pelvic fins gave it an exotic, almost regal appearance which rarely left the observer unimpressed. Thomas glided towards it, attempting to study it at close quarters, but sensing his looming presence, the John Dory flicked its tail, turned on a hairpin and disappeared into a narrow gap in the rock.

Mike had more success when he spotted a small colony of bright red coral, protruding from its foothold on a sheer rock face. He hovered motionless before it, admiring the delicate network of finger-like branches, decorated with tufts of fine, feathery white coral polyps. The sight was both uplifting and encouraging, but Mike's joy was marred by the sad knowledge that a thoughtless collector, like the one presently on board the *Sampiero* Corso, would willingly rip it from its hold if he happened across it. Mike could only cross his fingers in the hope that this particular colony might remain undetected for many years to come and thus avoid the ignominious fate of being turned into tourist trinkets in some backstreet jeweller's workshop.

The narrow rock corridor soon gave way to open sand and Mike again spotted the flattened boulder with its resident marbled moray eel. Knowing that the anchor was close by, he checked his run-time against the schedule and saw that they were now 19 minutes into the dive. A quick exchange of signals with Thomas confirmed that there were only three minutes of bottom time remaining. Once Thomas had reeled in the last few metres of line and freed it, Mike dislodged the anchor from the rock fissure and transferred it to a wide patch of sand, from where it could easily be pulled free from the surface.

Thomas flashed up two fingers to signal the number of minutes left before they would be obliged to begin their ascent. Mike checked his computer and confirmed the signal before adding a thumb up sign to suggest rising up the anchor line in advance. With an elegant sweep of his hand, Thomas invited him to lead the way. Mike unclipped the scooter from a 'D' ring on his harness and waited for Thomas to do the same. After a reciprocated nod of agreement they activated the DPV's and began to follow the shallow gradient formed by the looping anchor line. Thomas saw a small shoal of barracuda slowly circling in columnar formation to his right and couldn't resist the temptation to veer off and cut through the middle of them, sending them scattering in all directions, like an explosion of silver shards. He made a victory roll before banking and returning to join Mike, who could only shake his head and smile at his indulgent behaviour.

The anchor line was now starting to rise steeply and they were obliged to slow their ascent by turning off their DPV's. They arrived at the 20 metre stop slightly ahead of schedule and immediately reached for the nitrox regulators which were strapped to the body of their sling tanks. Looking towards the surface, they could see the RIB in a shimmering patch of daylight, somewhat distorted by the thermocline above them. Mike checked his watch and saw that the run-time was now 24 minutes. It was time to rise upwards and commence a lengthy decompression schedule.

The last stop was invariably the longest one and starved of visual distractions there was little to do besides deploy their surface marker buoys, monitor their instruments and wait patiently for the dissolved nitrogen in their tissues to escape back into the atmosphere through their lungs. The nitrox in their sling tanks helped to speed up the elimination process, but only by a matter of minutes.

Mike entertained himself by observing the prism effect caused by the cillia of a passing comb jelly and watched a school of silvery anchovies appear from nowhere and then with a sudden burst of acceleration disappear just as swiftly into the grainy backdrop of blue.

Thomas came towards Mike, tilted his head and began to point at his sling tank. Wondering if there was a problem, Mike looked down and realised that Thomas was in fact pointing to the unusual object which he'd found earlier. With all the distractions, he'd almost forgotten about it and now, under Thomas' curious regard, he reached down to pull it free of the restraining bands. He found that he could make out more of the details now that it was illuminated by the light of the sun and his senses were no longer impeded by the effects of narcosis. Thomas drew close and examined the instrument with equal interest, expressing his opinion by pointing to it and then to his own submersible pressure gauge. Mike nodded his agreement, took out his knife and carefully scraped away more of the light scaling of growth that was covering the glass face. He saw the word *Tiefenmesser* written at the centre of the dial and a unit of measurement displayed at the base of the curved scale: mWasser. At first Mike was unsure what the unit represented, but he knew that *wasser* was the German word for water. As he began to work out the connection between the measurement and the scale, the startling reality of what he could be holding in his hand suddenly dawned upon him. It was, as he and Thomas had suspected, a depth gauge, but certainly not one intended for use by any diver. And that left one intriguing possibility.

Bertie and Hubert tied the RIB alongside the jetty and walked over to the terrace of the restaurant where Monica and Anna were sitting. Monica looked up from her laptop screen as they approached the table and leaned back into a wide wicker chair, shading her eyes against the glare of the midday sun. Sitting opposite her, Anna replaced her *café-crème* on a white porcelain saucer and closed a folder of documents.

'How is it out there?' asked Monica.

'It's much better,' replied Bertie. 'The wind has dropped considerably and it looks like the swell has eased too.'

'Do you think it would be safe for us to go out then?'

'I can't see why not; as long as we just take basic equipment.'

'I can live with that. I don't suppose we'll be attempting any lifting today, so let's do as you suggested and take a look at the second site in 445R. If that doesn't look promising then we can always return to the Roman site and forage around the exterior of the hull.'

'OK. Well if everyone is agreed, we'll start loading the excavation equipment. Do you want to take the grids?'

'If it makes things easier, we'll do without them. We can temporarily peg out the area if we find anything interesting and then set up the quadratic grids on our next visit.'

'Let's do that then. Obviously we'll have to leave some of the other equipment in the truck as well, but I think it should be safe enough.'

'I'm sure it will, but try not to leave anything on display just the same; I'd hate to have to try and replace anything out here.'

'Don't worry, Hubert and I will take care of everything. Just finish up what you're doing and meet us at the jetty in 15 minutes.'

'What the hell is that boat doing over there?'

'They came while you were in the water. I couldn't exactly stop them could I?' said Jeannot, feeling unjustly accused. 'I tried to tell them that there was nothing to see in this area, but they were obviously determined to dive here anyway.'

'So you spoke to them did you?'

'Well...yes, they came here first.'

'And what exactly did you tell them?' demanded Santorini.

'I told them that we were diving for red coral. What else could I say?'

Santorini looked away, shaking his head in frustration. He could not argue with Jeannot's actions but it did little to settle his mood. After completing yet another fruitless dive, his patience was beginning to wear thin.

'Pascal, isn't that the hire boat that we saw beside the archaeologists yesterday?' he asked, staring intently at the two divers seated in the small orange RIB.

'I think so...yes it is!'

'I thought so. Perhaps those archaeologists aren't what they seem after all,' he said, narrowing his eyes. 'What exactly did those two say they were doing out here Jeannot?'

'Well they asked if there was a wreck here and...'

'A wreck! They we're asking about a wreck? God give me strength.'

'Well it appeared as if they just wanted to find a wreck to explore. They weren't asking about any specific wreck.'

Santorini threw his fins across the boat and dropped his tank heavily onto the deck.

'Are you trying to tell me that you think a couple of weekend divers have just by chance come out here to this precise spot, close to a kilometre offshore, in 50 metres of water, just to find a random wreck to explore?'

'They're not weekend divers,' said Jeannot, shaking his head. 'They're properly equipped for deep decompression diving and if you want to find any kind of depth around here, you *have* to go far from shore.'

'And that's supposed to make me feel relieved is it?'

'He's right Jean-Claude. Just take a look at all the gear they're wearing,' said Michel, peering at the RIB through binoculars. Santorini scowled.

'From now on anyone who takes an undue interest in this area must be regarded as a threat. I want those two stopped before they get a chance to nose around down there and I want to make damned sure that they don't come back here again. Quickly, haul in the anchors.'

'Too late,' said Michel, 'they've just gone over the side.'

It was unquestionably a wreck; there could be absolutely no question about that. It was too early to determine the age of it with any great accuracy, but the size, design and construction were consistent with the time-frame that they were interested in. Moving slowly around the perimeter, they identified the exposed structural ribs of the hull and settled down next to the best preserved of them.

The nozzle of the water suctorial swept gently back and forth, skimming the top layer of sand and silt away from the exposed upright timber. Streams of sediment were drawn up into the nozzle and blasted out into a collecting sieve some distance away. A small crater began to form as the substrate was progressively stripped away, exposing the sculpted surface of a supporting cross-beam. Striped mullet, ornate wrasse and gilthead bream appeared as if from nowhere, swirling and darting around the newly formed crater, in frenzied competition for the bounty of tiny crustaceans and molluscs that were being unearthed. Bertie pulled the nozzle away to check his progress, chasing away the unwanted intruders before returning it to the spot which he was working on. He deepened the crater by another few centimetres and then pulled the nozzle away again. Through the milky suspension he saw a bright flash amongst the invading shoals of foraging fish. At first he thought that it was just the reflection of the floodlights from the shiny flank of a seabream, but as the sediment began to settle, he saw that it wasn't any part of a fish at all. It was a partially buried piece of metal; a distinctly bright gold metal.

'That wasn't a bad dive at all,' said Thomas as he slipped off his fins. 'I was surprised at how much there is to see down there.'

'Yeah, you and me both. At times it was just like being in the tropics, especially with all those amazing sea fans - and the eagle ray was just the icing on the cake.'

'What were those two big fish that were chasing that shoal of sardines towards the end of the dive? They looked like Spanish mackerel.'

'Same family. They were Albacore.'

'Did you see how fast they moved?'

'All the Scombridae family are endothermic in that their bodies are warmer than the surrounding environment. Many of the fastest predatory fish have that adaptation which allows them to benefit from a faster metabolic rate.'

'You should tell that to Monica. She'd be most impressed.'

'Maybe I will,' smiled Mike.

'I think this site is perfect for deep air training anyway,' said Thomas.

'Yes, it's an ideal spot, but we need to find more sites like this. After all, we'll be in competition with a lot of other exciting destinations worldwide.'

'True. Perhaps we should try going further out. Maybe check out those islands we saw on the chart; the *Îlots des Moines.*'

'That would be nice,' agreed Mike, 'but unfortunately it's illegal to dive there; it's a conservation area.'

'That's a shame,' said Thomas, chewing his lip. He looked down absently at the equipment lying on the deck and his eyes came to rest on the piece of wreckage which Mike had discovered.

'What exactly is that thing you brought up with you?'

'I think it's an old depth gauge - a German one.' Mike pulled the broken pipes free of the sling tank and passed the instrument to Thomas. 'Here take a look.'

'That's an odd thing to find way out here.' Thomas held the instrument in front of his face and read the name that was printed on the dial behind the shattered glass face.

'*Tiefenmesser.* Well I suppose it would mess your teeth up if someone hit you in the face with it.'

'Maybe we should put it to the test,' said Mike.

Thomas smiled, and then a look of puzzlement came over him when he noticed the scale.

'Hey wait a minute; did you say that this was a pressure gauge or a depth gauge?'

'I'm pretty sure that it's a depth gauge,' replied Mike.

'It must be in feet then.'

'No, it's in metres.'

'But that's impossible, the scale goes up to 260. I've never seen an analogue gauge that goes anything over 100 metres. And nobody could have been diving anywhere near those depths when this old relic was in use.'

'I didn't say that it was a diving depth gauge.'

Mike watched Thomas frown, open his mouth to speak and then close it again as he thought the problem through.

'You mean to say that it came from a submarine?' he asked tentatively.

'A U-boat I think. I'm not certain, but with that manufacturers name, if that's what it is, we should be able to find out.'

'But how could it have ended up here?'

'Well that's what I've been trying to work out. I can only guess that the gauge got damaged somehow and an engineer decided to throw the defective part overboard once he'd replaced it. The only problem with that scenario is the fact that the pipework got ripped away along with it. I can't imagine how that could have happened.'

'Maybe there was an accident, or....' Thomas suddenly turned his head in alarm.

'Oh shit! Looks like we've got company.'

'Why haven't they surfaced yet? It's been nearly an hour since they went in.'

'Like I told you, they're properly equipped for extended deep dives,' said Jeannot as he squinted through a pair of binoculars. 'I can see their surface marker buoys now, so they must be decompressing.'

'How can they stay down for so long?' asked Santorini in frustration.

'They're using twin cylinders and separate sling tanks; probably filled with nitrox.'

'Can't we do the same?'

'It's not that simple,' replied Jeannot. 'Twin cylinders and slings can't be safely used on standard buoyancy jackets because they lack the necessary attachments and can't provide enough lift. Besides, even if we had the proper equipment, we'd still need to get specialised training and neither of those things come cheap. The bottom line is that unless you're prepared to make a major investment, we'll have to make do with what we have.'

Santorini scowled, knowing that it would be unwise to make a large investment without being certain of a return. On the other hand, he could not just sit back and allow someone else to work his patch unchallenged. The simplest and most inexpensive solution, he realised, was to remove the threat of competition altogether.

'They've just surfaced,' announced Michel.

'Good, let's go and pay them a visit.'

The *Sampiero Corso* advanced against the rolling swell while the two anchors were hauled aboard and secured. Once liberated from her restraints, she turned to starboard and crabbed towards the small RIB, gradually closing in on her stern quarter. The throaty diesel engine rattled noisily as she came to a halt beside the RIB and held her position against the wind. Santorini stood imposingly at the wooden rail and glared down at the two occupants.

'*Qu'est ce que vous faites ici*? - What are you doing here?' he challenged.

Mike and Thomas exchanged nervous glances.

'We're diving, why?' asked Thomas.

'You're not from around here are you?'

'No – I'm from Marseille originally...and he's British.' Santorini looked from one to the other.

'Are you working with the archaeologists?'

Thomas baulked at the question, realising to his surprise that they had been watched.

'No, why do you ask?'

'So you're friends of theirs then?'

'Well no, not really. We only met them yesterday.'

Santorini eyes were full of suspicion, as he probed the Frenchman's face for signs of a lie.

While Mike was following what he could of the conversation, he discreetly eyed the *Sampiero Corso* and its crew. The big bearded man speaking to Thomas was almost certainly the person who Monica had dealt with. He was dark, built like an ox and had the appearance of a man who might kill you as soon as look at you. Mike noticed with interest the tattoo on his left forearm. It was the same head and shoulder design of a black slave wearing a headband which he'd seen on the Serena beer label in Bonifacio. Underneath it was written a single word in Corsican: *Libertà*, which was close enough to the French word for him to understand what it meant. The rest of the crew had the dark, surly looks that were typical of Mediterranean men from rural backgrounds, but their weathered faces betrayed none of the warmth and timidity which was generally associated with them. Mike dropped his eyes and scanned the decks, looking for signs of red coral or the mesh bags and tools which might be used to collect it. There was no sign of either, and more surprisingly, the diving equipment that most of them were using was basic to the point of being dangerous. It was certainly not the sort of material which he would expect professionals to use, even in shallow water. Perplexed, he turned his attention back to the conversation.

'Are you here on vacation?' asked Santorini.

'No,' replied Thomas. 'We're doing some research because we're thinking of setting up a diving business here.'

'You're wasting your time,' scoffed Santorini. 'This is no place for diving and no one will pay you to come here. Go to Bonifacio or Porto Veccio.'

'Well actually, with what we're doing, we can operate anywhere where there is deep water. We're not particularly interested in shallow diving.'

Thomas quickly realised from the bearded man's darkening complexion that his advice was not in fact a suggestion.

'Am I not making myself clear?' Santorini's jaw muscles twitched as his blazing eyes flicked between Mike and Thomas. He glanced down at their equipment, thinking of sabotaging it, when something caught his eye.

'What's that thing there?' he asked pointing down at the deck. Thomas followed the line of his outstretched arm and saw the gauge that Mike had found.

'You mean this?'

'Yes. Let me see it,' demanded Santorini, beckoning with his hand.

Thomas shot Mike a worried glance and was met with a resigned shrug. He picked up the gauge and passed it to Santorini, who held it in front of his face and studied it with great interest. Mike noticed a brief look of disbelief come over him before his eyes narrowed and he fixed Thomas with a piercing stare.

'Where exactly did you find this?'

'Tell him I found it just beneath the boat,' said Mike, needing no translation.

Thomas saw from Mike's unwavering expression that he was not prepared to play ball with them. The situation was becoming uncomfortably tense, and knowing that he would be unable to lie convincingly, Thomas thought carefully before he replied.

'He says that he found it beneath the boat.'

Santorini's eyes bored into Mike's as he addressed him directly.

'What else did you find down there?'

'*Rien* – Nothing,' replied Mike, calmly shaking his head.

Santorini grunted and stared at the gauge in his hand. His face reddened and his left eye began to twitch as he lifted his head and addressed Thomas.

'Listen well *Pinzuti*. You and your *Rosbif* freind are not welcome here; you are trespassing on our territory. These fishing grounds have belonged to our families for centuries and only *we* can exploit them if we choose to. Take my advice and look for somewhere else to dive, or you will find yourselves in much deeper water than you anticipated. Here in Corsica, when we settle our disputes, we don't rely on the courts to hand out punishment.' Santorini drew his finger across his throat to illustrate the point. 'You would do well to bear that in mind.'

Thomas stood in bewildered silence as Santorini confiscated the gauge, fixed him with a final vitriolic stare and then ordered the helmsman to break away.

Mike came over to join Thomas as the *Sampiero Corso* motored back to its original point of anchorage.

'I take it that we we're not invited to a cocktail party then?' asked Mike.

'If we were, then I would seriously think about writing my will before going.'

'Who are they?'

'Local thugs I guess; we didn't really get round to introductions. Anyway, I don't think we'll be diving around here again.'

'Why's that?'

'Because he made it quite clear that if we wanted to visit his ancestral fishing grounds again, he would gladly supply us with a pair of concrete diving boots.'

'Ancestral fishing grounds? That's nonsense. This area is within the national park boundaries.'

'Yeah? Well you can argue the toss with him if you like, but I quite like my knee-caps on the front of my legs, thanks.'

'If you want my opinion there is something down there which he doesn't want us to find. Their story about looking for red coral just doesn't ring true. I had a good look at the equipment they're using and there was no sign of any tools or collecting bags.'

'That doesn't prove anything,' said Thomas. 'They could have stowed everything away before they came over.'

'What about the gauge then?'

'What about it?'

'Well he got pretty fired up when he saw it and he didn't give it back did he?'

'Here we go with the conspiracy theories again,' said Thomas, rolling his eyes. 'It was just a piece of valueless wreckage. And besides, if I made a living from red coral and someone started moving in on my patch, I'd get pretty pissed off too.'

'You think it was valueless?' asked Mike.

'Well it might make a nice paperweight, if you polished it up.'

'Thomas, it was a depth gauge from a German U-boat.'

'You don't know that for sure. And even if it *is* true; what does it prove?'

'Probably nothing,' replied Mike, 'but you have to admit that our big, hairy Neanderthal friend's reaction to seeing it was pretty strange. I mean, why would he be so keen to know where we found an apparently worthless piece of wreckage, unless it had some value to him?'

'I don't know. Didn't you say something about him being a collector of Second World War memorabilia?'

'Yes, but his reaction was hardly one of delight was it? I still think there has to be something bigger at stake. Pull the anchor line up and I'll record a GPS position when it goes vertical.'

Thomas could not believe what he was hearing.

'Are you seriously thinking of coming back here?'

'I don't know; but if I do, I'll need a fix on our position.'

Thomas muttered to himself as he strained to haul the anchor up from the depths. Mike recorded a waypoint on the GPS when it broke free and then began to make his way back towards the shelter of the small bay. Halfway there he turned to look over his shoulder and was surprised to see the *Sampiero Corso* dropping anchor over the site which they had just vacated.

'Hey Thomas, take a look where our friends are now.'

Thomas shaded his eyes and looked out over the stern.

'I don't believe it. They've gone back there haven't they?'

'Yep, it certainly looks that way.'

'Do you think they're going to dive there now?'

'I'd bet my best pair of surf shorts on it.'

'They must be out of their minds doing repeat dives to those depths,' said Thomas, shaking his head. 'Maybe you're right. Maybe there is something down there that they think is worth risking their necks for.'

'Well it's their funeral,' said Mike, 'and I guarantee that they won't find anything.'

As they reached the entrance to the bay Mike glanced to his right and saw a familiar figure waving to him from a black and yellow RIB.

'Hey look, there's your pal Hubert and the rest of the merry crew. Let's go over and say hello.'

'It has to be around here somewhere. If this is what I think it is, there can be no question about it.'

Santorini held the gauge up so that everyone could see it. Four faces frowned in concentration as they tried to spot something which might give them a clue as to what they were looking at.

'It's German all right,' said Pascal, his crooked nose almost touching the glass face as he examined the dial. 'It's some kind of gauge.'

'Obviously! And although my German is about as useless as a Frenchman with an assault rifle, I *do* know what *wasser* means,' said Santorini. 'Anyone else here remember that from school?'

'I don't even remember going to school,' said Michel with a smirk. The others burst into laughter.

'I think it means water,' said Jeannot, after the noise died down.

'Exactly! I'm glad to see that not all of you were out stealing motorbikes when you should have been in class.'

Michel and Pierre swapped knowing smiles.

'That's the first bit. Now does anyone have any idea what this M might stand for in front of the word *wasser*?'

Three blank faces stared back at him. Jeannot had a good idea, but decided to give someone else the opportunity to answer.

'Hah Jean-Claude, you know some clever things,' said Michel finally, 'but I think I speak for all of us when I say that we don't have a clue what you're trying to tell us.'

Santorini looked to the skies and let out a sigh.

'It's a depth gauge,' he said after a pause, 'the M stands for metres.'

There were raised eyebrows and low mutterings as Santorini passed the gauge around.

'It must have come from the submarine. And this time we know for sure that it could not have floated to where it was found.'

'Maybe,' said Pierre, 'but if there's any truth in the story, it could still have been blown far away from it.' There were nods of agreement.

'Yes, I've taken that into consideration,' said Santorini. 'But now, at least, we have a realistic point from which to start searching. We know that the depth gauge was found in this spot and even if it fell a good distance away from the site of the explosion, we can still be reasonably confident that the wreck is at this moment lying within a 300 metre radius of the point where we are standing right now.'

Santorini's men stared at the surrounding sea as if might give a clue as to the wreck's presence below them.

'We're now going to concentrate all our efforts in this area. We have two more dives to do and we'll do them right here, just in case those two clowns are keeping quiet about anything else which they might have found down there.'

'Hey there. How are things going?' asked Hubert, while peeling off the top of his wetsuit.

'All good thanks,' replied Mike. 'I'm surprised to see you lot out here after the bad weather this morning.' Hubert slipped on a pair of dark sunglasses and with his wet, spiked blonde hair, Mike thought that he looked more like a rock musician than an archaeologist.

'Yeah, it was touch and go for a while,' said Hubert, 'but it soon calmed down.'

'Did you get much done?' asked Thomas.

'Quite a lot actually; we're really glad we made the effort because we've made quite a significant find this morning.'

'Don't tell me that you've stumbled across Captain Blackbeard's lost treasure?'

'Not exactly,' laughed Hubert, 'but you might be closer to the truth than you think.'

'Sounds intriguing,' said Mike.

'It certainly beats sucking mud out of amphorae.'

Monica put down a clipboard and came to join Hubert.

'Hi you two. Did you have a good dive?' she asked.

'It was pretty cool, thanks,' said Thomas. 'We saw an eagle ray, I finally got to see a john dory and then we had a very close encounter with a fat, bearded walrus.'

'Oh, that's...unusual,' said Monica with a confused smile. 'Don't walrus live in the poles?'

'They do. This was just some low life bottom feeder,' replied Mike.

'I see,' said Monica, clearly no wiser. 'Excuse me for just one second.'

She turned to speak to Hubert in hushed tones of Swiss-German.

'Hubert, can you please try to be a little more discreet about this find.'

'What? Oh come on Monica, these guys are professionals; they're not going to go...'

'Those decisions are mine to make Hubert,' said Monica, cutting him short. 'You know that you should always consult me, whatever you think is right. We don't really know who these two are and we can't be totally sure that they can be trusted.'

'Fine,' said Hubert, prickled. 'Much as I think you're over-reacting, I'll keep my mouth shut.'

'That would be much appreciated.'

'You'd better ask Bertie and Anna to keep those artefacts out of view then,' he said, with a curt jerk of the head.

'Sorry are we disturbing anything?' asked Mike, detecting a slight tension in the air.

'No, not at all,' replied Monica, 'we're just discussing work.' She flushed and found herself nervously brushing her fingers through her hair. Hubert went over to speak with Thomas at the bow.

'So you've made a find, have you?' asked Mike.

'We've found *something*,' said Monica evasively, which is quite a relief after the way the day started. I was afraid, this morning that we weren't going to get anything done at all.'

'Yes, the sea was still a bit choppy when we jumped, but by the time we surfaced it was just a light swell.' Mike watched Monica filling in notes that weren't entirely necessary. 'So this find of yours. Is it from the period that you were telling me about yesterday?'

'It's too early to tell at the moment. We'll have to send a lot of material to the laboratory for testing.'

'It all sounds positive though; you must be pleased.'

'Yes, there is definitely cause for optimism. If we get positive results, we'll almost certainly get increased funding, which means that we'll be able to excavate the site fully.'

'And how much time would a project like that take?' asked Mike, for reasons that were not entirely without self-interest.

'It's difficult to say. Initially I would have said a month, but we could now be looking at an extended project, which could well stretch into winter.'

'That's great news,' said Mike. The prospect of staying in Corsica through the low season had just become a little more attractive.

'Yes, well we're a long way from that situation yet,' replied Monica, with characteristic reservation.

'Hey Mike, what was the name that was written on that gauge again?'

Mike turned to see Thomas and Hubert looking expectantly in his direction.

'I...don't remember; I didn't get chance to write it down on my slate. Wait a minute though; what was it that you said about being hit in the teeth?'

'Oh yeah! I said it could mess your teeth up - teeth messer,'

'Yeah that's it, teefmesser, or something like that,' agreed Mike.

'I think you mean tiefenmesser,' corrected Monica. 'It's the German word for depth gauge.'

A wide smile crept across Mike's face as he turned to face Thomas.

'What did I tell you? Now there can be no doubt.'

'No doubt about what?' enquired Monica.

'We found a depth gauge. A German depth gauge right next to the place where your friends from the *Sampiero Corso* are diving.'

'Is that so unusual? There are many German divers who come here.'

'Yes, but first let me ask you something. What would *mWasser* mean on a German depth gauge?'

'*Meter wasser*; metres of water in English,' said Hubert.

'Exactly what I thought,' said Mike nodding. 'And have you ever seen a diver's depth gauge the size of my hand which has a range of 270 metres?'

'270 metres!' exclaimed Monica, 'No it can't possibly be a diving gauge. Is it modern looking?'

'Not at all. It was an analogue depth gauge and judging by the growth on it, it had been down there for a good number of years.'

'Then it must be from an *unterwasserboot*...a U-boat,' said Hubert, intrigued.

Mike turned towards Thomas, his eyebrows raised and a smile of triumph lighting up his face.

'But how would it have got there?' asked Monica.

'Initially I thought that it had been thrown overboard, but I'm starting to think that that there might be another explanation.'

'Do you have it with you?' enquired Monica.

'Well, here's the interesting bit. The fat bearded guy from the *Sampiero Corso* took it from us. He came over after we surfaced to find out what we were doing there. When he spotted the gauge he demanded to see it and then flew into a rage and warned us never to dive there again. Pretty unusual don't you think?'

'Yes, they did seem a little strange,' said Monica. 'So what do you conclude from all this?'

'I think they're searching for something. They say that they're collecting red coral, but I don't believe that for a second. As soon as we left the site where we found the gauge, they took our spot and dived immediately after us. There has to be something down there that they're afraid we'll find.'

'Have you thought about drugs?' asked Hubert. 'Maybe they're trying to locate a drop. It's common practice for ships smuggling narcotics to avoid customs by ditching water-tight containers overboard and then giving the coordinates to divers to pick up later.'

'Yes, that's a possibility I suppose, but the fat man's reaction to us finding the gauge, tells me that it's not quite so clear cut as that.'

'Maybe there's actually a U-boat wreck out there then,' suggested Hubert.

'That's what I'm starting to wonder. Unlikely as it might seem, it's about the only explanation which seems to make any sense.'

'Maybe we should risk going back there at first light,' said Thomas. 'If there really is a sunken U-boat in the area, we should be able to find more wreckage from it.'

'Might I suggest something before you decide to go off and risk another confrontation,' asked Monica.

'All suggestions are welcome,' said Mike.

'There are public records available for U-boats which went missing in action during the war and there should certainly be some documentary evidence to support the losses recorded in this area. You might also consider speaking to local fishermen and some of the older local inhabitants to see if they know anything. After all, if a U-boat went down close to shore, there is a good chance that someone would know something about it. Either way, it's definitely worth doing a little research before you decide to do anything rash.'

'That sounds like good advice to me,' agreed Mike. 'Do you happen to know how we might get hold of that information?'

'Well I would imagine that there's a war records archive where you can make enquiries. Having said that, I might be able to get you the information more quickly through our department at the university. We have professors of military history there who have access to all sorts of information, and if they don't have exactly what you want, they will certainly know where to get it.'

'How about Professor Bergmann?' asked Hubert smiling. 'He was always quite fond of you wasn't he?' Monica flushed and glared at him.

It was widely known amongst Monica's contemporaries that the elderly professor had once tried to seduce her in his quarters, during the course of a private tutorial. The damning red hand mark which appeared on his cheek directly afterwards, left no one in any doubt as to what she had thought about his advances. Monica rose above Hubert's taunts and cleared her throat.

'I'll send a few E-Mails out and see what comes back Mike. There's no harm in asking.'

'Thanks Monica. That would be fantastic,' beamed Mike.

Thomas caught Hubert's attention and rolled his eyes. Hubert smiled knowingly.

'Well it looks like we all have cause to celebrate tonight,' said Mike looking from Hubert to Monica. 'How about we all go out for dinner together? Surely you're not going to back out on us again?'

Hubert spoke up in support of Mike.

'Yeah Monica, we should do that; we've definitely earned it today.'

'That's easy for you to say, since you have a day off tomorrow.'

'True, but we don't have to stay out late. Besides, we haven't been out together since we arrived.'

Before Monica could make her excuses, Hubert rallied for support.

'Hey Bertie, Anna, you want to go out and celebrate with us tonight don't you?'

The young couple exchanged glances, shrugged and nodded.

'Sure, why not? Once we've finished writing up of course,' agreed Bertie.

Monica sighed in resignation.

'OK you win, but this is not going to be a wild drinking party. We'll go to a restaurant, have a quiet evening together and if anyone wants to carry on the festivities afterwards, that's up to them.'

'That's fair enough,' agreed Hubert.

'Good, that's settled then,' said an upbeat Mike. 'The next question is...where are you staying?'

'We're just outside Propriano,' replied Hubert. 'Do you know Propriano at all?'

'No, I've never been there. What about you Thomas?'

'I've been through it, but I don't really know it well.'

'Why don't we meet near the harbour then?' suggested Monica. 'It's easy to find and there are plenty of bars and restaurants around there.'

'We could meet at the *Bar Nautique*,' suggested Hubert, 'it's on the left hand side as you go down the Avenue Napoléon; you can't miss it.'

'Do they serve food there?' asked Monica.

'No...but we could meet there and have a drink before we decide where to go.'

'Very well,' said Monica, wearily.

'I'm sure we'll be able to find it,' said Mike. 'What time do you want to meet there?'

'How about 8pm?' suggested Hubert.

Monica, Bertie and Anna nodded their agreement.

'That suits us too,' said Mike.

'The *Bar Nautique* at eight it is then.'

Mike was about to wind up the conversation when he realised that an opportunity presented itself.

'Maybe we could swap phone numbers Monica, just in case there's a change of plan.'

Monica hesitated, unsure whether Mike was being practical or just unashamedly forward. She chose to respond in an equally elusive manner.

'Very well Mike; I'll give you our field number. One of us has the operations mobile with them at all times,' she said with a wry smile, omitting to tell him that it was invariably her.

Mike accepted the number with resigned grace and gave Monica his personal number in return.

'Just one thing before you both go,' said Monica, her expression solemn. 'I would like to impress upon you the importance of not speaking to anyone about the work which we're doing here. I'm sure that you're both aware that it is impossible to close the site to the general public and unfortunately we have learned from experience that not everyone is interested in preserving our cultural heritage. The only realistic protection that we have against theft and vandalism is absolute discretion.'

'Of course Monica, we understand your position perfectly,' said Mike, 'and you can rest assured that we won't breathe a word to anyone.'

'Thank you. I would appreciate that immensely.'

'Well I suppose we'd better leave you to your work then. We'll see you all later.'

'Yes, see you both tonight.'

Thomas untied the boat and quickly pulled on a black wetsuit hood while Mike was waving farewell. As the RIB began to pull away, there were hoots of laughter as he began to leap around on the sponsons, throwing his arms around and making high pitched noises like a ninja fighter. Mike turned to face them, his eyes raised to the heavens and his hands spread wide in apology.

'OK, that's it for today. Let's pack up; I'm tired and I need a drink.'

'You're not the only one. I've seen enough sand and rock to last me a lifetime,' said Pascal. 'I really thought we might have more luck diving where those two found the gauge, but it was just as barren as everywhere else.'

'Well let's look at the positive side,' said Santorini. 'If we'd found any wreckage, then the chances are that they'd have found it too.'

'Do you reckon they knew something about the submarine?'

'Who knows?' replied Santorini, as he passed a cigarette lighter to

Michel. 'It sounds like Jeannot was so drunk the night he spoke to Pierre, that he could have told half the town.'

'If they do know about it, you can be sure that they'll come back again,' said Michel, blowing a cloud of cigarette fumes into the wheelhouse.

'Yes, that's what worries me,' said Santorini, his eyes narrowing. 'Those two may be idiots but they are certainly dangerous ones. If they ignore my warning and return here during the week, there is every chance that they'll discover the wreck before us. They are better equipped than us, they can cover more area and they have more time on their hands too.'

'And we'd be none the wiser if they did find it,' pointed out Michel.

'We're too close now to let this slip through our fingers,' said Santorini, staring fixedly out of the wheelhouse door. 'We need to be better organised so that we can stay ahead of the competition. The only way we can be certain of doing that is to keep watch over the bay during the week.'

'But we can't be here all the time,' grumbled Pascal, 'we have work to do.'

'I'm not suggesting that we should *all* be here. One of us would be enough.'

Santorini tapped the cigarette lighter against his lower lip.

'Michel, do you need to work next week?'

'Well, Pascal had some stuff for me to do on the farm, but I guess it can wait.'

'That's easy for you to say!' barked Pascal.

Michel smiled, eager to take a rest from the back-breaking work.

'Surely you can do without him for just a few days?'

Pascal snorted in annoyance.

'The work's already behind schedule,' he complained, 'but I suppose I can get by if I have to.'

'Good, then this is how we'll work it.'

'I've got an idea how we can search for this U-boat without being seen,' said Thomas as they were making their way back to the villa.

'Go on, humour me.'

'Well the problem we have at the moment is that we need to use a boat, and that makes our presence pretty obvious.'

'Yes I would have to agree with your logic there, but unless you fancy doing a great deal of swimming, I can't really see any way around the problem.'

'Well obviously we'd need a boat to get out to the site initially, we just wouldn't be able to leave it anchored there; otherwise we'd be inviting trouble.'

'Yes, I don't think I mentioned that I have an allergy to Corsican neckties.'

'To what?'

'Never mind; carry on.'

'Anyway, I was thinking that what we need is someone to take us out on the RIB, drop us off over the site and then pick us up again once we surface.'

'You mean like a drift dive?'

'Yes, except we wouldn't actually be drifting and the boat would stay well out of the way until we needed it.'

'Yes interesting idea, but there are a couple of flaws that I can see in your cunning plan.'

'Like what?'

'First of all, we don't happen to know anyone who is free to help us and secondly, if we end up surfacing a long way from the RIB there is a good chance that we won't be spotted at all.'

'I already have someone in mind to help us out and we won't need to be spotted.'

'Why not?'

'Because we'll have a mobile phone with us.'

'This just gets better. Would that be one of those brilliant new underwater ones that you can use to communicate with Humpback whales?'

'Listen before you mock. I'll simply place my normal mobile phone inside a waterproof pouch and then put that in my underwater camera housing so that we can take it with us on the dive.'

'Thomas, I'm impressed. Scary as it seems, I can tell that you've given this some serious thought.'

'When faced with the risk of a severe beating, I can become quite resourceful.'

'Evidently. So who are you planning to ask to drive the boat; surely not Hubert?'

'Why not? It just happens to be his day off tomorrow, so I think I may have to buy him a few drinks tonight and casually drop it into the conversation.'

'You sly devil! Do you think he'd go for it?'

'Well he told me that he was very interested in doing a technical diving course and I'm sure that if we offered to teach him for free, he'd be most cooperative.'

'You've got this all figured out haven't you?'

Thomas shrugged and smiled.

'I don't know though,' said Mike, 'is it really worth taking the risk?'

'It would be if we found it. Anyway there'd be no thrill in it if there wasn't some element of risk.'

'You've changed your tune haven't you?'

'Well I can't say that I'm totally convinced of your theory, but since the depth gauge is obviously genuine, I'll give you the benefit of the doubt. Anyway, I don't think I could live with myself if I missed the opportunity of discovering a virgin U-boat wreck. If there's a way to search for it without drawing any unwanted attention, I can't see why we shouldn't give it a go.'

'In that case we have some serious planning to do.'

'Do you think everything will be safe back there?'

'I'm sure it will. We covered all the partially excavated pieces; besides no one's going to find anything at night.'

'I realise that,' said Monica, 'but now that the skeleton of the wreck is exposed and it's clearly pegged out, I just can't help thinking that someone might come across it early in the morning, a spear-fisherman for example.'

'Even if someone did stumble across the dig, I doubt they'd know what it was,' said Bertie, 'and there wouldn't be much time for them to take anything anyway. Think about it. The site has remained undisturbed for three thousand years; a day or two more shouldn't make a hell of a lot of difference.'

'I'm sure you're right, but if anything did go missing, I'd never forgive myself.'

'Well we can't watch the site around the clock Monica. You have to accept that there are factors which are simply beyond our control. There's no point in beating yourself up over this. Anyway, we should be celebrating our good fortune tonight rather than fretting about what might go wrong. Why don't you go and take a nice long bath and try to relax a little before we go out.'

'But I still have some work to do.'

'Don't worry, I'll take care of the writing up.'

'Would you? I'd really appreciate it if you could.'

'It would be my pleasure. Just promise me that you'll try to forget about work tonight.'

'I'll do my best.'

Bertie and Monica looked up in surprise as Hubert suddenly burst into the study, holding a sheet of paper in his hand.

'Hey listen to this!' he said excitedly. 'I was surfing the internet for information about missing U-boats in the area and I came across this local news article from 1995.'

He cleared his throat and began to read out loud.

'A German dive research vessel is presently operating in the area between Les Iles des Moines and l'Anse de Roccapina, fuelling speculation that it is searching for a missing U-boat, rumoured to have been sunk there during the Second World War. Claude Poitevin a survivor of the Maquis resistance movement says that the story gained popularity in 1943 when...'

Monica fixed Hubert with a contemplative stare.

'I think maybe I ought to send that E-Mail I promised Mike.'

'At last! I was wondering whether to call the rescue services.'

'Do I look OK?' asked Mike, fussing over his clothes.

'Do you seriously want me to answer that question?'

'What about the shirt though? Too flashy?'

'Not if you happen to be a pimp. Just put on a normal shirt and Monica will never suspect that you're an idiot. And get a move on; the taxi is due any minute.'

'At least I'm making an effort. Your only criterion for deciding what clothes to wear is how bad they smell.'

'At least I don't take two hours to dress. Now go away and take that cloud of aftershave with you.'

Thomas picked up a glass of pastis from the terrace table and swirled the rapidly melting ice cubes around in the pale yellow liquid. He took a sip and rolled it around his tongue, savouring the cool taste of liquorice and aniseed which so reminded him of the warm summer days of Provence. As he was gazing out to sea, he heard the distant rumbling of car tyres rolling over loose chippings.

'Hey Mike, the taxi's here. Get a move on, you old woman.'

Thomas quickly drained his glass, ambled over to the taxi and installed himself in the back seat. Moments later Mike came rushing out of the villa wearing a half buttoned up shirt and stuffing a leather wallet into his back pocket. He slammed the kitchen door shut and trotted over to the waiting taxi.

'*L'Avenue Napoléon à Propriano s'il vous plaît,*' instructed Thomas, as Mike joined him.

The driver nodded and set off back up the track.

The sun had all but disappeared by the time they'd covered the 30 or so kilometres north along the N196 to Propriano. Mike's initial excitement at the prospect of visiting a new town was quickly dulled by the banality of its approaches. Propriano had none of the natural beauty of Bonifacio or the affluence of Ajaccio and the functional nature of its architecture reflected its heavy dependence on the port for its prosperity. Not all of it was unappealing though and Mike's mood lifted when he saw the bustling activity along the main drag.

'This is a bit more like it.'

'Keep your eyes open; we're on the Avenue Napoléon. The bar should be somewhere here on the left.'

'There it is look! *Le Bar Nautique*,' said Mike pointing.

'*Arretez ici, s'il vous plaît!*'

The taxi stopped at Thomas' request and Mike paid the rather exorbitant fare demanded by the driver.

'I don't think we'll be calling upon his services again,' he said as they walked towards the bar entrance.

'Me neither, but I'm not going to let it spoil my evening,' said Thomas. 'It's time to get *complètement pété.*'

'Steady on there Thomas. Just remember that we may well be diving tomorrow; you'd better go easy.'

'Oh well, just a little bit *pété* then.'

Mike sighed as Thomas pushed open the door to the bar. A blast of air conditioning met them as they stepped into a brightly lit establishment decorated with various objects of a vaguely maritime theme. They walked towards the bar, scanning the crowd for familiar faces, but were at a loss until Thomas heard his name being called.

'Look there's Hubert.'

'Yep and it looks like he's already hit the juice. Hey Hubert, are you here all on your own?' asked Mike, shaking his hand.

'Yeah, but the others will be here soon. They do a little too much thinking in the evening for my liking, so I usually get out of there as soon as I can. What can I get you both to drink?'

'I'll have a beer please,' replied Mike.

'Same for me thanks,' said Thomas.

Hubert nodded and turned towards the bar.

'There's someone here that I think you might be interested in meeting.'

'Oh yeah – who's that?' asked Mike.

Hubert attracted the attention of the barman; a portly man with a balding head and a thick black moustache. He finished serving a young girl and came over to where Hubert was standing.

'*Deux demis François, s'il vous plaît.*'

The barman nodded his head, pulled two glasses of foaming draught beer and placed them on the counter in front of Hubert.

'François, I'd like you to meet two of my friends, Thomas and Mike.'

François leaned over the bar and gave firm handshakes to Mike and Thomas while greeting them with a formal *enchanté*.

'These are the friends that I was telling you about; the ones who are researching the story of the Roccapina submarine. I wondered if you could tell them what you told me earlier.'

François gave them both an enquiring regard before nodding his head and leaning over the counter towards them.

'So you are journalists then?' asked François.

Mike looked to Hubert for an explanation, but all he got was a smile and a shrug. Thomas realised that he was going to have to bluff it.

'We're not journalists as such; we're travel writers, and we like to pick up stories of interest from the places that we cover.' Mike soon picked up the thread.

'We're writing a review of Southern Corsica at the moment - resorts, hotels, bars, that kind of thing.'

François' enthusiasm grew, as Mike had intended.

'Well I'm not sure that there's a great deal to tell,' began François. 'All I know is what I heard from the elder fishermen and even then it was some time ago.' François paused and cleared his throat.

'Rumour has it that late on during the last war, some old men witnessed a submarine being attacked and sunk by a British bomber in the Roccapina area. No one really knows if the story is true or not, because there were no other witnesses around to back up their claims and besides the men had been drinking heavily at the local Auberge. The following day though, some of the local fishermen reported seeing a dismembered corpse and bits of floating debris out at sea, which they presumed had come from a shipwreck. After that, the story was pretty much forgotten until a few years ago when a local fisherman was trawling out in Roccapina and pulled up a radio mast in his nets. The strange thing is, that shortly afterwards his boat was reported as missing and a few days later it was found washed up on the rocks in Sardinia; the body was never found and the radio mast disappeared too. Maybe it was just coincidence, but a week later a team of German researchers came down here and started diving over the same area. They stayed for a couple of weeks and then left again. That's about all I know.'

'You say that the old men claimed to have seen the attack in Roccapina. Were they in the bay or on the road above it?' asked Mike.

'Well obviously it was at night; and I doubt if three old men, drunk as they were, were going for a midnight swim; do you?'

'No, I suppose not,' said Mike, feeling slightly foolish.

'Didn't anybody else hear the attack?' asked Thomas.

'I don't know, but you have to remember that it's pretty isolated out that way.'

'Last question,' said Mike. 'Do you know if anyone has been searching for the wreck recently?'

'Well stories come and go, but I did hear a couple of weeks ago that someone found a strange piece of wreckage while diving in Roccapina.'

Mike and Thomas exchanged knowing looks. They had heard just about all that they needed to know.

'Thank you for all your help François,' said Mike.

'You're more than welcome. Now if you'll excuse me, I have clients waiting to be served.'

'Yes of course, thanks again.' Mike turned towards Hubert with a wide grin on his face.

'You have some excellent contacts.'

'François knows everything which happens around here,' nodded Hubert. 'I searched the internet this evening and found a newspaper report about the German research divers that he was telling you about. I showed it to François and he gave me the whole story.'

'Hubert, you're a genius.' Mike shook his hand and gave Thomas a high five.

'Gentlemen we are in business!'

'This calls for a celebration,' said Hubert, holding out his glass.

'*Prost!*'

Mike and Thomas tapped their glasses against Hubert's and quenched their thirsts with a generous draught of chilled beer.

As they were congratulating each other on their combined detective work, the main door swung open, allowing the noise of the busy Avenue to reach their ears. Mike turned to see Bertie and Anna standing at the entrance to the bar. They glanced around uncertainly until Hubert shouted over the noise of the music and beckoned them over. Mike's eyes remained fixed on the entrance where Monica entered a few paces behind them, shivering momentarily as she was hit by a blast of cold air conditioning.

She was wearing a light, floral summer dress cut close to her figure; simple but no less stunning on such a delicately sculpted frame. Mike was rooted to the spot, his eyes tracking her every movement as she skirted delicately around the tables and strolled towards Hubert. He felt his pulse racing as she turned towards him and managed to compose himself in time to welcome her with a broad smile and a kiss on both cheeks. He pulled away and there was an awkward moment as Monica was left pausing in mid-air for the third kiss to which she was accustomed. Mike clumsily jerked his head back to plant a third kiss on the proffered cheek while cursing the peculiarities of the custom.

'We give three kisses where I come from,' she explained with a smile. 'One is too intimate, two feels too formal and four is just plain messy, don't you think?'

'Well to be honest, I've only just got used to giving two, so the extra one just seems like a bonus.'

Thomas, forewarned, greeted Monica with three carefully planted kisses.

'Just stick with the handshakes Mike,' he suggested with a wink.

Mike ignored the taunt and returned his attention to Monica.

'You look stunning.'

Monica smiled shyly.

'Thank you. You don't look too bad either.'

'That's only because I stopped him from wearing an awful Hawaiian shirt,' remarked Thomas. Mike glared at him.

'Sounds like he's very lucky that he has you to take care of him Thomas,' said Monica laughing.

'Now hang on a minute, before you get any ideas. Thomas is not an ideal housemate and he is certainly no lifestyle guru. Not unless you consider a life of eating fast food, watching heavy-metal videos and drooling a worthwhile aim.'

'I do have some bad habits as well,' said Thomas with an impish grin.

'Well you're obviously a very cultured man,' said Monica smiling. 'Now before you two get into a fight, can I offer you both a drink?'

'Don't be silly Monica,' said Mike, flustered. 'I'll get the drinks.'

'No, I offered first,' said Monica insistently. 'If you don't wish me to buy you both a drink, I'll just have to get my own.'

Mike could see from the determination in Monica's eyes that she was not going to back down.

'In that case I would be happy to accept your kind offer; I'll have another beer please.' Monica turned towards Thomas.

'I love you Swiss women; I'll have another one of these please,' he said, holding up his glass.

Monica laughed and turned towards the bar where Anna, Bertie and Hubert were standing.

'Hey Monica. Like the dress - very classy! Did you put it on for anyone special?' teased Hubert.

'Yes I did actually; I put it on for *me*,' she replied curtly.

Hubert shrugged and watched her reach for her purse.

'Hey, just put that on my tab Monica.'

'Thanks, but I'm ordering for Mike and Thomas too.'

'I don't believe it,' exclaimed Bertie, 'my impressions of the English gentleman have just been shattered.'

'Well, actually, I insisted on buying the drinks, despite Mike's protests.'

'Why would you do that?' asked Hubert.

'Because there is absolutely no reason why I shouldn't; and I'm certainly not going to let stereotypical behaviour stand in my way.'

Hubert and Bertie exchanged surprised glances while Anna smiled in admiration.

'Why shouldn't we buy drinks for men? You fear it because it deprives you of the notion that you are the providers.'

Bertie held up his hands in submission.

'Please feel free to express your right to freedom from male domination...actually it's your round Anna; I think I'll have a rum and coke.'

Anna slapped Bertie on the arm and scowled, much to Hubert's amusement.

Monica caught the attention of François and placed her order.

'Monica, we were thinking of going to eat at *La Portigliola* if that's OK with you,' said Hubert. 'They're just down the road and the seafood's fantastic.'

'That's fine with me, as long as everyone else agrees; I'll check with the boys.'

'OK.'

Monica paid her bill and Mike suddenly appeared beside her.

'Let me help you carry the drinks at least.'

'Thank you.'

Mike caught the odour of her fragrance and drew close, lingering over the deliciously heady aroma. Monica turned towards him, holding a glass in each of her hands and her hips brushed against him. The contact was electric and Mike was surprised at the childish thrill which it gave him. He looked deep into Monica's striking, light blue eyes to see if she had felt a similar reaction, but after a scintillating second she broke away from his gaze and adopted a troubled look. Mike quickly realised that he had prematurely breached her comfort zone. Cursing his lack of tact, he attempted to return the situation to normal.

'Let me take those glasses from you or you'll spill beer down your dress.'

'Ah...thank you,' said Monica with a relieved smile.

As Mike walked away, Monica breathed a sigh of relief. For a moment there she was afraid that Mike was going to try to kiss her. She was greatly relieved that he'd not had the audacity to do so, especially with her colleagues standing so close by. She could have read the situation wrongly though, she realised, and thought it wise to give him the benefit of the doubt. After all, there was no point in letting it spoil the evening ahead. She picked up her glass of wine and calmly walked the few paces over to where he and Thomas were standing.

'*Prost!*' she said, holding her glass out towards them. Mike and Thomas followed suit.

Monica took a sip of wine and set her glass down on a table.

'Hubert suggests going to a restaurant called *La Portigliola* if that's OK with you both. Apparently they do good seafood, but I haven't been there myself, so I can't personally recommend it.'

'It sounds fine to me,' said Mike.

'Anywhere that sells food sounds good to me,' said Thomas, 'I'm ravenous.'

'Good, well that's settled then; I'll let the others know. In fact, why don't you come over and join us rather than standing there all by yourselves?'

Mike and Thomas agreed and went to join Hubert, Bertie and Anna around a high table.

'So did Mike tell you the good news Monica?' asked Hubert, pushing his sunglasses up into the thick blonde tufts of his hair.

'No, what news is that?' she asked, turning towards Mike.

'Well, Hubert has been doing a spot of investigating for us and it turns out that there's a local rumour about a U-boat which sank off Roccapina during the war.'

'Yes I know, Hubert already showed me the article.'

'Ah, but we've had the full story since then,' said Hubert, smiling broadly.

'Well? Are you going to keep me in suspense all evening?'

Hubert gestured towards Mike who began to recount everything which François had told them.

'Well that's certainly very intriguing,' admitted Monica when Mike had finished.

'It's pretty exciting,' agreed Mike, 'but if you happen to speak to François about this, just be careful what you say, because he thinks we're journalists.'

Monica looked from Mike to Hubert, who shrugged and nodded.

'You lot are unbelievable,' she said, with a half smile. 'Well, just you be careful what you do with that information.'

'We'll try,' said Thomas unconvincingly.

'Incidentally, I've sent a couple of E-Mails to some of my colleagues in Zurich Mike. If I get any replies, I'll let you know.'

'Thanks, that's much appreciated. We'll need all the information that we can get.'

There were a few minutes of idle chatter before Hubert started to grow impatient.

'Is everybody ready to go yet? I'm starving.'

Thomas drained his glass and placed it on the table.

'I'm ready now!'

Mike followed suit while Monica discarded her glass, still half full on the table.

'There's no rush Monica.'

'It's fine Mike; I'm ready. The wine wasn't particularly good anyway.'

They left the bar and slowly walked the short distance to *La Portigliola*, further along the Avenue. The night was alive with the background throb of busy traffic, the boisterous cries of the young thrill-seekers of Propriano and the lilting voices of head waiters, touting for business. Thomas and Hubert reached the restaurant first and paused outside to check that everyone was following before they entered. Mike arrived close behind and held the door open for Anna, Bertie and Monica.

Looking around the restaurant's interior, Mike guessed that the building had been used as a warehouse at some point in its distant past. In keeping with the feeling of old-worldliness, the vaulted ceiling and arched recesses were illuminated by restored ships lanterns which cast irregular concentric patterns of light on the exposed stonework. On the dark mahogany tables, the flames of thick, white candles flickered over the polished surface to recreate an atmosphere of nineteenth century merchant France. The small gathering seated themselves on chairs made from old cognac casks, three either side of a large oval table. The girls sat facing each other, Anna being flanked by Bertie and Hubert and Monica by Mike and Thomas. They ordered an *aperitif* from the pretty waitress and began to study the menu.

'Hey Mike do you want to share a *ziminu* with me as an *entrée*,' asked Thomas.

'I don't know. What is it?'

'It's the Corsican version of *bouillabaisse* - the speciality of Marseille; I want to see if it compares with the best.'

'If we share it, will I get to eat any of it?'

'Of course! If it's anything like a *bouillabaisse* it will be impossible to eat quickly, even for me.'

'Hmmn, fish stew? I'm not so sure that I'm convinced. What are you having Monica?'

'*Gambas à la Provençale* and then a *daurade grillé*.'

'Now that sounds pretty tempting...ah wait a minute, *tianu de sanglier* - wild boar stewed slowly in its own juices, that'll do for me.'

The waitress returned shortly afterwards and took their order. Thomas, being considered the closest thing to a local, was nominated to choose a regional red and rosé wine to complement the various dishes. When the order was complete, they chatted amiably while picking at slivers of *tome* cheese and garlic marinated olives which had been left on the table as an *amuse geulle*. The wine soon arrived and Hubert quickly filled the glasses so that he could propose a toast.

'To friendship and our mutual success. Long may they both continue!' There was an enthusiastic clinking of glasses as the party seconded Hubert's toast.

'Hmm, this red is a little bit rustic,' commented Mike.

'Well the rosé is delicious,' said Monica.

'What can I say? Corsica has almost everything, but it's not Bordeaux,' said Thomas in his defence.

'So what success are you lot celebrating anyway?' asked Mike, looking around the table. 'You're being very secretive about it all.'

Hubert, Bertie and Anna deferred to Monica, who paused, weighing up the amount that she was willing to tell.

'Let us just say for the moment that we have made an important find. It's too early to say how important, but we believe that it has the potential to create huge excitement amongst archaeologists, anthropologists and historians alike.'

There was a reverential quiet around the table.

'That's all very nice,' said Thomas, 'but what we're about to find will cause huge excitement amongst wreck hunters, Nazi historians and probably a few murderous Corsicans as well.'

The table erupted into raucous laughter.

Thick clouds of smoke swirled around the tar stained strip-lights, which clung morosely to the sagging ceiling tiles of *Le Bar des Chasseurs*. The sound of drunken revelry was surpassed only by the animated voice of a television presenter commentating on a local football match that was being screened on a large wall-mounted television in the corner. The game had attracted more than the usual amount of customers and the crowd had become more boisterous as glasses emptied and the competition intensified. Santorini was in no mood for niceties and egged on by his companions, roared scathing abuse at anyone who dared to step out of line.

There was an explosion of outrage as a penalty was conceded by the Ajaccio team and the whole room came to its feet to shout futile protestations at the referee. Pierre entered the bar in the moment of quiet just before the kick was taken. He was halfway across the room when the whole place suddenly exploded with cries of jubilation as the ball went flying over the crossbar and whistled into the crowd. Pierre cursed, ignoring the television completely as he pushed his way through the flailing arms and strewn chairs towards the bar. When he reached it, he slumped down onto the bar stool next to Michel.

'Salut Michel, salut Jean-Claude,' he muttered.

'Salut Pierre,' they replied.

'Looks like you need a drink,' said Santorini. Pierre nodded.

'I'll have a beer.'

'It's on the house, you sure you don't want anything else?'

'No, I'm not in the mood; just a beer.'

'Suit yourself.'

'I've just seen something very interesting out there,' said Pierre, jerking his head towards the door.

'Oh yeah, and what's that?' asked Santorini. Pierre beckoned him in close.

'I just saw the archaeologists. They were with the *Pinzuti* and the *Rosbif*.'

'Where did you see them?'

'They were going into a restaurant - *La Portigliola* on the Avenue

Napoléon.'

'When was this?' Santorini winced as a burst of outrage from the crowd blanked out Pierre's reply.

'What did you say?'

'Not long ago; about twenty minutes I suppose.'

Santorini stared in silence at the counter before turning towards Michel.

'Michel I want you to follow them. I want you to find out where they're all staying.'

'Why is it always me who has to do this shit, why don't you ask Pierre?' said Michel in irritation.

'I'm asking you because Pierre's just got here. You're supposed to be the expert anyway. I'd do it myself if I didn't have a business to run.'

Michel took the last cigarette out of his packet before crushing the empty box and throwing it scornfully on the bar. He lit the cigarette and put on his jacket, his eyes blazing with anger.

'You owe me one Jean-Claude,' he said pointing his finger at Santorini.

'I owe you nothing. If it wasn't for me you'd still be in prison.'

Michel ignored his comments and pushed his way through the crowd towards the door.

A group of musicians walked in from the street and began to serenade the clientele with a selection of Latin ballads. Monica's table were already in high spirits after a delicious main course washed down by yet another bottle of the local rosé. Hubert and Thomas added improvised percussion to the songs by using spoons as maracas and even the normally timid Anna joined in the fun. When the band approached their table, Thomas jumped up and sang La Bamba with them, his enthusiasm far in excess of his ability. Hubert joined him with the spoon maracas, taking a flower from a nearby vase and holding it between his teeth. When the song had finished the musicians shook hands with everyone and posed good-naturedly for photographs. They were rewarded with generous tips before they moved on again, retreating with parting smiles and bows.

Since her earlier reservations in the bar, Monica had started to enjoy herself too, due in no small part to her fondness for the local rosé. As the evening wore on she became less inhibited in her conversation with Mike and spoke freely of her childhood spent in the historic town of Bern and its surrounding countryside. Mike learned that she had once been an accomplished swimmer and had learned to dive with the University of Zurich sub aqua club, unaware that the experience would lead to an interest in Maritime Archaeology years later. She graduated from the University of Zurich with a doctorate in Classical Archaeology and after being offered a permanent position within the department, was given the opportunity to combine the disciplines of both interests.

In return, Monica learned of Mike's childhood spent in the West-Midlands, watching the underwater documentaries of Jacques Cousteau and David Attenborough while dreaming of diving on the Great Barrier Reef. When he left school, he took a degree in computer studies at his father's insistence and soon those early dreams began to seem like a distant memory. Mike told her how he'd found his first job in London and despite his efforts to make the most of it, soon became bored with city life and began to yearn for something different. It was during a visit to the London Aquarium that he was reminded of his boyhood aspirations and it struck him then, that the only thing which realistically prevented him from going on to fulfil them, was a little step into the unknown.

Monica had first thought of Mike as a kind of drop-out, but she soon began to realise that in his own way he was as passionate about his profession as she was. She listened to his stories of diving with whales, sharks and manta rays with the same avid attention with which she'd listened to her professors talk about the discovery of the first traces of agriculture in Syria, Anatolia and Greece and the emergence of the first truly civilized race, the Sumerians of Mesopotamia.

In some ways Mike reminded her of her father; a banker by profession and a passionate amateur ornithologist in his spare time. When Monica was young, he would take her around the lakes and tell her the names of all the migrating birds and explain where they had come from. She particularly liked the white storks because her father had once told her that they had brought her with them when they came on their long journey northwards from Africa. She knew even then that it wasn't true, but she loved him for it all the same. His death from a stroke when she was sixteen came as a terrible shock for all. Her mother never fully recovered from his death and although she put on a brave face, she rarely ever smiled again.

Monica watched Mike's face light up as he talked about his underwater adventures and subconsciously felt herself as a small child again, listening to her father's stories. When she suddenly became distant and melancholic, Mike noticed the change.

'Are you all right Monica? I'm sorry I get a bit carried away when I talk about diving; I hope I wasn't boring you.'

'No, no - not at all. It's very interesting. I'm just a little tired that's all; I'm not really used to the wine.'

Mike smiled and nodded.

'I don't suppose that you get much time to go out and socialise when you're working on such important projects.'

'No, but that's probably me rather than the actual workload,' she admitted.

'I understand that. When you enjoy what you do, it can be incredibly fulfilling, but on the other hand, there's always the danger of excluding yourself from everything else around you.'

The waitress came over to clear away their empty dessert dishes. Hubert and Thomas were still laughing and joking and competing unsuccessfully with each other to get her telephone number. When they both finally admitted defeat, Hubert asked for the bill.

'Hey, how about we go to another bar. There's one just down the road that I know.'

'Sounds good to me,' said Thomas, eager to carry on partying with Hubert.

'We'll go just for one drink,' agreed Anna and Bertie.

Monica declined the invitation despite Hubert's protestations.

'I'm sorry Mike. Please don't be offended if I don't go, but I'm really not in the mood for it.'

'Well at least let me escort you home.'

Monica considered his offer and decided to accept. By now she no longer felt pressurised by his presence and she knew that she wouldn't feel comfortable walking back to her lodgings alone. Thomas winked at Mike when he caught wind of it, but Mike dismissed his inference with a resounding shake of the head.

They left the restaurant and Mike arranged to catch up with Hubert and Thomas once he'd escorted Monica home. The small group joined the throng of people wandering along the avenue outside and soon Hubert stopped outside a crowded bar. Monica winced as the door opened and a loud blast of electronic music spilled out into the night. It made her very glad that she'd chosen to cut the evening short and go home. After saying goodbye to Thomas and her colleagues and watching them disappear inside the bar, she gestured to Mike to continue walking along the avenue. Mike fell in beside her and after a few steps offered her his arm. Monica hesitated for a second and then with a gracious smile, looped her arm through his.

Several people came out of the restaurant opposite the terrace of the brasserie where he had been sitting patiently for the last half hour. None of the faces he'd seen so far looked familiar and he was just starting to wonder if he'd arrived too late, when he spotted the head of the tall blonde archaeologist framed in the doorway. The statuesque Swiss man led a small group out of the restaurant and then turned to walk up the avenue. Michel identified each member of the entourage in turn, smiling when he saw the *Pinzuti* and the Englishman amongst them. It looked as if his patient vigil was about to pay off.

After downing a last mouthful of whisky, he placed a few coins in the saucer in front of him, pulled his leather jacket from the back of the chair and slipped his arms into it. He retrieved a smouldering cigarette from the ashtray, placed it between his lips and pulled a pair of shades down over his eyes. When he judged that a wide enough gap had opened up, he left the brasserie and followed the group from the opposite side of the avenue. They stopped outside a bar and Michel melted into the crowd from where he could watch them unseen. To his annoyance the group split, four of them entering the bar and two walking on. But the couple who remained would serve his purpose adequately enough.

Michel followed the pretty Swiss archaeologist and the Englishman at a discreet distance, up the *Avenue Napoléon* and along the *Chemin des Plages*. After a few minutes they turned into a poorly lit road, an *impasse*, which ended at an old stone farm building with a terracotta tiled roof. He followed and watched them approach the entrance of the building. He extinguished his cigarette and crept closer to the grounds, using the cover of a partially demolished wall to position himself where he could observe them unseen. The young couple paused and he saw the Englishman kiss the girl on both cheeks. There was laughing and then the Englishman gave the girl a final peck and let go of her hand. The pretty archaeologist waved goodbye as the Englishman turned to walk away. She entered the house and Michel was forced to retreat deeper into the undergrowth as the Englishman passed within a few meters of him. When the coast was clear, he flicked his eyes towards the secluded house and let his mind begin to wander. He imagined silently breaking in and finding the girl half undressed; helpless. There were untold things that he would like to do to her – to humiliate her, just for the hell of it. '*Salope*,' he whispered under his breath. Maybe another time when he had less pressing matters to attend to. He reluctantly tore his mind away from thoughts of the girl, stepped out into the shadows and began to follow the Englishman back along the *impasse*.

Mike was already on a high when he entered the bar and the pulsating rhythm of the music seemed to match his mood. He was met by Hubert, who flung a fraternal arm around his shoulder before pressing a beer firmly into his hand. Bertie and Anna were backing out of the next drink and rapidly heading towards the door. Seeing Thomas laughing along with Hubert, Mike pulled him aside and asked him how much he'd had to drink.

'Well I'm trying to moderate but it's not easy as you can see,' he shrugged. 'The good news is that if we can stop him from killing himself, Hubert has agreed to be our helmsman tomorrow.'

'Great, but if you both carry on like this, there isn't going to be much point.'

'Don't worry; I've revised my plan. We're buying all the drinks tonight in return for Hubert's services. He's drinking rum and coke and I figured that if we just stick to coke he'll never notice.'

'Hmm, it's worth a try I suppose. Will he recover from the hangover though?'

'No problem - the man's a beast.'

Mike chuckled to himself as he watched Hubert trying to pick up any girl who passed within his grasp.

'I think you're right. I'll get the next round in.'

Mike ordered drinks at the crowded bar and returned to find Thomas and Hubert seated at a table towards the back of the room.

'Looks like his persistence paid off then,' said Mike, looking at the young girl who Hubert had just cornered.

'Yeah, she hasn't tried to run away from him yet,' agreed Thomas. 'Speaking of which - how did you get on with your date?'

'If by that you mean Monica; fine. She's going to be a hard nut to crack alright, but I think that she's warming to me.'

'Hubert reckons that you don't have a chance in hell. He says that she's not interested in men; she's too occupied with her work.'

'Well, from where I'm standing it doesn't look like Hubert is any expert on seduction. I wouldn't be surprised if he was planning to club that girl and drag her back to his room.'

'Judging by the way she just knocked back that vodka, I don't think he'll need to.'

'You're probably right.'

Mike glanced around at the buzzing crowd and felt distinctly out of place in his sober state. He knew that it would all be a lot more tolerable if he had a few drinks inside him, but if he let his guard down now they would be forced to abandon the following morning's dive. It could be weeks before Hubert would be free to help them out again. He sighed and checked his watch - it was 12.30am. He would stay another hour and then call it a day.

The young girl in conversation with Hubert was joined by two of her friends and Mike watched distractedly as Thomas began talking to them. He sat back in his chair and tried to keep a low profile, but Hubert soon spotted him and dragged him to his feet. He was pushed towards the three girls and forcefully introduced to them. Not wanting to appear a stick-in-the-mud, Mike played along with Hubert and struck up a conversation with the tallest of them. She was pretty enough, but not really his type; far too young and self-conscious for his liking. Still, he had time to kill and it had been a while since he'd held a lengthy conversation in French.

Over the next few minutes he tried his best to keep the conversation flowing, but in the end his lack of vocabulary was less of an obstacle than the banality of the exchange. It soon became clear that he and the girl had wildly differing interests and Mike was relieved when she was distracted by a call on her cell phone.

'Let's make this the last one shall we?' said Mike, as Thomas returned from the bar with yet another round of drinks.

'Hang on, just give me a bit more time,' said Thomas, 'I think I might get on the scoreboard here.'

'Well you'd better go for broke, because after I've finished this drink I'm out of here; with or without you.'

Thomas blew his cheeks out in irritation.

'Just give me half an hour.'

'OK half an hour starting from now.'

Mike childishly began timing on his wristwatch and shooed Thomas away.

Thomas muttered under his breath and slinked over to where the girls were standing.

While Thomas was distracted, Mike drew his chair up close and decided to amuse himself by eavesdropping on their conversation. At first Thomas began talking his way around the subject, like a shark circling a shoal of mackerel. His intended prey, a pretty, dark skinned girl, listened attentively as he described the beautiful location of the villa and the fact that it belonged to the Corsican side of his family. It was a great place for a party, Mike heard him say, and she and her friends were very welcome to stay the night there. It would be lots of fun and quite safe, he assured them.

Mike took a sip from his glass and struggled to contain his laughter when he saw the look of disbelief which appeared on the girl's face. He leaned closer and strained to take in every word as she spoke.

'Well I don't normally make a habit of going off to isolated places with random men who I've only just met in a bar and I think that my brother would probably have something to say about it too. In fact, why don't you go and ask him? He's the guy standing over there with his friends from the rugby club. You could always try and convince him that you have my best interests at heart.'

Mike nearly fell off his stool, choking as coke went up his nostrils. Thomas stood rooted to the spot, his mouth open wide with disbelief. He turned to see Mike contorted with spasms of laughter and hid his face in his hands. The dark skinned girl spoke a few short words to her tall friend who picked up her handbag in readiness to leave. The two then turned towards the third girl, who was still talking to Hubert.

'Chantale, *tu viens ou quoi?* - Chantale, are you coming or what?'

'Non, *je reste un petit peu* - No, I'm staying for a short while.'

The two girls raised their eyebrows and pursed their lips in a show of disgust before walking away.

'Are you ready to go now?' asked Mike, with an infuriating grin.

'Just don't say a word,' warned Thomas.

They finished their drinks and said goodbye to Hubert, who in the presence of Chantale made only mild protestations at their departure. Since he now knew where Hubert was staying, Mike arranged to pick him up at one o'clock the following afternoon. Hubert promised that he would be there and locked thumbs with Mike and Thomas in a show of camaraderie before they headed for the exit. Once outside the bar, they quickly spotted a vacant taxi cruising towards them. Stepping out from between parked cars, they flagged it down and within seconds were in the back seat moving swiftly away. Unseen behind them, a man wearing a dark leather jacket and seventies style shades ran out into the road and kicked a parked car in frustration.

5

It was obvious that the discovery had caused quite a stir if her E-Mail inbox was anything to go by. There were urgent messages from Corte, Zurich, Athens and Texas all clamouring for her attention.

Monica yawned, took a sip of coffee and tried to rub the tiredness from her eyes. She eased the stiffness from her neck muscles with a gentle rocking motion of the head and then returned her attention to the screen. With a click she opened the first message. It was from her project coordinator in Zurich giving details of the collection and transportation arrangements for the excavated artefacts. She made a note of it, placed the file in her work in progress folder and quickly scanned through the other messages. There were requests for photographs and wood samples, enquiries as to the condition of the artefacts, offers of assistance and messages of congratulation, including one from the Head of the Archaeology Department in Zurich. It was encouraging to see that other people were as excited about the find as she was. Still, she would much rather be spared the drudgery of sifting through countless messages in her inbox each morning.

With a sigh, she quickly dealt with those which needed a brief reply and then deleted them from her list. The ones which required a more detailed answer, she filed away into sub-folders so that she could tackle them later in the day. Towards the bottom of the list she came across an E-Mail from the Department of History in Zurich. It was a reply from Professor Rieder, a highly respected historian who had been one of Monica's lecturers during her freshman year. The subject of his E-Mail read: *Re U-boat enquiry.*

Monica had almost forgotten about the requests which she'd made on Mike's behalf and the reply took her somewhat by surprise. Her studious expression softened as she thought about the previous evening and aware that the content of the message would be of great interest to Mike, she opened it with a certain amount of trepidation.

Dear Monica,

I am so very pleased to hear from you after such a long time. I do occasionally get news of your exploits from other members of staff and they tell me that you are starting to make a name for yourself in the world of maritime archaeology. Well done to you. I am afraid though that as far as your question is concerned I have little to offer you. I have been unable to find any information regarding a missing U-boat in Corsica, although there are several confirmed losses in Sardinia and the Tyrrhenian Sea. This is not to say that there are definitively no vessels of the type missing in Corsican waters; after all there was significant activity in that area during the Second World War and one or two U-boats do still remain unaccounted for. Unfortunately, without supple-mentary information such as the U-boat number, the date of loss or the names of crew members, any further research will prove difficult, if not impossible. However, should you wish to continue your research, I am including a list of sources which you may find useful. If I can be of any further assistance in this matter, please do not hesitate to contact me.

Kind Regards

Helmutt

Monica closed the message with a sigh. She was in two minds whether to give Mike the information or not. He'd clearly become so excited about the idea of finding a U-boat, that she now felt loathed to disappoint him. She chewed the end of her thumb as she considered what to do. The simplest solution was perhaps to tell Mike the parts of the truth that he wanted to hear - that there had been U-boat activity in the area and that a small number of the vessels which went missing in action, still remain unaccounted for. Once Monica's mind was made up, she quickly typed a reply thanking Professor Rieder for his help and then filed the message away.

It was nine thirty in the morning and the temperature was already above 30 degrees. Mike pulled the bed sheets over his head in an attempt to lessen the invasive hiss of cicadas but soon threw it off again as the heat became unbearable. He reached for a plastic bottle beside his bed and swallowed an unsatisfying mouthful of tepid water. With a groan he threw his arm over his eyes in the faint hope that sleep would take pity on him. It didn't. Suffering from a thirst which could no longer be ignored, he rolled to a sitting position, pushed himself to his feet and padded groggily through the hallway to the kitchen. He found a half bottle of water in the fridge and took several lunging gulps from it. The icy coldness made him wince, but he persisted in drinking, finishing most of the bottle before he stopped to breathe.

As his senses started to return, memories of the previous evening began to filter through to him. He remembered spending a good deal of time talking to Monica and accompanying her home after dinner. She had looked so stunning in that summer dress and despite an awkward start to the evening, he had a feeling that he'd made a good impression on her. After that there was the episode in the bar and Mike chuckled to himself as he recalled Thomas being sent packing by one of the girls from Propriano. And of course there was Hubert, drunkenly pouncing on hapless young girls. Thoughts of Hubert reminded Mike that he and Thomas had an appointment to keep. They were supposed to be hunting for a U-boat later today and they hadn't even started working on a plan.

Throwing off his lethargy, he walked over to the laptop, fired it up and left it to load while he armed himself with a mug of steaming coffee. He pulled his admiralty chart down from a bookshelf, rolled it out on the table and activated the hand-held GPS. After plotting the positions of the *Sampiero Corso* and his own anchorage point from the previous day, he used the latitude scale of the chart to measure the distance between them. After conversion it came to just under 241 metres. With a top speed of around 3.5 kilometres per hour, Mike calculated that the DPV's would cover that distance in just over 4 minutes. Next, using the compass rose of the chart, he made a note of their relative headings so that he would have the basic elements needed to navigate between the two points. The second part of his plan required an effective search strategy.

Using the same dive schedule as before, Mike noted that they would arrive at the second waypoint with 15 minutes left to search the area before they would have to begin their ascent. In order to make the most of that time, he opted to employ the use of a classic sweeping 'U' search pattern that would gradually progress in a westerly direction, towards the place where he had found the gauge. By trial and error he discovered that with the DPV's they would be able to cover an area of approximately 100 metres square in the time available. It seemed like quite a large area until he plotted the square on the chart and saw how miniscule it looked in comparison. His optimism was further dented when he worked out that they would need to do at least eight similar dives just to be sure to have covered all the area within a 150 metre radius of the point where he had found the gauge. The U-boat may have been huge, he realised, but then so was the area in which it might conceivably be lying.

With a sigh of frustration, he slumped back in his seat and pinched the bridge of his nose. He began to understand how a team of divers lacking the technical resources which he and Thomas had at their disposal, might easily have given up hope of ever finding the wreck. It was a daunting task even for them with their combined wealth of knowledge and experience. Humbled, yet undeterred, Mike transferred all the information to his slate, put on a pair of shades and stepped out onto the terrace. He braved the stifling heat and stood looking out to sea, trying to imagine the vast underwater plateau which lay beneath its surface. It felt almost as if he was being drawn into some strange and compulsive game; a huge puzzle for which he had found only one single piece. The winning prize was out there somewhere, he felt sure of it, but without a little luck along the way, the odds of finding it did not appear to be stacked in his favour.

The road had already begun to melt under the heat of the morning sun. Shimmering mirages appeared and disappeared again on the smooth tarmac, like pools of mercury seeping into the ground. There was a holiday feel in the air as brightly dressed tourist advanced towards the coast's most popular beaches, eager to expose their pale bodies to the elements. The traffic was unusually busy for the time of day, but Michel was in no rush. He could easily have gunned the 900cc red Honda Fireblade past the slow moving traffic at break-neck speed if he'd had a mind to, but today he was content to just take in the scenery and relax; after all he would probably be doing a lot of it this week.

He took a left turn and began to negotiate the uneven track which led down to Roccapina Bay. Arriving at the bottom ten minutes later, he parked off the exit road in the shade of a large juniper bush. He locked his helmet to the bike and set off walking towards the beach. He was wearing a pair of cut-off denims, a plain blue polo necked shirt and a weathered baseball cap. Over his shoulder, he carried a rucksack containing bread, *salamu* sausage, water, a bottle of *rouge*, a book, a newspaper, a pair of binoculars and a 9mm Glock semi-automatic handgun.

From the beach, he glanced up towards the promontory and spied the path which led to its summit. He approached and began to climb up the steep incline. The view over the bays to either side became ever more spectacular as he progressed. He pushed on to the top and paused to admire the beauty of the rugged coastline and imposing mountains to the east. It made him proud to think that this was what he was fighting for: his homeland, his heritage and the freedom for him and his countrymen to enjoy it. He strolled over to the Genoese watchtower and sat down on a patch of coarse heather, from where he could look out over the bay.

He removed the baseball cap from his head, took a sip from his bottle of water and then poured a trickle directly onto his scalp. After moistening his neck and face, he pulled the binoculars from his rucksack and scanned the shimmering blue expanse ahead. When he'd reassured himself that there were no boats anchored out in deep water, he placed the binoculars to one side and pulled a cigarette from the packet in his top pocket. He lit it and turned to the first page of his book.

Over the next hour several boats motored in and out of the small bay below. Michel casually tracked the progress of one or two of them, but there was nothing to arouse his interest until he spotted a yellow and black

RIB coming in at speed from the north-west. He trained his binoculars on it and grunted when he saw that it was the boat belonging to the archaeologists. There were three people on board and Michel quickly established that the tall blonde man was not amongst them. No doubt still nursing a hangover, he thought to himself.

He followed the RIB's progress until it came to rest in the outer entrance of the small bay and dropped anchor there. His attention was drawn towards the pretty girl with the wavy hair and he smiled to himself, knowing that she could have been easy pickings the previous evening. She was wearing a two piece swimming costume with the top half of her wetsuit hanging down limply from her waist. He could clearly see the nipples of her shapely breasts pressing against the tight lycra of her top and was surprised at the voyeuristic thrill which it gave him. She would definitely be worth spending a little time with, he thought to himself. The source of his amusement soon disappeared when the girl pushed her arms into the sleeves of her wetsuit and pulled it up over her torso. Michel watched the two women strap on SCUBA equipment and fall back into the water with familiar ease. They disappeared beneath the surface leaving the dark haired man to wait alone on the boat. Michel shook his head in disgust. In Corsica, at least, the roles were clear; the men went out to work and the women looked after the home. He spat on the ground and returned his attention to his book. It was going to be a long day.

'Hey Thomas are you awake?'

'Huh...what time is it?'

'It's time to get moving; it's ten thirty.'

'Ah shit. Why didn't you wake me before?'

'I haven't been up too long myself. Anyway, quit talking and drag your ugly butt out of there; we need to get a move on. We've got gear to load, tanks to fill and we have to be at Hubert's place by one.'

Thomas stepped out of his room fully dressed.

'Come on then, let's go.'

Mike did a double take.

'Did you actually take any of those clothes off before you went to bed last night?'

'Of course. Do you think I'm dirty or something? There's no way I'd sleep with my flip-flops on.'

'Lord preserve us! Have you got your gear together?'

'Yep, everything's in my bag and ready to go.'

'Amazing. Well if you're ready, I'll grab mine and meet you by the car. Don't forget your phone!'

'You nag like an old woman,' grumbled Thomas.

Mike finished packing his kit bag and placed it outside on the terrace. He stuffed his wallet, GPS, chart and phone into a backpack, locked the villa and threw the keys into the outside store. Forty minutes later they arrived in Bonifacio and waited patiently for the dive centre to fill their cylinders. Mike made use of the time by explaining his plan to Thomas.

'First I want to take a look at the site where the *Sampiero Corso* was anchored; we still don't know for certain that they haven't found a wreck and if they're drug smugglers, we should be able to spot their containers. If we find nothing at all, then we'll use the DPV's to take us to the area where I took the second reading; the place where I found the gauge.'

'Is that realistic?'

'Yes, don't worry, I've already worked out the distance and heading. It'll take around four minutes to reach the waypoint and then we'll have 15 minutes left to search the area for more wreckage.'

'Are you sure that we'll be able to find the right spot?'

'Not one hundred percent, but even if we can't, we can still run the search as if we had; it's only a point of reference after all.'

'I guess so. Are you planning to use DPV's for the search too?'

'Yes, according to the manual they should normally last between 40 minutes to an hour on full power and that's more than enough time to complete the search and get us out of the area.'

'What if one of them dies?'

'That's just one of the many things which could potentially go wrong, but I'm confident that we could still get clear of the area by linking together and using one DPV between us. We'll still be able to use our fins to help us along after all. It might be a little clumsy, but I'm sure it's feasible.'

'Let's hope so. Anyway, I suppose we still have the mobile phone if it goes really pear shaped.'

'Exactly. And even if that fails, we can always ditch our gear and swim for it.'

'I'd rather not think about that option thanks. So what happens when we finish searching?'

'We start heading towards the promontory; the nearest point of land. We'll be about a kilometre away from it, and we should be able to cover that distance in about 15 to 20 minutes. Once we've switched to breathing nitrox, we'll have 28 minutes of decompression time still to complete in any case, so we might as well do it on the move. Of course that means that there is a reasonable chance that we can make it all the way to shore without surfacing.'

'That would be ideal. No one would have any idea at all where we'd been diving.'

Mike nodded.

'It probably won't be quite as simple as that, so we'll have to remain flexible.'

'Well much as it pains me to say so, I'm impressed with your planning.'

'It's mostly common sense really,' said Mike.

'Well you must be more common than I thought.'

Mike flashed him a warning stare.

'Oh look, our cylinders are ready,' said Thomas, quickly getting to his feet.

Soon the car was loaded and they were speeding their way towards Propriano. Once they reached the town centre, they edged their way along the *Chemin des Plages* until Mike spotted the small *impasse* which led to the old farmhouse where Monica and her colleagues were staying. They approached it, parked on the driveway and knocked on the door. There was no answer. Thomas waited a few seconds and then began to bang on the door with his clenched fist. Mike was just about to pull out his mobile phone when he heard the sound of approaching footsteps. Hubert answered the door wearing a dressing gown; his hair matted and his eyes barely open.

'Oh, it's you two,' he said raspingly, 'sorry I must have overslept. Come on in.' He motioned them inside with a jerk of the head and ushered them towards the kitchen.

'Make yourselves a coffee or something; I'll just go and get myself sorted out.'

Hubert went back to his room and they heard him speaking to a girl in hushed tones of French. Mike and Thomas glanced at each other and smiled.

'Looks like you picked the wrong one again,' chided Mike.

'I don't remember seeing *you* with anyone this morning,' retorted Thomas.

'That's because I'm interested in quality, not quantity. Anyway I'm still ahead in the stakes, whichever way you look at it,' said Mike, smugly. Thomas sneered.

From inside the house came the sound of someone taking a shower. Mike groaned, knowing that they weren't going to be leaving as promptly as he had hoped. He occupied himself by making coffee while Thomas found an old copy of *Le Monde* to leaf through. After a quarter of an hour, Hubert entered the kitchen with a groggy looking Chantale trailing just behind him.

'Guys, I think you've already met Chantale.'

Mike and Thomas restrained their smirks as they greeted Chantale. Mike offered coffee to everyone while Hubert busied himself making toast. When it popped, he offered a piece to Chantale, who took one look, shook her head and pulled out a packet of cigarettes.

'*Ca vous derange si je fume?* - Do you mind if I smoke?' she asked.

Mike and Thomas shook their heads in a manner which suggested politeness rather than willing. Hubert looked a mess and Mike could tell from his puffy eyes that he'd had little in the way of sleep.

'Do you think you're going to be OK on the boat today?' he asked.

Hubert laughed. It was the sort of question he might have expected from Monica.

'Me? I'll be fine. I feel a lot better than I look.' He chewed reflectively on a piece of toast and then turned towards Chantale, who was absently blowing smoke at the tip of her cigarette.

'Do you have anything planned for today?'

Chantale shrugged her shoulders and continued to stare at her cigarette. Mike thought that she looked bizarrely out of place in the rustic kitchen, dressed in the same glitzy, black and silver clothes which she'd been wearing the previous evening.

'Do you mind if she comes along with us?' Hubert asked.

Thomas and Mike turned towards each other with the same concerned expression.

'Personally, I don't mind,' said Mike diplomatically, 'but the boat will be crowded and overloaded with four people on board, especially with all our heavy equipment. Maybe Chantale could stay on the beach until you've dropped us off and then you could pick her up afterwards. As long as you have your mobile phone with you I can't see it being a problem.'

Hubert nodded and then asked Chantale if she wanted to tag along. Chantale agreed on the condition that she could stop off at her apartment to get changed. Mike groaned knowing that further delays would be inevitable. Thomas was in less of a charitable mood.

'Look Chantale, you're welcome to come with us, but we don't have a lot of time because we have something important to do. We'll gladly drop by at your place, but we can't hang around for long. Any more than 15 minutes and we'll have to leave without you.'

Chantale curled her lip in silent protest. Hubert tried to smooth things over.

'You won't need much anyway, just a bikini, shorts and a tee-shirt.'

Chantale inhaled deeply on the remains of her cigarette and then dropped the butt into the dregs of an empty beer can.

'Oui, d'accord. Allons-y. – Yes, OK. Let's go,' she said testily.

Hubert shook his head in exasperation.

'Right let's make a move then,' said Thomas impatiently.

'Wait, I just need to get my wallet,' said Hubert, 'and my phone. Have you got everything Chantale?'

Chantale nodded her head and checked through her handbag to make sure. Hubert disappeared momentarily and then returned, stuffing his wallet into his back pocket.

'OK, I'm ready.'

Chantale gave directions to her apartment and left them to wait outside while she changed. Exactly fifteen minutes later she returned wearing a short summer dress, stacked espadrilles, a fake Gucci handbag and matching shades. Her makeup had been refreshed and the sickly sweet aroma of a liberal dousing of perfume followed her into the car. Mike opened the windows in a vain attempt to flush it away. After a brief stop to pick up food and water they drove directly to Roccapina, arriving at the parking area shortly before two. Mike stepped out and took Hubert aside so that he could quickly run through the plan with him.

'Right, this is where the boat is moored,' said Mike pointing to the chart. 'If you and Thomas can stand ready, I'll bring her to the beach to load her. We need to do it as quickly and discreetly as possible, so try to keep everything in the dive bags. Once we're loaded you can both jump aboard and I'll let you take the helm. I want to go around this headland to the south because there's a rocky bay behind it where we can kit up out of view of everyone. Once we're ready to move, I'll activate the GPS and you can simply follow the navigational directions until we reach the waypoint. We'll be keeping our heads down in the boat so we'll have to rely on you to count down the distance as we begin our approach. When we're within 0.1 nautical miles of our target, slow down and that will be our cue to lie face-down on the sponsons. When you hear the waypoint alarm sound, drop into neutral and we'll roll over the sides. Wait 5 seconds and then continue your course for another 200 metres or so. After you've checked behind to make sure that we haven't had to abort for any reason, you're free to go and pick up Chantale or moor up in the bay as you wish. One thing though; it's vitally important that you keep your mobile phone with you at all times because that's how we'll contact you when we need you to pick us up. Here, take this waterproof pouch to keep it dry.'

Hubert stared at him in disbelief.

'Are you trying to tell me that you'll be diving with a mobile phone?'

'Yes, but it will be kept inside a watertight sleeve which will in turn be placed inside a camera housing. I'd better take your mobile number now, before we forget.'

Hubert, still shaking his head in disbelief, gave Mike his telephone details.

'You're serious about this aren't you?'

'Absolutely. Do you have enough charge and credit on your phone?'

'Yes, I've got enough, sure.'

'Good. Try not to use it any more than is strictly necessary; we'll be almost completely dependant on you if an emergency arises. You can expect our call to come within an hour of submersion. Once we've contacted you we'll explain our position and simply guide you towards us. If for any reason the delay exceeds 70 minutes, consider us in danger and begin searching for us immediately. Is any of that unclear or shall I run through it again?'

'No, it's all quite clear; completely crazy if you ask me, but I'll go along with it.'

'That's all we ask. Any last questions before we start?'

'Just one thing; when you've finished all this rushing around, do you think that we might have a little time to relax?' Mike laughed.

'Yes, of course Hubert. You never know, we may even have something to celebrate.'

'That would be nice. Actually I was wondering something; if you do find this U-boat wreck, is there any chance that I could dive it with you?'

Mike chewed his lip.

'We'd have to teach you the proper techniques first, but sure, I think you'd pick it up pretty quickly.'

'I've dived at those depths before.'

'I don't doubt it, but there's a safer and more rewarding way to explore deep sites than just jumping in with a single cylinder on your back and hoping for the best.'

'Well I'm always willing to learn.'

'That's what keeps us ahead of the pack.' said Mike with a smile.

Hubert sent Chantale off to find a spot on the beach and then helped Mike and Thomas to move the gear to the edge of the beach. Soon the orange RIB was fully loaded and under Hubert's guidance was carving a smooth V shaped wake through the centre of the limpid waters of the narrow bay.

By now there was a constant stream of tourists, looking red faced and breathless as they walked from one side of the promontory to the other, admiring the view. Michel was sick to the back teeth of them, with their garish clothes, loud irritating voices and sickly smiles as they tried to share their holiday bliss with anyone within spitting distance. He had stopped returning their syrupy *bonjours* some time ago and at one point had even thought about taking out his hand gun and cleaning it in an attempt to keep them at a distance.

Five hours had passed since he'd taken up his position by the watchtower and no boat had gone anywhere near the search area. The heat was starting to make him feel irritable and he was already beginning to regret turning down the work at Pascal's farm. The sound of an outboard engine leaving the small bay below caused him to stir and he picked up the binoculars and walked towards the edge of the plateau. He pressed the lenses to his face and centred in on the moving craft. His brow tensed in sudden concentration when he realised that it was the orange RIB being used by the Englishman and his *Pinzuti* friend.

He spread his legs and pinned his elbows to his chest, adjusting the focus of the binoculars until he could clearly see the three people on board. Studying each person in turn he quickly identified the Englishman and the *Pinzuti* and was surprised to see the tall blonde archaeologist with them. It explained why he hadn't seen him with his three colleagues that morning.

He tracked their progress and watched them approach the black and yellow RIB, anchored at the tip of the southern headland. The tall blonde swapped a few words with the skinny girl on board and then pulled away again, disappearing behind the next headland. Michel let the binoculars fall from his face and waited. Five minutes passed and the boat did not reappear. Maybe they had taken the warning seriously after all, he thought. He continued to scrutinise the area for a further minute, grunted and then returned to his post by the watchtower. With his eyes still trained on the headland, he took a swig of water and lit a cigarette. After a while he yawned distractedly and leaned back against the base of the watchtower. His attention turned towards two young female tourists wearing skimpy bikinis who passed by to his right. One of the girls was topless and Michel watched as she and her friend stood facing out to sea. He stared lustfully at the firmness of their tanned buttocks, hidden ineffectually by brightly coloured G-Strings. The topless girl pointed at something and Michel watched her ample breasts being lifted outwards and upwards with the movement. In his mind, he was placing his hands all over them. The two girls soon sensed Michel's intrusive stares and turned their heads, exchanging concerned words when they noticed his unwanted attention. They turned to walk away, scowling reproachfully at him, but Michel was unperturbed. He grinned and waved at them, without the slightest remorse. They were fortunate that they had not been in a more secluded area, he thought to himself as he touched the barrel of the Glock in his backpack. Suddenly, from the corner of his eye, he glimpsed movement out to sea and the smile dropped from his face. The unmistakable white wake of a fast moving boat was clearly visible, moving rapidly towards the area which he was supposed to be surveying. He cursed loudly and grabbed the binoculars, pushing himself quickly to his feet. Scanning downwards from the horizon, he picked out the thin white wake and tracked it to the right until he saw the vessel forming it; a familiar orange RIB. He pulled the binoculars from his face as if he did not trust what he was seeing, but there was no mistake. The hire boat had returned to the search area.

Hubert guided the RIB around the headland and dropped anchor in the protective enclave of the bay which lay behind it. With no beach it was virtually deserted, save for the handful of intrepid tourists who had struggled over the rocky headland to escape the crowds. Thomas took a good look around the steep coastline and pointed out the terrace of the villa, perched high up amongst dense vegetation.

'Is that where you two are staying?' asked Hubert. 'There you are living like millionaires and I'm stuck in a farmhouse with a bunch of academics.'

'I'll swap if you like,' offered Mike.

'Ah! And that would be because you appreciate rustic architecture would it?' asked Hubert.

'Well I'm actually starting to grow rather fond of Swiss designs,' replied Mike smiling.

'Everyone has their taste I suppose.'

'Yeah, it's not his fault he's English,' laughed Thomas.

'OK, fun's over,' said Mike. 'We need to run through the details of our search plan.'

'Fire away,' said Thomas, picking up his wrist slates.

'Right. I'm planning to time our progress as we're searching so that I'll know our approximate position at all times. Since we have good visibility, we'll do a 'U' pattern consisting of seven search lines roughly 17 metres apart running in a north south axis. Each sweep will take 100 seconds and our timing will determine our position along each axis to give us a fix. That will allow us to plot the position of anything which we find onto the chart afterwards. Thomas, I'd like you to keep track of compass headings and the elapsed time of each sweep. I'll be timing as well, but I'll also be keeping a tally of the line number, monitoring our dive schedule and acting as spotter.'

'No problem,' said Thomas, scribbling on his slate.

'I'll be positioned behind you and slightly higher in the water for a better angle of view, so we'll need to communicate using sound signals. I thought that we could use two strikes of the cylinder to indicate time to turn, three for slow down and five for an instant stop.'

'OK, just give me a moment to write those down,' said Thomas. 'What are the times of the sweeps again?'

'A minute and forty seconds to cover each of the 7 position lines and 17 seconds gap between them.'

'I have to say that this is the most complicated simple plan that you've ever devised,' said Thomas, when he'd finished writing.

'Well unless you can come up with a better one?'

'I can, but it involves girls, beer and pizza,' replied Thomas, much to Hubert's amusement.

'Exactly, so unless you have any constructive comments, I suggest we start getting ready.'

Hubert helped Mike and Thomas to strap on their heavy rigs and watched with interest as they clipped on their accessory equipment and ran through their final checks.

Once they had adopted a low seating position, Mike confirmed that they were ready to move. Hubert acknowledged, hauled the anchor in and fired up the engine. Following the waypoint heading indicator which Mike had activated on the GPS, he gently accelerated away, leaving the protective cover of the bay behind and heading for open sea. He advanced cautiously against the buffeting waves, counting down the distance to the waypoint as they progressed. Once he had approached to within two hundred metres of it, he eased back the throttle. Mike and Thomas pushed themselves up into a kneeling position and Hubert watched them roll their chests onto opposite sponsons in readiness to launch themselves over the side. With the weight of the cylinders pressing down on their chests, Mike and Thomas were greatly relieved when the waypoint alarm sounded and they were finally able to roll off the sponsons and into the weightless embrace of the sea. Having put only a small amount of air in their buoyancy wings, they submerged instantly and stabilised four metres below the surface. Mike spotted Thomas to his right and exchanged OK signals with him when their eyes met. Beyond Thomas, Mike saw the RIB drifting momentarily before the prop began to spin again, churning up the water and powering away. A startled shoal of slender garpike darted to and fro near the surface, like silvery arrows. Mike and Thomas quickly ran through bubble checks and exchanged descent signals before dropping rapidly through the column of water. They pierced the thermocline at 20 metres and continued to descend without a second glance.

At 33 metres Mike could already see the bottom and he executed a neat pirouette to get a 360 degree view of the sea floor. It was quite evident that there was no wreck of any description within the area. He paused at 38 metres and tried to spot any other man-made structures; drums, containers, chains, netting, anything in fact which might have indicated its use as a drop off zone for contraband. There was nothing except a wide, undisturbed patch of sand; a featureless plateau that tellingly, made a particularly unsuitable environment for red coral to flourish in. Mike joined Thomas at 42 metres and they both agreed to move on. After consulting the compass which he had mounted on top of his DPV, Mike indicated the direction to follow with a straight arm. Thomas unclipped his own DPV and fell in beside Mike as they began to move away.

The topography was mundane at first, with large expanses of barren sand broken up by the occasional rocky outcrop, but as they progressed the sea floor began to shelve away and the ridges became more pronounced. Mike kept an eye on his watch and four minutes into the run, signalled his intention to stop. Thomas stared into the distance and thought that he recognised the outline of a rock further ahead. Mike followed his lead and soon they were both staring in triumph at the familiar rock crevice which had previously served as a hold for their anchor. Thomas kneeled down on the sandy patch next to it and nearly jumped out of his skin when a starry ray, which had been hiding beneath a layer of sand, burst forth in a flight of panic. Mike chuckled to himself as Thomas regained his composure and settled back down on the sand.

Once he had sighted along the compass bearing and set his watch, Thomas signalled his intention to move away. Mike rose above him and began to scan the area to either side as the whirring DPV's began to pull them through the water. He barely noticed the shoals of jacks, bream and dentex that passed him by as his eyes tried to penetrate the gloom. Every dark ridge which appeared from the sombre background seemed to have the misleading appearance of a wreck and Mike struggled to prevent himself from getting carried away. His heart skipped a beat when an unusually regular shape appeared in the sand, but on closer inspection, it turned out to be the outline of an enormous turbot, lying motionless on the seabed. He would have liked to have taken a closer look, but unfortunately there was no time for such distractions.

Four sweeps came and went with little incident and Mike was starting to lose enthusiasm when he suddenly spotted a tall dark shape in the distance. The more that he stared at it, the more he was convinced that it was something other than just a ridge. Thomas was about to turn away and Mike knew that he had to make a decision. Unable to resist the nagging doubt in his mind, he tapped his cylinder five times and saw Thomas swing around to face him. He gave a rapid OK and *wait there* sign and left Thomas watching in bewilderment as he turned away and shot off into the distance.

Michel watched the RIB slow almost to a stop and then inexplicably accelerate away again. In the fraction of a second preceding it, he thought he saw a blurred movement, as if the bow had struck an underwater obstruction. With his elbows locked against his chest he could see that there was only one person on board and the sight of sunlit blonde hair left him in no doubt as to that person's identity. Perplexed, he immediately began to scan the area behind the boat to see if the Englishman and the *Pinzuti* had entered the water. But apart from the creamy wash of the boats propellers, there was not a ripple. Cursing loudly, he nervously ran his thin nicotine stained fingers through his coarse dark hair. He bit down hard on his lip, trying to think everything through, but having seen no sign of either the *Pinzuti* or the Englishmen since they had disappeared around the headland, he had little to go on. The only certainty in his mind, was that if they were now diving over the search area, then they would have to return to the surface at some point and their presence would be exposed when the boat came to pick them up. It was a perfectly reasonable assumption to make and yet contrary to what Michel would have expected, the blonde archaeologist seemed to have no intention of waiting around. In fact, he was now heading back towards the bay at full speed.

The uncertainty unnerved Michel and he ground his teeth in frustration as he watched the RIB pass beneath him and disappear into the bay, its decks now clearly empty. He cursed himself for having broken the cardinal rule of effective surveillance; he had allowed himself to become distracted.

After spending the next fifteen minutes anxiously scrutinising every movement between the promontory and the search zone, he heard the sound of an outboard engine roaring up the channel to his left. He moved towards the edge of the plateau and saw the orange RIB once more emerging from the bay below him. Determined not to be caught out again, he pressed the binoculars to his face, but the sight which met his eyes only served to confuse him further. The tall blonde archaeologist was again at the helm, but this time he was not alone. There was a pretty young female passenger standing beside him. Michel had never seen the girl before, of that he was certain. Someone with her curvaceous physical attributes would not easily have escaped his attention. He lingered momentarily over the plumpness of her breasts and then checked himself, tearing his eyes away. His weakness had already cost him dearly today.

He watched the blonde archaeologist allow the girl to take control of the boat and slip his arm around her waist. When Michel saw him reach up to cup her breast and kiss her on the base of the neck, there was no need for any further explanations. Michel spat on the floor in contempt. If she was Corsican, then she was a traitor to her race as far as he was concerned. Seething in hatred and more than a little envious, he watched them disappear around the headland to the south. He gradually regained his composure and lit a cigarette as he tried to evaluate the situation. The girl was almost certainly just what she appeared to be; a mere amusement; eye candy. The tall archaeologist had probably gone to join the Englishman and the *Pinzuti,* diving behind the headland and was taking the girl along for the ride. It certainly didn't look like he was too concerned about leaving anyone stranded out at sea. He continued to stand and stare at the headland for some minutes and then moodily returned to his post by the watchtower. One way or another he would soon know for sure.

As he approached the dark mass, Mike already began to have his doubts. Bathed in the eerie diffused daylight which filtered down from above, the shape of it just didn't seem regular enough to be man-made. Large fan corals and long whip-like strands of organic growth, delayed Mike's diagnosis by breaking up the general outline, but even so, he soon came to the conclusion that it was just an unusually large granite pinnacle. In its isolation the strangely sculpted monolith had become a small microcosm in itself. Silvery clouds of bait fish darted about beneath red, sponge encrusted ledges to escape the prowling schools of jacks, tuna and grouper which silently stalked them. Mike's frustration at being misled was confounded by the disappointment of being unable to explore the amazing diversity of this unique underwater oasis at his leisure. But with its position noted on his slate, he could at least console himself with the knowledge that he would be able to find it again.

Reluctantly, he turned away and sped back towards the search line, to find Thomas agitated and pointing nervously at his watch. Mike shrugged and wrote - *SORRY FALSE ALARM* - on his slate. Thomas, unimpressed, held his hands up in frustration and consulted his compass before continuing along his original heading. Mike took up position as before, hoping that he wouldn't be tempted to investigate any more false leads. Using selective vision to filter out any further distractions, he passed stunning gorgonian sea fans, colonies of brightly coloured tubular sponges, huge conger eels and marbled cuckoo wrasse without a second glance. The effort of concentration eventually started to dull Mike's senses and just as it seemed like they were merely going through the motions of the sixth sweep, his attention was suddenly attracted towards something unusual sticking out of the sand to his left. He hesitated for a second and then convinced that the object merited investigation, alerted Thomas using the agreed stop signal. Thomas twisted around to face him and followed the direction of his pointing finger. There was a dark half moon shape protruding from an otherwise flat expanse of sand. Side by side, Mike and Thomas swam over to investigate.

Much of the object was still buried in sand and Mike had to agitate it back and forth to free it from its sucking hold. When he pulled it clear, a startled octopus, which had taken up residence inside it, squirted a cloud of black ink at him and darted out from the opening. Mike recovered his composure, waited for the clouds of sand and mud to disperse and then held the object out at arms length. It was somewhat distorted, but otherwise clearly identifiable as a bucket. Mike cleaned the silt away from the outside surface with his hand and in the light of his flashlight saw that it was painted red with a single word written clearly across it in white lettering: *Feuer*. A smile crept across his face as he presented it to Thomas in triumph. The word was German and Mike had a pretty good idea what it meant. Since it was unrealistic to take the bucket back to shore with them, Mike simply wrote down the word on his wrist slate and noted the object's position relative to the search line.

After checking his watch, Mike realised that there was not enough time left to complete the final search line. He conferred with Thomas and they quickly agreed to terminate the search and begin an immediate ascent. Within seconds they were rising up through the water column, still peering into the distance with the faint hope of spotting a large dark, cigar shaped object lying on the seabed below. At 20 metres they paused and switched to breathing nitrox. Mike gave Thomas the heading which would take them back towards shore and aligned his body with his compass in readiness to move away. With only the surface visible as a reference above them, all their attention now became focused on their instruments to ensure that they completed their decompression schedule as accurately as possible while slowly advancing towards the coast.

After 45 minutes of continual use, Thomas' DPV began to lose power and Mike allowed him to grip one of his cylinder valves to help him along. By now they could clearly see the sea floor beneath them and knew that they were approaching the shore. A ridge appeared, which ran parallel to their heading and slowly began to shelve up towards them. They spent the last few minutes of their 6 metre decompression stop staring down at the teeming variety of fish life which it attracted. Amongst the usual schools of salema, sea bream and damselfish they spotted stingrays, several larger species of wrasse and a free-swimming moray eel. The flickering displays of silver, gold and blue drew ever closer as the ridge continued to rise up towards the surface. Once their computers indicated that their decompression schedule was complete, they calmly swam up diagonally towards the surface, emerging to the sound of cicadas, the smell of pine resin and the warmth of the afternoon sun on their faces. They were staring up at the promontory.

'Oh man; what about that for navigation?'

'Not bad,' admitted Thomas, 'but without my steady hand and perfect compass technique we would have been on our way to Sardinia right now.'

'I think you'll find that Captain Cook's voyages of discovery weren't dependant entirely on his compass technique.'

'Well obviously! The star ship Enterprise didn't have a compass.'

'What are you talking about? No! Captain James Cook, you idiot.'

'I know...Captain James T. Kirk...boldly goes where no man...'

'Oh shut up and get your phone out will you.'

'Temper, temper,' teased Thomas, as he brought his camera case to the surface. He opened the clear plastic casing and took out the transparent waterproof pouch which contained the mobile phone.

'Where did you disappear off to down there anyway?'

'Oh yes...sorry about that. I saw this huge dark shape that looked just like a wreck so I went to check it out.'

'Well, you might have told me. What was it anyway?'

'It was fantastic; a huge isolated rock pinnacle, teeming with life. I would have dragged you along, but it just seemed simpler if I went alone so that you could keep our position on the search line.'

'Yes, well I do like to think that my contribution is valued,' said Thomas as he selected Hubert's number through the thin plastic pouch. 'Try not to make a habit of doing it.'

'OK,' replied Mike, feigning guilt.

'Hi, is that Hubert's water taxi service?'

'It is indeed. How may I help you?' chuckled Hubert.

'Well you could certainly save us from a long swim. We're right on the end of the promontory.'

'Really? Incredible! OK hang on, I'll be there in five minutes.'

Hubert pocketed his phone and approached Chantale who was sunning herself at the bow.

'That was Mike and Thomas. I'll have to take you back now.'

Chantale nodded and replaced her swimsuit top while Hubert started up the engine and accelerated around the headland. When they were close to the beach, he left Chantale to wade towards the shore while he motored back up the channel. Once he had cleared the moorings, he opened up the throttle and raced towards the tip of the promontory. He edged around the rocky shoreline and spotted two pairs of arms being waved up ahead. He approached and glided to a halt beside beaming faces.

'Need a lift anywhere guys?'

'Yeah, we'd like you to take us somewhere a bit less damp.'

Hubert laughed as he hauled out their heavy equipment with surprising ease and placed it at the bow.

'So did you find anything?' he asked as Mike and Thomas climbed aboard.

'We certainly did,' replied Mike. He flipped over his wrist slate and showed Hubert the word that he had scribbled on it.

'First things first; what does this mean?'

'*Feuer* – it's German for fire.' He looked to Mike for an explanation.

'As I thought. We found a fire bucket.'

'Is that what it was?' asked Thomas.

'Yes. And fire buckets don't get thrown overboard unless they are totally unusable. This one clearly wasn't. They're generally kept below decks and filled with sand to extinguish oil fires.'

'So do you think it came from the U-boat?' asked Thomas.

'Well, all I can say, is that if the engine room of a U-boat blew apart at the surface, a depth gauge and a fire bucket are two of the things which you might expect to be blown clear by the blast. And if our U-boat sustained that kind of damage, then there is absolutely no doubt that it sank straight to the bottom of this bay.'

Michel had to wait nearly fifty minutes before he caught sight of the orange RIB again and when he did, he was far from impressed. It emerged from behind the headland with the blonde archaeologist at the helm and the girl by his side, yet there was still no sign of either the Englishman or the *Pinzuti*. He approached the edge of the plateau so that he could follow the RIB's movement, but it soon passed out of sight in the narrow bay below him and he was forced to run back along the footpath to find a more suitable vantage point.

Breathing heavily from the effort, he was just in time to see the girl jump out of the RIB and make her way towards the beach. To his annoyance, the tall archaeologist powered the RIB around and retraced his path back out of the bay. Cursing loudly, he ran back towards the plateau, pushing his way past ambling tourists to see the RIB pass below him and follow the foot of the promontory around to the north-west. It reached the point where it would disappear from view again and Michel quickly ran down a narrow track at the end of the plateau, slipping on loose stones in his haste. He pushed through dense thickets and emerged gasping for breath on a small ledge facing west, arriving just in time to see the RIB slow down and drift in towards the shore. There seemed no sense to the RIB's movements until he spotted a flash of sunlight on polished metal and saw two dark silhouettes floating in the water. Peering down through his binoculars, he was so dumbfounded to see the Englishman and the *Pinzuti* at the base of the headland that he nearly overbalanced and fell.

He watched them transfer their equipment to the RIB, unable to understand how they could have arrived there without him being aware of it. It was inconceivable that they had been dropped off there right under his nose. Apart from the brief distraction of the two women tourists, his surveillance of the area had been virtually uninterrupted. As Michel was wracking his brain for a plausible explanation, he caught sight of the propulsion units that the Englishman and the *Pinzuti* were using and it occurred to him that they might have reached the promontory underwater. In truth, he had no idea what sort of distances they could cover with such equipment, but if, as he suspected, they were substantial, then the implications were daunting. Difficult as it was to imagine, Michel had to accept the possibility that the two divers had been dropped over the search area and then left to make their own way back to shore. All the time he had been looking for a boat; a stationary vessel that would betray the presence of divers, but now that method of surveillance was called into question. The problem was that he could not be certain. He hadn't actually seen the Englishman and the *Pinzuti* enter the search area and until he had, he could take no action against them. He cursed as the boat moved off, briefly visiting the yellow and black RIB off the southern headland before heading back into the bay. Perhaps he had been outwitted this time, but the next time he would be ready for them. He returned to the watchtower and pulled out his mobile phone.

'Oui?'

'It's me...Michel,'

'Where are you?'

'In Roccapina. The Englishman and his *Pinzuti* friend were here diving this afternoon.'

'Where?'

'They just surfaced, close to shore. The Swiss archaeologist was driving the boat; the tall blonde.'

'Hmm, they all seem very friendly at the moment don't they? Did anyone go near the search area?'

'A few boats passed by; that's all.'

'You sure you didn't fall asleep or disappear off to a bar at any time?'

'Of course not! What do you take me for?'

'OK, don't throw your toys out of the pram. Where are they now?'

'They went back towards the beach. It looks like they've finished for the day.'

'Are you on the motorbike?'

'Yeah. Why?'

'Because I want you to find out where the Englishman and the *Pinzuti* are staying.'

'Of course. No it's perfectly all right; you should go, I wouldn't want anything else.'

'I feel awful abandoning you all like this; if there were any other way.'

'There is absolutely no reason why you should feel bad about it; if it was me in your situation, I wouldn't hesitate.'

Bertie, still in shock, stared into space and nodded.

'You must go Bertie,' agreed Anna, staring up at him with her arms clamped around his waist. 'If it came to the worst and you weren't there, you'd never forgive yourself.'

Bertie frowned, his jaw muscles trembling as he struggled to contain his emotions. The phone call had come completely out of the blue. His father had seemed well enough when he'd said goodbye to him in Zurich a few weeks ago, but now he'd been rushed into hospital, fighting for his life following a massive heart attack.

'Go and get your things packed and I'll get an airline ticket organised for you,' said Monica, leaving no room for argument.

Her words seemed to have the desired effect. Bertie, still rooted to the spot with shock, took a deep breath and nodded, relieved to have the decision taken out of his hands.

'Thanks Monica, I'll try to get back as soon as possible,' he said in a strained voice.

'Don't even think about that now. Just go and get your things together. Forget about what is happening here; you'll have far more important things to concern yourself with when you arrive in Zurich. We'll manage here one way or another. Just let us know how things go when you get there.'

'Thanks, I will.'

Anna accompanied Bertie to his room, leaving Monica to contact the airport in Ajaccio. With characteristic persistence, she managed to get him booked onto a ten thirty flight to Marseille, with a connecting flight to Zurich at 3am the following morning. After she had given Bertie the flight details, she returned to the kitchen, feeling utterly drained. It was a quarter past six in the evening and they would have to think about leaving for the airport within the hour. Unable to relax, Monica began to prepare a light meal for them all. It was as much to occupy her mind as to relieve the acidic emptiness which she felt in the pit of her stomach.

'Well, for once I have to say that I'm glad we have a beach lover amongst us,' said Mike, watching the sun descend towards the promontory. 'I don't normally like to hang around on beaches, but I must admit that this is a welcome relief after all that activity.'

'It's an almost perfect end to the day,' agreed Thomas, 'There's just one vital ingredient missing and I'm going to see if I can put that right now. Anyone want a beer?'

'Do sharks eat seafood?' said Mike. Thomas grinned.

'Hubert?'

'Excellent idea.' He turned towards Chantale. '*Tu veut une bière aussi Chantale?* - Do you want a beer too Chantale?'

Chantale declined the offer and asked for an orange juice instead. Thomas nodded and set off on his mission. Chantale, who was lying between Mike and Hubert, sat up and lit a cigarette. She blew out a stream of smoke and turned towards Mike.

'*Tu parles Français, non?* – You speak French, don't you?'

'*Oui, un peu* – Yes, a little,' replied Mike modestly.

'*Bien, alors tu peux me parler en Français. Tu viens d'ou en Angleterre?* - Good, you can speak to me in French then. Where are you from in England?'

Mike entered into a polite conversation about the peculiarities of his nationality, something which Chantale obviously found more interesting than he did. After trying to explain that the English didn't actually put jam on their roast lamb and didn't eat desserts for starters, he tried to cut the exchange short, but found Chantale to be unusually persistent. With her back facing towards Hubert, Mike began to feel uncomfortable when he noticed her eyes playing across his torso. She was completely unabashed and looked him firmly in the eyes when she smiled, making it quite obvious that she was interested in more than just conversation. She was reasonably pretty, with a lean curvaceous body and was obviously quite aware of how powerful an attraction it was for men. Mike was by no means a stranger to the admiring glances of women, but Chantale's interest was unwelcome, especially with Hubert in such close proximity. As Chantale was cooing over the attractiveness of his accent, Mike glanced past her and was not surprised to see that Hubert was starting to get annoyed.

'Chantale, why don't you leave Mike in peace, can't you see that he doesn't want to talk?'

'Yes he does,' she snapped. 'How is he going to learn French if he doesn't practice?' she said turning her back on him. 'You don't mind talking to me, do you Mike?'

Mike closed his eyes and sighed. He really didn't want to become embroiled in their bickering and he certainly didn't want to upset Hubert. Fortunately he was saved from further embarrassment when Thomas reappeared, carrying four bottles.

'Ah Thomas your timing is impeccable,' he said, with a smile of relief.

Thomas raised a questioning eyebrow as he distributed the drinks. He could see that Chantale was annoyed about something, but then she had been churlish for most of the day.

'*Santé!* – Cheers!' said Mike, clinking bottles before taking a welcome swig of cool beer.

'To the success of our mission,' said Thomas, holding out his bottle to receive a second blessing.

With Thomas sat between Mike and Chantale, Hubert began to relax again. He sat cross-legged and stared contemplatively at his bottle, twisting it around with one hand.

'Do you know that there is a much quicker and easier way for you to find your U-boat?'

Mike and Thomas' heads turned in unison.

'And what's that?' asked Mike.

'A sounding profile,' he said, raising his eyebrows. 'The technology is now available to locate undersea objects, even quite small ones, very quickly and easily.'

'When you say *quickly*, what does that mean exactly; minutes, hours or days?'

'Well that obviously depends on the scale of your search and the size of whatever it is you hope to find. It also depends to some extent on the topography, depth and technique being used.'

'OK, so given that we're looking for a very large submarine at a depth of between 50 to 60 metres in an area of say 500 metres square, how long would it take to find?'

Before Hubert could answer, Chantale interrupted and asked them to speak French so that she could join in the conversation. Hubert held up his hand to her.

'Just wait a second Chantale, this is important,' he said sternly. Chantale tutted loudly and angrily blocked out any further conversation by listening to her MP3 player. Hubert rolled his eyes and continued.

'If you were using sidescan, you'd be able to locate it in just a few hours.'

'You're kidding me - that fast?'

'Absolutely, but that technology requires an onboard computer and for the best results a submersible towfish probe.'

'Right, so eliminating that extravagant option what other technology is available?'

'You could use multibeam sonar, which would eliminate the need for a towfish. You'd still need a transducer and a computer though. That's the method that we're presently using to map the area ourselves; it takes a little longer than sidescan but the end result is better.'

Mike sat up and gave Hubert his full attention. 'How long would that method take to locate the wreck given the same parameters?'

'I would say, approximately half a day.'

Mike glanced at Thomas, the next question burning on his lips.

'Do you think there is any chance that Monica would let us borrow the equipment?'

'I'm afraid that you would have to borrow the entire boat...and Bertie with it,' laughed Hubert. 'Somehow I doubt that Monica would agree to part with either of them...but you could always ask.'

Mike sighed in frustration, aware that his relationship with Monica was not nearly strong enough to win him any special favours.

'Right, now that you've shown me the sweets and then cruelly snatched them away again, are there any practical sounding methods which we could use?'

'You could try a fish finder. Most of them are limited to a two dimensional representation of the sea floor, but some of the more advanced ones now display a simplified 3D image. They're not really designed for mapping, but over a small area they could probably get the job done. Of course you would have to buy one and set it up on your boat, or alternatively charter a vessel which already has the equipment installed.'

'Let's say that we were prepared to invest. What would be the chances of success?' asked Mike.

'It's difficult to say with the size of the area you're talking about, but if you organised the search using a GPS receiver, I think you'd find what you were looking for in a matter of days. Of course, you need to be aware that there is a far greater risk of confusing your target with natural formations using this method, or even missing it altogether.'

Mike picked up a handful of sand and let the grains pour out between his fingers. After a moment's reflection he turned towards Thomas.

'I don't know about you Thomas, but personally I'd prefer to continue searching underwater for the moment. After seeing that huge rock outcrop and all those ridges down there, I think that we'd just end up chasing our tails.'

'I think so too. And we'd also have to conduct the search under the cover of darkness.'

'Good point,' agreed Mike, 'and it would be totally impractical to consider doing deep dives at night each time we stumble across something which looks vaguely like a wreck.'

'I was only telling you what is possible, not what is practical,' said Hubert in his defence.

'Yes, of course,' said Mike. 'Thanks for the information, but I think we'll have to carry on as we are for the moment.'

'Well just remember that I won't have another day off for a good while now.'

'Yes I appreciate that.'

Thomas decided to run an idea past him.

'What are the chances of Monica allowing you to drop us off in your RIB? After all, we know that we can make our own way back to shore now.'

'Not a chance,' replied Hubert, laughing. 'There's only just enough space for our own equipment - and even if you wanted me to pick you up from the beach, there's no way that I could just abandon everyone at the site without a support vessel. No, you'll have to find a way to use your own boat.'

'In that case, I suppose we'll have to take it in turns to dive solo,' said Thomas resignedly.

'Wait...there could be another solution,' said Mike, nodding. 'You're right Hubert; we should use our own boat, but if we could get you to drop us off in exactly the same way as you did today and then tie our RIB alongside yours, we could make our way back to it under our own power. Of course, we'd be in a spot of bother if you weren't immediately available to come and get us in an emergency, but then we'd still have the security of the mobile phone.'

Hubert picked at the label of his beer bottle.

'It all sounds a bit risky to me, but if you really want to go ahead with it, I'm sure that we could work something out.' Mike broke into a smile.

'Right, we'd better have a look at the chart to check the distances then,' he said, pulling a waterproof sleeve from his kit-bag. He slipped the chart from its protective cover and spread it out on the sand. With the edge of a piece of paper he marked the distance between the search site and the headland where Monica's team were working and then measured it against the latitude scale.

'Look, there really isn't a great deal of difference between going to the end of the promontory and the headland. It's only about 130 metres further, which would take...' Mike made a quick calculation; 'around an extra 2 minutes by DPV or five finning; that's hardly worth worrying about.'

Hubert stared contemplatively at the chart.

'Maybe we could do it in the intervals between dives,' he suggested. 'I'm pretty sure that Monica wouldn't object to that, just as long as I'm back on the boat when she needs me.'

'I'd certainly be happy with that arrangement,' agreed Mike.

'Perfect! It sounds to me like we have devised an excellent plan through a combination of gritty English determination and Swiss efficiency,' said Thomas getting to his feet. 'However, to be perfect it will need a little bit of French style and flair...which I will of course provide.'

Thomas smiled and made a low sweeping bow. In a flash Mike made a grab for his shorts and tried to pull them down. Thomas stumbled backwards laughing and managed to wriggle free. Hubert joined in the fun and helped Mike to chase him down the beach and straight into the sea.

From behind his newspaper, Michel watched all four of them leave the beach and head towards the car park. Their movement was slow because of the heavy bags which they were carrying and it made them that much easier to keep track of. Once they had reached the gap in the juniper bushes, which served as an entry and exit point to the beach, he rose to his feet, picked up his backpack and tucked his newspaper under his arm. He followed them into the car park, where he saw them congregate around a silver Peugeot estate and begin to load their bags into the trunk. He opened the newspaper and folded it in half at a crossword puzzle. As he neared the Peugeot, he pulled out a pen and filled out a line of empty squares with the registration number. After he'd passed by, he disappeared behind a line of parked cars and doubled back on himself, heading quickly towards the exit road.

The Fireblade was still standing nicely in the shade where he'd left it. He started the engine and turned the bike around so that it was facing the road, letting it tick over as he watched the exiting cars make their way up the track. Six vehicles passed him before he finally saw the silver Peugeot pulling out. The last two digits of the registration plate made it impossible to miss. The hire car was registered in department 78 of the Paris area, whereas the registration plates of private vehicles in Corsica carried the number 20. Michel let the Peugeot pass him by and waited until it had disappeared around a bend before he pulled out and began to follow it up the dusty track.

Five minutes later it reached the junction with the main road and turned left towards Propriano. Michel let two closely spaced cars pass by before pulling out and tucking in behind them. Over the roofs of the other cars, he kept his eyes trained on the Peugeot, ready to accelerate at a moments notice. There were many unmarked tracks which snaked their way up and down the hillside on either side, but the Peugeot continued along the N196 all the way into Propriano.

When they reached the Avenue Napoléon, Michel was surprised to see the car turn left and enter the maze of back streets in the old quarter. He had to accelerate rapidly in order to stay in contact with them as they made several tight turns in succession. They came to a sudden stop beside a small block of apartments and Michel was obliged to pull over. He watched from a distance as the young girl stepped out of the car, followed closely by the blonde archaeologist. There was a heated exchange between them and Michel watched with interest as the girl pushed away from his grasp and marched defiantly towards the entrance to the building. The blonde archaeologist returned to the car and slammed the door behind him as he climbed in. The Peugeot began to move away and Michel waited as long as he dared before pulling out onto the road again. He paused momentarily by the apartment building and through a windowed stairwell watched the girl insert her key into a door on the second floor. He glanced at the street number of the building and then sped off after the Peugeot in time to see it rejoin the Avenue Napoléon. It continued along the Chemin des Plages and then made a left turn into the *impasse* which led to the farmhouse.

Knowing exactly where they were going, Michel pulled over to the side of the main road and walked the short distance to the farmhouse grounds. Taking position behind the crumbling stone wall which he'd used as a surveillance post the previous evening, he spotted the silver Peugeot parked outside on the drive. Retreating into the cover of the undergrowth, he satisfied an urgent craving for a cigarette and waited patiently for the Englishman and his *Pinzuti* freind to leave.

'That's very strange,' said Hubert, walking around with a confused frown. 'There's almost always someone here at this time of day. It's in the early evening that we usually work on the conditioning of the artefacts and complete all the documentation.'

'Perhaps they had to go out,' suggested Mike.

'Well the truck isn't here, so I guess you're right. I still find it strange though.'

'Look, there's a note here on the table,' said Thomas pointing.

Hubert picked up the piece of paper and read the hastily written message, his face clouding with concern.

'It's Bertie; he's had to fly home. His father was rushed to hospital with a serious heart problem this afternoon. Anna and Monica have taken him to the airport in Ajaccio.'

'Oh shit!' exclaimed Mike.

'Poor Bertie,' said Hubert, shaking his head. 'I hope he'll be OK.'

Thomas and Mike stared glumly at the letter in Hubert's hands.

'Can I offer you two a drink or something?' asked Hubert.

'Thanks, I'll have a glass of juice if you have any...or just water,' said Mike.

'Sure, no problem.'

'The same for me thanks,' said Thomas.

Hubert went to the fridge and found a couple of half cartons of juice. He looked at them quizzically and then mixed the two together, pouring the resulting yellowish liquid into three glasses. Mike and Thomas sipped their drinks with caution before deciding that Hubert's blend of orange and apricot juice was surprisingly good.

'Do you want to hang around for a while, or do you need to get going?' asked Hubert.

'I think that we'd better make a move,' said Mike. 'I wanted to ask Monica if we could do a trial run tomorrow, but I guess it can wait. If you see her, tell her I'll try to contact her later.'

'I will.'

'We need to get the tanks refilled anyway,' pointed out Thomas.

'If you want your tanks filling, we've got a compressor here,' offered Hubert.

'Thanks, but I think we'll leave it this time,' said Mike, 'we need to get nitrox in any case.'

'Well if you do want to use it anytime, just ask.'

'Thanks, we'll definitely take you up on that next time,' said Thomas. 'Shall we make a move Mike?'

'I think we should; before it gets dark.'

Mike drained his glass, set it down on the table and walked towards Hubert with his hand extended.

'Hubert, thanks for all your help today. When you get some spare time we should arrange for you to come over and run through a few exercises with the twin tanks in the bay. There's also some reading to do, but I think you'll find it quite interesting.'

'Great, I'll look forward to that.'

'Good. Well, perhaps we'll see you tomorrow sometime. Please give our regards and best wishes to Bertie when you hear from him and say hi to Monica and Anna for us.'

'Yes, I'll do that, of course.' Mike and Thomas finished their drinks.

'OK, let's make tracks.'

Michel quickly stubbed out his cigarette when he saw the Englishman and the *Pinzuti* leave the farmhouse and walk towards the Peugeot. He grabbed his rucksack and ran hunched over along the length of the boundary wall until he emerged at the *impasse*. He turned and walked swiftly back towards the main road pulling the collar of his jacket up as the Peugeot approached from behind.

Once he reached the junction, he sprinted towards the Fireblade with the ignition key ready in his hand. The engine was still warm and started immediately, giving him time to strap on his helmet. The Peugeot turned to pass in front of him and he calmly counted off ten seconds before easing the bike out from between two parked cars. At a cautious distance, he followed them through the town centre and back onto the N196. He was starting to grow weary of travelling back and forth along the same route, but until he knew for sure where the Englishman and the *Pinzuti* were staying, he had little choice. Santorini was a difficult man to please and had little patience with those who failed him.

Each passing kilometre took Michel further from home, steadily increasing his frustration and progressively eating into his fuel supply. He had been unaware of just how low his reserves had become, until in the rapidly fading light he glanced down and saw to his consternation that the fuel warning light was illuminated. Cursing loudly, he jerked his body back and forth in frustration, having no idea for how long it had been lit. He felt sick to the stomach knowing that he could now end up stranded miles from anywhere, powerless to give chase to the Peugeot. He wracked his brains trying to think of any place along the way where he could refuel, but this was a remote stretch of road. The next place he knew of was at least 20 kilometres away and if the Peugeot had not turned off the main road before then, he would be forced to make a stop there. In his anxiety, Michel could almost feel the fuel siphoning away as the kilometres passed, antic-ipating the jolting loss of power which would result when the Fireblade's cylinders ran dry. He found himself willing the Peugeot to indicate and pull off the main road, but it resolutely refused to do so. With a mixture of relief and anger, he finally saw the lights of the garage through the trees up ahead. Forced into a race against time, he accelerated wildly towards the rear of the Peugeot and then braked forcefully, swerving dangerously into the forecourt. He remained seated on the bike with the engine still running and rammed the nozzle of the nearest pump into his fuel tank. When the meter read 10 euros he pulled out a note from his pocket and thrust it at the flustered attendant before accelerating away, leaving him choking in a cloud of blue smoke. A large truck had passed by while he was refuelling and now he struggled to overtake it against the oncoming traffic. When a gap finally appeared, he accelerated fiercely around it and found himself going head-on with an approaching car. The oncoming driver slammed on his brakes at the last moment and Michel leaned hard to the right, just managing to squeeze in front of the truck. Horns blared angrily behind him as he weaved in and out of opposing lanes, trying to force a way past the cars ahead of him. He began to realise that something was wrong when he found himself behind a white Ford Escort; the same one which he'd seen directly in front of the Peugeot when they left Propriano. In frustration, he checked his mirrors, overtook it and gunned the bike ahead of a further three cars before he eased off the throttle in resignation. He'd lost them. Sickened and demoralised he doubled back on himself, staring in vain down every possible exit road before shaking his head in disgust and racing back towards Propriano.

It was there, lingering in the background, every time Mike turned a corner. The glare of a single headlamp, one, sometimes two cars behind him. It wouldn't normally have attracted his attention, but he'd come to accept that motorcyclists in this part of the world had little, if any, patience. They seemed to see cars as mere obstacles on a testosterone fuelled racing circuit. And yet the one lurking behind him seemed unusually reluctant to test his nerve against slower moving vehicles and more surprisingly had even allowed one or two of them to pass.

Mike had caught a fleeting glimpse of a red bike racing around the old quarter of Propriano when dropping off Chantale, but he'd been too busy following directions to take much notice. Maybe his mind was playing games with him, but that persistent single headlight seemed to nag at him every time he rounded a bend. There were few exit roads along this stretch of the N196, which meant that most of the traffic was heading in the same direction, but for his own peace of mind Mike was thinking about missing the turning to the villa and continuing on towards Pianotolli.

While he was deliberating, the motorcyclist suddenly accelerated towards him and unexpectedly pulled off the road into a garage forecourt.

Mike breathed a sigh of relief and chastised himself for being so paranoid. The turning for the villa was now just ahead and he indicated right before pulling off the main road. As the Peugeot bounced down the uneven track, Thomas awoke from a brief slumber and glanced around sleepily. He yawned as Mike pulled up outside the villa.

'I must have drifted off back there,' he said, pushing open the car door. 'It was a hell of a lot quieter without those two bitching at each other.'

'Yeah, Chantale's a bit of a handful isn't she? Hubert definitely got more than he bargained for there.'

'Well it looks like he won't be seeing much of her again anyway.'

'No and I don't think that it's any great loss do you?' said Mike as he retrieved the keys from the store.

'Not really. I got the impression that Hubert was quite fond of her though.'

'To be fair, she did have some interesting qualities. It's just a shame that her personality wasn't one of them.'

'She's far too used to getting her own way if you ask me,' said Thomas.

'I think Hubert realised how much trouble she'd be. He was definitely starting to get tired of her antics towards the end of the day.'

Mike unlocked the door of the villa and lowered his equipment bag onto the kitchen floor.

'She's just very young and a bit too selfish. Like we all were at her age.'

'True. I must admit that I broke a few hearts when I was younger.'

'That's hard to imagine with your present success rate.'

'You're incredibly shallow Mike. Relationships aren't just about sex; there's far more to them than that.'

'I'm sorry,' scoffed Mike, 'but I find it difficult to imagine you having romantic, candle-lit dinners with anyone in front of an open fire.'

'Actually I was thinking more along the lines of having someone to drive you home when you're drunk and lend you money when you're skint. You can't underestimate the free shampoo either.'

'And they say that romance is dead. It's no wonder you can't get laid.'

Thomas was about to protest when Mike's mobile began to ring. Mike fished it from his pocket and glanced at the name displayed on the screen.

'Speaking of romance,' he said, his eyes glinting. He stepped back out onto the terrace.

'Hello, Mike Summers Global Enterprises.'

'Oh...Mike, is that you?'

'Yes indeed Monica. How are you?'

'I'm fine thanks. Listen, I'm sorry to disturb you so late in the day, but I've got a favour to ask you.'

'A favour? What do you need?'

'I suppose that you heard about Bertie?'

'Yes, we were at your place when Hubert got the note; he's flying back to Switzerland isn't he?'

'Yes, we just dropped him off at the airport. The problem is that we're going to be one person short for a few days. We could get someone in from the archaeology department, but we really need someone with good diving skills. Hubert suggested you and...well I was just wondering if you might be interested in helping us out for a while.'

'I'd love to, but I'm afraid that I don't know the first thing about archaeology.'

'That's not a problem. We really just need you to act as an assistant. You'll either be supporting us at the surface, or in the water setting up equipment and transporting materials back and forth from the lifting cradle. It doesn't require any specialist knowledge and if we do need to move any really delicate articles, you won't need to be directly involved. I wouldn't want to put you in that situation anyway. So what do you think?'

'Well I'm flattered that you've asked me and of course I'd love to be able to help you out if I can, but do you have any idea how long you'll need me for?'

'That's the only problem I'm afraid; I really don't know how long Bertie will be away. He's planning to give me a call from Switzerland when he has a better idea of his father's condition. If it's any help, I just spoke to the head of the archaeology department and they have agreed to let us pay you on a daily basis. It won't be a great deal I'm afraid, but it should go some way to compensating you for your time.'

Mike thought that the opportunity of working in close proximity to Monica for a few days would be compensation enough.

'That's not a problem. I really wasn't expecting to get paid. I was just thinking about the delays to our own project.'

'Yes I understand that you have other priorities and I don't want you to be inconvenienced in any way. Obviously I can't guarantee how long we'll need you for, but if you have to pull out at any stage, we'll understand.'

'To be honest we've started to get a little bit sidetracked, so the break might not be a bad thing. It would give Thomas the opportunity to find out about the legal side of things; he's been putting it off for long enough.'

'Well if you're absolutely sure that it'll be OK, we're going to need your help tomorrow. Is that too short notice?'

'No, that should be fine. In fact we were unsure about what we were going to do tomorrow because of a slight logistical problem. In fact it's something that I wanted to talk to you about and...well it looks like I'll have the perfect opportunity now.'

'I see,' said Monica, uncertainly. 'Let's keep that for tomorrow then shall we?'

'Of course. So where do you want to meet?'

'Well we generally leave from Tizzano which is just up the coast from Roccapina, but we could pick you up from the beach if you prefer.'

'No, let's meet in Tizzano; I'd like to have a look at the place. It might be of use to us at some point in the future. Where will I find you?'

'We'll meet you on the jetty. Tizzano is very small, so there's no way you'll miss us.'

'Good. What time shall I meet you there?'

'Can you make it for nine?'

'Sure. Is there anything that I need to bring?'

'Just bring your wetsuit, mask and fins. We have everything else on board. We'll even provide lunch.'

'Perfect! Well if there's nothing else that I need to know, I guess I'll see you tomorrow in Tizzano.'

'Thank you so much Mike, I really appreciate this. See you at nine then. Bye.'

Mike punched the air and walked across the terrace towards Thomas who was busily rinsing off his equipment with a hosepipe.

'Guess who that was.'

'Hmm, let me think now. You've got a huge grin on your face and sickly loved up eyes so it must be someone you've got the hots for; Chantale?'

The smile fell from Mike's face.

'Very funny! You know that she was coming on to me don't you? On the beach, right in front of Hubert.'

'Really? I didn't notice.'

'It was when you went off looking for the beers. I'm sure she was doing it just to piss Hubert off.'

'What did she say?'

'She decided that she was going to teach me French, but she was just using that as an excuse. She started to come on to me and then Hubert got annoyed with her and they ended up having a go at each other. I was quite glad when you came back.'

'Is that why she wouldn't talk to him in the car?'

'I don't suppose it helped. Anyway let's forget about that now, I've got more important things to talk to you about. As you no doubt guessed, that was Monica on the phone and she's asked me to help them out on the dig for a couple of days while Bertie is away.'

Thomas took a moment to respond.

'I take it that you've already accepted.'

'Yes,' admitted Mike.

'So what am I supposed to do while you go off chasing your bit of skirt?'

'While I'm helping them out,' corrected Mike. 'Look Thomas, there are other things beside the diving that we need to research here and this is as good an opportunity as any to make a start. We need to find out how to go about registering and running a dive business, what costs we'll incur and what the legal requirements are. Only you can find out that information Thomas and if we're serious about doing this, we need to know sooner rather than later.' Thomas breathed a sigh.

'I suppose so, but I don't even know where to start looking for that kind of information.'

'I'm no expert either, but I do know that it's there if you are prepared to make the effort to find it. Why don't you start with the chamber of commerce, or the department of employment, or even a business advisory service? If you're really stuck just go to a library; there are bound to be some self-help guides for this kind of thing. Unfortunately Thomas, there's a lot more to running a business than just having an idea.'

Thomas nodded resignedly and tried, with difficulty, to show some enthusiasm.

'OK, I'll see what I can do. Maybe I can get some advice from some friends of mine.'

'That's not a bad place to start.'

'I'll need the car for all this. Are they coming to pick you up?'

'No, you'll have to drop me off in Tizzano tomorrow morning. Do you know where it is?'

'Yeah, it's about 30 kilometres from here; you have to go inland via Sartène.'

Mike went to fetch his guide book and leafed through it until he found a map of Southern Corsica.

'Yes, there it is. Hmm, it's a bit of a detour isn't it? Maybe it would be better if I went by boat.' He rolled out his admiralty chart and checked the distance along the coast.

'Look, it's only about 13 kilometres by sea; I might as well take the RIB. Do you think you could drop me off at the beach at 8.20 tomorrow morning?'

'No lie in then?' groaned Thomas. 'Well I suppose it's better than doing a round trip to Tizzano. I expect you'll need picking up in the evening as well?'

'Yes, but I'm not yet sure when that will be. I'll call you in the afternoon to confirm the time.'

'I'll look forward to it,' said Thomas, with undisguised sarcasm.

'Maybe you could get the tanks filled as well while you're in town.'

'Sure, don't worry; you just go off having fun with Monica while I break my back carrying the twin tanks on my own.'

'Do I detect a little resentment there Thomas?'

'Yes. There'll be payback for this, just you wait,' said Thomas, skulking off to his room.

'See you bright and early then,' Mike chirped. When he was alone, he grimaced, feeling a sudden pang of hunger. He stared glumly at the fridge and walked towards it, prepared for disappointment.

When he arrived it was almost empty. The acrid odour which infused the gloomy interior was all the more noticeable after a day spent breathing clean salt air and the dreariness of it reflected his sombre mood. He avoided eye contact with Santorini as he crossed the room, anticipating the inevitable recriminations.

'Ah at last! Did you have to follow them all the way back to England?'

Michel ignored the remark and sat down at the bar.

'*Un whisky s'il te plait* - A whisky please.'

Santorini could see that Michel was in a foul mood and eyed him warily as he served the whisky.

'*Et alors?* - And so?' he finally prompted.

Michel calmly lit a cigarette and exhaled the smoke through his nostrils. He tapped the smouldering tip against an ash tray as he answered.

'I followed them to Propriano and then back towards Bonifacio, but I had an electrical fault on the bike, so I had to stop.'

'So you lost them?'

Michel raised his eyebrows and shrugged.

Santorini looked ready to explode, but remained silent, his reddened face and tightly clenched jaw, comment enough. He turned his head to one side and made small nodding movements as he fought to regain his calm.

'What did they do in Propriano?' he asked, his eyes blazing.

'They dropped off the archaeologist and the girl.'

'The girl...what girl?'

'There was a girl with him...his girlfriend I think; although she probably isn't anymore.'

'Explain,' demanded Santorini curtly.

'She was alone on the boat with him when the other two were diving. They were fondling each other like teenagers. After the dive they were all on the beach together. They left in the Englishman's car and I followed them to Propriano. The girl got dropped off and that's when I saw her arguing with the archaeologist.'

Santorini tilted his head back and stared up at the ceiling.

'So they dropped this girl off at her apartment. Did you make a note of where it was?'

'Yes.'

'Well at least you got something right.'

Michel glowered at the remark.

'And after that they dropped off the archaeologist and went back towards Bonifacio I suppose?'

Michel nodded, exhaling cigarette fumes across the bar.

'So where did you lose the *Rosbif* and the *Pinzuti*?'

'Just before the turn off to Roccapina.'

Santorini snorted and shook his head.

'So, we've learned nothing new; except that the archaeologist has or perhaps *had* a girlfriend,' said Santorini, pacing back and forth.

Michel sucked his cheeks in and flicked the ash from his cigarette.

'Right, I want you to pay the girl a visit; find out what she knows.'

'You want me to use my powers of persuasion?' asked Michel, his eyebrows raised.

'No, I want discreet information gathering,' countered Santorini.

'But I don't even know her name; or any of the others for that matter,' protested Michel, 'and why would she want to co-operate anyway?'

'We'll get the names. And you'd be surprised at how easily people are prepared to give up information when they think it will get them out of trouble.'

'You've lost me completely. What are you talking about?'

'Listen carefully and I'll explain.'

'You'll need to pack all the usual equipment plus four sets of dive gear.'

'It's already taken care of,' replied Hubert, 'and I've done the inventory as well.'

'And the laptop?'

'It's in the cab.'

'I'm impressed Hubert. That day off has obviously done you some good. Anna, are all the containers prepared?'

'Yes. Actually I noticed that we're starting to run short; we might have to get hold of some more if the labs don't return the others this week.' Monica nodded.

'Remind me to give them a call later today.'

'I will.'

'Is there anything else which Bertie usually takes care of that we might have overlooked?'

'I think we've covered everything,' replied Anna. 'I know his routine quite well by now.'

'I'm very grateful that you do. Well, we'd better get started then, I suppose.'

After Monica had helped Hubert and Anna to load the truck, she made a quick tour of the house to check for any items which might have escaped their notice. She walked through the kitchen which doubled as an office, the spare bedroom which had been transformed into a makeshift laboratory and the lounge which served as a storeroom, her eyes searching every corner before she was satisfied that everything had been accounted for. With her mind finally at rest, she exited through the kitchen door, locked it behind her and walked towards the cab of the truck, unaware that she and her two colleagues were being watched and photographed through a high power lens.

'Come on it's nearly eight o'clock. We need to leave in five minutes.'

'OK, OK. I'm getting up.'

'That's what you said ten minutes ago.'

'Well this time I actually mean it.'

'Look, I'm leaving with or without you in five minutes from now, so if you want the car, you'd better get a move on.'

Thomas opened his bedroom door and stepped out into the hallway, wearing board-shorts and an inside out tee-shirt. He yawned and rubbed his eyes.

'OK I'm ready now. Come on Don Juan, let's go.'

Mike ignored the jibe and turned on his heel, walking out through the kitchen door and onto the terrace. Thomas picked up a scrap of bread from the kitchen worktop and drank the rest of Mike's abandoned coffee before following him. Soon they were making their way down to Roccapina accompanied by the sound of a lame pop song which crackled in and out of tune on the radio. Mike turned the music off and breathed in a lungful of cool, rosemary scented morning air, his mind buzzing as he anticipated the day ahead.

They reached the empty parking area at the foot of the valley and Thomas watched while Mike pulled on his wetsuit and packed the rest of his belongings into a dry-bag.

'I'll give you a call later when I'm about to leave Tizzano,' said Mike. 'Don't forget to take your phone with you.'

Thomas nodded and gave a half-hearted salute before climbing back into the Peugeot and making his way towards the exit. As Mike walked down towards the beach, he heard the sound of loud rock music slowly fading into the distance. After a brief pause to admire the beauty of the narrow bay under the soft glow of the early morning light, he entered the water up to waist height and slipped on his mask and fins. With the dry-bag slung over his shoulder, he set off swimming towards the moorings, watching damsels, salema and mullet scatter away as his flailing arms agitated the surface.

Soon he was at the helm of the RIB, emerging from the narrow bay and rounding the end of the promontory. He pushed the throttle forward and the outboard engine began to roar, sending the hull skittering across the *Anse de Roccapina* and on towards Cape Zivia and Tizzano.

The first part had been easy. He'd approached the postman confidently enough to unsettle him and prevent him from paying too much attention to the details of the badge which he'd briefly flashed at him. He gleaned two names from the three letters which the postman was about to deliver: Monica Huber and Bertie Horschwitz. At present it was impossible for him to tell who was who, but he felt confident that he soon would.

Once the postman had left, Michel took up position behind the boundary wall and set up the tripod of the Nikon D80 camera which Santorini had entrusted him with. He focused the 300mm telephoto lens on the main door of the farmhouse so that he could take frontal shots of the archaeologists as they left the house in turn. It didn't take long for his first opportunity to present itself.

He ditched his cigarette and rattled off several shots of the tall blonde archaeologist as he walked back and forth from the truck. The high-speed, automatic shutter whirred and clicked as his two female colleagues came to assist him. Soon he had head and shoulder shots of three out of the four archaeologists who he believed to be living there. The exception was the tall dark haired man, who for some reason was absent, but Michel already had the shots which he needed.

When the truck and its three occupants had departed, Michel collapsed the telescopic tripod and packed it into his rucksack along with the telephoto lens. After attaching a standard 35mm lens to the camera, he walked back up the *impasse* and along the main road taking several random snapshots of buildings and tourists on the way so that the photographs would not arouse any undue suspicion when they were developed. Once his morning's work was complete, he recuperated the Fireblade, made his way out of town and sped south towards Roccapina.

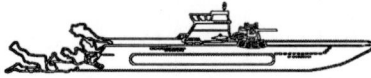

6

'What time is it now?'
'Twelve minutes past eight,' replied Hubert, looking down at his sleek titanium watch-cum-dive computer.
'Right on schedule; well done everyone.'

Hubert pulled away from the lights and joined the traffic that was heading towards Sartène.

'I take it there's no point in keeping the details of our find from Mike anymore?'

'No...I suppose not,' said Monica after some thought, 'but I should have a word with him first, just to make sure that he fully understands our position.'

'I'm pretty certain that we can confide in him,' said Hubert, 'and to be fair he's been very forthcoming with us.'

'Yes, well he hasn't *quite* got the same security issues as us, but I do take your point. Either way, I'd appreciate it if you let me decide what information to share with him.' Monica turned towards Anna and smiled. 'I don't suppose that's going to be a problem for you.'

'No, my English stops at asking where the toilets are,' she giggled.

'That won't be much use on our boat then!' chuckled Hubert.

'None at all!'

Monica waited for the laughter to die down.

'I'm hoping that we'll be able to continue doing our hourly rotational system so that everyone gets a two hour break on the surface. We'll obviously be doing all the excavation work ourselves with Mike acting as assistant, but it's unfair to ask him to do all four dives. Once he's understood the principle of it, we'll let him take a turn doing surface watch. Apart from anything else, he'd probably welcome a break from the monotony. What do you both think?'

'That sounds fair to me,' agreed Anna.

'No objection,' said Hubert.

'Excellent. In that case we should be able to operate almost as effectively as we did when Bertie was here.'

'We'd better not tell Bertie that or he might go off in a sulk and never come back,' joked Hubert.

'It would take a hell of a lot more than that to keep him away from this find,' countered Anna.

'I can vouch for that; I almost had to force him to the airport,' agreed Monica.

'Such dedication!' said Hubert, shaking his head.

For the remainder of the journey Monica quietly leafed through her notes, listening with one ear while Anna excitedly quizzed Hubert over the girl she had seen him with the previous day.

Twenty minutes later, they arrived in Tizzano as the soft hues of the early morning sun were being gradually forced into retreat. A small fishing boat chugged lazily up the calm inlet accompanied by a squadron of scavenging gulls, swooping noisily in its wake. Monica's team began loading the RIB, a task which had by now become more of a shared morning ritual than an arduous chore. The approaching whine of an outboard engine reverberated around the enclosed bay, the tone gradually dropping as it was throttled back. Hubert was the first to catch sight of the familiar orange RIB skirting around the end of the jetty.

'Hey look, there's Mike,' he said, rising to his full height.

Monica and Anna stopped what they were doing and stared in the direction of the approaching RIB. Mike raised his hand in salute and pulled up alongside the jetty. Monica checked her watch, impressed that he'd arrived with time to spare.

'Good morning fellow workers,' chirped Mike, as he secured the RIB and came over to join them.

'Morning Mike. I didn't expect you to be coming by boat,' said Monica.

'I didn't plan to, but when I saw how short the distance was by sea, it just seemed simpler that way.'

'Yes, I'm afraid it's a bit of a haul by road. What were the sea conditions like on the way?'

'Quite good; a gentle breeze, not too much swell and heaps of flying fish.'

'Good. Well it seems a bit silly to have to go back that way again, but I'm afraid that's what we'll have to do.'

'That's no problem; I really wanted to see Tizzano and I'm certainly not disappointed.'

'Yes it's a lovely spot isn't it?' said Monica, her eyes sweeping the view. 'Well since you're here, perhaps you could give Anna a hand to finish unloading the truck.'

'My pleasure.'

Mike took up position next to Anna and passed the equipment which she was unloading to Monica, who was standing at the edge of the jetty. At the far end of the chain, Hubert was busily positioning and stowing the equipment in every conceivable place around the RIB. Soon the truck was empty and the RIB so full of equipment that there was barely enough space for them to sit. Hubert lashed netting over the loose items and then took up position at the helm while Mike, Anna and Monica squeezed themselves into small gaps between the sponsons and the central console. Once everyone was settled, Anna slipped the lines and Hubert gently eased the RIB away and began to pick his way through the flotilla of small boats which were moored at the edge of the channel. They soon emerged into open sea and Hubert gradually opened up the throttle until they were powering towards the tip of Cape Zivia. Monica, who was sitting close to Mike, leaned towards him so that she could speak to him over the drone of the twin outboards.

'Mike, I just need to have a quick word with you if you don't mind.'

'Sure, go ahead.'

'It's about security. I've already mentioned that we've made a significant find here, but to be honest that's an understatement. It's an exceptional find; probably the most important of our careers, and it would attract a lot of unwelcome attention if news of the discovery got out too soon. I'm saying this because you're going to be placed in a position of trust.'

'I take it you're asking me to keep my big mouth shut.'

'Well that's not really the way that I would put it, but there is some truth in that, yes. You see the remains of the wreck that we have found in Roccapina contain some very valuable artefacts and although most of them don't have any great intrinsic worth, they're incredibly rare. As a consequence, their value to a collector would be inestimable and much as it grieves me to say so, there are certain individuals who would stop at nothing to get their hands on them. My other concern is that if the media gets any idea of what we've found here, they'll be around us like flies, making it impossible to work normally. Worse still, they would expose our position to the general public and then we would be at the mercy of every amateur souvenir hunter under the sun. We can't possibly protect the site day and night, so it would be a bit like leaving the doors of a museum open, with all the exhibits left unguarded.'

'In some of the places I've lived, they'd take the doors as well!' said Mike. Monica smiled.

'So do you now understand what we could be up against?'

'Yes of course Monica, and believe me I have absolutely no intention of leaking any information; even under threat of torture.'

'Not even to Thomas?'

'Especially not to Thomas; he'd want to come and see it for himself.'

'Well I just want to be sure that you understand how incredibly important this is to us.'

'I do and you can count on my absolute discretion.'

'Good,' said Monica, smiling. 'Let's leave it there then.'

'So what exactly will I be doing today?'

'You'll be assisting us, which basically means fetching and carrying equipment while maintaining a general safety watch. You'll be handling lights, tools, cameras, containers and anything else which we might need during the course of our work. We'll also show you how to use the lifting basket, so that you can send things up to the surface and request things from the boat. There are some specialised hand signals which you'll need to learn, but of course for complex communication, we'll use slates.'

'Are you sure that there's no risk of me damaging any of your pieces?'

'That's very unlikely because we take great pains to protect any fragile objects before we attempt to extract and move them. Sometimes it takes days to prepare a single item.'

'You need a fair bit of patience to be an archaeologist don't you?'

'Patience, dedication and sheer stubbornness will get you a long way in this field,' agreed Monica.

'Then you'll be glad to know that at least one of my faults could prove to be a benefit to you.'

Mike observed the pretty dimples which appeared on Monica's cheeks as she smiled. When she broke eye contact with him, he turned to face the shoreline.

'Looks like I'm back where I started from.'

'Yes. I think perhaps it would make more sense if we picked you up from the beach tomorrow.'

'That would certainly make things simpler,' agreed Mike. 'As long as you'll be needing me again, of course.'

'I'm fairly certain that we will. I can't see Bertie getting back here before Thursday at the least. I'll know before the end of the day in any case; Bertie said he'd call me as soon as he'd spoken to the doctor.'

Mike nodded and glanced up at the Genoese watchtower as they passed the promontory. There was a dark, kite-like shape fluttering silently above it.

'Hey look, there's a sea osprey up there. I think he's got a catch too.'

Monica smiled.

'You sound just like my father,' she said before she could check herself. Her face lit up and then clouded over almost as quickly.

'You were very close to him weren't you?' said Mike, remembering how fondly she had spoken of her father when they were at the restaurant together.

Monica glanced up in surprise at the remark. She felt an irrational urge to snap at him, but when she looked into his eyes, she faltered, seeing that there was only sincerity and genuine concern. She managed a brief nod and then looked away. Mike respectfully left her to her thoughts. It was quite clear that her grief was locked away inside her even now.

'We're almost there,' he said softly, as they approached the headland.

From his vantage point high above the bay, Michel spotted the yellow and black RIB almost a mile before it reached the promontory. He calmly attached the telephoto lens to the camera body and then screwed it into the base of the tripod. Through the viewfinder, he picked up the line of the bay and scanned to the left until he caught sight of the RIB again. Once he had it in his sights he zoomed out so that he could monitor its approach.

Picking up the binoculars again, he continued his general surveillance of the bay. The small orange RIB was not at its moorings when he'd arrived and it unnerved him to think that it might now be hidden somewhere, waiting to try and catch him off guard again. He lit a cigarette and paced from one side of the plateau to the other, peering down into the bays on either side. When the yellow and black RIB came close enough for detailed observation, he homed in on it using the camera's powerful telescopic lens. To his surprise, he counted four people on board and immediately began to search for the dark haired archaeologist who had been absent earlier in the day. The tall blonde was at the helm, as usual, with the skinny light-haired woman to his right. The pretty girl had her back to him, obscuring his view of the person behind. He centred in on the back of her head, waiting for her to move and when she did, he twitched in surprise. Deep lines were etched into his brow as he lifted his head and nervously scanned the bay, afraid that he might have missed something. Tugging nervously at a thick clump of his dark, wiry hair he tried to make sense of the situation, but there was no immediate solution which sprung to mind. As the yellow RIB continued its approach, he composed himself and moved back into position behind the camera. Realising that there was an unexpected opportunity to get the photograph which he needed, he returned his eye to the camera viewfinder and centred in on the RIB. He selected his target and was just about to press the shutter release when to his astonishment he saw the Englishman pointing directly at him. The pretty girl turned to face him too and Michel recoiled from the camera in confusion. Surely they could not see him from there, he reasoned and even if they could, they would have no idea who he was or what he was doing there. It was then that he heard a shrill cry above him. He turned to see a large bird of prey settle on the Genoese watchtower and begin to devour the plump sardine which it clutched in one of its talons. Michel closed his eyes and cursed in annoyance, but there was no time for further delays. He whipped his head around and within seconds had the camera lens focused on the Englishman's head. With the trained reflexes of a sniper, he stopped breathing, lowered his heart rate and calmly fired off two shots. He was satisfied, but not nearly as much as he would have been if he'd seen the head of his target jerk backwards with the impact rather than turn away calmly, oblivious to his contempt.

'This is our diver to surface communication system. It's very simple as you can see. That bell on the 'A' frame is operated by a weighted rope which drops down to the sea floor. There's a slate attached to the end of it, which we use to pass messages up and down. If you want to send a message up to the boat, you write on the slate and ring the bell. Whoever is on the surface will then haul up the line and read it.'

'Ingenious,' said Mike.

'Wait, we're not finished yet. This is an underwater chime,' said

Monica, holding up a cylindrical metal tube that was suspended from a thin line. 'If you're on the boat and you need to get a message to someone in the water, you write on the communication slate and lower it down as before. Once you've done that, you hang this tube below the surface and strike it with the metal rod that is attached to it. Underwater, it makes a strange metallic ringing sound that's audible for quite some distance. Once we hear the sound, one of us will come over to read your message and then add a reply or acknowledgement as necessary. Then you'll hear the bell on the 'A' frame ring, which is your cue to lift the slate back up to the surface.'

'Just like underwater E-mail.'

'Something like that,' said Monica smiling. 'We all find it very useful and it avoids too much ascending and descending, which as you know is a contributory factor to decompression accidents.'

Mike nodded.

'I expect you run close to the limits doing this kind of work.'

'We do take a lot of precautions, but yes there is a tendency to try and make the most of the time available.'

'I think we're all tempted to take silly risks when there's something at stake. I've had one or two close shaves myself while searching for lost equipment and trying to free jammed anchors.'

'Well it's funny you should say that; you might just find yourself doing the same thing today,' said Monica with a glint in her eye.

Mike eyed her inquisitively.

'You'll see what I mean later; it's not what you think.'

'I'm not sure what I think.' Monica remained tight lipped.

'Well I suppose that this would be a good time to teach you our hand signals.'

Mike listened attentively as Monica ran through the various signs and signals which they would use while working underwater, most of which were demonstrative in nature and easy to learn.

Once Monica was satisfied that Mike knew what was expected of him, she asked Hubert to take the first surface watch while she, Mike and Anna began to suit up. Both Monica and Anna clipped canvas pouches containing their excavating tools around their waists before putting on their buoyancy jackets and running through their pre-dive checks. Mike waited for them to roll backwards off the sponsons before entering the water himself. The three of them came together at the surface and remained close to the RIB as Hubert began to pass down larger pieces of equipment. Monica took the underwater camera and strobe, Anna the range finding frame and Mike took charge of the floodlights.

'Keep them submerged at all times when they're on,' called out Hubert as he started up a small generator mounted on the 'A' frame. Mike felt a humming vibration in his hand as the floodlights flickered on and slowly grew in intensity until they lit up the sea floor ten metres below.

Monica and Anna dropped beneath the surface and Hubert began to pay out the floodlight cable as Mike followed close behind. They regrouped at eight metres and swam in formation towards an irregular flattened mound located on the port side of the RIB. As he neared it Mike noticed a number of black and yellow gradated pipes which formed a latticework over the area to form a rigid reference grid. To his untrained eye, there was at first little to see which might indicate the presence of a wreck, except for a few regularly spaced stumps of wood which he presumed to be the structural ribs of the keel. By following their progression, he was able to make out the perimeter of the wreck and was surprised at how large it was.

As they glided over the central part of the grid, Mike began to see shards of pottery and exposed sections of seemingly complete objects protruding from little pits which had been dug into the substrate of sand and silt. Monica and Anna paused next to separate grid squares just a few metres apart, their movements being carefully controlled to avoid damage to anything which might lie beneath them. Pivoting on the very tips of their fins, they adjusted the position of rubber mats lying on the seabed and used them to support the load of one steadying hand. Their free hands were used to locate and replace the excavation tools which they kept in the pockets of their waist pouches to help them free the artefacts from the binding silt.

Anna began to scoop away fine sand from around a dark rounded feature while Monica concentrated her attention on a pale elongated object which lay beneath a layer of heavy silt. She gave Mike a one handed signal which resembled a starburst to tell him that she required light on her subject. Mike acknowledged and concentrated the powerful beam of the floodlights on to the buried object, indirectly picking out the dazzling blue pink and green striations of a pair of rainbow wrasse which were waiting to profit from their activities. He watched in fascination as Monica gradually teased sand and silt away from the edges of her subject using only a tiny spatula and a stiff brush. Occasionally she would waft away lighter particles of silt from the area using a flexible plastic card or blast more resistant patches with a concentrated jet of water from a large plastic syringe.

Little by little the pale coloured stick was painstakingly exposed until a joint was visible, separating it from a flat section of brown-green metal. Mike had already guessed that it was the base of a blade and as the minutes passed by he watched the object became recognisable as a dagger with a carved handle. He became so engrossed by the whole process that Monica had to remind him on more than one occasion to keep the lights steady. Working with extreme caution, Monica gradually undercut the dagger and eased it free from the silt so that it was visible in its entirety. She then took a small PVC tablet from her tool belt, wrote a code and number on it and placed it next to the dagger. Clearly relieved to have the opportunity to stretch her aching arms, she gave Mike the hand signal for camera and frame and took temporary possession of the floodlights while he went to fetch them from the perimeter. When he returned, Monica swapped the floodlights for the range finding frame and carefully placed it over the dagger so that the PVC tablet and part of the grid would be visible in the camera's field of view.

After placing a further measuring aid beside the dagger and attaching the camera body to the frame, she peered through the viewfinder and adjusted the position of the strobe lighting. When everything was arranged to her satisfaction, she took three separate shots at different aperture settings to guarantee a wide range of exposures. With the dagger's position now permanently recorded, she was free to remove it from the hold of the sediment for good. She carefully removed the camera and frame and passed them to Mike, who returned them to the sandy area beyond the perimeter. Mike spiked the stand of the floodlights into the sand nearby so that they would continue to illuminate the general area. He returned to Monica's side and was handed a slate with some dimensions written on it. Monica gave Mike the signal for container and having been briefed on the procedure, he acknowledged with an OK sign and made his way back towards the RIB.

When he was directly beneath it, he attached the slate to the bell rope and jerked it sharply downwards. There was a dull ringing sound and looking up Mike saw a distorted Hubert appear at the side of the boat and draw the slate up to the surface. A minute later, a wire mesh lifting basket was lowered down to him with a weighted container inside it along with Monica's returned slate, which had been wiped clear and written over.

The new message read:

You're wasting your time Mike – she's not interested in men!

Mike smiled to himself as he erased the message and took out the container. Before he rang the bell to signal his departure, he wrote a reply on the communications slate: *Sorry to disappoint you Hubert, but neither am I!*

He swam back over the grid towards Monica and returned her blank slate before handing her the container which she'd requested. While Mike was watching Monica prepare to transfer the dagger to the container, Anna gained his attention and requested the camera and frame. Monica signalled to Mike that she was able to carry out the delicate operation alone and he went to recuperate the camera and frame from the perimeter. While Anna was positioning the frame, he retrieved the floodlights and watched her run through an almost identical sequence to Monica after excavating what appeared to be a dark ceramic bowl. Once Anna's photo-graphic records were complete, she wrote down the dimensions of the container which she needed. While Mike was waiting, Monica attracted his attention and handed him the newly excavated dagger, now safely cushioned between two layers of foam inside the protection of the plastic container. He noticed that a synthetic paper label had been attached to the lid, complete with an identifying reference number. Monica indicated that the container was to be taken back to the boat and lifted to the surface in the basket. Mike nodded and turned his attention back towards Anna. She was just about to hand him her slate when her body suddenly began to convulse. Without warning, she panicked and made a desperate bolt for the surface.

'Did everything go as planned this morning?'

'More or less. I got most of the photographs and a couple of names as well.'

'Good. Any movements out in the bay?'

'Nothing to concern us; but I'm not sure what's happening on the archaeologists RIB,' said Michel, kicking a branch with his foot as he walked back and forth with the phone pressed to his ear.

'What's the problem?' asked Santorini.

Michel walked away from a young couple who were in hearing range of his conversation.

'It's the Englishman; it looks like he's working with them on the RIB today. The dark haired archaeologist is absent and I think the Englishman is there to replace him.'

'Was he with them in Propriano?'

'No, they must have picked him up on the way. There was no sign of the Peugeot in the car park this morning and the hire boat isn't moored up in the bay any longer.'

'What about the *Pinzuti*?'

'I haven't seen any sign of him.'

There was a pause as Santorini considered the situation.

'Well he can't be using the hire RIB otherwise the Peugeot would be in the car park, unless of course the Englishman dropped him off before going to meet the others.'

'Maybe the Englishman took the boat and the *Pinzuti* took the car.'

'We're just guessing here,' said Santorini in frustration. 'They could have taken the boat back to the hire company for all we know. Look, there are several possibilities, but as long as no one is going near the search area there's no reason to get excited. Just stick around and find out if they are still using the hire RIB or not.'

'But I could be waiting here for hours,' Michel protested.

'We need to know,' said Santorini firmly. 'Look, if you haven't seen any sign of the boat by six, I'll ask Pierre to come and relieve you. Does that make you feel any happier?'

'Not a lot, but I'll live with it. Tell him to bring cigarettes.'

'Why didn't you tell us that you felt sick Anna?'

'I didn't feel too bad until I got in the water and then it just slowly got worse.'

'You should have abandoned the dive as soon as you felt ill.'

'I would have done, but I didn't want to slow our progress.'

'Anna we all want things to go well and I admire your dedication, but there are limits. I don't want anyone putting their health at risk to keep us on schedule. You could have had a decompression accident or a serious lung injury if Mike hadn't been around to stop you shooting to the surface.'

'I know and I feel really stupid. I've vomited through a regulator before without a problem, but this time I don't know what happened. I just panicked.'

'You should have cut the dive short before it even got to that stage,' said Monica sternly. 'You'll be taking the next surface watch in any case, so let's just see how you feel in a few hours time.'

'Thanks Monica. I'm really sorry.'

'It's Mike that you should thank, if anyone.'

Monica turned and crossed to the other side of the deck, pushing wet coils of hair behind her ears.

'How is she?' asked Mike as Monica sat down next to him.

'She's feeling much better now. Thanks for what you did back there.'

'Oh...that was nothing. When you've worked as an instructor for a while, you take those kinds of things in your stride.'

'Well thanks all the same.'

'No problem.' Mike took a sip of water to wash the taste of salt from his mouth. 'I really enjoyed that. I was expecting to see a load of rotten old wood and some smashed up pottery, but that dagger you excavated is amazing.'

'Yes, this is a very fortunate find and we're anticipating even more surprises as we go deeper into the hull.'

'How old is this wreck?'

'It's from the Bronze Age. We estimate that it's at least 3,000 years old, maybe more.'

'So does this mean that you've found what you were looking for?'

'It's too early to say yet, but we have excavated a sword with a design similar to the ones carved on the *menhirs* at Pagliaju.'

'Isn't that proof enough?'

'Not really; it certainly suggests that an invading force settled here during the period which we are interested in, but as yet we have nothing to indicate that the wreck is linked to the Sea People. In any case, it will still be of tremendous historical interest even if we can't establish the link; nothing like this has been discovered since the Uluburn wreck.'

'Excuse my ignorance, but what was the Uluburn wreck?'

'Sorry, there's no reason why you should know. It's the wreck of a 3,300 year old Bronze Age vessel that was found in Turkey in the 1980's. Apart from its age it was remarkable because of the extraordinary value of its cargo. It sank while transporting just about everything which was considered to be of great value to Bronze Age civilisations: finely worked weapons, gold and silver jewellery, ebony, ivory, fine ceramics and copper, tin and glass ingots. It's highly likely that the cargo was destined for a person of great power and influence; possibly royalty. The crew and vessel were identified as being of Canaanite or Cypriot origin although two passengers are thought to have been Mycenaean. The great diversity of the origins of the different artefacts is a surprising testament to the flourishing trade routes which were in existence at the time. In fact we have now come to appreciate that the Bronze Age civilisations were far more sophisticated and knowledgeable than we thought.'

'That's fascinating,' said Mike. 'What do you think it was that brought the Sea People to attack a country as powerful as Egypt?'

'Well, the Sea People were in fact a collection of separate tribes with vastly differing origins. Many came from the Mediterranean Basin and some from the Black Sea but others are believed to have come from as far away as the British Isles. At the time, Egypt was a great source of envy for the more arid countries of the eastern Mediterranean. Apart from the vast wealth which it had accumulated through its trading networks, it was blessed with a reliable water supply and regular harvests from the fertile valley of the Nile. The yearly inundation guaranteed the Egyptians food and water when the rest of the Mediterranean Basin was suffering from widespread drought. We know that a complex climate change was taking place at the time and neighbouring countries such as Libya and Chad were starting to dry out and become desert lands. Under these circumstances it is easy to understand why the Valley of the Nile began to attract such widespread attention. The Egyptians themselves were of course aware of the problem, but since their fertile lands were surrounded mostly by desert, they were relatively safe from overland attacks and the vulnerable coastline was protected by an impressive naval fleet. In fact they had no real reason to fear the Sea People at all until around 1280BC when they started to settle in Libya and join forces with the Meshwesh during the reign of Seti I. Ramses II was so concerned that he had a series of fortresses built along the northern coast as a precaution, but it was not until long after his death that a serious invasion was attempted. The Sea People and their Meshwesh allies finally launched a combined attack during the reign of Ramses III when there was widespread economic unease in Egypt. Unfortunately for them, they had wildly underestimated the strength of their opponents and as depicted in the Medinat Habu temple carvings, they were soundly defeated and chased back into the sea.'

'Sounds like they got what they deserved,' said Mike. 'So if I understand correctly, the Shardanes then split up from the other tribes and reverted to an opportunist existence.'

'Yes, that's what all the evidence suggests. And being outcasts they would have had to use force to establish themselves elsewhere.'

'Like Corsica, for example?'

'That's what we aim to find out.'

'I'm really frustrated that I don't know more about this period in history; it sounds captivating.'

'It is...and that's probably one of the main reasons why I specialised in Prehistory. There were so many incredible civilizations that came and went during the last 5,000 years that some of them still remain undiscovered today. We tend to concentrate on the achievements of the Egyptians because their legacy is so evident, but in fact they were greatly influenced by the technical advances arising from all around them at the time, particularly from Persia and Mesopotamia. The wheel for example, considered the most important invention in history, was virtually unknown as a form of transport in Egypt until the Hittites attacked their armies using horse drawn chariots during the New Kingdom. You may also be surprised to learn that the practice of mummification does not have its origins in Egypt. The oldest known example is the famous Black Mummy of the Libyan Desert which was discovered by professor Mori in 1958 and was the handiwork of a great Central Saharan civilization which once dominated vast areas of North Africa. In fact as little as 6,000 years ago, parts of the Sahara Desert were covered by fertile savannah plains able to support animals such as crocodile, rhinoceros and giraffe. We know this because the Central Saharans depicted them in their cave paintings, which can still be found scattered over an area extending from Libya to Mali.'

'You said that the invading peoples who came here and carved their images into the *menhirs* also built towers using heavy blocks of stone.'

'Yes, the Torri, they were funeral towers in fact.'

'So, if they were Shardanes, could they have learned their building techniques from the Egyptians?'

'I wouldn't like to guess, but I think it's unlikely. Many cultures were building impressive stone monuments at the time, probably because it was the most obvious way to flaunt technological prowess. Of course many of the structures served religious or administrative purposes, but ultimately they were an early form of Propaganda; intended both to impress and intimidate.'

Mike leaned back and stared up at the mountains wondering how such a primitive race had managed to carve huge granite blocks, drag them over rough terrain and then lift them into place using only the rudimentary Bronze Age implements which they had at their disposal.

'Do you have any idea why the vessel sank?,' he asked.

'Well it's only conjecture, but I think that the boat may have been overloaded. The bow is pointing away from the bay which suggests that they were heading out to sea and we think that as they followed the headland around, they may have turned side on to the waves and capsized. We've noticed that the cargo is concentrated on the port side which is consistent with violent rolling. Judging by the unusually large quantity of goods and weapons onboard they must have been planning to stay away for some time.'

'How much of the cargo have you been able to recover so far?'

'We've already lifted around thirty pieces and we've really only just scratched the surface. I expect that there will be enough excavation work here to keep us busy for at least another six months.'

'It sounds like you're going to be kept busy.'

'There's no doubt about that,' said Monica.

Mike glanced at the plastic containers which contained the two freshly unearthed artefacts.

'So what happens to all the articles once you've brought them to the surface?'

'Well there is not a great deal that we can do here apart from keep them immersed in water until they can be preserved using the appropriate technique. Drying anything out which has been in water for a long period of time can have quite catastrophic consequences, as can exposure to higher levels of oxygen. We generally sterilize the water which surrounds them to prevent micro organisms from changing the chemical composition and then we send the protected articles to the university in Corte. From there, many of them are sent out to specialist laboratories for specific treatment. For example, the dagger blade which we just excavated is bronze and the handle is made from carved bone. The bronze part will almost certainly be stabilised and decontaminated by electrolysis, which is particularly effective on ancient metals due to the large number of chlorites which they contain. The bone handle has a porous structure and will most likely be treated with polyethylene glycols and freeze dried at low pressure; a process which is called lyophilization. The wooden bowl which Anna excavated can be treated in the same way, but there are also several other techniques which are effective in preserving semi-porous substances, such as high pressure resin injection and Gamma ray exposure.'

'So archaeology is not just about digging in the mud with wellies on then', said Mike with a grin.

'No, that's just the fun part,' smiled Monica.

Hubert who had been chatting with Anna glanced at his watch and then said a few brief words to Monica. She nodded and turned towards Mike.

'Well it looks like we're ready to go back into the water. Are you happy to continue what you're doing?'

'Yes, I think I've got the hang of it now.'

'Good, well Anna is going to stay on the surface this time. Her English is not too good as you know, so if she sends any messages in Swiss-German, just bring the whole slate with you.'

'I'll do that,' said Mike.

'Perfect,' said Monica. 'Now let's start working on that anchor.'

Capitaine Benoit Villeneuve of the *Brigade de Gendarmerie de Propriano* was sitting at his desk, reluctantly sifting through a large pile of documents in order to prepare his monthly incident report for the *Commandant du Groupement* in Ajaccio. Sitting beside him, Lieutenant Guy Lechaux was attempting, with little success, to guide him through the intricacies of the new internal computer system.

'Do you know Guy, in two months time I will be happy when I can take my retirement and leave all this new technology behind. I much preferred the old days when we went out to talk to people, typed up our reports on sheets of paper and filed them away in grey cabinets. At least you could find them again when there was a power cut.'

Guy smiled at the old battler whom the garrison affectionately called *Le*

Taureau - The Bull.

'Yes *Capitaine*, but I'm afraid that those days will soon be gone. Information has always been our greatest tool in the fight against crime and nowadays that is best treated and stored on a computer hard drive.'

'Yes it's inevitable I suppose, but I still think that crime is best solved or at least prevented by men on the ground. We may now have technology on our side, but do we solve more crimes because of it?'

'On the whole no,' admitted Lieutenant Lechaux, 'but that's because we have more sophisticated criminals to contend with. Think about it - fraud, theft, counterfeiting, money laundering, it's all done by computer these days. And the scene of the crime is more likely to be a computer terminal than an actual physical place. Like it or not, we now have to patrol the highways of information as vigorously as we once did the backstreets of town. It may be tedious, but it's the only realistic way that we can stay ahead of modern criminals.'

'Well all I can say Guy, is that I'm pleased that it's you who'll be taking my place when I'm gone; we need someone who can keep on top of these things. Just remember though, that when the bullets start to fly around here, they are *real* ones.'

Lieutenant Lechaux knew that these words of caution referred to an incident which took place three years ago and which *Capitaine* Villeneuve still took as a personal affront. The *caserne* at Propriano was attacked by Corsican separatists while Villeneuve was still inside the building and although no one had been hurt in what was primarily a show of force, it was a stark reminder that anyone who represented the French establishment in Corsica was a potential target for extremism.

The *caserne* at Propriano, like every other on the island, had been put on high security alert ever since 1998 when Claude Erignac, the Prefect of Corsica, had been shot dead on a busy street while going to a concert with his wife. A period of great unrest had followed, as the French government stood firm against the aggressive tactics of the separatists, but it was ultimately the Corsican people who would settle the issue. In 2003 they were finally allowed to vote on their future status and after the referendum was narrowly won by the anti-independence lobby, the violence gradually faded away. *Capitaine* Villeneuve, had never forgotten what happened that day, however, and convinced that they were still sitting on a dormant volcano, he never allowed his men to become complacent.

'Right Guy, so I have to click on the type of crime first, then enter the report number which will then call up the details of the victim and also the *Agent de Police Judiciaire* who investigated or recorded the crime; is that right so far?'

'Yes *Capitaine*, and then we fill in the action taken here and click on the present status, which for this one will be...pending.'

'Yes...well unless the pick-pocket becomes a born-again Christian and turns himself in, it's going to remain pending.'

'True, but it's better to put pending rather than unsolved because it looks better on the reports and...well you never know.'

'This is exactly what I mean Guy. We are becoming more like backroom administrative staff rather than defenders of the public interest,' sighed the *Capitaine*. 'I really don't know why I should care anymore now that I'm on my way out, but I dedicated my life to this job and I can't help feeling that we now pay more attention to statistics than we do to establishing effective policing methods.'

'I understand what you're saying *Capitaine,* but unfortunately it's all about political accountability these days. The government wants to see crime figures drop so it looks like they have the nationalist problem in hand. We're just a cog in the wheel. We make the situation look better to keep them off our backs and they're happy when they get statistics which show that their policies are effective.'

'And what use is that to the man on the street?' asked Villeneuve with barely repressed contempt.

'Well the powers that be would say that it makes people feel safer in their homes, and let's face it, any government would want to encourage that belief, especially in the present climate of unrest. We both know that we are virtually powerless to prevent a properly planned terrorist attack, but it would be pointless and irresponsible of us to publicise the fact.'

'Well let's just be thankful that for the moment at least, the violence seems to have calmed down. I wouldn't like to go back to the tension that we worked under ten years ago; I nearly lost a third of my men through stress back then. All of us lived in constant fear for our families and colleagues.'

'I know *Capitaine*, I was here at the time,' pointed out Lechaux.

'Yes of course you were,' said Villeneuve dismissively. 'Do you know Guy, even now, I'm fairly certain that there are still people out there who would like to see my head on a plate.'

'No *Capitaine*, I don't believe that; not after all you've done for the community. You should go away from here with peace of mind and make the most of your retirement; you've certainly earned it.'

'Thank you Guy.'

'I presume that you'll be staying in Propriano?'

'Well it's home now, I suppose. I really can't see myself going back to Lyon, or any other big city for that matter. I've grown to love this place over the years and I've made some good friends here. I've never known such a fiercely loyal people in all my life. Of course, it took a long time for them to accept me, but now that they have, I feel like I belong here. In any case my wife loves the place and if I took her away from here, she'd be unbearable.'

Lieutenant Lechaux smiled, aware that the *Capitaine*'s wife had a reputation for being more formidable than her husband when the mood took her.

'Right Guy, let's finish this damned report later,' said Villeneuve decisively. 'I'm getting peckish and the chef has promised to make *boeuf bourgignon* today. I always work much better on a full stomach.'

It took two thirty litre lift bags to take the weight of the huge rounded boulder. The bright yellow membranes billowed out like hot air balloons as they were inflated to within two thirds of their capacity, lifting the tapered end of the boulder clear of the sea floor. A few more litres of compressed air was all that was needed to lift the main body free of the sand and silt which had ensnared it for the last 3,000 years.

Taking care to vent the excess expanding air as the lift bags rose upwards, Mike and Hubert gently pushed the heavy load horizontally through the water towards the RIB. Once they had positioned themselves beneath it, Hubert disconnected the shackle from the lifting basket and transferred the cable directly to the eyes of the main, load bearing harness. He wrote rapid instructions on the communication slate and then rang the bell above. Within seconds his message was drawn up to the surface. A moment later, the slack was taken up on the cable and Hubert started to deflate the lift bags. As he did so, the load settled vertically under its own weight until it was suspended by the cable, four metres above the seabed. Anna, who had now recovered from her earlier nausea, came to join them beneath the boat as they commenced a cautionary safety stop. In her hand she was carrying a freshly excavated artefact, protected by a small, labelled container. When the 3 minute stop had elapsed, they rose to the surface and Anna immediately handed her container to Monica . She passed up her equipment and hauled herself aboard with Mike following close behind. Hubert remained in the water to watch the boulder rising upwards as Monica turned the lifting winch handle. When it was half a metre below the surface, Hubert asked Monica to stop winching so that he could remove the two limp lift bags. He handed them to Mike along with his equipment and then pulled himself into the RIB. Monica continued to turn the winch handle until the boulder was clear of the boat's sponson and then gently swung the gantry arm inboard. With Anna's help, the flattened boulder was carefully eased down onto a square of rubber matting.

'Well I've freed some anchors in my time, but never one that has been stuck in the mud for that length of time!' said Mike, shaking his head. 'It's a pretty rudimentary design isn't it?'

'Yes, not the most effective either,' agreed Monica. 'It's one of the earliest and most basic types of anchor and as you can imagine, it would have been fine in calm conditions but very poor in rough weather.'

'Hmm, it's really just a big weight isn't it? When you pointed it out to me during that last dive I had no idea what you were trying to tell me. It wasn't until you cleared the mud from the hole in the tapered end that I finally began to realise what it was.'

'They're actually quite easy to identify once you know what you're looking for and since the rock composition and designs are all slightly different, lost anchors like these prove very useful in recording the movements of ancient civilisations. The most famous example of this is the ancient Chinese-style stone anchors which have been found in several unusual places around the globe, including California, which has led some experts to suggest that Asiatic races visited America long before Columbus did.'

'Really? That would be one hell of a voyage,' said Mike impressed, 'but isn't there some evidence to suggest that the Vikings were the first people to discover America?'

'In truth, America was discovered and colonised by a Siberian race over 12 thousand years ago, but you're right, the Vikings were undoubtedly the first European race to have landed there. Eirik the Red discovered Greenland, which is technically part of the American continent, in 982 AD and not long afterwards his son Leif describes visiting a temperate land to the south-west, which he called Vinland. Most historians agree that Vinland was most probably Newfoundland and the recent discovery of Nordic artefacts and a settlement in *l'Anse aux Meduses*, or Meadows as it has come to be known, proves that at some point the Vikings did attempt to set up a permanent colony there.'

'Why is that not more widely known?' asked Mike.

'That's a good question. Personally I think that we like to stick with the historical accounts that we are most familiar and comfortable with.'

Mike nodded and stared down at the huge stone anchor that was now lying at his feet. He somehow doubted that this crudely hewn piece of rock would be instrumental in solving any new theories.

'I once saw a Roman anchor in a maritime museum and I remember being surprised that it was made mostly out of wood.'

'That's right, both the Romans and the Greeks used hardwood anchors, but they were not made entirely of wood. They had lead stocks and fluke braces to help them sink more rapidly. Wooden anchors were actually more durable than you might expect. The fact that one survived long enough to be discovered and displayed in a museum is a testament to their resilience.'

'Hmm, I never thought of it like that.'

Monica put her notes to one side.

'Just excuse me for a second.'

'Of course.' Mike watched Monica help Hubert to soak some sacking material in sea water and place it over the anchor before wrapping it in a plastic sheet.

'Why do you need to do that?' he asked when they had finished.

'It prevents salt crystals from forming and damaging the surface layer,' explained Monica. 'Also, because the anchor is made of limestone, it's vulnerable to acidic erosion and keeping it wet will reduce the acidity which results from the decay of organic matter.'

'I didn't realise there were so many factors to consider.'

'This is a very specialist field, and unfortunately, amateur archaeologists who lack the proper knowledge to conserve submerged artefacts can cause them irreparable damage.'

A mobile phone began to ring. Anna answered it and spoke in rapid tones of Swiss-German before holding the phone out to Monica.

'Bertie,' she said.

Mike listened in to the guttural exchange, hoping to gain some insight as to the content from Monica's expression. After much nodding and a brief smile, Monica wound up the conversation and switched off the phone. She spoke to Hubert and Anna before turning towards Mike.

'Well that's good news at least. That was Bertie on the phone. His father's condition is now stable and he's hoping to fly back tomorrow afternoon.'

'Oh...good,' said Mike, uncertainly.

Monica picked up on Mike's hesitancy and realised that he might not entirely welcome the news of Bertie's return. She placed a consoling hand on his shoulder.

'Mike, I'd just like to say on behalf of all of us that we think you're doing a fantastic job. I really do appreciate you helping us out like this.'

Mike glanced up at her and smiled.

'Thanks Monica. It may not look that way, but I'm actually enjoying myself.'

'Good, I'm glad to hear it.' There was the barest hint of a frown on Monica's face as she turned to help Hubert connect the high pressure hoses to the empty cylinders. Soon the gentle sound of water lapping softly against the hull was drowned out by the regular throb of the compressor, mounted on the 'A' frame. When Monica sat down again, Mike took the opportunity to draw close to her.

'Monica, I have a favour to ask you.'

'OK go ahead, but no promises.'

'We'd like Hubert's help to continue searching for the U-boat. We just need him to drop us off over the search site and tie our boat up next to yours. It shouldn't take more than fifteen minutes.'

Mike watched Monica's face stiffen.

'Surely you mean that you need him to drop you off and then pick you up again?'

'No, just drop us off. We'll be using the DPV's to get back to the coast. We tried it yesterday and it worked fine.'

'Have you spoken to Hubert about this?'

'Yes of course. He said he'll help us out just as long as you agree to it.'

'So let me see if I've got this right; you want Hubert to take you out there, drop you off...and then return here directly and tie your boat up alongside ours. Is that correct?'

'That's correct.'

'So when you've returned to the coast with the DPV's, how will you make your way back to the RIB?'

'Hopefully we won't be too far away from you when we hit the coast. We'll be following a compass bearing that should bring us here directly.'

'It sounds absolutely crazy to me, I mean, what happens if you don't make it?'

'Well if we're not too far out we'll swim to shore, otherwise we'll obviously need Hubert's help.'

'And what if he's underwater?'

'He won't be, because we'll do it when he's due to go on surface watch.' Monica sighed.

'And how will he know where to find you in an emergency?'

'We'll phone him and then he can drop a message down to you and come to get us.'

'I'm sorry, did you say *phone him*?'

'Yes, we'll be taking a mobile phone with us in a watertight case. It works fine; we've already tried it.'

Monica shook her head in disbelief.

'I don't know who's the craziest between you and Thomas.'

'They do say that madness is very close to genius,' said Mike, smiling.

'Well I can't see any practical objections,' said Monica, chewing her lip, 'and if I don't agree, I expect you'll probably go and do something even more dangerous.'

'Does that mean it's OK then?'

'I know I'm going to regret this...but I suppose so, yes.'

Mike punched the air in triumph, gave Monica a hug and kissed her neatly on the cheek.

'Thanks Monica you're a star.' Monica didn't know which way to look. Mike strolled over towards Hubert and slapped him on the shoulder.

'Hubert we've got the green light; you're hired as a stealth skipper.'

From the promontory, Michel watched the Englishman relieve the archaeologists of their equipment after they had completed their fourth and final dive of the day. He'd long since stopped speculating as to why he was working with them. It was enough to know that he was there where he could keep an eye on him and not making a nuisance of himself elsewhere.

He placed the binoculars by his side and picked up his book, scanning disinterestedly through a few pages before casting it aside and giving in to the growing urge to smoke his last cigarette. Breathing several puffs in rapid succession, he paced around the plateau like a caged animal, glancing at his watch and cursing, knowing that it would be at least another 20 minutes before Pierre came to relieve him. When the cigarette had burned down to the filter, he stamped it into the ground and picked up the binoculars again. The archaeologists were now taking their equipment apart and stowing it away, ready for the return journey. He watched them moving around like ants on a tiny black and yellow leaf, working with the same industrious cooperation. Typical of the Swiss, he thought to himself. When he grew tired of squinting through the lenses, he retrieved his book and had barely read through the next couple of pages when his mobile phone began to ring.

'Pierre, I was starting to think that you weren't coming. Where are you?'

'I've just arrived at the car park.'

'Good, you'll find me by the watchtower up on the promontory. Did you bring cigarettes?'

'Yes, don't worry. I'll be with you in a moment.'

'Hurry up then, they're about to leave.'

Michel switched off his phone and looked from the headland to the search area. Apart from the archaeologist's RIB there was no other vessel in sight. He walked back along the footpath to check that the orange hire boat was still missing from its mooring and then returned to the watchtower to pack his rucksack. Pierre arrived shortly afterwards.

'Salut Pierre.'

'Salut Michel,' said Pierre, stooping to catch his breath. 'Here I expect you'll be wanting these.'

Michel took the packet of cigarettes which Pierre held out to him and tore away the plastic covering. Within seconds he had a lighted cigarette between his lips.

'That's the RIB over there by the headland,' said Michel, pointing with the lighted cigarette.

'Yeah, I see it.'

'There are four people on board. The tall blonde archaeologist with the two women and the Englishman; the one who we saw on the hire RIB with the *Pinzuti* the other day. Here take the binoculars.'

'Yes, I recognise him,' said Pierre, peering through the powerful lenses, 'and the others as well.'

'Good! All you need to do is follow the Englishman and find out where he's staying. He may get dropped off on the beach here, or he might go off with the archaeologists and return in the hire boat. Then again, he may not come back here at all. Wait until nightfall and if there's no sign of him by then, there's not much more you can do. Keep an eye out for the *Pinzuti* too, because there's a chance that he's taken the hire boat. If you see him before the Englishman, you can follow him instead.'

'So to make it simple, I follow either the Englishman or the *Pinzuti*, whoever I see first?'

'That's about it.'

'OK leave it with me.'

The twin outboard engines of the yellow and black RIB suddenly burst into life and the two men watched it nose away from the headland and accelerate towards the north-west.

'Well that eliminates one possibility,' said Michel, 'you just need to sit tight now.'

An onshore wind had developed since they'd left Roccapina obliging them to huddle down against the chilling spray that was being whipped up over the bow. Mike pulled his wetsuit back on and Hubert put on a windcheater which he kept tucked away under the instrument panel. By the time they reached Tizzano they were tired, cold and drained of enthusiasm. Mike helped to tie up the boat and transfer the heavier items to the truck. The stone anchor proved particularly difficult to manipulate while the RIB was rocking by the quayside and after several attempts, the four of them resorted to lifting it physically from the extended gantry and lowering it onto protective matting in the back of the truck. The rest of the equipment quickly followed and soon there was only light material left.

'You should start heading back before this wind gets any worse,' suggested Monica.

'Yes you're probably right,' agreed Mike. 'Will you pick me up off the beach tomorrow then?'

'Yes, just before nine if possible.'

'No problem. I'd better get going then. See you all tomorrow.'

Mike waved and walked over to the hire boat. Before firing up the engine, he pulled out his mobile phone and skipped through the menu until he found Thomas' number. He dialled and waited for the connection.

'Thomas, it's me.'

'Mike, where are you?'

'I'm just about to leave Tizzano. What about you?'

'I'm at the villa. How'd it go today?'

'Yeah - good, listen I'm going to be back in Roccapina in half an hour; can you come and get me?'

'Let me see now. Yes, I suppose so; I'm not really doing anything special at the moment.'

'Oh, well I don't want to put you to any trouble or anything. I just thought that it might save you from a punch in the face later.'

'Well since you asked so politely. I'll try my best to be there - bye.'

Mike rang off and returned the mobile phone to his dry-bag. Thirty minutes later he was in Roccapina, rounding the promontory and making his way up the small bay towards the visitor moorings. The beach was virtually empty save for a lone figure sitting conspicuously in the centre of it. Thomas' sturdy features and close cropped hair were easy to recognise, even from a distance.

Once Mike had secured the boat, he jumped over the side and swam until he found footing in the shallows. He slipped off his fins and trudged up onto the beach.

'Brrr, that wind is cold,' he said shivering. He pulled off his wetsuit and rummaged in the dry-bag for his tee-shirt.

'It does look a bit lumpy out there this evening,' agreed Thomas, as he stuffed the remains of a hotdog into his mouth.

'Yeah, it was pretty uncomfortable coming back, but I was pushing it a bit. How'd you get on today?'

'Quite positive really. I've got lots of information from the chamber of commerce and I've arranged an appointment with an enterprise advice centre tomorrow.'

'Well that's most impressive. Looks like you're well on your way to becoming a high flying city boy.'

'Yeah, maybe I should get a pin-striped wetsuit. I'll tell you something though; it's surprising what doors open up to you when you tell the locals that you're half Corsican. They want to know all about your family connections and which part of the island they're from and then they reel off the names of about half a dozen people who might be related to you. Before you know it, they're telling you all the local gossip and scandal as if you've known them for years. I tell you, one bloke was almost marrying me off to his daughter by the end of the conversation.'

'Well it's nice to see that you're finding your roots again, and we need all the help we can get. In fact, perhaps you should take him up on his offer; we'd get a great local contact and you'd be guaranteed to get laid.'

'Yes, well unless she's the local beauty queen, I think I might just ignore your business advice thanks.'

'Suit yourself. So, in general, everything looks quite positive does it?'

'It does, but I'm starting to realise that running a business in France can be quite costly. We need to be absolutely sure that we're going to make enough money to cover all the hidden charges.'

'That's after we've paid off our drinks bill right?'

'Well obviously there's an order of priorities.'

'Perfect; that's our business plan sorted out then. Now perhaps we can go and discuss all this back at the villa before I freeze to death. I've got some good news too.'

The orange RIB carved across the backs of the incoming waves and rounded the promontory just below his vantage point. In the dimming light Pierre tracked its approach, his eyes narrowing when he spotted the Englishman at the helm. Only an hour had passed since the black and yellow RIB had departed and Pierre was relieved that he would be spared having to wait around in the chill of the wind until nightfall.

When the RIB passed out of view, Pierre quickly packed away the binoculars and began to make his way back along the promontory. Halfway down the steep footpath, he stopped in his tracks and hid behind a rock when he spotted a familiar figure, sitting alone on the beach. The binoculars confirmed what he had first thought; it was the *Pinzuti* – no doubt come to pick up his *Rosbif* friend. Now with two targets to follow, Pierre continued his descent, staying on the blind side of the path and taking care to avoid exposing his presence by sending loose stones cascading down the incline. He arrived at the base of the footpath in time to see the Englishman walking up the beach to greet his friend.

While the two were distracted in conversation, Pierre quickly crossed the beach and disappeared into the cover of bushes behind it. Following a small trail which led through coarse scrub and low-lying sand dunes, he made his way to the parking area. It was almost empty and the silver Peugeot was easy to spot, parked as it was close to the entrance to the beach. After a quick glance at the registration plate, Pierre returned to his own car and drove to the top of the track. Before he reached the junction with the main road, he pulled over, killed the engine and got out of the car. Through the binoculars, he peered down towards the bay and spotted clouds of dust billowing up from the tyres of a car. As it neared, a flash of silver in the dying light confirmed that it was the Peugeot estate. Pierre's rugged face became set with determination. He lifted up the hood of his car, propped it open and waited for them to draw near.

Fortunately the one hour processing laboratory was still open and with a request for priority treatment and a flash of the police badge, the assistant agreed to develop the films immediately. By the time that Michel had returned from the bar next door with something soothing inside his stomach, they were ready for collection. He thanked the assistant, stepped outside and pulled the photographs out of their small protective folder. Quickly flicking through them, he selected the four most suitable shots and discarded the rest in a nearby waste bin. Now he was going to make up for his earlier errors. He rode his motorbike into the back streets of Propriano and parked it in a secluded alleyway. Once he was sure that he would not be overlooked, he locked his helmet to the bike, opened the seat cover and took out a peaked cap from the luggage space beneath. He slipped off his jacket to reveal an official looking blue cotton shirt and a dark neck-tie which he checked and adjusted in his wing mirror. After a furtive glance up and down the street he stepped out onto the lamp lit pavement and began to walk along it. Just ahead of him, an old man opened his front door to let out a cat. Michel dropped his head and hurried past him. A few meters further on, he stopped opposite a modern apartment building to confirm that the lights of the right hand, upper floor apartment were on. They were. He crossed the road and approached the main entrance of the building to study the names that were written beside the intercom buzzers. Tracing his finger down the list he soon found the one that interested him: *2ème étage droite / Moret* – 2nd floor right / Moret.

With a smile of satisfaction he drew in a breath and calmly pressed the button.

'*Oui, qui c'est?* - Hello, who's there?'

'Mademoiselle Moret?'

'*Oui*'

'Gendarmes, I would like to ask you some questions. Please open the door.'

'Gendarmes?' answered a surprised voice. 'Just a minute please.'

There was a buzzing sound as the latch was released. Michel quickly scanned both sides of the street, opened the door and climbed swiftly up the stairwell to the upper floor. He paused to assume a more authoritative posture and knocked firmly on the door of the right hand apartment. It opened on a chain lock to reveal a confused looking Chantale.

'What's this about?'

'Allow me to enter and I will explain,' said Michel, briefly flashing his police badge.

Chantale's brow furrowed with concern as she detached the chain and allowed him to enter. Her hair was wet and she was wearing a towel robe cinched tightly around the waist. Michel glanced at the contours of her breasts and tried, with some difficulty, to keep his mind from wandering onto dangerous ground. Forcing himself to look away, he cleared his throat and pulled a small notebook and the freshly developed photographs from his lapel pocket. He selected one and showed it to her.

'Do you know this man?'

Chantale's eyes opened wide with surprise when she saw the image.

'Yes, that's Hubert...but I hardly know him. What's he done?'

'Where did you meet him?'

'In a bar, just two days ago. Has something happened to him?' Michel saw the fear in her eyes and his confidence fed on it.

'Let me ask the questions Mademoiselle. What were you doing on a boat with this man in Roccapina yesterday?'

'N-nothing he just asked me to come along with him. He was driving the boat for friends of his...they were diving.'

Michel selected the picture that he had taken of Mike on the RIB. 'Do you know this man?' Chantale frowned in utter confusion.

'Yes that's Mike; one of the two friends he was with. Look, what's going on; are they in some kind of trouble?' Michel ignored her question.

'What was the name of the other diver?'

'It was...Thomas I think; yes that's it - Thomas.' Michel made a note of the names.

'Did they mention anything to you about what they were doing out in the bay?'

'No, they were all speaking English...I couldn't understand what they were saying. Look, please tell me what this is all about.'

'Did they say anything about a wreck?'

Chantale frowned and shook her head.

'A wreck? - No, I don't know anything about that.'

Michel's jaw muscles flexed in annoyance. It was obvious that the girl was going to be of little use to him. He checked his notes to see what other information he might be able to squeeze out of her.

'Do you know Monica Huber or Bertie Horschwitz?'

'No I've never heard those names before.' Michel showed her the remaining photographs.

'So you've never met any of these three people?'

Chantale hesitated.

'Yes I saw these two in the bar with Hubert,' she said pointing to the photographs of Anna and Bertie, 'but I didn't speak to either of them. I think they're his colleagues.'

'And this woman?' Michel asked, pointing to the photograph of Monica.

'I think I saw her briefly on the boat; she's probably a colleague of his as well.'

Michel bit his cheek, aware that he was reaching a dead end.

'When are you likely to see...Hubert again?' asked Michel, checking his notes.

Chantale's face became harder. She was beginning to resent this intrusion into her personal life.

'I'm not.' she said defiantly, 'We had a fling, that's all. And now it's over. Now are you going to tell me what this is all about, or do I have to make a call to your superior.'

Michel nursed a desire to slap her across the face.

'There has been an allegation of drugs trafficking and we are making routine enquiries. That is all that I can say at present.'

Chantale looked genuinely shocked. Michel was about to press home his advantage when a telephone began to ring in the next room.

He begrudgingly allowed her to answer it, listening with one ear to the conversation as he considered his next move.

Chantale picked up the phone and began speaking with one of her friends. She was about to cut the call short and ask her friend to call back, when she caught sight of the Gendarme in the mirror of her wardrobe. She watched in disbelief as he took a pair of her panties from a chair and slipped them into his pocket. The initial shock of what she had just witnessed, quickly transformed into humiliation and outrage. She tried to keep the emotion out of her voice as she prolonged the conversation while studying the Gendarme more closely. Something about him was definitely not right, she decided. The investigation appeared genuine enough, but she was aware that Gendarmes rarely worked alone in these matters. On closer inspection, she noticed that he was wearing ordinary shoes rather than the plain leather boots that were standard issue. More surprisingly, there was no gun belt and holster around his waist. And no serious Gendarme would ever be separated from his firearm while on duty, especially when investigating a drugs related issue. Chantale narrowed her eyes and wound up the conversation with her friend, having decided that she would challenge the Gendarme to confirm his identity.

As the Peugeot approached, Pierre closed the hood of his car and walked towards the driver's door while wiping his hands on a dirty rag. He glanced at the faces of the Englishman and the *Pinzuti* through the window of the Peugeot as it passed, before climbing back into his car and pulling out behind them. The Peugeot approached the main junction with its right indicator flashing and Pierre drew close so that he could quickly take its place when it moved off. He scanned the road as it turned and cursed as a speeding Citroen XM arrived from the left, preventing him from pulling out directly behind it. When the Citroen had passed, he saw a van approaching from the same direction and swerved out in front of it, causing it to brake sharply behind him. He ignored the insulting gesticulations from the driver and stared fixedly at the road ahead. The Silver Peugeot twisted and turned around the hillside causing anxious moments each time that it slipped out of his view.

Soon they reached a relatively straight section of road and Pierre hovered dangerously close to the Citroen in front, edging out into the middle of the road. He suddenly saw its stop lights illuminate and was forced to brake hard to avoid slamming into the back of it. Pumped up with adrenaline, he was about to overtake, when he realised that it was in fact the silver Peugeot ahead of it which was holding up the traffic. The Peugeot's flashing indicator told him that it was about to turn right onto an unmarked exit road with which he was not familiar. When it finally pulled off the main road, the Citroen accelerated away sharply and Pierre hesitated, not wanting to expose his presence to the occupants of the Peugeot. He bought himself some time by stalling the engine, causing the van driver behind to blast his horn in protest. Once he felt sure that the Peugeot was far enough down the track, he re-started his engine and began to follow. The irate van driver accelerated fiercely around him, but Pierre took no notice. He paused briefly at the top of the track and opened his window to check the names that were written on the post boxes. None of them were English sounding names. He continued down the track, listening intently through the open window for the sound of the Peugeot's engine. After a blind left hand bend he heard the sound of tyres crunching over gravel and glimpsed glowing brake lights through the dense vegetation. He cut the engine and pulled over so that he could continue his approach on foot. Walking on the soft undergrowth at the side of the track, he crept around the bend until he had a clear view of the silver Peugeot, parked outside a small villa that was set back in the trees. There were voices coming from the terrace and under the cover of darkness, Pierre approached until he could hear the unmistakable sound of English being spoken. His face cracked into a rare smile.

'So did you learn anything about archaeology today?'

'Yeah, archaeologists are very smart and have the patience of saints.'

'It was a bit tedious then was it?'

'No I wouldn't say that. They kept me quite busy actually. It was like being at an operating table, assisting a couple of surgeons.'

'It would have to be an autopsy then,' said Thomas. 'What was the wreck like?'

'Well, if you didn't know it was there, you could quite easily have passed it without noticing it. Most of the wreck is buried in silt; in fact the only real clue to its presence is what's left of the wooden ribs, sticking out from the sand.' Thomas nodded.

'I once dived on an ancient Greek wreck and it looked just like a rubble tip. All the amphorae were smashed and fused together. In fact there was virtually nothing left of the original structure at all.'

'Fortunately this one seems to have fared a little better,' said Mike. 'They've exposed part of the hull with a suction lift and are now excavating the interior by hand. Pretty much everything that was in the holds when it sank is still there, encased in sand and mud. There's hardly a day goes by without them discovering something new.'

'You mean something old,' corrected Thomas.

Mike rolled his eyes.

'So did they find any weapons yet? I quite fancy a bronze age axe on my bedroom wall if there's one going spare.'

'Something tells me that they would not be overly keen to give up a priceless artefact just to indulge your warped fantasies.'

'Well if you don't ask you don't get,' said Thomas with a shrug.

'You wouldn't either way and besides I'm not allowed to give you any details about what I saw.'

'Are you serious?'

'Absolutely. I made a solemn promise to Monica not to tell a living soul. Don't fret about it though; there really wasn't much that would interest you anyway.'

'So no skeletons with sabres and gold earrings then?'

'I think you may have read a little too many Tin Tin adventures when you were a kid Thomas.'

'There's nothing wrong with showing an interest in history!'

'Or reality for that matter,' muttered Mike. 'Now on a more serious note, I spoke to Monica today about getting Hubert to take us out into the bay.'

'Did she go along with it?'

'Yes, she agreed on the condition that it doesn't interfere with their work.'

'Excellent! So when can we start?'

'Very soon. I'll only be working with them for another day because Bertie is flying back tomorrow.'

'Is his father OK now?'

'He's doing well from what I heard. His condition isn't critical any more and he's recovering quickly.'

'That's good news. So all being well, we should be able do a run out the day after tomorrow.'

'I don't see why not. As long as we're properly prepared,' said Mike. 'Did you get the cylinders filled?'

'Y-yes.' said Thomas with a guilty look on his face.

'Thomas, where are the cylinders?'

'They're still in the dive shop; I forgot to collect them.'

'Well if you're going to Bonifacio tomorrow, you can pick them up can't you?'

'It's a big ask, but I'm sure that I can pull something out of the bag. What about you; are you taking the boat again in the morning?'

'No, they're going to pick me up off the beach at 9am, so you'll have a bit of a lie in.'

'That's a strange definition of a lie in.'

'How long did you have to wait before he turned up?'

'Not too long. Just over an hour I'd say.'

'Hmm, that sounds about right,' said Santorini, sucking in his cheeks.

'What does?' asked Pierre.

'That's about the time that it would take to go by RIB to Tizzano and back. I think the Swiss may be using it as a launch base, which would explain why the Englishman chose to go there by boat. By road it's over three times the distance.'

'I guess that would make sense,' said Pierre nodding, 'Do you think all this surveillance is worthwhile though? I mean, no one has been near the search site since Sunday.'

'Perhaps, but we wouldn't even know that if we hadn't been watching. The Englishman and the *Pinzuti* remain a threat as long as they have access to a boat and diving equipment. We have no idea what they know or what they are capable of. And until we do, we need to keep a very close eye on them.'

'I suppose so,' conceded Pierre.

The door chime sounded and Santorini looked up to see Michel skulk into the bar and walk towards the counter.

'At long last,' he growled, with a glance at his watch. Michel slumped onto the bar stool with his face set like stone.

'Did you get lost or something?' asked Santorini, probing for a reaction as he placed a whisky on the counter in front of him. Michel shrugged dismissively, drank the whisky straight down and asked for another.

'Bad day I take it?'

Michel nodded once and pulled a cigarette from his top pocket. He helped himself to Pierre's lighter.

'Did you have a fight with someone?' asked Santorini, narrowing his eyes.

'Why do you say that?' he asked, defensively.

'Because you've got scratches on your face.'

Michel placed his hand on his cheek and felt a sting of pain as he touched two elongated welts.

'I had a disagreement with the ex,' he said, frowning.

'Ah! So that's why you're in such a good mood,' chuckled Santorini. 'What about the photographs; did you get them developed?'

Michel pulled the photographs from his shirt pocket and threw them onto the counter. Santorini picked them up and studied them one by one.

'There are names on the back of two of them,' said Michel, staring at his rapidly emptying glass.

'So the Englishman's name is Mike and the tall blonde archaeologist is called Hubert,' said Santorini as he flipped over the photographs. 'No surnames?'

Michel shook his head.

'What about the *Pinzuti*?'

'I didn't see him, but I have his name.'

'Where did you get this information?'

'From the postman...and the girl.'

'Good work Michel, you should try and get a job with the police,' laughed Santorini.

Pierre smirked and chinked Michel's glass with his own.

'Good. So now we have names and we know where everyone lives.'

Michel looked up sharply and turned towards Pierre, who raised his eyebrows in acknowledgement.

'If any of them step out of line now, we'll be ready to teach them a little about Corsican hospitality.'

'Surely you're not going to get too involved in this ridiculous search?'

'They just need me to skipper the boat,' replied Hubert, chewing reflectively on a piece of toast. 'Having said that, if they find what they're looking for, I'm definitely not going to miss out on the chance to dive a U-boat wreck.'

'Well let's face it, that's not likely to happen is it?'

Hubert took a sip of coffee and leaned back against the kitchen counter.

'What makes you so sure?'

Monica sighed in exasperation.

'I asked Professor Rieder in the History Department to run a check on all U-boats that went missing in the area. He told me that according to the official reports, there aren't any.'

'Maybe there are no official recordings,' Hubert conceded, 'but there must be a good few U-boats which went missing without trace.'

'Perhaps, but there's no credible evidence to support the theory that one of them ended its days here.'

'In my opinion there is. There's no disputing the fact that Mike found a German depth gauge and of course there's the newspaper article and François' story. Add to that the piece of wreckage which they found on Monday and to my mind you have a reasonable argument.'

Monica eyed him warily.

'Another piece of wreckage? You didn't tell me about that.'

'Well there were more important concerns at the time, but yes they found a fire bucket - a German one, within 100 metres of the place where they discovered the gauge.'

'That can't be directly linked to a U-boat though can it? It's a coincidence I'll grant you, but certainly not proof beyond doubt.'

'Well how many excavations have we undertaken on far less convincing evidence?' countered Hubert.

'That's different. As professionals, we sometimes have to make educated guesses based on scant information, otherwise we'd only ever discover anything purely by chance.'

'And isn't that exactly what Mike and Thomas are doing?' said Hubert, raising his eyebrows.

Monica sighed.

'All I'm saying is that your theory relies heavily on a local legend which is probably both misleading and inaccurate, so I suggest that you exercise a bit of discretion before getting carried away.'

'I'm not getting carried away. I'm just helping out a couple of friends, without judging their motives. Maybe you should try to be a bit more supportive after all the help that Mike's been giving us.'

'I'll accept that we owe Mike a favour,' agreed Monica, 'but that's no reason to let our work suffer because of it.'

'That's not likely to happen,' said Hubert. 'Apart from anything else, you're the last person that Mike would want to upset.'

'And why is that?' asked Monica.

'Are you kidding me? You do realise that he's crazy about you, don't you?'

'That's ridiculous Hubert!'

'Is it? Come on Monica; surely you've noticed; he can hardly keep his eyes off you.'

Monica became flustered.

'You must be imagining things. I've done nothing to encourage him.'

'No because you're always hiding behind your work. Don't you realise that if you carry on like this you're going end up missing out on all the good things in life? There's no reason why you can't combine both your professional and private life; you just need to find someone who understands and respects how important your work is to you.'

Monica stared at him.

'And you believe that Mike is that person, do you?'

'I have no idea, but you won't find out unless you give him a chance.'

'That's easy for you to say. You're not the one who'll end up disappointed.'

'We've all made mistakes Monica, and painful as they can be, they're a learning process. Look, I'm not trying to push you to do anything that you don't want to do. All I'm saying is that you should perhaps have a little more faith in people.'

Monica folded her arms and gave Hubert a sideways glance.

'You make me sound like a real cold fish.' Hubert smiled.

'I'm sorry; I really don't mean to Monica. I'd just like to see you happy, that's all. My advice is to give Mike your support as a friend and see where it takes you. Let him and Thomas have their little adventure and if it all comes to nothing, we'll all have a good laugh about it and there will be no harm done.'

'Well I hope for their sakes that you're right.'

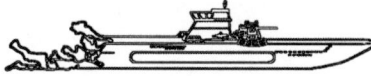

7

The cool morning air buffeted against Michel's jacket as the purring red Honda Fireblade tore along the winding tarmac road. Leaning expertly into the curve of a snaking bend, he passed the sleepy town of Sartène and slowed to make a right turn onto the D48 which would lead him down to the coast. He flashed past the turn off's to the ancient Megalithic sites of Stantari and Pagliaju and eased off the throttle when the road began to narrow. Soon he arrived at the mouth of the natural inlet which led to the port of Tizzano and he paused to take in the beauty of the coastline before him.

With the inconveniences of the previous evening now put well behind him, he felt his confidence returning. His surveillance work had been a success and he was back in Santorini's favour; so much so that Santorini had offered to compensate him for his commitment directly from the coffers of *Libertà Corso*. It was a gesture that Santorini rarely permitted and Michel felt honoured to have been rewarded with such a privilege.

On approaching a small hotel near the jetty, he parked the Fireblade in the shade of an outbuilding and strode off towards a hilltop with his backpack slumped over one shoulder. When he reached its highest point, he took out the binoculars and began to scan the bay before him. Within seconds he had spotted the archaeologists black and yellow RIB, moored alongside the jetty beneath him. He smiled to himself as he sat down on the thick carpet of coarse grass. Santorini had been right.

He lit a cigarette and relaxed while he waited for the archaeologists to arrive. Fifteen minutes later his patience was rewarded when he spotted the familiar white truck making its way carefully along the edge of the inlet. On approaching the foot of the jetty it turned away and then reversed back along the wooden planking until it was level with the black and yellow RIB. The team of archaeologists stepped out of the truck and began to unload their equipment. Michel remarked that they were still without their dark haired colleague and as yet there was no sign of the Englishman either. When all the equipment had been transferred to the RIB, Michel watched the tall, blonde haired archaeologist park the truck out of the way and return to take position at the helm. The twin outboards rattled into life, the mooring lines were cast off and the RIB picked up speed as it rounded the jetty and made its way out towards open sea. There was clearly no point in waiting around any longer. If they were going to meet up with the Englishman, they obviously planned to do it further along the coast; perhaps even in Roccapina. To find out, he realised that he would have to arrive there ahead of them. Returning quickly to the Fireblade, he kicked it off of the stand and prepared to push his riding skills to their limits.

Mike sat on the beach, sharing the peace of the morning with a handful of keen sunbathers. A lone fisherman was perched on a large rock at the base of the promontory, staring meditatively into the shallows. Mike watched him land a juvenile seabream and after making a cursory examination, throw it back into the water in disgust. To his right an early tourist was skirting his way around the edge of the beach, heading for the path which led to the summit of the promontory. For some reason Mike thought that there was a familiar look to him. As he was following the walker's progress, he heard the familiar drone of outboard engines echoing around the steep sides of the inlet and he rose to his feet to see the yellow and black RIB emerge from behind the promontory. As it approached the shore, he waded out into the water to meet it and was greeted by Monica's radiant smile.

'Good morning.'

'Morning Monica, hi Hubert, hi Anna,' he called as Monica relieved him of his dry-bag.

'Hello Mike,' they replied cheerily as he flopped over the sponson and pushed himself up into a seating position. Hubert waited for Mike to settle before gently turning the boat around and heading back up the channel.

'Welcome back. Did you have a pleasant evening?' asked Monica.

'I wouldn't describe it as pleasant. I spent most of it trying to get to grips with French administration. And it's not just me; Thomas seems to have problems with it as well.'

'I know exactly what you mean. You wouldn't believe the amount of paperwork that was required for us to secure a permit to excavate within the boundaries of the national park.'

'I can imagine,' said Mike, nodding. 'Is the excavated material going to remain in France?'

'Yes, in fact it was a condition of the permit being granted. We've agreed that the collection should stay here in Corsica, although we do have the liberty to take pieces away for research and analysis as and when required. If, as we hope, the link to the Shardanes can be substantiated, they will construct a dedicated museum close to one of the nearby Megalithic sites.'

'That sounds fair to me.'

'It is. And the good thing is that here in Corsica, they take their heritage very seriously.'

'That certainly seems to be the case,' agreed Mike.

The drone of the engines fell away as they neared the excavation site. Hubert followed the directions indicated by the GPS screen and picked out familiar transit markers to guide him towards the anchoring spot.

'You'll be diving with Hubert and Anna this morning,' said Monica. 'It's my turn to do surface watch.'

'No problem,' said Mike as he began to prepare his equipment.

Hubert and Anna were first to enter the water and Monica handed them the camera, strobes and stand. Mike entered shortly afterwards and as usual was given the lighting rig. When the three of them were ready to descend, Mike turned to give Monica a parting salute and watched her smiling face fragment and distort into a profusion of abstract forms as he dropped beneath the surface.

The lighting rig in his hand hummed and flickered into life, illuminating tiny pin-pricks of microscopic zooplankton that were floating invisibly around them, like a thin transparent soup. He followed Hubert and Anna to the scattered remains of the wreck and settled himself down at a point equidistant from each of their chosen work areas. Anna teased compacted silt away from the edges of a small cylindrical object while Hubert, to his left, began excavating a partially damaged amphora. A large cuckoo wrasse came to chase away a small gathering of red and blue headed ornate wrasse to guarantee being first in line when the free food was served. Mike was amused to see Hubert swatting at it each time it obscured his view. The jerking movements caused his fins to drag over the sand behind him and as they did so Mike noticed a sudden flash of dull greenish gold. He edged closer to Hubert and made fanning movements with his hand to investigate further. Sure enough, he was soon looking at a curved metallic surface, like a large bowl or plate. He attracted Hubert's attention by gently tapping him on the shoulder and pointing to the exposed metal. Hubert gave Mike an OK sign, shifted his position and immediately returned to his work.

Feeling somewhat foolish for having drawn Hubert's attention towards something which appeared to be of little interest to him, he returned to his original position. He continued to watch Hubert's painstaking work until he was distracted by the sound of nearby muted squeals. Turning his attention towards Anna, he saw her gesturing energetically for the camera. He left Hubert to work under natural light and brought the camera and stand over to her. While he illuminated her work area, Anna centred her find in the metal range finding frame, adjusted the strobe angle and fired off a few shots. Once she had finished, Mike moved in closer to the object and could just about make out a series of engravings on the cylinder in the form of pictograms. He stared at Anna in astonishment and mimed the crooked arms of an Egyptian dancer. Anna smiled and nodded enthusiastically. Mike looked on in fascination as Anna gently lifted the cylinder in her fingertips and rotated it against the light. The encrusted silt fell away from it as she wafted it gently through the water, revealing the details of the carefully carved indentations. She pulled out a small zip-lock bag from her utility belt, placed the cylinder inside and then gave Mike the dimensions of the container which she required to protect it.

By the time that Mike had collected the container from the boat and watched Anna prepare the cylinder for transport, they were running out of dive time. Mike signalled the approaching limit by pointing at his watch and Hubert and Anna brought their work to a close before following him back towards the boat. Anna placed the small container in the lifting basket and joined Mike and Hubert, in conducting a precautionary stop.

While they were waiting to surface, Anna and Hubert swapped messages on their work slates. Mike could not understand their writing, but he could certainly see the excitement in their gestures. After what must have seemed a very long three minutes, they surfaced, and almost as soon as Anna had taken the regulator from her mouth she began to chatter incessantly. Monica listened attentively as she helped Anna to lift her equipment over the sponson. Mike and Hubert followed and as soon as everyone was settled, Monica hauled up the lifting basket and took out the plastic container. The suspense was palpable as she opened it and pulled out the zip-lock pouch. Without a word she went over to the helm and pulled her laptop out from the dry compartment. She booted it and placed it on a crate, studying the cylindrical object in the palm of her hand while she waited. Mike, Hubert and Anna gathered around her as she opened a file containing hundreds of images of pictograms surrounded by oval borders. She stopped by one image in particular and then checked it against the engraving on the cylinder. It was a perfect match. She looked up and smiled in triumph as she uttered a single word: 'Merneptah!'

Michel's reflexes did not let him down. He raced ahead of the morning traffic at breakneck speed and descended the poorly surfaced track which led to Roccapina using all the skills which he had learned as a young Motocross racer.

On arrival at the car park, he parked in an area that was screened off by bushes and killed the engine. The casing and exhaust ticked and pinged as the overheated metal began to contract. Michel pulled on a cap and walked quickly towards the gap in the bushes which led to the beach. He stopped abruptly when he caught sight of the Englishman sitting on the sand, facing out to sea. With one of his questions answered, there was a further and more important one which rose to prominence. Skirting along the bushes to his right, with his back to the Englishman, he walked towards the footpath which led to the top of the promontory. He began to climb and was soon high enough to see the moorings, one of which was occupied by the orange RIB. Now things started to become a little clearer in his mind. The Englishman had taken the RIB to Tizzano yesterday as Pierre had suggested and that was why there had been no sign of it in the bay. Today it looked as if there had been a change of plan and the Englishman was waiting to be picked up from the beach.

Michel continued to climb until the sound of outboard engines alerted him to the arrival of the archaeologist's yellow and black RIB. From his elevated position, he watched it enter the bay and approach the shore where the Englishman was wading out to meet it. Shading his eyes from the glare of the morning sun, he watched him climb aboard and take a seat as the RIB came around and made its way back up the channel. He continued along the footpath and arrived at the watchtower in time to see the archaeologists drop anchor in their usual spot by the headland to the south. It was such a short distance from the beach that Michel wondered why the Englishman had not had the sense to meet them on the beach in the first instance, but then the stupidity of foreigners had always been a constant source of amazement to him. Placing the binoculars by his side, he turned his face towards the sun. Unless the *Pinzuti* turned up to take the hire boat for a spin, he had 8 hours to kill until the Englishman would be returned to the beach. Things could be far worse, he thought as he placed a cigarette between his lips. With the weekend only two days away, he might as well enjoy being paid to do very little. If luck was on his side, he'd soon be rich enough to make it a full time occupation.

Anna had obviously found something of great importance. Mike watched bemused as the three of them hugged while talking excitedly in undulating tones of Swiss German. Once the hysteria had died down, Monica noticed the mystified look on Mike's face.

'I'm sorry Mike; I sometimes forget that you can't understand us.'

'There's no need to apologise. I gather it's good news then?'

'Yes it's very good news. Anna found a steatite cylinder seal bearing the cartouche of Merneptah, the fourteenth son of Ramses II.'

'Are you still speaking Swiss-German? Because none of that made any sense to me.'

'OK I'll try again,' said Monica laughing. 'Are you ready for yet another history lesson?'

'Well I'll give it a go. I'm getting pretty good at pretending that I understand.'

Monica smiled and cleared her throat. When she began to speak, it was with the authority of a lecturing professor.

'As you may know, Ramses II was one of the most notorious and powerful Pharaohs in the history of Egypt. He had many sons amongst his hundred or so offspring and since he lived to be nearly ninety years old, when the average life expectancy at the time was only forty, he outlived all but one of them: Merneptah. Merneptah was probably around 60 years old himself when he became Pharaoh in 1212BC, and consequently his reign was very short. As I've mentioned previously, the Sea People had been a constant threat along Egypt's Mediterranean coast and when Ramses II died they no doubt considered that the time was favourable to launch a full scale attack. But in the fifth year of his reign, Merneptah's armies fought a bloody battle against the Sea People and their Libyan allies and in defeating them proved that Egypt was still a powerful and resourceful state, even without the influence of his illustrious father. Of course this was not the end of the Sea People, because as I mentioned yesterday, it was around 25 years later that Ramses III eventually repelled them from the borders of Egypt for good.'

'OK so far, but what exactly is it that you've found and how did it end up here?'

'It's a royal seal bearing the cartouche of Merneptah.' Monica pointed to the cylinder through the plastic pouch. 'You can see his name written in hieroglyphics here.'

Mike saw an oval shaped frame which enclosed an image of a cow and what looked like three flags.

'It looks like they made a spelling mistake.'

'What?'

'Just kidding,' chuckled Mike. 'The carving's surprisingly clear isn't it?'

'It's in excellent condition,' said Monica. 'The name means *beloved of Ptah,* the god of creation and craftsmen. The seals were used in much the same way as their modern counterparts. They were rolled over soft materials such as clay or beeswax to create a rectangular image which effectively became a security stamp.'

'So how did it end up in the possession of one of the people in this wreck?'

'I'm not entirely sure, but it may have been a war trophy or even a counter-intelligence weapon.' Monica noted Mike's startled reaction. 'If the people who once navigated in that vessel were involved in the battle against Merneptah at Perire, then it is likely that they took it from a fallen Egyptian general. If an invading army had this seal in their possession and fully understood its potential, then they could have used it to confuse the enemy by distributing false commands.' Monica carefully turned the cylinder over in her palm. 'Of course, after the death of Merneptah, it would have been of no further use to anyone, except perhaps as a memento.' Mike was astounded.

'You mean to tell me that this little cylinder had the potential to change the course of history.'

'No, I doubt that very much Mike. Brute force was more the weapon of choice in those days. The battle at Perire lasted all of six hours.'

'Well, does it at least prove that the vessel belonged to the Shardanes?'

'*Prove* is not the word that I would use, but it does strongly suggest that, yes. To be certain we would need to find a link which identifies the Shardane's culture rather than one which was prevalent at the time.'

'So that means more digging then?'

'That's what we archaeologists do Mike. We prod, poke and dig until something turns up.'

'Like private detectives!'

Monica laughed and her eyes sparkled as they caught the sunlight reflected from the sea.

'That is probably the best way to describe us, yes: underwater detectives.'
She glanced down at her watch and raised her eyebrows.
'Speaking of which, it looks like it's time to do some more probing. Are you OK to stay on the surface for this one Mike?'
'Sure, no problem; I think my brain could do with the rest.'

'*Oui, Guy Lechaux, qui parle?* – who's speaking?'
'It's the desk here. Is *Capitaine* Villeneuve there?'
'Not at the moment; who wants him?'
'It's France Telecom. They have a distraught customer who rang about a fault on the line.'
'So what does that have to do with us?'
'They say that their customer, a young lady, has been trying to get in contact with her sister since yesterday evening. They'd arranged to meet, but the sister didn't show up and was not answering her mobile phone. When the young lady found out that there was a problem with her sister's land line as well, she started to get a bit worried. Especially as she didn't show up for work this morning either.'
'Has anyone tried knocking on the door? Maybe she's ill.'
'Well actually a France Telecom line technician passed by the apartment to try and repair the fault, but he says that no one's answering the door. That's why they thought we should be informed.'
'OK, just take a note of the address and get the telephone numbers of the customer and the technician who's on site. It's probably nothing, but I'll send someone round to check it out; just to be on the safe side.'

The meditative rhythm of lapping waves was suddenly broken by the metallic ring of a bell. Mike started and quickly went over to the gantry to winch the lifting basket to the surface. Looking over the side of the boat he saw the rising bubble columns and distorted forms of Hubert, Monica and Anna as they commenced their safety stops below the RIB. When the lifting basket emerged, Mike saw that it contained a large section of the amphora which Hubert had been excavating along with a slate which had the words *please keep submerged* written on it. He winched the basket back down a couple of metres, locked it off and then cleared some space on the deck. Shortly afterwards Monica and her two colleagues rose to the surface and Mike relieved them of their equipment and helped them to climb aboard. As soon as they had removed their regulators from their mouths, an animated discussion followed and Mike was surprised when Hubert suddenly walked towards him and held his hand out.
'Put it there Mike.'
Mike locked hands with him although he was not entirely sure why Hubert was suddenly expressing this bond of friendship between them. He

stared at him in anticipation of an explanation.

'Well done Mike, you have discovered the most important piece of the dig so far.'

'I'm sorry, you've lost me completely.'

Anna and Monica stood beaming at him.

'Do you remember that exposed patch of metal you showed me earlier?' asked Hubert.

'You mean that bowl thing I saw behind you?'

'Yes, except it wasn't a bowl. When I finished excavating the amphora I started to work on it and as I exposed more of the metal I slowly began to realise what it was.'

Hubert watched Mike's impatience grow.

'Oh come on, what was it?' Mike blurted, unable to contain himself any longer.

Monica stepped in to put him out of his misery.

'It's a bronze helmet, almost totally preserved.'

'Really? That's fantastic,' exclaimed Mike, 'but surely it's not the most exciting thing you've discovered; I mean that dagger you excavated yesterday was pretty impressive.'

'We're not just interested in the physical attributes Mike. As archaeologists, were far more interested in the historical significance of each piece. We've been hoping above all else to find an intact Bronze Age helmet and now that we have, thanks to your keen eyesight, we may well have found the vital link which we've been searching for.'

'All I did was spot a piece of tarnished metal. What's so important about a helmet anyway?'

'It's the most crucial identifying feature of the Shardane's battle dress,' explained Monica. 'The style of weapons that the Sea People used varied greatly because of the number of differing tribes that they embraced, but we do know from the battle scenes depicted in the Medinat Habu temple bas reliefs that the Shardanes consistently wore horned helmets; probably so that they could identify each other in battle. One of the main reasons why we think the Shardanes and the Torréens are one and the same is that several of the warriors who have been carved into the menhirs in Southern Corsica are depicted wearing the same type of helmets, albeit with the horns removed. Consequently, if this helmet matches the bas-relief images in Luxor and has either the remains of the original horns or the fittings into which they would have been attached, there will be almost indisputable proof that it was in fact the Shardanes who settled in Corsica and built the Torri from which the name Torréens was derived.'

Mike suddenly felt his head reeling. In the space of a week he had chanced upon two vital pieces of wreckage. One that might lead to the discovery of a missing U-boat and another that could prove instrumental in solving a 3,000 year old mystery.

'Are you feeling OK Mike?' asked Monica, placing a concerned hand on his shoulder.

'Yeah...yeah I'm fine. I'm just a bit overwhelmed that's all.'

'Well I'm glad to see that our work is having such an effect on you.'

'Nobody is more surprised than I am. I hated history when I was at school.'

'In that case I'm glad that we've managed to convert you. In fact it's a pity that we can't have you working with us permanently; you do a great job and you seem to bring us luck.'

Mike shrugged with typical modestly.

'Hey Mike, I think Monica just paid you a compliment,' chuckled Hubert. 'It's quite a rarity; she must like you.'

Monica scowled and slapped Hubert on the arm. Mike laughed along with Hubert as she began to scold him in her mother tongue. Fortunately Hubert was saved from further abuse when the mobile phone began to ring. Monica answered it and after a short conversation, passed the phone to Anna.

'That was Bertie, he's just arrived and he's on his way to Propriano,' she announced.

Seeing Mike's subdued reaction to the news, Monica bit her lip and stared out to sea in quiet contemplation. It was undoubtedly a relief to have a valuable and talented member of her team back, but Monica reluctantly had to accept that it would be at the expense of someone who, despite her efforts to the contrary, she had found herself growing particularly fond of. In quiet resignation, she dealt with the conflict in the only way she knew how. She retreated into the protective shell of her work.

'Hubert can you give me a hand with the amphora?' she asked.

'Yes, of course,' replied Hubert, rising to his feet and following her towards the stern of the boat.

By the time that they had finished transferring it from the lifting basket to the protection of a lined container, the next dive was upon them. Mike, Hubert and Monica kitted up, leaving Anna to keep watch on the surface. Soon the three of them were in the water facing each other.

'Right, let's go and see if we can rewrite a piece of history.'

'Lieutenant Lechaux?'

'*Oui, je vous écoute* - Yes, I'm listening.'

'Officer Bertoli speaking. I'm at the apartment in the *Rue du Château*, the one that you sent me to investigate.'

'Yes, is everything OK there?'

'Not really sir. I got the concierge to open the door and I'm afraid that there's a body inside; I think it's the tenant.'

'*Merde!* Right, stay where you are and get everyone out of there. Don't allow anyone to enter until forensics arrive and don't touch anything. Is that clear?'

'Yes, perfectly sir.'

'Good, I'll be there as soon as I can.'

Lieutenant Lechaux closed his eyes and held the bridge of his nose. This was the last thing which *Capitaine* Villeneuve needed just a couple of months before he was due to retire, but there was not much he could do about that now. He made a call to forensics, ordered a car and went directly to *Capitaine* Villeneuve's office.

'*Entrez!*,' bawled Villeneuve, when he heard the knock on the door. 'Ah it's you Guy. Good, I wanted to speak to you about this damned computer.'

'I'm afraid that it will have to wait sir.'

'Why, what's happened?'

'A body has been found at the *Rue du Château*. We think it's a young girl who went missing yesterday evening.'

'Do we know the cause of death?' asked *Capitaine* Villeneuve frowning.

'No sir; not yet. Look, I'm sorry to bring all this upon you but...'

'Oh come now Guy. There's no need to apologise on my behalf. The timing is undoubtedly regrettable, but I think a bit of real police work is just what I need right now. Have you contacted forensics?'

'Yes sir, they should be leaving any moment.'

'Good, well I'll get my things together and you can fill me in on the details in the car.'

Monica and Hubert worked in tandem on the partially excavated helmet, its form now clearly evident in the clogging mud. Using a stiff brush, Monica teased away encrusted silt and oxidised copper deposits to reveal the hidden details of the finely worked surface. The helmet was almost intact, but it soon became clear that if it had once been decorated with animal horns, they had long since disintegrated in the unforgiving environment. Hubert continued to remove the substrate from the outer edges of the helmet, while Monica concentrated her efforts on the area where she expected to find mountings for the horns. Unable to tell how resistant the thin bronze plating of the helmet would prove to be, she worked with the same intense concentration and self-discipline as a surgeon, conscious that the slightest inept manoeuvre could have catastrophic consequences. The quality of early bronze depended greatly on the quantity and purity of tin and copper that was used in the initial casting process and Monica was well aware that the growing scarcity of tin was a major factor in its fall from favour when primitive iron was being introduced. She could only hope that the blacksmith who'd made the helmet had been provided with the luxury of access to a plentiful and reliable source of each.

Monica ceased brushing for a moment and looked from one side of the partially exposed dome to the other. After a few more delicate strokes with a small, fine haired brush, she attracted Hubert's attention and pointed to symmetrical irregularities on either side of the helmet. Mike watched as she placed upright forefingers on either side of her temples and broke into a wide smile.

Michel lifted his head from his newspaper and scanned the area in front of the bay. It was quiet, as it had been for most of the day. He glanced towards the yellow and black RIB in time to see three divers surfacing beside it. By now he was quite used to the archaeologist's routine and casually checked his watch, knowing that in almost exactly half an hour, they would be hauling up the anchor, ready to leave.

The Swiss seemed to him to be as reliable and predictable as their famous clocks. In fact he wouldn't have been surprised if they had a cuckoo clock chiming on the boat to mark the beginning and end of each dive. He smiled to himself as he pictured the scene. He really couldn't imagine living in a country which had such a confusing mix of culture and languages, especially one that seemed to survive by making watches, chocolate and penknives. But he had to admit that there was one quality of theirs which he greatly admired; their uncanny ability to make money out of other people's. He picked up the binoculars to make a cursory inspection of the four people on board and then returned his attention to his newspaper. Around 25 minutes later he heard the outboard engines starting up and he rose to walk to the opposite end of the promontory. As expected, the RIB entered the channel below him and deposited the Englishman on the shore. The *Pinzuti* was there too, he noticed, sat waiting for him on the beach. Michel replaced the binoculars in his rucksack and began to make his way down the steep footpath. After a quick glance to reassure himself that the hire boat had not moved from its moorings, he arrived at the beach and followed the Englishman and the *Pinzuti* to the parking area. Once he had seen them drive to the main road and turn right, he opened up the throttle and sped off in the opposite direction. He already had the taste of the first whisky on his tongue.

It had been an incredibly successful day and there was excitement on the faces of everyone in the team. Monica knew that they would now have to go public with their find, but the rewards would be wide reaching status within the archaeological community and a virtual guarantee of work and funding for the rest of their careers. There would be requests for interviews, seminars, lectures and guest appearances all over the world. And no doubt one or two hotly contested debates with some of their envious contemporaries. She expected no less.

Hubert slapped Mike on the shoulder and handed him a bottle of water.

'I hope that your luck extends to finding this damned U-boat as well,' he said, 'then we'll really have something to celebrate, eh?'

'I don't think luck will come into that one,' said Mike. 'It's purely a matter of methodical searching. If it's there, we'll find it.'

'Say what you like, but I still think the Gods are smiling on you at the moment. I wouldn't normally be so superstitious but...' Hubert beckoned

Mike closer. 'I've got a feeling that the ice queen is starting to thaw,' he whispered. 'If she's finally going to fall for your charms, then I would have to believe in divine intervention. There could be no other explanation for it.'

Hubert laughed loudly and slapped Mike on the shoulder again.

'What are you two laughing about?' asked Monica with suspicion in her voice.

'Erm, nothing Monica. I was just saying to Mike that we've really appreciated his help.'

'Yes, of course we have. I hope that you've enjoyed working with us too Mike.'

'Oh absolutely, it's been fascinating. The time has just flown by.'

Hubert excused himself and went to start up the engines.

'Yes, we always feel like we're chasing our tails too,' said Monica. 'There never seem to be enough hours in the day to do all that we would like.' Anna raised the anchor and the RIB began to move away. 'By the way, if you're stuck for something to do at any time, you're more than welcome to come and help us out on a voluntary basis.'

'Thanks for the offer, but unfortunately I have other things that I need to attend to. We really need to put some work into our business plan.'

'Yes of course Mike; I understand perfectly and if there's anything that I can do to help you, I'd be more than pleased.'

'Thank you. I'll bear that in mind.'

Mike looked up and saw that they would soon be approaching the beach. Encouraged by Hubert's comments he decided to throw caution to the wind.

'Monica I really have enjoyed working with you and...well I might not be able to see you on a professional level, but I was wondering if you might consider seeing me on more of a social basis.'

Monica raised her eyebrows and tried to suppress a smile.

'Are you asking me out Mike?'

'Um...yes I suppose I am.'

'Well that's very sweet of you...and I'm very flattered, but I don't think that would be a good idea.'

'Oh, I see. I'm not your type then?'

'No it's not that,' laughed Monica. 'The problem is that I don't really have any free time and so I don't have room for any kind of social life.'

'But surely you have a day off from time to time?'

'Yes I do, but I use them to catch up with my paperwork. You see it really would be much better for you if we just remained friends.'

Mike breathed a sigh of resignation and mustered a smile.

'Well the offer is there Monica. If you change your mind, you have my mobile number.'

'Yes I do,' she said, smiling. 'Looks like this is your stop.'

Mike heard the engines being throttled back and knew that it was time to back out gracefully. He retrieved his dry-bag from the central console and was about to jump into the shallows when he remembered that he'd brought something along for Hubert.

'Hey Hubert I forgot to give you this,' he said, handing over a deep decompression diving manual. 'When you've finished reading it we'll get you trained up.'

'Oh fantastic. Thanks Mike, I'll make a start on it right away.'

'See you tomorrow then.'

Mike shook Hubert's hand and planted three kisses on Anna and Monica's cheeks.

'Thanks again for all your help,' said Monica as Mike slipped into waist high water.

'You're welcome.'

'Hi Thomas!' shouted Hubert as the RIB began to back away from the beach. Mike turned to see Thomas at the water's edge holding a large ice cream in one hand while waving with the other.

'Hi Thomas, how did it go today?'

'I can't say that I enjoyed myself, but I got most of the information that we need. What about you?'

'Fantastic. We excavated a bronze helmet today. I guess I shouldn't really be telling you this, but it could be one of the most important finds in Corsica's history.'

'Why's that?'

'It once belonged to a Shardane.'

'Australian was she?'

'Very funny. It's the name of an ancient tribe actually.'

'I see. Do you want an ice cream?'

Mike shook his head dispairingly and trudged off towards the car park. They drove back to the villa and were soon sat outside on the terrace sipping ice cool Pastis and picking at ripe black olives. Mike unfolded his maritime chart on the table and pointed at two crosses which he had pencilled in over the search grid.

'Look, this is the place where I found the gauge and this is where we found the fire bucket. They both border on this grid sector to the north, so I suggest that we concentrate our search there tomorrow. If we find more wreckage in that sector then we can pretty much eliminate all this area to the south.'

'And if we don't?'

'Then we'll have to search all of the sectors systematically, so we'd better hope I'm right.'

'I have absolute faith in you,' said Thomas, crossing his fingers. 'Actually I don't care what we do; just as long as I don't have to deal with those damned bureaucrats again.'

Mike smiled as he took a sip of Pastis and rolled it around his tongue.

'This mark here is where we jump,' he said, pointing to the chart. 'Once we've hit the bottom, we'll sweep eastwards until we reach this point and then start heading back to shore. The pencil line is our return heading, which I've corrected for tidal set and drift so that it will lead us straight to the RIB; in principle at least.'

'I'll give you the benefit of the doubt on that; mainly because I'm not really sure what you're talking about.'

'You don't need to. Just use the compass heading as you normally would.'

'That's what I like to hear. What about the dive profile? Are we going to use the same one again?'

'Yes, I can't see any reason to change it. Did you remember to pick up the nitrox cylinders?'

'Yes of course; they're in the car. And before you ask, I've also put the DPV's on charge.'

'Somebody pinch me.'

'Is that it then?'

'Yes, I think we've covered everything for now.'

'Good. Well if your corporate presentation is over, I've got an important appointment with the shower,' said Thomas, draining his Pastis.

'I don't think anyone will stand in your way,' said Mike. 'And make sure that you get plenty of rest tonight. Tomorrow is going to be a big day.'

'Her name is Chantale Moret; aged 22; living at the present address and employed as an Administrative Assistant. She was single with no previous record.'

Capitaine Villeneuve looked down at the lifeless body of the young girl in the body bag, her nudity barely concealed.

'What was the cause of death?'

'There were large amounts of barbiturates and alcohol in her stomach, but the actual cause of death was drowning,' said the Head of Forensics. 'We found her lying in the bath when we arrived and on further investigation discovered that her lungs had water in them, which confirms that she was alive when she was immersed. As far as we can tell, the alcohol and barbiturates were forced upon her, and at some point she appears to have been bound, gagged and sexually assaulted.'

Villeneuve's brow furrowed in consternation. Lieutenant Lechaux shifted uncomfortably by his side.

'Did you find any fingerprints?' asked Villeneuve.

'No *Capitaine*. No fingerprints and no sign of forced entry, but we did find some shoeprints on the bathroom tiles: size 37. The girl had intercourse, probably forced, as we found superficial tears, skin tissue beneath the fingernails and microscopic blood droplets on her clothes. Her face was also badly bruised. We've taken samples to make sure that all the DNA profiles match before we run a check on the database.'

'That would seem wise under the circumstances,' agreed Villeneuve. 'What are your thoughts Guy?'

'I have the impression that this murder wasn't planned,' said Lieutenant Lechaux. 'If it was, then the killer has made a very poor attempt at covering up.'

'Yes it all looks very amateurish doesn't it?'

'It certainly does. And with no evidence of a forced entry, it's likely that she either knew her killer or considered him to be someone who posed no threat. The apartment appears relatively undisturbed and nothing, as far as we know, has been taken, which leads me to think that we might be dealing with a rejected lover or possibly a sexual predator. I'd tend to go for the former because of the amateurish nature of the killing.'

'Yes I'm inclined to agree with you there,' said Villeneuve, stroking his moustache. 'Officer Bertoli, have the neighbours been questioned?'

'Yes sir, the lady next door says that she heard some loud music and banging noises on Tuesday evening, but she also said that it was not unusual as the girl often had men in her apartment. She was not very complimentary about her sir.'

'Yes well that's not a great deal of help is it?'

'No sir; sorry sir.'

'Have the deceased's family been informed?'

'It's being taken care of as we speak.'

'Good. Right, let's begin working with what we have. Lieutenant, I need you to check telephone calls, mobile phones, diaries and letters. I'll organise a team to track down friends, family and colleagues and if we can get the DNA profile checked against our records Henri?'

'Yes *Capitaine,* we'll make it our priority,' said the Head of Forensics.

'Excellent. We'll also need press coverage with a photograph of the deceased and our incident desk telephone number. Can you deal with that Lieutenant?'

'Yes *Capitaine*. I'll have it organised for tomorrow's press.'

'Perfect, are there any other suggestions gentlemen?'

'We could check her E-mail account sir.'

'Ah Lieutenant Lechaux; you and your computers. Well I suppose that it can't do any harm. I'll leave that to you boffins then shall I?'

'I'll take care of it sir.'

'Good, we'll make an immediate start and put all our findings together tomorrow morning at nine.'

Things did not seem to be going quite so well this morning. The black and yellow RIB had arrived from the north-west as usual, but as it passed the foot of the promontory and continued towards the southern headland, Michel saw to his annoyance that the Englishman was no longer a member of the four person crew. He'd been supplanted by the tall, dark haired archaeologist who had now, it appeared, returned from his leave of absence. With the orange RIB still tied to its moorings and no sign of either the Englishman or the *Pinzuti*, Michel knew that he would have to remain on his guard. Things could have been so much simpler if he'd sabotaged the RIB when he'd had the occasion, but Santorini had given him strict instructions to observe without interference.

An hour passed and Michel stirred when he heard an outboard engine burst into life down in the bay to his left. Stubbing his cigarette into the ground, he leapt to his feet and grasped the binoculars in one hand. Walking briskly over to the edge of the promontory, he looked back towards the moorings but his view was obscured by dense foliage. He waited, knowing that there was only one way for the vessel to go. His pulse quickened when he saw flashes of orange through the gaps in the trees. Within seconds the hire RIB emerged into the clearing beneath him and even by the naked eye Michel could clearly identify the two passengers. He pressed the binoculars to his face and tensed the muscles in his arms and legs as he studied the decks. They were loaded with diving equipment, and not the type that was intended for use in the shallows. He anxiously tracked the progress of the Englishman and the *Pinzuti* as they advanced towards the headland and approached the yellow and black RIB which was anchored close to the point. A rope was thrown and a conversation took place between the crews as the two vessels were drawn together. Alarm bells began to sound when he saw the tall blonde archaeologist step over into the smaller RIB. Michel watched in frustration as they broke away and disappeared from view behind the headland. It was the exact same sequence of events which had taken place earlier in the week, minutes before he had seen the orange RIB speeding towards the search area. He'd undoubtedly made a crucial mistake back then by allowing himself to become distracted, but this time he would not repeat the error.

The single 75 horse power outboard engine of the orange RIB churned the turquoise waters of the narrow inlet into a swathe of white foam as it powered away from the moorings. Mike crabbed across the channel and hugged the coastline to the south, gradually throttling back as they hit open sea. The black and yellow RIB soon came into view, anchored in its usual spot, just short of the tip of the headland. As they neared, Mike saw that Monica and her team had already surfaced from their dive. He asked Thomas to stand ready at the bow while he shaped his course to come alongside.

'Hey Hubert are you still drunk?' teased Thomas when Hubert missed the securing line which he'd thrown.

'Ha Thomas! Why don't you talk less and learn how to throw a rope properly!'

'Hello boys,' called Monica, looking up from the clipboard that she was busily writing on.

'Hi Monica,' they both replied. Bertie and Anna added their greetings.

'Hey, welcome back Bertie. How's your father doing?' asked Mike.

'Thank you, he is much better now,' Bertie replied. 'He was quite bad when I first arrived in Switzerland but now he has returned to the house. The doctor says he must take rest.'

'Well I'm pleased to hear that he's getting better.'

'Thank you.'

Mike turned his attention to Monica.

'Have you managed to free the helmet?'

'Hmm, not yet I'm afraid. It's still clogged up with silt. We're having to remove it all very carefully as we can't risk having any weight inside it when we transport it.'

'I'm sure that you guys will pull it off.'

'I hope so; we've put a hell of a lot of work into it.'

'I can imagine,' said Mike nodding. 'Well, I don't want to delay you any more than is strictly necessary, so is it still OK for us to borrow Hubert?'

'Yes, as long as you can do what you need to do now. We'll be diving again in forty minutes and I'd appreciate it if we could have him back here before we jump.'

'I don't think that will be a problem. We're more or less ready to go.'

Monica nodded and spoke briefly with Hubert, who quickly finished up what he was doing and came over to join them.

'So where would you like me to take you today gentlemen?' he asked with a smile.

'Oh, just drop us off over the nearest U-boat please,' replied Thomas.

'I'll see what I can do.'

Hubert stepped across into the smaller RIB and untied the painter.

'See you all later,' shouted Mike as they began to pull away.

'Have a good dive and good luck,' replied Monica.

Hubert took the helm and guided the RIB around the headland and into the rocky bay which lay behind it. When they were out of the way of prying eyes, Mike and Thomas began to strap on their bulky equipment. After several minutes spent rehearsing moves and checking gauges, valves and instruments, they positioned themselves towards the bow of the RIB and turned to face Hubert.

'OK, let's do it.'

The four men sat around a simple formica topped wooden table, lit by glaring overhead fluorescent lights, busily consulting the documents and handwritten notes which were sprawled across the table in front of them.

'We've narrowed the time of death down to 7.45pm give or take a quarter of an hour,' said Henri, the Head of Forensics. 'We've pretty much ruled out any possibility of suicide now, as a more thorough examination of the victim's mouth and throat has confirmed that the drugs and alcohol were forced upon her. The victim clearly tried to put up a fight, as is demonstrated by the bruising to the face, lacerations on the inner thighs and the skin tissue that was found under her fingernails. As for the lab evidence; the DNA profile of the semen matches that of the other tissue samples found at the scene of the crime, so we are obviously dealing with a single suspect. Unfortunately no match was found on the database, but we have identified the assailant's blood group and found fibres which we believe came from his clothing.'

'Thank you Henri,' said *Capitaine* Villeneuve with a curt nod. 'Please keep us informed of any further progress. Guy?'

'We checked everything that we could find sir, but most of the victim's communications were with female friends and offered no insight. We still have a couple of male acquaintances to interview today and I'll obviously keep you informed of the outcome. A press release has been prepared this morning and should be out in time for the evening newspapers.'

'Very good Lieutenant. Officer Bertoli?'

'Sir, we've interviewed most of the people living nearby, but no one seems to have seen or heard anything untoward on the evening in question. There was one old gentleman who claimed to have seen a Gendarme pass by around 8pm, but I checked and we had no one present in the area at the time.'

'Interesting,' said Villeneuve, taking notes. 'Henri, do you by any chance have details of the colour and type of fibres that you found in the apartment?'

'I'm afraid that I didn't take note *Capitaine*, but I could easily check.'

'Please do so and let me have the information as soon as you can. Good; well from my team's research we have one lead which looks very promising indeed. According to accounts from two of the victim's friends, she met a man in a bar on the Avenue Napoléon on Sunday evening and apparently spent the night with him. He was tall, well-built, blonde, in his late twenties and of Swiss origin. The two friends say that he claimed to be an archaeologist, working in the local area. On the following evening - the Monday, one of the girls spoke with the deceased over the phone. It appears that *Mademoiselle* Moret had an argument with the Swiss man that same day and reportedly said that she was unlikely to see him again. The same friend also spoke with her on the evening of the murder and recollects that she appeared unusually subdued and distant, though not unduly anxious. Unfortunately, neither of the two friends could remember the Swiss man's name, but they did say that he was there with some of his colleagues. I've got someone working on it as we speak and I'm reasonably confident that with such specific information *Les Renseignements Généraux* will have something for us later today. Naturally, I'll keep you all informed.' Villeneuve paused and scanned through his notes. 'Well gentlemen, it seems that we're making progress. Are there any questions or further information which any of you would like to volunteer before we conclude?'

The three men looked up from their notes and shook their heads in unison.

'In that case I won't keep you from your work any longer.'

'Three, two, one, mark!' called out Hubert as he eased back the throttle. Mike and Thomas' movements were in perfect synchrony as they rolled off opposite sponsons and disappeared below the swirling surface. Hubert counted off five seconds before he turned to look over his shoulder. Seeing nothing but the widening wake of the RIB he traced a wide arc around the area and then started back towards the headland.

Beneath the surface, Mike checked his descent and hovered until the shroud of fine bubbles had cleared. He caught sight of Thomas a few metres away and swam towards him. After they had completed their pre-dive bubble check, they quickly exchanged signals and began a rapid descent through the shifting blue columns of penetrating sunlight. For a minute or so the constantly changing pressure on their eardrums was the only way of sensing their descent through the blue void, but indistinct shadows soon began to sharpen into definite forms beneath them and signs of life began to appear as if from nowhere.

A startled pair of cruising silver crevalle jacks were temporarily distracted from their pursuit of a shoal of anchovies as Mike and Thomas passed them by. On the sea floor below a starry ray shot out in alarm and skittered away, sending pearly razor fish darting head first into the sand. Mike and Thomas slowed their descent until they were hovering motionless a couple of metres above the sea floor. Their tiny computer screens informed them that they were at a depth of 46 metres. Coarse sand and elongated ridges of rock spanned out and disappeared into the distance all around.

Having opted to navigate, Mike lost no time in sighting along the compass which he'd attached to his DPV. After a brief exchange of signals he and Thomas were soon moving away. As they progressed northwards along the first position line, the rocky ridges gradually began to increase in size, creating an interconnecting maze of deep passages. Mike took his eyes briefly away from the compass to glance at a solitary longfin gunard and a swift moving school of Atlantic mackerel before two consecutive ninety degree turns brought them around and onto the second position line. They dissected a school of pink dentex and caught glimpses of painted combers, darting for cover amongst the sponge encrusted rocks.

The third sweep came and went without incident and the fourth had barely begun when Thomas alerted Mike with the audible stop signal. Mike paused his timer and left a marker on the seabed before following Thomas towards a dark uneven patch in the sand. From a distance it looked like an isolated slab of rock, but on closer inspection Mike saw that it was a man-made structure about 2 metres square. It consisted of a flat ribbed grid of metal with protruding bolts, some of which still held the remains of dark wooden panels. Mike wafted away some of the sand that was obscuring them and after probing the splinters of wood wrote a note on his slate. Thomas read the word *decking* and understood that the panels must once have been bolted onto the hull of a steel plated vessel. A small moray eel which had made its home beneath the wreckage slid its head out to inspect the strange looking intruders. It must have decided that it didn't like what it had seen, because it quickly retreated beneath the wooden panels and remained there peeping out warily from the shadows.

Mike noted the position of the wreckage relative to their progression along the search line and scanned the area in all directions before he gave the signal to continue.

At the start of the fifth sweep they encountered a large stingray which skirted elegantly around them when they intersected its path. When they reached the northern extremity of the sweep, they came almost directly upon another piece of wreckage; a tangle of pipework and gauges which had been ripped away from their supports. The faces of the gauges were shattered and obscured with marine growth, much like the one which Mike had found a few days ago. Thomas tried to unscrew one of the gauges but found that it was firmly attached. He suggested using his marker buoy to lift the whole structure to the surface and recuperate it later, but Mike was against it for several reasons, not least of which was the fact that it might lead Hubert to the wrong conclusion. With no other option, Mike marked the position of the find and chose to abandon it and continue the search.

After two more right hand turns they began to head southwards along the sixth search line. A small group of barracuda were slowly rotating in a vertical columnar formation ahead, their flanks emitting silver flashes in sequence as they caught the light, like the rotating mirrored spheres of dance halls. Mike glanced at his compass and his heart jumped when he heard Thomas signalling yet another stop. He turned to see him pointing towards a small dark object that was half buried in the sand, its outline too regular to be natural. Mike noted the time and his position before veering off to investigate.

There was something oddly familiar about its appearance and on closer examination, Mike noticed the telling presence of eye holes and the shredded remains of laces. Thomas tentatively prised the heel and sole of the boot free from the sand and let the silt fall away from it. As he was doing so, Mike was left wondering if it could have belonged to a member of the U-boat crew. If it was, then there was an outside chance that it could still have the owners name written inside it. Intrigued, he took the boot from Thomas, turned it upside down and agitated it to remove the deposits of silt which had accumulated inside. A murky brown cloud emerged from the boot and Mike heard a slight clinking sound as if something had fallen out from it. He distanced himself from the ballooning cloud of silt and examined the top of the boot. On the dark leather interior he searched in vain for signs of writing. As he was reaching for his flashlight, he heard muffled shouting and looked up to see Thomas pointing wide-eyed at the place where he had just upturned the boot. The cloud of silt had now begun to disperse and on the sand he saw a collection of irregular sized white sticks. The largest of these objects had a jagged edge where it had been shattered, exposing a distinct honeycombed core. A wave of nausea passed over Mike when he realised that he was staring at a human tibia. He dropped the boot in horror and felt a sickening surge of adrenaline as the full shock of the discovery sank in. Experience told him that in this heightened state he was in danger of letting the narcosis cloud his judgement. He needed no reminding that loss of self-control at these depths could easily result in a fatal accident. With an effort of will he regained control of his breathing and examined the boot again. There was no writing inside it. He shook his head and signalled his intention to move on. Thomas was in full agreement.

The gruesome remains had brought home the sober reality of what they were searching for: the last resting place of an unfortunate U-boat crew who had been caught up in the horrors of war. Neither of them had seen much direct evidence of death on the hundreds of wrecks which they had explored. In fact it was such a rarity to find human remains of any kind that they had barely considered the possibility. Now Mike and Thomas were fully aware of what might be waiting for them if they were fortunate enough to find the U-boat. All the evidence so far suggested that it had met a violent end and they did not need to be munitions experts to understand that a serious explosion inside a submarine would leave few if any people alive. Those that were lucky enough to survive the initial blast could only have hoped for a miracle as the cold sea swept in to claim its share of unfortunate souls.

Mike and Thomas continued their search in sober introspection, silently questioning their motives for wishing to explore a wreck that was also a graveyard. What they had originally perceived as an amusing and exciting adventure suddenly took on the appearance of a morally questionable escapade.

They had barely begun the seventh sweep when time began to press, forcing them to abandon the last leg of the search. After a brief exchange of signals, they left the sea floor and rose towards their first stop. While reflecting on their discoveries, they switched from air to nitrox and prepared themselves for the long haul back towards the coast.

It was almost beyond belief. The Englishman and the *Pinzuti* had been diving in the bay right under his nose all along. They had blatantly ignored the warnings to stay away from the area and clearly thought that they could get away with diving there unseen. There could be no doubt in Michel's mind now. They knew what was down there and had the determination, means and knowledge to find it. Even worse, they could have already located the wreck and were presently stripping it of whatever valuables it contained; stealing Michel's share of the haul. Shaking with fury and frustration, he stared at the empty spot in the sea where he had just seen them roll into the water from the moving RIB. If he'd not been paying careful attention to the whole operation he might easily have missed it. Those two were clever all right. Far too clever for their own good. But now they would pay the price. They had to come up to the surface some time, and when they did, he would make them wish that they hadn't.

Thirty minutes had elapsed since they left the search area and their decompression schedules were now complete. The sea floor had been visible for the last fifteen minutes or so and the gradually rising incline reassured them that they were slowly but surely approaching the shore. Mike decided to ascend and signalled his intention to Thomas, who acknowledged and rose up alongside him. When they reached the surface they found themselves close to shore, but to their dismay, the black and yellow RIB was nowhere to be seen.

'We've drifted south of the headland,' said Mike. 'We're in the bay where we started from; look there's the villa over there.'

'Yes I can see that,' said Thomas. 'We'll have to use the DPV's on the surface to pull ourselves back towards the RIB.'

'OK let's start moving.'

Mike followed Thomas' lead and soon they were rounding the rocky headland close to shore. They were making good progress until Mike felt a sudden loss of power in his DPV. He shouted and grabbed hold of Thomas' ankle before he went racing ahead.

'I've lost power,' he explained. 'The battery must be flat.'

'We still might be able to reach the RIB if you hold on to me.'

'Maybe, but we're going against the current and the charge in your DPV will be running low too. It might be better if you stay here with the gear and I go ahead with the DPV. I'll get there much faster without the weight of the equipment and then I can come and pick you up with the boat.'

'Yeah, I suppose that makes sense,' said Thomas reluctantly.

'You can't argue with logic,' said Mike, smiling. He clipped off the redundant DPV and freed himself from his harness before pushing the entire floating rig towards Thomas. Freed of constraints, he took Thomas' functioning DPV and set off towards the RIB at a surprisingly fast pace. He reached it in less than a minute and was met by four very surprised faces.

'Mike, are you OK?' asked Monica, concerned to see him alone.

'Yes I'm fine thanks; we just had a slight hitch in our plan; nothing serious.'

'Did you finally get rid of that deadbeat friend of yours then?' asked Hubert, who was busily stowing cylinders into racks.

'Unfortunately not,' laughed Mike. 'He's a lot tougher than he looks. I tried to leave him for the sharks, but I think he may have bitten one or two of them.'

Monica laughed and took the DPV from Mike as he pulled himself out of the water.

'So where is he then?' she asked.

'He's waiting back there, but there's no rush. How was your morning anyway?'

'Excellent. We finally eased our prize from the mud and managed to get it up in one piece.'

'That's fantastic news. I'd advise you to keep quiet about it while Thomas is around though, because if he sees it, he'll want to try it on.'

'If he does, he'll wish that the sharks really had got him,' she warned.

'I think I'd prefer the shark odds myself,' chuckled Mike. 'Well, I suppose I'd better go and pick him up; he'll only sulk otherwise.'

Mike jumped over into the smaller RIB and started up the engine.

'See you in a minute or two.'

He cast off the lines and slowly accelerated away, rounding the headland to find Thomas up ahead, lying flat on his back across the two fully inflated rigs, like a shipwrecked sailor adrift on a raft.

'I guess you weren't too worried then?'

'Why should I be? I've got your equipment here as insurance.'

'Damn, I knew there was a flaw in my plan. Pass the gear up then.'

Thomas handed the sling tanks and the remaining DPV to Mike and then helped him to wrestle the two twin sets aboard. Once Thomas had hauled himself out of the water, Mike gunned the boat back around the headland to join the others.

'Hey Thomas, do you need some help with your navigation?' asked Hubert.

'No, I just need to find a more competent diving companion,' said Thomas.

'Any more of your cheek and you might have to find one,' said Mike in retaliation.

'So, in between your bickering, did you manage to find anything interesting?' asked Monica.

'Are you sure you want to know?' asked Mike.

'Yes of course. We archaeologists are naturally curious.'

'Well, it looks like we're getting very close. We found a section of decking, some gauges and a boot.'

'A boot? Was there something particular about this boot which made you think that it might have come from a U-boat?' asked Monica.

'Well it still had its owner's foot inside it,' said Mike, soberly.

Monica screwed her face up, unsure if she had heard correctly.

'You mean to say that it had a human foot inside it?' she asked incredulous.

'Yeah, well what was left of it. It was just a collection of bones really.'

'You really ought to inform the police about that.'

'I'm not sure that the police would be too impressed; I mean just imagine the scenario - *Excuse me sir, but I'd like to report the discovery of a dismembered foot which I believe once belonged to a crewmember of a German U-boat.*'

Thomas and Hubert began to laugh, but Monica was unimpressed.

'You have no tangible proof that it came from one of the U-boat's crew,' she said, sternly. 'That boot could have belonged to someone who was recently murdered and dumped at sea.'

'Judging by the state of decomposition and the amount of silt that we found inside it, it's been down there for decades, so if there is a murderer, he's probably in his grave by now. Besides, I'm definitely not going back down there to recuperate it and I certainly don't want anyone else snooping around the area if I can help it.'

'Well, that's up to you Mike, but I still think that it should be reported.'

'OK, If it makes you any happier, I promise that we'll report it if we *don't* find the sub.'

'Let's hope that you don't have to keep your promise then,' said Hubert with a grin.

'Don't you have any work to do?' Monica scolded.

'I'm sure that I can find something,' said Hubert with a smile and a sly wink to the boys.

'Actually, I think we'd better make a move as well,' said Mike. 'There are a couple of things which we need to do this afternoon.'

'Before you go...I was wondering if you wanted to come over to our place tonight?' asked Hubert. 'I've got some questions about that manual you gave me, and if you like, I could put some meat on the grill and chill some beers so that we can make an evening of it.'

Mike and Thomas glanced at each other and nodded in agreement.

'Sure, we'd love to.'

'Have you decided this all on your own Hubert, or do the rest of us get a say in this?' asked Monica, incredulous.

'Don't worry; I'll take care of everything.' He turned to suggest the idea to Bertie and Anna and got the green light.

'Looks like we have a majority decision,' he said with a smile of satisfaction.

Monica shook her head in irritation and turned towards Mike and Thomas.

'Well it looks like we'll be seeing you both later then.'

'Don't look so happy about it,' said Mike.

Monica broke into a half smile.

'Don't worry, by tonight I'll be just plain old irritable.'

'Well I promise that we'll be on our best behaviour.'

'And I'll just behave like myself,' said Thomas, grinning.

'We wouldn't expect anything less,' said Monica.

'So what time do you want us there Hubert?' asked Mike.

'Seven thirty will be fine.'

'OK. In that case we'll see you all later.'

After the orange RIB had broken free, Mike and Thomas gave parting waves and headed back towards the shore. The trauma of their earlier encounter had now been put well behind them and in buoyant mood they laughed and joked as they planned their evening ahead.

At first he thought about doing it alone without consulting Santorini, but he soon realised that it was unlikely to win him any favours. He'd been criticised in the past for his over zealous approach when taking matters into his own hands and knew from bitter experience that it was better to get clear directives from Santorini and receive his support, rather than be left out in the cold when things got out of hand. He pulled out his mobile phone and dialled the emergency number. There was a delay before the line connected.

'*Oui.*'

'It's me.'

'I take it there's a problem.'

'Yes.'

'OK, keep it brief and no names.'

'They ignored the warning. They were out there today searching for the wreck.'

The line went quiet for a moment.

'Are you sure?'

'I'm absolutely certain.'

'Does anyone else know what they were doing?'

'Yes, the tall blonde; maybe his colleagues as well.'

'Then we need to be discreet. We can't afford to risk anything permanent; just make it clear to them that this is a matter of life or death. Do what you have to do.'

The line went dead.

Michel frowned; it was not the response which he'd been hoping for, but disappointed as he was, he understood Santorini's reasoning; a murder enquiry would draw too much attention towards the *Sampiero Corso* and that would put an end to their activities in the bay. The alternative was to make the Englishman and the *Pinzuti* so afraid for their lives that they would leave the area for good.

As Michel was putting the finishing touches to his plan, he spotted movement beside the black and yellow RIB. He trained the binoculars on it and was astonished to see the Englishman being helped out of the water, alone and without equipment. At first he thought that he might have missed something, but a few minutes later, when the Englishman took the orange RIB around the headland and returned with the *Pinzuti* and two sets of equipment, the situation became clear. Unlikely as it seemed, they had somehow made the entire journey to the coast underwater. It was a stark reminder of just how serious a threat they posed.

Michel watched the two of them exchange words with the crew of the larger vessel before they broke free and made their way back up the channel towards the beach. As they passed beneath him, he searched in vain for evidence of salvaged material amongst the piles of equipment on the deck. When they had passed out of view, he quickly gathered up his things and made his way back along the promontory and down the steep footpath. He arrived at the beach and mingled into the crowds, watching from a distance as they began to unload the RIB. Knowing that they would be preoccupied for some time, he went to the car park to check that the silver Peugeot was there. When he found it, he walked towards the Fireblade, parked in the shade of a pine tree. Out of the view of prying eyes, he mixed a little mineral water with earth to make a paste and then splattered it over his number plates and the surrounding frame. From under the seat compartment, he took a shoulder harness and slipped it on beneath his dark denim jacket. After a quick glance around, he discreetly slipped the Glock into the leather holster and stashed his backpack into the empty compartment. Finally he pulled on a balaclava followed by his black full-face helmet. He pulled down the dark visor, started up the engine and felt it purring beneath him like a panther. In his heightened state, he nursed a desire to open up the throttle and make the engine roar. With every nerve in his body tingling, he took a couple of deep breaths and slowly let out the clutch.

Mike tied the boat up and swam to shore to help Thomas wrestle the heavy gear up the beach to the car. Once they had packed everything away in the trunk, they sat on the edge of it, exhausted and drinking thirstily from a bottle of water.

'We must have been damn close to it today,' said Thomas.

'I think it's lying in the section north of the one that we just searched.'

'Are we going to have another crack at it tomorrow?'

'Yes, definitely. It will be our last chance before the weekend.'

'We'd better dump the gear off at the villa and go to Bonifacio then. We can get our stores while they're filling the tanks.'

'That's a good idea,' said Mike, getting to his feet. 'Let's make a move while time's on our side.' Thomas climbed in behind the wheel and Mike jumped in beside him. When the engine was running, Mike pushed a CD into the player and they set off up the dusty access road to the jangling guitar sounds of the Clash's *I fought the law.*

'We're going to find this damned U-boat if it kills us,' shouted Thomas, grinning like a maniac as he played drums on the wheel. He slapped his hand into Mikes and began to blast the horn in time to the music. They soon reached the junction with the main road and turned right, heading towards the villa. A red Honda Fireblade pulled out onto the road behind them. As Mike and Thomas were busily singing out of tune to the music blasting from the speakers, the motorcyclist accelerated fiercely towards them and began to rev his engine, lifting his front wheel off the ground and moving rapidly from side to side. Thomas stopped singing and stared into the rear view mirror. Mike turned around in his seat to see a spinning tyre tread just inches away from the rear window screen.

'What the hell's he doing?' shouted Mike. 'Why doesn't he just overtake us?'

'I don't know. He must be fucking crazy,' yelled Thomas, trying to keep his concentration on the road.

Mike glanced ahead and saw that the downhill stretch of road in front of them was clear on both sides for a good two hundred metres before it veered off to the left. He snapped his head back in alarm when he heard the bike accelerate and draw level with Thomas' open window. The motor-cyclist lifted his visor and began to shout obscenities, through a black balaclava.

Mike saw Thomas' eyes suddenly grow wide with fear.

'What's he saying?' Mike shouted over the music as the biker continued to rant and rave. Thomas turned to face Mike and was about to explain when a handgun appeared next to his head.

'Thomas, watch out!' warned Mike.

Thomas whipped his head around and instinctively slammed his foot on the brake pedal when he saw the gun barrel pointing at his face. The rear end of the Peugeot began to swerve violently and he tried desperately to correct the sliding movement as the motorbike shot away to get clear of him. Mike's left shoulder crashed into Thomas and then his right smashed against the passenger door as the car veered wildly out of control. He raised his arms instinctively as the nearside wing of the Peugeot slammed into the barrier and the rear splayed into the road. For a fraction of a second the car was airborne and then it came crashing to the ground again with a sickening crunch. Mike felt the air being forced from his lungs as it began to roll, throwing heavy cylinders around just inches behind his head. The window screen exploded into fragments in front of his eyes and in the blinding chaos, he anticipated the fatal blow which might come at any second. He glimpsed a flash of blue sky passing beneath him, followed by grainy tarmac, all with surreal clarity, as if he was watching a scene from a movie. His vision began to cloud over and he suddenly found himself submerged in the stunning blue light of the deep canyons of the Red Sea, the faces of friends and lovers smiling at him from the shifting shadows. And then there was a final thunderous roar in his ears as he watched a monstrous wave rise up and come crashing down over him, plunging him into a deep, dark oblivion.

A small team of Gendarmes arrived and quickly cordoned off the area to prevent the suspect from bolting. Under cover of fire, Officer Bertoli approached the main door and rang the bell. He waited several seconds and then tried again. There was no reply. He spoke into his radio and began to walk around the outside of the building, peering inside the few windows which had not been shuttered. Seeing no sign of life, he concluded that the house was empty and walked back to the unmarked blue van. He picked up the VHF radio handset and selected the emergency operations channel.

'Papa Romeo Zero Four to control over.'

'That's Bertoli,' said Lieutenant Lechaux, to the operator. 'I'll take it.'

'Papa Romeo Zero Four, this is control, go ahead.'

'Control, we are at the scene but the building appears to be empty. There are no vehicles outside and the doors and windows are all locked, over.'

'Papa Romeo Zero Four, your message is understood. We request that you remain at the site and stay out of view until the suspect returns. We are expecting his arrival at any moment, over.'

'Roger, Control. We will contact you when we have a visual. Papa Romeo Zero Four - out.'

Lieutenant Lechaux returned the radio headset to the operator and was about to leave the control room when the emergency coordinator called after him.

'Sir, we have a caller on the line reporting a serious road accident on the N196 between Roccapina and Pianotolli.' Lieutenant Lechaux stopped in his tracks and sighed.

'Do we have any bikes in the area?'

The operator checked his log.

'Sir, we have one in Propriano and another further north on the N196.'

'OK, send the bike from Propriano on priority and get an emergency response team and an ambulance out there. You'd better inform Ajaccio as well in case they need air support.'

'Very good sir; I'll deal with that now.' Lieutenant Lechaux nodded his head wearily.

'If there are any further developments, I'll be in my office.' He left the control room feeling drained and resigned to the fact that it was going to be another long evening.

The reaction had been far more severe than he'd anticipated. When the Peugeot had slammed on its brakes and dropped behind, he realised that he'd been just seconds away from death. If he'd applied his own brakes at that precise moment, the Peugeot would surely have rolled right over him and crushed him. Glancing down at his wing mirror, he could see that the Peugeot had now skidded to a halt on its roof. He braked sharply and turned side on to the road so that he could see the full extent of the damage. The roof had caved in on the driver's side, one of the front wheels was buckled in against the axle and the rear hatch door was hanging off on a single hinge. It looked bad; very bad.

As Michel was staring transfixed, a car came down the hill behind the wrecked Peugeot and braked sharply to avoid slamming into it. The sound of yet another car coming around the sharp bend at the bottom of the incline stirred him from his trance-like state. He had to get out of there fast. It was likely that one or both of the Peugeot's occupants were seriously injured or even dead and as each second ticked by, the odds of him escaping unseen were growing slimmer. He slipped the clutch and accelerated away, rapidly picking up speed on the downhill stretch of road. Once he'd disappeared around the sharp bend at the bottom of the incline, he raced on towards Bonifacio, determined to put as much distance between himself and the accident as possible.

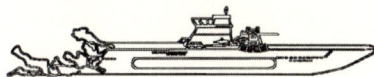

8

The first thing that he noticed when he came round was that his face felt heavy and swollen. For some reason his arms were hanging above his head and when he tried to bring his hands towards his face, it was against the pull of gravity. It slowly dawned on him that he was hanging upside down, suspended by the seat belt, with his head resting just an inch or so from the buckled roof of the car. There was a smell of fuel, but no smoke, which reassured him that for the moment at least, he was not in any immediate danger.

Ignoring the ache in his right shoulder, he tentatively began to feel for injuries. There was some soreness when he touched his ribs and a few cuts and bruises to his face, but no sign of any serious bleeding or broken limbs. He had been extremely fortunate, he realised. When his own immediate concerns had been attended to, he slowly turned his head to the left. The bloody sight which greeted him sent renewed waves of nausea pulsating through his body. He let out a cry of anguish and struggled to free himself from the restraint of the seat belt. Pushing off the roof of the car with his right hand to relieve his weight, he stabbed at the seat belt release with his left. It sprang open and he slumped downwards, banging his head on the roof of the car as he fell. The passenger door was buckled and would not give way when he tried to kick it to open. In desperation, he punched away the shattered remains of glass from the frame of the front windscreen and wriggled out through it, ripping clothes and skin from his back as he went.

He emerged from the mangled wreckage and was helped to his feet by motorists arriving at the scene. They tried to calm him, but Mike was beyond any attempts at restraint. He fended them off and limped around to the other side of the car where he tried to wrench open the driver's door. It too was jammed shut. Unperturbed, he kicked in the window and lay down flat on the floor so that he could reach his arm inside. Through the shattered glass, he pressed two fingers against Thomas' carotid artery, but could feel no pulse.

'Stay with me!' he shouted, as he pressed them in deeper. He withdrew his hand when he spotted blood streaming from Thomas' ear and scalp, forming a dark red pool on the roof. His heart sank, knowing that Thomas had almost certainly suffered severe head injuries. The cassette player was still playing in the background in surreal and macabre contrast to the events which were taking place. Mike hesitated, unsure whether he should try to move him, but he soon decided that if there was no pulse, he could not make the situation any worse. Scrambling to his feet again, he kicked in the remains of the front windscreen and wriggled inside. He cradled Thomas' head as best he could and ignoring his own pain, reached up to unclip the seat belt. When the catch sprang open, Thomas' body slumped down heavily and Mike withdrew so that he could drag him clear.

A police motorbike arrived at the scene and the officer dismounted and began to push back the crowds. Mike continued to shout at Thomas while he checked in vain for signs of a pulse. Knowing that Thomas' vital organs were slowly becoming starved of oxygen, he opened his airway so that he could begin administering rescue breaths. The accumulated blood and mucus in Thomas' throat gurgled as Mike's exhaled air escaped from his lungs between breaths. Now Mike quickly located the tip of his sternum and measured two fingers up from it. He locked his hands together and quickly executed fifteen compressions over the mark. The police motorcyclist was now speaking urgently into his radio, but made no attempt to interrupt Mike. A man carrying a leather bag suddenly broke through the ranks and spoke to the Gendarme.

'Je suis medecin – I'm a doctor,' he said confidently. The Gendarme allowed him to join Mike kneeling in the middle of the road. The doctor placed a hand on Mike's shoulder and asked him to discontinue the heart massage while he felt for a pulse. Mike knew that he would not find one, but the doctor's expression gave nothing away as he pulled out a flashlight and shone it directly into Thomas' retinas. Next, the physician put on a pair of latex gloves and Mike saw the frown of concern on his face when he felt the swelling behind Thomas' neck and head. Mike struggled to hold back tears as the doctor took off the gloves and looked him directly in the eye. He placed a consoling hand on Mike's shoulder and slowly shook his head. In his heart Mike already knew it, but the finality of that gesture extinguished any last hope that he might have clung to. He curled up and rested his head on Thomas' shoulder as great sobs shook his battered body. His desolation was coupled with the terrible guilt which he felt at being left alive and virtually unhurt.

'Go ahead and make the arrest. When he's out of the building, go in and search his room. We're looking for a blue cotton shirt and anything which looks like it has blood or stains on it. We also need a sample of his footwear. Don't let him speak to the others and bring him straight to the interview room when you get back. Is that understood?'

'Yes sir,' replied Officer Bertoli. 'We're going in now.'

Officer Bertoli ended the call and picked up the two way VHF radio.

'Victor Seven to all units. Stay in position. We're about to make our approach.'

Bertoli and a fellow officer stepped out of the unmarked blue van and walked swiftly towards the open backed truck that was being unloaded by the four unsuspecting archaeologists. He glanced at the printed copy of the passport photograph which Lieutenant Lechaux had provided him with and matched it to the tall blonde man who was standing in the rear of the truck. The four archaeologists looked up in surprise when they saw the Gendarmes approaching.

'Can I help you?' asked Monica, taking an authoritative step towards them. The two officers ignored her and went straight to the rear of the truck.

'Are you Hubert Dorfmann?' asked Bertoli.

'Yes, why?' asked Hubert, his face a mask of confusion.

'We need to speak to you at the *Gendarmerie* sir.'

'But why? I haven't done anything.'

'This is routine sir. We need your assistance in the investigation of a crime.'

'If this is anything to do with our work,' interrupted Monica, 'we have permits from the ministry of...'

'This is nothing to do with your work,' said Bertoli, cutting her short. 'We just need to speak to Mr. Dorfmann...alone.'

'I'll just go along with them Monica. There's obviously been some mistake,' said Hubert climbing down from the truck.

'I think that we deserve an explanation at least,' protested Monica.

'I'm sorry but we cannot discuss the nature of the crime as yet,' replied Bertoli.

Officer Bertoli's assistant pulled out a pair of handcuffs and began to open them. Hubert recoiled.

'Surely there's no need for that,' he exclaimed.

'I'm sorry sir, but it's just a precaution.'

'Hubert winced and reluctantly allowed the officer to put on the cuffs.'

'I'll get in touch with the embassy,' said Monica determinedly. 'You're not going to be interviewed without a lawyer present. Where's he being taken?'

'To the *Caserne de Gendarmes* here in Propriano,' said Bertoli. 'We will also need to search the premises and ask you all some routine questions.'

'This is ridiculous,' said Monica. 'Do you have a search warrant?'

'Yes we do - and I might also remind you that we have the power to arrest any one of you for obstructing police duty, should you be thinking of making this more difficult than it needs to be. If you have nothing to hide from us, then we will not keep you any longer than is absolutely necessary.'

'Fine, but I categorically forbid you to touch any of our archaeological finds,' said Monica indignant.

'I doubt if that will be necessary,' said Officer Bertoli. He pulled out his two way radio and called in his men. Hubert was escorted away by two armed officers while Bertoli led a small team into the house. Monica, Bertie and Anna were confined to the kitchen and questioned.

The road was almost at a standstill as the traffic backed up westward. A patrol car arrived on the scene and two Gendarmes immediately debarked and began to seal off the area. Officer Florent spoke briefly with the Gendarme who had first arrived at the scene and then questioned the doctor who had tended to the casualty. Finally he was directed towards Mike, who he found sitting quietly by the roadside with his head in his hands. He introduced himself and guided Mike towards the patrol car so that he could take a statement from him. In his state of shock Mike had difficulty recounting what had happened and the language barrier only made matters worse. His eyes kept drifting back towards the inert body lying in the road, now covered with a plastic sheet. It seemed impossible to believe that Thomas, who was so full of laughter and enthusiasm could suddenly be reduced to a lifeless corpse.

Feeling tired and nauseous in the aftermath of the accident, Mike's concentration started to drift away and recognising the signs, Officer Florent tried to keep him alert.

'You say that there was a motorcyclist?' asked Officer Florent, mimicking the twisting throttle action of a motorcycle with both hands held out in front of him. Mike nodded.

'And he threatened you with a gun?' he asked, pointing to his pistol. Mike nodded again and rested his head in his hands. Officer Florent persisted.

'Did you see his face?'

'No, he was wearing a hood.' Mike did not know the word for hood and used his hands to shield his face, leaving a gap for the eyes. Officer Florent nodded his understanding.

A wail of sirens announced the arrival of an ambulance, escorted by another patrol car. A helicopter arrived on the scene shortly afterwards, the throb of its rotor blades adding to the cacophonony as it began to circle overhead. Mike felt a strange sense of guilt at all the commotion. He had become the centre of attention and yet had never felt more isolated and vulnerable in his life. He wanted to disappear; to hide from the world around him; to be left in peace so that he could begin to come to terms with what had happened. But it was no longer for him to make the decisions.

He remained seated in the car while he was checked over and treated by a medic. Once he had been given the all clear, Officer Florent enlisted the help of a colleague to drive them to Propriano. Through the window, illuminated by flashing blue lights, Mike watched Thomas' body being rolled onto a stretcher and transferred to the waiting ambulance. When the double doors closed, it felt as if a curtain was falling over a chapter in his life. The ambulance pulled away and Mike followed in the back seat of the patrol car, wondering if anyone would ever be able to make him smile again.

Lieutenant Lechaux and *Capitaine* Villeneuve sat across the table from their suspect, scrutinising every detail of his behaviour. Officer Bertoli, removed the handcuffs, attached them to his belt and stood guard at the door of the interrogation room. Hubert rubbed his wrists and matched the stares of his two interrogators, his eyes burning with injustice.

'Can you please now tell me why I'm here?' he asked angrily.

Lieutenant Lechaux casually slid a photograph face down towards the middle of the table. Looking Hubert dead in the eye, he flipped it over and studied his reaction. He opened his mouth to speak, but didn't get the chance.

'That's Chantale!' Hubert blurted, with a genuine look of surprise on his face. 'What's going on here?'

Lieutenant Lechaux leaned back in his chair and frowned, glancing sideways at his superior. *Capitaine* Villeneuve cleared his throat.

'Mademoiselle Moret's body was found last Wednesday afternoon in her apartment on the *Rue du Château*,' he said solemnly. 'The previous evening she had been beaten, raped, forced to ingest prescription drugs and then drowned.'

Hubert could only stare in shock and disbelief at the two men in front of him.

'Where were you between the hours of 7pm and 10pm last Tuesday evening Mr. Dorfmann,' asked Villeneuve with a penetrating stare.

Hubert's eyes opened wide with sudden understanding.

'You think that I had something to do with this? I hardly even knew the girl.'

'Please just answer the question Mr. Dorfmann,' advised Lechaux.

Hubert shook his head in disbelief.

'I was with my colleagues all evening. They can vouch for me if you ask them.'

'Rest assured that we are already questioning them,' said Villeneuve. 'Did you leave the house at any time on Tuesday evening - or were you alone for any length of time during those hours?'

'I didn't leave the house at all. And if I was alone for any length of time, it would only have been for a few minutes.'

'What was your relationship with Mademoiselle Moret?' asked Lechaux.

'There was no relationship. We met in a bar on Sunday evening, we spent the night together; the following day as well and then that was it; finished.'

'But you were disappointed that it ended so abruptly were you not?' asked Villeneuve probingly.

'Not particularly; we were hardly suited.'

'Yet your short relationship ended with a bitter argument didn't it Mr.

Dorfmann; an argument which resulted in aggressive behaviour and insults. Was there another man perhaps? Was it jealousy that made you want to kill her?'

Hubert was ill at ease with the line of questioning and decided that it was time to make his position clear. After all, he had nothing to hide.

'Look I'm truly sorry that Chantale has been murdered, but she was just a girl who I met in a bar. She was young, slightly drunk and up for a bit of fun. She was by no means innocent and old enough to know what she was doing. Yes we slept together, but there's nothing wrong in that is there? The following day she was moody, demanding and selfish and I'm a little too old to put up with that kind of behaviour so we parted company. I don't know how you found out that we had an argument, but in any case it's irrelevant because I was not at her apartment on Tuesday evening and I have witnesses to prove it.'

Sensing that the interview was losing impetus, Villeneuve decided to play his trump card.

'We've extracted a DNA profile from the killer's body fluids and traces of skin tissue which we found under the girl's fingernails. Are you prepared to give us a tissue sample for comparison?'

'If it will get you guys off my back then I'll be more than happy to do so.'

Villeneuve sighed and rearranged his notes on the table. There was a knock on the door and Officer Bertoli opened it a fraction to retrieve a note that was passed through the gap. He handed it to *Capitaine* Villeneuve who read it and then slid it towards Lieutenant Lechaux.

'Well it seems that your colleagues have substantiated your claim that you were at your place of lodging on Tuesday evening,' said Villeneuve, neglecting to add that his shoe size was found to be substantially larger than that of the prints found in Chantale's apartment.

'We have a couple of tests to run on you and a few more questions to ask before we release you. However, you must understand that you are still considered a suspect in a murder enquiry and I must therefore ask you not to make any attempt to leave the island until we give you clearance to do so. Is that understood?'

'Yes, perfectly,' replied Hubert, relieved.

'Then I shall leave you in the hands of Lieutenant Lechaux as I have other matters to attend to.'

The most important thing now was not to draw undue attention towards himself. It was not the first time that he'd been placed in this position and he knew perfectly well what to do. On arrival in Bonifacio, he bought a bottle of water and a small transistor radio from a local petrol station. After cleaning his registration plates, he pushed the black balaclava inside an empty oil container and threw it into a litter bin. He briefly considered disposing of the handgun as well, but since no bullets had been fired, there was nothing to link it to the accident, and it would be good to have around in case he ran into trouble.

He parked his motorbike next to several others in the centre of town, locked his helmet to it and then blended into the crowds. Down a quiet backstreet, he found an empty table at a nearby cafe terrace and ordered a whisky from the waiter. While he was waiting, he lit a cigarette, switched on the radio and tuned in to the local traffic news. The congestion on the southbound section of the N196 was mentioned several times, but it was not until he was on his second whisky that he finally heard the report which he'd been listening out for:

Due to a fatal accident west of Pianotolli, the N196 is now at a virtual standstill with tail-backs extending in both directions for over 5 kilometres. With delays of up to three hours expected, Police are warning motorists to stay away from the area until normal service has been restored.

Michel held the bridge of his nose and swore under his breath. A fatality meant that the Gendarmes would now have interviewed witnesses and would probably be aware that there was a motorbike seen at the time of the accident. Worse still, if one of the occupants of the Peugeot had survived and talked, they would have a description of the clothes that he was wearing and would know that he was armed. Without making a lengthy detour over the mountains, Michel realised that it was no longer safe for him to return to Propriano on the Fireblade. It was time for him to bite the bullet and call Santorini. He pulled out his mobile phone and dialled the emergency number.

'Oui?'

'It's me again.'

'Have you completed the job?'

'Yes, but there have been some unfortunate complications. I need someone to come and fetch me.'

'Where are you?'

'Bonifacio.'

Michel heard Santorini sigh.

'I'll see if I can free myself. I'll call you back when I arrive so that we can arrange a pick up point.'

'OK, I'll be somewhere near the centre.'

Michel finished the call and slipped the phone back into his jacket pocket. He ordered another whisky, lit a cigarette and prepared himself for a long wait.

Capitaine Villeneuve stared at his notes in frustration. He'd felt certain that the murderer would prove to be someone who the girl knew and yet all their investigations had so far drawn a blank. Hubert Dorfmann had seemed to fit the profile perfectly, yet with no links to the evidence and a cast iron alibi, Villeneuve had to concede that his involvement in the murder now seemed highly unlikely. After all that talk about good solid detective work earlier in the week, he now wished that he could press a button on the computer keyboard and see the name of the murderer appear on the screen in front of him.

The problem with the case was the motive. If they weren't dealing with a rejected lover then they had to consider the possibility that the motive for the murder was rape. Yet Villeneuve knew that rapists generally left their victims alive, and those that didn't were usually more concerned about covering their tracks than trying to hide their crimes. It was almost as if the rape was incidental; as if the murderer had intended to humiliate the girl, to punish her for some perceived disappointment. And then there was also the question of access. If the girl hadn't known her killer, then how did he get into the apartment? Villeneuve was troubled by the sighting of the Gendarme close to the scene of the crime. Certainly, the testimony had come from an older gentleman with failing eyesight, but the intriguing thing was that the blue cotton fibres which forensics had found in the girl's apartment were of a similar type to those used in the manufacture of uniform shirts. It stood to reason that anyone disguised as an Officer of the Gendarmes who had a nerve to do so, could easily gain access to any apartment which they chose. It was a worrying thought.

Villeneuve's concentration was interrupted by a knock on the door.

'*Entrez!*'

'*Bonsoir Capitaine,*' said Lechaux with a brief nod as he entered the room. Villeneuve noticed the emergence of crow's feet at the corners of his eyes, presently accentuated by a frown of concern.

'Ah Guy, is that mess on the N196 sorted out yet?'

'Yes sir, more or less. The wreckage is being cleared and the traffic should be back to normal in a couple of hours. The body has been transferred to the morgue and the survivor is presently receiving treatment in hospital. I understand that he's unhurt and will be discharged shortly.'

'Have the deceased's family been contacted?'

'We've passed the information on to the Commissariat in Marseille sir.'

'Good, well I suppose that's all we can do for one evening.'

'Well actually,' began Lechaux, 'the accident on the N196 was not as clear cut as it appeared.'

'What do you mean Guy?'

Lieutenant Lechaux chewed his lip, reluctant to be the bearer of more bad news.

'I've just spoken with Officer Florent who took statements from the casualty and witnesses who arrived at the scene just after the accident took place. The survivor is an English tourist called Mike Summers who claims that he and his friend, Thomas Casanis, were driving along the N196 when they were threatened by a motorcyclist with a hand gun. Mr. Casanis, who was driving at the time, braked hard when he saw the gun being pointed at him and consequently lost control of the vehicle. Although we have no eye witness accounts of the incident, Officer Florent confirms that the pattern of tyre marks appear to support Mr. Summer's statement and at least one person reported seeing a motorcyclist leaving the area directly after the accident took place. Obviously we'll be checking the car for mechanical faults as a precaution. Unfortunately we couldn't obtain a detailed description of either the bike or the rider, so we are presently stopping all motorcyclists in the area and searching for weapons.'

Villeneuve massaged his temples as he stared at his desk.

'Does the survivor know of anyone who might have had reason to harm either of them?'

'Well actually sir, Officer Florent is having trouble with the language and we were thinking that with your English being quite good...well we were wondering if you might interview him personally.'

'Y-yes, I don't see why not. It's not particularly convenient right now, but then when is it ever? Where is this...English person now?'

'Mike Summers sir. He's at the hospital; just about to leave in fact.'

'Well ask Florent to bring him here and I'll have a chat with him. My English is a bit rusty and could do with a bit of practice.'

'Very good sir, I'll get Florent on the radio right away.'

'I suppose I'd better give the wife a call while I think of it too; otherwise there might be another murder for you to investigate,' said Villeneuve, with a crooked smile.

'I'll leave you to face the music then,' said Lechaux, smiling. 'Shall I get some coffee sent up to you?'

'Yes please. The stronger the better. I've a feeling that I might need to keep my wits about me tonight.'

The quays were lit by the shabby diffused glow of the surrounding street lamps which contrasted sharply against the dark waters of the harbour. Bright pinpricks of red, green and white navigation lights betrayed the presence of small fishing boats, moving back and forth between the pontoons and the open sea. Michel watched them disinterestedly while chewing on a slice of chorizo pizza, glistening with olive oil. His mobile phone began to ring and he quickly wiped his hands on a paper serviette before answering it.

'*Oui?*'

'It's me, are you ready?'

'Yes, where are you?'

'Outside the tobacconist on Avenue Sylvère Bohn. Be there in 5 minutes.'

'OK, I'm leaving now.'

Michel put away his phone and called over the waiter. He paid his bill and threw a few coins on the table before taking his leave. With his jacket lapels pulled up around his ears, he walked briskly along the side of the quays until he reached the main road at the end of the harbour. Looking from right to left, he spotted a red and white *tabac* sign and Santorini's white Renault parked beneath it. He darted across the busy road, opened the passenger door and clambered inside. Santorini hardly glanced at him as the car began to pull away.

'What happened?' he asked, as he checked his rear view mirror.

'There was an accident. I followed them on the bike and gave them a bit of a scare, but when the stupid *Pinzuti* saw the gun, he panicked and lost control of the car.'

'Why didn't you wait until they got to the villa?'

'I wanted to get in and out fast so they had no time to think; that's the way I always work.'

'So what's the problem? Why did you need to be picked up?'

Michel lit a cigarette before he answered.

'At least one of them is dead. Maybe both.'

'*Putain!*' swore Santorini. He smashed the steering wheel with the flat of his hand. 'Why are there always complications when I send you to do something?'

Michel continued to smoke his cigarette, unruffled.

'It was an accident. If you're not happy then send someone else the next time.'

'Don't take that attitude with me,' shouted Santorini. 'If either one of them survived, they will point the finger at us, thanks to you. They might not know who we are, but they do know where they can find us. The last thing I want right now is a boat load of interfering Gendarmes sniffing around us.'

Michel shrugged.

'So we just stay low to the ground for a while.'

'No! You're the one who'll be staying low to the ground. I don't see why we should all have to suffer because of your stupid mistakes. They'll be looking for *you*, not us. *We* all have valid alibis, so we have nothing to fear. We'll dive without you on Saturday.'

'Suit yourself, but I still get a share in the money,' said Michel with a look of indifference.

'Yes, you'll get your money, as long as you're a member of my team, but from now on you'll do things exactly as I tell you; or you're out!'

Michel made no comment. He opened the window and flicked out his cigarette butt with all the venom that he could muster. Much as he hated it, he knew that for the moment at least he would have to follow Santorini's orders. On his own, he was just a small time gangster, running petty rackets for loose change and forever looking over his shoulder. But as a member of *Libertà Corso* he was part of a criminal elite; a member of a powerful separatist organisation that had a formidable reputation and benefited from far reaching political influence. Michel was a survivor; an opportunist, and the noble cause which he claimed to be fighting for, also conveniently served his own self interest. Santorini was his ticket to a bright and profitable future.

'OK, I'll work the bar on Saturday instead.'

'There's no need; I've got it covered. But there is something else which you can do.'

Mike finished the hot chocolate which Officer Florent had kindly bought from the hospital vending machine and followed him through the exit doors to a waiting car. He was taken to the *Caserne de Gendarmes* and promptly ushered into a spartan interview room. Officer Florent invited him to take a seat on a plastic chair, facing two others across an empty table. Shortly afterwards, a tall, silver haired man with grey-blue eyes and a neat aviator style moustache entered the room. He walked towards the table where Mike was sitting, smiled and held out his hand.

'Good evening Mr. Summers, my name is *Capitaine* Benoit Villeneuve. I am here to ask you some questions about your accident.'

Mike raised a polite smile and shook his outstretched hand.

Villeneuve pulled one of the two empty chairs away from the table and invited Officer Florent to join him.

'I hope that you understand my English. It's been quite some time since I've used it.'

'Your English is very good.'

'Thank you,' replied Villeneuve. 'Before we start, may I first offer you my sympathy for the loss of your friend; a most regrettable incident.' Mike nodded.

'I understand that you have told Officer Florent here that the accident was caused when your colleague lost control of the car after being threatened by a motorcyclist brandishing a gun.'

'That's right.'

'Can you think of any reason why someone would want to harm either of you?'

'Yes, we were threatened a few days ago and I should have taken it more seriously. This is all my fault.'

Capitaine Villeneuve eyed him inquisitively.

'So you know who the motorcyclist was?'

'No, his face was covered, but I know that he's a member of a local gang.'

Villeneuve raised an eyebrow and smoothed his moustache.

'I think it might be better if you tell me the whole story from the beginning Mr. Summers,'

Mike explained the events which had led to their fateful encounter with the crew of the *Sampiero Corso*. Villeneuve listened carefully, but remained unimpressed.

'Well I'm no expert in these matters, but a search for a missing submarine? It all sounds a bit far fetched to me.' He stared at his notes and absently tapped his upper teeth with a pen. 'Can you give me a description of the leader of this gang?'

'Yes, he was quite portly with a dark beard and thick brown hair. I think his eyes were brown too and I'd say that he was in his fifties.'

'Hmm...was there anything more distinctive which might help us to identify him?'

Mike cast his mind back to the day when he and Thomas were approached by the crew of the *Sampiero Corso* and he suddenly remembered the tattoo.

'He had a tattoo on his arm. It was that black prisoner's head symbol, the one that you see everywhere, the one that's on the beer bottle.'

'Do you mean the Corsican flag by any chance,' asked Villeneuve. 'White background, black head with a scarf tied around it.'

'Yes that's it! I wasn't aware that Corsica had its own flag.'

'It certainly does; the *tête de Maure*. The Moors or Saracens were once frequent invaders of the island and traditional enemies of the Corsican people. When they were defeated, the Moor's head became a symbol of Corsica's victory over tyranny.'

'That must be why he had *Liberté* tattooed beneath it then.'

Villeneuve looked up sharply. 'What did you just say?'

'Liberté Corse - I think that's what it said; it was written beneath the tattoo.

Villeneuve's expression darkened and something close to hatred appeared on his face.

'Florent, would you please fetch me the file of Jean-Claude Santorini.'

'I'll get it straight away sir,' said Florent, his eye's widening.

'And more coffee,' shouted Villeneuve as he was leaving the interview room. Mike was left wondering what had provoked such a reaction.

'Is there something significant about the tattoo?' Mike enquired.

Villeneuve snapped out of his dark introspection and looked searchingly into Mike's eyes, wondering whether it was advisable to add to his concerns in his present emotional state. Sucking reflectively on his moustache, he decided that it was probably better to be frank with him.

'Libertà Corso, if that is what you believe you saw, is a splinter group of the FLNC, the militant nationalist extremist group.'

Mike was stunned into silence. He had heard about the ruthless reputation of the FLNC and now realised what an incredibly dangerous situation he and Thomas had unwittingly placed themselves in. It seemed incredible that fate had somehow conspired to put them into conflict with the most violent and dangerous group of men on the island. He slumped onto the desk and put his head in his hands as the recriminations began to eat away at him.

Officer Florent returned and placed a folder in front of *Capitaine* Villeneuve, who opened it and took out the first page. He inverted it and slid it across the table towards Mike.

'Is this the man who you saw on the boat?'

Mike studied the black and white photograph which was glued to the top left hand corner of the dossier and instantly recognised the gruff features of the imposing man who had snatched the depth gauge from Thomas' hands.

He looked up at Villeneuve and nodded solemnly.

'That's him.'

Villeneuve sat back in his chair and sighed heavily.

'You seem to have made yourself some powerful enemies Mr. Summers,' said Villeneuve, folding his arms. 'Jean-Claude Santorini is the founder and head of *Libertà Corso* and an extremely dangerous individual. I've spent the last twenty years or so trying to convict him for a chain of insidious crimes and although I have come close many times, he has always managed to evade justice. The last time that we had him in the dock, we had the evidence to send him to prison for a very long time and yet none of the witnesses turned up to testify against him and consequently the judge was forced to throw the case out of court. Two days later, following several death threats, the arresting officer, one of my best men, had to be transferred to the mainland after he and his family had their house burned to the ground. I am telling you this so that you understand the complexity of the situation. If we have difficulty convicting Santorini in what appears to be a watertight case, then what chance do we have of bringing him to justice on the basis of scant and circumstantial evidence? I can tell you now that without a credible motive it would be pointless for us to even begin making enquiries.'

'So you're going to do nothing?' asked Mike, incredulous.

'With all due respect, what do you expect me to do? We have very vague descriptions of a motorcyclist and his vehicle, no witnesses to the actual accident, no ballistic evidence and only the vaguest of motives based solely on your dubious theory of a missing U-boat. Believe me, if I thought that there was even the slightest hope of implicating Santorini and his gang in this case, I would not rest until I had them all locked up in a cell.'

Mike frowned and stared at the table in frustration. It looked as if Thomas' killers were going to get away with murder - literally. Under such unusual circumstances, he couldn't blame Villeneuve for his unwillingness to act and yet it still all seemed grossly unfair. There had to be something which the Gendarmes could do.

'*Capitaine*, I can't prove that Santorini is looking for a U-boat, but there has to be some reason why he's diving in very deep water out in Roccapina Bay. Believe me, it's not for pleasure. I've dived in the same spot and there is nothing of any interest there whatsoever. There has to be at least a possibility of something illegal happening out there, whether it be drug smuggling, arms trafficking or a hiding place for stolen goods. All I ask is that you keep an eye on them and perhaps, I don't know...arrange a random inspection or something.'

Villeneuve pulled at his moustache and considered Mike's words.

'It does all sound a little unusual, I must admit. If, as you say, they are diving in deep offshore water then there most probably is some criminal interest for them and of course that might explain the threats that were issued. Just one question though.'

'Yes?'

'What made you decide to go diving in such an isolated area in the first place?'

'Well, we were out exploring potential sites and we noticed that their boat kept anchoring over the same spot. We knew that they had SCUBA equipment on board and we just assumed that they were diving a wreck.'

'I see. Well, all that I can say is that we will keep an eye on them, but I can't promise you any more than that. Meanwhile, in your own interest, could I ask you to refrain from diving in the Roccapina area for the foreseeable future? These people are to be taken very seriously indeed.'

'At the moment there is nothing further from my mind.'

'That's perhaps just as well,' said Villeneuve as he closed the dossier. 'Rest assured that if you have any other concerns or feel the need to speak to me or my colleagues at any time, we will always make ourselves available to you.' He slipped his card across the table.

'Now unless you have any further questions it is getting rather late.'

'Not at the moment,' said Mike shaking his head.

'I expect that you'll be needing some transport then. We'll give you an official report to give to your car hire company so that you can get a replacement vehicle, but I'm afraid that most of the offices in town will now be closed. Can I get one of my men to give you a lift somewhere?'

'I think I might stay in a local hotel just for tonight. Could you recommend one?'

'Well there are several, but we often use the Hotel Bellevue when we have official visitors. It's convenient for the centre and is reasonably priced.'

'That will do just fine.'

'In that case I'm sure that Officer Florent here will be happy to take you there.'

Officer Florent nodded.

'Just one thing before we leave,' said Mike, 'I'd like to get my diving equipment back from the car. How can I do that?'

'Give me a call tomorrow and I'll let you know if it's been cleared by our accident investigation department.'

'OK, I'll do that. Thank you *Capitaine*.'

'It's my pleasure Mr. Summers,' said Villeneuve, shaking his hand. 'I can only express my deep regret at what has happened and apologise for being unable to put your mind at rest.'

'I understand,' said Mike as Villeneuve accompanied him out of the interview room. Mike followed Officer Florent to a waiting patrol car feeling more alone and isolated than he'd ever felt in his life.

Monica's body had only just succumbed to the welcome embrace of sleep when she was suddenly awake again, groping blindly for her mobile phone. She answered it more from a willingness to stop its relentless piercing tone rather than any desire to find out who was on the other end of the line. Her voice was unsteady from her forced awakening.

'Hello?'

'Monica, is that you?'

'Yes, who's speaking?'

'It's Mike.'

'Oh Mike, did you get the message we left on your phone...about the barbecue?'

'No, but just forget about that now. Look, I'm sorry to call you at this late hour, but something terrible has happened and I just need to speak to someone before I go mad. I don't know who else to turn to.'

'What's wrong Mike?' asked Monica, propping herself up on her elbow.

'I was involved in a car accident, except it wasn't really an accident and Thomas is...Thomas didn't make it.'

'What do you mean?' asked Monica, now fully awake. Thomas is...?'

'Dead, yes - murdered.' Mike choked up, his words reaffirming the stark reality of what had happened.

'Oh my God Mike. Where are you now?' There was a pause as Mike pulled himself together.

'I'm in a hotel in Propriano. I daren't go back to the villa.'

'Are you hurt?'

'Not badly...just a bit bruised.'

'Listen, why don't you come here. You can't stay there all alone in a hotel room.'

'I don't want to be a burden Monica; I know how busy you are.'

'Are you crazy? You've just lost your best friend! Either you come here right now or I'm going to come over there and get you.'

'OK. But only if you're absolutely sure.'

'Of course I'm sure. I'm not going to be able to sleep now anyway, so we might as well keep each other company.'

'I'll be there in a few minutes then.'

Monica ended the call, put on a dressing gown and went to the bathroom. Mike's words were fresh in her mind as she stared at her reflection in the mirror, unable to come to terms with what had happened. She splashed cold water on her face and dragged a brush through her hair, trying to quell her growing unease. By the time that Mike knocked on the front door, she was fully dressed and there was a fresh pot of coffee standing on the kitchen table.

'Come on inside Mike.'

Monica's eyes widened with concern when she saw the scratches which covered his face. Mike entered in his ragged blood-stained clothes, looking pale and withdrawn.

'You look awful Mike. Sit down and let me get you some coffee while you tell me what happened.'

Mike began to recount the events which had taken place since they'd last seen each other. Monica listened as she poured coffee into two mugs, sending concerned glances in his direction as the details of his terrifying ordeal unfolded. Mike attempted to explain what happened after he'd regained consciousness in the car, but the trauma of it began to tell and his chest heaved as he choked back tears. Monica came over and gently took him in her arms, pulling his head towards her chest as she felt her own tears rolling down her cheeks. They stayed that way for several minutes as Monica silently stroked his neck and ran her fingers through his hair.

'Were you at the Gendarmerie in Propriano this evening?' she asked finally.

'Yes they took me there to interview me after we left the hospital. Why?'

'Hubert was there too. He must have left just before you arrived.'

'What was he doing there?' asked Mike, surprised.

'It's been a pretty awful evening all round Mike. Hubert got arrested and taken away by the Gendarmes. He told us afterwards that they were questioning him about a murder, but it seems that it was all a mistake in the end. It was the girl that he met in the bar the night we all went out together, the one who was on the boat with him the following day. It was terrifying; the Gendarmes were waiting for us when we arrived back here. They questioned us all and then searched the house thoroughly. That's why we left the message on your phone.'

'Wait a minute. Are you talking about Chantale?' Mike's heart was now pounding in his chest.

'Yes, I think that was her name.'

'Oh my God,' exclaimed Mike. He stared dumbfounded into Monica's eyes. 'Why would anyone do that?'

'I don't know, but I really don't think that I can stand any more bad news today,' said Monica, frowning. 'Look, why don't you stay here tonight. There's no reason for you to stay in a strange place all on your own after what's happened, and to be honest I could do with the company. I really don't feel safe on my own at the moment.'

'None of this should affect your safety Monica. In fact my being here probably puts you in greater danger.'

'What makes you say that?'

'Because I've a feeling that someone's been following me.'

'Well if that's the case, then it's definitely safer for you to stay here amongst friends.'

'But where would I sleep?'

'We have a folding bed. You can set it up in my room, over by the window.'

'Are you sure that will be OK?' asked Mike, surprised at how suddenly Monica had taken him into her confidence.

'Of course it's OK,' replied Monica, decisively.

Mike didn't argue. These were hardly normal circumstances and if Monica was finally prepared to put her trust in him, he would do his utmost not to disappoint her.

'We are effectively searching for something very large which is lying on a relatively flat stretch of sea floor and this piece of equipment is ideal for those conditions. Fishermen have been using them for years to locate the wrecks and rock formations where the big fish are found,' said Jeannot, showing Santorini the digital echo-sounder which he'd borrowed from a friend. 'I don't know why I didn't think of it before. We'll be able to cover much larger areas with it and we'll spend less time in the water; In fact we'll only need to dive once we've found something that looks interesting.'

'I've seen these things before,' said Santorini, but I've never had the opportunity to use them. It looks quite sophisticated.'

'They're evolving all the time and this one is pretty good; but there are limitations. We'll see a cross-section profile of whatever we come across as we move along and that will give us a good idea of the terrain which is directly beneath us. As for the U-boat, unless we are lucky enough to go right along its axis, all that we'll see is a lump rising above the seabed. When we come across something like that, we circle around the area to build up a picture of the overall size and shape and if the dimensions compare with those that we're looking for, we just drop anchor and go down to take a look.'

'I have to admit that it sounds a lot more productive than our present system,' agreed Santorini, 'but how do we work out where we've been?'

'We input waypoint settings into the GPS to form a grid and then go back and forth between the position lines using the cross-track error function to keep us on course. I've programmed in the first set of coordinates so that we can make a start straight away.'

'Well it looks like you've been doing your homework on this one Jeannot and I'm pleased to see that you're taking this seriously.'

Jeannot remained silent. He was actually more interested in speeding up events rather than demonstrating his loyalty.

'It does all sound a bit technical though,' said Santorini frowning.

'The GPS can seem a little tricky if you're not used to it, but it's very easy to learn.'

'So how long will it take you to set up the equipment?'

'If we take my boat we can use it straight away, but if you want to use the *Sampiero Corso* I'll need time to install everything.'

'I see,' said Santorini, drumming his fingers on the counter. 'Then let's take your boat. It may well prove to be to our advantage.'

The morning didn't start particularly well for Michel. He was woken by an early call from Santorini and told to go out and read the local press. After dragging himself out of bed and throwing on the nearest clothes which he could find, he made his way down to the newsagent and picked up the early edition of the local newspaper. With a cigarette smouldering on his lips, he flipped over a couple of pages until he found the report of the car crash. The outcome was not favourable, as Santorini had wanted to impress upon him. The *Pinzuti* had been killed, the Englishman having somehow survived unscathed to relate his story to the Gendarmes. It was now likely that they would link the accident to the activities of the *Sampiero Corso* as Santorini had feared. Michel was about to shrug it off as a minor inconvenience, when an article on the opposite page caught his eye. His pulse quickened as he read the title:

Girl, 22 found murdered in her apartment on the Rue du Château.

Scanning quickly through the first half of the article he was relieved to find that there was no mention of a Gendarme being seen entering the building prior to the murder. He began to breathe more easily and a smile crept across his face when he read that several suspects had already been interviewed. If the Gendarmes had been doing their job properly, he thought, the tall blonde archaeologist would surely have been one of them.

He read on and was not unduly surprised to learn that the cause of death had been recorded as drowning. It was too much to expect anyone to be fooled by the staged suicide, but it had served to confuse and that was the best that he could have hoped for. No doubt the Gendarmes would now be turning round in circles trying to find some poor amateur to pin the blame on. He smiled to himself, but his mood quickly soured when he learned that samples of DNA, clothing fibres and shoe prints had been taken from the scene of the crime. The clothes he could get rid of if necessary, but there was not much that he could do about the rest. He'd not been expecting to kill the girl and as a result had taken few precautions. He touched his cheek and felt the traces of the girl's fingernails; now just furrows of hardened skin. It would have been better if he'd burned the place to the ground, he now realised. He'd considered it at the time, in fact, but disguised as a Gendarme, he ran the risk of drawing attention to himself when fire alarms and smoke brought people out of their homes. Still, he was confident that there was no record of his DNA on police files and as long as there was no link between him and the murder, he was off the hook. He grunted, folded up the newspaper and threw it contemptibly into a nearby litter bin. It was time to occupy his mind with more immediate concerns. The Fireblade needed recuperating from Bonifacio and there were one or two amusing little jobs to do which should keep him occupied for the rest of the morning.

There had been little rest for either of them during the night. Mike found himself drifting in and out of sleep; the slightest sounds causing him to sit bolt upright, ready to defend himself against a sudden attack. When he did sleep, his mind was tortured by images of carnage, as nightmares crept into his dreams. On at least one occasion, he found himself fighting his way through tangled bed sheets in an attempt to escape from the crushing innards of some mangled, blood stained wreckage. But there were also times when he awoke to see the concerned face of an angel watching over him, with a comforting hand ready to wipe away the perspiration from his brow.

As he lay there, watching the darkness slowly give way to dawn, he was not entirely sure whether that angel had been real or imagined. He lifted his head to see if Monica was still there, but pain seared through every nerve and muscle in his body. He lay back, wincing as each breath brought an accompanying dull ache to his ribs. There was stiffness in his joints when he tried to move them and his skin felt like it had been rubbed with sandpaper. As he was trying to loosen the tension in his aching muscles, he captured the faint scent of perfume drifting over from the double bed across the room. He closed his eyes, momentarily forgetting his discomfort and feeling a brief flicker of contentment before images of Thomas' bloodied face resurfaced in his mind. With a groan, he gingerly pushed himself to a seating position, eased himself to his feet and tiptoed into the bathroom. On his return, he saw that Monica's eyes were slightly open and staring sleepily at him. He approached and sat gently on the bed beside her.

'Did I wake you?'

'I was already awake,' she replied. 'Did you get any sleep?'

'A little, I think.' He brushed a lock of hair away from her face. 'I had some awful dreams though.' Monica took his hand and kissed it.

'I noticed. It's not really surprising after what you've been through. How are you feeling now?'

'Probably about as terrible as I look.'

'Come here,' said Monica warmly. She caught Mike's upper arm and pulled him gently towards her so that his head was resting on her chest. Mike felt his heart racing as a warm glow enveloped him, temporarily masking the aches and pains of his battered body. He lay there motionless for a while, content merely to breathe in the intoxicating perfume of her skin and feel the warmth and closeness of her body. Monica ran her fingers through his hair and in response he raised his head and drew closer. He placed his hand at the base of her neck and pulled her mouth gently towards him. Their lips had barely touched when Monica's alarm clock began to sound. Mike pressed his face into the pillow as Monica reached an arm out of bed to press the snooze button. She wriggled back under the cotton sheets and Mike pulled her towards him. Their legs entwined through the thin covers and Monica studied Mike's face in the growing light of dawn.

'I don't let many people get this close to me; you know that don't you?'

Mike nodded.

'I know and I feel very flattered. But you don't have to do this because of what has happened.'

'This is not exactly a charitable act Mike, but you're right, it has advanced things a little too quickly. We can forget that it ever happened if you'd prefer?'

'You're not getting away from me that easily,' said Mike, wrapping his arms tightly around her. 'I feel something for you that I haven't felt for anyone in a very long time and to be honest it scares the hell out of me. It's been like this ever since I first set eyes on you.' Monica stared back at him in silence. 'You do feel something too don't you?' Mike asked, almost pleadingly.

Monica didn't answer. She simply brought her lips towards his and kissed him in a way that put all his fears to rest. Mike ran his fingers through her hair and traced his hand between her delicate shoulders and along the length of her spine. The alarm clock repeated its electronic chirping and Monica gently pushed herself away from his grasp.

'Saved by the bell.' she said with a smile as she reached over to cancel it.

Mike propped himself up against the pillows and watched admiringly as Monica padded barefoot towards the bathroom. There was a lingering smile on his face as he listened to the swish of a shower curtain followed by the sound of water drumming against the old iron bath tub. The smile faded when he reminded himself that Thomas' body was now lying on a slab in a cold morgue while he was languishing in the warm comfort of Monica's bed.

Feelings of guilt began to eat into his conscience as the raw memories returned. How could he feel any happiness less than 24 hours after he had seen his closest friend being zipped up in a body bag? It seemed totally callous and disrespectful. Or perhaps inflicting a period of austerity upon oneself was merely the reaction which convention expected. Life had to go on after all, and shutting himself away was not going to bring Thomas back. Would he really be demonstrating a lack of loyalty by seeking happiness so soon after Thomas' death, or was it simply a means to blot out the enormity of his grief? Thomas, who was so full of life, would not have wanted Mike to remain miserable. On the contrary, he would have encouraged him to continue to celebrate life, to follow his dreams and most of all, to listen to his heart. Convention might well dictate a period of mourning, but Thomas would remain in Mike's thoughts until he had taken his last breath. And there could be no greater demonstration of loyalty than that.

As Mike was thrashing out an uneasy truce with his conscience, he heard the shower slow to a trickle and then Monica's soft footfall on the bathroom tiles. He watched her shadow temporarily eclipse the light beneath the door and wondered what the future might hold for them both. The only thing which he knew for certain was that for the present at least, she was the only ray of light which pierced the dark depths of his grief.

Monica returned to the bedroom with a white bath towel wrapped around her chest. She saw the fixed stare on Mike's face.

'Are you OK Mike?'

'Oh yeah...I'm fine,' he replied. 'Just thinking about things, you know.'

Monica came to sit beside him and Mike gazed up at her, astonished at how glowingly natural her beauty was. She took his hands in hers.

'Are you going to be alright today? You know that you can come with us if you wish.'

'Thanks, but I'll be fine. There are a couple of things that I need to take care of.'

'Well if you're sure.' Monica dropped her gaze. When she lifted her head again there was an anxious look in her eyes.

'You will be careful won't you? I'm not sure that I could take any more bad news right now.' She gripped his hands tightly and locked her fingers into his. Mike nodded, his eyes communicating his sincerity. He kissed the back of her hand and pulled her towards him.

'Don't worry,' he whispered into her ear. 'It would take a whole tribe of the fiercest Shardanes to keep me away from you.' Monica broke into a smile and rested against his chest. Mike winced at the sudden pain in his ribs and Monica quickly withdrew, apologising profusely. She used her arms to support her weight, planted a neat kiss on his lips and then sat back, staring at the alarm clock.

'I really need to go I'm afraid. Will you be around later?'

'Yes...if that's OK of course. I'm not sure that I want to stay at the villa for a while.'

'Well, you're welcome to stay here for as long as you need to. My colleagues will understand when I explain what's happened.'

'Thanks, I really appreciate that. So I guess that means I'll be sharing a room with Hubert then?' he asked tentatively.

'Only if you upset me,' replied Monica, as she stood up to slide a pair of bikini bottoms over her slender legs. 'So you'd better be nice.'

'I wouldn't dream of upsetting you; I've seen what you're like when you get angry.'

'Good, well just you bear that in mind,'

Monica turned away from him and let her towel drop to the floor. Mike silently admired her finely sculpted waist, toned shoulders and smooth honey-coloured skin. He let his eye run down the undulations of her spine to the fine downy hair of her lower back, deliciously exposed by the early morning light, like the soft skin of a peach. As Monica reached around to fasten her bikini top Mike caught a glimpse of her pretty upturned breasts and let out an appreciative sigh. Monica turned her head and smiled self-consciously.

'You're not supposed to be looking,' she teased as she slipped on a pair of denim shorts and pulled a white polo-necked shirt over her head. Mike shrugged as he watched her brush her hair and pull it neatly back in place with a band.

'At least I'm showing an interest.'

Monica stifled a smile as she grabbed her watch and phone from the bedside table and leaned over to plant a neat kiss on his cheek.

'Just you be careful,' she said as she prepared to leave.

'I will,' he nodded. 'I'll try to come out and see you later.'

'Sure, just give us a call and we'll let you know when we're likely to be out of the water.'

'No problem.'

'See you later then.' Monica gave him a final peck before turning to leave the room. Mike leaned back against the pillows and listened to the sound of the other team members milling about in the hallway. He kept his presence discreet to avoid any unnecessary embarrassment for Monica, stirring only when he heard the sound of the truck leaving the driveway. Determined to keep his mind active, he left the comfort of Monica's bed behind, took a quick shower and through necessity, pulled on the shorts which he'd been wearing the previous day. He was reluctant to wear the ripped and blood-stained tee-shirt though and borrowed one from Monica's wardrobe, certain that she wouldn't object.

There was a long list of things which he needed to do, but first and foremost he needed transport. He found the address of the car hire company in the telephone book and arranged to pick up a replacement car within the hour. To avoid any possibility of being followed, he kept his wits about him and walked to the agency using the back streets. Once he had submitted the police report and signed the necessary paperwork, he was issued the keys to a blue Volkswagen Passat. Next, he called the Gendarmerie to ask *Capitaine* Villeneuve if he could pick up his diving equipment. He was told that everything found inside the car had been cleared and was given permission to recuperate it. On arrival at the Gendarmerie, he went to the transport yard and after inspecting the equipment was disappointed to discover that both his and Thomas' twin sets showed signs of damage. The technician on duty asked Mike if he would take charge of Thomas' equipment and he readily agreed, hoping that he could put together at least one fully functional set from the two. His next stop was the dive centre in Bonifacio.

He stripped the four air cylinders from the units and returned them to the store, explaining what had happened and suggesting that they be tested. The technician agreed to give him two replacement cylinders and fill both of the nitrox slings so that they would be ready for use. An hour later he picked them up and made his way out of Bonifacio and back onto the main road, heading west. The next task on his list was to recuperate his belongings from the villa. He was not looking forward to it in the least. In truth he had no idea whether Santorini and his gang knew of the existence of the villa, but if he was going to stay one step ahead of them, he would have to assume that they knew almost everything.

He arrived at the point where the access track to the villa split off from the main road and continued past it until he reached a rest spot further ahead. After parking the car, he walked back towards the junction and strayed onto a partially overgrown footpath which he'd discovered a few days previously. It led him through sparse woodland and dense undergrowth until it skirted the perimeter of the villa grounds. Emerging from behind a large rosemary bush, Mike approached the villa from the far end of the terrace and advanced towards his bedroom window. He glanced inside and stopped dead when he saw open drawers with their contents strewn across the floor.

With his heart thumping in his chest, he carefully backtracked and made a complete circuit of the villa, discreetly checking each window as he passed. Every room had been turned over. He made a precautionary tour of the grounds, where he stumbled across a disturbed patch of soil and found several recently extinguished cigarette butts – a sure sign that someone had been watching them. Unsure if the intruder was still inside the villa, he cautiously approached the main entrance and saw splintered wood where the lock had been forced. With no means to protect himself, he grabbed a barbecue fork from the store to use as a makeshift weapon and gently pushed open the door. It swung freely on its hinges to reveal the chaos which lay within.

Mike's heart was in his mouth as he moved slowly from room to room; the eerie silence only adding to the tension. Thomas' bedroom was the last which he chose to visit and he loosened his grip on the fork when he found it unoccupied. Breathing a sigh of relief, he walked out into the kitchen and began to take stock of the damage. After a half hour spent clearing up the worst of the mess it didn't look quite so bad. The villa was intact, as were most of the furnishings and as far as he could tell, nothing had been stolen. If, as he suspected, Santorini's gang had been trying to find information relating to the wreck, then they would have been greatly disappointed. In fact the only clear indication that he had been searching for it at all, were the plotted marks on the maritime chart which he had just recuperated from the Gendarmerie. The break-in served as a stark reminder of what the gang were capable of though, and confirmed Mike's fears that it was no longer safe to stay there.

He returned to Thomas' room and smiled sadly to himself, unsure whether it looked any more untidy than when he'd seen it the last time. After cleaning up the worst of the mess, he packed Thomas' affairs and locked them in the store.

Increasingly conscious that one of Santorini's men might return at any moment, he quickly gathered his own belongings together and stuffed them into a backpack. Before he left, he took a last melancholy look around the place which had seemed to hold so much promise for them both and with a heavy heart, stepped outside and closed the shattered door on a future that was evidently not meant to be. He locked his thumbs into the straps of his backpack, trudged back up the footpath to the main road and made his way back to the car.

After taking a good look around, he threw his pack onto the rear seat, climbed in behind the wheel and pulled away. He drove the short distance to the track which led to Roccapina and began to make his way down to the bay. Halfway there, he was just emerging from a blind corner, bordered by thick gorse, when he saw a biker with a denim jacket and a black visored helmet racing towards him. As the gap continued to close, Mike froze with terror, knowing with terrifying certainty that he was going head on with Thomas' killer.

Capitaine Villeneuve stared dejectedly at the pile of letters in his in-tray. With a sigh he began to sift through them with the firm intention of working his way systematically through the backlog, but try as he might, he couldn't stop his thoughts from straying towards other matters; the murdered girl, the fatality on the N196 and most of all Santorini. The wretched man had been a constant thorn in his side ever since he'd arrived in Propriano and now it looked as if he was going to darken his last weeks in office as well. If there was one nagging regret during his long career, it was that he'd been unable to bring the most dangerous criminal in Propriano to justice. Quite what Santorini was up to in Roccapina, he had no idea, but he doubted that it would be anything serious enough to get him locked away. It would take nothing short of a miracle for that to happen while he was still *Capitaine de Gendarmerie.*

Villeneuve's introspective broodings were interrupted by a knock on the door. Lieutenant Lechaux entered carrying fresh coffee and a plate of croissants.

'Ah Guy, you must have read my mind.'

'I thought that you might be in need of sustenance sir; especially after our late evening.'

'Yesterday was quite a day wasn't it?' he agreed, nodding. 'There are times when I feel that my retirement can't come quickly enough.'

'You'll miss it all when you're gone though, won't you sir?'

'I dare say that I will Guy. In fact you might see even more of me if my wife has anything to do with it. She's already starting to complain about me getting under her feet. Maybe I need to find myself a hobby - perhaps I'll take up fishing again.'

'As I see it, you've never stopped fishing sir.'

Villeneuve laughed.

'Well Guy, the really big one has always eluded me, much to my regret. Somehow he's always managed to wriggle off the hook.'

'I presume that you're talking about Santorini sir?' Villeneuve nodded wistfully. 'That's by no means any reflection on you sir. I mean, what chance do we have when witnesses refuse to testify and judges are too afraid to pass sentence?'

'Yes, the cards *do* always seem to be dealt in his favour don't they?'

'It's not just Santorini; it's all the separatist leaders. Every Gendarmerie in Corsica has met with the same frustration at some time or another. We both know that the FLNC have sympathetic ears in high places, and when political pressure fails to protect them, the threat of violence can be equally as effective.'

'Unfortunately I have to agree with you. I was educated to believe that our judicial process is impartial, but my experience has demonstrated otherwise. The rich and powerful always seem to get the better of the system. It's enough to make the Statue of Liberty blush.'

Lieutenant Lechaux smiled.

'It's undoubtedly true that Santorini has connections, but even without them, his alleged involvement in the accident yesterday wouldn't impress the most scrupulous of judges. The evidence is circumstantial at most.'

'I'm quite aware of that Guy, but one day he'll slip up and that's when we need to be ready. I probably won't be around when he does, but there's no reason why you shouldn't have better luck than I did.'

'We can only try our best sir.'

Their conversation was cut short when the telephone on Villeneuve's desk began to ring. He picked up the receiver and frowned in concentration as he listened to a rapidly spoken message from the control desk.

'Yes. When was that? Good! Send everyone who is available.'
Villeneuve replaced the receiver and glanced up at Lieutenant Lechaux.
'Maybe our luck is about to change after all.'

Michel's morning had all been going to plan until some idiot in a blue
car had nearly forced him off the road. Whoever it was, had been very
lucky that he didn't want to draw any attention towards himself, otherwise
he'd have caught up with him and given him a close look at the blade of the
diving knife which was now stashed beneath his seat. It would have been
the second time he'd used it that morning. The razor sharp blade had
proved very effective at slicing into the rubber sponson of the orange RIB
while he'd been doing a spot of snorkelling in the bay. The resulting hiss of
escaping bubbles had been particularly satisfying to hear, especially after
the disappointment of drawing a blank at the villa. He'd been tempted to
wait around just to watch the Englishman's reaction when he found it, but
he felt that he'd spent enough time hanging around there already this
week. Besides, there was a good chance that the Englishman would not
show his face at all, especially after what happened yesterday.

After he'd recovered from his skirmish with the motorist, he
approached the main road, having decided that he would reward himself
with a complimentary three course lunch in one of the stylish harbourside
restaurants that were under the gang's protection. He turned left and was
casually making his way towards Propriano when the traffic suddenly
started to back up. At first he wasn't too concerned and simply overtook
the stationary cars in front of him, but a few hundred metres further on,
he saw traffic cones standing in the middle of the road and Gendarmes
diligently filtering the traffic. As he neared the blockade, he suddenly
noticed that they were only pulling over motorcyclists. Fearing the worst,
he thought about making a run for it, but quickly reconsidered, knowing
that all escape routes would now be covered. Under the circumstances, he
realised that it would be far better for him to remain calm. After all, they
had no proof that he'd done anything wrong and he no longer had the
Glock with him. As he approached the narrow line of traffic cones, a
Gendarme stepped out in front of him, and with his hand resting firmly on
the stock of his pistol, waved him over.

Mike never saw the motorbike swerve to avoid him. He dropped his
head and pressed his foot down hard on the accelerator. When he heard it
roar past, he looked up and saw the bike's single brake light through the
rear view mirror, glowing red in a thick cloud of dust as it skidded to a halt
behind him. When the dust cleared, Mike saw the motorcyclist spin
around in his seat and punch his index finger high into the air, beside
himself with rage. In the panic of the moment, Mike had completely

forgotten that he was no longer driving the conspicuous silver Peugeot. Eager to put as much distance as possible between himself and the motorbike, he skidded and bounced his way down the track as fast as he dared, knowing that if the biker gave chase, he might not reach the bottom alive. For once he had a desperate need to be around people and right now the hills above Roccapina seemed like the most desolate place on earth.

He reached a straight section of road and glanced anxiously at the rear view mirror. To his relief, he saw no sign of the bike in the swirling cloud of dust that was kicked up behind him. The safety of the beach was now just a few hundred metres away and Mike eased off the accelerator as he approached the busy car park. He found an empty space at the far end of it and after carefully scanning the area to make sure that he had not been followed, he cut the engine and took a moment to calm his nerves.

Feelings of nausea and claustrophobia welled up inside him, as he relived scenes from the accident. He forced himself to count to ten and only then did he allow himself to leave the car and sit down beneath the shade of a large pine tree. After taking several deep breaths, he pulled out his mobile phone and contacted the Gendarmerie to inform them that he'd spotted the killer heading towards the main road. He thought about mentioning the break in too, but there seemed little point when nothing had actually been stolen. Besides, he could hardly imagine the Gendarmes being too keen to interrogate Santorini over such a triviality.

He ended the call and dialled Monica's number as he walked towards the crowded beach. The phone was answered by Bertie who began by offering his condolences in stuttered English. Mike thanked him for the gesture and was told that Monica and the others would be out of the water in twenty minutes. The words seemed to restore his shattered morale.

He stripped off his tee-shirt and placed it in the dry-bag which he'd recuperated from the Peugeot. Leaving the noise of the beach behind, he waded out into the water and dived into its liquid embrace. He basked in the silent weightlessness of it, opening his eyes and swimming a few slow strokes close to the bottom before arcing his body upwards and breaking the surface to freshen the air in his lungs. It was a brief moment of escape from the harsh reality of the world above, but not nearly long enough.

Mike raised his head and saw the orange RIB, just a few metres ahead of him. He slowed his pace and his eyes widened with alarm when he saw that it was listing badly to one side and threatening to flip over at any moment. On closer inspection he saw that one half of the sponson chamber had completely deflated and he reached his arm beneath the rubber membrane to see if he could find the cause of the leak. A gentle squeeze told him all that he needed to know. Large bubbles welled up from beneath the flagging chamber and Mike felt the unmistakable edges of a straight slash. It was so big that he was able to push his whole hand inside it. He pushed away from the RIB and stared dejectedly at it, knowing exactly what had happened and why. Feeling that he could no longer contain the anger that had built up inside him, he put his face in the water and screamed silently into the depths, beating the surface to a froth with his fists.

Officer Bertoli and his colleague, Jean-Marc, were making their way across town when they heard the message come in over the radio:

Calling all available vehicles in the vicinity of the N196 eastbound from Propriano. Proceed to checkpoints at delta points three, seven and nine to intercept suspect on motorbike, believed to be armed. Report present positions and estimated arrival times, over.

Officer Bertoli immediately reported his call-sign and position. His transmission was acknowledged by the control desk and he was given a description of the suspect before being directed towards a checkpoint located close to Sartène.

'Put the Christmas tree lights on Jean- Marc.'

'OK, you'd better hold on to your hair piece.'

They raced towards the edge of town with their sirens blaring, narrowly missing the cars that were scrambling to get out of their way. In seven minutes flat they arrived at the site of the checkpoint to find a police motorcyclist already in place, slowing the traffic down and placing cones in the road.

'Go and help Franck while I interview those two,' said Bertoli flicking his head in the direction of two dismounted bikers who were standing at the side of the road, waiting impatiently to have their papers controlled.

'Yeah, that's it; you go and chase the glory while I play at skittles,' Jean-Marc grumbled, as he got out of the car.

'The whole is more important than the sum of its parts Jean-Marc,' replied Bertoli with a smile and an infuriating wink. He walked over towards the two motorcyclists and reached for his note book. Even from a distance, he could see that neither of the two matched the description, but his instructions were to interview and search everyone. He began to take down the details of the first of the two men and was joined a few minutes later by his colleague, Jean-Marc. Together, they'd interviewed a dozen or so persons, when a motorcyclist with a black helmet and denim jacket was pulled over and directed towards them. Bertoli watched from the corner of his eye as the motorcyclist dismounted and parked his bike to one side with the keys left in the ignition. He seemed reluctant to remove his helmet and Bertoli prolonged his current interview so that Jean-Marc would deal with the next person in line. Now it was the turn of the man wearing the black helmet and Bertoli beckoned him over, keeping one hand close to the stock of his pistol. The man walked over with a confident swagger, looking menacing in his dark jacket and opaque black visor.

'Take your helmet off please,' ordered Bertoli. The man obliged.

'Your papers.'

Michel handed over a fake driving licence and turned his head to one side in a gesture of disinterest. Bertoli raised an eyebrow as he wrote the name down on his ledger.

'What is your date of birth Mr. Bernard?'

Michel gave it correctly. It was his own, apart from the month, which had been changed.

'And your address?'

Michel reeled off the address which he had memorised.

'Where are you coming from this morning?' enquired Bertoli.

'Bonifacio,' was his monosyllabic reply. Bertoli nodded.

'And what were you doing in Bonifacio Mr. Bertrand?'

'Bernard,' Michel corrected. 'Just riding around.'

'Just riding around were you?' repeated Bertoli, sucking his teeth.

'Right. Direct me to your vehicle please.' Michel jerked his head towards the Fireblade.

'I'd like you to open the seat compartment,' requested Bertoli, escorting him towards the bike, with his hand still poised over the pistol. Michel obliged.

Bertoli stared with interest at the mask, snorkel and knife that were stashed beneath the seat.

'What were you doing with these in Bonifacio?'

'They've been there since yesterday.'

'Funny that; they're still wet. What did you need the knife for?'

Michel thought for a second.

'I was collecting sea urchins.' Bertoli raised his eyebrows.

'It's a little late in the season isn't it?'

Michel shrugged.

'Where were you on Tuesday evening between seven and nine o'clock?' Bertoli asked probingly.

'I was at home.'

'Do you have witnesses who can confirm that?'

'Yes.'

'How very convenient,' said Bertoli. He looked him directly in the eye and handed his papers back. 'OK you can go.'

Michel's eyes flickered with surprise. It appeared that he'd escaped more easily than he'd anticipated. He turned to walk away and was barely in his stride, when he heard a restrained voice behind him.

'Watch your back Michel.'

Mike sat on an isolated rock, staring fixedly at the sagging RIB while carefully analysing the week's events. There was now no doubt in his mind that he and Thomas had been watched, but it was more difficult to understand how anyone had been aware of their movements out in the bay. Mike was certain that there were no other boats in the area when he and Thomas had been diving and the only other possibility was that they had been watched from the coast. As he was thinking the problem through, he whipped his head around and stared at the promontory in sudden realisation. The logic was irrefutable; a watchtower, by its very nature, was built in an ideal spot for surveillance. All an observer would have needed to track their movements from the plateau above, was a good pair of binoculars. Mike put his head in his hands knowing that all their attempts to conduct a discreet search operation had been totally in vain. It just hadn't entered into his mind that someone might be so determined to prevent them from diving out in the bay, that they would be prepared to mount an intensive, military-style surveillance operation against them.

As he tried to think who he'd seen loitering around the area, he remembered the early morning hiker and it suddenly dawned on him why there'd been a familiar look to him. He'd last seen him standing on the decks of the *Sampiero Corso*. He narrowed his eyes and stared fixedly at the sabotaged RIB, his anger raging inside him like a bush fire. An important question was now running through his mind. Being fully aware of who and what he was up against, did he take the safe and sensible course of action and let the whole thing drop, or did he ignore the risks and try to fight back? He was in no doubt that he could repair the damage to the RIB, but to further incur Santorini's wrath by continuing his search for the U-boat now seemed nothing short of suicidal. And yet more than anything, Mike wanted revenge. Santorini and his thugs survived by spreading fear amongst those who could not defend themselves and the only way to remove their power was to refuse to be intimidated. For the moment Mike believed that he held the advantage. Santorini's men did not know where to find him and as long as it remained that way, there was a chance that he could beat them to the wreck. It presented a huge challenge and a considerable risk, but one that Mike would gladly undertake in order to strike a blow at those who had taken the life of his friend. Rising to his feet in sudden determination, Mike took a deep breath and plunged head first into the water.

Lieutenant Lechaux placed the report of the day's activities in front of *Capitaine* Villeneuve and poured himself a glass of water. He watched *Capitaine* Villeneuve frown and pull at his moustache; a sure sign that he was not impressed.

'So we've made no further progress with the Moret case then?'

'No sir. Unfortunately we've taken it about as far as we can at present. We've contacted and questioned everyone who we believe was linked to the girl and chased up every conceivable lead, but we seem to have reached a dead end.'

'What about the sighting of the Gendarme?'

'It's still open to discussion sir, but we really need a second eye witness statement to back up the old gentleman's story, otherwise we're going to have to discount it.'

'Damn!' said Villeneuve, tapping his pen on the table. 'So what options do we have left?'

'Well, at this stage we're treating it as a random killing, possibly the work of a psychopath. Forensics are of the opinion that we may have to wait until the killer strikes again to get any closer to identifying him.'

'That is most ungratifying,' said Villeneuve, 'and I don't think it's an excuse for abandoning our enquiries prematurely. I'd like you to keep a couple of men on the case; for the moment at least.'

'Very good sir; I'll see that it's done. I presume that you also read the report about our stop and search operation today?'

'Yes I did. Our response time was excellent, but once again the results are disappointing. Were you able to trace all the names that were recorded?'

'Yes sir; all apart from one.'

'What was the exception?'

'One of the motorcyclists had a fake ID and his vehicle's registration plates were untraceable. Bertoli, who interviewed him, gave us a description, but says that he searched him and found no firearm. As a precaution we've alerted all mobile units and asked them to keep an eye out for the false plates.'

'That's something I suppose, though hardly the result we were looking for.'

'No sir.'

'Did you manage to find time to speak to the *Brigades Nautiques*?'

'Yes sir. They've agreed to send a small surveillance team out to Roccapina tomorrow morning. I gave them the directive and asked them to find out what they could.'

'Good. Well let's just hope that they have better luck than us.'

Mike surfaced beside the RIB and rocked it gently to see if he could risk climbing aboard. Despite the list on the starboard side, it was surprisingly stable. He considered himself fortunate that the saboteur had not had the foresight to pierce both chambers, otherwise the whole thing might have been sent straight to the bottom.

After he'd hauled himself up onto the intact sponson, Mike leaned over carefully and started the outboard engine. Crawling on his stomach, he slowly eased himself towards the bow and released the line from the mooring buoy. Once it was freed, he clambered aft and opened up the throttle. The rigid part of the hull began to lift up out of the water and gain stability as he accelerated away. He steered towards an empty part of the beach and following a sustained burst of power, lifted the outboard clear of the water so that the hull came to a sliding halt in the soft sand.

There was consternation amongst the nearby holidaymakers as the RIB emerged onto the beach. Mike could only smile apologetically, and point to the damage. He jumped out and found a piece of driftwood, which he used to prop the hull to one side while he inspected the damage. There was a straight 15 centimetre gash in the tubing, just below the waterline. He found the repair kit in one of the lockers and read through the instructions.

The enclosed patches were a little too small and Mike realised that he would have to overlap three of them to seal the puncture completely. With no alternative, he set about cleaning and preparing the surfaces as best he could. Ten minutes later he applied the last of the patches and sat back, waiting for the adhesive to dry. He glanced at his watch and realised that he had no time left to meet up with Monica. With a sigh, he pulled his phone from the dry-bag and punched in her number. It was Monica who answered.

'Hi Mike, where are you? Bertie said that you were coming over to see us.'

'Yes that was the plan, but I had a problem with the boat; I'm just fixing it now.'

'Nothing serious I hope.'

'No, just a puncture, I'll have it sorted in no time. How's your day been?'

'Good thanks, we've found some more pottery and a tin figurine too; a religious icon we think.'

'That sounds like a pretty good haul,' agreed Mike. 'Listen Monica, I should be passing by in a half hour or so, but I guess you'll already be in the water.'

'Yes we're just about to get ready.'

'Who's next on surface watch?'

'It's Hubert's turn.'

'Good. Tell him I'll drop by when I've finished what I need to do.'

'OK I'll let him know. I'll see you later then shall I?'

'Yes. Actually I was thinking maybe we could go out for a drink together; I'd like to speak to you about something.'

'Oh, you're not getting all serious on me already are you?'

'Ah no,' laughed Mike. 'Not unless I find out that you own an island in the Bahamas.'

'Unfortunately not,' laughed Monica. 'Well if I can get my work finished up early, we have a date.'

'Excellent! See you later then.' Mike returned his phone to the dry-bag and stared down at his handiwork. The adhesive now appeared to have dried and Mike picked at the edges of the patches to make sure that they were holding. After a further fifteen minutes, he pulled out the foot pump and began to fill the empty chamber with air. It was hard work in the glaring heat of the sun, but the repaired sponson was soon firm to the touch. Mike scooped some water into his mask and slowly poured it over the patches to check for small leaks. When he was certain that the repair was holding, he patted the RIB's sponson with an affectionate smile. She was back in service again.

After soliciting the help of a couple of bystanders, Mike slid the RIB back into the water and pulled her clear of the beach. He thanked his helpers with a cheery wave and then quickly jumped aboard. Within seconds he had the engine roaring and was heading smartly up the channel and out of the bay. He paused next to the yellow and black RIB to tell Hubert that he would be returning shortly and then continued around the headland into the quiet bay which lay behind it. Once he had found a spot that was sheltered and out of view of the promontory, he circled around until he found a patch of rocks. He cut the engine, pulled on a mask and jumped over the side holding a length of rope. After securing it around a big smooth slab of rock, he returned to the surface to take in the slack and tie a loop to create a temporary mooring. Once the RIB was secured to it, Mike grabbed his dry-bag and swam towards the shore. After a short hike over the headland, he was back in the water and swimming towards the yellow and black RIB.

'Hey Mike, where did you come from?'

'I tied up in the bay around the headland and then walked here.'

'Why didn't you just come alongside?'

'Because I'm being watched Hubert. They sabotaged the RIB.'

Hubert's look of concern was replaced by a deep frown.

'Monica told me about the crash,' he said. 'I can't believe those bastards killed Thomas.'

'No, neither can I,' said Mike, clenching his jaw and staring bitterly in the direction of the bay. 'And I'm not going to let them get away with it either.' Hubert stared at him wide eyed.

'You can't mess with those fanatics Mike. They'll kill you as well.'

'Not if they can't find me. Don't worry; I'm not going to do anything stupid. I just want to find out why they're so desperate to find this U-boat and then I'm going to scupper their plans.'

'You mean you still want to continue searching for it, despite what has happened?'

'Right now, more than ever. But this time I'm going to make damned sure they don't see me.' He lifted his eyes and stared fixedly at Hubert. 'And I'm going to need your help. I understand if you don't want to get involved and I won't hold it against you if you refuse,' continued Mike, 'but at this present time, I have no one else to turn to. All I need you to do is skipper the boat - nothing more.'

Hubert thought carefully before answering.

'No!' he replied firmly. Mike's face slipped and he nodded resignedly.

'That's OK Hubert, I really don't blame you.'

'No, you don't understand...I'll do it, but when you find the wreck, I won't be content to just stay on the boat.'

Mike broke into a wide smile and thrust his hand out. Hubert clasped it tightly.

'Does that mean we have a deal?'

'We have a deal.'

Michel watched smoke drift away from the tip of his cigarette, still troubled by the voice of the Gendarme calling his name. He wasn't entirely sure whether he'd imagined it, or it was just a sneaky police trick designed to try and catch him out. Probably the latter, he thought. Fortunately he'd had the presence of mind to avoid a reaction and calmly walk away.

'Is something wrong?' asked Santorini, as he served him a whisky.

'No everything's fine,' replied Michel.

'I'd hate to see you when it's not then,' chided Santorini. 'How did you get on at the villa today?'

Michel took a sip of whisky before he answered.

'I didn't find a great deal. Nothing which showed that they'd found anything anyway.'

'No maps or notes?'

'No, I checked everywhere.'

'What about the boat. Did you look there?'

'Yeah, there was nothing there either. I put it out of action.'

Santorini drummed his fingers on the serving counter.

'Well there's nothing for it then; we'll just have to keep watching him. Have you seen any sign of him at all today?'

'No. From what I could tell, he didn't stay at the villa last night. Maybe he stayed overnight at the hospital.'

'I doubt that; they said in the newspaper that he'd escaped with minor injuries. Is there anywhere else where he might have stayed? What about the archaeologists place?'

'Yeah, that's possible.'

'Well we need to know for certain,' said Santorini. 'You'll have to try and find out tonight.'

'It's Friday night for God's sake,' exclaimed Michel.

'Yes, the perfect time to catch people moving around,' pointed out Santorini. 'Pierre will be out there too, keeping an eye on the villa. Anyway you don't have much to do tomorrow, so don't complain.' Santorini took Michel's empty glass away and wiped the mark from the counter. Michel took the hint and moodily stubbed out his cigarette before taking his leave.

The sound of tyres crunching over the driveway alerted Mike to the arrival of the truck. From the kitchen window he watched Monica pass equipment down to the others for transfer to the house. Not wishing to expose his presence to prying eyes, Mike remained indoors and helped place the equipment in the store room. Hubert clapped him on the shoulder as he passed by, while Bertie and Anna smiled shyly, unsure how to react to his loss. Once the truck was empty, Monica came to find him and when she was sure that they were alone, she wrapped her arms tightly around his waist.

'I'll be with you soon. I'm just going to have a shower to wash off the salt and then I've got a couple of quick reports to write up.'

'That's fine, there's no hurry.'

'Why don't you go and have a drink with Hubert while you're waiting.'

'Yeah, that's not a bad idea. I want to have a chat with him anyway.'

'I'll see you in a short while then.' Monica kissed him on the cheek and disappeared down the hallway. Mike watched her go and found himself staring into the space which she had just vacated. He was falling madly in love with her, he realised, and for once he felt totally at ease with it. He sighed inwardly and made his way to the kitchen where he found Hubert rummaging around inside the fridge.

'Hey Mike. It looks like you have a full head and an empty hand. Maybe I can help you balance things out a bit.' He pulled two beers out of the fridge and popped off their caps. '*Proscht!*' he toasted, handing a bottle to Mike and clinking his own against it.

'Our house is yours for as long as you need it.'

'That's very kind of you Hubert, but I don't want to get in anyone's way.'

'We're pleased to have you here. Monica is just not the same person as she was. She's smiling, she's happy, she's not so demanding; it's quite unnerving really. What did you do to her?'

'I didn't do anything. I just stayed in her room, that's all.'

'Millions would believe you Mike. Anyway whatever it is, keep it up; it's doing us all the world of good.'

Mike shook his head and smiled as he took a swig from his bottle.

'Did Monica tell you what happened to Chantale?' asked Hubert.

'Yes...she did. Sorry, I should already have offered you my sympathy.'

'Nonsense Mike. You have enough on your shoulders as it is; anyway it's not as if we were close or anything.'

'They took you to the *Caserne de Gendarmes* as well, I heard.'

'Yeah, what a strange coincidence eh? We can't have missed each other by much more than an hour.' Hubert stared contemplatively at his bottle. 'Can you believe that they thought I murdered her?'

'It's unbelievable isn't it? You must have been pretty damned scared.'

'Well I had a valid alibi, but you just never know what you're going to get caught up in.'

'Yeah, tell me about it,' said Mike, gloomily. 'So did they find out who did it?'

'I don't think so; it was probably some random psycho. I just hope that if they do catch him, they cut his balls off.'

Mike nodded his agreement. He also had a thirst for justice.

'Hubert, I need to ask you a favour.'

'Sure, go ahead.'

'I need you to get Bertie to show you how to use the multibeam scanner.'

'The multibeam scanner? Well I can do that, sure, but wh...ah, I can see where this is leading.'

'I'm going to have a word with Monica about it tonight. If she gives me the go ahead I want to start mapping as soon as we possibly can; maybe even by tomorrow evening.'

'That's pretty soon,' said Hubert raising his eyebrows, 'but if Monica agrees, that's fine by me. I already know the basics of the procedure already. I'll just need Bertie to run through the finer details with me.'

'If you could, that would be great. And I'd also like to arrange some advanced dive training for you. We need to run through some exercises, to familiarise you with the equipment we'll be using and give you an insight into the problems that we might encounter.'

'I'd love to, but when will we find the time to do that?'

'I'm still working on it. I think I can arrange something, but I still need to discuss it with Monica. If she agrees, we should be able to make a start tomorrow.'

'Sounds like it's going to be a busy day.'

'Busy and productive, I hope.'

'Well I for one am looking forward to it,' said Hubert, holding his bottle out towards Mike. 'To our success and to absent friends.'

Mike soberly tapped Hubert's bottle with his own.

'Thanks for your support Hubert; I really appreciate it.'

'There's no need to thank me Mike; it's what friends are for.'

'What are you two busy scheming about now?' asked Monica, her eyes narrowing as she stepped into the kitchen. She was wearing a smart pair of jeans and a cheesecloth top, showing damp patches on the shoulders where her wet hair touched it.

'Just boy's talk,' said Hubert dismissively.

Mike was unable to take his eyes from Monica's slender figure as she reached up to flick wayward coils of hair from behind her ears.

'Nothing that we girls would find interesting then?'

'Nothing about handbags and shoes I'm afraid,' teased Hubert.

'And probably not much more imaginative either,' said Monica. Hubert sighed.

'Are you sure that you know what you're getting yourself into Mike?'

'Who says he's getting into anything?' asked Monica, ruffled.

'Good luck,' said Hubert, rolling his eyes

'Are you ready to go Mike?' asked Monica.

'Yes, I'm ready.' He drained his bottle and left it on the table. 'Thanks for the beer Hubert.'

'Any time. Have fun.'

Mike and Monica left the house as night was falling and made their way up the *impasse* towards the main road. They walked to the centre of town and were soon sitting at a candle lit table on the terrace of a chic café, drinking crisp Sancerre from misted glasses and watching the world go by.

'Well this is quite romantic isn't it,' said Monica, as she popped a plump olive into her mouth.

'Isn't it just,' agreed Mike, taking a sip of the chilled wine and letting it swish around his palate. 'The wine's excellent too.'

'Well I don't suppose that you're going to whisper sweet nothings to me all evening so why don't you tell me what's on your mind?'

Mike chewed the flesh from an olive stone as he gathered his thoughts and then discarded it on a small white saucer.

'I still want to find the U-boat.'

The smile dropped from Monica's face. She sighed and shook her head.

'Isn't it bad enough that one person has been killed?'

Mike grimaced, the words tearing at a raw wound.

'I'm sorry, but I can't put Thomas' death behind me until I understand why he was killed. I sincerely believe that we were very close to discovering something extraordinary and until I know what it was, I won't be able to put my mind at rest. I know that it will involve an element of risk, but that's something I'm prepared to accept.'

'Well maybe it's easier for you than for me,' protested Monica, tears welling up at the corner of her eyes.

'I'm sorry Monica. The last thing that I want to do is to upset you, but this is what I feel it is right to do. There are risks, of course, but they will be greatly reduced if you agree to help me.'

'You want me to help you?' asked Monica, incredulous. 'What do you expect me to do? Go diving with you, so that we can both get killed?'

'No, in fact I won't even be diving myself. Not until I've found the wreck anyway.'

Monica shot him a questioning look.

'I think you'd better explain just what it is you have in mind.'

Mike took a sip of wine and stared at the candle flame, flickering inside a glass jar.

'I don't need your help directly; it's your permission I'm after. I'd like to use your boat and equipment to map the sea floor.'

Monica paused to consider the idea and then made a firm decision.

'No Mike, I can't allow that. It would be in conflict with my professional responsibilities. The RIB isn't mine to do as I please. Besides, Bertie is the only person who is fully trained to use the equipment and it's unfair to ask me to put either him or the boat at risk.'

'Well actually, Hubert knows how to use the equipment too. And he's already volunteered to help.'

'Is there anything else which you've arranged behind my back?' she asked, affronted. Mike winced.

'No, it's not like that at all Monica. Hubert is the only person I've spoken to about this. We talked about doing this some time ago, but we knew that you wouldn't agree to us using your equipment.'

'You're damned right I wouldn't.'

'Listen Monica, I don't want to interfere with your work and I don't want to put anyone in danger; which is why I plan to do the mapping at night.'

'At night? How will that work?'

'I'll meet Hubert in Tizzano at the end of the day and we'll take the RIB back to Roccapina at nightfall. No one will be any the wiser.'

Monica sat with her arms crossed, unable to think of any reasonable objections.

'I suppose that if I say no you'll keep searching regardless?'

'Probably,' admitted Mike.

'You know that there's nothing down there don't you?'

'Why do you say that?'

'I checked. I didn't tell you, but I did some research when you first came up with your theory. There were no U-boats sunk anywhere near that area.' Mike considered the information carefully.

'I still have to find out for my own peace of mind. There's got to be something there.'

Monica sighed resignedly, realising that nothing she could say or do was likely to change his mind. She now had a difficult choice to make - either stand up and walk away from Mike, or stand by him.

'OK, I'll help you if you make me a solemn promise.'

'What's that?'

'I don't want this all to drag on. You do it once and you do it properly. If you don't find anything then I want you to give me your solemn word that you'll stop all this nonsense.'

Mike took a few seconds to decide.

'Fine I agree. If we don't find any trace of the wreck by tomorrow night, you have my promise that I'll abandon everything.'

Monica searched his eyes and saw no reason to doubt his sincerity.

'In that case I agree.'

Mike breathed a sigh of relief.

'Do we need to shake hands on this?'

'I think that you can do a whole lot better than that Mike,' said Monica with a sulking sideways glance.

Mike reached his arm around her shoulders and gently pulled her towards him.

'You are, without a shadow of a doubt, the most wonderful woman I have ever met.'

Monica's chin was battling unsuccessfully against a smile.

'OK there's no need to go over the top.' Mike pulled her lips towards his. They kissed; hesitantly at first and then with an unashamed display of affection.

When they had settled their bill, Monica decided that she wanted to walk back to the farmhouse rather than take a taxi, despite Mike's protestations. Rather than admit his concerns about being followed, Mike walked arm in arm with Monica while discreetly checking the reflections in shop windows. After a while he began to notice someone lurking in the shadows behind and when he drew level with the next window display, he stopped abruptly. From the corner of his eye he saw the man following stop too. Retracing his steps on the premise of having missed something, he caught a glimpse of the man's face and realised to his alarm that it was the early morning hiker, the lookout who he'd seen in Roccapina just a few days previously. His instincts told him to get out of there fast, but he had to do it in a way which would not cause concern to Monica.

'Oh shit,' he exclaimed, while patting his pockets.

'What's wrong?'

'I think I left my keys back at the bar. You go ahead and I'll catch up with you.'

Before Monica could protest, Mike was gone. The man who had been following turned his face away as Mike hurried past.

Santorini winced at the sound of raised voices coming from a table where four men were gambling.

'Keep the noise down over there,' he bawled. The four men dropped their voices until the next round was played.

'So where did you see them?'

'They were on the Avenue as I was walking towards the archaeologists place. I followed them to a bar and tried to listen in to their conversation, but I didn't learn much because they were speaking English. I noticed that they've become very close though.'

'How close?'

'Well at first it looked like they were having some kind of argument, but after that they were all over each other.'

'Very interesting,' said Santorini, with a glint in his eye. 'That will most definitely work to our advantage if the Englishman tries anything clever. He might be foolish enough to risk his own life, but I doubt if he'll be too keen to risk hers.' Michel smiled.

'I'd be happy to deal with her for you.'

'Yes, I'm sure that we won't be short of volunteers for that,' said Santorini, grinning. 'So where did the Englishman go after that? Pierre says there's been no sign of him at the villa.'

Michel flicked cigarette ash onto the floor.

'I don't know; I lost him.'

'What do you mean you lost him?'

'It all happened very quickly. One moment I was following him and the girl back to the farmhouse and the next, he suddenly left her for no reason and doubled back. I managed to keep up with him for a while, but he was moving fast. He went into a multi-storey car park and then took one of the elevators. I lost him somewhere on the fourth floor.'

'Did you check to see if he drove out?'

'I searched a couple more floors and then went to the exit, but I didn't see him leave.'

Santorini stared into space.

'It sounds like you were spotted Michel. He must have known that you were on to him.'

'That's the impression I got.'

'Well it's not surprising really when you think about it. He's going to be pretty wary after what happened to his *Pinzuti* friend; especially if he thinks that we're going to take him out.'

'Maybe we should.'

'No. We've attracted enough attention to ourselves as it is. For now he stays alive, but we need to keep a very close eye on him. By that I mean finding out where he is and what he's up to at all times. That won't be easy because he's obviously being very cautious, so we need to find a way of staying one step ahead of him, and for that the girl may prove to be very useful.'

'It sounds like you have an idea.'

'Maybe,' said Santorini scratching his beard. 'Just hang on a second.'

'Right you lot. Out now!' he suddenly shouted at the four gamblers.

The men began to protest, but Santorini was having none of it. He lifted the bar hatch and stormed towards them.

'We're closing right now, so you'd better get out of here before I kick you out.'

The men grumbled as they stuffed crumpled notes into their pockets and filed out onto the street.

'I was getting sick of them anyway,' growled Santorini as he closed the shutters and locked the door behind them. 'Right let's go into the back room.'

Michel followed him into the kitchen and watched him prise up a floor tile and turn a handle which was lying beneath it. He stood aside as Santorini pulled a huge dresser clear of the stone wall to reveal a narrow vault behind it. The interior walls of the concealed room supported sturdy metal shelves that were stacked with all manner of arms, explosives and surveillance equipment which his gang had collected over the years. He fumbled through the contents of a plastic container and pulled out a small disc.

'Give me your mobile phone.'

Michel obliged, watching with curiosity as Santorini removed the back cover and stuck the metal disc to the underside of it. On a nearby shelf was a device with a digital screen which lit up when Santorini activated it. After punching a few buttons, he gave a grunt of satisfaction and handed Michel's phone back to him.

'Right, now call my phone and leave a message on it.'

Michel dialled the number and was surprised to see the small device come to life when he spoke into his phone. He left a message as instructed and then ended the call. Santorini pressed the playback button on the receiver and the whole of the conversation was repeated. Michel was impressed.

'It's an automatic voice recorder,' explained Santorini. 'The transmitter activates when it picks up a certain intensity of sound, such as when someone speaks directly into the phone. It stops recording when the sound level drops below the threshold for a period of twenty seconds or more. All you need to do, is get hold of the girl's phone and stick the bug inside it, just like I did with yours.'

'That's all well and good, but if the Englishman phones her, we won't be able to understand what they're saying,' pointed out Michel. 'She only ever speaks English with him.'

'You and I might not be able to understand, but fortunately for us Pascal's daughter works at the tourist bureau. I'm sure that he'll be able to persuade her to translate for us in exchange for a few euros and a couple of glasses of wine.'

'You never cease to amaze me,' said Michel, smiling.

Santorini raised his eyebrows.

'As soon as you've planted it, we'll be operational, so just make sure that you get the job done properly.'

'Consider it done,' said Michel.

Santorini eyed him warily and then with a sigh, opened up the mobile phone and pressed the transmitter firmly into his palm.

'Did you find your keys?'

'Er...yeah, luckily the waiter picked them up.'

Monica sensed that Mike was keeping something from her.

'You look as if you've been running,' she remarked. Mike nodded.

'I wanted to get back to the bar quickly, before they went missing.'

Monica raised her eyebrows and decided to let it drop.

'Hey Mike, do you have your chart with you,' asked Hubert, who was sitting at the kitchen table.

'It's in my bag, why?'

'Monica would like to take a look at it, if you don't mind.'

'Yes of course, no problem.'

Mike went to fetch the chart and then spread it out in front of them.

'Right let's see,' said Monica as she flattened out the creases, 'now I'm not saying that I believe there's a U-boat wreck out there, but I can certainly help you refine your search area, based on the relative positions of the objects which you found.'

Hubert gave Mike a discreet wink.

'That would be very helpful,' said Mike.

'Good, so we'll start by identifying the nature of the target. What you are essentially searching for is the centre of a large explosion. Now if we presume that all of your objects originated from a stationary vessel, were subjected to the same force and projected at roughly the same angle, then the distance which they would have travelled from their point of origin, can be determined by their density, weight and aerodynamic properties.'

'Yes, I think I'm with you so far,' said Mike.

'I'm glad someone is,' mumbled Hubert. Monica rolled her eyes and continued.

'Now there's obviously going to be some guess-work involved, but we are not concerned with exact figures, so let's begin with the depth gauge that you found. It's composed of a dense material, but light in overall weight. It also has good aerodynamic properties, so we could expect it to travel quite far, shall we say 300 metres?'

'I'd go along with that,' agreed Mike.

'Me too,' added Hubert.

Monica did a quick conversion and then took a compass and measured off the equivalent 1.6 cables on the vertical scale of the chart.

'Right, where did you find it?'

Mike pointed to a pencil cross on the chart and watched in growing fascination as Monica placed the point of the compass on the cross and drew a circle around it.

'Right next object.'

'A fire bucket,' said Hubert.

'OK, a fire bucket. Let's see; it would also be composed of a dense material, light overall, but not very aerodynamic, which means that it would soon reach its terminal velocity and decelerate. Any suggestions for distance?'

'Don't forget that it probably had sand in it at first,' pointed out Hubert, 'but I'd still say around 120 to 150 metres.'

'Good point Hubert, and I agree with your estimation. We found it here,' said Mike, pointing to another cross on the chart. Monica measured off a distance equivalent to 140 metres and drew a circle around the mark as before.

'They overlap,' exclaimed Mike excitedly. 'That means the wreck must be over this way.'

'Patience,' advised Monica. 'We still have other objects to consider.'

Mike watched as more circles were added to the chart, representing the distance travelled by the pipework, deck plates and boot which he and Thomas had discovered. By the time that Monica had finished, a distinct pattern had emerged.

'That's incredible,' enthused Mike as he gazed at the mass of interconnecting circles. 'They're all clustered around the same spot.'

'Which is exactly what you'd expect if your theory is sound,' said Monica, now intrigued. 'Most of the debris from an explosion would be positioned close to its centre with the space between projectiles increasing proportionally as you move away from it.'

She studied the pattern of intersecting arcs for a moment and then took a pencil and shaded in a small segment. 'This point here is within the radius of each of the circles. Now, if our estimations for the distances that each object travelled are reasonable, then this is where you ought to concentrate your search.'

'That's the sector that we were going to explore next,' said Mike in frustration. 'Damn it! I knew we were getting close.'

'We still don't know for sure,' said Hubert with caution in his voice. 'This is all just theory until we see that image on the computer screen. And we'll have to wait until tomorrow evening for that.'

'I take it you've agreed all this then?' asked Mike, glancing from Hubert to Monica.

'I've given Hubert permission to use the RIB tomorrow,' Monica confirmed.

'That's fantastic!' said Mike. 'I really appreciate this. Thanks so much Monica.' She smiled and rested a hand on his shoulder.

'Well that's about all I can contribute at this stage. I'm going to retire now and leave you two to formulate your plan.' She ruffled Mike's hair affectionately. 'Don't be too long.'

'I won't.'

'See you in the morning Hubert.'

'Yeah, *Guet Nacht* Monica.' Mike watched her leave the room.

'Well it certainly looks like you've melted the ice queen's heart,' said Hubert when Monica was out of hearing range. Mike shrugged.

'I can't take in what's happening to my life at the moment. It just seems to go from one extreme to the other.'

'You've certainly been through quite a lot recently.'

'And it looks as if there's more to come,' agreed Mike. 'Do you think I'm being irresponsible by going ahead with all this?'

'Well it's not what most people would call sensible, but I can see why you feel the need to do it.'

'I'm glad to hear someone say that. I have to admit that after what's happened, it's started to become an obsession. I know that finding the wreck won't bring Thomas back, but...and this is probably going to sound stupid...I still want to find it for *him*.'

'It doesn't sound stupid to me at all Mike. It's something that was important to you both; the kind of opportunity that comes along once in a lifetime. Thomas never got the chance to live out his dream and so you want to do it for him, to honour his memory in some special and very personal way. It's not a rational decision, it's an emotional one and it's quite understandable.'

Mike nodded. 'I think mostly that I need to reassure myself that his death was not in vain. I want it to be associated with something extraordinary; something that will keep his memory alive.'

'You know what? When we find the U-boat, we should have a memorial plaque made for Thomas and have it permanently attached to the wreck.'

'That's a fantastic idea,' agreed Mike, his face lighting up. 'That would be a really fitting tribute.'

'I'm glad you like the idea. But first we have to find it.'

'Let's crack on with this plan then,' said Mike.

'OK, firstly we need to set the outer perimeter of our search area. How far around this central point should we be looking?'

'We need to allow at least 150 metres to be sure.'

'Yes, that should give us a good margin for error; it's quite a big area, but with the technology we'll be using, we can afford to be conservative.'

Hubert measured off the distance, drew a circle around the centre of the shaded area and then boxed it off with vertical and horizontal lines. 'Right this is our area, 300 metres square. We can map it in thirty metre segments, so if we start 15 metres in from the perimeter we'll be able to cover it with 10 straight runs. Now comes the hard part. We need to program all the position lines into the laptop.'

Mike watched as Hubert marked in the vertical lines and named them from P1 to P10. He read off the latitude and longitude values of the northern and southern extremities of the lines while Hubert programmed them into the laptop. As the coordinates were entered, visible waypoint marks appeared on the digital chart.

'That's fantastic,' exclaimed Mike when Hubert had finished. 'But how do we keep a steady course between the marks? Does it give you a cross-track error value?'

'I guess that you've never seen this system before then?'

'No, this is all new to me,' admitted Mike. Hubert smiled.

'When the GPS is linked to the laptop, you'll see that there is no need, because the boat will be represented on the chart by a small triangle and the course to follow will appear as a fixed line. All we'll have to do to stay on course is to keep the triangle from straying away from the line as we progress. It's child's play.'

'You mean to say that we'll be able to see exactly where we are relative to the heading at all times?'

'Absolutely! That's the beauty of this system. Once you've put in the waypoint information you get a graphic representation of where you are and where you need to go. There'll be no need to worry about drifting off course because we'll see it happening in real time. In any case, the sounding beams overlap, so weaker scans will be strengthened as we pass in the opposite direction. If we mess up altogether, we simply go back and do the run again; in fact the more runs we do, the better the end result will be.'

'That's just incredible; I really couldn't have asked for anything better,' enthused Mike. 'What level of accuracy are we talking about?'

'More than enough for what we want. If we pass close to the wreck, we'll be able to see most of the details quite clearly.'

'Do you have any examples that I could take a look at?'

'Yes of course. Let's see.' Hubert searched the computer until he found a suitable file.

'Here we are; this is the Roman wreck that we were excavating recently.'

The image appeared on the screen as a multicoloured 3D landscape.'

'That's incredible. You can see the amphorae, the timbers and the overall structure of the boat quite clearly. Can it pick out small pieces too?'

'Yes definitely. Depending on the settings, we could probably get a reasonable image of something the size of a coffee mug.'

'Wow! Will we also get that level of detail on the sub?'

'No, unfortunately the signal will be too weak at that distance, but anything the size of an oil drum should show up reasonably well.' Mike nodded.

'So if Santorini's gang are actually smuggling drugs, we should be able to detect their containers.'

'If they're big enough, yes.'

'And then we could just hand the details over to the police and let them deal with it.' Hubert nodded.

'Looks like we have a watertight plan then.'

'Even U-boats spring leaks Mike,' chuckled Hubert.

'Evidently!'

'Well, I'm almost finished here and you're welcome to stay here chatting with me for as long as you like,' said Hubert, 'but there is a rather attractive woman waiting for you next door, and I know what I'd rather be doing.'

Mike grinned.

'Well no disrespect intended, but I have to admit that I would rather be looking at her face than yours. Perhaps I should call it a day.'

'It might be in your interest. If I know Monica she'll expect her favour to be returned,' said Hubert, smirking.

'I don't think I'll complain too much about that,' said Mike as he got up from his chair. 'See you in the morning then.'

'Yeah, sleep well.'

Mike wandered towards Monica's room and found her half asleep, facing away from him.

'Should I sleep in the camp bed again?' he asked tentatively. Monica didn't reply; she simply pulled down the sheets behind her to expose the smooth naked contours of her shoulders and back. Mike stripped off and slipped in beside her. He reached his hand around her waist and ran his fingers over the finely honed contours of her stomach before reaching up to cup the uppermost of her breasts. Monica placed her hand on top of his and then turned to face him. Their lips met and Mike let his hand glide down her spine until it came to rest on the soft firmness of her buttocks. At that moment Monica froze and Mike sat bolt upright as the sound of a door crashing open was followed by loud shouting and someone running along the driveway.

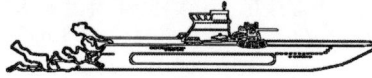

9

Officer Bertoli had a busy day ahead of him. His binoculars scanned the neat rows of shiny pleasure craft and came to rest on the *Sampiero Corso*. Santorini was standing on the pontoon beside it with three other men. Two of them were his usual sidekicks, but the third he'd never seen before. He watched diving equipment being transferred from the *Sampiero Corso* to a tattered RIB that was moored further along the quay, noting with interest that the new recruit held the keys to it. After jotting down the name and registration number of the ageing RIB into his notebook, he watched her lines being cast off, before the wizened newcomer took the helm and guided her towards the harbour exit, along with his three unsavoury passengers. Once they had disappeared from view, Bertoli went directly to the Harbourmaster's office and asked to check the berthing records. Within minutes he had all the information that he needed. *L'Espadon* belonged to a certain Jeannot Raspail, employee of the local port authority, who the Harbourmaster, a portly, dark bearded man, knew personally.

'Jeannot's a very quiet man. He works hard and keeps himself to himself. He's been known to drink a little too much at times, but he's never been any trouble to anyone.'

'I see. Do you know whether he has any financial difficulties?'

'Not as far as I know. He's a man of simple tastes and they say he has money stashed away. Is he in some kind of trouble?'

'No, not as far as I know; he just seems to be keeping the wrong company at the moment. I think I might have to have a little word with him before he gets sucked into something he'll regret; he sounds like a reasonable man.' Bertoli checked his notes 'Well, that's all the information I need for the moment; thanks for your cooperation. Obviously I'd appreciate it if you kept quiet about my visit.'

'Of course officer; anytime you need our help, we're always happy to oblige.'

'Thank you. In the meantime, what I would like you to do is to keep your eyes open for anything suspicious being unloaded at the port.'

'Could you be more specific?'

'Well, anything that looks like it has been lying at the bottom of the sea for a while; boxes, crates, barrels, that kind of thing.'

The Harbourmaster stroked the bristles of his beard and screwed his face up.

'Well I'm not sure exactly what it is you're after, and somehow I doubt that you're going to enlighten me; so I'll just keep my ear to the ground shall I?'

'That would be very useful,' agreed Bertoli smiling. 'Well I'd better be moving along. Here's my direct line if you need to contact me.'

Bertoli left the Harbourmaster's office and joined his colleague, Jean-Marc, who had been waiting patiently in the patrol car.

'You took your time.'

'I was working. Something that you know very little about.'

'That's probably because you keep sneaking off and leaving me to answer the radio.'

'It's called resource management Jean-Marc; I'm good at detective work, you're good at communications.'

'I know what you're good at and it has a lot to do with bulls and manure.' Bertoli chuckled.

'Say what you like but my methods get results, and this morning was no exception.'

'Why, what did you discover?'

Bertoli's eyes glinted with satisfaction.

'I may well have found a chink in Santorini's armour.'

Mike sat opposite Hubert and Monica at the kitchen table, pulling at the tip of a croissant.

'Did you get a good look at the guy last night Hubert?'

'Not really, it was pretty dark outside. I only saw him from behind; some small, skinny guy.'

'Was there anything else about him? His hair for example?'

'He did have an untidy mop of curls come to think of it. Why? Do you have some idea who he is?'

'No, just curious,' said Mike dismissively. 'What was he doing out there anyway?'

'I don't know; he was pretty close to the window, so I guess he was thinking of breaking in or something. It's really only by luck that I saw him in the first place. I was just going to get something from the truck and the next thing I know this guy is running down the drive like he's got a rocket up his ass. I chased after him, but he was already well ahead of me.'

'You must have given him a bit of a fright though. With any luck he'll think twice about coming back.'

'I hope you're right,' said Monica shuddering. 'I certainly don't fancy being around here on my own with some strange man prowling around outside.'

'You're right, we need to be a little more careful in future,' agreed Hubert. 'We'll have to make sure that all the doors and windows are locked at night and you girls are not left alone in the house.'

'That's a good idea,' agreed Mike, knowing that the man who Hubert saw last night was almost certainly much more than a thief.

'Well, I'm off to help Bertie and Anna finish loading the truck,' announced Hubert, pushing himself to his feet. 'Are you joining us on the boat today Mike?'

'Yes, I'll take the car and meet you at the jetty.'

'Do you want us to drop you off near the car park?'

'No, I'll walk thanks.'

'Suit yourself; I'll see you in Tizzano later then.'

'Yeah, see you there.'

'It will be nice to have you on the team again,' said Monica.

'Thanks. I suppose it will be a bit cramped, but I'll try to keep out of your way.'

'I'm not sure that I like the sound of that,' said Monica. She leaned over and stole a quick kiss from him. 'I'd better go too. I need to check over a few things before we leave.'

'No problem; I'll be in the bedroom if you need me.'

Mike went to pack some things into his dry-bag and a few minutes later, Monica put her head around the door.

'We're making tracks Mike; see you shortly. Try not to keep us waiting.'

'I won't.'

When Monica and the others had left, Mike waited five minutes and then left by the back door which led to an enclosed garden. After climbing over the perimeter wall, he cut through some private land and emerged on the opposite side of the *impasse*. Now he began to weave his way back along the sinuous escape route which he'd taken the previous evening. Once he'd reached the multi-storey car park, he took the elevator up to the 4th floor and then used the stairwell to descend to the basement. The hire car was in the dark corner where he'd left it. Within seconds he was making his way up the exit ramp and out onto the sunlit street outside.

He left Propriano, went east along the N196 and after passing through Sartène, turned right onto the D48. Speeding past the Megalithic sites of Stantari and Pagliaju, he soon reached the coast and made his way along the single track road which led to the tiny settlement of Tizzano. He went to the parking area, close to the jetty and saw Monica's team busily unloading the truck. For some reason there was an Officer of the Gendarmes standing beside them. As Mike was stepping out of the car, he noticed a red motorbike parked nearby, identical to the one which Santorini's gunman rode. He glanced around nervously and placed his hand near to the exhaust. The heat was still radiating out from it. The

proximity of the Gendarme reassured Mike enough for him to take a good
look at it. After noting down its details he turned to walk towards the jetty
and stopped dead in his tracks when his eyes met the cold stare of a killer.

The four men crowded round as Jeannot approached the starting
position and activated the first waypoint, some 200 metres away. They
watched in fascination as the RIB began to advance and a graphic representation of the sea floor began to form on the display of the fishfinder.

'I'll keep the heading, if one of you can keep an eye on the screen,' said
Jeannot. He needn't have asked, since Santorini, Pascal and Pierre were
already studying it transfixed as the sonar receptor began to record
everything solid which it encountered beneath the hull.

'Hey look, you can even see the fish,' exclaimed Pascal excitedly.

'Yes, you'd kind of expect that on a *fishfinder* don't you think?'
remarked Santorini cuttingly. Pascal's enthusiasm was nonetheless
unabated.

'Wow, we should get the lines out; there are some beauties down there.'

'We're not on a Sunday afternoon outing here,' Santorini reminded
him, 'just keep your mind on the job.'

Santorini shook his head and glanced back towards the coast where
he'd seen a small boat drop anchor earlier. It was just a few hundred
metres away and he could now see fishing rods protruding from the stern.
It seemed to him to be an unlikely spot for fishing and his gut feeling told
him that he was being watched. He could smell the police as easily as a fox
picks up the scent of a rabbit, and every nerve in his body told him that
they were nearby. Still, it was irrelevant as far as he was concerned; after
all they were doing nothing wrong. It would just make their salvage
operation more difficult once they had found the wreck. And at the
moment that was a problem which he would gladly be faced with. He
turned around sharply when he heard Pascal shout excitedly.

'Hey look there's something down there.'

On the LCD screen an isolated lump rose up off the otherwise flat sea
floor and then disappeared from view again. There was palpable
excitement as Jeannot swung the RIB around and retraced his path. The
four men crowded around the tiny screen in time to see the protrusion
appear and disappear once again. Jeannot began to circle around the spot
and soon an impression of a long thin mass lying on a north east / south
west axis began to form. He attempted to sound along the length of the
protrusion and as he did so a cross section of a long continuous mass
appeared on the screen. They was a flurry of excitement followed by a
torrent of objections from Pascal and Pierre as Santorini nominated
himself to be first to go down and see what was lying beneath them. He had
already decided some time ago that he was going be the first person to set
eyes on the wreck of the Roccapina submarine.

Michel arrived in Tizzano knowing that his plan to get hold of the Swiss woman's phone would have to be a little more sophisticated than simply stealing it from her room. After making his way to the jetty, he pulled over into the car park and behind the cover of bushes stripped off his jacket to reveal a blue cotton shirt beneath. He pulled on the peaked cap that was concealed beneath his seat locker and slipped on a pair of police issue shades. In the wing mirror of the motorbike he studied his appearance and smiled when he saw the face of a Gendarme staring back at him. After finding a spot from which to survey the approach road to the jetty, he settled down to wait.

He'd barely smoked his first cigarette, when he spied a familiar white truck making its way around the edge of the inlet. As soon as it had reversed back along the jetty and the occupants were busily transferring equipment to the RIB, he stepped out and walked confidently towards them. The pretty archaeologist was standing next to the truck and Michel let his eyes roam over her admirable curves before he spotted the mobile phone that was clipped to her belt. His fingers twitched as he rehearsed the skilful hand movements which had kept him in pocket money as a teenager. He approached the truck in an officious manner and walked around inspecting every detail of it. When he saw that he had the pretty archaeologist's full attention, he turned towards her and fixed her with an intimidating stare.

'What exactly are you doing here madam?'

'We're working,' she replied rather more bluntly than she had intended. She checked herself and softened her tone.

'We're archaeologists working on an underwater project in Roccapina. Right now we're loading our boat with the equipment we need to continue our work. Does that present a problem of any kind?'

Michel dismissed the question with a shrug.

'Do you have your permits with you?'

'Yes, but surely that's not necessary. We're working in association with the *Universita di Corsica Pasquale Paoli* in Corte. If you speak to the Head of Archaeology there I'm sure that he'll be able to tell you everything you need to know.'

'Perhaps, but it will take some time to get that information, so if you don't wish to be delayed, I suggest that you show me your permit...and your ID cards and the papers of your vehicle and vessel.'

Monica became exasperated, exactly as Michel had intended.

'This is ridiculous; it's just plain harassment.' Monica stormed off to find the paperwork and collect ID cards. When she returned and handed everything over to him, he purposely let some of the documents slip from his grasp. Monica bent down to pick them up and as she did so Michel took his cue and reached down at the same time so that he would bump into her. In the confusion, his dextrous fingers quickly released her mobile phone and pulled it from its holder. He slipped it into his pocket under the cover of the documents that were still in his hand.

'What's going on Monica?' asked Hubert, with Bertie close behind.

'We've got an over zealous official,' replied Monica in her native tongue, 'just carry on loading and let me deal with it.'

Hubert shrugged and returned to his work. Michel glanced up briefly when he heard a car arriving at the parking area. He distanced himself from Monica, pretending to make a call to check the authenticity of the licences. In reality he was completing his list of names and matching them with the photographs on the ID cards. Next, he turned his attention to Monica's phone, opening the back cover and placing the transmitter inside as Santorini had showed him. Once he had replaced it, he dialled his own number to record a missed call. With his work now almost complete, he turned to walk back towards the girl and froze when he saw someone in the distance, taking a close interest in the Fireblade. His concern turned rapidly to irritation when he saw that it was the Englishman. Fortunately he'd arrived too late to interfere with Michel's plan, but there was still one more thing which he had to do before his cover was blown. He walked briskly back towards the Swiss woman and thrust the papers into her hand. As he did so, he replaced her mobile phone in its holder.

'All is in order, you may go,' he said curtly.

He brushed past her and walked back along the jetty, leaving her standing with her mouth open in astonishment. A short distance away, Michel saw the Englishman turn towards him and stiffen, his eyes betraying his fear. Knowing that he could no longer hide behind his disguise, Michel walked directly towards him and reached for his gun.

'Forget it, it's just another ridge,' grumbled Pascal as he emerged at the side of *L'Espadon*. 'The whole sea floor is covered in them.'

Santorini cursed, staring hatefully at the sea as if he held it personally responsible for making his life difficult. The fishfinder might well work effectively over flat expanses of sand, but as Santorini had now discovered, rock ridges produced sounding images that could easily be confused with the wreck of a U-boat and they were presently in an area abundant with them. After several fruitless investigations, the optimism with which they'd started the day had rapidly drained away.

'There is at least one good thing with this method,' remarked Pascal. 'You don't use much air. It only took me four minutes to do the round trip.'

'Yeah, well just get back on the boat, because four minutes without finding anything is still four minutes wasted,' grumbled Santorini.

Pascal rolled his eyes and passed up the remainder of his equipment in silence. Jeannot stared at the decks avoiding the black looks which Santorini was aiming in his direction. He was now beginning to understand how a U-boat wreck might remain undiscovered for decades in an area such as this. It would blend in perfectly with the surroundings, lying undisturbed in a deep area which fishermen were no longer allowed to exploit. Barring a stroke of luck, he realised that they would now have to change their tactics radically, or return to a time-consuming regime of systematic searching. The problem which faced them was simple; they could not clearly see what was beneath them without sending someone down to take a look. And since divers could only cover small areas at a moderate pace and were limited by the amount of time which they could remain submerged at such depths, a manual search was by its very nature, slow and laborious. Jeannot had hoped that the fishfinder would help them to cover distances more rapidly, but it had proved to be at the expense of precision. What they really needed, he realised, was a combination of the two search methods. As the seed of an idea was forming in Jeannot's mind, Santorini's phone began to ring.

'I hope that you're calling me with good news Michel.'

'Of course.'

'So I take it everything is in order.'

'Yes, we're in business, but it was a close run thing.'

'Why's that?'

'The Englishman turned up just as I was planting the bug. Fortunately I had time to get the phone back to the girl before he could interfere.'

'Did the girl suspect anything?'

'No. No one saw me take the phone.'

'Did the Englishman recognise you?'

'Oh yes! He got the fright of his life.'

'So I suppose the rest of them know about you too now.'

'Probably.'

'Well it hardly matters now. Did you get the girl's number?'

'Yes. I'll text it to you in a moment.'

'Excellent. Where's the Englishman now?'

'He left with the others on the RIB. They're heading in your direction.'

'Good, we'll keep an eye out for him. I don't suppose there's much else you can do right now, so just keep your phone with you and don't stray too far.'

'OK, I'll speak to you later.'

Santorini ended the call and replaced the phone in his pocket. He was just about to join Jeannot at the helm when it began to ring again. He pulled it out and answered it directly.

'What is it now?'

'Santorini?'

'Who is this?'

'Be quiet and listen; I've got no time to explain. There's a warrant out for Michel's arrest and there are Gendarmes out searching for him as we speak. He's wanted in connection with the rape and murder of a young woman.'

'But that's impossible,' said Santorini frowning. 'How do you know this?'

'Don't interrupt. I'm not here to argue the point. If you don't get him to ground right now he will be caught, and this time there's a good chance that he'll go down.'

The command centre at the *Caserne de Gendarmes* was a hive of activity when *Capitaine* Villeneuve arrived. The vehicle yard was almost empty and the locker rooms were teeming with recalled officers, busily strapping on body armour while being briefed on the spot. Villeneuve proceeded to the control room and found Lieutenant Lechaux directing operations with a telephone in one hand and a VHF radio in the other. Lechaux raised his eyebrows in greeting and gestured to Villeneuve to wait for him in his office. Villeneuve acknowledged, resisting the urge to jump in and take command of the situation. It was time to stand back and allow Lechaux to find his wings.

He left the control room and walked along the corridor, pausing to return the salutes of three young officers who were running past him on the way to the stairwell. Once he arrived in Lechaux's office, he sat down and absently leafed through some reports which were lying on the desk. A moment later Lechaux entered, looking decidedly tense.

'You look stressed Guy. What's going on? It's like a war zone in here.'

'I take it you've not been informed then.'

'No, I've just this minute stepped through the door.'

'We've had something of a breakthrough on the Chantale Moret case.'

'Really? Has there been another murder?'

'No sir, we've received some new information. It seems that we've been barking up the wrong tree all along. We were closer than we thought, but unable to make the connection.'

'I think you'd better explain Guy.'

'Yes sir. There was a call for you early this morning, which I took in your absence. It was Mike Summers, the Englishman who was involved in the car crash.'

'Yes, go on,' nodded Villeneuve, impatient to learn more.

'He was calling from Tizzano where he went to join some friends of his. They're a team of archaeologists involved in excavation work in Roccapina.' Lechaux stopped and studied Villeneuve's face to see if he'd spotted the link, but all he got was a blank expression.

'Swiss archaeologists,' he added, raising his eyebrows.

Villeneuve's face lit up with sudden comprehension.

'You mean to say that he's a friend of that Swiss fellow; the one who we suspected of the Moret murder?'

'Yes exactly. But wait, it gets even better. Mr. Summers arrived in Tizzano a little later than his friends and saw a motorbike identical to the one which he saw the day he was involved in the accident.' Villeneuve sighed.

'This is not going to be another wild goose chase is it?'

'No sir, let me finish and you'll see why.'

'Go ahead.'

'Mr. Summers said that when he arrived there was a Gendarme at the scene, speaking with his Swiss friends. He was about to join them, when he realised, to his surprise, that the Gendarme was in fact a member of Santorini's gang in disguise.'

'How could he be so sure?'

'He said that he'd seen him several times before, and the description which he gave me matches a certain Michel Perotta.'

'Perotta eh?' Villeneuve's eyes narrowed as he repeated the name. 'I presume that you've already checked to see if we had one of our men posted there?'

'Yes sir. None of our officers were assigned to that area.'

'So let me see if I have this right. We have a member of Santorini's gang impersonating a Gendarme, an unconfirmed report of a Gendarme being spotted close to Chantale Moret's apartment at the time of her murder,' said Villeneuve rubbing his temples, 'and Mr. Summers is a friend of that Swiss archaeologist fellow.'

'Hubert Dorfmann, sir.'

'Yes, and Mr. Dorfmann had an intimate relationship with Chantale Moret.'

'Mr. Summers met Mademoiselle Moret too, sir. He confirmed that to me.'

'So that puts Mr. Summers into the murder frame.'

'Certainly, but don't forget that he volunteered all this information willingly. Personally I think that Perotta killed the girl.'

'But what reason would Perotta have to murder her?'

'Well it's hypothetical at the moment, but let's just say for the sake of argument that Mike Summers and Thomas Casanis began to interfere with Santorini's criminal interests.'

'OK, I'm listening.'

'So Santorini warns them to keep clear of Roccapina, but they don't take the warning seriously enough and consequently he begins to suspect that they're up to something.'

'Go on,' prompted Villeneuve.

'One of Santorini's men spots Chantale hanging around and thinks that she might be close enough to them to know what they're planning, so he sends Perotta to her apartment disguised as a Gendarme to find out.'

'I can see your logic, but would it really be worth killing someone for that information?'

'Well that really depends on what's at stake; but I don't think that Chantale actually had any information to give them. As far as I know she didn't speak English and Mr. Dorfmann was only with her for a brief period of time. My guess is that she frustrated Perotta with her lack of knowledge and he reacted violently.'

'Yes, Perotta is certainly capable of that,' agreed Villeneuve, 'but there are too many assumptions in your theory. I accept that it's a reasonable scenario, but we need some hard evidence to back it up. Have you checked Perotta's file for a DNA match?'

'Yes. Unfortunately we have no record for him sir; that's why we're trying to make an arrest.'

'So that's what all this commotion is for then?'

'Yes sir.'

'Well I hope to God that you're right Guy. How are we doing so far?'

'We've blocked all his exit routes from Tizzano and our units are closing in as we speak. Fortunately Mr. Summers got a good look at the bike, so we've issued descriptions of Perotta and his vehicle to all our men.'

'Excellent work Guy,' said Villeneuve, tapping his fingers on the desk, 'but we still need to find out what's at the root of all this killing. Is there any report from our surveillance team in Roccapina?'

'Yes sir, the *Brigades Nautiques* are certain that Santorini and his men are searching for something, but as yet they have no idea what. For some reason Santorini's gang aren't using the *Sampiero Corso* today; they're operating from a vessel which is registered to a Mr. Jeannot Raspail. According to the limited information we have on our files, Raspail has never been associated with Santorini before and has no previous record of criminal or political activity. We've given the team a description of Raspail and they believe that he's one of the men presently on board. Of course, it's quite possible that he's simply chartering his vessel to them.'

'Interesting,' said Villeneuve, nodding.

'Shall I ask the team to continue their surveillance work tomorrow?'

'Absolutely, this could now be part of a murder enquiry. Tell me. This person who owns the boat; what was his name again?'

'Jeannot Raspail, sir.'

'Do we have an address for him?'

'Yes, I believe so.'

'Good I think maybe we should pay him a little visit and try to find out what his involvement is in all this. Send someone with a bit of tact; we don't want him running into hiding or anything. He could prove useful to us.'

'Very good sir, I'll send Officer Bertoli when he reports back.'

'Excellent. Well I'd better let you get back to your work, before all hell lets loose. Unfortunately, I'll be out for most of the morning. I'm hoping to catch up with Mr. Summers at some point. Come to think of it, I'll take a swab kit along with me; after all he's now become a suspect in a murder investigation.

'This is madness Mike. You're trying to tell me that guy was not really a Gendarme and he may have been responsible for the deaths of both Thomas and Chantale? I'm sorry to tell you this, but I think you're losing the plot.'

'Please keep your voice down; I don't want the others to hear. Look, these are not just wild ideas Hubert; the Gendarmes had no idea that I even knew you until just now. As soon as they found out, they immediately asked if I knew Chantale. Before this I didn't even consider that her death could be connected to us.'

'That's ridiculous Mike; she knew nothing about our plans.'

'You and I both know that, but put yourself in Santorini's position. They probably saw her with us all day Monday, on the boat, on the beach, maybe even in the bar the previous evening. She would have looked like she was close to us; close enough to know what we were doing and she's exactly the kind of person who they would be able to put pressure on. Just think about how close the time of her murder is to that of Thomas. Is that just pure coincidence?'

Hubert massaged his temples and rubbed his face with his hands.

'No, no...it's not possible. I refuse to believe it.'

'Hubert, the Gendarmes checked their records and told me that they had no one assigned to this area. And something else - did you happen see the Gendarme leave?' Hubert frowned and shook his head.

'No, the last time I saw him he was walking away from the jetty.'

'Yes. That's when he saw me, taking a close look at his bike – an ordinary, civilian motorcycle. When I saw him coming at me, I ran off and hid behind some bushes. I thought he was going to kill me, but he obviously had other ideas. He changed back into his normal clothes, jumped on the bike and left.'

'Let's just get out of here Mike. I'm starting to feel nauseous.'

'OK but do me a favour. Let's just keep this to ourselves. I don't want to start everyone panicking. We'll just go back to the boat and tell them I'm being questioned over Chantale's murder; agreed?'

'OK Mike,' said Hubert, with a sigh of resignation. 'But I kind of wish that you'd left me in the dark as well.' Mike placed a comforting hand on his shoulder.

'Sorry to dump that on you, but I thought it was only right that you should know.'

'Are you two OK?' asked Monica, as they were walking towards her. 'You look like you've received bad news.'

'Well actually I have,' said Mike. 'The Gendarmes just found out that I know Hubert and now they're questioning me about Chantale's murder.'

'But surely you have an alibi?' asked Monica. Mike suddenly went pale.

'I did,' he said frowning, 'but I don't any more.'

'Oh...I see. Well you know that if you need any help from us; we're here for you.'

'I hope that it won't come to that, but thanks anyway,' he said glumly. 'Perhaps we should get a move on. I'm sure I've delayed you enough as it is.'

Monica nodded and gave instructions to move away. She sat close to Mike on the way to Roccapina, sensing that he was deeply troubled. When they were drawing close to the promontory, Mike glanced out to sea and went to join Hubert at the helm.

'Do you see those two boats out there,' he said pointing.

'Yeah, I see them.'

'Just keep an eye on them for me will you?' Hubert nodded.

When Mike sat down again his mobile phone began to ring. He held it up and was surprised to see *Capitaine* Villeneuve's name appear on the screen. After some deliberation, he answered it.

'Hello?'

'Is that Monsieur Summers?'

'Yes it is. How can I help you *Capitaine*?'

'Where are you right at this moment?'

'I'm on a boat; heading for Roccapina.'

'Good. Is there any chance that you could meet me at the villa where you and Mr. Casanis were staying?'

'I'll do my best. When do you want me to meet you there?'

'Would an hour from now be convenient?'

'Yes I should think so, but what's this all about?'

'I have someone with me who would very much like to meet you. It's Monsieur Casanis - Thomas' father.'

The constant ringing of the mobile phone was starting to get to Michel. He pulled it out of his jacket pocket and slowed when he saw Santorini's name on the display. He was in half a mind to turn it off, fearing that Santorini might have changed his mind about giving him the rest of the day off. In the end he relented and was met by an angry barrage of questions.

'Whoah! Slow down. What's all this about?'

'I'll give you slow down. What the hell did you do to get the Gendarmes out hunting for you?'

'What are you talking about? What makes you think they're looking for me?'

'Believe me Michel; you are in a shit load of trouble. I'll ask you this question once and once only. Answer me truthfully and I'll do what I can to help you out. Lie to me and you're on your own. Do you understand?'

'OK, what do you need to know?' asked Michel resignedly.

'Did you take someone out without telling me – a girl?'

'Yes,' he answered after a pause.

Santorini sighed, now knowing for certain that the phone call was genuine. It was not the first time that he'd been tipped off by an anonymous source and it always unnerved him when it happened. There were clearly well informed people out there protecting his interests, but useful as they might be, there was always the nagging doubt in his mind that they might one day turn against him.

'I'm not going to ask you any details; we'll sort that out later. Right now there's a whole army of Gendarmes out looking for you and they'll be closing in fast. You need to get off the road as soon as you can and take one of the overland routes. Ditch the bike if you have to and dispose of the gear. When the heat is off, get a message to me and we'll take it from there. Is that clear?'

'Yes.'

'Good, now get moving before it's too late.' The line went dead.

There was no doubt in Michel's mind that Santorini's warning was to be taken seriously. He rammed the phone into his pocket and quickly retrieved the Glock from the seat compartment, stuffing it into the waist belt of his jeans. The rear tyre of the Fireblade squealed as he let out the clutch, leaving a cloud of blue smoke behind as he accelerated away. His mind was in overdrive, visualising the road ahead as he tried to piece together an impromptu escape route. The main road to the north was definitely out of the question and Tizzano, behind him, was a dead end. His only option was to try to reach the junction of the D21, now about a kilometre away. If he could make the turning without being intercepted, he would then have a choice of overland routes which would lead him over the mountains and through barren moorland down towards the coast. Once he had made his decision, he quickly gathered momentum and was just passing the brow of a hill when a motorcyclist of the Gendarmes shot past in the opposite direction. He cursed when he heard the sound of tyres screeching to a halt behind him. With his position now compromised, he was painfully aware that he might never reach the coast alive.

Monica gave Mike a discreet peck on the cheek and held him by the pockets of his shorts.

'Are you going to be okay with this?'

'I think so. There's no doubt that it's going to be hard, but I suppose I owe it to Thomas' father to let him know what happened. It would just be a little easier if I didn't feel like everything was my fault.'

'It's natural that you have feelings of guilt, but you're not the reason why Thomas is not with us any more. He made his own choices in life and his father will undoubtedly be aware of that. All that he'll want from you is an honest account of what happened so that he can start coming to terms with his loss. Don't forget that he'll be feeling a great deal of guilt himself; it's a natural part of the grieving process.'

'Yes, I suppose you're right,' said Mike, glancing at his watch. 'Well I suppose I'd better get going; I've got to make a bit of a detour to get there. With any luck, I'll see you later this afternoon.'

'Take your time. Just give us a call when you're finished.'

'I will.' Mike gave Monica's hands a parting squeeze before slipping neatly over the side of the RIB, sending rings of cobalt blue scattering across the surface. He swam the thirty or so metres to shore and in the approaching shallows, found footing amongst the slippery sea weed, spiny urchins and razor sharp mussels that clung to a ledge beneath the surface. After climbing out onto sun-warmed rocks, he began to make his way along the fractured shoreline towards the sheltered bay at the other side of the headland. When he reached its highest point, he was greeted by the sight of the orange RIB floating high in the water on fully inflated air chambers. With a smile of satisfaction he dived into a shallow inlet and swam swiftly out towards it.

Once he had hauled himself aboard, he fired up the engine, cast off the temporary mooring and cruised along the coastline until he was positioned directly beneath the terrace of the villa. There were several other dwellings lower down the hillside which all shared the same access road and Mike was now studying the one closest to shore. The garden at the front boasted a large sloping lawn, surrounded by succulents and ended in a set of carved stone steps which plunged directly into the sea. Mike spotted an overgrown footpath that appeared to run around the perimeter of the property and join up with the access road behind it. He dropped anchor and swam towards a small beach that was lying at its foot.

On closer inspection, the path was not quite as well used as it appeared. Undeterred, Mike began to climb, his wet shoes slipping on the loose earth and his legs stinging as he advanced through bracken and thorny under-growth. Ignoring the discomfort, he pushed on and finally burst through onto the access road above, sticky and panting for breath. After a short pause he began to climb up the winding track under the heat of the blazing sun, nursing a strong desire to dive headfirst into every private swimming pool which he passed. Eventually the driveway to the villa came into view and Mike cautiously entered the grounds. After checking each window of the villa to make sure that nothing else had been disturbed, he pushed open the splintered front door and stepped inside.

Everything was as Mike had last seen it. The damage was minimal, but he suspected that Thomas' father might appreciate the villa looking a little tidier than it was at present. With 20 minutes to spare before he was due to arrive, Mike began to sweep the floors and run a cloth over the kitchen and bathroom. A quarter of an hour later, he was just emptying out the fridge when he heard the sound of car tyres crunching to a halt on the driveway outside. He downed a glass of water and took a deep breath to calm his nerves before walking out onto the terrace to meet his visitors. *Capitaine* Villeneuve was first out of the car and greeted Mike with a brief smile and a firm handshake. A second or two later, Thomas' father emerged from the passenger door and cast his eye over the villa before turning towards Mike and extending his hand in greeting.

'*Bonjour* Mike, I'm sorry that we have to meet under such sad circum-stances.'

'As am I, Mr. Casanis. Please accept my sincerest condolences.'

'Thank you.'

Mike saw the sadness in his eyes and lowered his head, painfully aware that his own grief was incomparable to it.

'Perhaps I can get you both something to drink? There isn't very much I'm afraid - just a little juice and water.'

'Water would be very welcome,' said Mr. Casanis. *Capitaine* Villeneuve declined the offer.

'Please take a seat,' offered Mike, gesturing towards the terrace.

'I'd like to have a quick look around the villa first, if that's OK with you,' said Mr. Casanis.

'Of course; you hardly need my permission.'

'I do while it's your home.'

Mike appreciated the gesture even though the villa had felt nothing like a home to him over the past few days. *Capitaine* Villeneuve followed Thomas' father into the kitchen, casting a suspiscious eye over the broken door frame as he passed through it.

'What happened here Mr. Summers?'

'I lost my keys,' Mike replied. He could tell from the look on Villeneuve's face that he was not convinced.

'The place looks unoccupied,' commented Mr. Casanis, while peering inside the bedrooms, 'aren't you staying here at the moment Mike?'

'No, I'm staying with friends. I don't really feel comfortable here after what happened.' Thomas' father nodded his head in understanding.

'I don't see any of Thomas' affairs either. Did you put them somewhere?'

'Yes, sorry; I put them in the store room for safe keeping. Would you like to see them?'

'No, not right at this moment thank you, but I'll be taking some of them with me when I leave.'

Mike nodded and escorted the two men back to the terrace where he served their drinks and joined them around the table.

They exchanged small talk for a few minutes and then *Capitaine* Villeneuve excused himself and left Mike and Mr. Casanis to speak in private.

'I'd almost forgotten how nice this place is.'

'Yes, the location is fantastic,' agreed Mike. 'I can sit here for hours just taking in the view.'

'You know that you're welcome to stay here for as long you need to. I don't want you to feel that you're being pushed out or anything.'

'Thank you, that's a very kind offer. I'm actually quite happy where I am right now, but of course that could all change.'

'It sounds to me like there's a girl involved.'

'Guilty as charged,' smiled Mike. He saw Thomas' glinting eyes in his father's and wondered if they shared the same mischievous temperament. Mr. Casanis poured himself a glass of water and Mike watched that familiar sparkle begin to fade.

'Thomas' funeral will be held in Marseille tomorrow at the *Sacré Coeur*. I don't expect you to be there Mike, but I would like to ask you one small favour if you wouldn't mind.'

'Yes of course. What do you need from me?'

'The funeral in Marseille is really only for family, but I would still like to hold a private ceremony here in Corsica when I return with his ashes. As you know Thomas lived for the sea and I think it would only be fitting if his ashes were scattered in the water, in this place which has become so special to us all. It will only be a small gathering as my wife is still too distraught to travel, but I'd be very pleased if you could attend the ceremony and perhaps say a few words if you feel up to it.'

'I'd be honoured,' said Mike, swallowing the lump in his throat.

'Thank you. There's just one other thing that I'd like to mention. *Capitaine* Villeneuve has kindly explained the circumstances of Thomas' passing to me so I don't need you to go over it all again; I'm sure that will be a relief to you.' Mike nodded. 'It sounds as if you are very lucky to be alive under the circumstances. I realise that you were just very unfortunate to find yourselves in the wrong place at the wrong time, but now that you know what these people are capable of, I hope that you will have the sense to stay well clear of them. I'm saying this because *Capitaine* Villeneuve told me about your attempts to locate a missing U-boat wreck, and I can just imagine how strong an attraction that would have been for Thomas. I don't know what your intentions are in that regard Mike, but I just want to point out that in my opinion, no matter how attractive the idea might appear, it's not worth risking your life over.'

'Don't worry, I don't intend to put my life at risk,' said Mike, with conviction.

'Well I certainly hope not; one death is hard enough to deal with as it is. This is all a matter for the Gendarmes to investigate now and I have been assured by *Capitaine* Villeneuve that they are making excellent progress. In fact he tells me that they may be closing in on a suspect as we speak.' Mike raised his eyebrows, wondering if that situation was due mainly to his efforts or those of the Gendarmes.

'Well I just hope that they catch him and lock him away for a very long time.'

'So do I. Of course, it won't bring my son back, but it might at least spare others from a similar fate.'

Mike nodded, but remained unconvinced that a single conviction would do anything to stop the violence.

'Thomas deserved better than that,' he said, with undisguised bitterness.

'Yes he did, but fate rarely takes that into account Mike. The most important thing is to accept what happened and try to move on. Neither of us can help Thomas any more so there's no point in beating ourselves up about it.'

'Yes I suppose you're right.'

'Well, that's about all I wanted to say Mike, except to thank you for being such a good friend to Thomas.'

'It was a privilege.'

'Thank you. Now perhaps you could show me Thomas' affairs.'

'Of course. I'll get them out for you.' Mike pulled the crates and bags from the store room and left Mr. Casanis to sort through them in private. He joined *Capitaine* Villeneuve who was standing by the car, listening to updates on the radio.

'Is there any news on the motorcyclist?'

'Yes, one of our mobile units spotted him heading towards Sartène earlier on. We've closed all the exits and there's a helicopter on the scene, so he has virtually no chance of escape. I expect that we'll have him caught within the hour.'

'I hope you're right,' said Mike, 'but will you be able to bring a conviction against him without a motive?'

'We won't need one if he can be positively linked to the crime scene.'

'How will you do that when nobody witnessed the accident and no evidence was left behind?'

'I'm not talking about the road accident Mr. Summers.'

'Ah, so you're talking about Chantale then?'

'Why do you assume that?' asked Villeneuve, with suspicion in his voice.

'Lieutenant Lechaux was unaware that I knew either Hubert or Chantale until this morning and it was clearly significant to him. It also set me thinking and I began to realise that Thomas' and Chantale's deaths could be linked.'

'Linked...how come?' asked Villeneuve, probingly.

For the same reason that you do. Their deaths are only separated by a couple of days and Thomas, myself and Hubert all knew Chantale. Since none of us murdered her, it's reasonable to assume that she was killed as a direct result of knowing us. Maybe Santorini intended to use her as a source of information. To find out what we knew about...well whatever it is they're searching for.'

Villeneuve snorted disdainfully.

'Your theory supposes a great deal.'

'Do you have a better one,' challenged Mike.

'Yes. There is now a more obvious link between Thomas and Chantale which we have not yet fully explored.'

'And what's that?'

'You! So perhaps you could tell me what *you* were doing between the hours of six and eight o'clock on Tuesday evening?' Mike shook his head and stared at the ground.

'I was here all evening.'

'Can anybody vouch for that?'

'Someone could have done if they hadn't just been killed in a car crash.'

Villeneuve glanced at Mr. Casanis over Mike's shoulder and let out a sigh.

'Look, I need a tissue sample from you in order to eliminate you from our enquiries. Don't take it personally. Everyone who's been linked to Chantale Moret has been tested.'

'I don't suppose I have a choice then?'

'It would not look good if you refused, put it that way.'

'Do I need to come to the Gendarmerie?'

'No, we can do it right here if you're willing.'

'Let's just get it over with then,' said Mike resignedly.

Villeneuve took a tube containing a cotton swab on a stick from his lapel pocket and asked Mike to open his mouth. He wiped the pad of cotton over the interior of his cheek and then returned it to its protective sheath.

'That should do it,' said Villeneuve as he pocketed the sample.

Mike felt strangely uneasy about having his genetic identity scrutinised and couldn't help fostering a certain grievance towards *Capitaine* Villeneuve for doubting his word. It was a relief when Thomas' father gave him an excuse to distance himself.

'Mike, I've taken most of the personal stuff that I want from this lot, but I'm limited to what I can carry so I'll have to leave one bag here. It can stay in the store room for now and I'll pick it up another time. As for the rest, you're welcome to take what you want before I dump it. I'm sure that Thomas would have wanted you to keep all these bits of diving equipment and to be honest it would make my life a little easier if you did.' Mike nodded.

'I've already recuperated some of the damaged stuff from the Gendarmes, but I'll happily take the rest. I'm sure that I can find good use for it; thank you.'

'It's the least I can do. Well that just about wraps up my business here, so unless you need anything from me, I'll leave you in peace again.'

They turned their heads in unison as *Capitaine* Villeneuve suddenly walked away and began shouting orders into his radio.

'What about the door?' asked Mike. 'Would you like me to repair it for you?'

'Yes, I was wondering what to do about that. Do you think that you could do it?'

'No problem, I'm pretty good at carpentry. There are some bits of wood that I saw in the store and one or two hand tools that I can use.'

'Well it looks as if you've found yourself a job then Mike. I'm sorry that we haven't had more time to talk, but the next time I'm here we must go out to lunch together.'

'I'd like that very much.'

'Good. Well, take care of yourself. Here's my number if you need to get in touch with me.' Mike took the card which Thomas' father held out to him. They were just about to shake hands when *Capitaine* Villeneuve approached, looking extremely anxious.

'I'm sorry Mr. Casanis but we must leave immediately. I have a very serious problem to attend to.'

'You want to do what! You're even crazier than you look.'

'No seriously, it can work,' stuttered Jeannot, 'if it's done properly of course.'

Santorini was incredulous.

'Wait a minute; you want to hang someone off the back of the boat at 35 metres and pull them along? What is that - some kind of shark fishing technique? It sounds like an accident waiting to happen. Have you thought about the prop, and decompression stops, and what if someone has a problem down there?'

'Of course there will be some considerations, but it's a technique which could definitely work.'

'Go on humour me. I could do with a lift today.'

'What we need to do is trail a tag line off the stern with a big float attached to the end of it; something like an empty oil drum. Then we attach the descent line to the float so that it clears the outboards and we keep it vertical by weighing it down with something heavy, like an anchor.'

'Yeah then maybe we can fish the submarine out of the sea,' said Santorini unfairly. Jeannot ignored the remark.

'In practice, what happens is that a spotter swims to the float and then drops down the line. We wait 2 minutes to give him a chance to descend to the bottom and then we start to move ahead, following the same position lines that we programmed in for the fishfinder. If we allow each spotter to search for eight minutes maximum at a time, we can avoid anyone having to do any unnecessary decompression stops. We'll need a rota, of course, so that when one person finishes another will be ready to take their place. That way we could search almost continuously and everyone would get a good thirty minutes on the surface between dives. Of course we'd have to put together an emergency signal in case anyone has to abandon; something that can be quickly released and will float rapidly to the surface, like a weighted SMB or lift bag. It could also serve as a marker if anyone spots the wreck. It's your decision, of course, but if done properly, I believe it will work.'

Santorini glanced up at him, wondering if this was yet another of his harebrained schemes that would end up being far more complicated than it sounded. He was tempted to pour scorn upon Jeannot's suggestions, but he had to admit that if his idea did work, it would speed the whole process up considerably and cut out the uncertainty that seemed to overshadow their present method.

'Have you ever tried this kind of thing before?'

'No,' admitted Jeannot, 'but it's similar to a technique used in drift diving, where a float is used to help the boat keep track of divers when strong currents are pushing them along.'

'So the float isn't normally attached to the boat then?'

'It is initially, but then it's released. The divers just hang onto the weighted line beneath the surface. Of course, what I'm suggesting is that we actually pull the float along.'

'And we'll be diving solo I suppose.'

'Yes. Otherwise we'd be wasting time and air.'

'That figures,' said Santorini. 'Well we can't try anything new today, so we'll just have to carry on as we are for now. Maybe we'll give your method a try tomorrow morning. I'll bring an empty beer cask to use as a float if you can put together the emergency signal.'

'I'll adapt one of my lift bags,' nodded Jeannot.

'In that case, I'll put the idea to Pascal and Pierre.'

Michel realised that he was never going to be able to shake off the Gendarme who was tailing him before he reached the junction. If he was seen leaving the main road, he would lose his prime advantage and if someone got close enough to see him take one of the forest tracks, then all his escape routes would be quickly identified and sealed off. He could not afford to let that happen.

In grim determination, he slammed on his brakes knowing that what he was about to do would have very serious consequences. His hesitation was quickly replaced by anger as he turned the bike around in a controlled 180 degree skid and turned head on towards the approaching Gendarme. As the rear tyre began to grip the road he steadied himself, opened his jacket and pulled out the Glock. The Gendarme began to reduce speed as the gap closed and Michel saw him fumbling for his firearm. There was no time for second thoughts as with composure and determination Michel took aim, squeezed the trigger and fired off a single shot. With an intuitive jerk of the upper body he leaned over at the last second and narrowly missed a fatal collision. He felt a jolt as his rear wheel clipped the other bike and the Glock was knocked from his hand. The Fireblade began to slew and Michel fought desperately to regain control of it as it veered off the road and plunged into the bordering bushes.

He was thrown into the air like a rag doll and landed with a heavy thump on his back. Startled but unharmed, he found himself looking up at the sky, surrounded by thick undergrowth. Pumped up with adrenaline, he immediately scrambled to his feet and forced his way back to the road, desperate to retrieve the gun before the Gendarme could stop him. He skirted along the edge of the road, darting from bush to bush until he saw the gun lying on the tarmac a short distance away. Keeping low to the ground he ran towards it and with surprising agility, picked it up mid-step and rolled neatly into the cover of bushes on the other side of the road. There was silence. He peered out from a gap in the foliage and caught sight of the Gendarme several meters away, sprawled awkwardly on the ground near his motorbike. Cautiously, Michel began to approach him, his gun held out at the ready.

The Gendarme saw him coming and flinched, trying desperately to reach for the weapon in his holster but Michel was already upon him. He kicked his hand out of the way and pressed the barrel of the Glock into his ribs, causing him to recoil in pain. He quickly undid the Gendarme's ammunition belt and pulled it free from his waist along with the holster and pistol. As he did so, he noticed blood oozing from a wound to his chest. Unperturbed, he pocketed the pistol and threw the belt into the bushes. Knowing that the Gendarme was no longer a threat to him, Michel picked up his BMW patrol motorbike and started the engine. With his advantage regained, he let out the clutch and roared away, leaving the Gendarme to his fate. He turned left onto the D21 only to see a patrol car pass the junction behind him with its siren blaring. It made no attempt to stop, but it was of little comfort to Michel. He knew that they would soon discover their wounded colleague and alert the other units to his presence.

The sound of more sirens in the distance quickened his pulse and with gritted teeth he pushed the bike and his nerve to their limits. Reaching a fork in the road, he hesitated when he was unable to judge the direction from which a siren was approaching. He chose to go right and immediately passed another patrol car going in the opposite direction. It screeched to a halt behind him and the sound of an approaching helicopter confirmed that his luck was thinning. With a kilometre still to cover before he could get off the road, he threw caution to the wind and used both lanes to negotiate the bends. After a close call with a bolting goat and the rear end of a tractor, he finally arrived with a screeching halt before the gate which would lead him to safety. The whine of patrol car sirens was rapidly growing in intensity as he dismounted and ran to open it. He snapped the lever up and wrenched the gate open only for it to jolt back into place again on a gleaming padlocked chain.

He cleared away the splintered wood and stood back to take a look at the repair. It wasn't a bad job at all considering the condition of the rusty tools which he'd used. Once he'd checked that the door could be locked, he glanced at his watch and made a call to Monica. The call was answered by Anna who explained, with some difficulty, that Monica would be surfacing soon. Mike thanked her, ended the call and prepared to make a move. After selecting a few bits and pieces of diving equipment from Thomas' affairs, he attached what he could to a buoyancy jacket and slipped the remainder into his dry-bag. He put the buoyancy jacket on, threw the dry-bag over his shoulder and began to make his way back down the access road. Soon he reached the steep path and scrambled down it to arrive at the water's edge covered in dust and carrying one or two more bruises than he had when he left. On arrival at the water's edge, he inflated the buoyancy jacket and filled his dry-bag with air, so that the weight of all the extra equipment would be supported as he swam back towards the RIB. Once he had hauled himself and his cumbersome load aboard, he freed the anchor and made his way back along the coast to the makeshift mooring. After another dip and a short hike over the headland, Mike arrived opposite the black and yellow RIB. He swam out to join Anna, who was alone on surface watch.

'Hello Mike,' she said in a sing-song voice as she helped him to climb aboard. She waited for him to settle and catch his breath.

'Your friend Thomas...it is very bad,' she said frowning. Mike nodded.

'Yes. Very bad Anna. Very bad.' Anna pursed her lips and nodded reflectively at the sea.

'Monica soon is here,' she said after a pause. Mike smiled.

'Thank you Anna.'

She continued to tap information into the computer and a moment later, they both started when the communication bell began to rang. Anna stood up and began to haul up the lifting basket while Mike peered over the side, watching her colleagues prepare to surface. Soon Monica, Bertie and Hubert were climbing out onto the RIB, with Mike and Anna helping to relieve them of their bulky equipment.

'Hey Mike, how did it go?' asked Monica, as she rose to her feet.

'It went well, I think. Thomas' father is a really nice guy. We spoke for a while, we sorted out a couple of things that needed taking care of and most of all we gave each other our support.'

'Good. How's he taking it?' she asked, as she began to peel off her wetsuit. Mike eyes involuntarily traced the contours of her sculpted body.

'He's doing well under the circumstances. It was difficult for him at times, as it was for me, but I think that we both feel better for having talked.'

'I'm sure you do. Is he staying for long?'

'No, I think he said that he's flying back today. The funeral is in Marseille tomorrow.'

'Do you intend to go?'

'There's actually no need. He's coming back in a few days with the ashes. He wants to hold a short ceremony and then scatter them into the sea.'

'That's a nice gesture,' agreed Monica. 'Please tell him that he can use our boat if he needs to. It would be our pleasure to help in any way that we can.'

'Thanks, I'll mention it to him. I'm sure he'll appreciate the offer. How's your day been anyway?'

'Pretty good thanks. We're still pulling things out of the silt and there's more beneath. We found a nice silver bracelet today; it's in a very good state of preservation.'

Anna approached and asked Monica a question. After a short exchange, Monica nodded and pulled back her wet hair.

'Sorry, you'll have to excuse me for a moment Mike.'

'No problem,' he said, as Monica went to join Anna at the computer.

'Hey Mike, are we all set for tonight?' asked Hubert, as he strapped on a fresh cylinder.

'We certainly are. I've got some extra gear for you too.'

'Hmm, what's all this stuff for?' asked Hubert as he rifled through a pile of clips, straps and other accessories.

'You'll find this stuff useful for securing and adapting the extra equipment we use for extended dives. Most of it belonged to Thomas, but I don't think he'd have objected to you using it.'

Hubert stopped handling the equipment as if it might be harbouring some unpleasant affliction.

'Is there a problem?' asked Mike.

'I don't know. It just doesn't feel right using Thomas' stuff.'

'Good,' said Mike. 'I want to take you well out of your comfort zone and believe me, you'll have to get used to a lot more unpleasantness when we start training. In fact you'll probably hate me by the time I'm finished with you.'

'Oh no; what have I let myself in for?' he groaned.

'No pain, no gain,' said Mike, with a smile. 'I presume that you've read through the manual I gave you?'

'Yes, it was quite interesting.'

'I'm glad you enjoyed it and I hope it made you conscious of how divers, even experienced ones, can get themselves into serious trouble when they're not properly prepared.'

'If you mean: *did it scare the living hell out of me?* - the answer is yes.'

Mike laughed.

'The most important thing to realise is that where deep wreck diving is concerned, over-confidence is your worst enemy. Without a proper understanding of your physical limitations and the potential risks involved, you are like a racing car speeding around a circuit without brakes. It's essential that you learn to recognise and avoid the most common hazards and understand how to get yourself out of trouble when things go wrong. Underwater emergencies can be demanding under normal circumstances, but just try to imagine how much more difficult they can become when nitrogen narcosis begins to impair your judgement. It's vital to understand that if you don't constantly monitor yourself, your equipment and your surroundings during a deep air wreck exploration, you will almost certainly run into trouble. And unfortunately, you won't be able to count on anyone else to help you out.

'You make it all sound so tempting,' chuckled Hubert.

'I just want to make certain that you fully understand the risks, because if we do find this wreck, it will be your decision entirely whether you choose to enter it or not.'

'Of course, but I'm afraid that you haven't quite managed to put me off yet. I'm intrigued though; would you really leave someone to their fate down there if things went wrong?'

'It all depends on the particular situation of course, but I certainly won't go near anyone who is in a state of panic; that would be suicidal. If you are unable to deal with your own or anyone else's problems quickly and effectively inside a wreck, the chances are that you'll find yourself caught in a downward spiral that may ultimately end in disaster for you both. There is what is known as the snowball effect, where one unresolved problem leads to another and then yet another, so that before you know it, you are heading towards an insurmountable situation.'

'Yes I can see how that might happen and obviously I have been in some tricky situations myself over the years, but up until now I've always seen another diver as someone who can help me out.'

'Yes and that's understandable in recreational diving, because you almost always use single cylinders. If, for whatever reason, you have an out of air emergency while diving with a single cylinder, you may have no choice but to solicit another diver's help, and since the donor won't need all his gas supply to complete a lengthy decompression schedule, he won't necessarily compromise his own safety by helping you.'

'That does make sense,' said Hubert nodding. 'So what do you do when you're faced with several problems at once?'

'You remain calm and solve them one at a time, in order of importance. For example, a continuous gas supply is more critical than a broken fin strap and disorientation is more deadly than a leaking mask. One of the golden rules of technical diving is that vital equipment is either duplicated or carried in substitute form, so any problems relating to it should be dealt with quickly and effectively. Once you are in control of your equipment, you can then start to tackle problems relating to your environment. Working your way systematically through your problems will also help you to focus your mind and that is ultimately what will get you through. Even the most desperate situations can and have been overcome through calm, rational thinking and sheer determination.'

Hubert nodded pensively and then glanced up as Monica approached.

'You two both look very serious. What are you talking about?'

'We were just running through a bit of theory,' answered Hubert. 'I think that Mike is trying to put me off deep diving for life.'

Mike smiled.

'Well if the theory hasn't already done it, then the practice will certainly make him think twice.'

'Monica, you need to be very careful of this man,' said Hubert, wagging his finger. 'I've started to realise that there is definitely an evil side to him. Just make sure that you sleep with a knife under your pillow at night.'

'Thanks for your advice Hubert,' said Monica smiling, 'I'll bear that in mind.'

'Well since you've already painted me as a villain, I might as well introduce you to one of my favourite pieces of training equipment.' Mike reached for his dry-bag and pulled out a standard diving mask, the lenses of which had been replaced by aluminium plates with a circle of small holes drilled around them.'

'Oh my god,' exclaimed Monica, 'that looks like some kind of torture instrument.'

'What are you planning to make me do with that?' asked Hubert, his concern mounting.

'You'll find out soon enough.'

Michel pulled out his hand gun, shielded his eyes and fired two bullets into the body of the padlock. The casing blew apart, springing the lock open and releasing the chain from the post. He wrenched it free and kicked open the gate. The low throb of an approaching helicopter was almost deafening as Michel bolted towards the bike, still upright on its stand. The tyres sent a spray of dirt and small stones flying backwards as he gunned it through the gate entrance and into the cover of trees. The helicopter screamed past overhead, sending a hail of dead needles cascading down from the swaying canopy above. Michel immediately dismounted and ran back to close the gate, throwing the chain aside and then dropping to the floor as a pursuing patrol car went racing past on the main road. The sound of wailing sirens and squealing tyres began to fade into the distance. Michel quickly sprang to his feet and remounted the BMW. He sped away along a service track, bordered with fir trees that would lead him up over a mountain pass that was inaccessible to most other vehicles.

Following one of the two parallel tracks worn by the tyres of four-wheel drive maintenance vehicles, he heard the sound of the helicopter backtracking up the main road behind him. He knew well enough that it would not take the *section aerienne* of the Gendarmes long to work out that he had left the public roads. They would now be checking every possible escape route along that stretch of the D21. It was essential to put some distance behind him before the patrols discovered the unlocked gate and began to search overland. If he could keep out of sight of the helicopters for a kilometre or two, he would soon have a good 30 minute advantage over the ground units and that was all the time that he would need.

Now covered in mud, the bike whined as it was put through its paces. Michel Pushed on through forest and scrub, darting for cover each time the sound of whining rotors drew too close for comfort. The road began to climb, snaking its way up a forested slope until it finally opened into a clearing beneath an electricity pylon, high on the top of a ridge. Michel remained in the cover of trees and glanced back down at the plain below to see a helicopter flying low across it. Soon he would be at the other side of the ridge and shielded from its view. Sensing that he was edging away from danger, Michel's arrogant smirk returned. He roared down the steep bank at the other side of the ridge and pushed on through woodland and rough pasture, at speeds approaching the limit of his daring.

The next ridge which he encountered was less elevated but no less significant a marker on his route to freedom. Michel came to a brief halt and let his eyes roam across the horizon. The sea shimmered in the distance like a sapphire set perfectly into the rocky coastline before him. He looked over his shoulder and listened intently. All he could hear was the quiet hum of the BMW beneath him and the pulsating chatter of a distant helicopter. He quietly congratulated himself and calmly set off on the final leg of his journey. Soon he would be within walking distance of the small coastal town of Portigliolo where he would be able to disappear into the crowds. Knowing that he would have to ditch the patrol bike soon, he looked for a suitable place to hide it. He passed through a stretch of woods and spied an abandoned farm building away from the track to his right. Standing on the foot-rests of the BMW, he forced it through thick clumps of fern and entered the roofless building through the empty stone doorframe. Once inside, he threw the bike to the ground and piled rubble from the collapsed roof on top of it. With the Glock and the police revolver still shoved into his waistband, he ripped off the blue cotton uniform shirt, zipped up his leather jacket and then set off on foot along a narrow walking track. He was now barely a kilometre from the coast and only twenty minutes walk from Portigliolo. Once there he'd be a fifteen minute bus ride away from Pascal's farm. Encouraged by his progress, he increased his walking pace and was just settling into a steady rhythm when a gun shot suddenly rang out from the cover of trees to his right. He dropped instinctively to the floor, fighting to free the Glock as he rolled lengthways into the undergrowth. With his heart pounding in his chest, he held the gun out at the ready as someone came crashing through the trees towards him.

Capitaine Villeneuve arranged for Mr. Casanis to be taken to the airport and then joined Lieutenant Lechaux in his office.

'Is there any news about Jerome?' he asked, pacing the floor nervously.

'He's undergoing surgery at the moment,' replied Lechaux. 'It looks as if he's going to pull through, but it was touch and go for a while. The bullet pierced his lung just below the heart. A couple of centimetres to the left and he would have been killed outright.'

Villeneuve winced at the thought.

'Are we any closer to finding that low-life Perotta?' he asked. Lechaux sighed and scratched his head.

'I'm afraid that we're losing ground on him sir. It looks like he went overland on an obscure access track. We found a gate with dents and splinters in it and a padlock and chain nearby which had clearly been shot apart. We can only assume that he knew exactly where he was going. Either that or he's extremely lucky.'

'Surely the helicopter ought to have seen him,' growled Villeneuve in exasperation.

'It was a forest track sir; he was hidden by the tree canopy. It was only after the ground units found the damaged gate that they had any idea where to look for him and by then he'd travelled a good distance. We've identified several routes which lead off from the main track, but all of them are inaccessible to our patrol cars.'

'Then we ought to be sending people out on foot.'

'Yes sir; we are doing, but it's taking time to redeploy the men and give them a proper orientation of the areas which we want them to cover.'

'So we've just got to sit around and wait have we? Hoping that something will turn up?'

'We're doing everything within our power sir, but at this point were open to ideas.'

Capitaine Villeneuve stood with his arms folded, staring fixedly at the ground.

'I think that we should post officers outside the homes of every known member of *Libertà Corso* and the FLNC in the area, particularly those close to Santorini. If he slips through the net he's bound to seek help from somebody within the organisation.'

'Yes, I would agree with you there, but we're already stretched as it is.'

'Then I'll arrange to get more help drafted in from Ajaccio. Until the reinforcements arrive, we'll just have to make do. I'll play my part by covering Santorini's bar until you can send someone out to relieve me. See what other volunteers you can muster.'

'Yes sir, I'll see what I can do.'

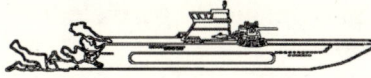

10

Mike and Hubert watched the others drive away in the truck. Once the jetty was clear, Mike reversed the Volkswagen along it and stopped beside the black and yellow RIB. He opened the trunk and pulled out a backplate, buoyancy wing and a pair of connecting bands. Hubert drew close as he demonstrated how to put together a working rig.

'This wing is a bit scuffed as you can see, but the main thing is that both chambers still inflate. I'll need your reg though because one of Thomas' was damaged beyond repair.'

'Of course. Take whatever you need.'

'There's a spare nitrox gauge in the dry-bag which we'll use to replace this shattered one,' said Mike. 'Here take this spanner and see if you can unscrew the old one.'

Mike attached the bouyancy wing, backplate and regulators to the double cylinders and after a few minor repairs, Hubert had a fully functional twin set. Mike lifted out his own rig and together they checked the pressure in the four main air cylinders and the two sling tanks.

'Right they're all good. Now I want you to use these clips and retaining bands to streamline your equipment and hold the hoses and redundant regulators in place. The last thing that we want is any of these getting snagged or damaged.'

Once Hubert had configured his equipment under Mike's watchful eye, they loaded the two twin sets onto the RIB.

'We'll start mapping when it gets dark, but until then we can begin your training.'

'OK, where do you want to go?'

'We might as well do it around here,' said Mike looking around the bay. 'It's nice and sheltered and we don't need much depth to start with. Let's see if we can find a patch of sand to anchor over.'

'I'll start up the engines.'

When Mike had slipped the lines, Hubert steered the RIB towards a quiet area beyond the moorings, coming to rest over a patch of calm turquoise water.

'This looks pretty good,' said Mike. 'I'll drop anchor here.'

Hubert nodded, let the boat settle once the anchor was released and then killed the engines.

'Well that was easy enough,' said Mike. 'Let's kit up.'

They pulled on wetsuits and strapped on their twin sets in the confines of the RIB. Hubert clipped on his sling tank followed by the reel and SMB under Mike's supervision.

'Bloody hell! It's not exactly light is it?' complained Hubert as he struggled to his knees.

'Well you *are* carrying around 40 kilos Hubert. It'll be a bit more comfortable when you're in the water, but it will still take some getting used to.'

'Jeez, I'll need to see a physio after two weeks of this.'

Mike smiled as he helped him to a seating position.

'Right Hubert, I want to run through some drills with you on the surface so that you can familiarise yourself with the position of the various controls. We'll do it by sight first and then I want you to try it while wearing the iron mask.'

'Is that what you call that thing? I knew it was some kind of torture instrument.'

Hubert followed Mike's instructions, reaching and stretching to practice gas and regulator switches, emergency shut downs, equipment releases and instrument location. When Mike was satisfied that Hubert had mastered the most important techniques, he asked him to repeat all the exercises with the low visibility mask on his face.

'That thing is horrible,' said Hubert when he was finally allowed to remove it.

'It's not meant to be nice,' said Mike. 'It serves a function - and that is to simulate conditions of low visibility and stress. You'll like it even less when we're in the water.'

'That's very encouraging,' said Hubert frowning. 'I'm getting pretty hot in this gear, so the sooner we get in the better.'

'Just bear with me, I need to explain a few exercises first.'

Hubert scooped some water over his head and listened carefully while Mike explained what was required of him. Once Mike had briefed him fully, Hubert needed little encouragement to slip over the side and plunge into the cooling water.

'Aah, that's better,' he said, with a relieved smile on his face. 'Do we really have to spoil it all by doing silly exercises?'

'We do if you want to dive the wreck.'

'Such sacrifices! Do people really pay you money for putting them through all this?'

'You'd better believe it; so let's get a move on before I start billing you.'

Hubert slipped beneath the water and after struggling to control his stability, completed the initial rotating bubble check. They continued their short descent and were soon kneeling on a large patch of sand. Mike immediately began to put Hubert through his paces. He demonstrated several exercises with and without the low visibility mask and then asked Hubert to repeat what he had seen. The first time that he wore the iron mask, Hubert was dismayed to discover that the holes in the lenses made it impossible to fully clear it of water. Braving the discomfort and relying purely on memory, he practiced regulator exchanges, gas shut downs, hovering exercises, SMB deployment, line laying and equipment removal, while almost totally blind.

After an hour of intense drilling, Mike suggested that they take a short break and Hubert raised no objections. They rose to the surface, released themselves from their harnesses and secured the heavy equipment to the side of the RIB while they climbed aboard. Hubert slumped down onto the deck in a heap and drank a whole bottle of water.

'That was good Hubert. I know that things got a bit tricky for you at times, but I was pleased to see you thinking the problems through.'

'I feel like a complete beginner again,' admitted Hubert.

'Everyone feels the same when they begin technical training. The equipment is unfamiliar for one thing and there is a greater emphasis on discipline, because at this level, failure to make the correct decision can have disastrous consequences.'

'I can appreciate that. I just find myself struggling to locate some of the equipment.'

'That's quite normal. It's not until you begin encountering difficulties that you feel the need to adapt your configuration. After that it's just a question of practice. Are you starting to feel more comfortable with the gear now?'

'Comfortable is not the word I'd use, but I'm certainly more confident with it.'

'Good, because the next exercise is really going to test your limits.' Hubert looked up wearily.

'I don't know why, but I get the feeling that you quite enjoy all this.'

'Well somebody has to have some fun,' said Mike with a smirk, 'but if it's any consolation I'll be doing the exercise as well.'

'Why does that not make me feel any better?'

'No idea,' said Mike with a shrug. 'OK Hubert, this is your challenge; I'm going to reel out a 15 metre sided square which will start and end at the anchor. At each of the first two right angle turns I'm going to tie in our sling tanks and at the third I'll be waiting to share my air with you.'

Hubert raised his eyes to the heavens.

'You'll be wearing the low visibility mask throughout the circuit and the exercise will start when I hand the reel to you. Whatever you do, don't put it down or you may not find it again. When I tap your arm, I want you to release yourself completely from your twin tank harness and then take up the slack on the reel. You can take a couple of breaths before you abandon your cylinders and then you'll have to reel yourself towards the first sling tank. When you reach it you must locate the regulator and then you'll be allowed a maximum of two breaths from it before you must reel yourself towards the next one. Use those breaths wisely as you'll need time to free the line from the cylinder. When you reach the second sling tank you'll repeat the process and then reel yourself towards me at the final turn. As soon as you touch me, I will share a single regulator with you while you reel us back towards the anchor. You'll obviously need to trust me to provide the air at that point as both your hands will be occupied. When you reach the anchor, you'll feel for your twins and once you've located them, I'll withdraw my regulator. As soon as you've strapped yourself back into the harness, you can deploy your SMB and reel yourself to the surface.'

'Just before we do this; there aren't any unspoken grievances between us are there?'

'Don't worry I'm not doing this to punish you,' Mike chuckled. 'I just want to see how well you cope with problem solving under stress.'

'I usually just have a couple of beers, but somehow I guess that's out of the question, so lets just get the humiliation over with shall we?'

'That's the spirit! Let's go.'

They slipped into the water again and quickly strapped on their floating equipment. On Mike's signal, they dropped below the surface. Hubert followed close by as Mike began to set up the circuit, relinquishing his sling tank for use as an obstacle at the first turn. Mike used his own for the second and then positioned Hubert at the third so that he could provide him with air during the last leg of the demonstration. When everything was in place Mike swam back to the anchor and clipped off the line. He reeled around the course in reverse order, first giving Hubert the line to hold and then tying in the two sling tanks before completing the square by returning to the anchor. Hubert's insides trembled as he watched Mike put on the iron mask, slip out of his harness and unclip the reel in readiness to begin the exercise. After taking two deep breaths Mike removed the regulator from his mouth, left the security of his air supply behind and reeled towards the first sling tank. When he encountered, it he calmly felt for the regulator hose and pulled it free from the restraining band. Without any apparent urgency, he took two breaths from the regulator while carefully freeing the line from the cylinder valve. In growing admiration, Hubert watched him abandon the cylinder and reel himself towards the second obstacle. Mike dealt with the following sling tank almost as easily as he had the first, before reeling himself leisurely towards Hubert as if he were taking a stroll in the park. Once Mike had made contact with Hubert's hand, he gave a calm out of air signal and Hubert responded by taking his regulator from his mouth and sharing his air. The regulator passed back and forth between them as they swam side by side towards the anchor. Once there, Mike unclipped the end of the line, felt for his equipment and secured the reel to his harness. After regaining control of his own air supply, he wriggled into the harness and pushed himself up into a kneeling position. To complete the circuit, he set up and deployed the SMB before using it to reel himself slowly up towards the surface. Hubert followed.

'That was a little too easy for you,' said Hubert as he surfaced beside Mike, 'you really ought to have had your arms and legs tied together.'

'You'd like to see me try that wouldn't you?' said Mike, grinning.

'Well maybe not now, but ask me again after I've done the exercise.'

Mike laughed.

'The trick is to try to remain calm and resist the urge to speed up your movements,' explained Mike. 'As any breath-hold diver will tell you, slow movement creates less of a carbon dioxide build up in your muscles and as a result prolongs the time that you can comfortably hold in a breath.'

'I noticed that you didn't breathe out while you were breath holding.'

'Yes, obviously that would be considered an unusual procedure in recreational diving, but as you know, your lungs are not at risk from expanding air unless you begin to rise, particularly in shallow water. At depth the relative gas volume change in your lungs is smaller, so if you had to do something like this in a wreck, god forbid, holding in your breath would not put you at significant risk.'

'It seems strange to be suddenly breaking all the standard rules of diving.'

'Yes, but don't forget that this is a discipline for expert divers with considerable knowledge. You wouldn't expect a glider pilot to be able to fly a commercial airliner would you?'

'No, but some of the scary flights I've been on in the third world do make me wonder.'

'I'd have to agree with you there,' said Mike. 'Well, you've seen what you need to do Hubert. Any more questions before you take up your challenge?'

'No, let's just crack on with it before I change my mind.'

They deflated their buoyancy wings and dropped down close to the anchor. Mike set up the circuit as before and carefully checked all the cylinders before handing the low visibility mask to Hubert. Unbeknown to him, Mike would be silently shadowing him during every stage of the exercise.

Hubert slipped on the mask and tried to clear a little water from it, to no avail. He closed his eyes and tried to control his breathing rate before the exercise started. When he felt the reel being pressed into his hands a brief surge of adrenaline scuppered any hope of relaxation. Holding onto one of the harness straps with the regulator in his mouth, he breathed deeply and appreciatively of the air on which his submerged body depended. It seemed madness to leave it behind and yet that was what he was about to do. Determined not to back out of the challenge, he clutched the reel with both hands in readiness to move away. There was no time for hesitation now. Hubert took a long, last deep breath and let the regulator fall from his mouth before swimming slowly towards the first obstacle. An eternity seemed to pass as he blindly reeled in the line, unable to judge the delay or distance until his next breath. It was with great relief that his fingers finally grasped the first cylinder and his hand closed around the regulator mouthpiece that was strapped to its side. While trying to control his rising anxiety, he yanked it free and took the first of his two permitted breaths.

Instead of the relief which he had expected, Hubert found himself fighting the immediate urge to take the second breath. Freeing the line from the cylinder valve as quickly as he could, he inhaled the second breath and reeled urgently towards the next stage. His lungs were now burning as he made contact with the next cylinder and rammed the regulator clumsily into his mouth. Again the first breath came and went too quickly and Hubert was unable to resist drawing the second. Realising that he was beginning to lose control of the situation, he scrambled to untie the line and after freeing it reeled even faster, swimming blindly into the obscurity. With no idea how far he needed to go, or even if Mike would still be there at the end of the line, waiting to administer that life giving gas, doubts began to creep into his mind. What if something had happened to Mike? What if this was all just an elaborate joke? Hubert felt a flash of resentment as his lungs started to cramp in an attempt to expel the stale air within them. All his instincts urged him to swim directly to the surface as an insistent mocking voice crept into his head: *You're not going to make it. You've failed. You're going to drown!* He panicked, inhaled water and bolted for the surface.

Officer Bertoli sat in the patrol car at the end of the pier and watched the incoming vessels through the open passenger window. It was a pleasant enough evening, a gentle onshore breeze helping the brightly painted fishing boats rock their way slowly back to port with their heavy catches safe in their holds. Through his binoculars, Bertoli spotted white flashes of spray shooting out from the underside of a bouncing hull. As the vessel neared, he saw that it was a heavily laden RIB. He tracked its progress, watching it speed past sluggish fishing boats as if they were firmly anchored to the bottom. When it had approached to within a few hundred metres of the pier, Bertoli scrutinised the four occupants and soon saw the unmistakable thick, dark mane of Santorini, blowing in the wind. But it was the sun weathered man with the white moustache and salt stained baseball cap who interested him the most.

'There they are...and there's my little mole,' he said, with his eyes still glued to the lenses. 'Take us back to the main entrance Jean-Marc.'

'Do you really think that you're going to bust them all on your own?' his colleague asked, as he started up the engine and set off back along the pier.

'I reckon I have as good a chance as anyone.'

'The boss wouldn't be too happy if he knew what you were up to. We're supposed to be out looking for Perotta.'

'Yeah? And who's to say he won't turn up here to meet them? Anyway, what's the point in listening to the old man? He hasn't even got close to convicting Santorini in twenty years.'

'Santorini's connected; you know that. I doubt if anyone can touch him, and if you try to put the heat on him alone, you'll probably end up in a ditch. This job's OK, but it certainly isn't worth risking your life over.'

'Well no one's asking you to get involved Jean-Marc. You just stay here in the car, listen to the radio and take in the scenery.'

Jean-Marc tutted and pulled over into a shaded recess close to the port entrance.

'Suit yourself. If I don't hear from you in an hour I'll report you as missing.'

Bertoli laughed and stepped out of the car.

'If you get too scared out here on your own, you can always make a call to your mother.'

He slammed the door shut before his colleague could retaliate and made his way over towards the quays. Slipping off his cap, he took up position behind a parked truck from where he could survey the scene unnoticed. Before long, he spotted Santorini's gang walking up the main pontoon before dispersing and going their separate ways. His eyes tracked the blue baseball cap as its silver haired owner entered the car park and weaved his way between the lines of vehicles. Crouching down low, Bertoli approached to within a few car lengths of him. He heard approaching footsteps and ducked as one of Santorini's men passed behind him. When he looked up again, he saw the silver haired man unlocking a car door and was forced to move swiftly. He emerged from a gap between two cars and called Jeannot's name just as he was about to climb into the driver's seat. Jeannot started and took a step back.

'Who's there?'

Bertoli approached and pulled out his badge. 'Gendarmes!'

Jeannot sighed heavily and leaned back against his aged Renault 5.

'What's the problem?'

'I need to have a little chat with you Mr. Raspail.'

'About what?'

'Well, I'm a bit concerned about the company that you seem to be keeping at the moment.'

'I don't know what you're talking about.'

'Have you really any idea what kind of man Santorini is?'

Jeannot dropped his head, realising that the Gendarme had the advantage over him.

'I've heard the rumours about him, just like everyone else.'

'Then I'm surprised to see you working alongside him.'

'I'm doing nothing wrong as far as I know, so what's your problem?'

'I'm reliably informed that you are actually quite an honest person, certainly not someone who would normally associate with a person of Santorini's reputation, so I can only presume that he has some kind of hold on you. And that usually means a debt of some kind or perhaps simply a desire for self preservation.'

'I'm just diving with them; for fun!'

'Yes, I can just imagine how much fun that would be,' scoffed Bertoli. Having read Mike's statement in detail, he now used the information to unsettle Jeannot. 'So have you found the wreck yet?'

He watched Jeannot's eyes widen with surprise and then snap back to their previous scowl.

'I don't know what you're talking about.'

'No I thought that's what you'd say; Santorini wouldn't want word of it getting around now would he? It's not illegal of course, looking for a submarine, but murder certainly is.'

'Murder? What do you mean murder?'

'Oh, you mean they didn't tell you about that? Don't you remember the English tourist and his friend, the ones who found the depth gauge?' Jeannot frowned. He wanted to say that he knew nothing about them, but his curiosity got the better of him.

'What about them?'

'The Frenchman was called Thomas Casanis. I say *was* rather than *is* because he's now dead. He was killed in a car crash on Thursday evening. Read the papers if you don't believe me. It wasn't an accident of course; far from it. He was killed by one of your new friends.'

Jeannot, initially shocked, now became suspicious.

'How do you know that he was killed by one of Santorini's men?'

'I know because the Englishman survived the crash and gave us a description of him,' he lied.

'Then why don't you arrest him?'

'We're trying to at this very moment. In fact he's now wanted in connection with two murders and an attempt on the life of an officer of the Gendarmes.'

Jeannot breathed uneasily.

'If you think that I'm going to stand up and testify against any of them you are sadly mistaken,' he said resolutely.

'I'm not asking you to testify against anyone. All I want you to do is feed me some information and tell me when Santorini finds what he's looking for.'

'But I have no idea if there's anything there. Why are you so interested in this wreck anyway?'

'Because we need to find out what motivated Santorini to order the killing of Thomas Casanis and Chantale Moret,' said Bertoli sternly. 'Look Jeannot, we're going to nail Santorini and his gang one way or another. We already have a boat out watching you and it's just a matter of time before we close in; so you can either cooperate with us now and get the benefit of our protection, or be arrested and tried along with the rest of the gang. You may be totally innocent, but I can't see you escaping a charge of accomplice to murder, illegal salvage, handling stolen goods...or even tax evasion if we choose to be difficult.'

Jeannot slumped against the car and put his face in his hands.

'Can you guarantee that I won't have to testify or make any statements?' he asked, knowing that Santorini's revenge was worse than any jail sentence.

'I personally guarantee it,' said Bertoli. Jeannot nodded his head wearily.

'OK I'll do what I can.'

'That's very wise,' said Bertoli. 'Now how close do you think you are to finding the wreck?'

'If it's there, we should know within a couple of weeks.'

'Good, here's my private phone number,' said Bertoli, handing him a card. 'Store it in your phone and then destroy the card...for your own safety.'

Pascal entered the bar, accompanied by his daughter Mathilde. He placed a protective arm around her shoulder and guided her through a small crowd of men towards the counter. Her expensive sunglasses and neat leather handbag were strangely at odds with her surroundings, but the same could not be said of her looks. She had inherited the narrow eyes, red cheeks and stocky build of her father and the matronly scowl of her mother. She wrinkled her nose at the sickly sweet odour of the smoke filled atmosphere as Santorini approached them.

'Ah Pascal, Mathilde, a good evening to you both. Did you happen to see *Capitaine* Villeneuve outside as you came in?'

'Villeneuve?' exclaimed Pascal. 'What's *he* doing here?'

'He's about to order a drink I hope,' said Santorini. Pierre, at the bar and several other men erupted into raucous laughter. 'I went outside and gave him the list, but I think he needs a little more time to choose.'

Pascal began to laugh along with the other men.

'You really like to rub salt into old wounds don't you?'

'Nothing gives me greater pleasure in life,' replied Santorini. 'What can I get you both to drink?'

'A beer for me please,' replied Pascal. 'Mathilde?'

'A Kir.'

Santorini served Pascal the beer and placed a glass of white wine over *Crème de Cassis* in front of Mathilde, whose disapproving countenance told of her desire to leave the bar at the earliest opportunity.

'Let's go in the back room,' suggested Santorini. 'Pierre, take the bar will you? And make sure that old fool Villeneuve doesn't enter my bar without buying a round.' The laughter at the bar began to fade away as Santorini escorted Pascal and Mathilde into the kitchen at the rear. He sat them down at the roughly hewn wooden table while he served himself a glass of Marc. Pascal declined the offer to join him.

'Mathilde, close your ears,' urged Pascal before turning towards Santorini. 'Michel's made it. He's staying at the hunting lodge up at my place.' Santorini breathed a sigh of relief.

'He has the luck of the devil that one.'

'And the cheek to go with it,' agreed Pascal.

'Are you being watched over there?'

'Funnily enough there was a car waiting outside the farm when I arrived. I thought that it was a bit unusual, so when I found Michel in the barn, I moved him up to the lodge in case they searched the place.' Pascal paused, looked over at Mathilde and then spoke in a whisper. 'He told me he shot a Gendarme.' Santorini looked up in consternation.

'He's in serious trouble this time then, and no doubt about it. As soon

as the heat dies down we'll have to get him out of here for good.' Pascal
nodded solemnly and then broke into a toothy smile.

'You'll never guess what happened to him while he was walking through
the forest to Portigliolo,' he said with a glint in his eye.

'What happened?'

'A gunshot blasted over his head and he heard someone running
towards him through the trees. He was ready to shoot his way out of
trouble when he suddenly sees this huge wild boar come flying out of the
bushes, chased by two dogs and a hunter with a twelve bore!' Pascal and
Santorini burst into hysterical laughter and slapped the table with the flat
of their hands.

'Oh, I'd have paid good money to see that,' chuckled Santorini. 'I can
just imagine the look on his face.'

'Yeah, we had a good laugh about it, but you don't know the best; he's
lost his curls and moustache.'

'No! Seriously?'

'Oh yes. When he got to Portigliolo he needed to disguise himself, so he
bought a pair of scissors and a shaver. He went into a public toilet, cut his
hair short and then shaved off his moustache. He's not too happy about it,
but I told him that he might as well get used to it, for when they send him
to prison.' Santorini roared with laughter again.

'Oh, I really must come and visit you soon so that I can see him in all his
glory. He must be as angry as a snake in a sack.'

'He is, but he said that he had no choice. There were police everywhere.
I tell you, he looks completely different now. I didn't even recognise him
when I saw him in the barn. I was almost ready to fetch my gun and chase
him out of there.' Santorini smiled and stared into the distance.

'You need to tell him to keep out of sight Pascal; you know what he's
like. He'll have to stay behind closed doors for at least a week and then
we'll have to find a way to get him out of here.'

'You're right,' nodded Pascal soberly, 'there's no way he can show his
face around here again.'

'Unfortunately there's nothing much that we can do about that,' said
Santorini.

Pascal looked sideways at Mathilde who was distractedly examining the
smears on her wineglass. 'Shall we listen to the recording now? Mathilde
doesn't want to hang around for too long if we can avoid it.'

'Of course; I've got everything ready here. Santorini lifted the recording
device onto the table while Pascal encouraged Mathilde to draw her chair
up close. He pressed the playback button and after some interference, a
ring tone sounded and a dialogue cut through the background static.
Mathilde listened with great concentration and soon began to shake her
head.

'That's not English; it sounds like German to me.' Santorini glanced up
at her.

'It's probably Swiss German then. We're not interested in that. Just
ignore it.'

The recorded conversation ended and was followed by another in English. Mathilde listened carefully and explained that it was an American professor interested in writing an article for an archaeological review. Santorini dismissed it and fast forwarded to the next conversation. Mike's voice suddenly broke through the background hiss. Mathilde frowned in concentration as she explained that the speaker was talking to a girl who spoke very little English and was attempting to arrange a meeting with a girl called Monica. She continued to translate, but the conversation proved to be of little interest to Santorini. He rapidly skipped two more dialogues before he reached the end of the day's recordings.

'Well we haven't learned anything new,' he conceded, 'but at least we now know that the device works.'

'It works incredibly well,' agreed Pascal. Mathilde coughed and buttoned up her jacket. 'Well if we're all finished up here, I'd better get Mathilde back. Shall we come at the same time tomorrow evening?'

'That suits me fine.'

Santorini pulled a 20 euro note from a wad in his pocket and slipped it across the table.

'Thanks Mathilde, you did well.' She smiled meekly and stood up, ready to leave. Santorini opened the door and ushered them outside into the noise of the adjoining bar. As they walked out into the animated throng, a red light began to flash on the recording machine. A crackling ring tone was followed by the sound of Monica's voice answering a rapidly spoken call from Mike.

Capitaine Villeneuve was fuming by the time he left *Le bar des Chasseurs*. He'd had to suffer the humiliation of Santorini's taunts, only to find out that Perotta had outwitted his entire operational staff. He returned directly to the *Caserne* and went to see Lieutenant Lechaux in his office. Lechaux looked up wearily as Villeneuve entered the room with a face like thunder.

'I hear that Perotta has escaped us Lieutenant.'

'It would seem that way at the moment, yes,' admitted Lechaux.

'We're going to be the laughing stock of the Gendarmes, you realise that, don't you?'

'I doubt that very much sir. The other garrisons are already sending us messages of support. The word has got around quickly that one of our men has been seriously wounded.'

Villeneuve grimaced, feeling a pang of guilt for allowing his wounded pride to overshadow more important concerns. He slumped down into an empty chair and sighed.

'You're right Guy. Sorry. I've had a damned awful day and I'm taking this all far too personally.'

'That's understandable sir,' said Lechaux, 'but we really can't fault the men. They've put a considerable amount of time and effort into this operation and they're as disappointed with the outcome as we are.'

'Yes I'm sure they are. Well I can tell you one thing, Perotta isn't hiding out at *Le bar des Chasseurs*; Santorini would have been a bit more discreet if he was.' Villeneuve ignored Lechaux's questioning glance. 'What about the other surveillance units? Is there any news from them?'

'They're updating us regularly, but we've had no sightings as yet.'

'At this late hour, I don't hold out much hope either, but I suppose we have to keep trying. I expect Santorini's associates are all well aware that they're being watched by now.'

'Probably,' agreed Lechaux. 'Incidentally, did you happen to see Pascal Cavaille in the company of a young girl at *Le bar des Chasseurs*? One of our units followed him there earlier.'

'Yes, they arrived just before I was relieved. The young lady bears a striking resemblance to him, which is rather unfortunate for her really. Do you think she's related? A daughter perhaps?'

'Well our files do show that he has a daughter of that age.'

'Then we need to confirm her identity and find out where she lives. Her presence there might be linked to Perotta.'

'I'll see that it's done sir.'

'Good. And while you're at it, I think we now have a good excuse to organise a few raids. We'll concentrate on Santorini's closest associates and see what turns up. If nothing else, forensics might be able to get a DNA sample from Perotta's house so that when we catch him, we'll have the evidence to nail him for the Moret murder. Either way, I want to send a clear message to them that we mean business.'

Hubert felt a regulator being rammed into his mouth as a firm hand gripped his weight belt and prevented him from reaching the surface. He inhaled deeply, relieving the desperate craving in his lungs and when his jerking breaths finally settled into a relaxed rhythm, he felt Mike gradually loosening his grip.

Still unable to see clearly, the increasing pressure on Hubert's ears told him that he was being taken back down to the bottom. He pinched his nose and blew against it to relieve the discomfort, realising that Mike was not going to let him take the easy way out. Still shaking from his ordeal, he felt the discarded iron mask and the reel being pressed firmly back into his hands. With great reluctance he put the mask back on and began to reel in the line while Mike fed him air from his regulator. His confidence gradually returned, allowing him to reach the anchor without further incident. After Hubert had detached the end of the line, Mike released his hold on him and watched him locate his abandoned equipment and finally regain control of his air supply. Hubert paused to breathe deeply and appreciatively of it before continuing with the exercise. Still starved of visual reference he was preparing to deploy his SMB when he felt Mike purging his regulator to simulate a malfunction. He groaned inwardly, knowing that he would now be expected to deal with the problem as a priority. After clipping the reel to his harness, he used the experience gained from previous exercises to switch regulators and isolate the supply to the one that was supposed to be leaking. Mike now left him in peace to prepare his SMB and send it shooting up to the surface like a missile. Hubert felt like he was being released from a hellish nightmare, when he was finally allowed to reel himself towards the surface.

'Damn, that was hard,' said Hubert as he pulled off the iron mask. 'It's impossible to judge where you are with this thing.'

'That's the whole point. If you'd done the same exercise with a normal mask you'd have had no trouble at all. As it stands, you failed to overcome the anxiety caused by your lack of orientation and consequently you are now a dead body floating in a deep wreck.'

'I always wondered what it would be like to be dead,' said Hubert, grinning.

'You'd probably look a lot better than you do now,' said Mike. 'But joking apart, the exercise is designed to show you where your limits are and make you realise how important it is to stay calm under pressure. You were dealing with several stress factors at once; lack of visual reference, the discomfort of a leaking mask, task loading and of course the overwhelming desire to breathe. Most divers, even experienced ones, find this exercise difficult, because it takes them out of their comfort zone. Anxiety is the number one enemy because it drastically reduces your capacity to solve problems. In your case, it was caused by uncertainty and the inability to overcome your desire to breathe. It's important to bear in mind that no matter how much your lungs feel like they are about to explode, your body can still function normally for quite some time. When you bolted to the surface just now, you were barely three meters away from me and yet the surface was a full six metres above you. Of course this was just an exercise, but if for some unfortunate reason you found yourself in a similar situation inside a deep wreck, that reaction would have been utterly futile.'

'You know what? There's something to be said about nice shallow dives in clear, warm water where you can just swim around, looking at the fish.'

'Does that mean you're no longer interested in diving the U-boat?'

'Are you crazy? Do you think that I'm going to give up just because I've been tortured and humiliated by a sadistic Englishman?'

'Well in that case, we'd better go find it,' said Mike. 'It'll be getting dark soon.'

'Nothing would give me greater pleasure.'

Hubert climbed out onto the RIB while Mike dived down to recover the two sling tanks. Once the equipment was lifted aboard and stowed, Mike and Hubert stripped off their wetsuits, dried themselves off and put on warm sweatshirts. Hubert clamped the sounding transducer in place beside the lifting gantry and connected the cable to the laptop. Once he had activated the GPS receiver and fired up the laptop, Mike saw a triangle appear on the digital chart, offset in the entrance to Tizzano.

'That's it, were in business,' said Hubert, when he was satisfied that all the devices were communicating with each other. Mike clapped him on the shoulder. 'Nice work Hubert; I'll get the anchor. Don't forget that once we're clear of the inlet, we need to stay well offshore.'

'I take it we won't be using the navigation lights either.'

'Not if we can avoid it. If anyone comes too close to us we'll just use a flashlight to warn them of our presence. Hopefully there shouldn't be much traffic at this time anyway.'

'Let's hope so, because Monica is going to fry your balls if anything happens to this boat.'

'Don't I know it!'

Mike stowed the anchor away in the chain locker as Hubert took the RIB towards the mouth of the inlet. The light was fading rapidly as they exited the harbour and headed out towards open sea. To the west a thin golden line marked the passing of the sun, like the dying embers of a fire. Somehow the transitory nature of the glowing skyline seemed to capture Mike's mood.

As the yellow haze darkened to orange and then indigo Mike pulled his eyes away and went to sit beside Hubert at the helm. The sea ahead was calm and the RIB flew across its ruffled surface as if skating on a sheet of ice. The twin engines hummed as they powered into the gathering darkness, leaving a silver grey trail in their wake.

'Were getting close now. We should start referring to the chart,' said Hubert.

Mike reached under the console and pulled the laptop out onto an upturned crate. He refreshed the screen and studied it through its protective plastic cover.

'The waypoint heading should read 127 degrees true if it's in sync with the GPS,' said Hubert.

'It does,' confirmed Mike. 'We're now 0.6 nautical miles away from it.'

'Excellent. I'll need your heading corrections as we make our approach.'

'No problem.'

Mike watched the red triangle track across the chart towards the activated waypoint.

'0.3 miles to go,' he called out.

'OK. Start counting me down.'

Hubert slowed to a crawling pace as Mike guided him to within a few boat lengths of the target.

'Were right over it now,' shouted Mike, as the waypoint alarms began to sound on both the GPS and the laptop. Hubert brought the RIB to a halt and then crouched down next to Mike. With a penlight clamped between his teeth, he pulled the waypoint list up on screen and activated one that was named P1 South. On the screen Mike saw a line appear, running due south from their present position. Hubert increased the scale of the chart and then went aft to lower the transducer into the water.

'Right we're recording. Keep the triangle moving along the line by telling me to go either to port or starboard and give me advance warning when we're nearing the end of the position line.'

'No problem; go right ahead.' Mike watched in fascination as an image of the sea floor began to form in a separate window in the upper part of the laptop screen. On the digital chart a wide band marked their sounding coverage as the RIB progressed. 'A little more to starboard,' he said as his eyes skipped between the sounding images and the chart.

'This is absolutely unreal Hubert... just unbelievable!'

'It will all be recorded, so just keep your eyes on our position,' said Hubert smiling to himself. 'Exercise some of that self-control you keep talking about.'

'Damned cheek!' said Mike. As they neared the end of the first search line, he began to count down the distance to the waypoint.

'Zero point zero three to go...point zero two...mark!'

Hubert put the engines astern and brought the RIB to a halt before selecting the next two waypoint markers on the digital chart. When they were active, he put the sounding window on full screen and reduced the scale to check that there were no gaps in transmission. A strip of continuous sea floor represented by a three dimensional image confirmed that everything was functioning perfectly. Even at such a reduced scale Mike could clearly see each detail of the stratified rock ridges that lay beneath them.

'That's just incredible,' he said, his eyes glued to the screen. 'It's a pity that there isn't a U-boat stuck in the middle of it though.'

'That would have been a little too easy,' said Hubert, grinning. 'I'm going to head west towards waypoint P2 South now and then we'll go north along the next position line.'

'OK, I'm ready when you are.'

Hubert moved away under Mike's guidance and was soon swinging the bow through 90 degrees.

As they were approaching the mid-point of the new line of soundings, Mike suddenly saw something unusual appear in the mapping window.

'Hey, there's something down there!' he shouted excitedly. Hubert remained at the helm and kept his course.

'Is it a complete image?' he asked.

'No it looks like part of something bigger to the west.'

'Then just ignore it for now. Are we still on course?' Mike was surprised by Hubert's seeming indifference, until he reminded himself that the position of the images was being automatically recorded using DGPS technology and they could therefore return to any feature which interested them at any point during the mapping process. He relaxed and continued to give heading corrections until they reached the end of the position line. Hubert put the engines into idle and came to join him.

'Let's have a look at that,' he said, scrolling back along the sounding profile.

'There it is,' said Mike, pointing at a mass of irregular forms. Hubert enlarged the window and increased the scale over the selected area. Even close up the detail was astonishing. 'It's definitely debris from the hull of a vessel of some kind,' confirmed Hubert. 'See those rounded spars, they're the ribs and you can just make out the panel sections joining them together.'

'Could it be wreckage from a U-boat?' asked Mike.

'It's impossible to tell at the moment; it really could be anything. We might have a better idea once we've finished the next sweep.'

Mike could not contain his excitement as Hubert activated the next set of waypoints and began to move away. Soon the RIB was heading southwards along the third position line and Mike's whole body became rigid with anticipation as they approached the point where he expected to find more wreckage. Sure enough, more twisted spars began to appear at the edge of the screen. Mike gasped and then almost immediately fell silent when the area of wreckage petered out into nothing.

'No, I don't believe it! Is that all there is?'

'Don't stop the course corrections,' called out Hubert. Mike sighed in frustration as he returned his attention to the chart.

'Go ten degrees to starboard,' he said flatly.

Hubert reached the end of the sweep and activated the waypoints for the following position line before he studied the recording.

'Hmm, there's not too much to go on is there? Let's just keep moving; we can always come back and enhance the details later.'

Mike agreed, but found himself unable to muster much enthusiasm for the next sweep. He watched ridges appear at the top of the sounding window only to disappear again at the bottom, as if they were travelling along a conveyor belt. Besides a tiny patch of debris at the very edge of the image, the sea floor seemed to be as barren as the surface of the moon. Soon they were heading south along the fifth position line and Mike was conscious that they had already covered close to 50 percent of the area. With only five more sweeps left to go, doubts began to creep into his mind.

'Go to port a touch,' he said, rubbing the tiredness from his eyes. He glanced up at the star filled sky wondering if this had all been just the result of an over active imagination. Perhaps he should have listened to Monica after all, he thought. He'd most likely caused the death of his friend and an innocent young girl, all because of a ridiculous and selfish obsession. A shooting star streaked across the night sky and as it faded, he had only one word on his lips...

'Sorry.'

'What did you say?' asked Hubert.

Mike dropped his head and rubbed his eyes before squinting at the chart.

'Er...go to starboard a fraction. OK we're there.'

Hubert eased the throttle back into neutral and crouched down to activate the next waypoints.

'Are you okay Mike? You've gone all quiet on me.'

'I dunno. I'm starting to think that this is all a waste of time.'

'You giving up so soon?' asked Hubert as he began to check the sounding profile. 'After all that crap you gave me about discipline?'

'Enough is enough Hubert. It's unfair of me to put any more people at risk, whether the U-boat is there or not.'

'Really? I guess you won't be interested in looking at this then?' Hubert continued to tap information into the laptop.

'Interested in looking at what?' asked Mike, frowning. Hubert smiled and turned the screen away.

'No, nothing. Shall we head back then?'

'Give me that!'

Mike pulled the laptop around and stared dumbfounded at the screen. The small, indistinct patch of debris from the previous sweep was now visible as the extremity of a substantial piece of wreckage.

'Holy shit! Where did that come from?'

'Obviously it was there all the time.' Hubert's toothy smile was lit up eerily by the yellow glow from the laptop screen. 'You see; persistence does have its rewards.'

'OK, don't rub it in.' Mike could hardly contain his excitement as Hubert centred in on the area of wreckage and enlarged it to the full size of the screen. Once again the detail of the image was remarkable.

'Look, that's machinery!' said Mike pointing animatedly. 'And those must be propeller shafts.'

'Probably, but there's not enough of an image here to make any accurate assumptions yet; we need to do at least another sweep.'

'Well come on then. What are we waiting for?'

'So you've made peace with your conscience then have you?'

'Hubert, has anybody ever told you how incredibly annoying you are?'

'Yes, Monica mostly.'

Mike was on the edge of his seat as they nosed their way northwards towards the point where they had seen the wreckage. The first man-made objects began to appear at the top of the screen and gradually consolidated into a single mass as the sounding display scrolled. Mike gasped and felt his pulse begin to race as he watched an elongated, cylindrical section of hull begin to form right in front of his eyes.

An electronic beeping sound cut through the background noise and Santorini reached into his pocket to retrieve his mobile phone. He glanced at the display and saw that he had received a message, with no name or number associated with it. Half-listening to the client at the bar who was relating a highly exaggerated story to him, he read the message and his expression darkened. Without offering any explanation, he walked away, leaving the customer open mouthed in indignation. He went to the kitchen, closed the door behind him and made his first call to Pascal.

'It's me. Don't talk; I'll keep this brief. There are unannounced visits planned for us all early tomorrow morning. Make sure that you clean the house and grounds. I'll explain later.'

Santorini ended the call and stared at the wall in contemplation. This was undoubtedly the work of *Capitaine* Villeneuve. He'd made the old goat look a fool last evening and this was obviously his way of exacting revenge.

Still, it was of no consequence now that he knew what to expect. It would almost be worth all the trouble just to see the look on his face when he realised that he'd been outwitted again. The tip-off had given him a firm advantage, but Santorini still felt uneasy about the manner in which he'd received the information. It seemed odd that the FLNC should go out of their way to help him, when *Libertà Corso* now operated independently of them. It was almost as if he was receiving support from someone who had their own particular agenda. Deep in brooding contemplation, he made a couple of further calls and then snapped his phone shut.

Monica was entering data into her laptop when her phone began to ring. She saw Mike's name on the screen and smiled as she brought it to her ear.

'Hey you, how's it going out there?'

'We've found it.'

'What do you mean, you've found it?'

'What do you think I mean? It's there, clear as a bell lying on the sea floor.'

'I don't believe it. Has Hubert confirmed what it is?'

'Yep, he's standing right next to me at this very moment with a huge grin on his face. Anyway, I just wanted to say don't go shooting off to bed yet because I want you to see this. We'll be there in just over an hour.'

'Well...OK, I'll see you when you get back. Be careful out there won't you?'

'Of course we will.' The line went dead and Monica noticed a strange high pitched squeal coming from the phone. She tapped it, frowned in irritation and replaced it on the desk beside her. Staring absently at the computer screen, she began to wonder what the consequences of Mike's discovery would be. In truth, she'd been expecting him to return with his tail between his legs, accepting that he'd let his imagination run away with him, but now that he appeared to have found the proof which he'd been searching for, she feared that there would be no reasoning with him.

With a sigh of resignation, she pushed her concerns to the back of her mind and continued to write her reports. An hour later, she stirred when she heard muffled voices in the hallway followed by a knock on the door.

'Hey Monica, are you in there?'

'Yes, I'll be out in a minute Mike. I just need to finish up something.'

'OK, we'll be in the kitchen.'

Mike left Monica in peace and rejoined Hubert, who was crouched over the laptop, busily running an enhancement programme over the mapping images. The detail of the multiple soundings which they'd taken over the main body of the wreck had now improved to the point where the whole thing looked like a scale model.

'Take a look at this,' said Hubert, turning the screen towards him with a smile of satisfaction.

Mike approached and stared at the image in awe.

'This is a work of genius Hubert. If I hadn't seen it all come together with my own eyes, I would never have believed that anything like this was possible.'

'I wish I could take the credit for it, but all I did was press the buttons,' said Hubert modestly.

Mike could now see that the U-boat had fallen between two parallel ridges and had rolled slightly to starboard in an upright position. On a reduced scale it became obvious that the trail of debris which they'd found lying some distance behind the wreck was all that remained of the obliterated stern. Hubert pointed out the starboard engine, which had been ripped from its mountings, causing the drive shaft, complete with its twisted propeller, to splay out from the hull like a broken limb.

'That's a gun isn't it?' asked Mike when a small, isolated piece of wreckage caught his eye.

'An anti-aircraft gun I'd say,' agreed Hubert after enlarging it.

Monica entered the room behind them and placed a hand on each of their shoulders. She stared fixedly at the computer screen, her brow furrowed in disbelief as she took in the unmistakable sleek lines of a U-boat.

'So what do you think Monica?' asked Hubert, grinning.

'Come on, where did you get this image from - the internet?' she asked, incredulous.

'Take a look at the coordinates if you don't believe us,' he countered.

Monica crouched down and studied the details of the image, clearly impressed.

'It must be over 60 metres long,' she said, passing a professional eye over it.

'About 65 I think,' agreed Hubert. 'It's hard to tell with any certainty because of the damage to the stern.'

'Yes, that must have been a substantial explosion. It's no wonder that you found pieces of wreckage so far away. It looks to me as if there are actually two areas of damage although one of them appears to be super-ficial,' continued Monica. 'See here? There are also signs of mechanical stress on this area in front of the tower.'

Mike took a back seat as Hubert and Monica began to dissect the image, drawing informed conclusions from the evidence which they found.

'Most of the force from the main explosion appears to have been directed upwards, outwards and to the rear,' said Hubert, 'which explains the scattering of smaller pieces that we came across some distance behind the hull.'

'Yes, I can see that. Could a bomb or torpedo have caused that scale of destruction?'

'I don't think the damage was caused by a torpedo; it's far too symmetrical and I have my doubts about a bomb as well. It's almost as if the explosion came from within the hull itself.'

'Maybe there was a secondary explosion,' ventured Monica.

'That's possible. But without knowing what kind of munitions they carried and where, we can't make a reliable assumption.' Monica nodded.

'What about the tower?' she asked pointing. 'Do you think this damage was caused by the same explosion?'

'I very much doubt it. The impact came from starboard, so it must have resulted from a separate, weaker explosion. I'm still unsure what all this stuff is here though. It looks like some kind of marine growth.'

'I think you'll find that it's a fishing net Hubert. I've seen similar results on other wrecks which we've sounded.'

'Ah yes, that would make sense.'

'What about depth charges?' asked Monica.

'Yes, I think that's probably what damaged the turret, and it could also explain the detached anti-aircraft gun over here,' said Hubert pointing. 'I'm pretty sure that it would have been mounted on the bridge originally.'

Monica nodded and then cleared her throat.

'Right, here's my stab at a scenario for what it's worth. The sub gets hit by a depth charge, takes in water and has to surface. The crippled vessel is then attacked, either by a destroyer or from the air and a lucky bomb lands right on the stern, blowing it apart and causing the sub to sink backwards. The bow rises into the air and the weight of it causes this buckling which you can see forwards of the tower. As it sinks the damaged stern hits the rocks first causing this prop shaft to splay and ripping the starboard engine from its supports. The rest of the hull slides down the ridge, causing these panels to be pulled away and leaving this trail of debris on the starboard quarter.' Monica finished speaking and then glanced at Hubert and Mike in turn. Mike nodded his approval, but Hubert was still busy thinking.

'Yes I agree with most of that, but I'm still not happy about the stern damage,' he said finally. 'I still think that it was caused by an internal explosion.'

'Well I've got most of the information that I need,' said Mike.

Hubert and Monica both looked at him in surprise.

'Sorry Mike, we didn't mean to leave you out of this debate,' said Monica.

'That's no problem; I've enjoyed listening to both of your opinions, but I'm more interested in the whys rather than the hows. I'm trying to figure out why this U-boat is apparently unaccounted for. I think we all agree that it met a sudden and cataclysmic end, which might explain why there was no distress call and no survivor accounts.'

'The transmitter could have been damaged in the blast,' pointed out Hubert.

'Yes, I realise that, but even so, if the aircraft or ship which attacked it survived unscathed, the crew would have filed a report somewhere. Obviously we could try to research all the reported losses in the area, but that would take time and it still wouldn't necessarily help us to identify the individual sub. It would be much simpler if we just dived the wreck first and identified her before carrying out our research.'

'Hey, before you two get carried away,' cautioned Monica, 'wouldn't it be better under the circumstances to just report the position of the wreck to the authorities?'

Hubert and Mike stared at her as if she had just grown a third arm.

'OK...I'll take that as a *no* then.' Monica blew a sigh and drummed her fingers on the table. 'Well I guess I'll leave you boys to plan your assault in peace then. I'm sure that you won't want me hanging around telling you how irresponsible I think you're both being.' Mike and Hubert lowered their eyes and wisely refrained to comment. 'Are you planning to use our RIB anymore Mike?'

'No we're done with it, and I can't thank you enough for letting us use it. The sounding equipment was absolutely invaluable, but now that we have an image of the wreck and accurate coordinates we can use the hire RIB.'

'Good, that will save me having to disappoint you then,' said Monica curtly. 'Right, I'm going to retire to my room. I'll see you in the morning Hubert.'

'Yeah, *Guet Nacht* Monica.' Hubert watched her leave the room and then turned to face Mike. 'Do you fancy a drop of Cognac to celebrate?'

'Excellent idea!'

Hubert went to fetch a bottle from his room while Mike continued to study the image on the laptop screen. He returned shortly afterwards and poured a generous measure of Cognac into each of two tumblers before handing one to Mike.

'*Gsundheit!*'

'Cheers!' replied Mike, tapping the rim of his glass against Hubert's. He swirled the golden liquid around the glass, breathed in the sweet, heady vapours, took an appreciative sip and let it roll around his tongue.

'Mmm, that hits the spot,' he said nodding appreciatively.

'Courvoisier - one of the best,' glowed Hubert.

Mike returned his attention to the computer screen.

'I've just been studying the wreck's layout and thinking about how best to enter it. It's unlikely that we'll be able to identify the sub from the outside, so we might as well plan a penetration dive directly. Obviously I'd prefer to take things a little more slowly, but unfortunately, time is a luxury that we have very little of.' Hubert nodded in agreement.

'I can't really see a great choice of entry points,' continued Mike. 'Submarines aren't designed with many openings, for obvious reasons. I'm hoping that this damage to the turret will allow us to access the central part of the vessel directly, because that will obviously make it much easier to explore the forward section.'

'Surely we could just enter through the damaged part of the stern,' ventured Hubert.

'Yes, that would be our next option of course; provided that there are no serious obstructions. It certainly won't be easy though. After an explosion like that, I'm expecting dislodged material, loose pipes, hanging wires and a generally weakened structure. I think the best course of action, to maximise our time and safety down there, would be for me to penetrate the hull alone and lay down a safety line while you explore the exterior and see if you can spot any alternative entrances. If I manage to get a good distance inside the hull, I'll try to open a hatch or see if I can find a perforation which I can squeeze through. Then, if everything looks straightforward and we've got enough time, I'll guide you through the inside of the wreck.'

'That sounds pretty good to me. So when do you want to do this?'

'The sooner the better. How about first light the day after tomorrow?'

'You mean a deep dive before I start work?'

'Well it's better than doing it after you've completed a day's diving.'

'I suppose that's true,' conceded Hubert.

'You'll be fine as long as you keep an eye on your computer and don't do anything silly. As for tomorrow, I'm going to be doing lots of research. I want to try and find out what type of submarine this is so that I can get a good idea of the internal layout before we start exploring it. After all, knowing what to expect inside a deep wreck can determine whether you'll have one of your best dives, or your last.'

'That's a pleasant thought to end the day with.'

'Well there's no point in kidding yourself it will be simple. Anyway you won't have worry about that side of things because I'll take care of everything. I'll put a comprehensive plan together and fill you in on the details tomorrow evening.' Mike drained the last drop of Cognac from his glass and then stood up. 'Here's another nice thought for you to chew on before you turn in. If it really is a U-boat, we'll almost certainly be entering an underwater graveyard full of the bleached bones of long dead German mariners.'

Mike lingered just long enough to see Hubert go green at the gills.

'Sweet dreams!' he trilled, with an evil grin plastered across his face. He left Hubert alone and went to join Monica in her bedroom. He found her awake, reading through some notes.

'Are you still working?'

'I'm just finishing up.'

'Good!' Mike walked over and sat beside her on the bed. He leant over and kissed her on the lips, gently at first and then with the hunger of desire.

'Mmm, submarines really do get your blood pumping don't they,' teased Monica as she put down her reports and pulled him closer.

'I love to explore the unknown,' smiled Mike as he pulled off the light cotton top that Monica was wearing and released the clasp of her bra.

Encountering little resistance, he slipped the straps over her arms and then gently nuzzled one of her shapely upturned breasts. Monica breathed in sharply and then began to moan softly, leaning back against the pillows as she tugged at his hair. Mike slipped his shirt over his muscular shoulders and ran his hand along the contours of her finely toned stomach. Soon their mouths were locked together and Mike began to slip Monica's panties over her thighs. She tensed and then rolled over to straddle him, pinning him against the bed by his wrists. She stared into his eyes like a viper, ready to strike.

'Let's get one thing straight. I'm not going to make love to you until I'm absolutely sure that you're not going to just disappear out of my life, either through macho selfishness or because you were stupid enough to go out and get yourself killed.'

'But Monica...I'

'No buts...you'll just have to wait.' She smiled in triumph and then turned out the lights. 'Goodnight!'

The peace of the early morning was disturbed by the sound of insistent banging on the door which led to the apartment above *Le bar des Chasseurs*. Santorini came downstairs, before the door was broken down.

'Who's there?'

'Gendarmes! Open up immediately! We have a warrant to search the premises,' ordered an *Officier de Police Judiciaire*. Santorini slipped the latch and opened the door. He was already fully dressed and surprised the Gendarmes by walking straight past them without complaint.

'Suit yourselves, you'll find me in the bar.'

'We have orders to search the bar as well,' said the young officer, determined to show his authority.

'Well you'd better get a move on then sonny. I haven't got all day; I've got a business to run here.'

As soon as Santorini had opened the shutters of the bar, two armed officers entered with their automatic pistols raised in readiness. Santorini followed closely behind and immediately began to slosh soapy water all over the floor. One of the officers ordered him to stop, but Santorini blatantly ignored his request.

'You have a warrant to search the premises, not to stop me from exercising my profession.'

'We'll arrest you for obstruction if you continue,' warned one of the men.

'Oh yeah, and I'll make a complaint against you for harassment,' bawled Santorini.

The two Gendarmes skated around the floors as they searched the adjoining rooms, much to Santorini's amusement. After a minute of fruitless searching, they glanced at each other, shook their heads and lowered their pistols.

'It's clean.'

'Who did you expect? Elvis Presley,' scoffed Santorini. The two men ignored him and made a swift exit. Out on the street they met two of their colleagues, who were looking decidedly pale.

'The man's a pig,' said one of them in disgust. Santorini smiled in silent triumph, knowing that they had found his little welcoming gift. After his tip off the previous evening, he had defecated into a plastic bag, sealed it and left it to sit overnight. Knowing that he would be woken early, he had slept fully clothed so that he could quickly slice the bag open and leave it in a cardboard box under the table when he left the apartment. Smiling contentedly, he began to open the rest of the shutters while whistling an

irritating tune and making a point of ignoring the scowls of the Gendarmes
who were now returning to the blue van that was parked across the road.

'Come back and visit any time boys,' he mocked as they prepared to
leave.

As soon as they were out of sight he immediately closed the shutters
again. The bar wouldn't be opening for at least another two hours.

'Raspail, *je vous écoute*,' chirped Jeannot as he picked up the phone.

'Bonjour Mr. Raspail. Officer Bertoli of the Gendarmes here. We talked
the other day.'

'You again! What do you want now...and why is there a car hanging
around outside my house?'

'It's nothing to worry about; we're still looking for Perotta and you've
obviously been linked to him.'

'But you said that I'd be protected,' complained Jeannot.

'I said that you'd be protected from prosecution, not from enquiries.
That's why I'm calling you in fact. Look, the pressure is on to find Perotta
and so there may be other people from my department wanting to question
you. If they do, just tell them that you've given all your information to me.'

'Why can't you just tell them to leave me alone?'

'It's not quite that simple. They have been given orders which I can't
overturn and to be honest there are also some office politics involved.
Everyone wants to take credit for catching Perotta. He's a high profile
criminal and he's just wounded one of our men, so there will be a lot of
praise for the person who arrests him.'

'And that includes you, I suppose.'

'I'm no different from anyone else.'

'It all sounds like a lot of nonsense to me.'

'Well, that's not really your concern, but what is important, is that you
don't leak any information to anyone else, because if you do, I'll no longer
be able to protect you. Is that understood?'

'I can live with it.'

'Excellent. Enjoy the rest of your morning Jeannot.'

'You're a slick operator,' commented Jean-Marc as Bertoli turned off
the phone.

'Stick with me and you'll learn a thing or two,' said Bertoli, winking.
'You have to be smart to get ahead in the services Jean-Marc. In two
months time Lechaux will be Captain and someone will have to take his
place.'

'And that someone will be you I suppose?' said Jean-Marc, rolling his
eyes.

'Why not? Someone has to; so you'd better be nice to me if you don't
want to spend the rest of your career kicking the homeless out of shop
doorways.'

'You should have been a pimp rather than a Gendarme.'

'So you like working with vagabonds then do you?'

Jean-Marc ignored him and stared out of the patrol car window.

'You know that this will all get back to him, don't you?'

'So what if it does? I'll just tell him what Jeannot told me.'

'Which is?'

'He's helping Santorini to find a lost outboard motor. Do you fancy a pizza?'

Mike watched Monica and her team leave for Tizzano and then sat back and fired up his laptop. Cradling a mug of coffee in one hand he began to work his way through the list of websites which Monica had forwarded to him, scouring the pages for any information relating to U-boat design and construction. He compared photographs and drawings against the sounding image of the wreck and soon concluded that they were dealing with a type VII U-boat, the most common and dependable of the *Kriegsmarine* fleet. Further reading helped him to narrow the choice down to one of two possible variations: the VIIB and the VIIC. The difference between them was a mere 0.6 metres in overall length and since the damaged stern prevented any accurate measurement of the wreck, it was impossible for him to narrow the field any further. Fortunately for Mike, the layout was almost identical in both variations and that would allow him to use the internal drawings of either type to formulate his plan.

After studying several photographic images of the interior of a VIIC U-boat, he began to appreciate the functional complexity of their design. It was clear that the crew would have had to work under very claustrophobic conditions during active service and Mike was mindful of the fact that he would be faced with even greater constraints when he was navigating through the wreck himself. Staring in dismay at the banks of hydraulic hoses, wires and pipes which weaved their way along every available space on the walls, he began to understand the true extent of the challenge which lay ahead of him. After a devastating detonation and over sixty years of submersion in a corrosive environment, many of those structures were now certain to be broken loose, close to collapse or hanging freely, ready to trap the unsuspecting diver. Even if the wreck was in pristine condition, Mike knew that with twin cylinders on his back and a sling tank strapped to his front, he would not have an easy time negotiating the confined passageways and narrow hatches which characterised the interior. To lessen the potential for snagging, he decided that it would be safer to leave the sling tank outside the hull and use it as a staging point, from which to reel away from. The nitrox was only needed for decompression purposes in any case and consequently the cylinder could be safely deposited and recuperated at some point prior to ascent.

Knowing that many of the potential problems could only be minimised through exhaustive preparation and familiarisation, Mike found an interior plan of a VIIC U-boat and began to study it in detail. His main

objective was to reach the central control room, the nerve centre of the
U-boat which lay directly beneath the conning tower. To access it from the
stern, he would have to traverse three major compartments; the electric
motor room, which served as the power source for the U-boat while it was
fully submerged, the diesel engine room, which operated during surface
and sub-surface cruising and finally an accommodation area; the Petty
Officer's quarters.

While studying the layout of the electric motor room and comparing it
to the sounding image, he realised that it was actually the starboard
electric motor which had been pulled out of alignment at the stern. He
knew from the images which he'd studied, that the gangway between the
two electric motors was very narrow and there was clearly a possibility that
the misalignment could have blocked the access to the other
compartments. It was a daunting prospect, but an unexplored wreck was
always likely to throw down a challenge before it gave up its secrets.

Once Mike had familiarised himself with the layout of the U-boat's
interior, he began to think about the extra equipment which he would need
to facilitate his progression through the wreck. The most challenging
obstacles which lay in his path were the circular steel hatches, that were
used to seal off compartments when water had breached the hull. Mike
knew that on a sinking vessel they would almost certainly have been
closed, and after more than sixty years of submersion it was unlikely that
they would open as easily as they once did. A small crowbar and a hammer
would be needed to tackle the more resistant of them and might also help
to dislodge any other heavy objects which he encountered along the way.
Wire clippers and a small hacksaw also came high on his list of priorities,
as they would be essential for stripping away the loose wires and
protruding pipework that seemed to swathe every surface inside the
wreck. There were other small but none-the-less important things that he
needed; new batteries for his back-up lights, chemical light sticks for
emergencies, protection for his head and hands and cable ties to hold,
repair and secure loose equipment.

Once Mike had prepared an exhaustive list of all the items that he
required, he leant back in his chair, closed his eyes and let the images and
plans which he had been staring at for the last two hours meld together in
his mind. He began to work his way through the wreck, section by section,
trying to visualise his route through the various structures, while
considering the problems which he might encounter and the solutions
which he would apply. The machinery, the compartments, holds and
passageways were each visited and examined as closely as if he was taking
part in an interactive virtual tour. When the spatial image had been firmly
fixed into his mind, his eyes sprang open and he stared into the distance.
It was time to take a trip to Bonifacio.

Leaving the farmhouse via the perimeter wall, he made his way through
the sinuous backstreets until he reached the multi-storey car park. Once
he'd recuperated the Volkswagen, he drove it to the car hire office and
changed it for a Citroen C5 Estate. Ignoring the disapproving expressions

of the staff, he drove into Bonifacio and stopped at the diving centre to buy chemical light sticks and drop the sling tanks off for refilling. While he was there, he enquired about the availability of helium and was given the address of a local gas merchant in Propriano. After purchasing a small crowbar, a hammer, a pair of strong wire clippers, a junior hacksaw and some cable ties from a local hardware shop, he went to a supermarket and armed himself with a supply of batteries for his back up lights. In the sports section, he picked up a pair of fingerless cycling gloves and a canoeing helmet, to serve both as head protection and a base on which to mount his caving lamp. It would be dark inside the wreck and Mike would need both hands free to operate his equipment.

Once all the items on his list had been accounted for, he visited the local library and spent a couple of hours reading up on the history of U-boat activity in the Mediterranean during the Second World War. When his eyes grew tired of translating from the large dictionary which lay open beside him, he pushed his chair away from the sloping, wooden desk and replaced the dog-eared reference books on the librarian's returns pile. He walked out squinting into the bright light of the afternoon sun and sauntered over to the shaded terrace of a local café-bar. While slaking his thirst with a cool beer, he looked out over the still waters of the harbour and considered the facts which he had learned:

Nazi U-boat's operated in the Mediterranean between 1941 and 1944 from their principal bases in Toulon, South of France and La Spezia, on the North West Coast of Italy. The fleet went into rapid decline when the Allies pushed westwards along the North East Coast of Africa and established an air and sea base on the strategic island of Malta. The newly developed technology of sonar gave the Allies the ability to seek out, track and destroy U-boats which would previously have remained undetected. The majority of the U-boats involved in the battle for the control of the Mediterranean were of the type VIIC and had entered through the Straits of Gibraltar. By the end of the war, virtually all of them had been put out of action.

Mike sat back and thought about the three drunken old men who claimed to have witnessed the aerial attack on the submarine all those years ago. Their story had been speculated over and ridiculed in the local community for more than half a century and with their tainted testimonies as their only proof, they'd almost certainly gone to their graves believing that their claims would never be vindicated. Mike felt a certain kinship with them now and was only sorry that they would not be around to milk the glory when he finally set the record straight.

'So will this system work?'

'It seems petty good to me. There's a tendency to rise up when the boat takes off, but you can still see the bottom well enough,' said Pierre as he stripped off his wetsuit. 'It's a bit strange being down there on your own though. You start to feel a bit edgy.'

'You'll get used to it,' said Santorini, while picking up a pair of binoculars and training them on the small boat which was loitering nearby. It was the same one which he'd seen the previous day, moored up in almost the same position, with two fishing rods protruding from the stern. The flash of a lens from the wheelhouse confirmed what he already suspected. He smiled and waved in their direction before raising an index finger in defiance.

'It looks like we have company again,' he said. 'They've obviously got nothing better to do with their time.' Pierre stared in the direction of the boat and spat into the sea. Seconds later, a yellow object broke the surface behind the boat.

'Stop the engines!' Santorini shouted.

Jeannot immediately put the engines astern and joined Santorini and Pierre, as they stared at the emergency signal, bobbing on the surface like a giant yellow man o' war.

'Pascal could be in trouble,' said Jeannot, 'keep watch while I get my gear on and take a look.'

'No wait!' said Santorini, 'I can see his bubbles behind the float. He's surfacing.'

Jeannot continued to put on his wetsuit while the other two stared transfixed at the floating barrel and the patch of effervescent sea that surrounded it. Soon a dark distorted shape flickered beneath the surface and gradually transformed into the stocky features of Pascal. Emerging to the sight of three concerned faces at the stern of the RIB, he spat out his regulator and pushed his mask up onto his forehead.

'There's something down there,' he shouted wide eyed in triumph. 'It's back there behind the lift bag. I couldn't release the damned thing straight away; I had to wrap my legs around the anchor so that I could free both my hands.'

'How long did it take you to deploy the signal?' asked Jeannot with sudden urgency in his voice.

'About thirty seconds, maybe more,' he replied.

'OK, climb aboard; we've got no time to lose.' Jeannot made a quick calculation in his head and returned to the helm while Santorini and Pierre helped Pascal out of the water. Once he was safely aboard, Jeannot spun the boat around sharply and headed towards the yellow lift bag. After a quick glance at the heading error on the GPS he went a touch to port and then retraced his path for a further 40 metres.

'I'm going down to take a look,' announced Jeannot as he began to put on his equipment. 'Keep the boat close to the marker and watch out for my SMB.' Santorini was about to protest, but Jeannot had already strapped on a compass and was ready to jump.

'OK, but if you find it, you come straight back to the surface - understood?'

Jeannot nodded and flipped back into the water. He dropped down rapidly, using the descent line beneath the barrel as a reference. The sea floor was just on the edge of his visibility by the time he reached 25 metres and became clear when he hit 40. He scanned the area around him and saw patches of sand and rock, but nothing which looked remotely regular in form. Glancing down at his compass, he began to follow the position line's reciprocal heading. He searched for two minutes, but saw nothing unusual. Cursing into his regulator, he continued unabated and after a few more powerful fin kicks, he glanced ahead and breathed in sharply when a long dark hull shape emerged from the blue haze to his right.

Lieutenant Lechaux listened with growing concern to the reports being submitted by the gathering of officers in the lecture theatre.

'I tell you they were expecting us,' complained one of the officers who was present during the raid of Santorini's apartment. 'He wasn't the slightest bit ruffled when we woke him up, in fact you would almost say that he was enjoying it all.'

'It's true, none of them seemed to be surprised by the visit,' said another.

'Has anyone talked about this operation to friends or family,' asked Lechaux, looking sternly about the room. 'I'm not looking to punish anyone; I just want to find out how this leak might have occurred.' There was an uncomfortable silence in the room. 'Look I don't expect anyone to admit anything in front of colleagues, so I'll ask you to please come and see me individually if you have spoken to anyone at all about it; even if it's only to your wife. Someone is obviously leaking information whether they intend to or not and it could cost us more than just a little embarrassment.'

There was a sudden shuffle of chairs as everyone in the room stood to attention. *Capitaine* Villeneuve entered the room and approached the podium.

'At ease gentlemen.'

Villeneuve spoke briefly with Lieutenant Lechaux before shuffling some papers and addressing the room.

'Good morning to you all. I've just this minute returned from the hospital and you'll be glad to hear that Jerome's condition is now stable. I presented him with the card that you all signed and he asked me to thank you all for your messages of goodwill. Jerome is as eager as ever to get back to work and he says that he would be here with us right now if the doctors would allow him. He's a very brave young man and a credit to the Gendarmes. I'm, sure that his example will inspire you all to redouble your efforts to bring Perotta in. He may well have given us the slip for now, but I'm convinced that he's still on the island. I've arranged for security to be doubled around the ferry terminals and airports and we shall maintain a 24 hour watch on the premises of all of Santorini's known associates.' There were muted sighs around the room.

'I know that this entails a great deal of effort from you all, but we owe it to Jerome, his family and the public at large, to do all that we possibly can to bring Perotta to justice. The newspapers are already looking upon this as a failed police exercise and I do not want to fuel their fires. Every

Gendarmerie on the island is behind us in this endeavour and I feel the weight of that responsibility, as I hope you do too. Lieutenant Lechaux and I expect nothing less than your total cooperation in this regrettable situation. If any of you are not prepared to give me your total commitment, then you ought to think seriously about changing your profession.' Villeneuve watched several heads drop around the room.

'There is one more thing that unfortunately I have to bring to your attention. Lieutenant Lechaux informs me that vital information is being leaked out of this garrison, right under our noses. It is for this reason that I have decided to restrict your advance knowledge of any further operations concerning this case. I want you all to remain extremely vigilant concerning the attitudes and motives of your colleagues, because much as I regret to say it, it is quite possible that we have an informant in our ranks.'

Mike walked from the rest spot to the villa to recuperate a slim, six litre cylinder which he'd left in the store. It was normally used for cave diving, because of its slender profile, but now he had other plans for it. The numerous hazards which he'd identified from the photographs and images of the U-boat's interior had convinced him that he needed something to give him the edge if a serious problem arose. Under normal circumstances, he would have been perfectly happy to breathe air at the proposed depth, despite the potential confusion that could arise from the effects of nitrogen narcosis. But the exploration of a U-boat was far from being a routine exercise and at some point his life might depend on keeping a cool head.

Mike knew that by adding an inert buffer gas to air, the physiological side-effects of the constituent nitrogen and oxygen would be reduced relative to their percentage in the mix. Helium had been used as a buffer gas in the commercial diving industry for decades and encouraged by its continued success, the more adventurous element of the recreational sector had been quick to follow.

When added to air, helium forms a mixture commonly known as trimix, which can be safely breathed well beyond the limits imposed by air. The major advantage, as far as Mike was concerned, was that breathing trimix would virtually eliminate the debilitating effects of nitrogen narcosis. There were other operational limitations to consider, however, not least of which was an increased risk of decompression sickness due to the need for a more complicated decompression schedule. With the correct training, most of the inherent dangers of breathing trimix could easily be overcome, but Mike could not change the fact that he would need to plan a separate profile to Hubert if he chose to go down that route. With Hubert's lack of decompression diving experience, it would have been both unfair and dangerous for Mike to leave him to his own devices, but he realised that there might be a way around the problem. The 6 litre cylinder could be filled with trimix and secured in the gap between his twin tanks, so that he could breathe from it in an emergency, without significantly modifying his profile. There was still a bit of creative planning to do and he had yet to run the idea past Hubert, but as he reached the outskirts of Propriano, his mind was more or less made up.

He followed the hastily written directions, which the dive centre had given him and arrived at the industrial estate where the Gas Merchant could be found. Clutching the slim cylinder in one hand, he was just making his way towards the warehouse reception when he glanced at a busy newspaper stand and stopped dead in his tracks when he saw the eyes of Michel Perotta staring back at him.

Jeannot emerged, peering anxiously over the peaks of the waves until he spotted the RIB in the near distance. He called out and saw three heads turn towards him in unison. The RIB's engines were immediately pressed into action and soon he was bobbing alongside it, ignoring the barrage of questions as he made haste to climb aboard.

'So did you see it?' asked Pascal, excitedly.

'Yes,' Jeannot replied, pushing his mask up onto his forehead and wiping the salt water from his moustache, 'I saw it, but it's not what you were hoping for. It's not a submarine.'

Looks of disappointment, anger and frustration spread across the faces of the three men.

'What was it then?' demanded Santorini, his eyes probing.

'It looks like some kind of coastal barge; the kind that's used to transport coal or ore. I can see how it might be mistaken for a submarine though.'

Santorini scratched the wiry tufts of his thick beard in annoyance.

'Is there any chance that the hatch which you showed us came from that vessel?' It was a question which made Pascal and Pierre suddenly take notice.

'I doubt that very much,' replied Jeannot. 'These types of vessels are simple in design. They're not built for rough sea passages. Besides, I'm pretty sure that it's the type of barge that we use around our shores.' Santorini grunted.

'I'm going down to take a look for myself,' he declared. Jeannot expressed only mild surprise.

'Suit yourself, but you're wasting your time.'

'That's for me to decide. Take me to the spot where you saw it.'

Jeannot shrugged and walked over to the helm. He guided the boat towards to the place where he judged the wreck to be lying and watched Santorini put on his equipment and jump over the side. While they were waiting for him to return, Jeannot remarked that Pascal kept rubbing his elbow joint.

'You got some pain there?'

'Yeah a little,' replied Pascal with a frown. 'I've got a numb feeling in my hand too.'

'That's odd. Can I see your computer?'

Pascal shrugged and handed over his wrist mounted computer. Jeannot took one look at the screen and breathed a sigh.

'You came up too fast.'

'I had to; otherwise we'd never have found the wreck again.'

'Well, you've put your health at risk for a worthless hulk of metal,' said Jeannot. 'Can you feel this?' he asked, as he began to poke and pinch Pascal's limbs. Just as he was about to deliver his prognosis, he heard Santorini shouting nearby and returned to the helm to retrieve him. There was a look of disgust on Santorini's face as he climbed aboard, throwing his equipment down heavily onto the deck. Jeannot was reluctant to approach him, but under the circumstances, he felt that there was little choice.

'We're going to have to call off the search for the rest of the day.'

Santorini stared at Jeannot in utter disbelief.

'Stop? Why in God's name should we stop now?' Jeannot swallowed and spoke with calm conviction.

'Because I believe that Pascal has the bends.'

'The bends? Nonsense! There's nothing wrong with you is there Pascal?'

'Well, there's a bit of pain, but it's not too bad; I think I'll be alright,' replied Pascal, sitting on the sponson, cradling his elbow.

'There's a good chance that the symptoms will get worse,' said Jeannot. 'It's your decision, but I would advise you to get him to a recompression chamber straight away.'

'Stand up and see if you can walk it off,' suggested Santorini.

Jeannot bit his lip, shaking his head in disbelief at Santorini's ignorance and lack of concern. He watched Pascal push himself to his feet with his left arm and then promptly stumble backwards.

'My legs seem to have gone weak,' he complained.

Santorini closed his eyes and held the bridge of his nose. 'OK, that's obviously not going to work; let's get him out of here and arrange to have him picked up.' Jeannot reached for the VHF handset.

'I've just received this surveillance report from the Brigades Nautiques,' said Lieutenant Lechaux, as he placed a document in front of *Capitaine* Villeneuve. 'Apparently Santorini and his men have now resorted to using unconventional and highly dangerous search methods.'

'Dangerous in what way?' asked *Capitaine* Villeneuve.

'Well it appears that they are towing each other along behind the boat, suspended beneath the water on a weighted line.'

'I see. That doesn't sound particularly safe does it?' commented Villeneuve.

'It's highly irregular according to our experts. And that's almost certainly why one of Santorini's men had an accident this afternoon.'

'Really? What happened?'

'I'm not exactly sure. The surveillance team picked up a distress call from *l'Espadon*. They were seeking assistance from the coastguard, for help with a suspected case of decompression sickness; a diving related emergency. The casualty was later airlifted to the recompression chamber in Ajaccio. I've just been in contact with the hospital and the Hyperbaric Physician on duty informed me that the person injured was Pascal Cavaille. He's undergoing recompression treatment as we speak, but they expect him to be discharged within the next couple of hours.'

'Interesting. Do you think that all this increased activity has anything to do with Perotta?'

'Somehow I doubt it. The surveillance team say that Santorini is well aware of the fact that he's being watched and apparently unconcerned.'

'Maybe he's being so blatant because he intends to salvage whatever it is he's looking for under the cover of darkness,' suggested Villeneuve. 'That's usually the way these things work.'

'Yes, that did cross my mind,' said Lecaux. 'Perhaps we should notify the Coast Guard and ask them to keep a close watch on the area after dark.'

'That's an excellent idea Lieutenant. Please see that it's done.'

Mike bought a copy of the newspaper and then proceeded to the gas merchant, where he had the slim caving cylinder filled with 60 bar of helium. After taking a detour through the back streets of Propriano he drove towards the *impasse* and parked the Citroen on the main road some distance away from the farmhouse. With the cylinder tucked tightly under his arm he made his way along the path which led to the rear of the farmhouse and slipped in through the back door. With time to spare before Monica and the others arrived, he read the newspaper, took a shower and then lay down on the bed exhausted. He closed his eyes and drifted off to sleep only to be woken an hour later when Monica entered the room.

'Oh, Mike. You gave me such a scare!' she said, startled.

'Sorry, I must have dropped off,' he said sheepishly.

'You just surprised me, that's all. I'm still not used to having someone in my room.'

'Is it a pleasant surprise at least?' Mike asked, his eyebrows raised.

Monica broke into a smile and came to sit beside him.

'I've had worse.'

Mike pulled her close and kissed her.

'I must be covered in sweat,' she said, pulling away self consciously. 'I really need to take a shower.'

'Don't worry. I love the smell of you, showered or not.'

'Well that's nice of you to say so, but I know which of the two I prefer,' she said, planting a rapid kiss on his lips. 'I'll only be a few minutes. Why don't you join Hubert and Bertie next door; they're taking a look at your U-boat.'

'Oh yeah? Perhaps I will,' he said, as he watched Monica getting undressed. 'I'm not in any great hurry though,' he said, grinning.

In playful mood, Monica pulled off her polo shirt and threw it at Mike's face before scuttling off to the bathroom. Mike sighed contentedly, threw on some clothes and then went to join Bertie and Hubert in the kitchen. He found them huddled around the laptop locked in animated discussion. Anna, who was busily rummaging through the contents of a cupboard, lifted her head and greeted him with a cheery 'Good Evening.'

Bertie and Hubert swivelled around in their chairs.

'Oh hi Mike...this is so great,' said Bertie excitedly, while pointing at the screen. 'I would like very much to dive this with you, but I think perhaps it is a little too deep for me.'

'Yes, it will be a very challenging dive,' agreed Mike. Bertie nodded regretfully.

'It's a shame...but perhaps if you have the possibility you could take some photographs for me, yes?'

'Actually, that's a very good idea Bertie. I could use Thomas' digital camera to take some shots of the interior so that we can study them later. And maybe you could get some exterior shots of the hull while I'm inside Hubert. We really need two cameras for that of course. Do you think there's any chance that we could borrow the field camera?'

'I don't know. I'd have to ask Monica...and you know what she's like.'

'I will talk to her with you,' offered Bertie. 'This is an unbelievable finding and it must be studied. I am sure that she will be understanding. I can also speak with the University if you want it.'

'Hey, hold on there a second Bertie; let's not get too carried away,' advised Mike. 'This discovery must remain a secret until we have positively identified the U-boat and found the right people to report it to. If its position is leaked too early it could be stripped clean before there's any chance to conduct any serious research on it. Also, I have a feeling that our friends from the *Sampiero Corso* would be less than understanding if they found out that we'd ruined their party.'

Bertie's brow knitted in concentration while Hubert translated for him. He finally acknowledged his understanding with a nod of the head.

'Yes...of course, it would be better to stay quiet, like for our *archäologische* finds.'

Anna appeared at the table with four tumblers and a jug of fresh juice. She spoke to Bertie and Hubert and then turned towards Mike with a shy smile.

'Would you like to drink something Mike?'

'Yes, thank you Anna,' he replied, helping himself from the tray. He smiled appreciatively and then turned towards Hubert.

'I've been doing quite a bit of research while you were at work today. This is definitely a Second World War U-boat of the type VIIB or VIIC. The two are almost identical, except that the VIIC is slightly longer due to a modification that was made to accommodate the newly developed sonar equipment. The VIIC were widely used in the Mediterranean and with major U-boat bases located in both La Spezia and Toulon they must have passed this area quite frequently. It's true that there weren't many U-boat losses recorded in this area, but operational accidents were not uncommon and there's always the possibility that this one simply slipped through the net.'

'Ah, I can see that the men have all become boys again,' said Monica as she entered the room, bringing the smell of scented body lotion and freshly washed linen with her.

'I'm afraid so,' said Hubert. 'In fact I'd invite you to join us, but we don't normally talk to girls.'

'Well that's not what I've been hearing,' she teased. Hubert shrugged and smiled.

'I'm sure that we can make an exception for you Monica,' said Mike. 'In fact I'd like your opinion on some new information which I've uncovered. I think I may have found the reason why the stern of the U-boat exploded with such violence.'

'I'm all ears,' said Monica as she pulled up a stool.

'Earlier today I discovered that both the VIIB and VIIC series had a stern torpedo tube in addition to the four located at the bow. The one ton torpedoes which they used were either kept in a locker under the deck plates or chained to the ceiling, from where they could be rapidly winched down into place. My guess is that your theory of a secondary explosion is correct and that the blast was the result of a detonating torpedo inside the hull.'

'A one ton torpedo?' whistled Hubert. 'That would have made one hell of a mess.'

'Yes, if a suspended torpedo of that capacity exploded inside the hull, it would certainly explain the extent of the damage which we observed,' agreed Monica, impressed by Mike's research.

'I'm glad you that you agree, but unfortunately the cause of the U-boat's demise won't get me any closer to identifying her and that's what I really set out to do. From what I've read, there are only a few items in the wreck which carry the U-boat's identification number: the ships log, spare machine parts and manufacturer's tags being the most obvious of them. Failing that, we'd have to try and find the name of one of the crew members.'

'This may sound stupid, but isn't the number of the vessel written on the hull?' asked Monica.

'Unfortunately not; that would have been too easy. At one time the U-boat numbers were actually painted on the conning tower, but that practice was quickly abandoned because it made them far too easy to spot.'

'Where do you hope to find the manufacturer's identification tags?' asked Hubert.

'From what I understand, they can be found on different types of instruments, the periscope being one of them, but the most obvious place is on the torpedo tube hatches. Once again the damage to the stern has eliminated any chance of finding the rear tube hatch and we have no way of knowing whether it will be possible to reach the forward ones.'

'So does that mean that you're counting on finding personal effects?'

asked Monica.

'I'm not counting on anything at present,' replied Mike. 'Every option has to be considered and that's just one of them. Most of the crew accommodation is forward of the control room anyway, so like the torpedo hatches, it's another unknown. I'm hoping that we might have some luck in the Petty Officer's quarters though, which will be accessible once we've managed to get past the electric motor compartment and traversed the diesel engine room. With a bit of luck, we might even be able to reach that section via the damage to the conning tower.'

'Um, do you have a plan of the wreck?' asked Hubert, 'because I'm finding this all a little hard to visualise.'

'Yes, sort of. I did a rough sketch in the library; here take a look.'

'That's better. So this is the control room is it?' asked Hubert, pointing to the large command section beneath the conning tower.

'Yes, that's right. And these are the P.O.'s quarters just next to it.'

'Through a watertight hatch,' commented Monica.

'Yes, that's obviously another concern.'

'Even if it's seized, we can still access that area through the engine rooms,' pointed out Hubert.

'Let's hope so,' said Mike.

'What about the section forward of the control room?' asked Monica.

'I'm ignoring that area for the moment. My first objective is to try to penetrate and explore the stern. Once I've done that, we can start to think about how to tackle the remainder of the wreck.'

'It sounds like a lot of dives to me,' said Monica. 'How do you plan to do all this without being seen?'

'I've got one or two ideas,' replied Mike.

'I'm not sure that I really want to hear the details,' said Monica. 'When are you planning to make a start?'

'Tomorrow. We'll dive in the early hours of the morning.'

Monica frowned and glanced at Hubert.

'I take it that you're involved in this?' Hubert shrugged and nodded.

'And what about work?'

Hubert began to rattle off an explanation in Swiss German.

'I'm sorry Monica, I should already have explained,' interrupted Mike. 'I spoke to Hubert without speaking to you first and I realise that was wrong. Look, I've planned an early start so that Hubert will have finished in plenty of time to join you for work. We'll be using my boat this time so there's no reason why we should delay you.'

Monica pursed her lips.

'Well apart from the fact that Hubert will be absent when we three are left to load everything, I think it's irresponsible of you to encourage him to put himself at risk. Don't expect my blessing.'

'This is my choice entirely,' said Hubert in Mike's defence. 'If anything, it's me who pushed *him* to let me take part.'

'Then you're both as bad as each other. Go ahead if you wish, but I want you fit and ready for work by nine,' she said with finality. 'If anyone needs me, I'll be in the lab.'

'Er...before you go. Is there any chance that I could borrow the underwater camera to take some shots of the sub?' asked Hubert.

Monica was about to launch into an angry tirade when Bertie spoke up in support of Hubert. After a short exchange Monica shook her head despairingly.

'Am I the only one who isn't completely obsessed with U-boats? OK...fine, you can borrow the camera, on the condition that if it gets lost or damaged, you replace it immediately. We cannot possibly work without it.'

'Of course Monica. I'll take personal responsibility for it,' Hubert assured her.

'I'll count on it,' replied Monica before turning swiftly on her heel and storming out of the kitchen. Bertie and Anna excused themselves and followed her to the laboratory.

'Well that was easy enough,' chuckled Mike.

Hubert's eyes drifted up to the ceiling and then settled on the folded newspaper that was lying on the table. He picked it up and stared dumbfounded at the photograph on the front page.

'That's him isn't it?'

'Er...yes,' replied Mike, looking around to make sure that they were alone. 'I should keep it to yourself if I were you.' Hubert began to read through the article.

'It looks like he got away then.'

'Yes, he seems to be making a habit of doing it. I'm not surprised that the press are starting to question the effectiveness of the Gendarmes. Still I suppose that one of them did at least get close.'

'Yeah, and ended up in hospital for his troubles by the sound of it,' said Hubert. 'Hey, check this out, the Gendarme leading the investigation is the same one who interviewed me: *Capitaine* Villeneuve.'

'You and me both,' said Mike.

'Ah, you got the old commander too did you?'

'Yeah, he was the one who first told me about Santorini.'

'He's quoted as saying here that the Gendarmes have been less effective than they might have been because of a security leak. What do you think that means?'

'It means that Santorini and his gang have inside connections.'

'What makes you say that?'

'Something that *Capitaine* Villeneuve said to me. He's been trying to convict Santorini and his gang for years, but he's never succeeded because the cases always get thrown out of court. The problem is that Santorini is a key figure in a separatist political organisation and he has contacts everywhere.'

'Even in the Gendarmes?'

'Why not? If his group can infiltrate the judicial and political circles, they can certainly get men inside the security services.'

'So do you think this guy Perotta will get away with it?'

'I doubt it; not after shooting a Gendarme. No one would be foolish enough to expose their political affiliations by attempting to protect Perotta now. I'm just glad that he's being forced to lie low. It will help to keep him out of our way.'

'Well I certainly don't want to make a habit of upsetting people like him,' said Hubert. 'We should just do a couple of dives on the U-boat and then turn the whole thing over to the authorities.'

'That's pretty much what I intend to do anyway. But first I want to identify the wreck and find out why Santorini is so desperate to find it. After that I'll be happy to pass the responsibility over to someone else.'

'I suppose that you've considered the fact that you won't be able to take any credit for the discovery?'

'Yes...but as it happens you gave me an idea when you suggested the memorial plaque. Thomas is going to take the credit for finding it.' Hubert eyed him warily.

'How will that work?'

'I'm thinking about asking Thomas' father to expose the U-boat's location along with supporting photographs and maybe even proof of her identity.'

'But surely that will put him in danger of reprisals?'

'Not if he says that he found the information amongst Thomas' personal effects.'

A smile crept across Hubert's face.

'What a brilliant idea Mike. You'd be out of the picture, Thomas would become a legend, and his father would look totally innocent. That's perfect revenge; Karma.'

'I take it you approve then?'

'Absolutely! Just think how much press coverage it'll get. Santorini will tear his hair out in frustration and the Gendarmes will be forced to re-examine the whole case.'

'That would be very satisfying, but before we get to that stage we've got some work to do and we need to get cracking. We've got the twin-sets to fill and there's a 6 litre cylinder which I need topping up until the pressure reaches exactly 200 bar.'

'Why does it need to be so accurate?' asked Hubert, surprised.

'Because it's got 60 bar of helium in it and I need a thirty percent mix.'

'Helium? Are you intending to dive with trimix?'

'Not if I can help it. I'm keeping it for emergency use so that I won't be hindered by narcosis if anything goes drastically wrong while I'm inside the wreck. I'm planning to mount it in the gap between the twin cylinders; come on I'll show you.'

Hubert followed Mike to the store room and watched him strap the thin cylinder into place using webbing bands and ties.

'OK, that seems secure enough. Fire up the compressor and we'll start filling the twins.'

Hubert nodded and began to connect up the high pressure hoses. While they were waiting for the cylinders to fill, Mike mounted his caving light onto the canoeing helmet and then looked for places to attach his newly acquired tools. The crowbar fitted under the straps of a dive knife which he kept on his right calf and the hammer, balanced the weight of it perfectly when mounted on his left. The wire-clippers, which needed to be more accessible, he attached to a retractable lanyard which could be secured to his harness.

'Are you sure you don't want to borrow my Swiss Army knife as well,' chuckled Hubert as he watched Mike distribute the extra equipment.

'Well unless I need to peel an apple, eat yoghurt or open a bottle of beer down there, I don't think that it will do me a lot of good.'

'Are you sure now? It's got a pair of scissors and tweezers too!'

'You Swiss really know how to put the fear of God into your enemies don't you? Thanks just the same.'

When the twin tanks were filled, Hubert carefully topped up the slim 6 litre cylinder and then re-checked the pressure in each.

'Right that's everything covered,' said Mike once he had run through his checklist. 'We'll keep all this stuff together and load the car in the morning. Now it's time to plan our profiles. Let's take another look at the laptop.'

Hubert followed Mike to the kitchen and sat beside him as he loaded his decompression software and pulled up a fresh file on the screen.

'Right, I'll customise the personal parameters to suit us both because I want to try to find a single profile that can be used for both air and trimix.'

'I like the look of this software,' said Hubert, impressed. 'It certainly beats working with dive tables.'

'It gives you a great deal more flexibility as well. It exploits the same algorithms as most dive computers,' Mike explained.

'So will my wrist-mounted computer give me the same result?'

'No, not entirely, because the model which you use is designed purely for air and since you'll be speeding up your decompression by using nitrox, your computer will start lagging behind. It can still serve as an effective back up though, because it will simply extend the profile beyond that which would normally be required to fully decompress.'

'Yes I see...I think.'

'Unfortunately I won't have the same luxury if I breathe trimix. The problem is that Helium is a lighter gas than nitrogen and moves in and out of the body tissues more rapidly. As a result, the first required stop for trimix is slightly deeper than it would be for air and consequently a standard wrist mounted computer would probably get me bent.'

'So how will we stay together if you have to make deeper stops?'

'I'm not yet sure that we can, but what I want to do is to plan the same deep stop on air that would be required for trimix and modify the following stages so that we can ascend together.'

'Won't that affect my decompression schedule?'

'It will extend it, but only marginally. Let's have a look.'

Mike entered the depth and time of the proposed dive and after selecting air as the primary gas, duplicated the file.

'Right, I've now got two plans with exactly the same parameters. I'll leave plan one as it is, but I'm now going to modify the primary gas in plan two so that it becomes a trimix blend with 30 percent helium.'

Mike tapped in the values and then clicked on the calculate button of both files. After a few seconds, an automatic decompression schedule appeared in each of them.

'Do you see the extra stop at 18 metres in plan two? That's to account for the faster rate of elimination of helium from the tissues. I'm now going to add that level to the air profile as a non-obligatory stop.' Mike modified plan one and hit the calculate button again.

'Look the 12 metre stop is now shorter for the air profile than it is for trimix, but that's no problem because I can simply extend it and recalculate.' Mike continued to experiment until he came up with a compatible profile.

'Excellent, this now seems to work fine Hubert. We've got a difference of just 3 minutes at the final 6 metre stop which makes our plan very simple; we'll both use this one profile and should the situation arise where I need to breathe trimix, we'll simply extend the last stop by 3 minutes so that we'll both be in the clear. Just a word of warning though, before we call it a day. If at any point things go badly wrong during the deep part of the dive and you're likely put your life at risk by attempting to save mine; think twice about it. And if there's any doubt in your mind, just remember one thing; if the roles were reversed, I'd look after number one.

'So how are you feeling now?'

'Not too bad. They stuck me in a metal coffin for a couple of hours and made me drink water until I almost pissed my pants, then they let me go. The doctor said that I should be OK now, but I can't dive for a few weeks.'

'What? That's means we're going to be two divers short now,' grumbled Santorini. Pascal nodded.

'I know, but he was insistent. I'm also supposed to stop drinking alcohol for a while.'

'Oh yeah? So what will it be...fruit juice?'

'Are you joking? I'll have a beer,' said Pascal, grinning.

'That's the Pascal I know,' laughed Santorini. 'Mathilde, a glass of white?'

'*S'il vous plait*,' replied Mathilde, standing silently beside her father.

'By the way, we went back and did a couple more sweeps after you left in the helicopter,' said Santorini, as he prepared the drinks.

'Did you find anything?'

'Yes and no. Pierre says that he saw something strange down there. Some kind of decking he thinks. We couldn't find it again, but it wasn't too far away from where the Englishman found the gauge. We're going to concentrate our search around there when we next get a chance.

'That sounds promising. Maybe we'll have better luck next week then.'

'Let's hope so.' Santorini jerked his head towards the door. 'Did you notice those two clowns hanging around outside?'

'No, I didn't.'

Santorini lowered his voice and glanced to his left. 'Don't look now, but I suspect that the misfit stood to your right is with them. I've insulted him plenty, but he still insists on hanging around. Let's retire to the kitchen. Are you ready Mathilde?'

'She's ready,' answered Pascal in her place. 'Come on Mathilde, I know you're keen to get this over with.'

Santorini lifted the bar hatch and escorted them into the back kitchen.

'Mathilde, close your ears for a minute please,' requested Santorini, when they were seated.

Mathilde sighed and pushed in the earphones of her MP3 player.

'Is Michel OK where he is?' asked Santorini.

'He's well enough. He'd prefer to be in the lodge of course, but it's just too risky now. Besides, he's slept in far worse places, I'm sure.'

'No doubt. It's unfortunate that he's out of action though,' lamented Santorini. 'We've got no one to keep an eye on the bay mid-week.' He chewed his lip reflectively and then glanced at Pascal. 'I don't suppose that you could do it?'

'That's really asking too much Jean-Claude. I have a farm to run and animals don't look after themselves you know. It's hard enough trying to find time at the weekend.'

'I figured as much, but I thought I'd ask anyway.'

'Sorry, but it's out of the question,' said Pascal firmly.

'Fair enough.' Santorini looked up and waved his hand in front of Mathilde's face. 'We're done. Let's listen to the recordings.'

Mathilde nodded and took out a notebook and pencil. Santorini lifted the recording device onto the table and pressed the playback button. Through the background hiss, the first conversation began to play. Mathilde frowned in concentration.

'It's English. The man says that he's found...something and then the woman asks what he means. The man says, what you think...it's there...lying at the bottom of the sea.' Pascal and Santorini exchanged worried looks as Mathilde continued.

'The woman asks if he's sure and if...someone called Hubert confirms it.'

'That's the tall archaeologist,' hissed Santorini.

'The man says that he does and that he's standing next to him with a...something on his face,' continued Mathilde. 'Then the man tells the woman not to go to bed, because he wants her to see it.'

Santorini frowned, staring silently into space.

'It sounds like the Englishman's found it,' said Pascal, with a look of disquiet on his face.

'It sounds like he's found something,' agreed Santorini, 'but it's not very clear what. Listen to the recording again Mathilde.'

Mathilde did as she was asked, but was unable to elaborate on her first interpretation.

'OK, just listen to the other calls,' growled Santorini.

Mathilde listened nervously to the other recordings, but they were of no interest.

'I don't like it,' muttered Pascal, when a beep marked the end of the days recording.

'Neither do I,' said Santorini, his eyes narrowing, 'It's too early to jump to any conclusions, but if he has found the wreck it may well work to our advantage.'

'How do you figure that?' asked Pascal, frowning.

'Mathilde, wait for us in the bar will you?' asked Santorini, while slipping a banknote towards her. He waited until she had left the room before turning towards Pascal.

'The thing is, we could spend hours fruitlessly searching for it by ourselves, undermanned and without the proper equipment, or we could just get the Englishman to take us to it.'

'But how can we do that? We don't even know where he is!'

'We just need to flush him out; get a nice tasty bit of bait to draw him into our trap.'

'I'm not following you.'

Santorini fixed Pascal with a stare of cold determination.

'Once we're certain that he's found it, we take the girl.'

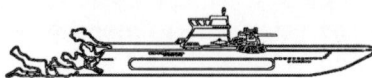

11

I t was bad enough eating cold food out of tin cans and sitting around for days on end in the same set of clothes. But the final indignity came when he ran out of toilet paper. He tried to light a cigarette to console himself, but it seemed that even that small luxury was to be denied him as the flame of his lighter flickered and died. He swore, threw it at a rock in disgust and pushed himself to his feet. He'd had enough of living like a wild animal, unwashed and unshaven, sleeping in a damp, cockroach infested cave and deprived of any contact with the outside world. In the growing darkness he stumbled down the hillside following the overgrown walking track which led to Pascal's farm. Ten minutes later he reached the shelter of a walled courtyard and rapped on a heavily weathered wooden door. He retreated into the shadows and waited.

'Who's there?'

'It's me,' Michel whispered hoarsely, when he saw Pascal's squat figure appear at the door.

'Who is it?' asked a female voice, deep within the house.

'It's no one, go back upstairs,' replied Pascal scathingly.

'Michel, what are you doing? I told you not to come down here unless there was an emergency.'

'There is; my cigarette lighter has packed up and I need some toilet paper.'

'Some emergency. Go and wait in the barn; I'll be out in a minute...and for God's sake keep out of sight!'

'Bring whisky,' Michel called out hoarsely, as he vanished into the cover of darkness.

When Pascal arrived at the barn, he found Michel lying prostrate on a bale of hay.

'Did you bring a lighter?'

Pascal threw a box of matches at him and watched him fumble in his haste to light a battered cigarette. Soon he was inhaling the fumes greedily.

'You're taking one hell of a risk coming down here,' growled Pascal, as he handed Michel a fresh roll of toilet paper and a half bottle of whisky.

'Yeah well, prison would be a step up from living like this. I bet they didn't even search the lodge anyway.'

'Yes they did. They had dogs with them as well, so it's fortunate for you that I thought to take you to the cave by tractor.'

'They'd be dead if they'd found me,' he said scornfully, as he unscrewed the cap from the bottle and swallowed a mouthful of whisky.

'Well I could have done without them crawling all over my land frankly. The wife was a nervous wreck this morning and she's been on tranquilisers all day. I just hope that you appreciate all this.'

'Don't forget that the reason why I'm here is because I've been doing all the dirty work,' barked Michel. 'Don't expect too much in the way of gratitude, because I'm the one who risks getting locked up, not you.'

Pascal sighed and stared at the floor.

'Jean-Claude talked about getting you away. He thinks it would be better if you left the island for a while.'

'There's no way that I'm going to leave Corsica,' scowled Michel. 'I'll see them all dead first.'

'Well the only other option is to get you into the mountains. You could join up with one of the militia groups and live under their protection. Jean-Claude says that he can arrange it.'

Michel scowled and threw away his cigarette butt. Pascal chased after it and stamped it out. 'Jesus Michel, this is a barn!'

Michel rolled his eyes and proceeded to light another one.

'Is there any news on the sub?'

'We have news, but it's not good. There's a possibility that the Englishman has found it.'

'What do you mean, there's a *possibility* he found it?' spat Michel.

'We listened to the recordings again this evening. The Englishman has found something out there, but we're still not sure what. Obviously there's a chance that it's the U-boat.'

Pascal saw the hatred burning in Michel's eyes.

'Tell Jean-Claude that I'll get the truth out of him one way or another; I've got nothing to lose now. I'll torture him until he begs me to kill him and when I get the truth out of him, I'll continue until he gets his wish.'

The night was moonless as Mike guided the orange RIB towards the glow of a flashlight on the beach ahead. Water dripped from his wetsuit after a brief nocturnal dip, but he still felt the benefit of the brisk walk over the rocky headland. When the keel of the RIB ground into the soft sand, he stepped out into ankle deep water and under the weak glow of the flashlight, helped Hubert to load the equipment on board. Soon the small RIB was heading back up the channel again, its navigation lights extinguished as Mike and Hubert disappeared into the darkness of the small bay. The outline of the promontory was barely visible as they emerged into the open sea and encountered the rhythmic jarring of an easterly swell.

'How are you feeling?' asked Mike, as Hubert eased the throttle forward.

'As well as can be expected at this ungodly hour.'

'What I mean is; are you still happy doing this?'

'At this present moment, no, but as soon as we're in the water, I'll be fine.'

'We won't be going over the side until dawn is about to break anyway, and you'll be surprised at how quickly the light intensity grows after that, even at depth.'

'It can't be any worse than diving with the iron mask.'

'Well maybe you'll now appreciate how useful those exercises were,' said Mike. 'Just be aware of the added complication that narcosis can bring.'

'I got plenty of experience of that in the bars of Zurich when I was a student,' chuckled Hubert.

'Well you'll get more than just a sore head if you lose it down there,' warned Mike.

'I'll be fine,' Hubert replied dismissively. 'Stand by with the anchor. We're getting close to the waypoint.'

Mike felt a shiver of excitement percolate his body. It was hard to believe that in half an hour's time he would be exploring the interior of an unexplored German U-boat. Three weeks ago the idea would have been impossible to conceive, but then things had changed dramatically since then.

Hubert nosed the RIB ahead until the GPS waypoint alarm began to sound. Mike, standing at the bow, immediately deployed the anchor and watched snaking loops being dragged downwards into the blackness which lay beneath. When the line went slack, Mike paid out another fifty metres and Hubert went astern to set the anchor in. Once all their equipment and instruments had been thoroughly checked, Mike and Hubert ran through the final details of the plan while they waited for the fist signs of the approaching dawn. Soon a band of lighter sky was just discernable over the mountains to the east as the darkness began to surrender its hold.

'I think it's time to make a move,' declared Mike as he flicked on a small pen light.

'OK, let's start kitting up,' agreed Hubert. There was a burst of activity as Mike and Hubert slipped into their harnesses and clipped on their sling tanks aided only by the glowing beam of the tiny penlight. Mike strapped on the helmet, making certain that the power cable was secured well out of the way of his regulator hoses. He touched the hammer, crowbar and wire clippers to forge their positions into his mind and then let his fingers renew their familiarity with the rest of his equipment. Soon, he and Hubert were sat motionless, facing each other on opposite sides of the RIB, a regulator held in one hand at the ready. They fixed each other in silent anticipation.

'Are you ready?' asked Mike.

'I think I need to use the toilet.'

'What?'

'Just joking...let's go.'

Hubert smothered the glare of his primary flashlight against his chest and rolled backwards into the dark embrace of the sea. After the initial disorientation, he saw the distorted glimmer of stars in the night skies above. A faint ring of blue on the outer edge of his circle of vision marked the rapid approach of the coming dawn. Mike turned his lamp beam on at the lower power setting and Hubert pointed his flashlight downwards to protect his night vision. After a brief round of preliminary checks they swam towards the anchor line and used it to guide themselves down into the black void.

As they passed the thirty metre mark Mike strained his eyes to see if there was anything visible beneath him. The beam of his head-mounted lamp merely illuminated the omnipresent fog of plankton and the descent line, disappearing into the darkness below. Brief flashes of light were intermittently reflected back from the flanks of scattering seabream and the iridescent eyes of a small shoal of errant squid. Mike hit 45 metres and was still looking downwards, when a solid mass unexpectedly came into view beside him. He slowed his ascent and put his lamp beam on full power before playing it along the face of the uneven structure. It was covered in a profusion of vibrant growth and Mike quickly realised that it was the face of one of the rock ridges which they'd seen on the sounding image. He checked to make sure that Hubert was still behind him and followed the rope and chain along the base of the ridge until he spotted the anchor, embedded firmly in a patch of sand and rock. Dismayed to see no trace of a wreck nearby, Mike placed his hand over his lamp lens to ease the backscatter. He stared into the distance all around, but saw nothing. Knowing that it would be imprudent to start searching randomly, Mike clipped his reel off onto the anchor chain and paid out fifteen metres of line in an easterly direction.

After a further check on Hubert, he began to swing in an arc, clockwise around the anchor. On full beam the head-mounted lamp picked out the rocky features well and Mike tried to resist the temptation to increase his speed. Scanning back along the line and out away from the centre of the circle as he progressed, Mike watched the compass needle slowly swing around on its axis. He had just passed over the top of a ridge and was about to check the time when a solid mass suddenly appeared in front of him. With calm composure, he played his torch over a textured structure, the surface of which was far too regular to be natural. Beneath the mass of clinging anemones, encrusting sponges and hydroids Mike realised that it was a torn fishing net and conscious of the danger which it presented, he quickly turned around to warn Hubert. Before he got the chance, Hubert grabbed his shoulder and began making squealing noises into his regulator. At first Mike feared that Hubert had been overcome by the effects of narcosis, but then it became apparent that he was trying desperately to draw his attention towards something. Mike followed the direction of Hubert's flashlight beam until his own head lamp illuminated something solid lying just a few metres beneath him. Looking up in surprise, Mike suddenly remembered the torn fishing net which Monica had identified on the sounding image and the reality of what he was staring at finally dawned upon him. His head began to jerk in all directions as he excitedly traced the smooth outlines of the steel hull of a German U-boat.

He fought to contain his burgeoning excitement, increasingly conscious that time was ticking away. The fishing net obscured the features of the bridge, making it difficult to tell with any accuracy in which direction lay the stern. A wrong decision at this point could prove costly and Mike paused, trying to think the problem through under the distracting effects of narcosis. In his mind's eye he pictured the layout of the vessel on the laptop screen with its bow pointing north-west and its stern towards the south-east. In sudden understanding, he swung his body around until he was lying parallel with the axis of the submarine. The lubber line of his compass settled between the south and east cardinal points, confirming without any further doubt that the stern was now lying dead ahead. He beckoned to Hubert and then began to swim away from the conning tower, using the deck beneath to guide him.

Brightly coloured gorgonian sea fans, sponges and bryozoans clung to the decks which had been their home for over half a century. A silver-grey conger slithered silently out of sight while schools of red striped cardinals scattered as the lamp beam encroached upon their territory. A diffused blue light was now starting to reach down to the wreck from above, picking out the details of its sleek form. Ahead of them, the sudden appearance of buckled deck plates and huge tongues of splayed metal announced their imminent arrival at the stern. Mike checked his watch and saw that there were now just 16 minutes left in which to attempt the penetration. He noticed that he was running short of line and quickly exchanged reels with Hubert. Immediately afterwards, Mike dropped his sling tank down amongst the scattered wreckage, clipped a line to it and promptly disappeared into the ragged remains of the stern. Thin columns of exhaled bubbles began to stream upwards, escaping from fractures in the damaged hull, like an inverted sieve. Hubert looked back along the decks towards the conning tower and was surprised to see that it was now visible, bathed eerily in the diffused grey-blue light which was filtering down from above. He decided that it was time to do a little exploring of his own and promptly set off back along the decks, smiling as his confidence grew.

Inside the wreck, Mike soon came up against the first obstacle. As he had suspected, the starboard electric motor was buckled upwards and inwards, blocking the passageway and restricting the access to a small gap on the port side. It looked big enough to squeeze through, but there were conduits and loose wires hanging ominously from the deckheads. After taking a quick snapshot of the area, Mike located his wire clippers and began cutting away at the loose cables while carefully bending pipes out of the way. He worked with the reel clipped to his harness and one hand gripping a valve wheel so that his fins did not disturb the light sediment. Soon he was able to squeeze into the narrow gap, using two fingers to pull himself smoothly through to the other side. Recalling his memorised image of the wreck's layout, he let himself glide horizontally, pushing away from a valve wheel and dropping head first towards an opening in the bulkhead. On the other side, he took his first look at the diesel engine room, virtually undamaged, but littered with debris and a shroud of fine silt. He took a snapshot of the interior, its dull grey-brown appearance, typical of a long submerged vessel.

Tiny shrimp scattered away from the invading light, the pink globes of their eyes retreating into the protection of dark recesses. A startled grouper dived into an impossibly tiny gap between the engine and the hull with an ease which exposed Mike's clumsiness. Skirting around a cluster of hanging wires, Mike saw a dome protruding from the thick layer of silt which lay between the twin diesel engines. He fanned it gently with his hand as he passed over it, to reveal what appeared to be a white porcelain bowl. Intrigued, he attempted to pull it free and felt his thumb sinking into a circular recess. The sediment began to fall away and when Mike saw what he was holding, he recoiled in horror and withdrew his hand. Empty eye sockets and a set of white teeth, smiled back at him from the thick carpet of silt. With his pulse racing, he instinctively wiped his hand on his thigh as if the curse of death might somehow be contagious. The sound of marching bands suddenly began to play in his head together with shouts of *Sieg Heil* over the amplified rantings of *Der Führer*. Mike recognised the signs of narcosis and took a few seconds to slow down his heart rate and regain control of his faculties. The aural hallucination gradually faded away and noting that there were only twelve minutes remaining on his schedule, he pushed on.

A large moray eel stared at him from the gap between the two engines, its jaws opening and closing to reveal a set of razor sharp teeth. Mike slowly continued his approach, watching its reaction closely, until with a wriggle of its muscular body it retreated effortlessly into an opening in the deck plates. At the far end of the diesel engine room he came across a partially closed hatch in the bulkhead which separated him from the Petty Officer's quarters beyond. He tried to open it by hand, but the hinges were seized by years of corrosion. Reaching down to his right calf, he extracted the crowbar and inserted it into the gap. A few strong pulls were enough to overcome the resistance and send a cloud of dense, reddish brown particles billowing outwards into the water. He felt something fragile collapse at the other side of the bulkhead as he wrenched the hatch open and through the brown fog his light picked out a set of white ribs, a pelvis and yet another skull. This time Mike was better prepared for the signs of lost souls and slipped through the hatch without a second glance.

More bones protruded from the silt around him, confirming that he was now in the Petty Officers quarters, a place where he might find some clue as to the identity of the vessel. He took three photographs of the interior from left to right and then glanced at his watch. Nine minutes remained. He began to look around with renewed vigour, examining several objects which were half buried in the silt. There were things which seemed oddly out of place on a submarine and he puzzled over the presence of a German infantry helmet and a mobile radio pack. From a detritus covered shelf he recovered a small square object and in the light of his headlamp saw that it was a silver cigarette lighter. He scratched the scale from the sides of it and uttered a cry of triumph when he saw that it was engraved. Eager to press on and make the most of his remaining time, he pocketed it and stared deeper into the hull. At the far end of the compartment, a hatch appeared in his headlight beam and from his memory of the layout, Mike knew that it was the only thing which separated him from the control room and a possible point of exit. He tried to turn the locking wheel of the watertight hatch, but like the previous one, it was sealed by years of corrosion. The seconds were ticking away rapidly and Mike knew that there would no longer be time for delicacy if he was to achieve the final objective of the dive. Emboldened by the knowledge that his return route through to the stern was now clear, he prised the lip of the hatch away with the crowbar and hammered at the locking wheel. It shook as the heavy blows rained down upon it and flakes of rust and brown smoke cascaded out of the seals. Mike felt the wheel loosening and after a few more heavy hammer blows, the locking mechanism finally gave way. Before he had time to congratulate himself, something came crashing down behind him, the line from his reel pulled up tight and the visibility suddenly plummeted to nothing.

Hubert was awestruck by the sheer scale of the U-boat. Gliding back towards the conning tower, he felt like pinching himself as he admired the perfect lines of the hull, projecting from the obscurity as if emerging from another world. Lost in the emotion of the occasion, he had to constantly remind himself that he was merely a temporary visitor in a potentially hostile environment. It was too easy to forget when the subtle effects of narcosis nurtured over-confidence.

With some reluctance, Hubert turned his attention towards the tasks which he'd been set. On reaching the starboard side of the conning tower he quickly located the damage which they had first identified on the sounding image. A dark opening at the base of the tower was surrounded by jagged tongues of protruding metal which had ripped into the fishing net and now held it fast. Hubert cut away large sections of it with his knife and let them drop harmlessly to the sea floor below.

Once the debris had been cleared, Hubert could appreciate the extent of the damage which the explosion had caused. Although there was a huge gaping tear in the outer hull, he soon discovered that it was only a relatively small elongated opening in the inner hull which had compromised the safety of the vessel. He aimed his flashlight beam into the dark mouth-like opening and picked out a ladder disappearing down into the darkness of the control room below. To gauge the size of the opening, he put his hand against it and found that it was just over four fingers wide. He realised that Mike would have no chance of fitting through it, even without his bulky equipment.

After locating the main hatch and trying without success to open it, he spent a further couple of minutes searching fruitlessly for an alternative entrance. He gave up, unclipped the camera and took a quick snapshot of the damaged area before turning his attention towards the impressive 37mm deck gun which he spied a few meters away in the direction of the bow. With no one around to see him, he found it impossible to resist the temptation to position himself at the controls and fire at an imaginary fighter plane, swooping down from above. To his great surprise a solid form did appear in the line of his sights and then promptly disappear into the gloom. He lifted his head and peered into the void, unsure if his mind was playing tricks with him. The shadow appeared again; closer this time - and the sight of an asymmetrical caudal fin left Hubert in no doubt as to what he was staring at. The slender bodied shark turned to make an exploratory incursion and Hubert was suddenly starkly aware that the only protection which the deck gun could now afford him, was that of a rudimentary barrier. The two metre blue shark cautiously began to circle him, its huge dark eyes scrutinising him as intensely as its olfactory, electromagnetic and lateral line sensors. Hubert remained motionless, studying its behaviour and watching for any signs of aggression. He was well aware that a blue shark should be treated with caution, especially if the observer had inadvertently intruded upon its territory. And there was no doubt in his mind that for a pelagic shark, the rich pickings of a wreck would certainly be worth fighting for.

Mike could barely see his hand in front of his mask. Working slowly but deliberately, he replaced his tools, tied the reel to the locking handle of the hatch and retraced the line backwards until his hand came up against something solid. He soon realised that a heavy fixture had fallen down onto the line and trapped it. With his right hand gripping the safety line, he began to explore the obstruction with his left. His impression was that it was some sort of metal case and to his consternation it proved far too heavy to lift. The daunting reality of his predicament fully hit home when he reached beyond the obstruction and found that it was lying directly in front of the hatch, effectively blocking his retreat. As he struggled to drag it clear, nitrogen narcosis began to fuel his anxiety and he realised that he was in danger of losing control of the situation. In a moment of lucidity, he remembered the emergency trimix cylinder and quickly located the regulator that was attached to his right shoulder.

The first breath brought cold logic to a mind that was on the verge of meltdown. He took a few seconds to think the problem through and consider his options. There was still a chance that he could escape from the conning tower once he had opened the hatch and he reasoned that if nothing else it would at least give the sediment in the P.O.'s quarters a chance to settle. In grim determination he followed the line back to the reel, unclipped it and then held the hatch's locking wheel firmly in both hands. With an almighty effort he wrenched the mechanism free and used the crowbar to break the hold of the watertight seal. The hatch creaked open and Mike was able to slip through the opening and emerge into the comparative stillness of the control room. The floor of its interior had the appearance of a mass grave, littered as it was with the bleached bones of long dead submariners that glowed eerily in the light of his lamp. The sight was by no means reassuring, but Mike had no time to dwell on the misfortune of others. His eyes were quickly drawn towards the mass of wires, conduits and instruments that were hanging loosely from the starboard side of the control room.

Deep in the midst of them was an oval shaped patch of blue light which clearly marked a perforation in the hull. Mike gauged the size of the aperture with his hand and swallowed his disappointment when it proved too small to serve as a viable escape route. After a vain attempt to widen it with the crowbar, he reluctantly abandoned the idea and moved on to his next option; the main hatch. At the top of the conning tower, it was easy enough to find, but when Mike tried to turn the locking wheel it resolutely refused to oblige. Heavy hammer blows advanced him no further and it was only when he noticed a glimpse of daylight penetrating a crack in the seal that he understood the reason why. The hatch's locking pins had been deformed by the blast and there wasn't the slightest hope of retracting them. Mike's heart sank, knowing that his survival now depended on his ability to remove the obstacle in the P.O.'s quarters and return the way he had come.

For the first time since he'd entered the wreck, Mike began to have real doubts about his ability to leave it alive. His thoughts turned towards Thomas and Monica, with the desperate feeling that he had failed them both. If only he'd been willing to move on and stop trying to prove a point, he could be lying comfortably next to Monica at that very moment instead of waiting to die, trapped inside the bowels of a dark, metal coffin. Wracked with guilt and self-pity he thought about writing a final note of apology to Monica, when from the back of his mind he recalled something that a survival instructor had once told him:

In a seemingly desperate situation there is one overriding factor which will determine who will make it through the ordeal and who will not...and that, quite simply, is the will to survive. If you ever find yourself staring death in the face, don't ever give up hope, because if you do, you're already as good as dead.

Mike suddenly felt anger burning somewhere deep inside his chest. He visualised the face of Santorini and focused the hatred which he felt for the man, channelling it into his mind and body. With an unhurried determination he pushed himself down the ladder and reeled back towards the hatch. As he passed over the floor of the control room, a skull with a broken eye socket stared up at him through the silt. He stopped in sudden surprise when he saw the collar of an intact uniform beneath the jaw of the skull. There were two metal letters attached to it in the form of double bolts of lightning and Mike understood their significance immediately. But intriguing as the presence of SS personnel on board a U-boat was, he had no time to contemplate the matter further. Moving swiftly on, he reeled back into the P.O.'s quarters and was relieved to see that the fog of suspended silt had partially lifted. He returned to the obstruction and in the growing clarity saw that it was a large metal cabinet which had broken free from the wall and collapsed to the ground. Planting both feet firmly on the deck, he dug his fingers into the silt beneath it and prepared to lift. He felt human bones crushing beneath his fins as he took the strain, but by now he was beyond all care. After taking a deep breath and focusing all his strength in his arms and legs he pulled with all his might. His muscles burned with the effort, but nothing moved. Not even a fraction.

Hubert watched for telltale signs of an arching back, a lowering of the pectoral fins and erratic swimming movements, but there was nothing in the shark's behaviour to suggest an aggressive intention. As his confidence grew, Hubert left what little protection the gun mounting afforded him and cautiously swam towards the bow. The shark loitered for a moment and then with a sudden flick of its tail, vanished into the shadowy obscurity with a speed which reflected its reputation as one of the fastest fish in the ocean. Hubert remained alert as he progressed along the forward deck, but there were no further sightings of the shark.

When he arrived at the bow, he stood upright on the deck and turned to look back towards the conning tower. It was barely visible, but the sight of the slender bow, emerging ghost-like from the grey-blue mist, was simply stunning. After recording the image with the field camera, he let himself fall back off the bow and executed a neat backward somersault until he was upright again, hovering in front of the torpedo doors. He took a snapshot of them and was surprised to hear a rhythmic clanging sound coming from somewhere deep inside the hull. A crazy idea passed through his mind - perhaps one of the crew members was still alive, trapped inside the hull of the wreck. He soon rejected the absurd notion, but try as he might he could not dispel the regular pinging sound that was careering around his head. After pondering several explanations through the background fog of narcosis, a worrying thought suddenly occurred to him. If the sound really was a desperate cry for help and not a narcosis induced hallucination, then the only person who could be making it was Mike. He glanced at his watch in alarm and seeing that there were only seven minutes of bottom time remaining, immediately began to work his way back towards the stern. If Mike was in trouble, he had to act quickly while there was still a chance of returning safely to the surface.

A minute later Hubert found himself peering into the dark interior of the wreck, not entirely sure if what he was about to do was prudent. Mike's earlier words of warning echoed around his head and yet he reasoned that his gas supply was adequate, the route would by now have been cleared of obstacles and there was a line laid down which would guide him safely through the wreck. With only five and a half minutes of bottom time remaining, there was no room for deliberation. Hubert dropped his sling tank, launched himself into the damaged stern section and lost no time in squeezing past the dislodged electric motor. Within seconds he was following the line downwards and gliding through the hatch which led to the diesel engine room. The sight of the skull smiling up at him from between the two imposing engines appeared ominous, but Hubert refused to be discouraged and pushed on with gritty resolve. On reaching the next hatch he was surprised to see puffy clouds of silt billowing out from it. The lifeline became unusually tight between his fingers and he could see that it was being pulled down against the lower lip of the seal. To get a better look at it, he reached his flashlight into the opening and was surprised when it came up against something solid. There was a small gap at the top and when Hubert turned off his flashlight he could see the glow of Mike's headlamp moving around behind it. Realising to his horror that Mike was trapped inside the next compartment, he tried to signal his presence, but at that moment the gap closed and the light disappeared altogether.

The situation clearly required technique rather than brute force. As Mike was wracking his brains for a solution, he suddenly thought about the huge stone megaliths which were dotted around the island. The people who had erected them did not have the benefit of modern machinery; they had achieved their astonishing feats by exploiting the scant resources which were available to them. Drawing inspiration from their example, he quickly amassed a collection of loose objects together and placed them on the floor within reach.

With the crowbar levered against the hammer and jammed under the cabinet, he managed to raise it a few centimetres. He picked up a rifle which he'd found nearby, pushed the barrel into the gap and then levered it up against a radio pack. The metal cabinet was lifted high enough for him to ram an infantry helmet beneath it and support its weight. With both hands free, he turned the radio pack upright and levered against it once more. The gap opened further and he was able to prop the underside of the cabinet up with the crowbar. Now he pushed the upturned radio pack into the larger end of the gap and while levering the rifle against his thigh, he slowly edged it deeper until it was almost half way along the underside of the fallen cabinet. Once again the visibility started to deteriorate and Mike struggled to find objects of a sufficient size to permit him to continue his levering technique. With the cabinet now propped up safely, he decided that it was time to take a risk.

He slipped off his harness, laid the twin set down beside him and with just a regulator in his mouth, squatted down under the raised end of the cabinet. Jamming his shoulders against the underside, he locked his elbows and began to flex his thigh muscles. He felt the cabinet lift and then settle down again on the radio pack. Drawing in a deep breath he prepared to push harder than he had ever pushed in his life. In his minds eye he pictured the scowl of Santorini, the sneer of Perotta and his friend Thomas trapped and bleeding inside the wreckage of the silver Peugeot. Tapping into the anger which had been lying dormant inside him, he pulled the regulator from his mouth and hit the mental detonator which commanded every muscle and sinew in his body to explode in unison. Like a firing piston, his shoulders extended upwards, pushing the cabinet backwards until it pivoted on its base and slammed back against the wall. As it did so, Mike was surprised to see a light and a torso appearing through the hatch at his feet. Before he knew what was happening, Hubert was there standing by his side, supporting the cabinet and urging him to put his equipment back on. Mike, keen to recuperate his precious gas supply, did not argue. As he moved towards his abandoned cylinders, the door of the cabinet fell open and a strange object fell out onto the floor. It looked like some kind of swim aid and Mike stared at it in curiosity as he replaced the regulator in his mouth and strapped on his harness. Once everything was secure, he located the reel and was just about to reel back through the hatch when he sucked on an empty cylinder.

The coastguard duty officer lifted his eyes from the crossword puzzle that had kept him occupied for the last half hour and listened intently as a call came in over the radio. He quickly pulled a notepad towards him, found a fresh page and answered the call.

'*Marie-Lou, Garde Côtière - à vous.*'

The skipper of the trawler Marie-Lou pressed the transmit button and reported the presence of an unoccupied boat which he'd spotted anchored offshore without lights.

The coastguard officer probed the trawler skipper for the coordinates of the abandoned vessel and then entered them into his computer. A waypoint marker appeared on his digital AIS chart alongside the transponder signal of the Marie-Lou. To his surprise they both fell within an area marked by a red circle and an attached dialogue box. He read the information, raised his eyebrows and with a shrug, cleared his throat and pressed the transmission button on his microphone.

'*Marie-Lou, Marie-Lou, Garde Côtière.*'

'*Garde Côtière, Marie-Lou,*' the skipper acknowledged.

'*Marie-Lou,* we have recorded your message and will take all the necessary action. Your assistance will not be required on this occasion. Many thanks for your call. Out.'

The duty officer read through the attached note once more and then with a sigh, threw his newspaper to one side and made a call to customs.

Mike cursed, having completely forgotten that he was still breathing trimix from the small sling cylinder. In mid-breath he switched back to his air supply and clipped off the redundant trimix regulator. He breathed in cautiously at first, knowing that a surge of narcosis would ensue after being temporarily relieved of its effects. Once he'd acclimatised, he began to reel in the slack line and wind himself towards the hatch. He spotted the abandoned rifle which he'd used as a lever and jammed it into the gap at the foot of the cabinet to keep it from falling forwards again. Hubert cautiously eased his weight from it and after a rapid exchange of signals, Mike urged him to return through the hatch. He pulled himself towards it and Mike kept the reel line clear of his fins as he slipped through the opening. Mike's eyes were again attracted to the strange swim aid which had fallen from the cabinet. He knew that he ought to disregard it, but curiosity got the better of him and in a split second decision he stashed it under his arm and quickly reeled himself out through the hatch.

Hubert was waiting for him in the diesel engine room and pointing urgently at his watch. For the first time since leaving the control room Mike was able to check his timer and was alarmed to see that they were now just thirty seconds away from the end of their planned bottom time. Hubert was already on the move when he looked up again and Mike decided to abandon the reel and simply follow the lifeline out. Ahead of him, Hubert glided swiftly through the next hatch, wriggled past the obstruction in the electric motor room and finned straight out into clear blue water. After a quick glance to confirm that Mike was following, Hubert recuperated his abandoned camera and detached the remaining reel from a rusting metal case, lying outside the wreck. Mike swam past him and unclipped the lifeline from his sling tank before tying it off around the exposed propeller shaft. Not wishing to waste a second more than was absolutely necessary, he looped his hand through the swim aid, grabbed hold of the sling tank valve and signalled to Hubert his readiness to make an immediate ascent.

Within a fraction of a second their buoyancy wings were inflated and they simultaneously left the sea floor. Mike hunched over to clip his sling tank to his harness and was surprised to see, a dark shape come suddenly hurtling towards him from the wreck. It took a second for him to register what it was; and when he did, he could only stare in bemusement as the blue shark spiralled up towards him, circled at a cautious distance and then shot off into the shadows like a vanishing spectre. Mike turned towards Hubert in astonishment and was met by a shrug and a smile. Hubert beckoned to Mike to stay close as he ascended in a rising arc, still clutching the reel that was attached to the anchor chain. Mike was impressed by Hubert's quick thinking, aware that by keeping the line vertical he would prevent them from drifting away from the site during their lengthy decompression schedule. His resourcefulness reaped instant rewards when they reached their first stop, and could see the underside of the RIB silhouetted against the dawn sky right at the limit of their vision. They switched to breathing nitrox just under a minute behind schedule and slowly moved towards it. Once they reached the anchor line, Hubert secured the reel to it and signalled to Mike to ascend to the next stop. While they waited for their bodies to adjust to the decreasing pressure, Mike had time to reflect on his terrifying ordeal. He felt delayed nausea as he replayed the events in his mind, knowing just how close to disaster he had come. Probing his actions and decisions, he searched for the vital mistake which had nearly cost him his life, but on reflection, he simply had to accept that even with the best planning and preparation there was always an element of risk when exploring a new wreck. If he was guilty of any negligence, it was to forget that he had been breathing trimix from a cylinder that was only intended for short term use. Still, all in all he could count himself lucky; he had remained calm under very difficult circumstances and improvised an efficient if rudimentary means of escape.

When they reached the 6 metre stop Mike studied the strange swim aid that was hanging loosely from his sling cylinder. On closer inspection it appeared to be some kind of inflatable life vest, although unlike any other which he'd come across. Hubert watched in growing curiosity as Mike examined the brass fittings, rubber mouthpiece and miniature cylinder that formed an integral part of it. As Mike was attempting to wipe a layer of grime from some writing on the rubber tubing, Hubert quickly intervened and scribbled an explanatory note on his slate.

Try not to touch it. We'll clean it up back at the lab. What is it anyway?
Mike wrote a reply .
It looks like some kind of breathing equipment.
Hubert nodded and continued his underwater correspondence.
I found something too!
He reached into a pocket, took out a coin and carefully scraped the surface of it with his knife. He then passed it to Mike, who turned it over in has hand in amazement. Although the coin was dulled by its long immersion, the bright flash of yellow metal where Hubert had marked it left him in no doubt as to its composition. When he looked up, Hubert was holding a slate out in front of him with a single word scrawled across it in large letters: *Gold!*

Before they had time to congratulate each other, the sound of a fast approaching motor launch made their blood run cold. Staring anxiously up at the surface they saw a large motor vessel surge past overhead and churn the water white as it came to a throbbing halt next to the RIB.

As soon as Mike's decompression schedule was complete, he distanced himself from the anchor line and slowly began to rise to the surface. With his eyes fixed firmly on the keel of the launch, he used breath control to momentarily break the surface and catch a discreet glimpse of the intruding vessel, before dropping below the water again. The motor launch was large, modern and well equipped. A French flag was flying at the stern, a machine gun was mounted threateningly on the bow and painted clearly on each flank was a single identifying word: *Douanes*. Mike recognised the word from airport immigration and quickly made the connection; it was a customs vessel. He breathed more easily, relieved that it was not Santorini's gang who had intercepted them. They were safe from harm, it appeared, although not entirely off the hook. A customs inspection now looked to be a distinct possibility and they were presently carrying compromising material.

He returned to Hubert's side and wrote a long message on his slate explaining the need to surface without anything which they had recuperated from the wreck. From his harness pocket, Mike pulled out a small mesh collecting bag and put the breathing device and the cigarette lighter into it. Hubert took a quick admiring look at the lighter and then tipped in a whole handful of gold coins. Mike shot a surprised glance at Hubert and saw him break into a wide smile. Shaking his head in astonishment, he placed Thomas' camera into the bag and held his hand out for Hubert's. He was met by a questioning look. Mike wrote a quick note on his slate explaining that customs would probably confiscate the film. With Monica's warning still fresh in his ears, Hubert sighed and reluctantly placed the camera into the bag. Once Mike had sealed it and tied it firmly to the anchor line, he gave the signal to ascend. They swam towards the RIB and surfaced empty-handed beside it. Above them, leaning over the rail of the motor launch, was a stern faced Customs Officer and a broody, shaven headed marine with a sub machine gun held across his chest.

'Put both hands in the air,' ordered the Customs Officer. Mike and Hubert did not argue.

'Now make your way slowly towards the port side of this boat.'

A small skiff appeared from the opposite side of the vessel and a marksman tracked their progress through the sight of his rifle.

'Pass up your equipment...slowly...and then come aboard,' ordered the officer.

Mike and Hubert handed up their masks, fins and sling tanks and then climbed the sturdy access ladder, straining under the weight of their equipment. The bearded Customs Officer shouted instructions to the men in the skiff, who immediately went to tie up next to the orange RIB. Mike and Hubert were allowed to sit down on a bench and take off their twin sets. The officer addressed two nearby marines.

'Search them!'

Once they were relieved of their cylinders, they were ordered to stand up and take off their wetsuits. Every fold of their equipment was searched and after several uncomfortably tense minutes, the two marines stepped back in turn and shook their heads.

'They're clean sir,'

The Customs Officer pursed his lips and flicked his eyes between Mike and Hubert.

'Can you please explain to me what you are doing diving in deep water over a kilometre from shore at this godforsaken hour of the morning?'

'I'm teaching a technical diving course,' replied Mike in stuttered

French. The bearded Customs Officer raised a doubting eyebrow.

'Does that require you to dive outside of daylight hours with no warning lights being displayed on your vessel?' Hubert answered in Mike's place.

'We arrived just before daybreak because Mike wanted me to experience conditions of low visibility. We had to go far from shore to find the depth and we were concerned that leaving the lights on would drain the battery and leave us stranded.' The officer narrowed his eyes. He was on unfamiliar ground and had difficulty finding a flaw in Hubert's argument. As he was considering his course of action, the skiff returned and tied up by the boarding ladder. A marine stepped aboard and handed the officer the ID cards which he'd found inside Mike and Hubert's wallets. The Customs Officer studied Mike's instructor card and sighed, realising that he was probably wasting his time. He handed the cards back to the marine.

'Check them out, just to make sure that they're legitimate,' he ordered. The marine gave a curt nod and went to the bridge.

'I take it that neither of you are French?' the Customs Officer asked in a more relaxed tone of voice.

'No I'm English and he's...'

'Swiss,' replied Hubert.

'I see; and what do you both think of Corsica?' he asked with the barest hint of a smile.

'It's beautiful,' replied Hubert.

'I'm glad you think so,' said the officer with obvious pride. He passed a curious eye over their twin-sets.

'That's quite a lot of equipment you're diving with. Is it all really necessary?'

'For this particular course, yes,' replied Mike.

'I'm a diver myself as it happens,' said the officer. 'In fact most of us are trained divers because we sometimes have to inspect the underside of hulls.' Mike felt his heart skip a beat.

'These depths would certainly be out of my range though,' continued the officer. 'Is there actually anything to see down there?' Mike and Hubert exchanged knowing glances.

'Yes, there's actually a surprising amount of life down there,' ventured Hubert. 'In fact we were lucky enough to see a blue shark this morning.'

'A shark? Weren't you afraid?'

'I was a bit apprehensive at first, I must admit, but I've seen far bigger ones. Besides, once you realise that domestic dogs are responsible for considerably more deaths amongst humans than sharks are, you start to understand how drastically exaggerated their reputation is.'

'Well I know which one I'd prefer to tackle,' said the officer, smiling.

The marine who had taken the ID cards, now returned.

'They're all in order sir.'

The officer took the cards from him, nodded pensively and flicked his eyes towards the other members of his crew.

'At ease gentlemen. Please help our guests with their equipment and escort them back to their vessel.' He turned towards Mike and Hubert and handed their cards back.

'I'm sorry to have troubled you both, but we have strict orders to search every vessel entering this area. I would strongly advise you both to find some other place to dive in future and ensure that you display adequate warning lights on your vessel.'

He escorted Mike and Hubert towards the boarding ladder.

'Well I hope that you both enjoy the rest of your stay in Corsica. My apologies again, goodbye.'

'Thank you...and goodbye,' they called as they stepped carefully from the ladder onto the awaiting skiff. They were accompanied back to the RIB where their equipment was returned to them. As the customs vessel was pulling away Mike and Hubert stared at each other in astonishment.

'I'm not sure how many more surprises I can take today,' said Mike.

'Me neither,' agreed Hubert. 'I nearly had a heart attack when I saw that boat stop above us. I was preparing myself for a very long swim.'

'Me too. I'm still amazed that a customs vessel spotted us.'

'Well they did say that they were watching the area, and they probably have sophisticated radar equipment on board.'

'Yes, I suppose they do,' said Mike. 'I wonder if they're here to keep an eye on Santorini.'

'I don't know, but I think we ought to get out of here before he *does* make an appearance.'

'I'm with you there. Let's get the anchor up and head for shore.'

'OK, stand by to take in the slack,' said Hubert as he fired up the outboard. 'And be careful with that damned camera!'

Mike smiled to himself as he pulled in the anchor line, stopping briefly to untie the mesh bag and then the reel. When everything was safely stowed, he joined Hubert at the helm.

'I didn't get a chance to thank you for helping me out down there. I'm not sure that I would have made it alone.'

'Don't be so dramatic; you were almost free by the time I arrived.'

'Perhaps, but I was still in difficulty. I really wasn't expecting you to put yourself at risk for me, so thank you.'

'Well I have to admit that it was nice to be the one who wasn't in the shit for once,' chuckled Hubert. 'What happened in there anyway?'

'I had to use the hammer to free the hatch which led to the control room and I suppose the vibrations must have dislodged the cabinet behind me.'

'That explains the tapping sound I heard then.'

'Ah, I was wondering how you knew I was in trouble.'

'Yeah, but at first I thought...well never mind.'

Mike shrugged and stared at the mesh bag, lying on the deck.

'Where did you find those coins exactly?'

'I tied the reel off around a metal case at the stern before following you inside the wreck. Afterwards, when I came back to untie it, I saw that the cover was almost torn off. It looked like an ammunition case so I glanced inside to see if there was anything interesting in there. I couldn't see because it was full of silt, so I just stuck my hand in and it came out full of coins.'

'You mean to say that there's a whole case full of them down there?' asked Mike, incredulous.

'That's what it looked like to me. Unfortunately I didn't have time to investigate further.'

'Well I suppose that explains why Santorini is so eager to find it.'

'Yeah! It looks like we beat him to it though, doesn't it?' smiled Hubert.

'There must be a hell of a lot more coins like that down there,' said Mike, deep in thought.

'That's probable,' said Hubert, nodding in a detached manner. 'Are you thinking of salvaging it?'

'I don't know,' Mike replied after some reflection, 'but it's certainly a tempting thought.'

'I'm sure that we'd be allowed to keep a fair percentage of the haul,' said Hubert, 'that's the way these things usually work.'

'Would you be comfortable doing that?'

'I handle priceless artefacts pretty much daily and to me their historic value is far greater than their market value. Having said that, given the opportunity to preserve history and make a bit of honest money at the same time, I'd be a fool not to take advantage.'

'Sure, but have you considered all the risks. After all, we're clearly not the only ones who know what's down there.'

'I'll take my chances. If we don't take it, Santorini certainly will. And he won't be interested in seeing any of it in a public collection. Besides, that was one of the most amazing dives that I've ever made and it would take more than a few ragged bandits to keep me from coming back.'

'Well that will save me having to blackmail you then. Let's shake on it.'

Hubert grinned as he locked thumbs with Mike.

'Did you get a chance to look at the damage to the conning tower?'

'Yes, I even got a photograph of it. There's an opening there, but it's too small to fit through.'

'I know; I saw it from the inside.'

'So you reached the control room then?'

'Very briefly, yes,' said Mike. 'Did you happen to notice how thick the metal was around the opening?'

'Well the outer casing was relatively thin, but the inner hull was much thicker, about the width of a thumb I'd say. Why do you ask?'

'The main access hatch to the bridge is completely seized, so I'm just wondering if we could force a way directly into the conning tower, to avoid having to go through the engine rooms each time.'

'We'd have to use something pretty substantial to make the hole any bigger.'

'Yeah, I don't suppose we'd get very far with a hack-saw,' agreed Mike. 'A few sticks of dynamite would probably do the job, but that's not the kind of thing you'd find in a supermarket. I'll have to think about it.'

'Did you see anything of interest while you were in the control room?'

asked Hubert.

'To be honest, I wasn't really in the right frame of mind to take in my surroundings at that point. There were a lot of skeletons in there, I remember that much, but now that you come to mention it, I did see something interesting – unusual anyway. There were foot soldiers and SS personnel on board when she sank.'

'How do you know that?'

'There were rifles and infantry helmets in the Petty Officer's quarters and in the control room I saw a uniform collar with an SS symbol on it. If I hadn't been breathing trimix at the time I wouldn't have believed my eyes.'

'Did you get any photographs?'

'Not in the control room. I took a few in the P.O.'s quarters, but I'm not sure that they'll reveal anything.'

'Well we can always come back and get some more.'

'I can see that you're really getting into all this Hubert.'

'It's the best fun I've had in a long time,' he said, grinning.

Once they had returned to the beach and transferred their equipment to the car, they took the RIB back to its temporary mooring.

'Watch out, here comes the boss,' said Hubert, while glancing up the coast to the north. 'I'd better let them know that we've finished.' Mike turned to see a black and yellow RIB hurtling across the *Anse de Roccapina*.

'OK, but do me a favour. Keep quiet about my little incident will you? You know what Monica's like.'

'Yeah, I doubt if our encounter with customs would impress her a great deal either,' agreed Hubert, as he throttled back the engine.

They came to a halt close to the excavation site and waited for Bertie to bring the larger RIB in. Once Anna had deployed the anchor, Hubert approached and tied up alongside. The two parties exchanged greetings and Mike and Hubert soon found themselves being barraged with questions. After they had recounted a highly edited version of their exploits, Monica and Bertie were keen to see the objects which they had recovered from the wreck. Mike pulled the breathing apparatus out of the mesh bag and handed it to them.

'It's some kind of emergency breathing device, but I'm not totally sure whether its purpose was to prevent the inhalation of toxic fumes, or to help the crew escape from a sinking vessel.'

'It is most interesting,' enthused Bertie as he examined it.

'I'm actually more interested in the writing that's on the back of it,' said Mike, 'I think it might be a name.'

Monica carefully turned the circular bladder over and studied the faded letters on its reverse.

'Yes look; there's an 'A' and that looks like an 'M' or maybe an 'N.''

'Is there any way of cleaning it up?' asked Mike, 'The name is important because it could help us to identify the U-boat.'

'Then we'd better try to restore it,' suggested Monica. 'Leave it with us and we'll make sure that it's properly treated.'

'You'd better take this as well,' said Mike, handing her the silver cigarette lighter. 'It's also got a name on it. You can just about make out the engraving.'

Monica found a magnifying glass and examined the lighter more closely.

'Yes, that's a nicely worked piece, but I'm afraid that the name won't be of much use to you.'

'Why's that?' asked Mike, frowning.

'Because it's a girls name - Petra; probably the owners sweetheart.' Mike blew his cheeks out.

'That's not the only thing we found. Take a look at these,' said Hubert with a crooked smile as he handed over the gold coins.

Monica took them and frowned as she turned them over in the palm of her hand. She uttered a few words of Swiss-German and Anna immediately went to fetch something from one of the holds. She returned carrying a small glass jar filled with a clear liquid. Monica dropped the coins into it and bubbles immediately began to form on their exposed surfaces.

'Just like soluble aspirin,' chuckled Mike, but no one was paying any attention to him. They were all listening intently to Monica's comments as she swirled the transparent liquid around the jar. Suddenly everyone began talking at once and Mike watched mystified as Monica's colleagues crowded around her. He went over to see what all the commotion was about.

'What's going on?'

Monica paused her Swiss-German monologue and turned towards him.

'Mike, the inscriptions on these coins are in Ge'ez; the ancient language of a civilisation which no longer exists. They must be well over a thousand years old.'

Capitaine Villeneuve stared dejectedly at the calendar on his desk. The 10th of September had been circled in red ink for many months now. It was supposed to be a date to look forward to; an opportunity to relax, pursue his interests, travel abroad and try to see more of his grandchildren on the mainland. Now only six weeks away, the date seemed more like a deadline than a point of departure to a more sedate and leisurely lifestyle. He sighed and pushed the calendar away when he heard a sharp knock on the door.

'Come in.'

Lieutenant Lechaux entered carrying a ream of paper in his hands.

'*Bonjour Capitaine.*'

'*Bonjour* Guy. Anything of interest there?'

'Yes sir. I thought that you might want to have a look at these.' Lechaux placed two hastily typed reports in front of him.

'Forensics eh?' commented Villeneuve as he picked up the uppermost of them and leafed through it. 'So it would seem that Mr. Summers is in the clear then.'

'Yes sir, but read on.' Villeneuve flipped the page over.

'Is this Perotta's DNA profile?' he asked in surprise.

'Yes sir. Forensics extracted it from a strand of hair that was found in his apartment. It's already been matched with the skin tissue which was found under Chantale Moret's fingernails.'

'Good Lord! So you were right after all.'

'It won't do us much good while he's still at large though,' he said with a shrug.

Villeneuve's jaw tightened.

'Well find him!' he said through clenched teeth. 'And this?' he asked, picking up the next report.

'It arrived just now sir. It's a report from the Coastguard. You asked them to intercept any vessel that was acting suspiciously in the Roccapina area.'

'Yes of course. Let's see what they have to say.'

Lechaux stood back, watching Villeneuve's moustache begin to twitch as he read the report.

'Oh for God's sake; do those two have no common sense at all?' They must have a death wish or something. As if my job isn't hard enough as it is. Right leave this to me Guy; I'm going to have strong words with that young man.'

Mike drove back towards Propriano with freshly filled cylinders of nitrox and helium in the trunk of his car and the angry words of *Capitaine* Villeneuve still ringing in his ears. The threat of being charged with interference in an ongoing police investigation was unpleasant enough, but it was far more disturbing to learn that their attempts to remain discreet had proved totally ineffective. If the Gendarmes were aware of their activities in the bay, then who else might share that knowledge? It didn't bear thinking about. Mike realised that he was being drawn into a situation which was far more complex and dangerous than he had anticipated.

The gold in itself was an enormous responsibility and Monica had made absolutely certain that he understood that. The astounding and controversial nature of the U-boat's cargo was certain to arouse unprecedented interest from all corners of the globe and provoke a great deal of diplomatic wrangling. After all, the U-boat was a protected German war grave lying in French territorial waters and carrying stolen gold from an ancient civilisation whose territories once overlapped the borders of several present day countries. Along with all his other problems, it now looked as if Mike could find himself caught at the centre of a political hornet's nest. Exposing the location of the U-boat anonymously was clearly no longer a realistic option and Mike knew that he and Hubert had an obligation to keep the coordinates secret until a sensible solution could be found. Once he had dropped the two films off for processing, he returned to the farmhouse and dialled Monica's number.

'Hello?'

'Hi, it's Mike here. Who's that?'

'Monica of course. It's so wonderful to hear your sweet voice again,' answered a falsetto male voice.

'Hubert I can tell your voice a mile away. You sound like an old queen.'

'Come on Mike admit it; you know it turns you on,' he laughed.

'Hubert, the thought of you wearing make-up and tights is enough to make a dung beetle sick.'

'You really know how to hurt a fellow don't you?' he chuckled. 'I suppose you want to speak to Monica?'

'No, it's actually you I need to speak to.'

'That's probably just as well, because everyone else is in the water.'

'Good. Listen Hubert, after what happened today, I think we need to increase our security. That customs inspection was a wake up call. If anyone finds out that we've discovered the wreck, and more importantly the gold, they'll do whatever it takes to get hold of the coordinates.'

'I realise that, but as far as I'm aware, no one knows that we've discovered anything.'

'Maybe not, but now that we know what's at stake, we can be certain that we're being very closely watched. If someone gets even a sniff of what we've found, I dread to think what might happen.'

'So what do you want to do?'

'The most important thing is to delete all the waypoints from the GPS and the laptop.'

'Sure, I'll do that right away. What about the files on the computer at the farmhouse?'

'I'll deal with them. I'll put the information on disk and then erase everything. When you get back here this evening, we'll find a way of coding the coordinates so that there's no accurate written record.'

'Is all this really necessary?' asked Hubert.

'Just look upon it as a kind of insurance.'

'Fine, if it makes you feel happier.'

'It does. And I also think that we should limit ourselves to just three more dives. That should give us enough time to put together a rough inventory before we hand over the coordinates.'

'Sure. I can live with that.'

'The only problem is that we'll have to do those dives without a boat.'

There was a pause.

'How do you propose that we do that?'

'We can use the same method that myself and Thomas perfected a few weeks ago. We'll arrange to get dropped off over the wreck and use the DPV's to return to shore.'

'I'm not sure I like the sound of that.'

'We'll be fine; trust me. We'll have extended battery power in the DPV's this time because we won't be conducting any searches.'

'So who's going to drop us off?'

'I was hoping that Bertie might do it, but I'll need to have a word with

Monica first.'

'Well if they both go along with it, I guess it'll be OK. Will we have a mobile phone with us?'

'Absolutely; we'll take every possible precaution. Just make sure that those positions have been erased and we'll talk more about it tonight.'

'OK, leave it with me.'

'See you later then.'

Hubert rang off. And in the *Bar des Chasseurs*, a flashing red light was extinguished when the receiver reverted to standby mode.

Monica cursed as she dropped her referencing documents onto the wet deck. It had been like that all morning; ever since she had set eyes on the Axumite coins. She just couldn't comprehend how they had ended up on board a Second World War German submarine.

In a lecture that she had given to the historical society in Bonn over a year ago, she remembered explaining to a captivated audience, that the wealth, influence and technological achievement of the Axumite civilisation in East Africa was considerable, but often sadly overlooked because of the proximity of their more illustrious neighbours, the Egyptians. Although they were directly inspired by them, the Axumites continued to build pyramids, erect obelisks and carve astonishing temples long after the Egyptian Empire had ceased to exist. Amongst their many achievements, one of the more interesting was that they were the first known African civilisation to mint coins in their own name and this had helped historians to record the extent of their vast trading influence. But the surprising thing about Hubert's find, was that although Axumite gold coins had been unearthed in archaeological digs as far away as India, large collections of them were almost unheard of.

Bertie placed the laptop to one side and came to Monica's assistance.

'Here let me give you a hand with those.'

'Oh thank you,' replied Monica. 'I just can't seem to hold my concentration today.'

'Yes, I noticed that you've been a bit distant. It wouldn't have anything to do with those coins which Hubert found would it?'

'Something along those lines,' she said smiling. 'How do you think they wound up on a U-boat Bertie?'

'Well, Ethiopia was under the occupation of the Italian Army during the Second World War and they were allies of the Nazis, of course,' he said with a shrug. 'Did you know that Hitler once ordered the SS to go to Axum to capture the Arc of the Covenant?'

'What, the original receptacle of the Ten Commandments? There's absolutely no proof that it exists.'

'Well, the guardian of the treasury of the St. Mary of Zion temple would probably disagree with you. In fact, most Ethiopians genuinely believe that King Menelik, supposedly issued from the union of King Solomon and the

Queen of Sheba, took the Arc from Jerusalem to Axum for safekeeping. And given Hitler's penchant for mysticism, it's not inconceivable that he shared that belief.'

'Granted, but he was probably more seduced by the thought of its value. After all it's described as being a fabulous receptacle of solid gold.'

'Exactly! And I think that's your key. He had a reason to send the SS there to look for it. They wouldn't have found the Arc of course, otherwise we'd know about it, but they certainly wouldn't have wanted to go back empty handed either. They probably looted everything they could lay their hands on.'

'Now that make's more sense to me,' said Monica, nodding excitedly. 'One thing that's been puzzling me is that gold coins weren't in normal circulation inside the Axumite territories; they were reserved for inter-national trade, to flout the wealth of the nation. However, gold coins have been found buried in the tombs beneath Axum's obelisks and if you take into consideration that 97 percent of Axum's underground chambers remain unexcavated, it's just possible that they stumbled across a hidden cache of gold.'

'It's a hypothesis that can't be ignored,' agreed Bertie. 'And don't forget that Mussolini succeeded in unearthing and transporting one of the largest obelisks to Italy in 1937. In fact it's only just recently been returned.'

'If we're right, it would explain why there's no written record of the gold being taken. After all, no one besides the Nazis would ever have been aware of its existence,' said Monica pensively. 'But why use a U-boat to transport it? Why not just fly it out?'

'Well, I suppose an aircraft could easily get spotted and shot down over the sea. A U-boat might have appeared to be the most discreet way to get it across the Mediterranean. It's not so unusual. After all, it's well documented that the Nazis used U-boats to transport stolen valuables from Europe to South America towards the end of the war.'

'Yes I realise that,' said Monica. 'I just find the scale of all this difficult to take in. It's clearly going to make headline news worldwide.'

'There's no doubt about that,' agreed Bertie. 'And it's all down to Mike's perseverance.'

Monica nodded.

'I think I've judged him a little too harshly over this whole affair. I first thought that he was a bit of a stubborn idealist, but I've since come to appreciate that he's just very passionate and determined.'

'I think you need that kind of blinkered belief to make the really big discoveries,' said Bertie. 'Just think what kind of opposition Columbus must have met when he decided to ignore popular opinion and sail towards what was considered to be the edge of the world.'

'Well I don't think he's quite in the same category, but I do see your point,' smiled Monica, surprised at the feeling of pride which she felt in Mike's achievement.

'We really should offer him all the help that we can,' pointed out Bertie. 'I'm sure the university would be delighted to be associated with such a controversial find.'

'Yes, I dare say they would, but they'd be far less enthusiastic if someone got killed in the process,' cautioned Monica. 'I'll certainly give it some consideration though.'

Mathilde looked from one disbelieving face to the other.

'Would you like me to listen to the recording again?'

Pascal reached for the unlabelled bottle of spirit and poured himself a large measure. Santorini's eyes burned into the wall opposite. He slowly shook his head, pulled a 20 euro note from a roll and placed it in front of her.

'Please wait outside. I need to speak to your father in private.' Mathilde, full of concern, stared at her father, who confirmed with a solemn nod of the head. She self-consciously gathered her things together and left the room in silence.

'Well that's it then; he's found it,' said Pascal, ruefully, when the door closed. He took a large swig of the potent marc and winced as it burned his throat and carried its fiery warmth to his stomach.

'Gold!' said Santorini, still staring at the wall transfixed, his head nodding almost imperceptibly. 'It had to be for that kind of money. I'll wager there's plenty of it too.'

'If there's any left,' said Pascal, miserably.

There were three distinct knocks on the door.

'Who's that?' barked Santorini.

'It's me...Pierre.'

Pascal let him in.

'Sit down and pour yourself a drink,' said Santorini, 'you're going to need it.'

'Why what's happened?'

'I still can't believe it,' said Pascal, picking up his glass. 'The story was true after all.' He took another gulp of marc and closed his eyes.

'I couldn't give a damn about the story,' spat Santorini. 'All I'm interested in is the gold.'

'What gold?' asked Pierre irritably. 'Will somebody please explain what's going on?'

'The Englishman found the U-boat,' explained Santorini. 'And gold.'

'How much gold?' asked Pierre, his eyes widening.

'We don't know yet,' replied Pascal, 'There has to be a fair amount though.'

'But when did he find it? I've been watching the bay all afternoon.'

'The call came in this morning,' replied Santorini. 'We think he found the wreck a couple of days ago, but it sounds like he's only just found the gold.'

'Then we need to act now before he takes the lot.'

'We'll have time,' said Santorini with assurance in his voice. 'Gold is heavy and it will take some time to strip it from the wreck, especially at those depths. Still, we can't just leave them to do as they please. Pierre, I need you to take my boat to the bay. Make sure you're in position at first light tomorrow and stay there until I say otherwise.'

Pierre was about to protest, but Santorini's withering stare quickly convinced him otherwise.

'I need time to work out a proper plan,' he continued. 'If we try to do this too quickly we'll make mistakes, expose the position of the wreck and risk losing everything. On the other hand we can't afford to delay for too long because for some reason best known to themselves, the Englishman and the Swiss are considering turning the whole thing over to the authorities. Why in God's name anyone would want to throw away a fortune in Gold, I don't know, but that's the kind of intellectual idiots we seem to be dealing with. Still I'd much rather be dealing with idiots than a rival gang; they're much easier to intimidate for one thing.'

'Are they the only ones who know where the wreck is?' asked Pierre.

'Yes, I'm fairly certain. The Englishman was going out of his way to keep the coordinates secret and that works in our favour. Once he's shown us where the wreck is, the information can disappear along with him.'

'And how do you propose to get him to do that?' asked Pierre.

'Simple. We kidnap the girl and keep her hostage until he complies. Once we've salvaged the gold, we'll dump their bodies out at sea and if needs be, we'll send Michel round to clean up the house. Another few murders here or there won't make much difference to him now.'

'Do we have enough people to do this?' asked Pierre.

'Five should be enough. We need Michel's help for the dives, so I'll have to think of a way that we can get him down to the port unseen. We'll need Jeannot's assistance as well.'

'I don't think that's a good idea,' said Pierre, shaking his head. 'He'll run a mile if he gets word of what you're planning.'

'Not if we don't tell him. He'll find out when it's too late to say no.'

'But what if he panics afterwards and goes running to the police.'

'Jeannot's no fool. He'll soon understand that it's in his own interest to keep his mouth shut; especially if we use his knife to kill our two guests.'

Pascal glanced up sharply, a mixture of surprise and admiration on his face.

'You're good Jean-Claude; I have to give you that.'

'It's always wise to take out insurance.'

'This calls for a drink,' declared Pascal as he topped up their glasses.

'What about the girl though?' asked Pierre. 'We'll have to take her when she's on her own.'

'Leave all that to me,' said Santorini. 'I've already got something in mind.'

Hubert took two bottles of Leffe beer from the fridge, popped their caps and offered one to Mike.

'Mmm, the first one is always the best,' he said, smacking his lips appreciatively.

'It certainly is,' Mike agreed. 'How are you feeling after your day's exploits?'

'I'm totally exhausted!' he said, glancing over his shoulder. 'Don't tell Monica, but I nodded off a couple of times while I was on surface duty.'

Mike laughed and clinked his bottle against Hubert's.

'Your secret's safe with me.'

'Thanks. What's this then?' he asked, pointing his bottle towards the laptop screen.

'It's the breathing device which I found inside the wreck. Amazingly, it seems that they were used to escape from submarines that were stranded on the sea floor.'

'Escape Lung,' Hubert, read from the screen. 'Did they actually work?'

'Not too well by the sound of it. They functioned like rudimentary semi-closed rebreathers and funnily enough the company which produced them now make modern diving rebreathers. The inflatable ring was placed over the head and then there were straps to secure it, just like the life vests on aircraft. When you breathed into the mouthpiece, the rubber ring inflated and functioned like a counter-lung in a rebreather. It was fitted with a carbon dioxide scrubber, a manual purge valve and a small cylinder of oxygen to replenish the supply.'

'Did they wear masks too?' asked Hubert.

'Apparently not,' replied Mike. 'They had to gather together in the control room, flood the interior, to equalise the pressure and then open the main hatch in total darkness.'

'You'd have to be pretty desperate to attempt that.'

'Well, when you consider that they were probably suffering from horrific burns and watching each other die slowly from oxygen starvation.'

'That would do it,' nodded Hubert. 'Did many survive?'

'Surprisingly, despite being instantly exposed to the dangers of oxygen toxicity, lung expansion injuries, drowning, decompression sickness and exposure, some of them did. One Petty Officer actually managed to escape from a U-boat that was stranded in 73 metres of water - an operational record which still stands to this day.'

'Incredible!' said Hubert, shaking his head. 'Do you think anyone could have escaped from our U-boat then?'

'Not a chance,' replied Mike, without hesitation. 'The main hatch is stuck fast and everything from the control room to the stern would have been flooded within minutes. Besides, we'd have known all about this wreck if someone had survived.'

'That's true enough,' said Hubert, leafing through Mike's notes. 'Looks like you've been doing quite a lot of research today. What else did you find out?'

'Mostly, I've been trying to locate places where the gold might have been stored during transportation. I don't think we'll find much in the bow section because most of the space below the deck plates there was taken up by trim tanks, the battery compartment and the fuel extension tanks.'

'The crate I found was amongst the debris behind the wreck, so it must have been stored in the stern.'

'I realise that, but there's not a lot of space there either. My guess is that they removed the stern torpedo from the floor locker and stored the crates there.'

'I suppose that would support your theory about the torpedo being chained to the ceiling then.'

'It does seem to fit the evidence,' said Mike. 'There are some other places where cargo could be stored. There's a large hold directly beneath the control room and they sometimes used the after heads as well.'

'What are heads?'

'Sorry, it's a marine term for toilet.'

'I see. And where are they on the plan here?'

'They're here, just before the P.O.'s quarters, opposite the galley.'

'That's the kitchen right?'

'Exactly. We must have passed them both this morning, which is frustrating because there's a hatch above the galley.'

'Never mind; we'll check it out next time. Is the cargo hold under the control room easy to access?'

Mike paused before he answered.

'There will be some complications. And to be honest, I'm not even sure that I want to try.'

'Why not?' asked Hubert.

'Because we'd first have to clear the whole area of silt to get the deck plates up and then we'd be faced with the dilemma of moving the skeletons.'

'Ah! Yes, that wouldn't be too pleasant...or entirely ethical, for that matter.'

'What wouldn't be ethical?' asked Monica as she entered the kitchen carrying a reference book under her arm.

'Grave robbing,' replied Hubert.

'Oh, is that what you were planning?'

'Definitely not,' replied Mike, knowing only too well what Monica's reaction would be.

'I'm glad to hear it,' said Monica. She placed the open reference book in front of them, along with one of the Axumite coins, now restored to its original golden sheen. 'Check this out; fourth century gold coin bearing the head of King Ezana of Axum.'

Mike compared the photograph with the gold coin lying on the page beside it. It was identical.

'Who was King Ezana?' he asked.

'Even by today's standards, he was a very powerful figure,' replied Monica. 'With the Axumite territories already extending into Eritrea and Southern Arabia, Ezana pushed on to gain control of the lands of Kush and parts of Sudan and Somalia. In fact the influence of the Axumite Kingdom was so great at that time, that along with Persia, China and Rome, it was considered to be one of the four greatest powers of the ancient world.'

'That's astonishing. I hadn't even heard of the Axumite civilisation before today,' admitted Mike.

'Yes, well our teaching of history is somewhat selective. You would have thought that a civilisation which produced some of the tallest obelisks in the world and were practicing Christianity while we were still dancing around fires in loincloths, would get a mention, but for some reason we still like to think of Sub Saharan Africa as a continent of savages.'

'They were Christians?' asked Mike in surprise.

'Yes, in fact it was King Ezana who adopted the religion for his country after being converted from paganism by the priest Frumentius of Tyre, later to became the Bishop of Axum. The coins that you see here were also a means of promoting the national religion. If you look closely at them you'll see that they have Christian symbols on them whereas the earlier ones show only pagan symbols.' Monica flipped over a page to show Mike some examples. 'The inscriptions around the perimeter are in the local Ge'ez and also in Greek, which of course was more widely recognised.'

'How rare are these coins?'

'They were quite widespread when they were in use, but now there are surprisingly few examples around. There was a lot of gold in Axum during Ezana's reign, in fact it was more abundant than silver, so the chances are that they produced large quantities, but up until now, only one large hoard has ever been found and surprisingly that was in Yemen, on the other side of the Red Sea.'

'So how much is one of these coins worth?'

'It's only a guess, but I would say around four to five hundred dollars per coin.' Mike whistled.

'So do you have any idea how such a large quantity ended up on board a U-boat?'

'I've actually been discussing that same question with Bertie. Since there is no record of any theft, we can only assume that either the Germans or their Italian allies, who were occupying Ethiopia at the time, discovered them in one of Axum's underground tombs.'

'But surely they couldn't have come all the way from Ethiopia by U-boat,' pointed out Hubert.

'No. They were probably flown as far as the North Coast of Africa and then transferred to a U-boat for the crossing. If they'd attempted to fly across the Mediterranean and got shot down, they'd have lost the gold forever.'

'Looks like they did anyway,' said Mike.

'They were just incredibly unfortunate. From a statistical and strategic point of view, the U-boat would have been their safest option.'

'It sounds reasonable,' agreed Hubert. 'Anyway, I guess it's unlikely we'll ever find out for sure.'

'Maybe,' said Mike, 'but someone out there definitely knows a lot more than we do.'

'I'm afraid I can't comment on that,' said Monica, as she closed the book, 'but if you want my advice on anything else, I'll be in the lab with Anna. She's working on that escape device you found.'

'Thanks Monica, I really appreciate all your help with this.'

'It's my pleasure,' she replied, with a gracious nod of the head.

Mike watched her leave the room in silent admiration.

'This is just like something from one of your training sessions,' said Hubert, while staring at the computer screen.

'What is?'

'All this groping around blindly while trapped in some dark underwater chamber; it's like something out of your twisted imagination.'

'Ah, the escape accounts. Yes, some of them are pretty amazing aren't they?'

'Unbelievable! Did you read the one about the guy who escaped from 40 metres just by holding his breath? Imagine that; waiting for the conning tower to flood in total darkness and then swimming blindly to the surface.'

'He must have had nerves of steel,' agreed Mike.

'If you think about it, it's kind of ironic that we're taking risks to go in the opposite direction.'

'Yeah, it does seem a bit odd,' agreed Mike. 'They were desperate to get out of the wreck and all we want to do is get inside it. Mind you, for a moment this morning, I definitely shared their point of view.'

'I can imagine why,' said Hubert. 'So when do we go again?'

'We'll give our bodies a rest tomorrow and then I think we should do another early morning start.'

'Any chance that I could follow you inside the wreck this time?'

'We'll see. Let me have a chance to speak...' Mike was cut short by the sound of Monica's voice coming from the hallway.

'Mike, Hubert, come and take a look at this!'

They hurried towards the makeshift laboratory at the rear of the farmhouse and crowded around Anna, who was leaning over a tray of yellowish liquid. In one gloved hand she held the escape lung and in the other a small paintbrush and a cotton wool swab. Having cleaned away the years of grime from the area where the name was written, she now covered it with a light powder.

'Damn it! Most of the letters are still illegible,' exclaimed Mike in frustration.

'Would you turn off the light please Hubert?' asked Monica, the faintest hint of a smile on her lips.

Mike watched perplexed as Hubert flipped off the overhead light. The laboratory was suddenly plunged into darkness and Monica turned on an ultra-violet light. Mike stared in stunned disbelief as the missing letters were suddenly revealed in their entirety.

'D. Kammerer!' he said breathlessly. 'That's incredible; you're absolute geniuses!' He put his hand on Monica's shoulder and squeezed it affectionately.

'Come on; let's see what we can find out about him.'

In jubilant mood, Mike led Hubert and Monica back towards the laptop in the kitchen and keyed in the web address of a U-boat information site. When the welcome page had loaded, he chose the *search by crew name* option of the integrated data base. They were all tense with anticipation as Mike typed in *Kammerer* and activated the search button. There was a short pause before a list of matches appeared on the screen.

'There are only three entries with that name,' he said excitedly.

'There he is!' exclaimed Hubert, pointing. 'Dieter Kammerer.'

Mike selected the name from the list and the service history of *Unteroffizier Dieter Kamerrer* instantly flashed up on screen. Mike hardly dared breathe as he scanned the information.

'Look! He saw active service in the Atlantic and then the Mediterranean. He went missing presumed dead in April 1943 at the age of 22. The last vessel he was assigned to was...that's it - U602!' Mike stared at Hubert in triumph.

'Let's see what it says about her,' said Hubert excitedly. Mike clicked on the link and a detailed list of general and technical information appeared before them.

'Look, I was right – it's a VIIC series,' said Mike, as he read through the list of statistics. 'So let's see; she was built in the Blohm and Vos shipyards in Hamburg, took part in patrols in the Atlantic and Mediterranean. Her last known port of call was Toulon on the 10th April 1943 and she was reported as sunk with all hands on 23rd April 1943 in...no! That's impossible!'

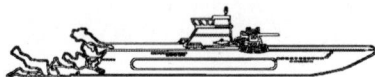

12

P ascal led the way along the narrow track in almost total darkness. He knew where every rock and depression was from the hours which he'd spent tracking wild boar and deer during the hunting season, but on this occasion, the wildlife had nothing to fear from his rifle. Michel walked behind him in silence, one steadying hand resting firmly on his shoulder. Pascal's tedious precautions frustrated him, but at least he was finally out of that stinking cave. Soon they arrived at the back door of the farmhouse and Michel was bundled into the hallway. Pascal ushered him through to the kitchen where they found Pierre, waiting in silence for their arrival. There was dry cured ham, *salamu*, bread, *brocchia* and red wine laid out on the solid chestnut dining table. Michel immediately pounced on the central platter.

'I take it you're hungry?' asked Pierre amused.

'So would you be if you were stuck in a godforsaken cave 24 hours a day,' said Michel through a mouthful of freshly baked bread smothered with soft goat's cheese. After they shook hands, Pascal poured Michel a generous glass of *rouge*. It was downed immediately and the glass pushed back towards the open bottle. Pascal raised his eyebrows and refilled it. Michel wiped his mouth with the back of his hand and lit a cigarette.

'So they've found the sub eh?'

'They've found it alright,' confirmed Pierre. 'And the gold as well.'

'How much gold?'

'We don't yet know for sure, but we're confident that there'll be plenty to go around.'

'How much have they salvaged?'

'They haven't had time to take much. I'll be paying them a visit tomorrow to find out.'

Michel bit off a large chunk of *salamu* sausage and chewed on it reflectively.

'Do we know where the wreck is?' he asked after the second glass of wine had disappeared.

'Not yet, but the Englishman is going to show us.'

'How come? Did you threaten to feed his balls to the fish?'

'No, we're going to threaten to kill his girlfriend instead; once we've kidnapped her that is.'

'Ah, now that sounds more interesting,' said Michel. 'I'd like to spend a little time alone with her.'

'Let's wait until we see the gold first shall we?' suggested Pascal. Michel shrugged.

'Jean-Claude wants you with us on the boat,' said Pierre. 'Pascal can't dive for another week and we need as many people in the water as possible.' Michel stared at the glowing tip of his cigarette.

'And how does he plan to shield me from the attention of the Gendarmes?'

'He's arranging to have a van parked down by the old fish market. You'll leave here in the trunk of Pascal's car at 6.30pm tomorrow evening and I'll meet you both down there at 7 sharp.'

'What happens then?'

'It all depends on the circumstances, but hopefully we'll go straight for the girl.'

'This doesn't make any sense to me at all. That first site claims that U602 was sunk north of Oran on the 19th April 1943 and yet this one here says that she simply went missing on that date.'

'Wait a minute, there might be an explanation here,' said Monica, pointing at the screen. 'U602 was mistakenly reported as sunk on the 23rd April 1943. It looks like she became confused with U453 which came under attack in that exact same area just a few days later. U453 survived the attack and returned to Toulon unscathed, while U602 was still missing in action. Someone has obviously jumped to the wrong conclusion.'

'Monica's right,' agreed Hubert. 'The British bomber crew who attacked U453 could not have known which vessel they were engaging. They would have reported an attack on an unidentified U-boat without being able to confirm whether they had destroyed it or not. The fact that U602's last radio transmission took place in that same area, four days before the attack on U453, has probably led someone to put two and two together.'

'You mean that U602 is still unaccounted for?'

'That may well be the case.'

'Even so, if U602 went missing off the coast of Algeria. How did she end up hundreds of miles away in Corsica?'

'Maybe she was heading back to base,' suggested Hubert.

'The Navigator must have made a serious error then. The quickest route to Toulon would be via the Balearic Islands, and if they were heading for La Spezia they should have passed north of Corsica.'

'Maybe the crew rerouted her for tactical reasons,' suggested Monica.

'Or perhaps there was a mechanical failure,' added Hubert.

'It's possible I suppose, but I still find it all a bit strange. Algeria just doesn't seem like the most logical place from which to ship such a valuable cargo. It was far too close to the Allied air base in Gibraltar for a start.'

'What we really need is a little more background research,' said Monica.

'Yes, and I'd like to get my hands on the official account of the fate of U602,' agreed Mike. 'Do you have any ideas where I could get hold of that information Monica?'

'I'll get in touch with my colleague in the History Department again. Now that we've discovered the U-boat's identity, he should be able to get hold of the additional information that we need.'

'Perfect. Do you think that you could do that tonight?'

'Sure, no problem; I'll send an E-mail right after I've finished up my work in the laboratory.' Monica glanced at her watch. 'Speaking of which, I'd better go and relieve Anna. I'll see you both later.'

'Thanks again,' Mike called after her.

When Monica had left the room, Hubert opened two more bottles of Leffe and continued to debate what might have caused U602 to disappear from one part of the Mediterranean and arrive inexplicably in another. As the bottles emptied, they began to compete with each other for the most inventive and outlandish explanation and soon found themselves reduced to fits of childish laughter. When theories about vortexes in the space-time continuum and irregular currents created by the mass migration of sardines had been expounded and declared as irrefutable conclusions, they both knew that it was time to call it a day. Hubert yawned and squinted sleepily at his watch.

'It's no wonder I'm tired,' he said, 'I've been up close to sixteen hours. Maybe I should turn in.'

'Yeah, I'm feeling pretty whacked myself,' agreed Mike, yawning in sympathy.

'So tomorrow will just be a normal day, right?'

'Yep, I'll put together a plan for the day after and hopefully we'll get the OK from Monica.'

'I'll leave it in your hands then. See you tomorrow sometime.'

'Sure thing. Sleep well.'

'Sleeping is never a problem; it's waking up again that's the difficult bit,' chuckled Hubert as he disappeared through the kitchen door.

Mike smiled and returned his attention to the computer screen. He absently browsed a few pages while he drained the last of his Leffe and then shut it down for the evening. Monica was tapping away at the computer in the laboratory when he put his head around the door.

'Ah, there you are.' Mike approached and passed his arms around her shoulders before nuzzling her neck. 'I'm just about to turn in. Have you got much left to do?' Monica stroked his forearm and kissed the back of his hand.

'Give me a minute or two and I'll join you. I just need to finish up here.'

'OK. I'll be waiting in bed.' Mike withdrew his hands, brushing the tips of his fingers along either side of her neck and pulling them through the silky coils of her hair.

Monica felt her skin tingle as Mike turned and padded softly out of the room. She quickly finished off the last of her reports, wrote an E-mail to professor Rieder and then shut down the computer. With a sigh of relief, she left the laboratory, walked into the bedroom and let her clothes fall to the floor. In the half light she saw that Mike was turned away from her. She slipped into bed beside him, placed her arm around his waist and pressed her body against his. Mike stirred and rolled over, his eyes half closed. Monica lifted her head to kiss him, but Mike merely murmured sleepily, smacked his lips and let his face fall back against the pillow. She stared at him in surprise for a few seconds before breaking into a wide smile and planting an affectionate kiss on his cheek.

'Goodnight Mike.'

Still smiling to herself, she rolled over onto her back and stared at the ceiling, a warm glow flushing the stiffness from her joints. Within minutes, her eyes were closed and she too had fallen into an exhausted sleep. The next thing that she knew, the alarm clock was chirping insistently and daylight was pushing its way around the curtains. She reached over to cancel the alarm and slumped back against the pillow, shielding her eyes from the light. Mike stirred, hooked his arm around her waist and pulled her gently towards him. Realising that she was naked beneath the sheets, he let his hand explore the soft, downy skin of her belly and then reached up to cup the smooth, firmness of her breasts.

'I don't remember hearing you come to bed last night,' he whispered, 'I must have fallen asleep.'

'Yes I *did* notice,' replied Monica with a teasing edge to her voice.

'I'm sorry Monica, I'm just feeling a little....'

'There's no need to apologise,' she said, cutting him short and lifting his hand from her breast. She turned away from him and smiled mischievously as she slipped out of bed and padded naked towards the bathroom. Mike was left ruminating as she closed the door behind her without a backward glance. Deciding that it was probably one of those intangible women's moments, he let himself fall back against the pillows. After a couple of minutes, the sound of shower jets drumming against the old iron bath tub slowed to a steady trickle and Monica reappeared wearing a bath towel wrapped around her torso. She sat on the edge of the bed and Mike reached over to place his hand in the curve of her hips. He watched her dress in silence, aching with the desire to pull her towards him and make love to her, right there and then.

'You have amazing skin,' he said, as she slipped a bikini top over the lobes of her breasts and clasped it into place behind her back. He delighted in seeing her lips curl into a smile.

'Thank you.' Monica pulled a polo shirt over her head and pushed herself to her feet. 'Enjoy your day,' she said, leaning over to kiss him.

'You too.'

She slipped out of his grasp and made her way towards the door. Mike moved towards the centre of the bed and listened to her voice mingle with others in the hallway. He closed his eyes and let the sounds resonate on the edge of his consciousness. Soon, he drifted back to sleep, but it wasn't long before his eyes sprang open again. Someone was moving clumsily around the house.

At first he thought nothing of it, but the sound of something smashing to the ground soon raised his suspicions. A quick glance at the alarm clock told him that the truck should already have left half an hour ago and in a sudden flurry of activity he threw back the sheets, rolled off the bed and quickly pulled on a pair of boxer shorts. He reached for the dive knife which he'd stashed under the bed and reassured by the feel of it in his hand, quickly began to move towards the door. His foot hooked a loose cable and he cursed when a bedside lamp came crashing to the floor. There was a moment of silence and then a fumbling sound from deep within the house.

Spurred into action, Mike bolted out of the bedroom, turning his head from left to right in an attempt to locate the source of the disturbance. He pushed open the door to the store room and glanced inside. Apart from a few pieces of equipment lying on the floor, the room was empty. Next he approached the laboratory and nearly kicked the door off its hinges. He entered with his hand gripped tightly around the knife handle and seeing that one of the dark blinds was swinging loosely on the far wall, he pulled it aside. The window behind it was open, the frame splintered where it had been forced. The courtyard beyond was deserted and Mike ran upstairs to check the grounds from the first floor windows. There was no sign of the intruder.

Still shaking from the ordeal, he returned to the laboratory to see what, if anything had been stolen. Containers littered the floor with their contents spilled and discarded. There were fragments of terracotta scattered around, indicating that some of the artefacts had been damaged. Mike sighed, knowing how much painstaking work it would have taken Monica's team to extricate and restore each piece. It would be soul-destroying for them to find it all reduced to worthless rubble. Not knowing what else to do, he found a pair of plastic tweezers and attempted to sort through the mess, doing his best to separate the shards of pottery and put them back into their respective containers. As he was replacing some instruments on the work bench, his eyes suddenly fell on the sample jar. Three round depressions in the cotton wool padding at the base of it, were all that remained of the 4th century gold coins.

'I need you to take the day off work tomorrow.'

'I can't do that. There's no one to replace me.'

'So what happens if you break a leg?'

'I...everyone gets delayed.'

'So let them get delayed. I'm telling you that we need your help tomorrow and believe me, broken legs can be arranged.'

Jeannot winced as a sharp burning pain signalled the reappearance of his old ulcer problems.

'Why all the sudden urgency?' he asked in exasperation. 'Why can't it wait until the weekend?'

'Because the submarine could be empty of gold by then.'

'Gold? What do you mean gold?'

'Well I'm holding three pieces of it in my hand right now. It doesn't look very German, I'll grant you, but it's gold all the same.'

'You mean that you've found the U-boat?' asked Jeannot, with suspicion in his voice.

'Not me personally, but somebody else has, and he's willing to show us where it is.'

Jeannot's curiosity got the better of him.

'Are you saying that this person has actually explored the U-boat and found gold on it?'

Santorini smiled knowing that Jeannot was already hooked.

'The proof is right here in my hand Jeannot. Come and see for yourself if you don't believe me.'

Jeannot was tempted, but a show of mistrust was an open admission of disloyalty and it was unwise to expose such a sentiment to Santorini. Besides it made little difference. Santorini seemed determined to make sure that he would be available, whether he liked it or not.

'OK, you win. What do you need me to do?'

'Now that's what I like to hear Jeannot. I knew that you wouldn't let me down. Now listen carefully.'

'*Je ne vous comprends pas monsieur, attendez un instant.*' The assistant in the control room put the call on hold and spoke to her superior.

'*Capitaine*, I have a foreigner on the line who I can't understand. I think he's English. Could I trouble you to take the call?'

'Yes, certainly. What's the person's name?'

'Monsieur Sommairs ...or something like that.' *Capitaine* Villeneuve's ears pricked up.

'Put him straight through to me will you?'

Villeneuve drummed his fingers on the desk while the lines were connected.

'Mr. Summers?'

'Yes, I'd like to report a robbery please.'

'Would you now? It's *Capitaine* Villeneuve on the line. Please tell me all about it.'

Mike cringed. *Capitaine* Villeneuve was the last person that he would have chosen to speak to. Any hopes that he'd entertained of reporting the break-in without drawing attention to himself, had just been irretrievably scuppered.

'Um yes, I'm at the farmhouse - where the Swiss archaeologists are staying. They're all out at work at the moment.'

'Yes, go on.'

'Well, there was a break-in this morning...and one or two things got damaged.'

'Has anything been stolen?'

'Er...not that I'm aware of. I think I disturbed them before they got the chance.'

'Did you see anyone?'

'No, I searched the grounds afterwards, but there was no one there.'

'I see, well I'd better send someone round to check the place for prints.'

'Is that really necessary? I mean, nothing was taken. I was really just hoping to get a report from you; for the insurance, you understand.'

'I'm afraid that's not the way we work here Mr. Summers. We're here to *fight* crime, not to document it. I'll send someone round within the hour. You'll still be there will you?'

'Yes, I suppose I can be here,' Mike replied, resignedly.

'They'll be over shortly then; Goodbye.'

Mike replaced the receiver with a deep sigh. He could well have done without such a frustrating start to the day. He took a shower, dressed, and within the next half hour, heard a sharp knock on the door. When he answered it, he was confronted by a surly officer of the Gendarme flanked by a bespectacled man and a stern looking woman, both wearing white lab coats. Mike knew then that *Capitaine* Villeneuve was fishing for something far more significant than the evidence to solve an attempted robbery. Images of Michel Perotta breaking into the house filled his thoughts as he guided the three visitors towards the laboratory and pointed out the broken window frame. The bespectacled man and the sour faced woman stared suspiciously at the small fragments of pottery which Mike had disturbed and pursed their lips as they listened impassively to his apologies for interfering with the evidence. Without a word, they unpacked their equipment and quietly set about their work.

Sensing that his presence was no longer required, Mike retired to the kitchen and continued his research on the laptop. An hour later the humourless visitors packed their instruments and samples away into metallic briefcases and exited with a curt *au revoir*. Relieved, Mike closed the front door behind them and was himself leaving by the back door almost immediately afterwards. He took the back street route to the multi-storey car park and from there made his way over to the villa, where he picked up the old tool box and a piece of wood from the store.

On his return to Propriano, he stopped to pick up the newly developed prints from the photographic store and flicked through the shots of the U-boat's interior, noticing things which had not been immediately apparent during the dive. In a separate pouch he found Hubert's shots and smiled when he came across a print of the blue shark, rapidly disappearing into the dark background. Hubert certainly wasn't going to win any prizes for artistic merit, he decided, but he'd shown surprising determination and discipline to return with any shots at all. After slipping the two pouches into his pocket, he checked the time and then pulled out his mobile phone. He drew in a deep breath and dialled Monica's number, wishing that he had a more pleasant reason for doing so.

'Hey Mike, what's new?' Monica chirped brightly.

'Hi Monica. Have you finished work yet?'

'Almost. This is our last dive. Why?'

'Good. I should have called you earlier I suppose, but I didn't want to mess up your day...the thing is, we got broken into this morning.'

'Broken into!' said Monica alarmed. 'Did anything get stolen?'

'Not much, but there's some damage in the laboratory. Fortunately I disturbed the intruder; otherwise it could have been far worse.'

'Jesus Mike, are you OK?'

'Yeah, I'm fine. We had the Gendarmes round to check the place over this morning, but I don't suppose anything will come of it. I'm just going back to repair the damage to the window.'

'What did they take?'

'I've no idea. I don't even know what was in there to be honest, but the coins have gone.'

'Damn it! They were probably the only things of any real value. The rest was just basic earthenware; nothing unique or even particularly saleable.'

'That's probably just as well, because some of it got smashed.'

'Is there a lot of damage?'

'Maybe five or six pieces.'

'Well the main thing is that you're OK. I'll sort everything out when we get back, so don't worry too much about it.'

'I'll try. Sorry for bringing you bad news.'

'That's no problem. I should thank you for saving us from worse. I'll see you when we get back.'

'OK, see you shortly.'

After a quick detour through the backstreets, Mike parked the car a short distance away from the farmhouse and entered through the back door. He spent the next hour fixing the broken window of the laboratory using the tools which he'd recuperated from the villa. When he'd repaired it to his satisfaction, he went to the kitchen and pulled out his internal plan of the U-boat. Taking each photograph in turn, he stuck them to the drawing, adjacent to their respective compartments and added notes and observations. While he was putting the finishing touches to it, he heard the truck pulling up onto the driveway outside. He went to offer his help.

'Hey Mike, is it true what I hear about you losing those gold coins in a card game?' asked Hubert, smiling.

'Damn it Hubert! You promised me that you'd keep quiet about my gambling problem.'

'Can't you two take anything seriously?' scolded Monica, as she placed a camera stand on the drive. 'We are talking about a robbery you know.'

Hubert rolled his eyes and continued to unload the truck.

'Why don't you show me the damage Mike,' suggested Monica, 'the others can finish up out here.'

'Sure, let's go inside. There are a couple of small pots which have been smashed,' he said, as they walked down the hall towards the laboratory, 'and it's likely that there are a few more dents and scratches in some of the other stuff as well.'

'OK, I'm expecting the worst; so let's just get this over with.'

Monica's face was impassive as she entered the laboratory and stared at the shattered fragments of earthenware.

'I tried to keep all the matching pieces together,' explained Mike.

'That was very considerate of you. When did this happen exactly?'

'About eight thirty this morning.' Monica nodded and studied the repaired window.

'Is that where the thief entered?'

'Yes. I've just patched up the damage.'

'Thanks for that,' said Monica. She frowned as a thought crossed her mind. 'Do you think this has anything to do with that person Hubert saw snooping around the place?'

'We can't rule it out.'

'I'd better call the Gendarmes to let them know about him.'

Mike shrugged without comment. Sensing his discomfort, Monica slipped her arms around his waist and pulled him close.

'Don't worry Mike; there was really nothing of any great importance.'

'It's kind of a pity about the coins though,' he said, chewing his lip, 'but then I suppose there is a positive side to it.'

'And what's that?' asked Monica, raising a quizzical eyebrow.

'It gives us a good excuse to go and get some more.'

As soon as darkness began to fall, Pascal made his way to the hunting lodge where he'd arranged to meet Michel. The forest in which the lodge stood afforded perfect cover and Pascal could find his way through it blindfolded. As he approached, he cupped his hands around his mouth and imitated the cry of an owl. The door of the lodge opened and a halo of cigarette fumes billowed out around Michel's head as he peered out into the darkness. Pascal shook his head in despair. Michel clearly had no idea how to remain discreet.

'*Salut Pascal. Tout va bien?*'

'Everything's fine Michel, get your stuff together; we need to get moving.'

Pascal passed a critical eye over the general untidiness while he waited for Michel to prepare himself. Soon he was ushering him out into the night and leading him silently through the forest, down towards the farm. They soon reached the boundary wall and skirted around it until they arrived beside a gate giving access to the main courtyard. Pascal's car was parked opposite, with its rear facing towards them.

'Right, I'll open the trunk and then I'll go inside the house,' whispered Pascal. 'That's your cue to jump in the back. I'll close the hatch when I return, so just make sure that you're inside. If for any reason there's a problem and you're not there, we'll meet back at the lodge in an hour. Understood?'

'Yeah, let's go.'

Pascal pushed open the rusting metal gate and casually walked towards the car. After pretending to look for something in the trunk, he left the hatch open and walked towards the house. A moment later, he returned to the car and went to close it. He saw Michel hiding under a blanket, holding out a cigarette and smiling at him from the darkness.

'Do you have a light?'

Pascal's jaw set in annoyance as he slammed the hatch down. He drove straight out of the farm and turned right onto the main road to Propriano. In the rear-view mirror he saw a car pull out of the verge and begin to follow at a distance. It came as no real surprise. Driving without undue haste, he reached the outskirts of Propriano and then gradually made his way towards the commercial port.

Once he was inside the port perimeter, he followed the signs until he reached the personnel entrance and then used the card which Santorini had given him to open the barrier. As it dropped down behind him, he glanced at his rear view mirror and saw the car which had been tailing him pull up sharply. A smile lit up his face as he watched the occupants jump out of the car and kick the barrier in frustration. Following Santorini's instructions, he made his way past a succession of deserted warehouses and entered a compound with several loading bays situated at one end. In the darkness he saw Pierre's car parked next to a large white van. He drove towards the two vehicles and extinguished his lights. Pierre stepped out of the other car and came over to speak with him.

'Is Michel with you?' he asked as soon as Pascal had opened the door.

'In there,' he replied, jerking his head towards the rear of the car. When they opened the trunk, they found Michel with a cigarette still held between his teeth.

'Do you have a light now?'

'Ask Pierre,' replied Pascal irritably, 'and for God's sake smoke it before you get in the van.'

Michel jumped out of the trunk and stretched.

'*Salut* Michel,' chirped Pierre, pulling a lighter from his pocket and throwing it to him. 'Did you have a pleasant journey?'

'Oh yes, I love to travel with the smell of pig shit in my nostrils.'

Pierre laughed, much to Pascal's annoyance, and pulled a mobile phone from his pocket.

'I'd better give the boss a call.'

Pascal and Michel listened in as Pierre announced their arrival and received his final instructions. After a brief exchange, he nodded, rang off and then turned to face them.

'We move in five minutes.'

'Here, you might find these interesting,' said Monica as she handed Mike some printed sheets. 'My colleague, Professor Rieder, seems very excited about the U-boat which you've discovered and he's been working flat out to try and get his hands on the relevant documentation.'

Mike frowned in concentration as he studied a scanned copy of an official report.

'This is incredible,' he said, squinting at the outdated typeset. 'This is an account of an engagement between a Wellington Night Bomber and an unidentified German U-boat approximately twenty miles north of Bonifacio. The Captain, Wing Commander Rossland, claims that the U-boat was permanently disabled and sunk with all hands on the 19th April 1943. Surely that can't be a coincidence.'

'It's certainly deserves some consideration,' conceded Monica. 'Professor Rieder explained that the report was never officially endorsed because there was no confirmation from Germany that they had a U-boat positioned in the area at the time.'

'Well that's not surprising seeing as U602 was reported as missing somewhere north of Algeria.'

'Something just doesn't add up here does it?' agreed Monica. 'Take a look at this. These are the original orders which U602 received from UbD, the U-boat control centre. She left Lorient on the 25th March and was ordered to Toulon where she stopped briefly on the 10th April. From there she was ordered to Tunis.'

'Tunisia!' exclaimed Mike. 'Now that would be an ideal place from which to make the crossing.'

'There seems to be no record of her actually leaving Tunis,' continued Monica, 'but she was expected to return to Toulon at the earliest opportunity.'

'Which would have placed her in the area around Corsica at the time when Wing Commander Rossland reported sinking an unidentified U-boat,' pointed out Mike.

'It would have done, had there not been documented proof that U602 communicated with the command centre on that exact date from a position hundreds of miles away.'

'I don't buy it,' said Mike, shaking his head. 'If I were a U-boat Commander transporting a sensitive cargo between Tunis and Toulon during wartime, I certainly wouldn't make a dangerous detour into the Western Mediterranean.'

'And yet that's what appears to have happened.'

'Unless the document was falsified.'

'Why on earth would anyone do that?'

'OK, I know this is going to sound crazy, but just bear with me for a moment. Let's say that U602 was making her way back to Toulon from Tunis and was unfortunate enough to be spotted by an enemy aircraft and sunk off the coast of Corsica. Before sinking, she has time to make a distress call and give an approximate position to UbD. The SS can't believe their misfortune when they realise that U602 and her precious consignment are lost, but when they look at a chart and see that she sank in relatively shallow water, they realise that there might be a chance to salvage some of the gold, especially now that they have developed rudimentary underwater breathing apparatus. To throw everyone off the scent, they record her last known position in an area where a few days later, another U-boat is seriously damaged and presumed destroyed.'

'You mean to say that the SS purposely wanted her fate to be confused with the attack on U453?'

'Yes - a smoke screen. And that's exactly what I'd do in their position.'

'It's a tempting argument, I have to admit,' agreed Monica. 'I think it might be of some help if we put all this speculation into context. I've been reading up on the history of the conflict in Africa during the Second World War and there are one or two things which happened in 1942 and 1943 which appear relevant. First of all, the Italians were in control of Somalia, Eritrea and Ethiopia, which gave the SS the perfect opportunity to loot valuables from East Africa. Getting them out of the country was more of a problem however. The British led Allies were in control of the Suez Canal, effectively blocking the access to the Mediterranean, so the SS would have had to drive or fly the gold over the Sahara, or undertake a long and dangerous sea passage around the Cape of Good Hope. In 1942 the British Army was slowly building up its strength in North Africa by using the Red Sea and the Suez Canal as a supply line. After Rommel's failure to take control of the Suez in 1942 they strengthened their supply lines and pushed westwards, slowly winning back territory in Egypt and gradually pushing Rommel's Afrika Korps back along Libya's Cyrenaican coast. At this point the American forces had also entered the war and after landing in Morocco and Algeria, began to push the German Axis forces eastwards, effectively blocking their escape. By the beginning of 1943, Hitler had lost most of Libya and Algeria to the Allies and was left desperately holding onto the country which lay between them: Tunisia. It proved to be a futile attempt because the port of Tunis fell on May 7th 1943.'

'So that's why they were there!' said Mike excitedly. Monica raised her eyebrows.

'It would be reasonable to assume that the Axis Forces were preparing an evacuation at the time that U602 was in port.'

'And taking their ill-gotten gains with them, no doubt.'

'That's a reasonable assumption. And to be honest, it wouldn't really be surprising. The Nazis were moving massive amounts of valuables towards the end of the war.'

'Yes, I've heard that. But what exactly were they doing with it all?'

'Hiding it away,' replied Monica. 'Actually, many historians believe that its purpose was to ensure the survival of the Nazi Party in the event that Germany was defeated.'

Mike's eyes opened wide with surprise.

'The operation was masterminded by Martin Bormann, Hitler's Personal Secretary,' continued Monica. 'His plan was to hide stolen valuables from the Allies using the established banking system. Accounts were opened with both European and South American banks which were then used to deposit large quantities of cash, gold and other valuables. Action Feuerland was the name of one particular operation which was set up in order to ship valuables from Europe to South America. The operation began in 1943 and involved the movement of bullion by trucks overland from France to Spain and then onward shipment by U-boat across the Atlantic to Argentina.'

'I've heard these stories before, but I must admit that I find the whole idea a bit far fetched,' said Mike. 'I mean, is there any actual proof that this happened?'

'Well some of the U-boats were definitely intercepted and captured by the Americans at the end of the war, but for some reason they've been unwilling to say exactly what or who they found on board. U977 was one of them, and it was known to be carrying war criminals when it surrendered in the Mar del Plata in 1945. But perhaps a better indication of the scale of the operation is the estimated increase in gold reserves which took place in pro-Nazi and neutral countries between 1940 and 1945. According to Professor Rieder's sources, there was around a 620 million dollar increase in gold reserves in Europe over that period with at least half being deposited into Swiss bank accounts. Argentina saw a 640 million dollar increase in their reserves and those in Brazil increased by 230 million. In fact it was in 1943 that the bulk of those movements took place. Add to this the 262 million dollar cache of gold found in the Merkers potassium mine in Germany at the end of the war and an estimated 250 million dollars deposited in the Vatican coffers by the pro-Nazi Croatian Ustachis and we start to get an idea of the scale of what was happening.'

Mike stared at Monica in stunned silence before shaking his head and letting his eyes drift towards the photographs of the wreck. Monica's phone began to ring and he listened with one ear as she answered it and switched to French.

'Yes that's right, were at the bottom of the *impasse*. Do you have any idea what it is? I wasn't really expecting to receive anything today. Well that's OK, just bring it along, I'll be here all evening; thanks.' Mike waited until she had ended the call.

'I just can't quite get my head around the scale of all this. To think that the gold on U602 might have been destined for the vaults of a South American bank.'

'It could just as easily have been deposited in a European bank. Toulon was ideally placed for either option. One thing is certain though; if the coins hadn't sunk along with U602 then they would almost certainly have been melted down into bullion.'

'But surely that would have decreased their value?'

'Of course, but it would also have eradicated any link with their origin. Even unscrupulous banks shy away from stolen valuables which are traceable. And where else would you obtain a large hoard of Axumite gold?'

'I see your point. You know this is all starting to come together; an uncharted wreck, the strange rumours, the gold, the SS uniform, the contradictory documentation, but there still seems to be one major piece of the puzzle missing.'

'Which is?'

'How Santorini knows about it.'

'Maybe he has some links with the Nazis. He's part of an extremist nationalist group isn't he?'

'I don't buy that. The Corsicans hated the Nazis.'

'Well, maybe Santorini doesn't know who he's dealing with.'

'Even if he doesn't. Why send in a bunch of amateurs?'

'The cost of a professional search and salvage operation would be astronomical, and it would also draw a lot of unwanted attention. Besides, if that newspaper article is to be believed, they already gave it a try. My guess is that Santorini was hired because he's local, he's got time, he'll keep his mouth shut and people are afraid of him.'

'You could be right,' said Mike.

'Yes, and when it comes to him breaking in and stealing from my laboratory, I think it's time to turn the whole thing over to the authorities.'

'But we don't know for sure that it was Santorini's men who stole the coins.'

'I'm no longer prepared to take the risk Mike. Do we have to wait until someone else gets killed before you accept that you're out of your depth?'

There was a look of deep hurt on Mike's face.

Monica screwed her face up, but she was determined to stand by her decision. There was an awkward silence as Hubert entered the room.

'Did I come at the wrong time?'

'No Hubert, come on in, this concerns you as well,' said Monica, cupping her face in her hands. 'Look Mike, I'm sorry; my remark was perhaps a little insensitive, but I have to draw the line somewhere. I'm not prepared to put the safety of my colleagues at risk any more, so if you don't speak to the Gendarmes right now, then I will.'

The tense atmosphere was interrupted by the chime of the door bell. Hubert moved to answer it.

'It's OK Hubert, it will be a delivery for me,' said Monica. 'Stay right here, because we need to sort this out, once and for all.'

Hubert nodded and returned to his seat. He waited until Monica was out of earshot before addressing Mike.

'I take it that you haven't managed to persuade her to allow Bertie to drop us off over the wreck then?' Mike glanced up despairingly.

'Never mind,' said Hubert, slapping him on the shoulder, 'we'll just have to put together a press release and see what mayhem it causes. It could be quite amusing.'

'I'm not sure I've got the heart for it. I think I'd rather just forget about the whole affair and let Monica deal with it as she pleases.'

'You're too involved in this to allow it to be taken out of your hands now,' said Hubert, as he leafed through the scanned documents on the table. 'What's all this stuff here anyway?'

'Oh, it's some information which Monica got from her colleague in

Zurich. There's some amazing stuff there; not that it really matters anymore.'

'Hey, humour me. These are copies of original records aren't they?'

Mike, sighed, poured himself a glass of water and began to talk Hubert through the documents which Professor Rieder had unearthed. After several minutes of discussion he became aware that Monica had not reappeared.

'Where did Monica go?' he asked. 'I thought she wanted to speak to us.'

'I've no idea. Did she come back inside the house?'

'I don't remember seeing her. Maybe she came in the back way. I'll go and take a look.'

Mike left the kitchen and returned several minutes later with a concerned look on his face. Hubert stopped leafing through the documents and glanced up at him.

'What's wrong?'

'I can't find Monica anywhere.'

Pascal threw the navy blue delivery cap onto the passenger seat and accelerated away up the *impasse*. The plan had worked brilliantly. The girl didn't even raise an eyebrow when he told her that she would have to check the condition of the goods; she just followed him out to the van like a lamb ready for slaughter. He switched on the radio to mask her muffled cries, as she thumped around helplessly in the back.

Behind the partition, Michel was binding Monica's hands and feet together, smiling as she tried to swear at him through the gag. The look of horror on her face, when the door had opened and she had been thrust inside the van, was almost worth all the trouble that he had been put to. He flicked his tongue suggestively at her while he finished taping her hands behind her back. Beside him, Pierre pulled her mobile phone from its holder and slipped it into his jacket pocket. Monica squirmed and bucked as Michel thrust his hand beneath her top.

'Stop screwing around Michel. You can play games once we've got the gold,' scolded Pierre. He pulled out his own phone and keyed in Santorini's number. Michel ignored his remarks and kept his hands where they were.

'Jean-Claude? – Yeah it's me. It all went as planned. Pascal spotted the Englishman in the house so he left the message there. We've got the girl's phone, yes. Don't worry, I know what to do. Good; we'll see you in an hour then.'

Monica trembled with fear as she strained against Michel's wandering hands and the bindings which cut into her wrists. She winced in pain as the van jolted and her shoulder crashed against the ribbed metal floor, her cries stifled by the rag that had been thrust into her mouth. Pierre stared down at her with dark pitiless eyes.

'This is what happens when you fuck around with Corsicans. Do you think that you can just come here and do what you like? This is our country and we've had enough of you self-righteous foreigners coming here and helping yourselves to our riches. So now your cretin of a boyfriend had better show us where our gold is or we'll gut you both and feed you to the sharks.'

Tears ran down Monica's cheeks and trickled into the grimy channels of the cold metal floor. Frozen with fear, she remained motionless, stirring only when she heard the familiar ring tone of her mobile phone. She lifted her head and looked on in helpless frustration as Pierre pulled it from his pocket and checked the name on the screen.

'*C'est lui*, - it's him,' announced Pierre, smiling. His face hardened as he answered the call.

'*Monsieur* Summers?'

'Who that?' answered Mike in stuttered French. 'Where's Monica?'

'Do you understand what I'm saying?'

'Yes...but who is this?'

'Be quiet and listen carefully. Do not interrupt. Go and stand outside the front door of the house. Do it now!'

Back at the farmhouse, Hubert watched in total bemusement as Mike stood up and walked towards the door with the phone clamped to his ear.

'I'm standing outside now,' said Mike, staring out fearfully into the darkness.

'Look down to your right. There's a jar on the floor. Do you see it?'

'Y-yes I can see it...but what's going on? Is Monica with you?'

'In the jar are your instructions. Read them immediately and speak to no one.'

Pierre ended the call, turned the phone off and replaced it in his pocket. On the floor beneath him, Monica's body shook uncontrollably as tears of desperation streamed down her face. In her misery, she wished that she'd never set eyes on Mike Summers.

Mike pulled the message from the jar and read through it in a state of numbness. He returned to the kitchen, slumped down into a chair and buried his face in his hands.

'What's wrong?' asked Hubert, his concern mounting. Mike, unable to answer, held the note out without a word. Hubert took it from him and read the first few lines.

'Oh my God, she's been kidnapped! This can't be true. How could...how did they find out?'

Mike was still in a state of shock. He stared fixedly at the ground, his stomach a writhing ball of snakes.

'We have to go to the Gendarmes right away Mike; we don't know what they might do.' Mike stared at him wearily.

'You read the note didn't you? If we go to the Gendarmes, they'll kill her for sure. And have you already forgotten about their security issue? It's out of the question.'

'So what do we do?' asked Hubert, chewing his thumb in anguish.

'I'll have to go along with them; I've no choice.'

'They'll probably kill you both, even if you do,' warned Hubert.

Mike breathed a heavy sigh.

'That's a risk I'll have to take. I'll just have to try to bargain with them - maybe get them to release Monica before I take them to the wreck.'

'Even if they agree, they'd never let you walk free.'

'Look, I got Monica into this and I have to do whatever I can to get her out of it,' said Mike, resolutely.

Hubert frowned and massaged his temples, trying to think the problem through. He reflected on the training sessions, the interior of the U-boat, Mike's close brush with death and the germ of an idea began to form in his mind.

'Why don't you give yourself a bit of insurance and plan an escape route?'

'An escape route?'

'Absolutely. An *underwater* escape route. Look, I've seen what you're capable of. On dry land you wouldn't stand a chance against these men, but down there it's a whole different ball game. You have an enormous advantage. Why don't you use your experience to give them the slip once you've led them to the wreck?'

'It sounds like you have something in mind.' he said, his curiosity aroused.

'Maybe,' shrugged Hubert. 'I was thinking that if you were somehow able to give them the slip while you were inside the wreck and surface a good distance away from them, I could come and pick you up with the RIB. You'd have to take a mobile phone with you, of course.'

Mike's eyes narrowed as he considered the idea.

'It would be even better if I could take a DPV with me, but they'd never agree to that.' Mike thought about what he'd just said and began to nod as a sudden flash of inspiration hit him. 'Let me have another look at those drawings.'

Hubert drew close as Mike spread his plan of the U-boat out on the table.

'The problem is that there's only one entrance to the wreck that we know of. To escape from it unseen, I'd have to lose them inside, hide and then wait until they had no choice but to surface. There's very little chance that they'll let me dive on twin tanks and they certainly won't let me take a DPV or a mobile phone, so I'd have to stash everything I need outside the wreck first.'

'Wait a second; how are you planning to lose them inside the wreck? There's only one direction you can go!'

'Yes, but they won't be able to see me once the visibility drops to zero. I'll just wait in the conning tower until they're forced to leave and then reel myself back out. With any luck they'll think I'm dead when I don't reappear.'

'That's a pretty shrewd plan, but they want to dive the wreck first thing tomorrow morning, so how are you going to find the time to stash the equipment?' Mike's eyes locked with Hubert's.

'Do you fancy doing a night dive?'

Lieutenant Lechaux had a tough call to make. Three of his surveillance teams had now reported losing contact with their marks and as a result, he had no idea where any of the gang members were. In the last few minutes one of the units had found the abandoned cars of two of the gang in the old commercial port and discovered that the *Sampiero Corso* was missing from its moorings. Lechaux knew full well that they had not all gone on an innocent fishing trip. After all, why would their cars be left in an abandoned part of the port when there was ample space in the marina parking area? No. Something serious was taking place and Lechaux believed that he knew what it was.

Capitaine Villeneuve had left the *caserne* hours ago and Lechaux had no intention of capitulating and seeking his advice. It was time for him to be positive, to trust in his own judgement and act with authority. The worst that could happen was that he would be made to look foolish. And he would much prefer that than to be considered incompetent.

He stared blankly at his untidy desk and then reached for the phone.

'Good evening, Lieutenant Lechaux of the *Gendarmes de Propriano* here. Could you put me through to the *Garde Côtière?*'

'Certainly sir,' replied the operator. Lechaux waited as the call was punched through.

'*Garde Côtière.* How can we help you Lieutenant?'

'Good evening. I'm calling because I have reason to believe that a known terrorist and murder suspect is being smuggled from the island.'

The *Sampiero Corso* glided gently into the secluded bay and dropped anchor close to shore. On a small beach nearby a pair of headlights flashed twice in succession. Santorini turned the *Sampiero Corso*'s navigation lights off and on in response before reverting to a single anchor light and cutting the engine. He went to the stern, pulled the inflatable tender towards him and carefully stepped into it. The small outboard motor stuttered into life at the second attempt and soon he was heading towards the small patch of beach that was illuminated by Pascal's lantern. The dinghy ground to a halt when it hit loose shingle and Santorini stepped out into knee deep water.

'*Salut* Pascal. Is everything OK?'

'Everything's fine,' assured Pascal as he helped Santorini to beach the tender.

'Did you take a good look around?'

'I checked; the place is empty.' Santorini nodded.

'Let's get moving then.'

Pascal led him towards the transit van and tapped on the side door. It slid open to reveal two crouching figures.

'*Salut* Pierre. *Salut* Michel.' Santorini tilted his head and broke into a smile. 'Nice haircut you have there.'

'You should get yours done too; it looks like a badger slept in it.'

Santorini chuckled and jerked his chin towards Monica.

'Bring the girl. I've got the dinghy waiting.'

Pierre and Michel hooked their arms under Monica's armpits and pulled her out of the van. They dragged her down to the waterline where they dumped her unceremoniously into the dinghy. She grunted as her head crashed against the wooden thwart.

'Pascal, wait here with Michel while I take Pierre and the girl to the boat. Park the van well out of the way. I'll be back for you shortly.'

As the inflatable tender was launched, Monica felt cold seawater from the sodden floor soaking into her clothes. The dinghy rocked as the two men climbed aboard, ramming their feet down on either side of her. The small outboard started up with a reluctant rattle and soon Monica heard the rhythmic slapping of waves as the tender began to move away. There was a gentle bump as it slowed and brushed against the stern of the *Sampiero Corso*. Santorini stood up to secure a line and then Monica was dragged out of the tender and up onto the main deck. From there she was bundled down the companionway steps and pushed into a dark cabin below the wheelhouse. The stench of sweat, mildew and spilt beer combined with the rocking motion of the boat to fuel Monica's urge to vomit. She stifled it, knowing that with a gag rammed into her mouth the consequences would be disastrous.

'Now watch over her while I fetch the others,' Santorini said to Pierre.

In the darkness, Monica saw Santorini's portly figure disappearing up the companionway steps leaving Pierre staring down at her like a carrion crow.

'Do yourself a favour and keep still,' he spat. 'You can't escape from here so don't even think about it.'

Monica turned her head away. She'd already established that struggling was pointless. Lying between two bunks, it was impossible for her to reach her bindings. She glanced around in the darkness, harbouring a desperate hope that she might find a sharp object and be left alone long enough to free herself with it. She heard the sound of the tender's small outboard engine speeding towards the beach and then a moment later struggling back with a full load. There were footsteps on deck followed by the sound of bottles being opened and passed around. Santorini descended into the cabin and told Pierre to join the others. When he and Monica were alone, he reached over and began to peel away the tape from her mouth.

'Don't make a sound or I'll replace it straight away, understood?' Monica nodded, her eyes blazing with resentment.

'Speak only when you're spoken to,' he warned, before removing the rag from her mouth.

'Now; who's he working for?'

'Who are you referring to?'

'Your boyfriend: Mr. Summers.'

Monica winced. Mike didn't seem anything like a boyfriend to her at present, but it seemed pointless to deny it.

'Look, this is all a big mistake. The only person who Mike has been working for is me. He found out about the U-boat purely by accident...I presume that's what this is all about?' Santorini stared at her without comment.

'He just stumbled across a few bits of wreckage and started asking around.'

'Nobody on the island knew anything about the gold,' said Santorini, 'not even us, until recently, so how did *he* find out about it?' Monica wondered if the source of his recent knowledge was the gold coins which were stolen from the laboratory.

'Mike knew nothing about the gold either until he found the wreck.'

'Do you want me to believe that he risked being killed just to find a large hulk of rusting metal?'

'He had no idea what he was getting into; if anything he just let his curiosity get the better of him...but that all changed when you had his friend killed. After that, finding the wreck became an obsession.'

Monica noticed that Santorini did not deny the accusation.

'You're lying. Someone must have told him about the gold. Why else would he go to such lengths to find it?'

'No, that's not true. Look, if it makes more sense to you, he's a diving professional and he knew that he could make a lot of money by taking clients out to explore the wreck of a newly discovered U-boat.'

Santorini's eyes bored into hers as he considered her words. The promise of money seemed to him to be a far more rational motivation than mere curiosity. In his experience people were prepared to do incredibly stupid things to get their hands on it.

'And then he found the gold, which made the process of getting rich look a whole lot simpler,' he ventured.

'It wasn't like that at all. In fact he was going to turn everything over to the authorities.' Santorini thought back to the recorded telephone conversation.

'Is that what he told you?' he asked, mockingly.

'It was my idea actually.'

Santorini snorted and shook his head in disbelief. Only a woman could push a man to do something so incredibly stupid.

'Well that's certainly not going to happen as long as I'm still alive,' he growled before ramming the rag back into Monica's mouth. 'Pascal! You're taking first watch down here.'

As Santorini climbed up the companionway steps and emerged into the wheelhouse, he was convinced that he would be doing the world a favour by tying the Englishman and the girl to an anchor and tossing them over the side.

He began to revise and adapt his plan on arrival in Tizzano, shortly after seeing the old tool box and the wheel jack lying in the trunk of the car. If everything went well, Mike now believed that he could get out of the wreck in advance of the others, make a clean escape and give Santorini and his gang a taste of their own medicine. But he only had one chance to get things right, and any failure on his part would probably get both himself and Monica killed.

'Two more miles to go,' called Hubert from the helm. As the black and yellow RIB sliced through a gently rolling sea at lightning speed, Mike stared up at the heavens, hoping that Monica's morale was holding out. A mile from the wreck Hubert began to reduce speed and Mike fired up the computer. The U-boat sounding appeared on the digital chart and under Mike's guidance Hubert approached a waypoint which he had placed at the centre of it.

'Go five degrees to starboard. Back 3 degrees to port. Hold it there and drop your speed.' Mike ran to the bow of the RIB and readied himself with the anchor. When the waypoint alarm sounded, Hubert put both engines astern and Mike stood clear of the loose coils of chain and threw the anchor into the sea. He watched it fall into the sucking blackness, dragging the snaking line behind it.

'That should put me pretty damn close,' he said.

'I've made up my mind; I'm coming in with you,' said Hubert after setting the anchor in.

'There's really no need Hubert.'

'I'm coming anyway. It'll make things go faster.'

'Suit yourself. You can take the car jack and the trimix sling then. You know what to do, don't you?'

'Of course.' Hubert pulled on his wetsuit and then attached an emergency stop tank to the RIB's winch. After fixing a chemical light stick to it, he lowered it 6 metres below the surface.

'We shouldn't need that,' said Mike.

'I know,' replied Hubert inexplicably.

Mike shrugged his shoulders and jumped over the side.

'Pass me the rebreather down please.'

Hubert lowered Thomas' rebreather over the side while Mike put air into the lift bag that would support it during the descent. The outside shell of the rebreather had been blackened with dark polish and attached to its harness were several items that were essential to the success of his plan.

'Right let's go,' shouted Mike.

Hubert strapped on his twin set, clipped the small trimix cylinder and the car jack to his harness and launched himself over the side. On Mike's signal they dropped down the anchor line and attached lime-green glowing light sticks at ten metre intervals as they progressed. Blue specks of bioluminescence streaked from their bodies like bright sparks of static electricity as they fell through the blackness. Mike's headlamp illuminated the anchor line beneath him and soon a lighter patch appeared out of the obscurity. It was the bridge of the U-boat. The anchor had fallen so close to the wreck that the chain was angled diagonally around the turret. Mike blew a sigh of relief into his regulator as he began to slow his descent.

To his right, Hubert's flashlight beam picked out teeming shoals of red cardinals and a huge wreckfish, but unfortunately there was no time to admire the spectacle. Mike carefully guided the suspended rebreather past the turret and pushed it deep underneath the curve of the hull. The ripped fishing net that now stretched out above him, would serve as a camouflage net to help keep it from view. He checked the rebreather over one last time, making sure that the cylinder valves and the mouthpiece cover were firmly closed before he deflated the lift bag and detached it. A large moray eel stared at him from a hole in the wreck and retracted warily as Mike pushed the rebreather into a gap beneath its lair. Please watch over this for me, he implored it, and smiled as the moray reappeared as if to carry out its sentry duties.

Above him, Hubert was hovering motionless, gripping a piece of jagged metal at the base of the damaged turret. Mike watched him unclip the trimix sling and push it as far inside the blast hole as he could reach before releasing it. There was a dull thud as the cylinder hit the floor of the control room deep inside the hull. Mike joined Hubert as he unclipped the car jack and placed it inside the jagged hole in the outer hull. Once he had opened the jaws to fit the gap, he braced himself and rotated the crank until he had forced away a sizeable flap of steel. As the metal buckled it sent strange pinging noises echoing around the entire length of the wreck.

Hubert released the jack and positioned it deeper, inside the mouth shaped perforation of the inner casing. He repeated the jacking process but made little progress against the thick steel which formed the watertight hull. The continued straining caused Hubert's breathing rate to increase and Mike decided to intervene. Hubert nearly jumped out of his skin when he felt his arm being touched and Mike realised that he was on edge. He signalled to him to ascend, but Hubert shook his head resolutely. Unwilling to waste time arguing, Mike took the crank handle from him and tried to open up the gap himself. The jaws of the jack were clearly jammed up tight and Mike pushed his head in closer to inspect the metal plating. As he did so, Hubert unclipped the lift bag from his harness.

Mike spotted a fracture line on one side of the gap and repositioned the jack close to it. After several rotations the crank came up hard and he braced himself against the hull and drew in a breath. He strained for several seconds and then heard a loud clanging sound. A fine orange cloud billowed out from the gap, and as it cleared Mike could see that the fracture had lengthened. He quickly worked either side of it and managed to widen the hairline crack a fraction more. There was still no overall effect on the size of the opening. Mike checked his watch and sighed. If his next attempt was not successful, he would have to abandon the idea altogether or risk compromising his plan for the following morning. In a last ditch effort he placed the jack into the hole diagonally and cranked it up tight. He strained again and heard more pinging sounds along the hull. After planting his fins firmly against the outer flap of steel he prepared himself for one last shot. He thought about Monica trussed up at the mercy of Santorini's gang and a rage began to burn inside him. The muscles in his shoulders flexed in anticipation and then he roared into the regulator and cranked with all his might. There was a dull cracking sound and Mike suddenly found himself falling backwards through the water.

His first thought was that the crank shaft had sheared off under the strain, but he soon realised that the entire jack was still in his hands. After adjusting his buoyancy, he returned to examine the hole again and discovered the reason why. A thick wedge of steel the size of a large roofing tile had fallen away from the inner hull where two fracture lines had intersected. There was no time to check if it was large enough to fit his body through, but measured against his hands, it looked like he might just be able to squeeze past.

Preparing for an immediate ascent, he turned around to look for Hubert and was surprised to find no sign of him. Assuming that he'd taken his advice and returned to the surface, he decided to follow suit. Soon Mike reached the light stick that was positioned at thirty metres and he reduced his ascent rate as he arrived at his first stop. Looking above, his concern began to grow when he saw no sign of Hubert's lights. Mike now found himself in a difficult situation. He could not cut short his decompression schedule to check to see if Hubert was safely back on the boat and a return to the bottom would seriously undermine his plans for the morning. Hubert was well aware that he should not have disappeared without giving notice of his intentions and Mike now had to prepare himself for an agonising wait and the prospect of a dangerous rescue attempt.

As he was considering his options, Mike looked down to check his instruments and saw the unmistakable glow of a flashlight further down the anchor line. A wave of relief passed over him as he watched it move and slowly grow in intensity. Hubert was obviously beneath him and ascending normally, if a little behind schedule. Relieved, Mike rose towards his next planned stop and tried to relax. When he looked down a minute later, he was surprised to see a glowing, medusa-like form several meters beneath him. He soon realised that it was a fully inflated lift bag and when he reached down, he discovered that his own was missing. Puzzled as to why Hubert would have taken it, he tried to attract his attention with a back-up flashlight. Hubert responded positively to his standard OK signal, but with further communication options being limited, Mike could only shake his head in annoyance and wait for a later explanation.

Mike's decompression schedule was completed shortly afterwards and he returned to the RIB alone. He quickly packed away his equipment, leaned over the sponson and watched Hubert's progress below the surface. A small group of semi-opaque squid darted back and forth in the greenish glow, their iridescent eyes glinting as they caught the light. The beam of Hubert's flashlight moved slowly towards the stern of the boat and paused at the drop tank. Mike frowned, unable to understand how Hubert could have run so low on gas that he was obliged to use the emergency supply. To his relief, Hubert surfaced immediately afterwards.

'Where the hell did you get to?' Mike asked, making no attempt to hide his annoyance.

'I went on a little detour.'

'Why the hell didn't you let me know?'

'Because you would have stopped me.'

Mike sighed in frustration.

'OK pass up your gear; I'm in no mood to argue.'

Hubert calmly passed up his equipment and then climbed aboard. When he had dried himself off, he went towards the gantry and began to winch up the cable.

'Did you manage to enlarge the hole in the conning tower,' he asked.

'Yes, I think it was more due to luck than anything else, but I eventually managed to break off a small piece of the inner hull. I'm just hoping that it'll be big enough for me to squeeze through.'

'Well Santorini certainly won't be able to follow if you can,' chuckled Hubert.

Mike watched in growing curiosity as Hubert winched the lift bag to the surface and collapsed it.

'It looks like you have quite a bit of weight under that. What exactly have you been...?' Mike stopped mid-sentence as the realisation hit him with the force of a baseball bat. 'No! Tell me you didn't.'

Hubert smiled and winched a bulging mesh bag clear of the water. Liquid silt streamed from it as he swung it inboard and settled it down on the deck. Mike drew close as Hubert thrust his hand inside and brought out a muddy crucifix. He reached over to rinse it off in the sea and then handed it to Mike with a grin of immense satisfaction. The golden reflections from Mike's flashlight left no question as to its composition.

'Hubert, that was an incredibly reckless thing to do.'

Hubert grinned and spat into the sea.

'Fuck them!'

13

Dawn began to break on the eastern horizon and a shaft of dim blue light slowly crept into the cabin of the *Sampiero Corso*. Monica blinked awake from a restless night and rolled over to allow the blood to circulate in her deadened right arm. When the painful throbbing eased and the feeling was restored, she cautiously lifted her head to take in her surroundings. There were dark shapes huddled in the bunks to either side of her and the stuffy air vibrated to the sounds of contented snoring. Pascal, who ought to have been watching over her, was slumped against the opposite bulkhead, breathing throatily with his eyes closed and his jaw slack.

Using her head and elbows to raise herself from the damp floor, she rolled onto her side and slowly drew her knees up towards her chest. Rocking back and forth, she used the momentum to push herself over onto her knees. She glanced up the companionway steps and saw a square of pale blue sky, a single star, briefly making an appearance as the boat rocked to port. The sight of approaching daylight gave her a glimmer of hope. If she could somehow manage to crawl up the steps and then out onto the main deck, there was a chance that she could attract the attention of a passer-by, or better still, find a sharp object and cut herself free so that she could swim to shore.

As she was easing herself up the side of one of the bunks, ready to push herself to her feet, the bleeping of an alarm clock sent a spike of fear tearing into the pit of her stomach. She collapsed back onto the ground with a grunt and stifled tears of frustration. A hand groped around on the shelf above her and the piercing sound ceased abruptly. Santorini yawned and sat up, rubbing his eyes vigorously. He looked around the cabin and then stiffened when he spotted Pascal slouching against the bulkhead. His eyes immediately darted towards Monica, lying beside him on the floor. His face clouded over as he picked up a shoe and launched it at Pascal's head. Pascal yelped and held his hand to his ear.

'Wake up you lazy son-of-a-bitch,' shouted Santorini. 'Next time it will be more than just a shoe. Now go and start the engine.'

Pascal shuffled up the companionway steps, muttering under his breath as he walked out onto the deck and lifted a hatch. There were muffled complaints from the men in the bunks as the growling diesel engine burst groggily into life, sending vibrations rattling through the thin wooden bulkhead which separated the cabin from it. Santorini turned Monica over so that he could check her bindings. She winced as her face was pressed against a pair of shoes and recoiled at the unpleasant odour which lingered inside them. Now beyond all pretence of dignity, she tolerated the injustice in silent rage. She was grateful at least that Santorini had prevented Michel from trying to rape her during the night. If he hadn't done so, she would have saved him the trouble of having to kill her.

'Pierre, Michel, get your backsides up and go and help haul in the anchor,' bawled Santorini. 'We're not on a pleasure cruise here.'

There were more groans and protestations as the two men threw back their blankets and rubbed the tiredness from their eyes. Santorini checked his watch as the two men climbed sluggishly up the companionway steps and walked towards the bow. Soon the growling cadence of the diesel engine increased and the *Sampiero Corso* began to yaw as it edged away from the coast. Santorini pulled out his mobile phone and punched in a number.

'Don't speak. You know who this is.'

Monica's head jerked up when she realised that he was speaking to Mike. Her hands trembled as she listened in to the conversation.

'I will not repeat this message. You will say *je comprends* only when asked. Do you understand?'

'I want to see Monica before I will agree to do anything,' Mike replied boldly.

Santorini was both surprised and angered by his demands.

'You'll get to see her this morning; now do not interrupt me again, otherwise *she* will pay the consequences. Do you understand?'

'*Je comprends.*'

'Good! You will go towards Sartène and then make your way towards Pagliaju. At 6.30am exactly, you will enter the site and walk amongst the rows of stones away from the main entrance. Remember that we will be watching you. If we see any sign of the Gendarmes, you and your friends will die. Do you understand?'

'*Je comprends.*'

The line went dead.

Mike placed his mobile phone and Hubert's recordable MP3 player in his pocket. He picked up Monica's tee-shirt and held it close to his nose, breathing in its delicate fragrance before placing it gently back on her pillow. His jaw set with determination as he reached for the keys to the

Citroen. Before he left the house, he went to Hubert's room and found him lying awake.

'I'm leaving now, so just make sure that you're on standby with the boat from 7am onwards. Leave a note for Bertie and Anna - I'm sure that you can think of something. And just remember that if you haven't heard from either me or Monica by this evening, contact *Capitaine* Villeneuve and tell him everything you know. Show him the gold if you need to.'

Hubert nodded.

'Leave everything to me, just go out there and do what you have to do,' said Hubert. 'I'll be anchored by the headland if you need me.'

Mike and Hubert clasped hands and fixed each other with an intensity which mirrored their resolve.

'Good luck!'

Mike nodded once and walked from the room. He stepped out of the house and went straight to the car. Soon he was racing eastwards along the N196 with one eye trained on his watch. He passed through the town of Sartène and then turned left towards Tizzano and the two Megalithic sites of Pagliaju and Stantari. The cool morning air filled the car with the sweet fragrance of myrtle and wild lavender, the peace of the surrounding *Maquis* strangely at odds with the events which were unfolding. The Citroen tore relentlessly along the quiet, deserted road, propelling Mike towards a fate which he dare not contemplate.

He slowed and turned right when he saw signs for Pagliaju and followed the track as far as the entrance gates. They were padlocked when he arrived and a solitary sign beside them informed him that they would not be open for another two hours. The time was now 6am and Mike understood that Santorini wanted him to enter the site alone. It seemed a simple enough task to scale the entrance gates, so he put on a shorty wetsuit and collected his buoyancy jacket and regulator from the trunk of the car. While the hatch was shielding him from view, he held the tiny MP3 player in his hand and set it to recording mode following Hubert's instructions. It would now be active for close to ten hours; more than enough time for what he needed it for. He placed it inside a latex surgical glove and then sealed the opening with a knot. After unscrewing the purge valve from the buoyancy jacket, he stuffed the glove inside the air chamber and then sealed it inside. Now it would secretly record everything that was said within range of its tiny microphone. He slipped his arms into the buoyancy jacket, wrapped the regulator hoses around his neck and began to climb over the gate.

On reaching the other side, he walked past the ticket booth and made his way along the path towards the main grounds. The low rays of the morning sun painted pale pink hues over the standing stones of the first *alignement*, accentuating the details of the carvings while casting long shadows across the meadow. Mike noticed the strange bas-relief figures which Monica had described, carved skilfully into the upright stones. The eyes of fierce warriors followed his progress with suspicion, their Shardane swords held at the ready as he passed before them. When he reached the next row of *menhirs*, he nearly jumped out of his skin when one of the stones appeared to challenge him. He turned to see a weapon pointing at him; more deadly than even the most skilfully crafted Bronze Age sword. The man holding the gun was familiar; one of the more discreet members of Santorini's gang and with a flick of the gun barrel, he gestured to Mike to keep moving along the path. Mike continued until he reached the perimeter, where he was searched and then ordered to pass through a gap in the fence. From there he was led along a trail bordered by thick scrub which terminated in a clearing, where a white van was waiting. A side door opened and Mike was prompted to enter at gunpoint.

'Where are you taking me? Where is Monica?,' he asked as the van began to move away.

'You'll find out soon enough,' was all that he received as a reply.

The windowless van jarred as it crept along a potholed track and then accelerated smoothly away when it reached the main road. Mike sat in quiet contemplation, staring fixedly at the regulator in his hand. A short while later, the van slowed and came to a halt. The man with the gun sat motionless, staring dispassionately at Mike, averting his eyes only when the side door slid open to reveal the face of the ruddy cheeked driver. His expression was less intimidating than that of the gaunt man who had been guarding him, but the bulge under his jacket told Mike that he was none the less threatening.

Mike was ordered out onto a dusty road at gunpoint and a quick glance at his surrounds told him that he was now in a secluded part of Tizzano. An inflatable tender with a small outboard motor was waiting in the shallows of the rocky shoreline and Mike was directed towards it with a prod of a gun barrel to his ribs. Despite the shaved moustache and military haircut, Mike had no problem in identifying the helmsman; it was Perotta. Bile rose into his mouth at the thought of sharing a confined space with him, and the hatred mirrored in Michel's dark eyes signalled that the feeling was mutual. Mike approached with his head held high, determined not to be intimidated. As he climbed aboard, clutching his regulator in one hand, he realised that an opportunity presented itself.

'Ah Mr. Perotta. I never did get the chance to ask; did you get a kick out of raping and murdering Chantale Moret?' he asked as the boat was pushed clear of the shallows. Michel smiled at Mike as he opened up the throttle and swung the boat around.

'Not half as much as I will enjoy killing you and your pretty Swiss whore,' he replied with a malicious grin. 'There will be some regrets though; after all she gives really good head.'

Michel's colleagues sniggered, but Mike refused to rise to the bait.

'And what about Thomas Casanis,' Mike probed, 'did you sleep easily in your bed when you learned that you killed him too?'

Michel shrugged. 'That was actually more of an accident...but it all helps to rid the island of vermin.' Mike was incensed, but he consoled himself with the knowledge that Perotta had just admitted his guilt.

'The island will never be rid of vermin while there are still people like you on it,' he retorted.

Michel's expression darkened. He reached into a pocket and with lightening speed, pulled out a switchblade. Pascal quickly reached across and restrained him before he had a chance to use it. Mike, having braced his legs in readiness to leap backwards into the water, eyed him warily.

'Control yourself Michel,' advised Pascal, 'remember that we need him alive and unhurt.'

Michel scowled as he put the knife away. He looked away and then with surprising agility, flung his arm out and slapped Mike hard across the face with the back of his hand.

'Next time there will be no one around to protect you,' he warned.

Mike ignored the burning pain on his right cheek and turned his face away. They continued their passage in silence, keeping clear of the main moorings and heading towards the far shore, where the *Sampiero Corso* was lying at anchor. Michel guided the tender in towards her stern and Mike glanced up when a figure appeared at the rail. It was Santorini, his arms spread wide and his dark hair blowing in the breeze, staring down imposingly, like some demonic opera singer.

'Don't bother to tie up the boat,' he growled, 'Jeannot is waiting for us back at the jetty.'

Michel gave a brief nod. Mike was prompted to his feet. He stepped from the tender to the swim ladder and climbed up onto the stern deck of the *Sampiero Corso*, followed closely by Pierre.

'Did you search him thoroughly?'

'He's clean,' Pierre replied.

Santorini nodded, his dark eyes watching Mike's every movement.

'Sit down!'

Mike ignored the request.

'I want to see Monica.'

Santorini stared at him with the kind of disdain that a rottweiler might reserve for a yapping poodle.

'I'm the one who gives the orders around here,' he growled. 'First tell me who you're working for and then you'll get to see her.'

'I'm not working for anyone,' said Mike.

'Then how did you know about the wreck?'

Mike sighed and began to recount the events which had led to his discovery of the U-boat. Santorini listened intently, searching his face for the slightest sign of deceit. When Mike had finished speaking, Santorini narrowed his eyes, unable to find any inconsistencies between his and the girl's stories.

'If you are lying, I will find out,' he warned, 'and it will be much worse for the both of you when I do.'

'Then I have nothing to fear,' said Mike, matching the intensity of his glare. 'Can I see Monica now?'

Santorini glanced at Pierre and jerked his head in the direction of the cabin. Pierre nodded and pushed Mike towards the wheelhouse. When they reached the companionway hatch, Mike was told to descend. A muffled voice came from the darkness below as he entered the sombre cabin. When his eyes adjusted to the light, he saw Monica strapped to a chair with her ankles and wrists bound tightly together. The gag wound firmly around her jaw stifled her sobs as she stared at him wide eyed in fear and desperation. She turned her head away as tears welled up and began to roll down her swollen cheeks. Mike felt his throat tighten as feelings of guilt and remorse tore like barbed wire into his chest. He looked down at the floor and struggled to hold onto the resolve which he so desperately needed to ensure their survival. Knowing that Monica needed reassurance more than anything else at that moment, he masked his own distress and drew in a calming breath.

'Monica look at me,' he implored.

When Monica's frightened eyes met his, he spoke with calm determination.

'I'm desperately sorry that I got you into this mess. I know that everything looks bleak right now, but don't give up on me, because I'm going to get you out of here. Whatever happens, stay calm, and don't lose hope.'

Jeannot was deeply troubled as the *Sampiero Corso* made its way towards Roccapina. It was one thing to take part in an illegal salvage operation, but to be unwittingly involved in a kidnapping was another matter entirely. The way things were looking, he might even be considered an accessory to murder.

As soon as he had set foot on the boat, it was clear that something was wrong. The Englishman appeared to have about as much choice in his involvement with the salvage operation as Jeannot had himself. Quite what hold Santorini had over him, apart from the threat of violence, was unclear until he overheard the Englishman pleading with Santorini to release some girl or other and let her return to shore. Pierre and Pascal's repeated visits to the cabin below decks had already begun to raise his suspicions and now he intended to find out just what exactly he had become embroiled in.

He walked into the wheelhouse, casually dropped a lighter onto the floor and while bending to pick it up, glanced down the stairwell. The sight of the young girl being held captive below drove a wedge of ice into his heart. If only he'd known how much pain and suffering that godforsaken hatch would bring, he would have buried it in the sand, right there where he'd found it. Wracked with remorse, he looked out at the Englishman, sitting dejectedly by the rail of the stern deck. It appeared that one way or another, they had both been caught in Santorini's snare, struggling to free themselves from his poisonous hold. He now began to look upon the Englishman with empathy. After all, they were both men of the sea; practically minded, wily and tenacious, that much he had seen. Certainly, neither of them deserved to find themselves in a position like this. Deep in thought, Jeannot lit his pipe and walked out onto the stern deck. He leaned over the rail close to where Mike was sitting and stared towards the horizon.

'The girl is with you?' he asked in a quiet voice.

Unsure if the words were meant for his ears, Mike glanced sideways and immediately recognised the wiry old man who Thomas had nicknamed Don Quihote. Before he answered, he flicked his eyes towards the thin faced man who had been keeping a close eye on him from the opposite bench. At the present moment he seemed more interested in picking his toes.

'Yes, why do you ask?'

'I just wanted to be sure.'

'I was under the impression that you all knew.'

'I'm not here by choice,' Jeannot explained, still staring out to sea. 'They have me by the balls, just like you.'

Mike frowned but made no comment.

'If there is any way that...' Before Jeannot could finish, the thin faced man stirred.

'Jeannot, get away from there,' he shouted, 'Go inside and join the others.'

Jeannot stood up and gave Mike a despairing look.

'*Bonne chance*,' he uttered as he tapped his pipe on the rail and walked away. Mike's face remained impassive. Whatever he was about to say, Mike was alone in this. If it was true that he was not a member of Santorini's gang, then Mike hoped for his sake that he had a steady nerve.

The morning sun was beating down on the quays, bringing the stink of rotting fish from drying nets to the attention of Bertoli's disapproving nostrils. He was already feeling quite miserable as it was, having been posted to the harbour since midnight to watch for the return of the *Sampiero Corso*. It had proved to be a pointless exercise, and Bertoli was starting to wonder if he'd backed the wrong horse when fate suddenly smiled upon him. His mobile phone began to ring and his eyes widened when he saw the name of the caller on the display.

'Good morning Jeannot. I thought you'd forgotten all about me. To what do I owe the pleasure of your call?'

'Listen I can't talk for long,' whispered Jeannot, 'I have some important information to give you, but first of all I want your absolute guarantee that I will get protection and immunity from prosecution.'

'As I told you Jeannot, you have my word.'

'And whatever happens, I will not testify against Santorini.'

'That is both understood and accepted. Now tell me all that you know.'

'The wreck has been found and Santorini is heading towards it as we speak.'

There was a pause before Bertoli spoke.

'Well that *is* excellent news. Do you have the coordinates?'

'No, I don't. But you'll have no difficulty finding us. We'll be anchored off Roccapina.'

'I see,' said Bertoli, his mind racing. 'Is Michel Perotta on board by any chance?'

'You'll find out soon enough.'

'Well I'll arrange...'

'No wait!' interrupted Jeannot. 'That is not the reason for my call. Santorini has two captives on board. One is the person who found the wreck; an Englishman, and I think the other is his girlfriend. The Englishman is the only person who knows where the wreck is and Santorini is holding the girl hostage until he leads him to it.'

Bertoli paused as he attempted to piece together all the information.

'The name of this Englishman wouldn't be Mike Summers by any chance would it?'

'I don't know his name, but I've seen him before. He was the diving partner of the Frenchman; the one who was killed in the car crash.'

Bertoli chewed his lower lip and felt a trickle of sweat run down the back of his neck. The situation was clearly far more complex than he'd anticipated.

'Thank you Jeannot; that's all I need to know,' he replied with sudden resolve. 'Just hang in there and we'll have a team sent out shortly.'

Santorini adjusted his course, guiding the *Sampiero Corso* towards the GPS coordinates which Mike had given him. The decimals of the twelve digit latitude and longitude reading ticked away as he made his final approach and began to flash when the sound of the alarm marked their arrival. Mike felt a burst of adrenaline course through his veins as Santorini shouted the order for the anchor to be deployed. A length of chain rattled through the bow roller dragging a longer section of warp behind it. Santorini set the anchor in and let the boat swing around in the wind as he gathered his men together at the stern.

'Right, all of you. Listen carefully. The purpose of this first dive is to ensure that the U-boat, and more importantly, the gold, are both there. I doubt if our friend here would be quite so foolish as to try to deceive us,' said Santorini, with a glance in Mike's direction, 'but I've heard tell that the English are stubborn and for some reason value their own honour greater than that of their women.' The gathering cackled with laughter until Santorini held his hand up for quiet. 'If it's possible to take some of the gold back with us on the first dive, all's well and good, but our priority is to come back with the knowledge to salvage it properly. I want you to approach this task with the same organisation and discipline which you would exercise on one of our undercover operations; so just make sure you keep your minds fully on the job. Right, here's the plan. Michel, Pierre and Jeannot, you'll be going inside the wreck with our honoured guest and it will be your responsibility to watch over him while he leads you to the gold.

I'll remain on the outside to prevent any attempt at escape. Make sure that you have your spear guns loaded and ready to fire - and don't be afraid to use them if you think you need to. Pascal you will stay on board and guard the girl. If anything goes wrong while we're down there, I will send up this signal,' he said, holding up a lift bag. 'If you see it on the surface, do not hesitate; kill the girl immediately.' Santorini directed a warning glance in Mike's direction to underline his threat. Mike dropped his eyes, but not in submission. He was taking a long look at the lift bag.

'OK, are there any questions?' The gathering remained silent.

'Good! You can start getting ready then.'

Mike was given Pascal's mask, fins and weight-belt to complete his equipment. He held his breath as Pascal double checked the pockets and seams of his buoyancy jacket. Fortunately, the MP3 player remained undetected. Ten minutes later, all five men were fully equipped and ready to enter the water. Michel and Pierre jumped first and trained their spear guns on Mike as he entered the water behind them. Jeannot and Santorini entered immediately afterwards. Under Pascal's watchful eye, they made their way across the surface towards the bow of the boat and began to drop down the anchor line. Mike set his timer to zero and glided effortlessly through the water trying to ignore the malevolent presence which surrounded him. A solitary jack crossed his path and he found himself envying its freedom to simply disappear into the vastness of the oceans. Shafts of shimmering sunlight reached down from the surface above and seemed to dissolve without trace into the obscurity below.

Soon a long shadow began to form across the featureless haze and a dark ridge suddenly came up to meet them. Mike's relief at seeing it was not shared by the men around him. Their eyes searched in vain for signs of a wreck. An agitated Santorini appeared beside Mike, poking him in the side and vigorously demonstrating the palms upward gesture which expressed a desire to know what the hell was happening. Mike responded by consulting his compass and pointing in a south-easterly direction along the ridge. He sensed the annoyance and frustration of the men around him, but remained unperturbed; he knew exactly where the wreck was, and he also knew that a two minute swim at 48 metres would quickly eat into their precious air supplies and prolong their decompression schedule.

Two huge cuckoo wrasse provided a temporary distraction as they weaved their way between bright orange gorgonian fans. Michel playfully took aim at one of them and would eagerly have pulled the trigger of his spear gun had circumstances been different. The tension grew as narcosis began to play on the men's nerves and Mike was relieved when a distinct grey shadow finally began to loom up ahead. Sharp outlines gradually began to appear from the hazy backdrop, like the emerging details of a developing photograph. The impressive bow of the slender U-boat emerged dramatically from the gloom as if it were piercing a bank of thick fog. The sight was magnificent and Mike could well understand the muffled howls of excitement which he heard around him as he led the men down onto the gorgonian festooned decks. The tension soon eased as they admired the spectacle and Mike welcomed the distraction it afforded. There were still another 60 metres to cover before they would reach the entrance to the wreck. He had chosen to approach from the north west for that very reason.

A quick glance at his watch reassured Mike that everything was running according to schedule. When Santorini's men lingered, marvelling at the 37mm deck gun and the imposing sight of the conning tower, Mike had to increase his pace to push them along. He paused only when he reached the damaged stern section, hovering over the misaligned propeller shafts and pointing down towards the jagged entrance, gaping like the mouth of a giant grouper. He moved towards it unchallenged and glided effortlessly into the electric motor room. Soon flashlights were being switched on behind him, their wandering beams picking out isolated bursts of scarlet, yellow and orange as the red end of the light spectrum was restored to otherwise dull looking sponges. Red cardinals scattered away from the invading light into the maze of inert machinery, hiding in the anonymity of the shadows.

Mike found the going easy without bulky twin tanks and slipped past the first obstruction with ease. He turned to see the others bump and push their way through the narrow gap, clouding the otherwise crystal clear water with silt and particles of rust. At this rate he wouldn't have to make things a great deal more difficult for them, he thought. With a degree of satisfaction at the growing anxiety in their eyes, he turned and continued onwards through the first hatch and into the diesel engine room. Up ahead, his lamp picked out the dome of the skull, still lying where he had last seen it, in the narrow passage between the two dormant engines. As he passed over it, he reached down and rotated it so that its gruesome smile was directed towards his pursuers. The sight of silt smoking eerily out of its empty orbits had the desired effect. Directly behind him, Michel, clearly struggling to hold his nerve, rose upwards to avoid the skull's menacing stare, hitting his head on a light fitting in the process.

There was no doubt in Mike's mind that they were starting to lose their concentration along with their composure. He reached down to pick up the abandoned reel from the previous dive and paid out line as he pulled himself through the next hatch. Aware that he was now entering the place where he had almost been killed, he made a conscious effort to remain calm. Curiosity pushed him to shine his flashlight onto the metal cabinet which had almost been the cause of his demise. In its normal upright position, it gave the deceiving impression that it posed not the slightest threat.

A few meters behind Mike, Michel hesitated at the sight of the gaping jaws of a moray eel, lurking in a hole to his left. Jabbing fiercely at it with the spear gun, he forced it into retreat before bolting past and causing more silt to balloon up in the process. Mike shook his head at Michel's ineptitude and took advantage of the delay it afforded him to explore the area. Drawing upon his recent knowledge of the wreck's layout, he soon located the galley and the hatch in the deckhead above it. Unfortunately, with neither the time nor the tools needed to open it, he pushed away and searched for the aft heads on the other side of the passageway. At first there seemed only to be a solid continuous wall until Mike's flashlight picked out the edges of an open door frame. The narrow space within it appeared to have been stacked floor to ceiling with stores. Remembering what he'd learned from his research, Mike gently wafted away the shroud of silt which had gradually built up over the exposed surfaces. When he brought his flashlight up close to the small area which he had cleared, he could hardly believe his eyes. There, right in front of him was the metal handle of an ammunition case, identical to the one which Hubert had stumbled across outside the wreck. Knowing for certain that no U-boat carried that amount of spare ammunition, Mike was left with a single awe-inspiring conclusion.

A clanging sound nearby drew his mind back to his present situation and he moved away from the area, reminding himself that there were infinitely more important matters at stake. He turned to see two of his pursuers inside the compartment, staring apprehensively at the collection of human bones on the floor. It was time for him to make his move. Looking deeper into the wreck, he caught sight of the hatch at the end of the Petty Officer's quarters and fixed its position in his mind. Turning swiftly around, he aimed his flashlight beam into the eyes of Michel and began to agitate the silt with his fins. In a flash, he extinguished the blinding light and with four powerful kicks, bolted towards the control room hatch, sending more clouds of silt billowing up into the passageway in his wake. In the semi-darkness he heard a spear clunk harmlessly against the bulkhead to his right. Within seconds he passed into the safety of the control room and turned swiftly to slam the steel hatch shut behind him. He quickly engaged the locking wheel and heard distant crashing sounds as his pursuers groped around blindly in the ensuing chaos. Mike knew that if they were unable to remain calm, they would be fortunate to escape from the wreck alive. But he felt little sympathy for them as he switched on his flashlight and moved away into the relative calm of the control room.

His first action was to tie the reel to the conning tower ladder, so that he could easily locate it again should he be forced to make his way back through the wreck. On the floor nearby, he found the trimix sling which Hubert had dropped from the blast hole in the turret and he opened the valve to check that it was working. It was. The first breath of trimix brought instant clarity to his mind. He ditched the regulator and air cylinder from the buoyancy jacket and looked up to see a shaft of natural light entering from the enlarged hole in the turret. As he was rising towards it there was a dull clanging sound and he turned in surprise to see light coming from the control room hatch. He extinguished his own light when he saw a figure emerge from it, accompanied by a voluminous cloud of silt. In the darkness, he quickly pulled himself up the ladder and thrust the sling tank through the pierced hull. Holding it at arms length, he pushed his head and one shoulder through the jagged gap. His chest became pinned by two tongues of sharp metal which cut painfully into his flesh. Retreating back into the wreck, he glanced down the ladder and saw that the person who had entered the control room was frantically searching the area with his flashlight. Mike's heart skipped a beat when the beam suddenly shone upwards and centred on him. Now there was no time for reflection; if he didn't get out straight away, he would be skewered like a roasting pig. In a split second he changed his position, breathed out to reduce his chest volume and darted cylinder first into the gap. He got half way out only to struggle when his buoyancy jacket snagged at the pocket. Reaching down with one hand he ripped it away and then pushed down hard on the outside of the hull to pull his legs free. He was almost clear when one of his fins suddenly jarred. A hand seized it from behind and was now pulling him back into the wreck.

Lieutenant Lechaux raced into *Capitaine* Villeneuve's office with barely a knock on the door. Villeneuve was caught with his mouth open and a cup raised halfway towards his lips. A few drops of coffee spilled onto his desk and he scowled as he blotted them up with a serviette.

'I'm sorry to burst in on you like this *Capitaine*, but we've just received some vital information.'

'That's all very well Guy, but I do have a telephone you know,' replied Villeneuve irritably. 'What's so important that it can't wait? Is there news on Perotta?'

'I can't say for sure sir, but we have now been reliably informed that Santorini and his gang are on board the *Sampiero Corso*. They're heading towards Roccapina and they have two captives on board.'

Lechaux watched *Capitaine* Villeneuve raise his cup, hesitate and then set it down on the saucer again.

'Captives you say! What the hell is he up to?'

'As far as I understand, Santorini is forcing them to take part in some kind of salvage operation.'

'Do we have any idea who these captives are?'

'We have reason to believe that one of them is Mike Summers. The other is a female, possibly Mr. Summer's girlfriend.'

Villeneuve stared at him in disbelief.

'That boy is determined to get himself killed,' he fumed. 'I warned him several times to keep clear of Santorini, but he obviously thinks that he's some kind of vigilante.'

Lechaux waited patiently for Villeneuve to finish his tirade.

'Sir we need to act quickly to prevent this from getting out of hand. I need your authority to launch a full air and sea operation.' Villeneuve picked reflectively at his moustache.

'Do we know for certain that this information is reliable?'

'We're about as sure as we can be sir. Officer Bertoli was contacted by Jeannot Raspail who is on the *Sampiero Corso* as we speak. It turns out he's not a member of Santorini's gang and wants nothing to do with the abduction. Bertoli told me that he's been grooming Raspail for some time in order to get to Santorini. Raspail won't testify against the gang but he's agreed to trade information in exchange for our protection.'

'Bertoli had no right to make any such deal without my backing,' complained Villeneuve.

'Perhaps not sir,' agreed Lechaux, 'but under the circumstances, I think we might make an exception.'

'Yes I suppose so,' said Villeneuve, exasperated. 'He's a rebel that one, and no doubt about it, but I have to admit that he gets results. You have the green light Guy...just one thing though.'

'Yes sir?'

'Do an old man a favour and see if you can arrange for one of the choppers to pick me up. I want to be there when our boys put Santorini in irons.'

Without a second's hesitation, Mike reached down and released the strap of his fin. It slipped free of his foot and disappeared back into the hull along with the hand that was gripping it. Now clear of the wreck, Mike scanned forward and aft to ensure that he had not been seen by Santorini and then dropped down beneath the curve of the hull. He quickly recuperated the rebreather from its hiding place beneath the torn fishing net, switched on the gas supply and then hooked himself into the harness.

Aware that the nitrox mixture in the rebreather would be lethal at his present depth, he continued to breathe from the trimix sling, which he clipped onto the harness. There was movement nearby as a moray eel swam past with graceful undulations of its muscular flanks. Mike smiled, wondering if it was the same one to which he had entrusted the care of the rebreather the previous evening. He promised himself that if he and Monica got out of this mess alive, he would bring down a whole tuna and feed his loyal sentinel by hand.

While hugging the contour of the wreck, he used his remaining fin to swim to the top of the turret. As he passed the blast hole, he saw Perotta, struggling with his equipment while attempting to follow Mike through the gap. Seeing him stranded there, totally at his mercy, Mike was tempted to finish him off for good. It would have been easy enough to do, but unlike Perotta, Mike was not a cowardly murderer, and rather than destroy life, he was determined to use every vital second of his remaining time to preserve it.

Now hidden behind the coaming of the bridge, Mike caught sight of Santorini in the distance, spinning around erratically near the stern. At first he was confused by the strange jerking movements, but all became clear when he saw a long, slender shadow moving swiftly through the water nearby. Even from a distance, its sleek outline was unmistakable, and a smile quickly spread across Mike's face. He unclipped the DPV from the rebreather harness and pointed it towards a column of barracuda that were slowly circling overhead. A flick of the switch sent him hurtling upwards, scattering the silvery arrows out from a central point like a detonating firework. Looping high over the wreck, Mike was barely noticeable as he moved towards the stern to position himself directly above Santorini and the tenacious blue shark that was buzzing him.

Pivoting vertically, Mike switched off the DPV, reduced his buoyancy and dropped into a steep dive. The shark immediately shot away into the distance, its sensitive lateral lines having detected something large and threatening approaching from above. Mike stopped his descent with expert precision, hovering undetected above Santorini's head. He swallowed his apprehension and hit the side of Santorini's face with the palm of his hand, wrenching the mask from his head. While Santorini struggled to replace it, Mike reached down and carefully unclipped his lift bag. A burst of air into the rebreather's integrated buoyancy jacket sent Mike rising upwards and away again, as if he had never been there at all. Beneath him, he watched Santorini turning about wildly, wondering from where the shark might attack him next. It was a source of amusement which Mike was unfortunately unable to stay around to enjoy; he now had to put his advantage to good use.

With the DPV whirring before him, he levelled out high above the wreck and used the ridge to guide him back towards the anchor line. When he reached it, he checked his depth, placed the mouthpiece of the rebreather between his lips and opened the watertight seal. Now undetectable from the surface, Mike let the trimix sling and lift bag fall from his hands and followed the early stages of his decompression schedule while slowly advancing towards the *Sampiero Corso*. Soon the underside of its hull came into view and he hovered beneath it, willing his timer to advance as he completed the last few minutes of his final stop. With only five minutes remaining Mike threw caution to the wind and decided to risk cutting his depth to three meters. He unclipped the hand drill and wide diameter spade bit which he had taken from the old tool box and positioned himself directly beneath the stern. With calm determination he pressed the point of the drill bit against the hull and began to bore into it.

Monica screamed through her nostrils until Pascal finally relented and removed the gag.

'What do you want?'

'I need to go to the toilet.'

Pascal scowled and pushed her roughly onto the bed so that he could release the bindings from her ankles. Once he'd removed them, he marched her towards the tiny cabinet which served as a latrine. Monica baulked at the stench of ammonia which met her nostrils when the door slid open.

'Do you want to go or not?' he asked, his eyes blazing with contempt.

Monica nodded weakly and was pushed inside without ceremony. Pascal took out his hunting knife and waved it in front of her.

'Don't try anything clever or I'll cut your pretty face into confetti,' he said before sliding the door closed.

Monica sobbed as she struggled to remove her underwear with bound hands. After relieving herself in an undignified manner, she looked around frantically and spotted a disposable razor on the floor. The blade was rusted through but it still looked sharp enough to cut. Placing her back against the wooden partition, she slid down it until she was sat on her ankles. She groped around on the floor until her fingers touched and closed upon the razor. Trembling with apprehension, she slipped it into the elastic trim of her panties.

'Have you finished yet, or do I have to come in there and drag you out?' Pascal shouted through the door.

'I'm coming out now,' replied Monica, using her thigh muscles to push herself back to a standing position. Pascal slid back the slatted door and stood to one side as she stepped out into the cabin. With a flick of the knife, he ordered her back to the bunks and pushed her face down while he re-tied her ankles and replaced the gag. He left her to struggle to a sitting position while he went above decks to continue his watch. The gruff voice of George Brassens began to resonate from a tinny cassette recorder in the wheelhouse. Monica retrieved the plastic razor from the back of her panties and bent the head until it shattered. She ran her thumb along the thin blade of metal which had been exposed. It barely cut her skin. Lying sideways on the bed, she brought her ankles up towards her hands and with the blade held tightly between thumb and forefinger, began to saw away at the coarse rope that was binding them together. Every few minutes she was forced to stop and quickly stretch out her legs again as Pascal put his head down the stairwell to check on her. After several minutes of painful work, she had succeeded in cutting halfway through the rope when she heard him dashing around frantically on the decks above. The music playing on the cassette recorder stopped abruptly and Pascal's reddened face appeared in the cabin.

'What are you doing?' he asked menacingly. Monica stared at him wide-eyed with fear, wondering how he could have known that she was trying to free herself, but Pascal merely turned his head to one side and narrowed his eyes in silent concentration. It was then that Monica heard it too; a strange grating noise which seemed to be reverberating through the hull. Pascal's head disappeared again and Monica heard him running back through the wheelhouse and along the side deck towards the bow. She twisted her body upright into a seating position and put her feet down between the bunks. To her astonishment, they landed in water. She looked around in alarm and froze when she spotted more water gushing through the gaps in the bulkhead which separated the cabin from the engine room. Realising that the boat was in imminent danger of sinking she howled into the gag and began to hop towards the companionway steps. The boat began to list and she stumbled onto the opposite bunk, banging her head against a locker as she fell. In rising panic she began to hack desperately at the rope around her ankles. The water quickly rose to the level of the bunks and began to soak into the mattresses. Suddenly Pascal came bursting into the wheelhouse with a gun in his hand and a determined look on his face.

'I'll kill you, you little bitch,' he shouted as he arrived at the hatch and began to negotiate the steep stairwell. He'd barely taken a step down it, when the bow of the boat suddenly rose up sharply, causing him to overbalance and stumble backwards. Losing his grip, he crashed out through the wheelhouse door, slid across the stern deck and plunged straight into the sea. Monica fell back against the bulkhead and struggled to her knees. She tried to launch herself out of the hatch to safety, but within seconds the opportunity had passed her by. Water came bursting through the stairwell pushing her back into the cabin and throwing her around like a rag doll. She gasped for air through her nostrils, kicking wildly with her bound feet in a desperate attempt to stay above the surface of the rising water. But the air pocket in the cabin was rapidly getting smaller and smaller. And then, to Monica's utter terror, it shrivelled to nothing and was gone.

The helicopter pilot of the *section aérienne* of the *Gendarmerie d'Ajaccio* could not believe what he was seeing as he approached the incident site. Expecting tough armed resistance and a prolonged stand-off, he'd been ordered to approach with caution, but now as he stared at the chaos below, it looked as if the battle was already over before it had begun. The Navigator sitting beside him relayed information to the control centre through his helmet mounted microphone.

'The vessel is sinking, repeat, the vessel is sinking. We have a visual on two...correction three casualties in the water. Two of them are wearing SCUBA equipment and the third is clinging to the vessel, about a hundred metres away. They appear to be unarmed and as far as we can tell, present no threat. We require immediate air sea rescue assistance and stand-by options for evacuation to hyperbaric facilities. Do you read; over.'

'Charlie Victor Zero Four we read you. A Coast Guard rescue helicopter with armed CRS unit will be with you in approximately zero six minutes and a fast launch of the *Brigades Nautiques* is now approaching from the south west with an ETA of zero one eight minutes. We will contact the hyperbaric chamber and request them to stand by; over.'

'This is Charlie Victor Zero Four, all copied and understood. Standing by.'

'Can we get any closer to the people in the water?' shouted *Capitaine* Villeneuve over the noise of the rotors. The Navigator turned around and pointed to his microphone and then to his ear.

'Oh yes, sorry about that,' said Villeneuve, pulling the microphone down towards his mouth. 'Can we go down and take a closer look?'

'I'm afraid that we can't get too close because of the downdraught sir,' replied the pilot, 'but there are some binoculars in the pocket to your left if you wish to use them.' *Capitaine* Villeneuve thanked him and pulled the binoculars out of a small locker. As the chopper circled the stricken vessel, he trained them on the two divers who were floating on the surface, a short distance away. One of the two men was floating horizontally, clearly in some kind of distress and Villeneuve's eyes opened wide with surprise when he recognised the dark, thick-set features and corpulent body of his nemesis.

'That's Santorini down there,' he shouted animatedly, while pointing through the cockpit window. The pilot and navigator winced as Villeneuve's voice blasted into their headsets.

'Oh sorry again,' said Villeneuve, meekly. 'He's one of the two divers down there in the water; the one floating on his back.'

The pilot banked towards the two men and began to circle in a wide arc around them. Villeneuve continued to peer through the binoculars and as the sun passed behind him, he was surprised to see a dark cloud of fluid mixing with the water next to Santorini's leg.

'Good Lord!' he said into the microphone, 'he's been wounded.'

With ten large holes pierced into the *Sampiero Corso's* hull, Mike knew that water would now be streaming into the engine room and dragging her stern deeper below the surface. Still shielded from view, he noticed that she was starting to list and he moved towards the bow, aware that she was rapidly becoming unstable. Seconds later there were crashing sounds from within as the hull forward of the beam rose clear of the water. Mike found himself staring through the surface at the upturned bow, towering high above him. He pulled his eyes away and burst into action, knowing that Monica might only have seconds to live. Activating the DPV's power switch, he tore around to the other side of the hull and saw the submerged stern deck slipping deeper into the water before his eyes. On the surface above him, there was a man treading water, but no sign of Monica. In a split second, he powered up into the submerged wheelhouse and straight down the hatch into the cabin below.

Through a mass of floating debris, he spotted Monica at the far end, flexing her body in a desperate attempt to swim free of the sinking vessel. Her wrists and ankles were still bound together, but of more urgent concern to Mike was the gag which prevented him from giving her a regulator to breathe from. Thinking quickly, he freed the second stage of the rebreather's emergency air cylinder and pressed the mouthpiece firmly against Monica's nostrils. At first Monica was terrified, but when Mike pressed the purge button and air began to stream around her nose, she found to her surprise that she could breathe from it without discomfort. Once she had regained her composure, Mike waited for her to inhale and then pinched her nose. Reaching behind her, he carefully peeled away the tape which was wrapped around her jaw and removed the rag from her mouth. He replaced it with the regulator and then cut through the bindings which secured her wrists and ankles. A spare mask was pressed into her freed hands and she gratefully strapped it over her head and cleared it.

The blurred features in front of her transformed into Mike's face and with tears in her eyes, she wrapped her arms tightly around him. Mike gently pushed her away and held up a cautionary hand; the vessel was in imminent danger of sinking and he needed to get her out of there as quickly as possible. Reaching behind, he released the rebreather's emergency air cylinder from its restraints and pressed it into Monica's hands so that she could move independently of him. He was about to reach for the DPV when Monica's eyes suddenly opened wide with terror. She bundled him to one side as a spear glanced off the side of his head and lodged into the wall behind her. Mike was unhurt, but thrown off balance and had no time to recover before his mask was ripped off and the breathing loop was pulled from his mouth. Monica tried to fend off the attack, but with no foothold and only one hand free, the best that she could do was to cause a diversion. It was enough to give Mike the time to release himself from the harness of the rebreather and push himself down beneath his attacker. Without clear vision and with only a lungful of air to sustain him, he now had to rely solely on his reflexes to survive.

He grabbed one of his assailant's legs and used it to pull himself swiftly up behind him so that he could get a hold on the valve of his cylinder. In a flash he reached over and equalled the contest by pulling off his attacker's mask. Cradling the cylinder between his knees and fighting the urge to breathe, Mike quickly slipped the mask over his own head and then pulled sharply on his attacker's regulator hose to rip it from his mouth. He took a quick breath from it and exhaled through his nose to clear the mask. A knife appeared and began to slash about wildly as in desperate need of air, his assailant attempted to dislodge him. With the mask clear, Mike could now see that he was fighting with Perotta and a burning rage welled up inside him. While he was dodging the lunging knife blade, a cylinder came hurtling in from Mike's right and smashed Michel in the side of the face. Mike looked around in surprise to see Monica holding it in both hands with a determined look on her face.

Spurred into action, he took a last breath from the regulator, inflated Michel's buoyancy jacket and then quickly turned off his air supply. Michel was propelled helplessly up towards the forward bulkhead, giving Mike and Monica an opportunity to make their escape. A sudden increase in pressure on Mike's eardrums told him that the *Sampiero Corso* was now falling through the water. He quickly unclipped the DPV from the rebreather, grabbed Monica's wrist and flicked the switch onto full power. The DPV pulled them down the inverted stairwell, through the wheelhouse and out into clear, open water. Mike's lungs were cramping as he reached for the single regulator that he and Monica would now have to share until they reached the surface. As he breathed from it, he looked down and watched the *Sampiero Corso* disappearing into the dark depths below, leaving thin streams of mercury like bubbles trailing behind in its wake. He glanced at his computer and saw that they had plummeted to over thirty metres in just a matter of seconds. He would have to make a small decompression stop, he realised, but after what he'd just been through, it was barely of any concern. The surface was clearly visible above them and there was a sense of reassurance at being lost in the infinity of the vast blue expanse which surrounded them.

As Mike was scanning the surface, he spotted a swordfish flashing by overhead and pointed it out to Monica. They watched it herding a shoal of silvery flanked sardines before it reached the edge of their vision and faded into the background. Monica beamed at Mike and wrapped her legs tightly around his waist. They remained locked together, sharing air from the single regulator as the DPV pulled them gently towards the surface. Monica made a precautionary stop at five metres and then swam to the surface, leaving Mike to clear his computer with the remaining air. Mike watched her rise, admiring her graceful movements as a stream of bubbles trickled from her mouth and ribbons of sunlight played over the contours of her body. When he saw her safely treading water at the surface, he returned his attention to his instruments and waited patiently for his body tissues to eliminate the excess nitrogen which they had absorbed.

Monica emerged into a world of chaos. Helicopters hovered noisily overhead, lifting people from the sea under the cover of armed patrol boats. She waved her arms above her head in an attempt to attract their attention, but she was away from the focus of their activity and went unnoticed. Suddenly between herself and the spectacle in front of her, she saw someone break the surface at speed. The emerging diver turned his head in all directions and then suddenly fixed his eyes on her. Monica froze when she realised who the diver was and her fear turned to terror when she saw the point of an armed spear gun rise above the surface. She looked down, desperate to get Mike's attention, but he was still monitoring his computer. In the distance, she saw Michel ditch his buoyancy jacket and weight belt and begin to advance towards her, propelled by powerful fin kicks. In panic, she began to swim in the opposite direction, but without fins, her progress was painfully slow.

Beneath the water Mike casually glanced up at the surface to make sure that Monica was not drifting away from him. To his consternation, he found that he could no longer see her and began to spin around, searching for her in all directions. From the corner of his eye he spotted a man wearing a wetsuit and fins, swimming rapidly across the surface nearby. He spun around and his heart skipped a beat when he caught sight of the spear gun. Knowing that Monica could be in grave danger, he flicked on the switch of the DPV and followed beneath the surface.

By now Monica was rapidly reaching the point of exhaustion. Glancing anxiously over her shoulder, she saw to her terror that Michel was steadily gaining on her. She shouted for help in desperation, sobbing as she swam for her life, but the power was draining from her arms. Finally, she could go no further and began to choke as she turned to face her executioner. She waited for the inevitable searing pain that would end her life, but to her surprise it never came. Instead, there was a loud grunt as Michel was thrown violently into the air as if he had been struck from below by a killer whale. Monica sobbed with relief when she saw Mike emerge in an explosion of water and proceed to batter Michel with the DPV.

He landed several forceful blows before Michel managed to recover and twist his body away. With the reflexes of a trained assassin, he quickly fired off a spear and Mike's shoulder jerked backwards as the shaft skewered his flesh. He cried out in pain as the DPV fell from his hand and realising his error, tried to claw it back. But Michel was not about to throw away his advantage. There was a smile of triumph in his eyes as he pulled the cord that was attached to the spear, locking the barb into Mike's flesh and dragging him howling in agony towards him.

'Now I'm going to kill you like I killed your idiot Pinzuti friend. And then I'm going to slice up your pretty girlfriend and leave her for the sharks,' he sneered. Mike grabbed the shaft of the spear and tried to kick him in the face, but Michel easily dodged his attempts and yanked the cord harder. As Mike was pulled closer towards him, he saw a flash of silver in Michel's right hand and knowing with certainty that a knife was about to be plunged into him, he swept his arm across his body to fend off the attack. Michel lunged, but Mike pushed his arm away with surprising ease, leaving him with a confused look on his face. Before he could recover his composure and attack again, Mike grabbed his wrist and twisted it with all his force. Michel howled but offered no resistance as Mike took the knife from his limp hand and cut the cord close to the spear that was lodged into his shoulder. Michel seemed to have no more fight left in him and Mike watched in bewilderment as he began to curl his body into a ball. When he began to scream in agony for no apparent reason, Mike finally understood what was happening to him. He had bolted directly to the surface from a considerable depth with his tissues still saturated with nitrogen. He was showing the signs of acute decompression sickness.

'Now you're going to wish that you'd drowned,' Mike shouted. 'You'll probably die anyway, but not before you've suffered the most excruciating pain imaginable. If you weren't such a murderous bastard I might even feel sorry for you.'

'Go screw yourself,' Michel retorted, in between cries of agony.

Mike turned around to look for Monica but saw no sign of her. The DPV was nowhere to be seen either. Presuming that she'd used it to make her escape, he began to swim one armed towards the circling helicopter in the distance. He flipped onto his back and tried to ignore a growing feeling of weakness as he kicked with his one remaining fin. The gash at the side of his head burned in the lapping seawater and there was blood on his hand when he touched his wounded shoulder. Moments later, the sound of an approaching power boat attracted his attention and he lifted his head to locate it. He pulled off his one remaining fin and waved it high above his head when he spotted a RIB powering towards him, sending sheets of white spray blasting out from the underside of its hull. As it drew nearer, he saw that it had the most sublime and welcome figurehead that he'd ever set eyes upon. Standing upright at the prow of a familiar black and yellow RIB was Monica, steadying herself with the bow line, like Boudichia leading a horse drawn chariot into battle. Within seconds she had spotted him and with an outstretched arm, was directing Hubert towards him. Now certain that their ordeal was finally over, Mike lay back in the water and blacked out.

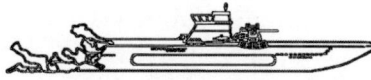

14

O fficer Bertoli left *Capitaine* Villeneuve's office with a smile on his face. The old boy had given him the usual roasting, but finished by putting a paternal arm around his shoulder while promising an award for his exceptional detective work. He'd even gone so far as to say that Bertoli's maverick ambition had reminded him of himself when he was a younger man. If only the old fool knew, Bertoli thought to himself as he stepped out of the *Caserne de Gendarmes* and casually strolled towards the public telephones. A quick glance up and down the road reassured him that he would not be observed as he stepped into a booth, pulled out a calling card and dialled the telephone number which was hand-written on its reverse. The call was answered on the third ring.

'*Oui?*'

'Achilles?'

There was silence on the line.

'This is Black Diamond,' prompted Bertoli.

'Ah, I had a feeling that you might be calling. Do you have my numbers?'

'Check your E-mail account. They're encoded as requested.'

'Excellent. I take it that the cargo is intact?'

'As far as I know - yes. But I can't guarantee that it will stay that way for long.'

'That goes without saying. What news of Santorini?'

'He's under observation in a high security hospital. He'll take the rap this time; unless, of course, you want to give him the Fairy Godmother treatment.'

'No. He can fight his own battles from now on. As far as I'm concerned, he's of no further use to our organisation.'

'As you wish. When can I expect the money?'

'You'll be paid within a week.'

'I'll count on it. You know how to contact me if you need me again.'

'Of course.'

'It was a very brave thing that Mr. Summers did,' conceded *Capitaine* Villeneuve. 'I just wish that he'd come to me earlier, before it all got out of hand.'

'If you'd believed his story about the U-boat in the first place, I'm fairly certain that he would have done,' pointed out Monica. 'Don't take that as a criticism. I was very sceptical about it myself. I think that it just got to the point where Mike felt that he was on his own.'

Villeneuve frowned.

'Yes I can understand his reaction, but his story *did* seem rather fanciful at the time. And even if we had believed him, we couldn't possibly have followed up such a line of enquiry. We don't have the resources for one thing.'

'Don't beat yourself up about it; I'm sure Mike holds no grudges against you.'

'No, he's a decent young man, and he has many other qualities that I admire too. I have to confess that without his dogged determination and guile, we would almost certainly have been unable to prove Santorini's involvement in Thomas Casanis' death.' He shook his head and stared out to sea. 'It's funny you know; I've been after Santorini for over twenty years and I always thought I'd bring him in myself - and yet it's actually a member of the public, who finally got the better of him. But that's the way life goes, I suppose. The important thing is that he'll stand trial and I'll gladly hand the plaudits to Mike if we get a conviction. And for once I'm pretty confident that we will; especially with the recorded evidence which Mike has provided. It still amazes me how he got it.'

'Oh, he's very resourceful...and very determined. I'd even go so far as to say stubborn.'

A glint appeared in Villeneuve's eye.

'I'm sure that one or two of my colleagues would describe me in the same way.'

Monica smiled and glanced at the white lilies in her hand.

'Mike told me that two of Santorini's men died.'

'Yes. Navy divers recovered the body of Pierre Meyreuil from the wreck yesterday and Michel Perotta died in transit to the recompression chamber. Santorini himself was a little more fortunate. The shark bite was superficial, but he got a spinal embolism when he rose to the surface too quickly; some kind of decompression accident I believe. They tell me he may never walk again.'

Monica nodded gravely.

'What will happen to the others?'

'Pascal Sorini will face charges of complicity to murder and kidnap. Since he wasn't a key decision maker, I expect he'll get a relatively light sentence. And as for Jeannot Raspail, it turns out he was never really a part of the gang at all. If he was guilty of anything, it was stumbling across a piece of wreckage from the U-boat and not being able to keep his mouth shut about it.'

Monica shook her head.

'Loose talk really can get you into a whole heap of trouble, can't it?'

'It certainly can,' agreed Villeneuve.

'There's one thing that I just can't quite figure out though,' said Monica, frowning. 'Hubert was the only person who knew where we were, but he says that he didn't contact you - so how did you find out what was happening?'

'Good old fashioned detective work,' said Villeneuve with a wry smile. Before Monica could press him any further, he turned and motioned towards the bow of the launch. 'Look's like they're surfacing.'

Monica watched Mike and Hubert make their way around the hull towards the swim ladder and climb aboard.

'Give me a hand with this dry-suit will you Monica, my shoulder is killing me,' said Mike after Hubert had relieved him of his equipment.

'Well the hospital did tell you not to dive until it was properly healed,' she scolded, before turning to face *Capitaine* Villeneuve. 'I told you he was stubborn.'

Mike rolled his eyes and winced as Monica pulled down on the watertight cuff of his dry-suit sleeve.

'Did you manage to get it done?' asked Thomas' father from the bench where he had been quietly cradling the urn which contained his son's remains.

'Yes, we bolted the plaque onto the guard rail of the bridge where everyone can see it,' replied Mike.

'Thank you both. I really appreciate all your efforts,' said Mr. Casanis, raising a grateful smile. 'It's really a pity that the wreck is so deep, otherwise I'd have gladly joined you.'

'If it's any consolation, we took a photograph of it for you; we'll make sure you get a copy before you leave.'

'You did? That's extremely thoughtful of you. Thank you again; both of you.'

'I only wish there was more that we could do,' said Mike, with a shrug.

Monica went to sit with Thomas' father while Mike and Hubert went to dry themselves off and change into more formal wear. Bertie and Anna joined the small gathering and soon they were all assembled on the open deck of the private launch, their faces warmed by a late afternoon sun. They listened in respectful silence as Thomas' father addressed them all, sharing memories and anecdotes from his son's life with honesty, humour and dignity. After he had thanked everyone for the kindness and support which they had shown him over the last two weeks, he invited Mike, as Thomas' closest friend, to step forward and say a few words in his honour. Monica squeezed Mike's hand as he left her side, took two paces forward and turned to face the gathering. He clasped his hands together and cleared his throat.

'What can I say about Thomas that hasn't already been said? He brought joy and energy into the lives of everyone he met, his enthusiasm for life was boundless and you couldn't find a more generous and loyal friend. The sea was in his heart, and it was there, surrounded by its many wonders that Thomas was at his most content. We've shared some amazing experiences over the years and I wouldn't swap any of those precious memories for all the gold in the world. There aren't really words to express how much I will miss him. Those kind of friendships only come along once or twice in a lifetime. Mr. Casanis you have every right to be proud of your son, and I can say with all sincerity, that the world above and below the surface will be much the worse for his loss. He was a very unique and special person.'

Mike looked up to see tears streaming down Monica's cheeks. She bit her lip and mustered a smile as he returned to her side and put a comforting arm around her shoulders. Mr. Casanis approached Mike and shook his hand firmly.

'Thank you for those kind words,' he said, his voice taut with emotion. 'Now it's time for him to return home.' With those words, he walked over to the hand rail, removed the lid from the urn and scattered his son's ashes into the sea. Monica threw the bouquet of lilies over the side, took Mr. Casanis' arm in hers and the small gathering stood in respectful silence as Thomas and the oceans became inextricably entwined for all eternity.

Later that evening Mike, Hubert, Monica and Thomas' father dined together at *Le Lido*, a busy seafront restaurant on the outskirts of Propriano. Monica wore a stunning black chiffon evening dress, diamond studs and an elegant white gold necklace bearing an arresting Viking rune pendant. They ordered a bottle of Champagne; and from their table overlooking the bay toasted Thomas' safe passage into a watery paradise.

'I hear that you've been invited to a press conference Mike,' said Mr. Casanis as he replaced his Champagne flute on the table.

'Yes...and it's probably just as well. I've got journalists hounding me for interviews at the moment and they're really starting to become annoying,' complained Mike.

'Well it's hardly surprising. The story *is* being reported all over the world,' pointed out Monica.

'I think they're more interested in the gold than the murders,' said Mike, scathingly.

'They report murders every day Mike,' pointed out Hubert.

'Yes I suppose they do.'

'What do you think will happen to the U-boat now?' asked Mr. Casanis.

'I presume they'll salvage the gold and then seal it up,' replied Mike.

'Actually there's been a lot of debate going on over the affair,' said Monica. 'As we thought, Germany wants the wreck to remain untouched, mainly because it's a war grave, but also because it's a military vessel and as such, it remains their legal property. Ethiopia understandably claims ownership of the cargo and would like its stolen artefacts to be returned, although there is no proof that they originated from there. The French have no legal claim over either the wreck or its cargo, but since both are located within their territorial waters, they insist on taking part in the salvage operation. Even then, they can't do a single thing without Mike's permission as Salvor. It stands to reason that the gold can't be left where it is, so there will need to be compromises on all sides. I'm presently negotiating with the French Minister for Foreign Affairs and the Ethiopian Embassy to get Mike accorded a percentage of the value of the cargo as a finder's fee. Once that is arranged they can sort out the minor details amongst themselves.'

'Do you think that you will have much success?' asked Mr. Casanis.

'As Possessor of the wreck Mike is legally entitled to a reward, and if they don't honour that, he can stop them from salvaging,' explained Monica.

'That may be true in theory, but could he do that in practice?'

'Well, we have taken out a little insurance, just in case they don't play ball,' said Hubert, with a smirk.

'Yeah, taken out is an accurate description,' agreed Mike laughing.

'I don't think I'll press you for the details,' said Mr. Casanis, with a wry smile. 'I suppose that when this all blows over, you'll be thinking of leaving the island Mike?'

'I don't have any concrete plans as yet; I'm just taking things day by day. But I do think that it would be safer for me to leave at some point, much as I'd like to stick around.'

'Actually I need to have a word with you about that Mike,' said Monica, her lips curling into a smile. 'I was intending to speak to you later, but this is probably as good a time as any. How would you like to join our team for a while; just until you decide what you want to do?'

'Are you serious?' asked Mike looking from Monica to Hubert and back.

'I've been given the budget to take on another person for a month, with the option of making the position permanent,' explained Monica. 'Bertie wants to spend more time in Switzerland to take care of his father which means that Hubert will be covering for him. You don't have to make the decision right now, of course; and I don't want you to feel any obligation, but we'd be more than happy to have you join us.'

'And we'd get the chance to do some great dives together too,' added Hubert.

'On your day off,' cautioned Monica, with a piercing glance at Hubert.

'Well much as I appreciate your offer,' began Mike, watching the smiles drop from their faces. 'I'm afraid that I'll have to disappoint you by accepting whole-heartedly.' Monica squeezed his knee reproachfully under the table as laughter broke out around the table.

'Well it looks like things might work out nicely for you after all,' said Mr. Casanis. 'How about we drink a toast to your future success?'

They readily agreed, touching the rims of their tall champagne flutes together at the centre of the table. 'Santé! Cheers! Gsundheit!'

After a sumptuous seafood dinner, followed by desserts, coffee and a fine local brandy, Hubert excused himself and left their company to meet with friends in the centre of town. Mike and Monica escorted Thomas' father to a taxi and wished him a safe return to the mainland, making promises to come and visit him in the New Year. Once they had waved him away, Mike took Monica's arm and suggested that they go for a stroll. He led her barefoot along the beach under a bright starlit sky as a crescent moon crept slowly above the horizon. They arrived outside the prestigious Grand Hôtel Miramar and Mike suggested that they finish the evening with a drink on the terrace, overlooking the sea. Ignoring Monica's protestations he pulled her inside and strolled up to reception.

'Good evening madam, we have a room reservation under the name of Summers.'

Monica stared at Mike open mouthed.

'Yes sir, please would you sign the register,' said the receptionist.

'I can't believe you did this,' said Monica, hiding her delight behind a reproachful stare.

'Well I just received a nice cheque for an interview I did with a German dive magazine and I thought that I should probably spend it on something worthwhile. And don't try to tell me that you have to work tomorrow, because Hubert's already told me that you've been given a week off.'

'Yes, well it *was* against my wishes.'

'Diligent to the end, but it makes no odds; I've decided that we're going to relax for the next couple of days,' said Mike as he took the key from the receptionist and led Monica up the marble staircase.

'And do I get a say in the matter?'

'No! Now let's not have our first argument, just accept that I'm right on this one,' said Mike with a smirk.

Monica huffed, stifling a smile as she glared at him through narrowed eyes.

Mike led her to the door of the suite, unlocked it and stood aside as she walked through into the sumptuous, softly lit bedroom, her mouth gaping and her eyes sparkling with delight. Long flowing net curtains gave way to an open, candle lit terrace on which was placed a table, two chairs and a bottle of Champagne on ice. For a backdrop, there was an unobstructed view over the moonlit *Golfe de Valinco* and the headlands which enclosed it either side. Monica walked out onto the wide terrace and leaned against the balcony, breathing in the sweet fragrance of jasmine and frangipani as she stared out to sea. She lifted her eyes towards the heavens and let out a sigh of utter contentment.

'I told them that we were newlyweds by the way,' said Mike, smiling as he loosened his tie and let it fall gently onto the silk sheets of the king sized divan. Monica slowly turned around to face him.

'Did you now?' she asked with a raised eyebrow. 'Well, I suppose in that case we'd better act the part.'

She slipped off the straps of her elegant dress and let it fall silently to the marble tiles at her feet. She was naked beneath, apart from a delicate pair of black lace panties. Soft moonlight caressed the side of her face and shoulders, the outline of her breasts and the deliciously smooth curves of her hips.

Mike raised his eyebrows and purred appreciatively.

'Now that is what I call a room with a view.'

Epilogue

The tall German, wearing the Pierre Cardin suit and the diamond studded Cartier watch, answered the telephone in his study on the second ring. He pushed his gold rimmed, designer reading glasses up his slender nose and brushed his fingers through his thinning but immaculately trimmed silver hair.

'*Hallo,*'

'Herr Blickmann?'

'Who is speaking please?'

'This is Achilles, Herr Blickmann.'

The tall German's eyes opened wide with surprise, his face flushing as his pulse quickened.

'It has been a long time,' he said breathlessly, loosening his collar. 'Is it true what I have been hearing?'

'Perfectly, Herr Blickmann. Your father's last resting place has at last been located, and I am reliably informed that the cargo has been left untouched.'

'Incredible! I've waited such a long time for this moment. I can hardly believe it has finally arrived.'

'Your excitement is understandable, Herr Blickmann.'

'So you've found it at last,' he said, savouring the words like a well matured Burgundy. 'Did that outlaw...what was his name...Santini...lead you to it?'

'Santorini,' corrected Achilles. 'Indirectly - yes. His greed and influence served our needs in the end, but unfortunately his incompetence has made the situation somewhat more complex than we anticipated.'

'In what way?'

'He managed to get himself arrested while attempting to salvage the gold. The wreck's position has therefore been compromised.'

'That is most inconvenient.'

'It is regrettable, certainly, but rest assured that I am taking all necessary steps to contain the situation.'

Blickmann's manicured fingernails drummed rhythmically on his polished walnut desk top.

'So, exactly how many people are presently aware of the U-boat's position?'

'More than I can safely control, so you will need to act swiftly. I've ensured that the coordinates remain classified for the moment and our security services are keeping a close watch over the site during the day, but I cannot guarantee that those measures will be anything other than a short term deterrent.'

'I see,' said Blickmann, tapping a pen against his lower lip. 'That will of course complicate the salvage operation, but I'm sure that we can find some way to work around the problem. Now if you could kindly give me the depth and coordinates, I'll have a team ready to depart Antibes tomorrow.'

There was a pause.

'I think that you might be forgetting something, Herr Blickmann.'

'Yes of course...your fee...a million was it?'

'A million in advance, the remainder on completion; my Bahamas account.'

Lightning Source UK Ltd.
Milton Keynes UK
09 June 2010

351UK00003B/120/P